N. Ross Yates

JOSEPH WHARTON

Joseph Wharton

JOSEPH WHARTON

Quaker
Industrial Pioneer

W. Ross Yates

BETHLEHEM
LEHIGH UNIVERSITY PRESS
LONDON AND TORONTO: ASSOCIATED UNIVERSITY PRESSES

Associated University Presses
440 Forsgate Drive
Cranbury, NJ 08512

Associated University Presses
25 Sicilian Avenue
London WC1A 2QH, England

Associated University Presses
2133 Royal Windsor Drive
Unit 1
Mississauga, Ontario
Canada L5J 1K5

The paper used in this publication meets the requirements
of the American National Standard for Permanence of Paper
for Printed Library Materials Z39.48-1984.

Library of Congress Cataloging-in-Publication Data

Yates, W. Ross (Willard Ross)
  Joseph Wharton: Quaker industrial pioneer.

  Bibliography: p.
  Includes index.
  1. Wharton, Joseph, 1826–1909. 2. Industrialists—
United States—Biography. 3. Quakers—United States—
Biography. 4. United States—Industries—History.
I. Title.
HC102.5.W47Y38   1987   338.7′6691′0924 [B]   86-81983
ISBN 0-934223-00-9 (alk. paper)

Printed in the United States of America

Contents

Illustrations

Figures

Maps

Preface

The earliest pioneers came bearing guns and Bibles.

The next added hand tools such as plows, pickaxes, bullwhips, and anvils.

A later wave was somewhat different. It comprised the industrial pioneers, who lived in cities and used machinery and capital instead of weapons and hand tools. Like the other pioneers, these were independent, ambitious, pugnacious, hardy, and resourceful. They employed chemistry, physics, biology, and the skills of engineering and banking; built canals and railroads; mined coal, iron, and other ores; established industries in chemicals, textiles, and metals; filled the land with inventions as dazzling as a display of fireworks on the Fourth of July; and amassed fortunes such as Americans had previously believed could only exist among nabobs of India. They made America a mighty industrial power and its people a great nation.

Joseph Wharton was one of the industrial pioneers. He lived as a boy in the period dominated by inventors or builders such as Cyrus McCormick, Samuel F. B. Morse, and Josiah White; matured during years marked by the rule of Asa Packer, Ezra Cornell, Cornelius Vanderbilt, and Elias Howe; and aged along with Andrew Carnegie, John D. Rockefeller, Henry C. Frick, Edward H. Harriman, and James J. Hill. "Robber barons," Americans called these later industrialists. The title discloses nothing of significance in their lives. They shared the values which made them a pioneering class, as well as a memory of thrills derived from penetrating the unknown; and each was among the first to appreciate the importance of his discoveries. None was typical. Each believed in the sanctity of individual difference and lived the belief.

Wharton's home city was Philadelphia; his parents were moderately wealthy Quakers. Philadelphia was at the time of his birth the most important manufacturing and commercial city in the country and had many industrial pioneers of Quaker heritage and comfortable means. But none other, excepting possibly an older brother, Rodman, who died young, was a Hicksite Quaker whose mother and father were ministers. Few if any of the others had as varied gifts and interests and impressed them on the land to form as large and sprawling an industrial empire expressive, as these things are, of the personality of the founder.

He became the first person in the country to refine metallic zinc on a commercially successful basis; began the nickel industry of the United States; led the iron and steel community in promoting the protection of American manufactures by high tariffs; helped to build up the small Bethlehem Iron Company into a major supplier of armor plate and guns for the U.S. Navy and put the company into a position to become attractive to Charles M. Schwab, who made it into the Bethlehem Steel Corporation; wove together an empire of mines and furnaces in New Jersey and New York and coke works in Pennsylvania and West Virginia and became the foremost producer of pig iron in the East; took control of the menhaden fishing industry of the eastern seaboard; encouraged Frederick W. Taylor in his work on scientific management; founded the Wharton School of Finance and Commerce at the University of Pennsylvania, the prototype of American schools of business; headed the board of managers of Swarthmore College for almost twenty-five years; mined for gold in Nevada and Idaho; and transformed a multitude of properties in the pinelands of southern New Jersey into a one-hundred-and-fifty-square-mile tract which bears his name and is today a preserve for one of the most interesting ecological sections of the eastern United States.

Today few traces of his work remain. But the importance of his accomplishments is not to be judged by the number and condition of artifacts. The natural progression of the scientific-industrial revolution, which Wharton and others pioneered, is marked by an effacement of the old by the new. The superseded theory and the obsolete machine are cast aside as being of no further use. The one gathers dust on the shelves of libraries; the other rusts and is gone. What endures is a memory of the accomplishment, and this is timeless. The discovery of antibiotics has not diminished the achievements of Pasteur, any more than fluorescent lights have dimmed the luster of Edison or space flight demeaned the invention of the Wright brothers. So, too, Wharton and his works survive in memory. They belong to the history of industrial pioneering and the problems which it raised for the American people.

No biography is more than an introduction to a life. I have tried to organize this one in such a way as to emphasize the links between Wharton and the industrial and financial practices with which his career was involved. This has necessitated minor digressions into the growth of the zinc, nickel, iron, and steel industries; the basic features of various industrial processes, such as those developed by Samuel Wetherill, Wharton, Bessemer, and Edison; and early forms of industrial management and the way of keeping accounts. I have attempted to present this material in nontechnical language and in such a way that the reader who is not interested may skip over it.

Many people have helped in the effort which has made this biography possible. Foremost are the staff of the Friends Historical Library of Swarthmore College which owns the Wharton Papers. Nancy Speers has processed those papers and was especially helpful, but others also provided much aid: Jane Thorson, Patricia Neiley, Albert Fowler, and the director, J. William Frost. Encouragement and access to further unpublished works by and about Joseph Wharton came from Catharine Morris Wright, Wharton's granddaughter, as well as from her son, Professor Harrison M. Wright of Swarthmore College, who also read the entire manuscript and made many useful suggestions for revision.

Robert Packer Fritz allowed me the use of the diaries of Robert Heysham Sayre, which at the time were still in the possession of the family. Jack Chamberlain contributed several memoranda concerning the Bethlehem Iron Company. Steven A. Sass, who was working on his history of the Wharton School, and I exchanged notes. Mrs. Jane G. Hartye, in charge of the papers of Frederick W. Taylor at the Stevens Institute of Technology, provided suggestions and access to materials. Professor Leonard Wenzel of Lehigh University helped in the interpretation of Wharton's meaning in the manuscript describing the process used in making nickel at the American Nickel Works in Camden. Mrs. Elke Haase Rockwell translated for me the manuscript of Dr. Theodor Fleitmann describing his process of refining nickel ores.

Staff of the Schwab Memorial Library of the Bethlehem Steel Corporation; the Batsto (N.J.) Citizens' Committee; the Moravian Archives at Bethlehem, Pennsylvania; the libraries at Lehigh University; the libraries of the American Philosophical Society, The University of Pennsylvania, and the Franklin Institute in Philadelphia; and the staffs of the manuscript rooms of the Library of Congress, the Historical Society of Pennsylvania, and the Sterling Library of Yale University were of great help.

I also want to thank the *Pennsylvania Magazine of History and Biography* for permission to use parts of several articles which I wrote for that journal, "Samuel Wetherill, Joseph Wharton, and the Founding of the American Zinc Industry" (vol. 98, no. 4, Oct. 1974, pp. 469–514) and "Joseph Wharton's Nickel Business" (vol. 10, no. 3, July 1977, pp. 287–321). The Office of Research at Lehigh University kindly awarded me a summer grant to help with research in 1980.

John Gera, Fritz Laboratory, Lehigh University, has prepared the maps.

Special thanks go to the American Philosophical Society for a grant from the Penrose Fund in support of research for this biography.

JOSEPH WHARTON

1

The Beginning of a Family

Joseph Wharton grew up in Philadelphia at a time when the city and its suburbs formed a center for scientific investigation and chemical manufactures. He profited from this background and used scientific knowledge to make fortunes in zinc, nickel, and iron. Yet he had no strong family tradition of science or manufacturing to support him. He was not among those Philadelphians who breathed the air of science and industry from the cradle on, such as Samuel Wetherill, a sometime competitor of Wharton for control of the zinc industry, and George T. Lewis, collaborator of Wharton in making zinc. Joseph was, rather, born to pure Quakerism slightly set off from a Quaker mercantilism. His parents were ministers in the Society of Friends and had no gainful occupation. They lived off fortunes inherited from relatives who had been rich Philadelphia merchants.

His background predestined young Joseph Wharton for no particular occupation. Everyone in the Society of Friends was supposed to have a vocation for Quakerism. True, membership in the Society meant virtual exclusion from careers in politics and the military. Also, few Quakers chose to study law; and teaching at the college level was generally frowned on. Subject to these exceptions, young Joseph Wharton had a free choice of livelihood; and, the Quaker religion being what it was, he could make that choice unencumbered by any numbing sense of guilt for being the bearer of unforgiven sins, such as inhibited some of the energetic, restless, talented youth tied to a Calvinistic theology in Puritan Boston.

1

There were, to be sure, some scientific and industrial interests among antecedents and relatives, particularly in the Fisher family. His mother's grandfather, Joshua Fisher, had experimented with the hydrograph and published a chart of the Delaware Bay which remained standard for nearly a century. Her first cousin, William Logan Fisher, had founded the Duncannon Iron Works on Sherman Creek in Perry County, Pennsylvania. Another of her first cousins, Thomas Gilpin, had with a brother of his operated a paper mill on the Brandywine and is supposed to have invented and installed there America's first endless papermaking machine. Her brother Thomas Fisher exhibited a book on mathematics and an elaborate panorama of human life called "Dial of the Seasons" at the Crystal Palace in the London Exhibition of 1851. There was a scattering of scientific and industrial accomplishments among other members of the Fisher and Wharton clans.[1]

But mercantile interests predominated. Joshua Fisher had founded a shipping house which endured for a hundred years. He was credited with establishing the first line of American packet ships sailing regularly between Philadelphia and London and had involved his four sons in the family business. One of these, Joseph Wharton's grandfather, Samuel Rowland Fisher, had become Joshua's successor. On the other side of the family, great-grandfather Joseph Wharton had also become a rich merchant and had brought a goodly number of his eighteen children into the business of buying and selling. One of them, named Charles—young Joseph Wharton's grandfather—had begun a career in the grocery line and moved from that into the shipping trade. He had become extremely wealthy and bought much land in Philadelphia, other parts of Pennsylvania, and New York.

These merchant ancestors and their wives were without exception descended from Quaker stock which had variously followed conscience, opportunity, and William Penn to America from the British Isles. The first Fishers had arrived in the *Welcome*, the ship bringing William Penn to the mouth of the Delaware. Shortly thereafter, the first Wharton had landed in Philadelphia from England. He was entirely unrelated to the noble Whartons of England who were variously Puritans, Independents, and Church of England people.[2] Quaker, too, were Wharton's grandmothers, both of whom were named Hannah and came from Newport, Rhode Island. Hannah Fisher's maiden name was Rodman. Her father, Captain Thomas Rodman, was a son of Samuel, who in turn was the offspring of Newport's first Thomas Rodman, a physician and surgeon who had come to Newport from Barbados in 1675. Charles Wharton married Hannah Redwood, who was descended from Abraham Redwood, a merchant who had removed to Newport from Antigua sometime between 1712 and 1718. The Rodmans and the Redwoods were among the old Quaker families of Newport and were, like the Fishers and Whartons of Philadelphia, closely associated with shipping.

These ancestors, like all Quakers, cherished simplicity but were not bound by any vow of poverty. Those who were ambitious, skilled, or lucky became wealthy. As far as the discipline of the Society was concerned, making money might be a way of providing others with occupation or the necessaries of life. The rules only said that Quakers ought not to spend money on frivolities. Still, what constituted a frivolity was subject to considerable interpretation. In class-conscious eighteenth-century Philadelphia a requirement of simplicity was interpreted to allow each to live according to his station. The wealthy Quaker merchants could build mansions, use the best fabrics in their clothing, lavishly entertain, and drive fine equipages, provided they did so without ostentation. The working out of the discipline resulted, for example, in the peculiar clothing by which Quakers came to be identified: a plain dress and small bonnet for the women; the shovel hat and shadbelly coat for the men.

Naturally, the Society allowed those who objected to such luxury to live in a simpler life if they chose. One who wanted the more Spartan existence was William Wharton, Joseph's father.

Charles's wife and William's mother, the former Hannah Redwood, died when William was six years old, leaving Charles with five children. A sixth had died in infancy; and one of the five, Joseph, the eldest, was to die at age eighteen. The remaining four included, in order of birth, Sarah Redwood, William, Charles, and Hannah. Sarah Redwood eventually married William Craig. Charles and Hannah married Hollingsworths.

Charles, the father, lived in a manner becoming a wealthy gentleman. He was tall and well formed, wore fashionable clothes, and walked with "measured gait." He had red hair of which he was ashamed and hid it under large curled and powdered wigs imported from England. Every morning a barber would bring in two wigs, freshly powdered, and take away the two which had been worn the day before. Charles lived at Number 136 South Second Street, near Spruce, in a mansion some thirty feet wide of red brick entered up a flight of high and broad marble steps. The double front of Robert Waln's big estate stood next door and beyond that, the mansion of David Lewis. In 1802 Charles purchased Bellevue, a large stone house set on 106 rolling acres several miles northwest of Philadelphia. Bellevue stood not far from Cliffs, the country seat of the Fishers.[3]

Joseph Wharton's mother Deborah in later life described young William's quiet revolt against his father's manner of living. William was not known to object to it until he reached adolescence. He was, she wrote, approximately seventeen years of age when he was called upon to go with his father and brother Charles for the purpose of choosing new clothes.

This was a time of trial to him, for he was "prompted by his religious convictions to change his dress & to withdraw from the divisions of the vain world," to use his own language. His brother chose a suit of the prevailing fashion. After which William asked to be shown some brown cloth, and desired his father to have a suit of it cut off for him. This was done without any remark & the cloth sent home. His brother soon appeared in his new clothes, but the brown cloth was laid by, until their father asked why William did not wear his. The fact was they were to be made by another taylor & after a new form. Isaac T. Hopper was the one chosen and his feeling manner on that occasion was never forgotten. When brought home they were supposed not to belong there, & on being brought into the parlour, were taken up & looked at by his younger sister

Hannah & laid down again [in] silence—William being present. The next day, a costume as plain as the one which he wore in mature age, was put on, and thus he appeared a speckled bird in the family. But from them he received no unkindness, his father saying, "he would not lay a straw in his way." That remark I heard him make to my mother, when she took me with her to make a call there, and was much impressed with the contrast between his plain garb & the general appearance of things, especially the scarlet dress of his sister Hannah. This change drew upon him many remarks & he was pointed out in the streets as "crazy Billy Wharton."[4]

Deborah did not face a choice similar to that of her husband-to-be because her mother and father, Hannah and Samuel Rowland Fisher, were already living simply. Samuel had followed this path before he met Hannah. This strange man charted courses which led him to wander from one edge of Quakerdom to another. He had a gift for buying and selling which he cultivated until it became almost an obsession. He seemed always to be able to make money even in adversity. So he faced the goddess Success, which confrontation led him to extremes of soul searching and sacrifice.

At the outset of the Revolution the Fisher children—Samuel Rowland, his brother Thomas, Miers, and Jabez Maud, and his sisters Lydia and Esther— were unanimous in nonbelligerency. In this they were heavily influenced by their aging father, Joshua, and were markedly different from the numerous Whartons, who took diverse stands of partisanship and neutrality. The Revolutionary authorities therefore labeled the Fishers Loyalist and treated them accordingly. Samuel Rowland, Thomas, Miers, and Lydia's husband, Thomas Gilpin, were among a group of Quakers who were arrested and imprisoned for a time at Winchester, Virginia. Thomas Gilpin died there under the harsh treatment.[5] After the return of the survivors to Phila-delphia, and following the British evacuation of the city, Samuel Rowland exhibited a stubbornness in opposing the revolutionary cause unmatched by most other Quakers. At a time when sentiment was feverish the authorities arrested him for having sent a letter behind the lines to his brother Jabez Maud, who was in New York harbor, unable to land. They charged him with "misprision of treason," alleging that the letter gave information to the enemy. The charges were insubstantial; under less emotional circumstances the case would probably never have come to trial. But Samuel Rowland was tried and, when confronted by the judge, further encouraged hostility to himself by refusing to recognize the legitimacy of the court. He was accord-ingly convicted and imprisoned in the old jail which stood on the southwest corner of Third and Market Streets. Here he remained for two years. During this time the fighting moved to the southern colonies and tempers in Phila-delphia cooled. The authorities indicated a willingness to release him, pro-vided that he cooperate with them to the extent of recognizing the justice of the proceedings against him. He refused, and soon found himself opposed by fellow Quakers and even members of his family. As Samuel Rowland recounted the experience in a diary, at one point a delegation from the meeting threatened him with being disowned. He was released only when a means was found of doing so while allowing both him and the authorities to retain their divergent opinions.[6]

Oddness followed Samuel Rowland Fisher into the postwar period. His sister Esther (Hetty) kept house for him until his forty-fifth year, when he married Hannah Rodman, who was beautiful and somewhat taller than he. This union, incidentally, released Esther from a vow to care for him and permitted her to marry a fiancé of many years' standing, Samuel Lewis. Samuel Rowland Fisher was throughout troubled by doubts concerning proper conduct and found relief in scrupulous adherence to the rules of the Society and in associating with traveling ministers such as Thomas Scattergood and Elias Hicks, who emphasized discipline and the simple life. Old Joshua Fisher had freed his three slaves and four of the five children of the slave named Sue; Samuel Rowland completed the manumissions by buying and freeing the fifth child; and he performed other charities for blacks. He supported Hannah in becoming a minister even though her good works reinforced a feeling of rivalry to excel her in exemplary conduct.[7]

He was the sort of person around whom legends cluster. Joseph Wharton recounted two. Wrote Wharton:

He had a habit of adding to the list price of all his goods what he thought a fair profit, charging no more for those more sought after. Naturally some goods were being unsold, among them a quantity of hatchets, at a time when blankets were eagerly taken. He therefore required that each buyer of blankets should purchase a proportionate quantity of hatchets, which a trader from Lancaster County refused to do, and so could have no blankets. The customer departed in vexation, but after a time returned professing readiness to take all the hatchets in the store, saying to my grandfather whose suspicions were aroused by this change that they were just what his people wanted to fight the Indians with. "Thou shan't have a hatchet" said my grandfather, and so the trader got his blankets without the hatchets.

The other incident related by Joseph Wharton of Samuel Rowland Fisher also concerned a sense of justice: "His commercial business involved his exportation of flaxseed every year to England: When the embargo preceding the War of 1812 took effect, his exportation of flaxseed for that year had been made, while most other cargoes of it were stopped. The scant supply of the highly prized American seed caused the price in England to rise higher than my grandfather thought just: he gave the surplus to establish negro schools in Delaware."[8]

A contrasting anecdote is to be found in the diary of the Philadelphia merchant Thomas P. Cope, who related an incident involving "a certain Dr.

Abm Chovet, of no inconsiderable celebrity." Dr. Chovet was once caught in a shower near Fisher's store and asked Samuel for the loan of an umbrella. Samuel replied, " 'I have none to lend but will lend thee my great coat & as I know thou art in the practice of using bad language, I must enjoin thee not to indulge in it whilst thou has my coat on.' " Now, Dr. Chovet's language was indeed more colorful than most, but he was not to be embarrassed, for he knew Samuel had a reputation of being somewhat sharp in trade. Dr. Chovet soon returned the coat. " 'Well, I hope thou didst not forget my charge,' 'No, I did not,' rejoined the Dr. 'I did not swear a single oath all the time I had your coat on, but in all my life I never felt such a propensity to lie.' "[9]

Samuel Rowland and Hannah Fisher settled at Number 110 Front Street (later Number 226) in a house built by old Joshua Fisher. On the rear of the lot Joshua had erected a warehouse, "separated from the house by a yard or garden in which excellent plum trees grew," as Joseph Wharton later described it.[10] Hannah and Samuel raised their family at Number 110 and the country estate of Cliffs. Sarah was born the first year after the marriage and was followed a year later by Deborah. Several years elapsed before the birth of twins, Rodman and Thomas, who lived only a few years. In 1801 another baby came along, whom the parents also named Thomas, the "Uncle Thomas" of Joseph Wharton's youth, who was destined to live out his life as a bachelor in Number 110 Front Street.

2

Hannah Fisher took pity on the motherless Wharton brood and often came to the pretentious Second Street mansion and to Bellevue with her children. Little Deborah and William Wharton frequently saw each other, but did not much play together, as William was five years her senior. He was, moreover, shy and introverted. As he grew to manhood he read much, especially the writings of primitive Friends and other religious literature, including poetry. He was particularly fond of the poetry of William Cowper.

He would have liked to be a farmer, he said later, but lacked physical strength and stamina. In fact, he became so engrossed in religious activities that he had time for little else. When not yet twenty-one he obeyed an inspiration to accompany the gospel minister Thomas Scattergood on a religious visit to New York and the New England states. He obtained the consent of his father and the Pine Street Monthly Meeting to which he belonged and set out with Thomas and another minister, Susanna Horne. They were gone seven months and traveled through eight states. William returned home more convinced than ever that he should live simply, devote his life to religious pursuits, and labor on the farm at Bellevue to the extent of his physical ability.[11]

Shortly after his return he found himself in love with Deborah. She had grown to be a woman as beautiful as her mother. Gentle and pious, Deborah favorably responded to William's attentions. They wanted to be married. William could afford it, having access to his father's fortune and possessing several legacies from relatives. Hannah favored the match and had probably done what she could to promote it. But Samuel Rowland Fisher objected.

According to a family tradition, his objection stemmed from a contemplation of William's wealth. Samuel believed that as a matter of principle an heiress such as his daughter should marry a less fortunate person than herself in order to spread wealth more equitably.[12] The substantial correspondence and memoranda left by William Wharton do not contradict the traditional reason, but nevertheless suggest a more complicated motivation. Samuel, wrote William, averred in refusing assent that the proposal of marriage came as a result of *"his wife's doings,"* saying, "I have no objection to William as a person, and I cannot name a reason for him not marrying Deborah. But I feel a stop in my mind, and it remains there after deliberate and dispassionate consideration; and I am under no apprehension that my mind will ever be changed."[13]

Samuel's intransigence put William's patience and charity to tests which they passed with far from perfect marks. He saw Deborah at meetings but avoided visiting at her home. Hannah had warned him against this, saying that "she was afraid her husband would use me roughly if I continued." "I never knew anything as deranged as this affair is," William complained.

In 1814 William took a trip to Western Pennsylvania and Ohio and returned as completely in love with Deborah as ever. In the autumn of 1815 he wrote jointly to Hannah and Samuel, again pressing his suit. Upon receiving the letter Samuel let William know of his decision. "I will bear thee no longer the censure I have born for breaking the match. My daughter is now old enough to judge for herself. I leave it entirely to her and will treat thee handsomely when thee comes to the house to see her." But in an interview with William on 11 December he said, somewhat rudely, "If this affair had been begun rightly, I should have been satisfied. I have not the least objection to thee, but still, the matter was wrong begun, and I will not give my consent to the marriage."

William was incensed. "He feigns to leave the way open by saying he will have nothing to do with it one way or the other, meaning he will do nothing to promote it nor nothing to prevent it," while at the same time he was doing his best "to influence his lovely daughter to dismiss me." Surely, William reasoned, Samuel was becoming a traitor to truth. What was he telling her? "If he pretends it is something unfit to be told me, because of its great criminality, it is a falsehood of the grossest and most heinous kind. . . . But if he affects it is a supernatural intimation of divine goodness revealed to him, of the impropriety of such a measure, I never did nor never will believe it." William had formed his own judgment, he wrote, "deliberately and dispassionately after a full & impartial investigation of the subject, his obstruction proceeds from his own unmortified, carnal, cruel & unregenerate will, for I do not believe it could proceed from a Christian spirit."

William wrote to a Newport relative, Charity Rotch, in a manner which is almost a caricature of a love-crazed youth of the Romantic period:

> Can I get rid of my affection for thee Deborah Fisher, Yes; but it must inevitably be at the sacrifice of my life, or what is dearer to me, for I fear not death, I dread life, at the sacrifice of all that gives life to life, my best principles, my best, my finest, most exalted and estimable sensibilities. If I attempt it, I must destroy what I appreciate most, I must part with forever, & bid a long farewell to the most tender & most amiable properties of the human heart; those feelings which promote in the highest possible degree, social intercourse, benevolence and love; Heaven forbid it, rather than undergo the latter, I pray God to cut short the tender thread of my life & number me to the silent grave. . . . behold the destruction, the ruin inflicted by the hand of a relentless cruel christian, a *christian* it is not possible, would not heathens be ashamed to own such a deed. Yes: it were better for the perpetrator indeed, if a millstone was hanged about his neck & be drowned in the depth of the sea. Think not, I have deceived you in appearing heretofore a mild and moderate person, but at this time expressing myself in such strong terms. You may suppose I have acted the part of an hypocrite in thus appearing what I was not; for although I now speak with an *emphasis*, & use expressions that may seem to indicate me a man of violent temper & disposition, I am not a man of such disposition; I am a *mild* & not a passionate man, my natural disposition of mind is easy & agreeable.

And still his pen ran on. He developed the same line of thought further, then concluded by indirectly admitting the injustice of much of what he had written: "No vain efforts of a refined imagination or of my wild & vagrant imagination can soothe the mental pangs & bodily pains my nature feels, or cure the throbbings of a broken heart."

An emotional explosion such as this, triggered by frustration, never afflicted Deborah. She calmly endured the separation, well knowing that her father would sooner or later let the marriage proceed. William's loss of composure when faced with frustration was again to appear in the crisis of the Hicksite separation.

Samuel Rowland Fisher never did give a formal consent to the marriage of his daughter. He only stood aside and respected the voice of the inward light speaking to her. As soon as William understood Samuel's position the courtship proceeded peacefully and without further disturbance. They appeared in the old Pine Street Meeting and promised themselves each to the other on 4 June 1817, daughter and son of the first families of the commonwealth and province; he "a gentleman of genial wit and gracious dignity"; she, a woman of "charm and singular beauty."[14] Theirs was a heritage of humble devotion and unaffected gentility.

As a wedding present Samuel gave his daughter the house at 130 Spruce Street. This was to be her home for the next seventy-one years.

2

From School to Farm

Deborah and William lost no time in beginning a family. Over a span of eighteen years Deborah bore ten children: Hannah, in 1818; Rodman, the oldest boy, in 1820; Sarah (Sally) (1821); Charles (1823); Joseph, the fifth child (3 March 1826); Mary (1828); William (1830); Samuel Fisher (1832); Anna (1834); and Esther Fisher (Hetty) (1836).

During these years family matters took up most of Deborah's time. William was the principal voice of the family in affairs concerning the Society of Friends.

1

A year after Joseph was born an event occurred which was to affect the range of his associations for his entire life. This was the dividing of Friends in the Middle Atlantic States into two mutually exclusive groups. The cleavage coincided with a spreading egalitarian spirit exemplified in Jacksonian democracy and a facturing of many established religions. But the Quakers were understandably little concerned with the weakening of loyalties to church and party on the part of non-Quakers. They regarded their internal separation as a family affair and variously viewed it as involving a proper balance between doctrine and discipline and a testing of the tolerance of prominent members of the Society.[1]

Issues and personalities were in fact intermingled, as the names of the parties indicate. Hicksites allowed themselves to be called by the name of the minister who most accurately symbolized their position, Elias Hicks. Their opponents did not object to being referred to by the name with which the Hicksites assailed them, Orthodox. The agreement on names was the only hint of tolerance shown by each society toward the other.

The contest was primarily fought within the formal organization of the Society. As Joseph Wharton in later life explained this organization to an acquaintance, it consisted of a "system of business meetings called Preparative, Monthly, Quarterly, and Yearly Meetings, each of those ranks, beginning with the Preparative, reporting to the next above it in rank. Usually but one Preparative reports to a Monthly, but several Monthlies in various adjacent localities report to a Quarterly, and several Quarterlies report in like manner to a Yearly. Now the Yearly Meeting also is but a local institution, and there is no general convocation or authority of any kind to bind together the several Yearly Meetings which collectively embrace all members of each branch of the Society. The organic law of each Yearly Meeting is expressed in the 'Book of Discipline' of each, and these are not exactly accordant." He went on to say that the responsibility for keeping the minutes of a meeting rested with a clerk or assistant clerk; and that no common repository for the minutes of the meetings existed.[2]

This decentralized system of meetings allowed disagreements such as that between Hicksites and Orthodox to be localized. In effect, the separation of 1827 did not extend to Quaker meetings in the South and in New England.[3]

Hicksites were the protagonists. In part they represented an equalizing voice which criticized the existence of class lines and the meddling of government in private affairs and encouraged active opposition to Southern slavery. In this way they anticipated future democratic sentiments. At the same time, they were reactionary in opposing education in the arts and sciences in favor of a simple, preferably rural, life. They objected to the toleration of high living carrying over from the eighteenth century and to the intrusion of what they called novel doctrines. They held that discipline, such as they alleged was practiced by the original Friends, and not doctrine, should knot the cords of membership in the Society.

Elias Hicks more or less summarized their position in his ideas and manner of living. A tall, straight, spare man with neither beard nor mustache, he had been born in 1748 on Long Island and lived there as a farmer. As his long hair turned white it accentuated a pair of large, clear, black eyes. He took up the ministry in early life, realized a gift of moving crowds, and spent much of his time traveling from one meeting to another, staying with Friends at each stop and forming a large following along the Atlantic seaboard. He emphasized the inward light to a point of insisting that it alone was sufficient for salvation and that the Bible was of secondary importance. His language in expounding his views was cloudy to a point that, as the Orthodox became more precise in their minds concerning what constituted true doctrine, he became an easy target of charges of departing therefrom. He denied the redemptive and healing powers of Christ, the infallibility of Scripture, original sin, and much else. Hicks also carried simplicity to an extreme. Quakers, he believed, should live apart from a sinful world and not partake of its pleasures. He rejected books, science, and public schools and advocated a rural life which would confine people pretty much to worship, work with the hands, and contemplation of the beauties of physical nature. He disapproved of internal improvements such as the Erie Canal and railroads. And he vigorously denounced slavery.[4]

He was not in any sense a typical political leader. Friends would have held anyone in contempt who might have tried to influence them by the usual political or administrative tactics. He was not even present at most of the events leading up to and including the separation crisis in the Philadelphia Yearly Meeting of 1827. Nor did Friends who carried out Hicks's ideas regularly refer to him as an authority.

Yet the attraction to Hicks was widespread and charismatic. He held no one under a greater spell than young William Wharton, who imparted his reverence for Hicks to his family so completely and convincingly that seventy-nine years after the separation Joseph Wharton uncritically described for Andrew Carnegie an incident occurring in the Fisher household when Deborah was a little girl. She was, Joseph wrote, "so near death from what was called quincy that the family was gathered in her bed room to await the last moment, when a visitor was announced: namely, Elias Hicks. . . . After sitting some minutes with the family he said that he was pleased to feel the spirit of resignation to the Divine Will which prevailed, and that he felt free to say that he believed the sacrifice would not be required at this time. Better symptoms appeared promptly, the child recovered, became the mother of ten children, and died after a most exemplary useful life at the age of nearly 93 years."[5]

Hicks was neither prophetic nor especially kind in his consideration of the Orthodox. He wrote on 14 February 1825, a long letter jointly to William and Deborah Wharton and Sarah and Thomas Fisher in which he stated in part, "I understand that our Orthodox, or more fitly, our antedox friends keeps [*sic*] up their struggle for power, what strange creatures men are. I have compared some men to our no-horned Cattle, for altho they carry, no outward visible weapons of war, being destitute of Swords, and horns, yet they are possest of as strong & warlike spirit as those that have good stout hornes, and besides that, they are hard headed creatures having a very hard bunch of bone on their heads which they cover with a soft bunch of hair, to deceive, for it makes them look innocent, yet I have heard of their knocking down large horned bulls."[6]

William was probably too young and wealthy to be counted as one of the top spiritual lights moving the Hicksites toward separation. Eminence belonged rather to men such as John Comly, a school teacher from Byberry Township in Philadelphia County whom Hicksites had hoped would be chosen clerk of the Yearly Meeting, Jesse Kersey, an eloquent but poor minister from nearby Chester County, and several others.[7]

Still, William did what he could to aid the cause. His support was substantial. He was a member of the committee which composed the Green Street Address, the principal document setting forth the reasons for separation; and he helped to advertise the separation to Friends in other parts of the country. Later he busied himself with arrangements for dividing the property of Friends and in establishing meeting houses at Cherry Street north of Fifth and at Ninth and Spruce.

Williams' attitude was not greatly different from that of the other

Hicksites. He later wrote down the speech he made at the closing session of the Yearly Meeting. He pleaded for reconciliation, he said, for it was not to be expected that Friends would always see eye to eye; but all should love one another. Yet he could not restrain himself from an attack of a sort making reconciliation unlikely. "Oh the wickedness which men and women may practice under the cloak of religious zeal and concern. . . . How many of the dead does this spirit of intolerance sentence to eternal misery, who will shine as Stars in the firmament of our father forever. . . . And now my friends near the close of this meeting I desire that we may join heart and hand to expel from our Borders this hydra headed Monster of Bigotry & intolerance and conduct the remaining business which may come before us in a peaceable & becoming manner."[8]

The separation put the Philadelphia Hicksites on their own and drew them closer together. They, after all, were the secessionists; and they rejected an overture from the orthodox to return, suspecting that this would have meant a submission contrary to conscience. Comly had rationalized their position by saying that they had not created the division, but had found it: "I am advocating that friends separate from the Orthodox as a means of healing it."[9] But no amount of rationalization could save Hicksites from the consequences of their departure. They had to prove to themselves and others the rectitude of their action by worship, manner of living, and promotion of worthwhile projects.

Thus, those who had been nearest in sentiment became farthest apart in living. After 1827 in the Middle Atlantic States, Indiana, and Ohio two Quaker societies existed, each avoiding the other and having its own institutions, elites, and, eventually, traditions. For the Hicksites the old Quaker landmarks such as the Arch Street Meetinghouse and the Westtown School were out of bounds, as was the soon-to-be-founded Haverford School. Intermarriage was not much of a problem because the young people of each group did not associate with the youth of the other.

The separation lasted for over a century. Joseph Wharton lived with it all his life. It effectively closeted him off from Orthodox Quakers more than from any other sort of people. He could count among friends and business associates, besides Hicksites, Episcopalians, Methodists, Presbyterians, Lutherans, Roman Catholics, Moravians, Unitarians, Jews, unbelievers, even a Mormon, a Swedenborgian, and Quakers who had fallen away in favor of some other religion or none. But few of his business associates and none of his close friends were Orthodox Quakers.

2

Deborah and William Wharton seemed to feel no traumatic effects from the separation. Hicks died in 1830. Even before that they avoided the name

"Hicksite" when talking with associates. As far as they were concerned, their communion was the Society of Friends; and Deborah and William busied themselves with its work. This involved meetings for worship, meetings for business, travel to quarterly and yearly meetings, a large correspondence, entertainment of visitors, and an enormous amount of committee work. A sample of committees of which Deborah and William were members includes those appointed to read and record marriage certificates; visit new members of the meeting; treat with delinquent members; "inquire into the cleanness from like engagements" of a member of another meeting about to marry a member of the Spruce Street Meeting; see that the rights of someone's children were secured "according to discipline"; "collect the cases of suffering that may have been sustained by our Members, in consequence of Military requisitions" (for the year 1834); aid the Indians of upper New York State; write a memorial against slavery; report on the status of education of children; oversee a primary school; and secure better qualified teachers.[10]

The Whartons were especially interested in education and were almost always assigned to committees dealing with the subject. They worked with others to have the city provide free public education for blacks and eventually were successful. William, wrote Deborah, "had that school under his special care for a number of years." He was also for a time a member of the corporation having charge of the schools established by William Penn. He was one of the first directors of the public schools in Philadelphia and served for twenty years as a school director.[11]

The house on Spruce Street was the principal abode. It was a typical eighteenth-century brick structure and adjoined a dwelling, now Number 338, in which Joseph Hopkinson composed the song, "Hail Columbia". Number 336 stood (and still stands) close to the northwest corner of what had been the old Almshouse Square. About the time of the Revolution the square had been broken up for dwellings. The house of the Whartons had a trellis for vines on the east side reaching to the roof. It was sufficiently large for a family of ten children and was often overcrowded with guests, especially at the time of Yearly Meeting, when Deborah and William worked hard to provide beds for out-of-town visitors.[12]

In 1834 Charles Wharton, then ninety years of age, gave William the family estate in the country, saying, "Billy, here are the keys of Bellevue and I want thee to go there with thy family and enjoy it, for I shall never go there again." "And truly we did enjoy it, young and old," wrote Deborah.[13] They passed most of their summers in the big stone house set among willows and giant oaks with whitewashed boles.

Bellevue lay about a quarter of a mile from the Schuylkill. It was reached by driving along the Ridge Road, then turning east on Nicetown Lane. Gardens and trees supplied flowers, vegetables, and fresh fruit. Cows grazed in the meadows; hired laborers tilled the fields and kept house, barn, and sheds in repair. Several servants assisted at housekeeping. A few blacks were hired from time to time, but most of the servants were Irish. The principal one was Margaret McGinley, a sturdy, capable, and motherly woman who remained with the Whartons for most of her adult life and died in their service. She managed the other servants and helped keep the children in order so that William and Deborah might go about their ministrations.[14]

While the children were still young Deborah and William saw the passing of the older generation. Deborah's mother Hannah had died shortly after the birth of her namesake. Samuel Rowland Fisher peacefully departed life in 1834. Charles Wharton, although enfeebled and suffering from loss of memory, kept to his old style of living to the end, and died in 1838. By that time the once great shipping houses of the Fishers and the Whartons had become memories. Deborah and William did not mourn their disappearance.

As parents William and Deborah were attentive, understanding, and gentle. Wrote daughter Esther, "Wise, kind, & tenderly affectionate, were the mother & father, indulgent as seemed to them proper, and most gently reproving, when reproof was necessary. Few harsh words were heard."[15] Spankings, if used at all, were rare. The parents taught by appeals to reason and by admonition and when these failed, punished by depriving children of simple pleasures. Their rule was never arbitrary. They saw to it that proper ways of doing things were known and regularly observed. Departures from the accepted ways were possible, but had to be justified. The elder children helped to care for the younger and were made to feel responsible for this.

Most pleasures were taken *en famille*, although visitors who chanced to be present were welcome to participate if they chose to do so. An activity of especial use to a biographer was that of writing letters. Postage in those days was expensive and delivery uncertain. Nevertheless, Deborah kept friendships alive with constant correspondence; and she taught her children to do likewise. Sometimes when the house was full of company she would write while others in the same room conversed. She aimed not so much at conveying news as "to show remembrance and love to the person addressed."[16] On evenings when members of the family gathered together Deborah or one of the daughters might get out an old letter considered especially informative or inspirational and read it aloud. After the children began to leave home, letters received from the departed were regularly circulated among those remaining.

The family was affectionate and closely knit. The children were normally robust, healthy, and handsome. Several, including Joseph, inherited Deborah's nearsightedness. They were regularly exposed to whatever illnesses were making the rounds; yet none except Joseph's youngest brother Samuel Fisher suffered permanent damage therefrom. Samuel Fisher died of an unrecorded illness or affliction in the winter of 1843 at the age of eleven. The rest lived to maturity, although not all to old age.

Several of the elder children made especial impressions on Joseph. Hannah and Rodman helped to raise him. They early followed the example set by William and Deborah in becoming active in the affairs of the Society of Friends and remained involved throughout their lives. Both had a common-sense approach to life and showed a large affection for Joseph, which he returned.

Sarah and Charles, the next eldest, were as different from Rodman and Hannah as from one another. Sarah was inclined to make acquaintances outside of the Society. She was the first of the children to be married and chose for a partner Abraham Barker, a banker, son of Jacob Barker, merchant, banker, and chief financier of the War of 1812. Jacob was at the time of the wedding living in New Orleans, being there engaged in various commercial ventures and attempting to raise sugarcane with the use of freed blacks.[17] He had earlier left the Society of Friends, and his son was not a member. Rodman and Charles violated the discipline of the Society by attending the ceremony and acknowledged their fault in writing to the Spruce Street Meeting. Sarah was at her request continued as a member of the Society.[18]

Charles, like Sarah, was little inclined to be active in the work of the Society, to which, however, he gave a lifelong loyalty. Charles was Joseph's closest companion. The two boys played together and attended some of the same schools. Charles was carefree. Attempts to infuse his thoughts and habits with discipline did not succeed. He would climb the trellis to the second-story window of the Spruce Street house, spend his pocket money freely, and procrastinate in doing his lessons. Charles grew to be the sort of person almost everybody likes but chooses not to confide in.

Joseph's correspondence contains far fewer references to his younger brothers and sisters. He was an idol for William, who was four years younger than Joseph. Mary, Esther, and Anna also admired Joseph. Mary's letters show a sensitivity to the passions, especially love, in which she reached a depth of feeling which Joseph could never appreciate. Esther, like Hannah, was sensible, forthright in giving opinions, and active within the Society. Anna, the youngest but one, was probably the most beautiful of the daughters.[19] She was the only one of the children surviving to adulthood who did not marry. She died of tuberculosis in 1863.

Joseph's early education occurred within the family and at various day and boarding schools maintained by members of the Society. At the ages of five, six, and seven (1831–33) he attended a school run by a person named Bowen. When he was eight and possibly nine years of age (1833–35) the master of his school was Thomas Conard. In the summers of 1834 and 1835 Joseph and Charles attended a boarding school on the Byberry and Bensalem Turnpike in Byberry Township operated by Henry Pike. When Joseph was nine his schoolmaster was named Griscom. At the ages of ten and eleven (1836–37) Joseph was back in Conard's school.[20]

In these establishments Joseph studied the subjects which Hicksite Quakers considered sufficient for formal education, namely, English grammar, reading, composition, arithmetic, and geography. He learned no Latin and Greek, such as he would have needed to qualify for entrance into most colleges, for the large majority of Hicksites considered these subjects and higher education as unsuitable and even undesirable.

In the measure that Joseph submitted to the instruction of these masters, his education was conventional and similar to that received by his brothers and sisters. But even a cursory reading of family letters written in the early 1840s suggests that they gained much knowledge outside of the schools. The play of their imaginations indicates widespread reading in the library of the parents, which was well supplied with most categories of science, history, and literature except fiction. Their facility in writing gives evidence of extensive supervised practice. Although music was forbidden, painting and drawing were allowed. Joseph became skilled at drawing. Possibly he and his brothers and sisters had tutors for such subjects. Sometime, too, he learned to sculpt, an accomplishment which might have been entirely forgotten if he had not in 1861 sent to Professor George J. Brush at Yale College "an electrotype copy of likeness of my parents which I cut in stone." When Brush praised the work, Joseph modestly replied that he no longer "sculpt." "The few things which I did in my youth were long ago given away."[21]

Joseph showed a proficiency in the arts and letters which occasioned William and Deborah to provide him with a somewhat greater measure of formal schooling than that offered to the other children. In the years from 1837 to 1840 he attended a private school headed by Frederick Augustus Eustis. Following this he came under the instruction of a Harvard graduate and Unitarian preacher named Wister. The Unitarian views concerning theology and moral philosophy were probably closer to the Hicksite persuasion than were those of any other denomination, except the Orthodox Quakers. Wister had ten or a dozen pupils and gave them the sort of instruction which would prepare them for college. Joseph studied among other things Latin and possibly some Greek, French, and German. He wrote later of Wister, "The two years spent under his kindly guidance were of great use to me, and a regard, which I am pleased to know from later intercourse was mutual, arose from this relation of instructor and student."[22]

The period of tutoring under Wister gave rise to an assertion that Deborah and William were preparing Joseph for college. Joseph himself in old age said as much. But nothing in the correspondence of the 1840s substantiates the assertion. It appears to have been an afterthought made some fifty years later, when Quaker attitudes toward higher education had changed. To be sure, William and Deborah placed a greater value on education than did most other Hicksites, but their valuation did not extend to encouraging young Joseph to go to a college or a university. Possibly they saw this as an option; certainly they did not promote it. None of the Wharton clan attended any institution of higher education, nor was there ever any question of them doing so.

Joseph Wharton's education in schools ended in 1842. He could and did receive formal training in after years by means of tutors, institutes, and chemical laboratories. Such opportunities were plentiful in Philadelphia. But when he left Wister's school the immediate and pressing question concerned the occupation which was to be his for life.

3

What was it to be? The answer was farming, the preferred occupation of Hicksite Quakers. Why? Possibly Joseph only wanted to do something different from what Rodman and Charles were doing. Rodman had come of age in 1841 and bought his way into partnership in the business of making white lead. Charles was getting started in the merchandising of china and related products. A boy with a lively imagination and an urge to be his own master and do something special, such as Joseph showed throughout his life, could not be content with mimicking the choices of his brothers. Farming was acceptable; he liked being out of doors; and his parents encouraged him. Farming suited his circumstances, and he took it up without much thought. He was so little concerned with justifying the choice that he never wrote out the reasons for others to see and preserve.

Here, as with schooling, a myth later developed to the effect that he went to the farm to recover his health. On one occasion Joseph himself wrote that he was "taken from school and sent to learn farming."[23] This belated rationale expressed a feeling of guilt for not having attended college. It is a response to a question, "Why did you take to farming instead of going to the university?"—a question which neither he nor his parents would at the time have thought to ask. In fact, his health was reasonably good. He had grown tall faster than he had filled out, which is a common feature of adolescence; and he was pale from spending the winter indoors. But he was suffering from no serious illnesses, broken bones, nervous breakdown, or anything of the sort. Although his mother frequently worried about his physical state, hers was only a normal concern for a boy who tended to neglect wraps in wet weather, medicine when sick, and proper food when not supervised.

Nor was Joseph "sent" to learn farming. That was not Deborah's and William's way. They counseled in such matters; they did not command. William wrote to his son, "In fact I thought it would invigorate thy constitution and long thy life, while as a concerned parent for the religious welfare of his son I was inclined to hope thy residence in the country would keep thee out of harms way, and away from many very dangerous temptations." Deborah agreed with her husband, although with less warmth. "It has always been a tryal for me to be separated from any of my dear children."[24]

Joseph undoubtedly found the approval of others gratifying. "Thy choice of a *calling* is approved by many," wrote his mother, who noted that a relative, William Rotch, also approved of his "choice" of being a farmer, calling it the "*most honorable* employment of all." Charles wrote an approval in his inimitable way: "I suppose we shall here [*sic*] of thy cutting loose pretty soon with some nice little country lass go it Joe while young The more I see of the City I am convinced that thee has made the true choice and if I could with civility and advantage I would yet turn but I am what I must be a china monkey."[25]

The decision in favor of farming having been made, William and Deborah had little trouble in selecting a suitable place for Joseph. They had friends in East Fallowfield Township, Chester County, named Joseph S. and Abigail Walton, who were active in affairs of the Society as well as being farmer and farmer's wife. The Waltons had a son, George, two and a half years older than Joseph, and two daughters, Lydia, born eleven days after Joseph, and Margaretta, three and a half years his junior. An unmarried sister of Abigail, Margaret Mann, lived with them. So, too, did an almshouse boy several years younger than Joseph named John Freal, as well as Jesse Kersey, whose wife had died. What better environment could there be for a young son of William and Deborah Wharton? They arranged to pay for his board, knowing that his initial contribution to the work of the farm would be slight.[26]

Joseph S. Walton was a mild-mannered, hard-working man of some education and considerable native intelligence. He and Abigail had moved inland from Byberry Township and in 1834 had bought a farm adjoining the property of the Fallowfield Meeting House at a crossroads called Ercildoun. The village was situated about three miles south of Coatesville. Farms and woodlands covered the rolling landscape. Friends predominated in the sparsely populated countryside and almost all were Hicksites who at the time of the separation had taken over the meetinghouse. In the years that Joseph Wharton stayed at the Walton farm the Fallowfield Meeting had approximately one hundred and fifty members. Some of these were ardent abolitionists. Joseph S. Walton and his family were not among these, although they abhorred slavery. Ercildoun became well known as a station on the Underground Railroad. Escaping slaves would come on foot or in wagons, singly on in groups. Friends would house and feed and if necessary clothe and arm them and send them to Downingtown or some other station on the route to Canada. Gideon Peirce, farmer, postmaster, co-elder with the Waltons, and general factotum of Ercildoun, was one of the chief operators of the station. Young Joseph came to know Gideon and members of his family and saw at first hand some of their work with the Railroad.[27]

Ercildoun was the final destination of Joseph Wharton on a day in the third week of June 1842. The trip from Philadelphia was an adventure in itself, as it involved traveling over Pennsylvania's first passenger railroad, the Philadelphia and Columbia. It may have been Joseph's first journey in "the cars," as passenger trains were then referred to. He found the trip exciting. Many years later, speaking before an audience, he recalled the arrangement at the start. The cars, he said, "were dragged by horses or mules from the corner of 11 & Market Sts., where Bingham House now stands, out to the foot of the inclined plane west of the Schuylkill River, were hauled to the top of the plane by a stationary engine and from there were taken by locomotives to the Susquehanna River."[28] The cars traveled a route which, years after the Philadelphia and Columbia had become part of the Pennsylvania system, became known as the Main Line. Joseph wrote of his trip on the cars to his sister Hannah, "The cars travelled faster than anything I have ever been in through a beautiful country. In the cornfields the straggling plants gathering up into regular rows at our approach was (dem'd fine)."[29]

From the time he reached the Walton farm and for the remainder of the year Joseph expressed unqualified enthusiasm for his situation. His letters contain no hint of homesickness. He enjoyed the sensation of being of the Wharton family but not in it and took delight in personalities, scenes, and occupations—all so different from what he had been accustomed to, even in the relatively primitive rural setting of Bellevue.

Joseph's first long letter was to Hannah, as his parents were attending a meeting at Fishing Creek in the northern coal regions. His hands and feet were blistered, he wrote, and his mother had put enough clothes in his trunk to furnish half of Fallowfield.

> We rise here at or before 4 o'clock and go to bed between 9 and 10. We have breakfast at 5, dinner at 12, and supper at 6. . . . Joseph's family consists of himself and wife, their son George aged 19 or 20, two daughters Lydia and Margaretta ages unknown (Lydia may be about 16 or 17 (most too old) and Margaretta 12 or 13, this is a mere guess), Margaret Mann, a little boy 12 years old named John Fraley or Faraday or some such name, Jesse Kersey who is here on a visit and Mister Joseph Wharton Equire, besides 18 pigs, 4 horses one of them a mare, 4 cows and a yoke of oxen. Our meals out here are much better than I expected, plenty to eat besides salt pork though they generally have it, as well as pie, on table three times a day. I drink about 2 quarts of milk a day and eat more than I did in town but that sinks into nothing compared with the feats of voracity which are every day displayed here.[30]

The family worked sixteen hours daily during the planting and harvest seasons but rested on first day unless weather conditions made labor necessary to save crops.

Joseph continued a description of farm life in a letter posted to his parents a week later:

> We have been busy making hay and hoe-harrowing the corn. Yesterday I took my first lesson in mowing by going around the fields with a scythe to cut off the weeds and bushes which was rather tiresome. . . . I have

already worn out a pair of boots. . . . I attended meeting last first and fifth days but not to-day as I have a slight bowel complaint which I think will be gone by tomorrow on account of the cholera mixture I have taken. Joseph Walton's hay is all in except one field of six acres that we expect to haul in tomorrow if it is a good day and some of his wheat is ready to cut. I have not had much time here to read, write, or draw: in the day we are too busy and in the evening too tired. . . . Jesse Kersey is well and more active than I expected. He went fishing yesterday and caught several catfish and he walks about the place a great deal.

The following week Joseph reported to his mother that the Waltons had put in twenty-seven loads of hay:

In the middle of the week the men were cradling wheat and on the 6th day we got several loads of it in, on 7th day they cut a little more wheat but could not keep at it steadily on account of the weather. . . . Since I came here I have learned to mow a little, to chop wood, to rake and bind wheat into sheaves, and to reap it with a sickle; this last acquirement cost me dearer than any of the others as I cut my left hand twice, the first time I cut the end of my thumb nearly off, and the second bared the bone of my little finger. The edge of a sickle is full of little teeth like a saw, which makes a cut with it much more painful than with a knife. Both cuts are now healing. Jesse Kersey went from here this afternoon to his grand-childrens' in Bradford Township. He attended Fallowfield meeting this morning, but did not speak. . . . John Freal (a little boy about 12 or 13 years old) and myself work together at everything, his superior practice makes up for the disparity of our strength and makes us about equally efficient. We feed the hogs, drive the cows in and out of the fields, catch the horses when they are wanted, take drink to the men working and help with the harvest, and when none of these things are to be done Joseph always finds something to keep us at work. Joseph's farm is I think kept better than any in the neighborhood and is about as good land as any. I like the way of living out here, perhaps it is only for the variety, but I think at present that I will continue to like it.[31]

Joseph's letters home during the remainder of that first summer on the farm continued to reflect a fascination for changing tasks as the seasons progressed. "We have been very busy today killing pigs and chickens and doing one thing or another," he wrote in mid-August. Later in the same month he sent a pair of hawk's claws to his brother William. On September 11 he wrote to his mother, "We began to cut corn last 4th day—and on 6th day we sowed 8 acres of wheat and harrowed it in. We have still about 4 acres to sow in the upper part of the cornfield but that cannot be done for about a week or two yet as the corn (which is not yet quite ripe in that part of the field) has to be cut and hauled away, and the ground manured and ploughed before the wheat is sown there." In October he complained of his hands being sore and cracked as a result of husking corn. On the thirtieth of the month he reported the arrival of the threshing machine. Two weeks later he noted the last five hogs were to be killed the next morning, and in the afternoon the men would begin to haul four hundred bushels of lime. By the Twentieth of November the threshing had been completed and an inch of snow had fallen. Ten days later the farm work for the year was over, and Joseph reported that George had left for London Grove to attend school there during the winter months.[32]

In several letters during the first summer on the farm Joseph cautiously reported concerning activities of the Underground Railroad. "Sixteen black men passed through here last week on their way to Canada, all well dressed and I believe also well armed." "The *blackbirds* continue to pass through here in large numbers every few days, sometimes a dozen or more in a band. I have heard that the reason of their unusual success this season is the pecuniary embarrassment of their masters many of whom, conscious that they must soon be sold out and their whole effects go towards paying their creditors, do not take the same pains to prevent the escape of the slaves or in pursuing them when they had effected it. One young woman came here by herself not long ago. She had travelled, alone I believe, the whole distance."[33]

With the departure of George for London Grove and the ending of outdoor work for the season Joseph found time beginning to drag. He foresaw the possibility of several months of being snowbound in the company of persons with whom he had no intellectual companionship and for whom he had little emotional attachment. "I do not care much about being out here in the winter," he wrote.[34] Perhaps he realized that his parents would sympathize, that his mother especially wished him back within the family circle. Sometime shortly after 11 December he returned to 130 Spruce Street and remained there for slighly more than three months.

4

The members of the family did not neglect Joseph in his absence from Philadelphia. He received letters from them all; but the one who wrote regularly was his mother. Deborah was determined that her children should feel their membership in the family wherever they might be. "The cords of love which bind thee to thy mother's heart I believe cannot be broken," she wrote Joseph. "On the contrary may they grow stronger and stronger is my desire, and this will be the case if we follow after that which is good, for nothing but wrong doing weakens them."[35]

She was especially attracted to Joseph, who of all the children was most like her. His strong will, keenness of intellect, power of concentration, energy, willingness to work, disposition to lecture others, and tendency to express life in terms of a few simple, philosophic themes reflected qualities found in her. Margaret Mann, writing to Deborah at the beginning of Joseph's second year on the farm, observed, "He is so calm, and so gentle in disposition that I often see in him the . . . image of his Mother."[36]

Deborah regularly lectured Joseph on spiritual and physical welfare. "I shall think often and much of thee, and my most ardent desire for thee is, that thou mayst so demean thyself that thy Heavenly Father may be felt by thee to be thy friend. If he is on our side, who can make us afraid?" "And thou Solomon my son know thou the God of thy father, serve him with a perfect heart and with a willing mind." "Thy willingness to be doing something useful was gratifying. I never could see any pleasure in idleness. Indeed the retrospect of idle hours was always painful. We may be doing good in some way all our lives, 'if not for ourselves, for a neighbor.' " She cautioned him to regard his health. He was always to dress warmly; not to put his head out of the window of cars; not to get into the front car or sit over an axle; not to eat too much fruit; not to ride a horse to Philadelphia. She sent him ice skates which he requested but "with regret," because she wished he would give up the "*dangerous sport* of ice skating."[37]

Sometimes Joseph teased her by reporting happenings which he knew would worry her. He wrote in detail of his trek from Coatesville to Ercildoun at the beginning of the second year on the farm. Because of mud and snow on the road he had balanced himself walking on top of a fence. To this, Deborah replied, "It is dangerous for creatures who have no wings to attempt aerial passages. I hope thee wilt never have the temptation to try the fence again."[38] His teasing was always innocent, never such as to cause her any real alarm.

His second year on the farm was uneventful. The correspondence shows a continuing interest in rural life and an improvement of proficiency in performing farm work. He wrote somewhat more than formerly about the people with whom he lived, describing, for example, a trip he and George took to attend the Yearly Meeting in Philadelphia and of Joseph Walton's work with Indian affairs in upper New York State.[39] Charles visited the farm during a slack period between harvesting of early and late summer crops. At home, in the beginning of the year Joseph's brother Samuel Fisher died and his sister Sarah married Abraham Barker; and late in the year Sarah had her first child. "Sally is a mother, and thyself an uncle," wrote Deborah, "and of course among the new appellations I take that of Grand-mother—venerable indeed is the sound."[40] These events made no visibly great impression on Joseph. Still, as the year drew to a close he eagerly anticipated a winter vacation at home and laid plans to study French, which in fact he did.[41]

By the time he returned to the Waltons in the early spring of the third year his interest in farming had begun to wane. He was now eighteen years of age and maturing fast. Undoubtedly during the winter he had renewed acquaintances with school chums who were now, like Charles and Rodman, going into business or manufacturing and had listened to their talk of exciting chances for service and also for making a fortune. Farming was enjoyable in a way, and he took pride in his improving skill. "I will almost 'make a hand' through harvest this year," he wrote to his mother.[42] But farming was no longer able to fill the variety of activities which he craved; and he missed the company of boys and girls educated to city ways.

He was restless rather than restive. In the course of the summer he and a cousin, Bill Hollingsworth, exchanged several letters written in French. When Joseph's father and Rodman commissioned him to buy a horse he showed a zest for the business similar to that which he had displayed for farming in his first year with the Waltons. He relished receiving from his mother and younger brother William detailed accounts of the anti-Irish, anti-Catholic riots of May, which had occurred near the Spruce Street house. In June he found diversion in a diet free of salt, meat, and milk. This adventure jarred the members of his family into a prompt show of displeasure. His mother lectured him at length, ending with, "Indeed if the present system is pursued I shall think thee stands in need of guardianship." Charles and Rodman acted the roles of reproving elder brothers. "There is one thing blessed certain that we will have to throw thy system of living to the chickens when we get hold of thee and we don't own half starved Sinners in these parts," wrote Charles. Rodman adopted a mock legal stance: "Whereas we the assembled wisdom of the Wharton family, being in full and secret conclave met have Resolved that inasmuch" as Joseph Wharton is pursuing a vegetarian diet we will "cause all such teeth . . . to be skillfully extracted & thrown to the dogs. And *secondly* applaud and commend our said brother and friend Joseph Wharton for the strictness and propriety and self denial which he has exercised and displayed upon this solemn occasion."[43] Given Joseph's restless state of mind, these remarks were undoubtedly gratifying. He stopped the dietary experiment.

He wrote to his sister Mary during the August lull in farm work, "I do feel lonesome here sometimes, especially in the evening when there is nothing to do. At these times instead of taking a walk with thee to Abraham's or to the Wood's the last resource is to go out into the moonlight and sing 'Oft in the stilly night' or some other lively and reviving air. . . . I visit very little here except at Gideon Peirce's so on first day after I am tired of reading I am thrown on my own resources very often, and on rainy days it is the same— rather worse indeed."[44]

He capriciously complained to his mother of the rustic ways of the Waltons and their neighbors. "I have been reading Paul and Virginia which I find very interesting. It seems to be a great source of chagrin to all the family on these wet days that none of them can read it—they look into it and admire the pictures, but that is the 'ne plus ultra' of their ability and they lay it down again just as wise as when they took it up." The people in the neighborhood, he wrote, "are some of them coarse and rough and some, fanatic reformers and enthusiasts—neither of these are the ones to suit my fancy." He wrote of George Walton, "George proposes that he and I go together to Baltimore Y.M. next month but my answer is that Charley and I planned to go to Hartford Co. this fall and I must stick to that. The truth is that I don't think George would be a very desirable travelling companion."[45]

Yet Joseph had traveled without complaint with George the year before; and the inference that members of the Walton family were practically illiterate was little short of libelous. Joseph Walton and his children were well educated for the times. In his first year on the farm Joseph Wharton had read a book on agricultural chemistry which he had undoubtedly obtained from Joseph Walton. The book was *The Muck Manual for Farmers* by Samuel Luther Dana and may well have been the first book on chemistry which Joseph Wharton ever read. But the Waltons had a small library, consisting principally of books on religion such as were usually found in Quaker households. Very likely the only periodical to which they subscribed was the *Friends Intelligencer;* and they were disinclined to speculate on timely subjects which Joseph found exciting and which had no immediate connection with farming or Quakerism. What was lacking to Joseph was not the proximity of intelligent, educated, and mannerly people but companionship, such as is based on a community of interests. The Waltons and their neighbors had not changed from the time when he first found and enjoyed them. He had grown apart and felt the tug of interests which no place as small and isolated as Ercildoun could satisfy.

Still, as long as he remained in the country he did not give up the idea of being a farmer. He only proposed to his mother that he change farms for the next year. He wrote to her that he had talked with Clement Biddle, a friend of the family who farmed in Birmingham Township near West Chester, and ascertained that Clement might need another hand for the 1845 season. "I shall probably see a rather different system of farming at Biddle's if I get there."[46]

Go to Biddle's? The proposal has the pathetic aspect of a man trying to warm his hands at a dying fire. The proposal had no real chance of being acted upon. Several members of the family, especially Rodman, recognized that Joseph had been mistaken in his choice of an occupation. In late September Rodman wrote to urge Joseph from continuing further on the farm: "If therefore thy disposition to be a farmer still continues, I should think it a very unwise step for thee to leave it." Then he added, "With a small probability of loss in the Country, there is scarcely a chance of anything beyond a mean living, with comparatively small anxieties, as small a field of usefulness. Any one for instance by ordinary care may become a good plowman, but anyone cannot fill with propriety many as advantageous a station open to thy choice." Rodman pointed out that he was losing an assistant and was at the same time considering branching out from making white lead to include other things.[47]

Deborah and William concurred with Rodman, differing from him only in putting greater emphasis on the desirability that Joseph should make up his own mind. Wrote William, "Rodman inclines to favor thy undertaking some other employment more lucrative—and I do not feel like dissuading thee from thy choice." Make a "*deliberate* and not *precipitate* decision."[48]

The precise time at which Joseph made his decision is unknown, but when he left the Waltons in December his career as a farmer was ended.

3

A New Beginning

Did he rejoice in his freedom from the farm? Probably not, for he had liked the life. He was not one of those youths who were seeking to escape what seemed to be a continuous, monotonous round of hard work and poverty. There were thousands of these who came from the hinterlands to staff the new manufactories which were springing up in villages and cities. These young men and women sometimes clashed there with immigrants from Europe. Together the old and new Americans provided brains and muscle that their descendants might be prosperous. An industrial revolution was under way and was, within the lifetime of youths such as Joseph Wharton, to make of Americans a wealthy people and of the United States a world power.

Philadelphia was one of the centers of this revolution. The old port city laid out by William Penn with its cobblestone streets, brick houses, brick sidewalks, and decorous, neatly dressed inhabitants had become ringed by industrial suburbs with their noise and smoke, rutted lanes, crowded frame and brick buildings, and restless peoples: Moyamensing, Southwark, Kensington, Port Richmond, and other places up and down the Schuylkill and the Delaware. Here manufactories received raw materials coming in along rivers and canals and, somewhat later, railroads, and sent textiles, chemicals, leather goods, and machinery to all parts of the world.

The industrializing of New York City and Baltimore differed only slightly from that of Philadelphia. These were coincidentally the places in which the Hicksite revolt had occurred and from whence it had spread westward. In these cities lived the most influential Hicksite Quakers, doing business and often amassing wealth as they moved into positions of leadership in banking, business, and industry. Thus was the Hicksite drift in favor of farming and the simple life turned back. The new city with its factories, banks, railroads—and problems—was to make demands on prosperous Hicksites for education, governmental services, business transactions, and social accomplishments which denied the values preached by Elias Hicks, Jesse Kersey, and their brethren. The old values would be heard of less often as a new class of urban ministers and elders adjusted to novel modes of conduct on which the discipline was silent.

1

Joseph Wharton's return to Philadelphia was symbolic of what was happening in the world of the Hicksite Quakers. In a sense he represented their failure to sustain the rural ideal of an earlier generation. His retreat from farming in no way embarrassed or hampered him in personal growth or membership within the Society. His parents made no objection to him or his brothers engaging in manufacturing or commerce. Their fears were more for the moral purity of the children and represented a parental concern which transcends historic periods. Later, Joseph may have faced some problems in adjusting his conduct as an industrial pioneer to his Hicksite conscience. But in the 1840s he was not concerned with matters of this sort, however much wiser heads might have anticipated them.

Joseph had only within the previous year become physically mature. A little over six feet tall, weighing about 145 pounds, straight in posture, quick of movement, strong in arms and legs—he had the sort of physique necessary for giving effect to intelligence and ambition. He disciplined his body by exercise, regular hours of work and sleep, and diet so as to remain as much as possible in perfect health. He was also good company for men who enjoyed outdoor sports, excepting sports involving the use of firearms. He already hiked and swam well; and in the years after his return from the farm he learned to ride horseback, row, and sail. The sense of well-being which he achieved through the physical side of his nature is amply demonstrated by his willingness to impart the messages of health and vigor to those closest to him in love, whether they asked for the advice or not.

He derived satisfaction from being again among friends and relatives. He could now consolidate his powers for work in some direction other than farming. Rodman provided guidance and inspiration.

Joseph did not immediately enter his brother's employ as Rodman had suggested several months earlier. The brothers worked out another plan: Joseph lacked two years of his majority; when he attained the age of twenty-one he might enter into partnership with Rodman in the business of making white lead and other chemicals; until that time he ought to gain more experience in business methods in some larger establishment.

Accordingly, Joseph became an apprentice in the countinghouse of the Quaker mercantile and importing firm of Waln and Leaming. The firm was a partnership between Lewis and William Waln and their brother-in-law Jeremiah Fisher Leaming. Theirs was a busy, prosperous establishment located in the old city, in sight of the tall masts of sailing vessels which entered and left the port almost daily. At Waln and Leaming's Joseph learned methods of bookkeeping and accounting. Before the end of his two years he became head bookkeeper in charge of about eight hundred accounts. He asked to go into sales, thinking thereby to extend his experience into other fields, but his success in the countinghouse was such that the Walns discouraged him.[1]

This check probably made little difference to Joseph, as he was gaining auxiliary training of other sorts. As an apprentice Joseph was unpaid and received a monthly allowance from his father. The sums ranged from four to fifty dollars, an irregularity suggesting payment for duties performed. Such was apparently the case, for the correspondence shows that Joseph was beginning in a small way to help Rodman in management of a sort which provided a model for the Wharton business empire of later years.[2]

2

The family estates consisted of property inherited from relatives, mostly the two grandfathers. Charles Wharton and Samuel Rowland Fisher had extensively speculated in land in and about Philadelphia and in farther away places in Pennsylvania and New York. Charles Wharton had provided for the division of his holdings among William and the other children. Samuel Rowland Fisher had died intestate; his properties were parceled out between Deborah and her brother Thomas. Legal title was thus variously vested in William and Deborah; and a few properties were jointly held by one or the other with relatives outside of the immediate family.

Most of the properties consisted of land, although there were a few holdings of stock in canal, bridge, and turnpike companies, for example, the Falls Bridge Company, The Schuylkill Navigation Company, the Belmont and Eastern Turnpike Road, and the Conshecton and Great Bend Turnpike Road.[3] Most of the Philadelphia lands lay within the original city and consisted of unimproved and improved lots and ground rents, that is, income-producing privileges reserved from sales of lots. The upstate Pennsylvania and New York properties were scattered, varied, and in part unexplored. A farm called Fairfield of a little more than 186 acres bordering the Allegheny River contained beds of coal and salt. These had been leased on occasion to private parties. The deposits of salt and coal had never been adequately surveyed. Another farm, called Craig Valley or Bear Gap, consisted of slightly more than 296 acres located along Roaring Creek in the anthracite region near the Susquehanna. The Bear Gap farm contained water power of undetermined value. Other farms and forested areas, some with known or suspected resources of timber, water power, coal, and iron, lay in Indiana, Greene, Pike, Carbon, and Northampton counties of Pennsylvania and in Broome and Otsego counties in New York.

Whatever the legal title of these estates might be, the members of the family considered their management to be the unique concern of William; and he was supposed to use them in such manner as to provide for the financial needs of himself, Deborah, and the children. In sum, the estates collectively comprised a family property which was the basis of a household economy such as might have met the approval of Aristotle and a long line of thinkers from his time to that of the Quaker merchants of the eighteenth century.

Indeed, a model for William Wharton existed in the way in which Deborah's grandfather, Joshua Fisher, had conducted his shipping trade. Joshua had owned the business and had acted as banker and underwriter for his sons. As the sons grew older they had purchased property in their own names or begun businesses with loans from Joshua and thus gained independent estates. The tax rolls of the province for 1774 indicate Joshua's dominance. By that time all of the sons were well established. Yet Joshua had held the property. He paid in taxes £325.7.4, whereas Thomas paid only £4.0.0 and Samuel Rowland nothing; and the names of the other sons—Miers and Jabez Maud—did not appear.

Household economies of this sort were the rule before banks, insurance companies, and other institutions for financing projects and socializing risk became widespread. A household economy operated on the basis of paternal control, mutual trust, and preferment for members of the family over others. The father judged the needs of his dependents according to family traditions concerning the proper portions to be allotted to wife, sons, daughters, the elder and the younger, and so forth. The only realistic remedy against paternal abuse of this power was that of leaving and striking out on one's own. Contracts and other legal paper, excepting sometimes a last will and testament, were generally not used. Promises to pay involving only members of the family could be and often were altered to alleviate the distress of a borrower facing a run of bad luck. Merit, as evidenced for example by an unusually gifted younger daugher, was expected to give way before status in the receipt of benefits, unless the members of the family voluntarily agreed to sacrifice some of their rights to the advantage of the gifted person. As for employment in the family business, sons and other relatives were always to be preferred over outsiders; and in normal circumstances the elder sons were conceded to have prior rights over the younger as successors to the father in managing the family property.

The Wharton family economy conformed to this pattern with some modification in the scope of operations as the decade of the forties progressed. The books of William Wharton show that before 1845 the family fortune was occasionally providing banking services for Rodman; William's brother-in-law Thomas G. Hollingsworth; Sarah's husband Abraham Barker; the firm with which young Charles Wharton was associated, Wright and Wharton; and another concern called Elijah Davis and Company. After 1845 banking services were restricted to members of the immediate family and their spouses; and by the end of the decade William Wharton was sometimes using commercial banks to obtain cash needed for family use.

William's outlays to members of the family variously took the form of gifts, loans, or advances. These might consist of cash, land, mortgages, or other properties. William seems to have tried over the years to equalize gifts among his sons. Loans included charges of interest and had to be repaid, although the date of repayment was frequently unspecified. An advance was a charge against the estate of William Wharton. An advance carried no requirement of interest. When William died, the member of the family to whom an advance had been made would have that amount deducted from his inheritance.

Several transactions illustrate the application of gifts, loans, and advances. When Rodman came of age in 1841 he bought his way into partnership in the business of making white lead with an advance or loan of five thousand dollars from his father, a capital which by March 1842 had been increased to $9,433.88. When Charles attained his majority in 1844 William made him an advance of three thousand dollars in order to buy into partnership with Robert Wright; and two years later Charles obtained another advance of eight thousand five hundred dollars. At the time William died, Joseph had received advances to a total of $23,104.83 which, he noted, was "to be deducted from my share of his estate."[4]

The difference between a loan and an advance could be of considerable importance. Rodman died two years before his father, leaving a modest estate for the support of a wife and two children. Joseph, who became his father's executor, found that the grants William had made to Rodman exceeded Rodman's share of the estate. Were these grants loans or advances? If loans, said Joseph, they would have to be paid back with interest, which would impose a hardship on Rodman's wife and children. If advances, nothing would have to be paid back; for, assuming the assent of the other heirs, any advance in excess of Rodman's share could be considered as a gift. Joseph found that the entries in his father's books were ambiguous. No one could say whether William had intended the grants to Rodman to be loans or advances. Joseph solved the problem by recommending that they be considered as advances; and to this, the other heirs agreed.[5]

The decision shows the way in which this system of banking could be used to strengthen family ties. Another transaction also helps to indicate the range of possibilities. Deborah's brother Thomas proved to be an inept businessman and about the time of Samuel Rowland Fisher's death found himself heavily in debt. Rather than allow Thomas's inheritance to go to his creditors at depressed values, William Wharton bought the properties at prices sufficient to allow Thomas to pay his debts and retain a modest sum on which to live out the remainder of his days in genteel poverty, pursuing hobbies in science and mathematics.

In general the family fortune could serve as a financial cushion for members of the family who were hard pressed. It occupied a place which in the outside world was filled by putting up properties of various sorts as securities for loans. The sons might go into business for themselves or enter into partnerships with others; and the daughters might marry men who did this and thereby extend to their spouses the same benefits enjoyed by the brothers. Hard times never hit all members of the family at the same instant or to the same degree. If one was in need of cash, the family fortune was there to supply it; and if the coffers were low, money could be raised from the other members. Stocks, bonds, mortgages, notes, ground rents, parcels of land, and cash could be passed back and forth as needed. In this way finances could be largely kept within the family, and the welfare of each made to depend on that of all. Outsiders who did business with members of the family knew this and recognized that, however hard pressed a member was, his credit was always as good as the prosperity of his brothers and brothers-in-law.

The limit to these advantages was rather obviously set by the financial soundness of the family property itself. By the time Rodman entered into the business of making white lead, the Wharton family property was suffering from William's one-sided attention to religion. Wrote Deborah after her husband's death, "He scarcely took the needful care of the good things or possessions, such being very irksome to him."[6] In addition, since 1834 his health had begun to decline. He found traveling painful and at times, impossible. His estates were suffering from neglect and losing value at a time when the maturing of sons and daughters presented the family with its greatest need for income. William had lost money on stocks, suffered when fire destroyed insufficiently insured property, overlooked opportunities for building on vacant lots, lost property through failure to pay taxes, maintained an inadequate surveillance over tenants, and failed to collect rents on several remotely located farms. Some of the distant properties were unattended and others were in the hands of agents whom he rarely if ever saw. Possibly they cheated him: The books do not say.[7]

William became persuaded to allow his eldest son to manage the estates. Rodman worked from an office in the old Fisher house. The salary he received from his father—five hundred dollars a year, increased in 1848 to one thousand—would have gratified many a land agent and indicates the amount and difficulty of work. The correspondence of Rodman and the account books of William Wharton show some of his strategies and activities. He evaluated properties for their short and long range potentials for producing income. This often involved surveying, searching and correcting titles, and answering to controversies aroused by these activities among people who contested the Wharton family claims. He had to visit distant properties and put them under the care of reliable agents, with whom he had to keep in constant touch. Matters concerning boundaries and taxes put him in contact with local government authorities. He closely watched internal improvements, especially those involving railroads, which might enhance the value of his father's lands. For example, letters to an agent named Edward Shoemaker in the years 1846 and 1847 contain a running commentary on the financing and beginning of construction of the western portion of the Central Railroad, which eventually became part of the main line of the Pennsylvania system.[8] A possibility that a party of German immigrants might settle near some of his father's lands once led him to advertise their availability in a Pennsylvania-German publication, *Der Deutchen Democratin*.

With such information at his disposal Rodman made decisions concerning which lands were to be immediately sold and which were to be retained untenanted or to be rented, leased, improved, and so forth; and all such decisions inevitably led to others and to various dealings with tenants, lawyers, contractors, real estate men, government officials, and persons in various trades and professions.

Everything that Rodman did in connection with the family estates was subject to review by his father. William sometimes initiated action, but most of the time he followed his son's advice and allowed him a free hand. William and Deborah signed the necessary papers. Rodman sometimes found himself overworked, for he also had his white lead business to manage. He accordingly relieved his situation by employing Joseph as an assistant. At first Joseph was little more than an errand boy; he was not yet twenty-one and so could not be held legally responsible. But two months after Joseph attained his majority, Rodman's horse unexpectedly reared and fell over backward on its rider; and Rodman found himself confined to bed with a broken leg.[9] From that time on, Joseph was his brother's eyes, ears, and feet, traveling to inspect the properties along the Allegheny and Susquehanna and other places and performing services of many sorts. Under Rodman's tutelage Joseph began to receive the breadth of experience in business which he missed at the countinghouse of Waln and Leaming.

In this way Joseph began an apprenticeship which eventually resulted in his becoming successor to Rodman in managing the family property. Charles, who by virtue of being older had a prior claim to the position, willingly ceded his right to Joseph. Charles had little taste for business and had as early as 1845 assented to Joseph being Rodman's aide.[10]

The effect on Joseph of helping to manage the family property was profound. He lived too long in the atmosphere of the family economy not to be deeply influenced by it in dealing with others. Although he could not slavishly follow it and expect to succeed in the hard-fisted outside world, he could and did honor many of its rules. Elements of paternalism, a sense of service, beliefs in the importance of blood relationships and cooperation, and charity in the enforcement of contracts remained with him, sometimes to heighten but more often to diminish the impersonality and acquisitive spirit of an economy dominated by individualism, capitalism, and competition.

The effects appeared in another way. Fifty years later he found himself the owner of almost all of the assets of an industrial empire which he could manage much as William and Rodman had administered the family estates. It was, as it were, an artificial family of which Joseph was the head and the managers in charge of mines, fleets, farms, furnaces, and factories were the sons; and he could and did on his death leave this "family property" as an undivided whole to be administered by the oldest available male among his heirs.

3

Rodman was Joseph's early model as a businessman. The older brother had a business sense at least as keen as that of Joseph. An early death put a stop to a career which might have surpassed that of Joseph in the variety and importance of accomplishments. Rodman displayed qualities of persistence, industry, and imagination in establishing a manufactory in white lead which could conceivably have become the basis of a large industrial complex. Joseph found Rodman's spirit of enterprise a challenge to his own, in much the same way as the youngest brother, William, in time drew inspiration from Joseph in founding companies for making steam railroad and electric railway equipment.

Nothing in the surviving records tells of Rodman's education, apprenticeship, or early connections with the business community. Certainly he had an interest in chemistry and had learned enough of it to be accepted as a partner by Samuel F. Fisher and George T. Lewis, both of whom were slightly older than he and belonged to families long established in the chemical industry. Rodman needed no college education in order to learn how to manufacture chemicals. He had only to conform to the prevailing practice, which was that of learning on the job, reading in European journals and books, perhaps paying for instruction from one of the private laboratories owned and operated by a new breed of professionals, and supplementing all this by attending lectures at the Franklin Institute, with which the chemists were in one way or another connected.

The science of chemistry was still in its infancy. The periodic table of elements had not yet been developed. Chemical notation, so familiar to schoolchildren of later generations, was still being worked out. Most of the leaders in the new science were to be found in European universities, especially those in Germany. Within the United States formal instruction in chemistry usually occurred in connection with the study of pharmacy and medicine. Few schools or colleges as yet had chairs in the subject. The University of Pennsylvania was one of the exceptions—a not surprising situation, inasmuch as Philadelphia was foremost among American cities in promoting the science of chemistry and the manufacture of chemicals. Leading firms such as those of the Wetherills, the Lennigs, and the Lewises specialized in making white lead and a related line, including red lead, litharge, lead acetate, acetic acid, and perhaps other acids such as sulphuric and nitric.[11]

Even in Philadelphia the most readily available place for studying chemistry was not the university, but private laboratories. These were maintained by persons who had received advanced training at the universities of Marburg, Heidelberg, Berlin, Paris, or at a European institute or university of comparable excellence. The interests of the professional chemists ranged widely over subjects now classifiable under the headings of physical, organic, agricultural, and biochemistry; geology, mining, and metallurgy; physiology and medicine. They made studies under contract for a clientele including individuals, private firms, and government agencies, studies that might focus on almost any product for which there was a market, such as ores, metals, fertilizers, soap, paint, food products. In addition the chemists did independent research in the more basic aspects of their science. They lectured on their findings, notably at the Franklin Institute and before members of the American Philosophical Society, organizations enjoying an unquestioned leadership in promoting the useful arts and sciences in the Middle Atlantic states. They published papers in the journals of these organizations and, a few years later, in the *American Journal of Science*, founded by Benjamin Silliman at Yale. Some of them wrote books. Frequently, too, they accepted auxiliary positions in industry and sometimes became heads of mining or manufacturing concerns of their own.

These chemists gave instruction to paying students. A few of the laboratories had lecture halls for the purpose. Many persons whose names later became famous in the annals of American chemistry spent time in one of the Philadelphia laboratories, men such as Wolcott Gibbs of Harvard, Robert E. Rogers of the University of Virginia, J. Lawrence Smith of the University of Louisville and the Smithsonian, and Charles M. Wetherill of Lehigh.

The most noted of the laboratories was that of James Curtis Booth. He was a native of Philadelphia who had studied at the Rensselaer Polytechnic Institute and several famous laboratories in Germany at a time before the German universities recognized chemistry as a serious course of study. Booth returned to the United States in 1836, accepted a position as Professor of Applied Chemistry at the Franklin Institute, opened a laboratory, and soon became the most widely known chemist in the area. His special interests centered on the assaying and refining of ores and metals. In 1849 he became melter and refiner for the U.S. Mint in Philadelphia.

Another famous laboratory, established somewhat later than that of Booth, was operated by Frederick Augustus Genth. A native of Germany, Genth studied under Liebig at Giessen and took a doctorate at Marburg. He arrived in Philadelphia in 1848 and shortly thereafter opened his laboratory. He, like Booth, was especially interested in mineralogical and geological subjects.

Booth and Genth later contributed to the education of Joseph Wharton and to his work in nickel. In the 1840s Joseph had not yet come under their influence; and it is impossible to determine whether Rodman had formal instruction from Booth or other chemists. All that can be said is that Booth, Genth, and their colleagues maintained a level of excellence which persons engaged in the study of chemistry and in the chemical industries of the city felt obliged to meet.

In view of Philadelphia's preeminence in chemistry and the chemical industry, Rodman was leading to strength in deciding to make a career in the manufacture of white lead, then mostly used for making paint. The skilled labor and technical know-how were available. At the same time, he faced formidable competition from established firms.

He showed wisdom in his choice of partners. Rodman had business ability and access to capital. He needed expertise and got this from James F. Fisher and George T. Lewis, Hicksite Quakers like himself, both of whom were to become wealthy industrialists. The partners probably first operated at the Lewis family works on Pine between Fifteenth and Sixteenth streets; but in 1846 they decided to build a factory on Gunne's Run in Port Richmond north of the city. Rodman supplied money for this with a loan or advance from his father. The partners named the factory the Aramingo Works. It was small, employing from six to a dozen workers, but profitable. Rodman had extensively traveled in connection with sales, and the firm had customers from the New England states to Maryland.

Beginning in 1845 Joseph ran errands for Rodman in the business of making white lead in addition to helping with the management of the family estates. Then in 1847, by prearrangement with all concerned, Rodman terminated the partnership with Fisher and Lewis and entered into business with Joseph. The firm was called R. Wharton and Brother. The effective date of the new partnership was 4 March 1847, the day after Joseph's twenty-first birthday, although the new arrangement had actually begun at least a month earlier: The first item in the account of R. Wharton and Brother is dated 2 February.

According to the terms of the partnership, the firm was to rent the Aramingo Works from Rodman for three thousand dollars a year. Joseph contributed a capital of ten thousand dollars, which was used to buy the equity of Fisher and Lewis. Each of the brothers received an interest on his capital at an annual rate of 6 percent, with additional profits being divided on a basis of two-thirds to Rodman and one-third to Joseph.

By the time the partnership went into effect Joseph was working full time for Rodman. Two months later, following Rodman's accident, Joseph had to substitute for Rodman in the varied activities of the white lead business as well as in managing the family estates. The accident did not stop the progress of the business. While Rodman was still in bed he and Joseph laid plans for expansion. For that purpose they obtained capital from another member of the family, Hannah's husband Robert Haydock. On 1 September a new partnership was formed among the three. The firm's name was changed to that of Rodman and Joseph Wharton. Robert Haydock was a silent partner, contributing twenty thousand dollars and having neither responsibility for the debts of the firm nor power of managing its affairs. Each partner was to receive 6 percent a year on his investment with additional profits being divided among them in a proportion of one-half to Rodman and one-fourth each to Joseph and Robert.[12]

The new capital came in time to permit the brothers to take advantage of a novel opportunity which, if it paid off, might make them almost immediately wealthy. This involved the refining and marketing of cottonseed oil.

It was Joseph's first venture into the mysteries of chemical experiments.

4

The seed of the cotton boll had both enticed and puzzled a scattering of entrepreneurs for several generations. The seed was known to contain an oil which could be used for many of the same purposes as the products of the flax plant and the olive tree. A steady market for linseed and olive oil existed. Chemists had proved by laboratory experiments that the extracting and refining of cottonseed oil could be done. A large and cheap supply of the seed existed, especially after the surge in cotton production resulting from the invention of the gin. Farmers used the seed for fertilizer or allowed it to rot in the fields. The stage seemed set for beginning a new and profitable industry. The only remaining problem was how to produce marketable oil at a cost sufficiently low to undersell linseed and olive oil.[13]

Various attempts had been made in the southern states to solve the problem. One difficulty was that of decorticating the seed, that is, separating it from the cotton fibers which clung to it after ginning. In France this difficulty had been avoided by using Egyptian cotton, whose seed was clean. But the varieties grown in America lacked this feature. Another difficulty was that of extracting the oil. The kernels were hard and resisted attempts to take it out by simple processes of crushing, pressing, and filtering. No one in the United States had as yet been able to overcome these difficulties.

The venture of Rodman and Joseph Wharton in cottonseed oil began in the summer of 1847 when George T. Lewis approached the partners with a query. A chemist named Martin Hans Boyé had invented a new and cheap means of refining the oil. Lewis believed the process was feasible and had agreed with Boyé to promote it. Would Rodman and Joseph be interested in working on the problem of extracting the oil from the seed?

The proposal was attractive. Boyé was one of Philadelphia's leading scientists. Son of a Danish chemist, he had studied at the university and a polytechnic institute in his homeland and had arrived in the United States in time to help Booth establish his laboratory. Boyé had worked with Henry D. Rogers on the Geological Survey of Pennsylvania and published a number of scientific articles. He was by 1847 approaching the middle point of a distinguished career.

The details of his process are unknown, although Joseph Wharton later drew a rough sketch which provides a general idea. The sketch, entitled "apparatus for clarifying cotton seed oil," shows the crude oil being successively heated and filtered through three stacks containing bone black.[14] Boyé was said to have patented the process, but the U.S. Patent Office has no record of this. In all likelihood he intended to apply for a patent as soon as the work of Rodman and Joseph proved successful. By thus delaying an application he could keep the secret of his method from being pirated by competitors at least until his own business was established. This would explain Joseph's later activity in trying to sell Boyé's nonexistent "patent rights."

The Wharton brothers favorably responded to Lewis's inquiry, and an agreement was worked out. The Whartons would give their undivided attention to the project. They would provide space for experiments in the southern wing of the Aramingo Works and bear all the expense with the option of quitting at any time they found their attempt to be unsuccessful. If they succeeded, each party to the agreement would put up an equal sum of money to refine and market the oil on a large scale and would divide profits equally. Boyé would continue his experiments and give the Whartons whatever advice and information they asked for.

Work began in September and continued for about a year and a half. Joseph directed the project, which was carried on in addition to normal factory operations. For a time a man named J. Smith Lewis assisted Joseph.

The challenge which Joseph faced could, it seemed, be met in one of two ways. One way was through engineering and involved inventing machinery adapted to the peculiar properties of the seed of the cotton plant for decorticating, hulling, grinding, and filtering. A gentleman of Petersburg, Virginia, had eighteen years ealier tried this approach and failed. The other way, and apparently the one which had been tried more often, was that of chemically treating the seed, using existing mills such as those for grinding sugar cane or flax seed.

Joseph chose the chemical approach. For machinery he used bark and oil mills and in various ways treated the seed of Sea Island cotton grown in Georgia. An excerpt from his notes indicates some of his experiments in trying to remove the fibers:

No. 1. ¼ peck cotton seed weighing 18 oz. well stirred for 7 minutes with common commercial sulp. acid (Geisse's) was almost entirely cleaned of fuz, a little remaining only on the ends of the seed.

No. 2. The same quantity of seed well stirred for 21 minutes with the same quantity of the acid belonging to George [Lewis] & Rodman was imperfectly cleaned.

No. 3. The same quantity of seed well stirred for 10 minutes with 3½ oz. of Geisse's sulp. acid was imperfectly cleaned.

No. 4. 3 oz. seed well stirred for 15 minutes and afterwards standing 3

hours with excess of nitric acid (about 1½ oz.) was very little
affected.

No. 5. ¼ peck (18 oz.) seed well stirred for 15 minutes with mixture of 2
oz. sulp. acid & 2 oz. nitric acid and afterwards standing 3 hours
was very little affected.

Experiments made by Lewis to obtain a maximum of oil from the crushed
kernels were also chemical in nature, as a report of one of Lewis's attempts
indicates:

1st. 2 bush. were put under the chasers (without having been rolled) &
tempered with 2 quarts of water, the 1st quart, ½ hour after being
under, the 2d ¾ after—tempered 1¼ hours—results of 1st pressing
1½ galls.—the cakes of above, were broken & thrown under chasers a
quart of water put on, tempered 1¼ hours—yield 1½ galls. making
equal to 6 quarts to the bushel.

While conducting experiments such as these Joseph also worked on other
possibilities for reducing costs. He and Rodman persuaded a farmer to feed
cottonseed cake to cattle to determine if it would increase the milk the cows
gave and improve the quality of the beef. Although the experiments were
highly inconclusive, they tended to support both possibilities. Wrote Joseph,
"The cake meal yielded is about equal to the seed worked and after trial by
three milk men is counted worth ½ the value of flax seed cake."

As a result of his experiments Joseph estimated that the lowest possible
cost of producing one gallon of crude cottonseed oil was 60½ cents. This, he
noted, took into account resale of the bags used to transport the seed and
the value of cottonseed cake. Having obtained this estimate, he asked Boyé
for a figure representing the cost of refining one gallon of the oil. This was
the final test. If Boyé's estimate was sufficiently low, a bright future would
open up for the partners.

Boyé's figures were disappointing. He computed the costs of refining one
gallon of oil at 66.3 cents and 74⅔ cents, depending on the quality of oil
desired. That, together with Joseph's figure of 60½ cents for producing crude
oil, would have made the total cost between $1.26 ⅚ and $1.35 ⅙ per gallon.
This would have been for oil suitable for making excellent soap, but not of the
light color of good olive oil.

Joseph noted that the price of olive oil was $1.25 a gallon. He concluded
that the methods worked out by the partners were unprofitable. The attempt had failed.

By the fall of 1849 Rodman desired to drop the project. Joseph wanted to
try an alternative, that of exploring the possibility of establishing a mill in
the South, where costs of manufacture might be lower. He wrote for advice
to Jacob Barker, Abraham's father, who was in the vicinity of New Orleans.
Joseph received the discouraging reply that planters would be unlikely to

buy stock in a factory for processing cottonseed oil, at least until the factory proved to be profitable. Also, Jacob wrote, New Orleans was too far from markets and growers alike.[15]

On hearing this, Rodman and Robert Haydock insisted on retiring from the business. About this time, too, Rodman developed another interest. He had invented a process for manufacturing kegs and barrels and wanted to expand his plant to take advantage of this. On 17 October 1849, William Wharton advanced the money and eleven days later Robert Haydock and Joseph sold to Rodman for one dollar each their interest in the invention.[16]

Joseph had a final idea which he wanted to explore, that of selling Boyé's patent rights to others, especially to southern mill owners. Robert and Rodman made over their interest in the project to him; and Joseph on 24 November contracted afresh with Lewis and Boyé. The essential item was that if Joseph succeeded in selling patent rights in the Mississippi Valley he would be entitled to one third of the profits therefrom.

When Joseph was contemplating ways of making money by introducing the manufacture of cottonseed oil into the South, did he consider the fact that southern mill owners used slave labor? Probably not. The surprise he registered several years later on discovering that fact indicates his ignorance concerning life in the South. Nor did he at this time receive any encouragement to learn about it. He failed to interest southern mill owners in Boyé's patents, and the project was finally completely closed out.

By 1870 others had overcome the obstacles which faced the partners with a result that a large and profitable business developed. Quantities of cottonseed oil went to Italy, where it was used to adulterate olive oil, until the Italian government put a stop to the practice by means of increasing the tariff. Within the United States cottonseed oil became widely used for making soap, shortening, oleomargarine, and many other products.

The breakthrough came as the result of choosing the engineering approach to taming the cottonseed. A linter was developed for removing the "fuzz," which became an important byproduct. Other new machinery included improved huller, screen, crusher, kettle for cooking, and press.[17]

In selecting the chemical approach Joseph and Rodman had taken the wrong track. The high point of wisdom in their venture appeared in the decision to give it up.

4

The Vigor of Youth

When in the autumn of 1849 the venture in cottonseed oil ended, Rodman and Joseph dissolved their partnership. Rodman continued in the business of making white lead and other chemicals, now supplemented by manufacturing kegs and barrels. Joseph found an opportunity to go into the manufacture of bricks. Their parting was amicable. Rodman sensed that Joseph had come to the end of a period of tutelage and must, like a pupil passing from a lower to a higher grade, move on. Joseph saw less clearly. He reasoned with himself: He had met a girl, fallen in love, and wanted to save money for marrying; he earned too little working with Rodman; the business of making bricks seemed to offer a surer chance for wealth than did that of making white lead.

What he did not see behind these rationalizations was the true nature of his ambition, now full-grown and seeking substance on which to feed. He moved too quickly, thought too widely, and felt too painfully the shortcomings of others to work well as a member of a team. Like Rodman, he was not impulsive. Both of the brothers acted rationally and deliberately. They were alike in another way. Each in his business concerns quickly reached a limit of tolerance for the ideas of others. Headstrong to an advanced degree, each felt compelled to be master.

Hannah, who had tended Joseph as a boy, divined what Joseph still confusedly felt. She expressed it kindly, almost maternally: "I only judge thee by the fruits, and it has occurred to me that much of the beauty of thy life is hidden and smothering under a great weight of strength and learning which thee finds it necessary to administer to others for their good."[1]

The business of making bricks offered an opportunity to escape from under the dominion of the older brother. Although Joseph was still not his own boss, he was also no longer a junior partner, but an equal.

1

In beginning the manufacture of bricks Joseph was, like Rodman with chemicals, leading to strength. Philadelphia was built of bricks; no other material came so cheaply or served so well. Because of this Joseph, again like Rodman, found his chosen field crowded with competitors. Each maker of bricks was seeking the technological advances which would enable him to cut costs and undersell other manufacturers.

The problems which had to be solved in order to achieve savings were clear enough. Bricks had customarily been fashioned by forcing wet clay into molds, then removing the molded bricks and stacking them to dry before carting them to the kiln. Because wet clay when cold chilled the hands of the molders they could not work in winter or on cold mornings in spring and autumn. Space was needed for drying bricks. Time was lost in the drying, especially in rainy weather. Some of the finished bricks were porous and weak because insufficient pressure had been applied to the clay in the molds.

Of the several possible ways of solving these problems the one which seemed most promising to inventors of the 1840s was that of forcing dry clay into molds under pressure. A person who could perfect a machine for doing this could conceivably make possible year-round operations and turn out a product of a uniform high quality with less hand labor than was needed by the older method. A number of inventors attempted to build such a machine and received patents for the results of their work. One of the most successful was a man named Thomas Culbertson.

The 10 October 1846 issue of *Scientific American* contains a description of Culbertson's machine,[2] copied from a story in a Cincinnati, Ohio, newspaper:

A frame of fourteen moulds, one brick to each is drawn by the power of steam between two press rollers, the lower one of which enables the frame to support the pressure of the upper roller, and being run through backwards, and forwards equalizes the pressure over the entire face of the brick. These, after undergoing in this mode a pressure of nearly one hundred tons to each brick, a pressure which covers clay, apparently perfectly dry, with a coat of glossy moisture, are raised above the surface of the mould by parallel levers, and are then delivered over to a bench or table by self-acting machinery, whence they are taken in barrows to the stacker at the kiln.

The dry clay is shovelled into a hopper, and if more of the material is pressed into a mould that serves to make a brick, a knife which ranges with the surface of the mould, shaves off the surplus.

Two hands shoveling, two more taking off, and one at the barrow, constitute a gang of five persons who turn out from 30,000 to 35,000 per day of ten hours. As brick makers' days are from sun to sun, say twelve working hours per day, during the season, from 46 to 50,000 bricks, per day, may be made by a single machine.

Joseph had agreed to enter upon the manufacture of bricks using Culbertson's machine about a month before he finally gave up trying to sell Boyé's patent rights. Joseph had known Culbertson for several years.

Culbertson operated a brick works with a partner named James B. Imlay across the Delaware at Pea Shore, about three miles north of Camden. Here Culbertson had installed his machine and, having perfected it to his satisfaction, wished to capitalize on it by selling the patent rights to others. He proposed that Imlay find another partner and continue using the machine as a model for purchasers to inspect.

Imlay sought out Joseph who, after investigating the potential for success, agreed to the proposal. Imlay's equity in the works was apparently small, as Joseph supplied the purchase money, $9.600. This was about the same as his equity in the white lead business. But that was not the only cash that was needed. Ten thousand dollars had to be raised to pay Culbertson for the use of his machine. Joseph managed this by changing partners. Within a few months of the agreement with Imlay, the latter retired in favor of Joseph B. Matlack, owner of several brickyards. By the beginning of spring, 1850, the firm of Wharton and Matlack was operating. Joseph had the management of the works at Pea Shore, including construction of buildings and kilns, installation of equipment, purchase of clay and other raw materials, and supervision of the manufacture. He and Matlack shared the work of selling bricks. Wrote Joseph in March 1850 to his sister Mary, "I am still busy preparing my brick works and expect to start in a week or so. My prospects still look good but I may be infatuated as many another has been."[3]

Joseph nevertheless heavily counted on the business being a success. He was convinced that his firm had the best brickmaking machine on the market. If he and Matlack could show sufficient enterprise and imagination in sales and reliability in supply they ought soon to be one of the largest manufacturers of bricks in the Philadelphia area. Joseph again wrote to Mary, "There has been a great deal of building to do at the place—kilns, wharves, sheds, etc. and as I had no regular master hands in any of the departments I have been on the ground every day myself to direct and superintend. It has been very pleasant to me to be so much in the country and in so beautiful a place and now I have the satisfaction to think that nearly or quite every thing is well planned and well done and that the place will work and pay."[4]

Business that first summer was brisk. In July a fire leveled a number of blocks in downtown Philadelphia. Subsequently Joseph was able to write, "We sold 500 to 600,000 bricks this morning which is a very agreeable circumstance. They are to rebuild Brock's property on the wharves which was recently burnt down and blown up."[5] Most of the money received from this and similar sales went to pay costs of improving the works. In September Joseph wrote to Mary, "My business will probably pay considerably more than my expenses though I do not keep a horse & wagon and take half holidays semi occasionally but as it is now I can't tell till winter how I will come out."[6]

Meanwhile Culbertson, in partnership with George Scott, was trying to make money from the patent. He knew of the desires of Wharton and Matlack to expand and encouraged them to install more machines. Wharton answered by proposing a scheme of a sort which became characteristic of his later attempts to raise money at little risk to himself. He proposed that a new company be formed which would use two machines. Wharton and Matlack would give Culbertson and Scott ten thousand dollars worth of stock in the company in exchange for the right to use the second machine. Wharton and Matlack would then sell this right to the company for cash. As a result of these arrangements, Culbertson and Scott would have to make their money from the profits of the new company, distributed in the form of dividends on shares of stock; but before any dividends were issued, the company would have to pay Wharton and Matlack for the patent right which they had bought from Culbertson and Scott. Thus, if the new company succeeded, all investors would profit; and if it failed, Wharton and Matlack would be out nothing and might obtain some money for the patent right. Wharton commented on Culbertson and Scott's reaction to the plan, "They thought it a hard offer but will think of it and do it I think or something like it."[7] The scheme did not come off, and by November Joseph and his partner were considering other ideas for raising money for expansion.

The year 1851 was disappointing. The economy went into one of its periodic slumps, and the construction industry suffered. Wharton used the months of depression in developing ideas for improving the works. He wrote to Uncle Thomas Fisher, then in London, asking him to send specimens of "the most marketed and meritorious" styles of brick, including tubular and waterproof bricks. "If any of the patentees of brick machines distribute engravings of their machines I should like to have them and should like a specimen of draining tile." A large hotel, he added (probably the La Pierre House), was being built with "our" bricks adjacent to the Academy of Natural Science. "It will be the finest in the city, probably."[8]

Although the economy recovered in 1852, the traffic in bricks remained slow. The partners still needed ten thousand dollars to pay for another machine and had no immediate prospect for raising it by selling bricks. They conceived an idea of helping Culbertson sell patent rights and proposed canvassing the southern states. With Culbertson's approval they set out on 24 January 1853 for a tour of four weeks across Maryland, the Carolinas, and Georgia.

The trip grossed them several thousand dollars. Still, disappointments outweighed profits. In Washington they failed to sell the patent to the architect who was planning an addition to the capitol building. Richmond and Wilmington proved to be empty of possibilities. Charleston was much better, and the partners developed several elaborate plans in collaboration with local contractors and manufacturers. One after another these plans fell through. The partners' only successes were in Augusta and Macon, Georgia, where they sold several patent rights at greatly reduced prices.[9]

The principal advantage to Wharton of the southern tour was an exposure to a way of life completely different from anything he had previously known. The ignorance of a lawyer in Georgia and the lack of initiative on the part of brickmakers in South Carolina shocked him. "I think that every driving man I have met in the South was from the North." He found that not all the slaves were on plantations. A lumber mill in Charleston was using slave labor, and so were brickmakers. "The owner doing nothing except going a few times a year to his brick yard and collecting the money from his factor." He concluded that the slaveowners he met represented a degeneration of reason and will contrary to what should be the natural condition of mankind.[10]

At the same time, the slaves seemed happy and contented. He speculated in a letter to his father on the condition of slaves being sold south as compared with those escaping to freedom in the north: "When I was at Fallowfield troops of blacks northern bound used to pass through but their probable fate as to the body I don't consider much better than that of these. The first would while enjoying a nominal freedom suffer much from privation and cold in Canada and many take to drink. These go to a congenial climate and if like all I have seen so far enjoy good bodily health and contentment."[11]

His observations led him to a conclusion that immediate abolition of slaves would be disastrous to both blacks and whites. He wrote to his mother:

> I am satisfied that the institution of slavery cramps and weakens very greatly the negroes of the South; the contrast between the thrifty productive appearance of country and town at the North with the slovenly desolate air of many parts indeed most parts of the South that we have passed through is as great as I expected to see it but on the other hand I believe the slaves are in general well treated and have quite as much physical comfort and health as northern laborers with a great deal less labor and the relation between master and slave seems less harsh and more domestic than we northern folks are led to believe. . . . It is plain that without the blacks the whole south would be a desert until repeopled, as they [the whites] are too careless to work for any more than enough to keep from starving if left to themselves.[12]

Wharton reflected that most southerners he had met realized the depressing effect of slavery on their civilization and wanted to do something about it but were inhibited by the attacks of abolitionists. "I feel more disposed than formerly to let them [the southerners] work it out their own way and at any rate try to avoid insulting any who may be trying to do their best with their position." "I believe slavery to be a curse to the land that maintains it. . . . But it exists and I think must be removed by the action of those who have it and not by others and the removal must be prepared for by systematically showing the blacks that as they sow they must reap."[13]

In later years, even to the time of the Emancipation Proclamation, Wharton did not swerve from this position.

2

As the brickmaking business of Wharton and Matlack continued an uninspiring existence, changes were occurring in the family of Deborah and William Wharton which increased Joseph's restlessness. The immediate family was breaking up. Within a period of three years four of the children were married and left home. By 1852 the only ones remaining at Bellevue and on Spruce Street were Joseph and his sisters Anna and Esther, who were not yet of marriageable age.

The first of the four to go was Joseph's younger sister Mary. On 30 April 1849, she became the bride of a New York city merchant named Joseph D. Thurston and went there to live. Joseph missed her, but not as much as he did relinquishing to the married state his brothers Charles, Rodman, and William. Joseph had worked and played with these; had traveled with them and their friends by horseback through the pinelands of New Jersey and the mountains of Pennsylvania and northern New Jersey; played chess and billiards with them; joined a boat club, the Camilla, and rowed and sailed in races on the Schuylkill; aided Rodman in putting the stamp of the Wharton business personality on young William; and with the brothers and their girl friends attended dances, heard Fanny Kemble read Shakespeare, attended lectures by Thackeray, Emerson, and others and concerts by artists such as Jenny Lind, and enjoyed long walks, picnics, and sleighing parties.

Members of the family had thought that Rodman would be the first of the sons to be married. He was the first to be able to afford the responsibility of a family and had been courting ever since Joseph had gone to live on the farm. Rodman had been engaged to a girl named Marianna, who had broken with him in order to marry the Wharton brothers' good friend Thomas Mott, only living son of James and the prominent Hicksite Quaker minister Lucretia Mott.

While Rodman continued his search, Charles met and fell in love with Mary Lovering, whom he married less than a week (3 May 1849) after his own sister Mary had stood up in meeting with Joseph Thurston. That was characteristic of Charles, whose heart pointed more directly and surely to happiness than did his head. Charles only dabbled in the things which Joseph regarded as serious. Charles knew this and once wrote to Joseph a few sentences which admirably sum up his outlook on life: "I am an enigma to myself, with disposition to do good but lacking energy. I want balance, judgment. This I hope will come. I'll meet it quite halfway. . . . I feel there is a much greater object than this rush, this drowning of nature almost, for money. Give me success enough for independence, then I will make my family the happiest in the world."[14]

Charles toyed with athletics and activities aiming at intellectual improvement, such as studying French and practicing the flute. He read books mostly for pleasure and enjoyed the opera, the theater, games, the company of women, and gay parties. He met his future bride through her younger brother, Joseph Lovering, who kept blooded horses at his parents' estate of Oak Hill near Germantown. The father, Joseph Shallcross Lovering, was a wealthy manufacturer of sugar who pampered his children. He, his wife Ann Corbit Lovering, and three children were members of the Cherry Street Meeting. The daughter Mary had a sister, younger by a year, who was quiet and serious. Mary was gay and socially inclined and shared most of Charles's tastes. She married him at a time when his prospects in business were not much better than those of Joseph. The couple lived for a time at Oak Hill and in 1852 moved to New York City and stayed there for several years while Charles and his partner went about their occupation of merchandising.[15]

Rodman, who cared little for the lighter sorts of social entertainment, was more attentive to women like himself who worked on projects sponsored by the Society of Friends. He assisted Dorothea Dix in trying to persuade the legislature of the Commonwealth to establish a hospital for the insane and pursued other projects for aiding the unfortunate, one of which issued in the founding in 1851 of the Catherine Street House of Industry for providing a temporary shelter for the homeless poor.[16] In the course of these activities he met Susanna Dillinger Parrish, a dedicated social worker and daughter of Joseph and Susanna Parrish. One of her brothers, Edward, was to become the first president of Swarthmore College. Rodman and she were married at a meeting held in the home of her parents on 6 June 1850.

Next came William, four years younger than Joseph, who proved to be more romantically impulsive even than Charles. While still nineteen he fell in love with a non-Quaker girl named Anna Walter, daughter of Edward and Hannah Ann Walter of Philadelphia. Joseph wrote concerning the pair. "Bill looks handsomer than ever before which is not saying much as his looks before were rather coarse. This change in him I looked for and expect to go much further as he is just emerging from the state of 'Hobbledehoy, neither man nor boy' when every one looks disagreeable." Anna, Joseph continued, "looks better from having improved in disposition and in health, the latter owing to daily horseback rides. She will be one of the handsomest and finest women in Philadelphia in five years, perhaps the very handsomest." The brothers wholly accepted Anna. "Bill probably could never have got a nicer wife if he had waited for years," wrote Joseph. Although William had scarcely the means to support a family, he and Anna refused to wait. They were married on 4 June 1852. William at his request was continued as a member of the Society of Friends.[17]

That left Joseph as the only single male. He, too, would have liked to be married. It was expected of him as a member of the Wharton family and of the Society of Friends, although these considerations probably had no place in his reasoning. He was naturally inclined to women, enjoyed their company, and liked being admired by them. Yet he hesitated. He told Charles and other members of the family that he could not afford a wife and family;

that he must be able to support them before he had a right to gratify his desire to enjoy married life.[18] He did not specify the details for judging how much his income ought to be or how secure should be his position, probably because these were less important to his idea of "affording" to be married than he would admit. Actually, his income and prospects seem to have been about equal to those of Charles at the time of marriage to Mary Lovering and certainly much greater than those of William.

In fact, the rationale of "affording to be married" was a blind behind which he hid from himself a passion to succeed as a businessman. The whole bent of his education as a Quaker and a son of Deborah and William Wharton emphasized the primacy of the vocation of husband and father. He would not repudiate this training by a blunt assertion that ambition should come first. Yet that ambition was there. He had nurtured it and become convinced that nothing ought to be permitted to stop its normal course. Thus he was caught holding aims which could doubtfully be reconciled. His perplexity was, moreover, complicated by an uncertainty of success. He had experienced the joys of family life from birth. Ambition was new, untried for its ability to withstand the distractions of a wife and children. Truly, work ought to come first for the satisfaction of ambition, but would it always?

He was in this state of mind when he found a woman with whom he felt himself to be in love. This was Mary Lovering's sister Anna, born 19 December 1830. Anna was several inches shorter than Joseph, slim, pretty, and dark-haired, with a pure, fresh complexion.[19] She preferred plainness in dress, was always neat, and carried herself erect, and for these reasons impressed some people as being prim. She coupled a reserve in the presence of slight acquaintances with a love of conversation amounting to gaiety among members of the family and friends. She avoided the opera and the theater on principle, yet she liked music and sang and played the piano well. She was highly intelligent, and her parents had given her an education such as might prepare her for any social occasion.

Her father, Joseph S. Lovering, was an industrial pioneer of great ability. That especially attracted Joseph Wharton, who in later life often turned to the elder Lovering for advice. Joseph Lovering had developed a method of refining sugar without the use of blood and after many trials had established himself as one of the leading manufacturers in the field. In 1852 the Lovering refinery was located at Number 27 Church Alley and was an imposing brick structure ten stories high.[20]

Joseph Lovering had married Ann Corbit in 1827. Both the Loverings and the Corbits came from Wilmington, Delaware, and had predominantly Quaker ancestors. Although Joseph and Ann followed the Hicksite persuasion, they were atypical of the first generation of members of the Society. They were rich, had received good educations, and enjoyed some pursuits which were on the borderline of acceptability for stricter Friends. Joseph played the violin and owned a piano. He understood French, carried on his firm's correspondence in that language and tutored Anna in it after she left school. Both Joseph and his wife read the daily papers and were interested in public affairs. Their large mansion of Oak Hill was fronted with white, fluted pillars and stood amid meticulously kept lawns and gardens. A pond large enough for swimming was nearby. A conservatory, of which Joseph was especially proud, contained grapes, lemons, oranges, palms, and many flowers. At Oak Hill the Loverings entertained large gatherings. He was dignified and imposing. A white beard extending past his collarbone accentuated a longish face highlighted by a large, straight nose and widely spaced eyes. A full wig hid his baldness. She was short, quick-witted, and charming, albeit given to hypochondria, which variously exaggerated and obscured some real physical weaknesses. For a month or two every summer the Loverings went to a fashionable resort, such as Cape May, Saratoga Springs, Yellow Springs, or Newport. There they entertained guests whenever Ann's real or imagined state of health permitted.[21]

Ann and Joseph were possessive parents. They hated to think of their daughters marrying and leaving home. They probably adjusted to Mary's union with Charles because of Charles's likable and compliant nature and willingness to spend much time with the Loverings. When Charles and Mary left Oak Hill for New York Joseph Lovering became more possessive than ever of Anna. He looked with dread on the time when she might also marry and tried to capture her sympathy by dwelling on his own mild ailments and the prospect of loneliness on the part of him and his wife living without the children nearby. Yet both he and Ann liked Joseph and admired his ambition.

Anna for her part responded favorably to Joseph's attentions. Whether or not she loved at first sight no one can say. She and Joseph saw each other often before their engagement and fully explored their reciprocal likes and dislikes. They shared intellectual pleasures and an aversion to fashionable social life; and they differed on the subjects of physical exercise, ambition, and the practice of charity. Anna had no skill in sports. Her involvement was a means of showing consideration for persons with whom she was playing and nothing more. She did not mind losing in billiards to her father and swam poorly, and then only to please Joseph. She had no real ambitions beyond those of leading a devout, pure life, helping people around her to do the same, and, when married, making her husband happy and raising a family. On the subject of charity she disagreed with an idea of Joseph that the best method was that of providing work for people in order that they might help themselves. Instead, she adhered to the principle of compassionate giving to people in need. As she lacked the missionary spirit of a social worker, she found an outlet for this belief in practicing private charities.

The engagement took place in early Septmeber, 1849. By that time Anna was sure of her love for Joseph. In subsequent months she had ample time to consider his faults and reflect on her choice. A normal period for an engagement was a year. Hers and Joseph's lasted for more than four. Theirs was, in fact, a strange relationship. Both wooed without outward show of passion. No one would have been surprised if the engagement had been quietly ended. Time and again Joseph's temperament clashed with Anna's. Yet not once did either seriously consider any outcome to their engagement other than that of marriage.

3

Most of the period of the engagement coincided with Wharton's involvement in the business of making bricks. That necessitated fairly frequent separations from Anna, which resulted in many letters passing between them. One might suppose these to be love letters, but they are not the amorous exchanges of ordinary passion. They are rather expressions of the tastes and temperaments of a man in love but determined to succeed in business and a woman who loves more deeply than he and does not well comprehend the consequences of her lover's ambition.

Joseph was easily the more versatile in expressing ideas. His letters frequently contain contrasts of banter and serious discourse. He was adept at the little things of love—the sighs, kisses, exchange of looks, compliments. He sometimes accompanied his letters with simple gifts, such as a translation of a love poem by Schiller, a daguerreotype of himself, a pair of engravings of horses, a feather from Newport, and a sketch of himself wearing a pair of spectacles which he had recently purchased. But then came the lectures stressing the need for work, vigor, and self-discipline. One in particular, written a week after their engagement, manifests a compensation for his fear that love and marriage might interfere with ambition. The compensation takes the form of an insistence that Anna possess the same qualities of stamina and determination as Joseph himself:

> Do not be afraid. It is certain that human beings cannot *live* on love alone much less be happy, without the extension of their faculties. . . .
>
> *We* must endeavor to and *we will* work and advance not only without injuring thereby our love for each other but to its maintenance and improvement. . . . I shall not calculate on retaining thy love if I become (I had better say remained) self indulgent and indolent nor do I believe that mine for thee would last with any real warmth if I should see thee so.
>
> We are not by our engagement absolved from duties and permitted to enjoy ourselves but have made our duties more stringent and various and must perfect the love that we have found so sweet if we neglect them.
>
> The same rule will hold for men and women free, engaged to be married or married; if they live for ease and enjoyment instead of labor and self denial they go to the devil for certain and without any chance of salvation but retracing their steps.
>
> But we want to be happy, and everlasting straining and labor looks so dreary—that is humbug.

I have found happiness to come from exertion of my faculties and no where else and the more I am active and the more faculties I use the more satisfied and happy I am and it is evidence that this must be so and not otherwise for a human being is a collection of faculties capable of acting on and being acted on by the outward world (By this I mean both the mental and physical world external to themselves) and so contrived that this action produces health and growth and a certain quiet pleasure connected with them while their idleness causes their disease and death accompanied by ennui, hypochondria and the like.

Whoever looks for happiness in repose will find a miserable short lived counterfeit only.

I think that thy parents' education of their children and example to them has been faulty in this respect. I think the standard of exertion has been a great deal too low and consequently neither your bodies or minds are as healthy and strong as they ought to be—not so capable of exertion and enjoyment as they ought to be. I suppose that thy father from his labor in his business and thy mother from her bad health found ease and repose agreeable and were therefore indisposed to deny them to their children.[22]

This is not an isolated example of his inner emotional conflict. Sometimes the preaching took the form of a soliloquy. He described to Anna an evening of intellectual give-and-take with Hannah and Robert Haydock. He had read *Punch* while Hannah sewed. Robert read aloud an amusing poem of Robert Browning, whereupon Joseph recited the "Ballad of the Dutchman's Pig Supper." This was followed by a reading of a favorable criticism of William H. Furness's translation of Schiller's "Song of the Bell." Then Hannah had recited verses written "long ago" by Robert Biddle and others. Joseph ended the recital of these performances, "I do wish such a circle could be got together now. Whenever I see a specimen of intelligent sprightly and enterprising society it makes me despise and abjure more strongly than before the frivolous and pitiable details of fashionable and semi fashionable life in which people waste the essence of their existence.

"To avoid a criminal neglect of duties absolute vigor is necessary not merely life enough to drag one languid day after another but energy capable of throwing off fruits daily and hourly and if this is not laid up in youth there is small chance of its being gained afterward."[23]

He wrote that he preferred the country to the seashore and especially to the city, which represented all that was vain, foolish, and wasteful: "Waltzes, quadrilles and the like seem to me to be at home nowhere but in cities. They are to me suggestive of nothing but society. . . . The preachers and poets allow theirs [energy] to escape in steam as if direct from the boiler without passing into the engine. These are desponding and melancholy at the thought of their wasted fire and generally cut a dismal figure in the world. Others go off in violent, sudden and destructive deeds."[24]

"Do! do! do!" he wrote again.[25]

His concern for his own future, expressed in the form of a zeal for educating Anna, never abated. He set himself up as her teacher and guide and pursued the occupation with all the vigor at his disposal. "My dear it is quite essential that thy strength and vivacity should be built up now in thy youth, that thee may have not only the habit of doing properly what lies before thee but that the ambition and vigor for longer affairs may not be found wanting when the trial comes."[26] "My dear thee don't know how ardently I desire thy development and improvement nor how much it would add to our harmony and peace if I should see thee always wide awake and active minded. Thee must excuse me for saying that at present thee is often absent minded and sluggish. If thee says that I also need improvement I admit it but reply that I worked on myself—trying to develop myself— eagerly for several years before I knew thee and now can no more be comfortable without urging thee onwards than I could be with one arm burning or mortified though the other was comfortable."

This last was written in late October 1853, less than a year before the marriage took place.

In another way, too, he did his best to prepare Anna for recognizing the importance of business. He did this by example rather than by preaching. Time after time he made engagements or tentative engagements which he broke, not carelessly, but deliberately. Each time he conscientiously but briefly wrote her in advance of the change of plans. "I cannot leave my business so I shall not come this morning to get my likeness taken." "I can't come to ride with you today." "I am sorry to say there is no prospect of my being able to dine with thee today."[27]

Anna took Joseph's preaching and tendency to break appointments un- ruffled. Her moral sense conformed more closely to the queries of the Society of Friends than it did to Joseph's sermonizing. Feeling no burden of ambition, she had no thought of binding herself to any discipline outside the Hicksite Quaker tradition, much less to translate any discipline into a morality of vigor. The specifics of Joseph's arguments for her welfare seemed of slight importance. Perhaps she sensed what was bothering him. Anyway, he seemed to her to be like her father in always missing the important things. Later, when she had been married almost nine years, she wrote him about it: "If thee only knew the one hundred and one thoughts that are constantly passing and repassing through my little brain, I think, some- times, thee would be *somewhat* surprised, notwithstanding thee thinks thee knows me from A to Izard. *I* think thee knows me from A about as far as *D*."[28]

The main point, she reasoned, was that he cared. She eagerly read his letters. Let him assault her with words! She acknowledged his remarks but refused to join battle.

Anna looked on life not as a working out of ideas but as a succession of details. Traffic in the great issues concerning the condition of the world and its denizens was best kept for leisure time. The important thing in living was to deal rightly with every concrete event as it happened. Words could come later. In a manner of speaking, bad breath was more repulsive than poorly phrased sentiments. She was more concerned that Joseph not eat onions, which she detested, than that he stop lecturing her.

Her love letters to Joseph are models of decorum. They almost invariably begin, "My dear Joseph" and end with "Thy attached friend." However she might have privately addressed her betrothed, in writing she never used pet names or other of the badinage of love. Her thoughts were sensible, never sentimental, and unlike Joseph she rarely moralized. She described her activities, gave news of friends and relatives, and sometimes analyzed the behavior of others. She wrote regularly in a fine, feminine hand and complained that he did not respond with the same regularity.

In the summer of 1850 Anna spent a month with her parents and other relatives at Cape May. She enjoyed the leisurely, fairly sedentary life, consisting as it did of meals, conversations with friends, walks along the shore, and short periods each day reserved for bathing, bowling, riding, and the like. Her letters to Joseph are filled with details. She described a shore landing of passengers from the *Kennebec:* ". . . two or three little row boats put off from her, filled with people, one woman among the rest. The tide was very low and they could not get to the beach. A carriage went out to the little boat and took a number of the passengers, and the rest were carried in, on the backs of men, I suppose the boatmen." She described accidents, for example, of two people almost being drowned and one being wounded in the pistol gallery; of the boiler of the steamship *America* blowing up; of the oddities of various people, such as of a woman enamored of a new fad "which permits Ladies to smoke cigars. There is one lady here from Memphis who walks on the piazza, with a cigar in her mouth, puffing and smoking as a gentleman would." Her principal complaint was that the Tomkins Hotel at which she and her relatives were staying was not the most popular spot that season. Many of the people with whom she would have liked to talk were going to Harwood's Columbia House. "Mr Harwood, . . . I understand, hires a man to stand at the landing and send people to the Columbia, and to say that there is small-pox and whooping-cough at this house." Also, she noted, the United States Hotel was having its first season and taking some of the guests.[29]

Joseph liked to read these details, but he disliked being part of them. Anna wanted him to look nice, he wrote to his mother, which he found difficult, "owing to my aversion to prim clothes and my great tendency to perspiration." He then ungenerously characterized the Tomkins House: "The whole place is like a big caterpillar's nest in an apple tree. There is a great deal of squirming about and very little done but eating."[30]

Anna studied German at Joseph's suggestion and they exchanged several letters in German and French. She knew that he like lectures by intelligent men and described to him those which she heard. She once wrote concerning Ralph Waldo Emerson, "He is full of originality and humor, made me laugh heartily and at the same time was so calm and quiet that he apparently did not know he was saying anything worthy of applause. His manner, although somewhat awkward and unattractive at first, is more agreeable to me than Thackeray's, because it is void of all conceit. He speaks very slowly, as if he was thinking and weighing each word before uttering it, and not as if reading from a book before him. Perhaps he lacks enthusiasm in expressing his thoughts and ideas."[31]

Once Anna's devotion became fixed on Joseph it never wavered. She endured the four years and more of their engagement without complaint. The delay in getting married meant putting off the moment of separating from her parents, but this was for her scarcely an important consideration. Marriage and being with one's husband came first, however sorrowful parents might be on seeing a child leave home. Anna put her trust in Joseph and would in all likelihood have married him at any time, provided it could be done with her parents' consent and in meeting.

4

The coincidence of the long period of engagement and the protracted attempt to make money from bricks suggests an idea that each of these supported the other. If Wharton had succeeded or even been able to see a real possibility of success he could have "afforded" to get married; and at the same time the commitment to marriage shored up his hope of and effort to make money from Culbertson's machine.

The hard fact was that his hope was misplaced. The brick business was failing to provide bright prospects. And yet he doubted. Was it really as arid of opportunities as it seemed? Or were they there, and he had failed to see them? Then came the disappointment of the southern trip. In March 1853 he wrote in desperation to Charles and received from the older brother a characteristically sympathetic and optimistic reply: "The business looks blue, well that's bad but mine did ditto for 4 years, got me down to 2000 dolls, with a *family*, think of that. Postponing your marriage is perfectly o.k. There is no comfort with a family and lacking the where withall. But you can be happy as you are and rid of responsibility till fortune smiles, as she will upon energy. Don't spend any more money, at the brick works. Study the closest economy at it, and push ahead."[32]

Charles's advice did not allay Joseph's doubts concerning his own ability. He wrote in September to Anna, "I have done very little good in the world and am mortified therefor and also that I can't get enough money to feel safe in marrying."[33] The failure to see a future which could satisfy his ambition oppressed him. He could stand the strain no longer and finally took the action which ambition itself demanded. A sense of relief underlies his remarks to Joseph Thurston following a January snowstorm: "I believe a snow storm makes the gay gayer and the sad sadder. I am so nearly balanced that it has no effect on me either way. . . . I have been on two famous sleighing parties at night both to Isaac R. Davises and both royal fun. . . . Enclosed is a notice of my departure from brick making; what will come next, ' 'Mighty only knows.'"

That was written 4 January 1854. Three weeks later he wrote Anna from New York, "My dear I think it is nearly time for us to get married."[34] Another prospect for work had turned up. He and Charles and some other Philadelphians of their acquaintance were buying into a zinc operation near Bethlehem, about sixty miles to the north, and he was to have a share in managing it. He wrote Anna on 28 January, "Yesterday morning I visited the ruins of Harper's buildings, the Great Republican Chas. Illins' office, the Pa. & Lehigh Zinc Co.; bought 1500 shares of its stock, accepted the post they offered me, wrote to Charley & Abm, lunched at Hannah's, visited Paul Duggan's casts of the Elgin marbles and other statuary, dined at Han's at 6."

For a few weeks the prime obstacle to marriage seemed to be removed. Then something happened, the details of which are missing. The opportunity for managing the Pennsylvania and Lehigh Zinc Company temporarily vanished. On 22 March Joseph wrote to his sister Mary, "I do not expect to go into business this year but intend to look after father's affairs and set his accounts in order, a dreary work but much needed. I am to have $1,500 for it and if Anna's family and my own make no objection I have some intention of getting married this year. I do not see the way very clear pecuniarily but am resolved to end this unprofitable suspense."

The timing of events permits a thought that being relieved of the burden of brickmaking was as instrumental in bringing an end to the lengthy courtship as was his desire to enjoy to the fullest his love for Anna. His future prospects were as unsure as they had ever been. Yet now he was resolved on marriage. He set aside the question of whether fate had cheated him or his powers had failed. He would enjoy the married state, and agreed with Anna that until something turned up they could live with the Loverings.

The Minutes of the Spruce Street Monthly Meeting record that the marriage of Joseph Wharton to a member of the Cherry Street Meeting was performed on 15 June at Oak Hill in the presence of sixty witnesses, all being members of the two families.[35]

He and Anna honeymooned at Chicago and Niagara Falls, a luxury which he certainly would not have allowed himself if he were still making bricks. Years later he wrote of the honeymoon to his sister Esther: "We used to stroll about into all sorts of difficult places in search of the romantic and picturesque. We walked hand in hand. We breakfasted in Syracuse or Utica or some foreign city on cherries and cakes purchased and eaten in the street as we marched up & down the town on a voyage of discovery. We clamb [sic] to the top of Crow Nest. We got up to see the sun rise (but looked at it out the window and didn't stay up), and in short consulted ourselves much more than others as to the manner in which we should have our good time."[36]

Even as he honeymooned with Anna, events were happening to provide the chance he sought. The job of managing the Pennsylvania and Lehigh Zinc Company was about to materialize. It would be the first of several ventures resulting in fortune and a generous measure of fame.

5

Venture in Zinc: Making Oxide

Several events of 1854 gave direction to Wharton's life. A Consolidation Act passed by the legislature of the commonwealth made twenty-nine municipalities into one, and the old city of Philadelphia was no more. In its place appeared an industrial metropolis of almost half a million people joined to New York, Baltimore, Washington, and points west by railroads and canals.

Cholera scourged the country that year and in July carried off Rodman, leaving behind a widow and two children, Susan Parrish, aged four years, and an infant son of two months, William Rodman. Joseph was now the unquestioned administrator of the property of Deborah and William Wharton which, however, came to an end two years later when the elder William died.

These two events had substantial meaning for Wharton, yet the importance was small by comparison with that of a third event, his removal to Bethlehem to take over management of the works of the Pennsylvania and Lehigh Zinc Company. This was his introduction to mining and metallurgy, which became the center around which his career orbited. And the introduction to mining and metallurgy occurred within a community contributing to him opportunity, wealth, and power for the next forty-six years.

1

Zinc was the metal which took him to Bethlehem. At the time of his partnership with Rodman no zinc industry existed in the United States. It was even new in Europe, where it tended to lag behind a demand for zinc products. Brass, an alloy of approximately 70 percent copper and 30 percent zinc, had always been much wanted. Metallic zinc or spelter as it was called in the trade was proving useful for roofing, packaging, and the galvanizing of iron. Zinc oxide, also called zinc white, could substitute for white lead in making paint and had the advantage of being nontoxic. Other uses of zinc and its products were being discovered with increasing regularity.

Why was the industry tardy in developing? The answer is to be found in

70

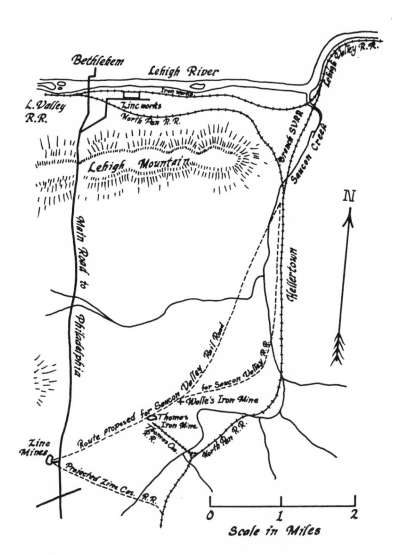

MAP 1. BETHLEHEM AND THE SAUCON VALLEY. On 29 January 1861 Joseph
Wharton sent to S. F. Fisher, President of the Lehigh Zinc Company, a freehand
drawing, shown here as he drew it except for the lettering. His purpose was to
indicate a possible spur route, called the Saucon Valley Railroad, which would haul
ore from the zinc mines at Friedensville to the oxide works (Zinc works) on the bank
of the Lehigh River in South Bethlehem. The spur route could also have served to
carry ore from Wolle's iron mine to the mill of the Bethlehem Iron Company (Iron
works). (The Thomas Iron Mine was owned by the Thomas Iron Company at Hokendauqua, which lay about ten miles up the river from the Bethlehems; the Thomas
Iron Mine had its own spur route, as the drawing shows.) Also on the map are the
routes of the North Pennsylvania Railroad connecting South Bethlehem with Philadelphia, the main line of the Lehigh Valley Railroad along the southern bank of the
Lehigh River, the old turnpike between Bethlehem and Philadelphia over which the
zinc company was hauling its ore, and the site of Hellertown, at which Wharton and
others later formed the Saucon Iron Company. (*Courtesy of the Friends Historical
Library, Swarthmore College.*)

several peculiar properties of zinc. At ordinary temperatures zinc is relatively inert; but as the temperature rises to about 434° C., the melting point, it becomes active. In the presence of oxygen it catches fire and burns brightly, forming the dense white smoke known as zinc oxide. If the heating is continued in the absence of oxygen, at about 940° C. the zinc is volatilized. Now, this temperature is below that needed to release zinc from its ores.

And so, for thousands of years pure zinc remained unknown to Western civilization. Brass could be made by heating copper in a bed of a peculiar earth which today is known as the zinc ore of calamine. By such treatment the copper was hardened as zinc vapors penetrated it and changed its appearance so that it resembled gold. But when calamine was heated in furnaces used for refining iron or other metals, nothing of importance appeared to happen. At a sufficiently high temperature the zinc was either oxidized and escaped with the smoke or, if a strong reducing agent such as carbon or iron was present to take up the oxygen, evaporated as pure zinc vapor.

Additionally, when finally metallic zinc became known in the West, its affinity for other metals presented the problem of finding a proper retort to refine it in. What was needed was a chamber built of a material with which zinc would not interact. Manufacturers discovered that clay could be used; but then, a whole series of technological advances was necessary before usable clay retorts, or muffles as they came to be called, were found.

Portuguese and Dutch traders brought pure zinc to Europe from the Orient sometime in the seventeenth century. As its utility and properties became known, exploration for its ores and development of furnaces for making it proceeded. The most common ores were given the names blende or sulphuret of zinc; calamine or carbonate of zinc; and electric calamine or hydrated silicate of zinc. Blende was the most widely distributed. Calamine and electric calamine were considered the most desirable because they contained fewer obnoxious impurities. Most European countries had deposits of one or the other of these sorts of ore, and in the later eighteenth and early nineteenth centuries the industry developed with the most important centers being found in England, Belgium, Poland, Silesia, some other parts of Germany, and Spain.

In a memorandum prepared in 1860 to induce congressmen to increase the duty on zinc, Wharton described the method used for refining zinc ores:

> The process of making zinc, though theoretically rather simple and everywhere the same, is actually carried on in at least three different manners, each of which requires great adroitness and judgment in the workmen, and thorough system, skill, and good management in the master. The origins of these methods are shown by their names. They differ in the construction of the furnaces and the shape of the retorts: the English plan, which is now almost abandoned, uses for retorts, pots similar to glass pots, but tightly covered; the Silesian plan, which is largely followed,

employs retorts shaped like a thick book set on its flat edge; the Belgian plan, which is now adopted in Belgium, England, Spain, and parts of Silesia & Germany, has plain cylindrical retorts open at one end. This latter is for most localities the best plan yet known.

In all these systems of making zinc, the process is substantially the same, and is as follows; viz. The ore is first calcined, finely pulverized, and mixed with pulverized coal. This mixture is then placed in air tight retorts (varying in their shape as above shown), set in furnaces, each furnace containing as many retorts as can be properly heated and tended; the furnace must be strongly built, and yet so formed as to allow full access to all the numerous retorts for the purpose of charging, cleaning, and replacing them; the retorts must be air-tight, strong, and capable of withstanding the fieriest heat, yet at the best they are destroyed in a large factory at the rate of thousands monthly. The furnaces are so strongly heated as to bring the retorts with their contents to a full white heat, which causes the carbon of the coal to take oxygen from the zinc ore, thus liberating the metallic zinc, which at that temperature can only exit as a vapor. This zinc vapor escapes into condensers attached to the retorts where it cools sufficiently to assume the liquid form, and whence it continually trickles, or is drawn at certain intervals according to the construction of the apparatus. This operation combines the processes of reduction and distillation, and does not succeed without great care, since a bad material for the retorts, a variation in the heat of the furnace, or wrong proportion of the ingredients of the charge, a want of skill or punctuality in the workmen, or an accident to a furnace may cause considerable loss almost imperceptibly; in fact a difference of one-third of the entire yield may readily occur between the quantities produced by two sets of workmen unequal in skill, but consuming the same quantities of materials and having in all other respects equal advantages.

European producers began by making spelter rather than oxide, since the demand for pure zinc products appeared first. When the market for zinc oxide finally was opened, they burned spelter. Some oxide shipped to R. Wharton and Brother was made by burning spelter, a shipment which Wharton later claimed marked the introduction of zinc oxide into the paint industry of the United States.[1] But oxide made in this way was expensive. An opportunity existed for someone to find a cheaper means of producing it directly from the ore.

The zinc industry began in the United States with the incorporation in 1848 of the Sussex Zinc and Copper Mining and Manufacturing Company and, a year later, of the New Jersey Exploring and Mining Company. These used surface ores found at Sterling and Franklin Hill, New Jersey. Before the American Revolution the deposits there had been mined for copper and abandoned when copper was not found. Identification of the deposits as ores of zinc was made in 1824. Some little consisted of red oxide of zinc, but most contained iron to which the name of Franklinite was given. Franklinite was complex and unknown in Europe. The Sussex Company devised a furnace for making zinc white from the red oxide which followed the European practice of first making spelter and then burning it. The product was of good quality and was in 1850 duly commended by the American Association for the Advancement of Science. The two companies then combined to form the New Jersey Zinc Company, which proceeded with the commercial manufacture of zinc white and the grinding of it with oil to make paint.[2]

But the New Jersey Zinc Company had trouble with its ores. The difficulty was explained by Wharton in a letter to Professor Brush: "The reason why the New Jersey Zinc Co. does not make Spelter I take to be that their ore consists in the main not of that handsome foliated red oxide which can be had as specimens, but of grains or crystals of Franklinite imbedded in a matrix more or less scanty of red oxide and of calamine in very variable proportions. Such an ore contains two substances very destructive to the muffles (which are too expensive to be wasted) viz. iron, and lime; these both make fusible Silicates with the substance of the muffles and eat it into holes through which the zinc vapors escape and are lost."[3] Franklinite was later to prove valuable as a source of spiegeleisen, used in the Bessemer converter for making steel. But in the early 1850s, as far as making zinc was concerned, Franklinite was intractable to the available technology. Whoever could find and exploit easily mined deposits of the commoner ores of zinc in a place handy to labor, fuel, clay, and markets would have a natural advantage.

2

Such ores existed and were recognized and used by a man of unusual inventive talent, Samuel Wetherill.

The ores appeared to the naked eye as a strange outcropping in a field near the Bethlehem Pike, about fifty-five miles north of Philadelphia. A creek called the Saucon flowed nearby and gave the locality its name. A traveler northward bound could continue on the pike past the Saucon Valley deposits to South Mountain, a ridge several hundred feet high running east and west about a mile away. He could cross South Mountain and descend to the Lehigh River, where a bridge provided entry into the quaint Moravian town of Bethlehem. Or, if the traveler wished to avoid a steep climb and descent, he could use a route later taken by the railroad and follow the Saucon Creek northeastward to a pass through which it flowed to join the Lehigh. The traveler would then journey upstream along a narrow, level plain to the bridge which took him into Bethlehem. (Please see map on p. 71.)

Bethlehem was the oldest town in the Lehigh Valley. Moravians coming mostly from Germany had settled it in 1741 as a missionary outpost. They had built in the wilderness large stone houses to accommodate their communal mode of living; and they had transplanted there a culture rich in an appreciation of art, education, and music. In the second half of the eighteenth century Bethlehem had been an economic and military center of considerable importance. Easton, the seat of Northampton County, lay at the confluence of the Lehigh with the Delaware eleven miles to the east and was by comparison a hamlet; and so was Allentown, a settlement lying near a bend in the Lehigh about six miles to the west. Bethlehem had served as a hospital for the Continental Army during the American Revolution, but with the coming of peace, had steadily lost influence. Easton and Allentown grew to equal it in size, then surpassed it. The Moravian elders did not care. They conscientiously tried to preserve the purity of their flock by keeping non-Moravians out, which they could easily do because the church owned almost all the land in and about the town. During the opening decades of the nineteenth century Bethlehem was a church village, subsisting on a farming-artisanal economy, and situated in a prosperous agricultural region largely peopled by Pennsylvania Germans.

Bethlehem was not to be allowed to remain isolated for long. The Lehigh and the Delaware rivers formed a natural highway for commerce between the Appalachian mountains and Philadelphia. In the 1820s Josiah White and the Lehigh Coal and Navigation Company built the Lehigh Canal, which joined the Delaware Division of the Pennsylvania Canal to connect the newly opened anthracite fields in the mountains with Philadelphia. The Lehigh Canal ran along the southern border of Bethlehem. Its development made possible the refining of ores of iron scattered in parts of the valley. Soon mines were opened and ironmasters were building blast furnaces. David Thomas, supported by the Lehigh Coal and Navigation Company, came over from Wales and established a commercially successful operation for reducing iron ores with anthracite. His company, the Crane Iron Company, lay about eight miles up the Lehigh River from Bethlehem at a place called Catasauqua. Several years later Thomas formed the Thomas Iron Company a few miles further upstream.

The pressures of industrialization were too great to be resisted. Less than a decade before Wharton came to Bethlehem the Moravian leaders sold most of the congregation's enterprises and much of its land to private citizens and had the town incorporated as a borough. Some of these leaders, possessed of small amounts of capital, helped to encourage industries which, however, were still located outside the borough limits. The leaders included such men as Charles Augustus Luckenbach, who managed the sale of Moravian farm lands on the southern bank of the Lehigh and the renovation of the old Sun Inn within the town along lines set by modern resort hotels, and Augustus Wolle, who dealt in real estate and merchandising and was soon to undertake the building of an iron furnace on the southern bank of the Lehigh opposite the town.

In the hands of men such as this, the development of lands across the

Lehigh from Bethlehem was rapid. In 1854 Asa Packer of Mauch Chunk (now Jim Thorpe) was building the main line of the Lehigh Valley Railroad through the area. Work was about to begin on another line, the North Pennsylvania road, which would connect Bethlehem with Philadelphia. The place of junction of the Lehigh Valley and the North Pennsylvania was the narrow plain on the southern bank of the Lehigh, a natural site for industries and soon to be known as South Bethlehem.[4]

The strange outcroppings in Saucon Valley had for many years invited the attention of the curious. A farmer had about 1830 sent a wagonload of the unknown mineral to a Mr. Trexler, ironmaster of the Mary Ann furnace in neighboring Berks County. Wharton later wrote to his wife of the man, the event, and the sequel:

> This morning I had a visit from a Mr. Trexler, an iron maker from Reading, to whose father, also an iron maker, the first zinc ore from our mine was taken for trial. The old man was one of the old fashioned sort; he grew rich by working hard and making his men work hard; when any man applied to him for work he challenged him to a wrestling match. If the man conquered he was employed, being strong enough to be a profitable servant. If the master conquered, the applicant was doubly defeated for he got no work there. His blacksmiths had to work from 5 a.m. to 8 p.m. and lay on well while they were at it. Well this old *gentleman* examined the ore enough to find that he could not make iron of it, pronounced it worthless and had it dumped out in the woods (several wagon loads which had been labouriously mined and hauled 30 miles) where it is yet.[5]

In 1845 Jacob Ueberroth, who owned the property on which the ores surfaced, took samples to William Theodore Roepper, a Moravian who was fairly typical of the talent hidden within the church village of Bethlehem. Born in Germany, Roepper had come to Bethlehem to help administer the estates of the congregation. In addition to being an expert accountant, he was familiar with the chemistry and metallurgy of his day. He made collections; conducted experiments; published some of his results in the *American Journal of Science;* carried on correspondence with Silliman and Brush; and was possibly the person who later introduced Wharton to those two scientists. Roepper was also an accurate and superb map maker; taught at the girl's school and the Theological Seminary; was organist and musical director of the Moravian Church choir; and was one of the leaders of the Philharmonic Society, the principal instrumental group. He had considerable diplomatic skill and was counselor to many.

Roepper tested the mineral from Ueberroth's farm in the local brass foundry of Lehman & Brothers and pronounced it calamine of excellent quality. He then tried to interest Robert Earp, a Philadelphia merchant, in mining the ores. Earp leased the Ueberroth farm and sent nine tons of the ore to England, where it was tested in English furnaces, which were not hot enough. Word came back that the Saucon ores could not be used. There they lay, identified and unexploited, when Samuel Wetherill came to examine them.[6]

That was in 1852. Wetherill was employed by the New Jersey Zinc Company, where he had gone after a period of work with the family firm in Philadelphia. His grandfather and namesake had founded the firm, which specialized in making white lead, in 1789. Samuel's interest in working for New Jersey Zinc reflected his belief in the potentiality of zinc oxide replacing white lead in the manufacture of paint.[7] Samuel was heavyset and affable and a few years older than Wharton. Enterprising, generous, and gregarious, he easily adapted to people with whom he had to live and work. People liked him; and he responded by flattering their interests. He loved horse racing, tolerated gambling, and dabbled in politics and religion. He was also imaginative and knew his chemistry. As an inventor he was a perfectionist, although when he changed hats and became a businessman, he seems not to have allowed considerations of quality to reduce his chances for profit. He was on balance a better inventor than a businessman and indeed in describing his occupation put himself down as "inventor."

While at New Jersey Zinc he developed what the industry needed, a process for making zinc oxide directly from the ore. He placed on the grate-bars of a furnace a layer of anthracite coal, lighted it, and over this white-hot fuel spread a layer of about six hundred pounds of mixed crushed ore and anthracite dust in proportion of two parts ore to one part coal. The result was a rapid reduction of the oxide of zinc in the ore to zinc vapor and an almost simultaneous reconversion of the metallic vapor into oxide. A fellow employee of the company, Samuel T. Jones, invented an easy way for collecting the oxide, which was released in the form of a heavy white smoke. A fan blew the smoke upward into a tower, where it passed into muslin bags. The oxide condensed out and adhered to the inside of the bags, while the impurities passed through the mesh into a stack. This "tower" or "bag" process became a standard companion of the Wetherill process.[8]

The New Jersey Company had not yet decided on using Wetherill's invention when it received a visit from Earp. Would New Jersey Zinc take over Earp's lease of the Ueberroth farm? The company sent Wetherill to investigate the Saucon deposits. Wetherill promptly ascertained their value and acquired the lease for himself. He then tried to transfer it and his process to the New Jersey company on terms which the company was unwilling to accept. He resigned and, although threatened with legal action, set in motion the train of events which resulted in Joseph Wharton coming to Bethlehem.[9]

Wetherill sought a partner and found one in Charles T. Gilbert. The course which the partners followed in establishing their enterprise reflects the state of existing laws and politics, which made obtaining a charter for a combined mining and manufacturing concern difficult and expensive. The partners planned for separate concerns for each sort of undertaking: a mining company to exploit the deposits and oversee the enterprise; and a partnership of Gilbert and Wetherill to accomplish the manufacture of zinc oxide and other products. The arrangement had an added advantage from the point of view of the partners of absolving them from any share in the financing or risk taking. These burdens would be borne by the company, which would raise money by selling shares of stock and by borrowing and which would absorb any loss.

The company was chartered in 1853 under the laws of Maryland and named the National Mining Company, but was reorganized several months later under the laws of New York as the Pennsylvania and Lehigh Zinc Company with an authorized capital of one million dollars. Most of the subscriptions to the stock came from New York City. The first president, Thomas Andrews, was from there. The Pennsylvania and Lehigh Zinc Company took over the Ueberroth lease and other properties and contracted with Gilbert and Wetherill for the manufacturing. The partners constructed the oxide works on the bank of the Lehigh at South Bethlehem, completing them on 13 October 1853, at a cost of eighty-five thousand dollars. According to their contract, they were to manage the works for a period of twelve years, producing four tons of oxide per day, for which the company would pay them a standard price, that is, fifty dollars a ton, the company furnishing the ore at the works. In separate actions they also built for the company a barrel works and a paint mill across the river down the bluff from the borough of Bethlehem, using water power from the canal.[10]

Almost immediately the enterprise was pronounced a success. A New York publication, The Mining Magazine, noted in November 1853 that stock of the Pennsylvania and Lehigh Zinc Company was selling at 5½, a good figure. The editors praised the quality of the oxide and acclaimed the inventive talent of Samuel Wetherill.

It was about this time that several Quaker manufacturers of white lead and related products in Philadelphia became interested in the Pennsylvania and Lehigh Zinc Company. What happened next is obscured by an absence of records and correspondence. This silence later permitted a story to develop to the effect that Joseph Wharton observed the zinc deposits while on a horseback trip through the area and from this arranged to take control of the company.[11] This is unlikely. Nothing in the surviving correspondence or other documents supports it. Possibly Wharton traveled to inspect the mines and contributed some ideas; certainly he bought some stock; but at this stage of his career he lacked the money and reputation to be able to superintend the transactions leading to the reorganization.

What happened was that in the winter of 1853–54 control of the Pennsylvania and Lehigh Zinc Company passed from the original investors in New York to a small group of Hicksite Quakers in Philadelphia. Charles Illins replaced Andrews as president and was himself soon replaced by Samuel F.

Fisher. The full roster of members of the new board of directors has not survived, but it included at least Fisher, George T. Lewis, Charles and Joseph Wharton, and probably the Philadelphia manufacturers Charles Lennig and Henry B. Tatham, who were certainly directors by May 1855. The directors contracted with a brother of George T. Lewis, James T. Lewis, granting him a monopoly of the right to sell the company's products. They reorganized the company under a General Mining Law of Pennsylvania.[12]

The position with the Pennsylvania and Lehigh Zinc Company, of which Joseph Wharton wrote to Mary in January 1854, was probably that of manager. The failure of the position to materialize in all likelihood resulted from some afterthoughts on the part of the directors concerning its necessity. There is no evidence that Wharton later replaced anyone. But if the members of the board thought they could get by without someone on the scene of operations to protect their interests, events of the next several months sufficed to change some minds. In May the oxide works burned to the ground and were immediately rebuilt at great expense. Other signs appeared that the management of Gilbert and Wetherill was sloppy and wasteful.[13] Clearly, the interests of the partners were not always identical with those of the company. Someone was needed to supervise Gilbert and Wetherill and protect the investment of the stockholders. Joseph Wharton was able, available, and willing; and he went.

3

He arrived in Bethlehem on Saturday, 9 September 1854, without Anna. That was a slight which she would not forgive. She had wanted to accompany him, but he had said no, giving as reasons a lack of knowledge of living conditions in Bethlehem and a need for him to devote all of his time to the new job.[14] Bethlehem was, he said, not to be a place of permanent residence: He would go there for several days or weeks at a time as needed and for the rest work out of his office at 110 Front Street on company business and the management of the family property. He had recently bought a house at 33 South Twelfth Street into which he and Anna would move as soon as it was put in order. Until then, Anna could live at Oak Hill; he would be with her there when not needed in Bethlehem and would in any event write letters telling of his accomplishments in and about the company's property and the Moravian town. His only concession to her desire to be with him was a promise that she might accompany him at some future time when he had become settled in both work and living quarters.

Having thus freed himself from Anna's distracting presence, Wharton wrote her long letters about the town, its people, and his work which expressed his great enjoyment of the new scenes. He lived at the Sun Hotel, whose rooms were large and comfortable; ate of ample and succulent provender served in its dining room; and in the evening conversed with other businessmen in its parlor; for the newly renovated Sun had outdistanced the other hotel in town, the Eagle, as a social and business center for local residents and out-of-towners involved with railroads, mines, furnaces, and manufactories which were collectively reshaping life in the Lehigh Valley.[15] He wrote Anna of boating on and swimming in the Lehigh River; of pleasant walks and horseback rides along the canal and out to the mines; of the merry girls from the boarding school who were almost always to be seen on the streets; and of the music floating out of open windows. "Today I dined on boiled pork and sour kraut which 'went pretty fair' but 'I dunno' as I should like it as a regular thing," he wrote. And again, "The Dutch folks up here are a source of perpetual amusement and satisfaction to me. They are so quaint—the country ones I mean and so simple minded and have such inexpressibly funny ways of saying what they have to say." "To tell the truth . . . I am perhaps more comfortable here than thee would care to have me as the place and people are now become quite familiar to me."[16] Anna was hurt and envious. He did not improve matters by continuing to write her about the need for energy and vigor. She became sharply critical of his neglect and won permission to accompany him on his fourth and fifth trips. Subsequently she wrote, "I have taken quite a fancy to the place, and enjoyed my visits there exceedingly."[17] Later she made several more trips to Bethlehem, but most of the time during his first three years of employment with the Pennsylvania and Lehigh Zinc Company he left her behind. He wanted to be free to serve his ambition and would rather have her at Oak Hill or Twelfth Street. And there she stayed.

Wharton did not waste time. The work at Bethlehem kept him busy, as it involved supervising all operations from the mining of zinc ore to the marketing of the oxide, and, for a time, paint. He had the task of hiring a competent miner and other persons to dig, concentrate, and calcine the ore and haul it to South Bethlehem. The hauling was done by pack mules, which wound in long trains over the mountain to the furnace. He also had responsibility for constructing and maintaining the company's property in South Bethlehem. This included, in addition to supervising Gilbert and Wetherill, directing the barrel works and the paint mill. "I bought out our Paint Grinder's contract today for the Co. at a saving to the Co. of 7000. I wish it was for myself," he wrote Anna on 8 February 1855. Shortly thereafter he rented the paint mill to others. Finally, the company established a farm for supplying the mules with pasture and providing material such as rye to be ground into flour for making a paste with which the kegs used for shipping zinc oxide were lined.[18]

Shortly after coming to Bethlehem, he hired an assistant, Richard W. Leibert, the son of the proprietor of the Sun Hotel, James Leibert. Richard Leibert remained as Wharton's assistant for the entire time that Wharton was employed by the Pennsylvania and Lehigh Zinc Company.

Most of Wharton's management was routine. The one aspect which was not involved Gilbert and Wetherill. Wharton quickly saw that the partners, and especially Wetherill, were using the company for their own purposes. They ingratiated themselves with local businessmen by buying supplies and services which they did not need and were lax in controlling the workers. Wetherill had improvised a racecourse along the river and met there with employees at noon for horse racing. More importantly, the partners were trying to increase the quantity of output at the expense of quality. Their contract called for four tons of oxide daily, which was to be equal in quality with the best "French" (Belgian) product. The partners had built a manufactory capable of making ten tons daily, although this could be done only by sacrificing quality. Gilbert and Wetherill were apparently willing to make the sacrifice, or so Wharton thought. Also, and most importantly for Wharton, Wetherill was using the company's property in an attempt to invent a process for making spelter. This would have been commendable if Wetherill had been experimenting for the benefit of the company, but clearly he was not. Wetherill was prospecting for ore in the Saucon Valley and was having some success. With an independent source of ore he could go into the business of making spelter for himself. He might, in other words, end by serving the Pennsylvania and Lehigh Zinc Company as badly as he had served New Jersey Zinc.

Wetherill's experiments provided Wharton with an additional anxiety. Wharton was himself thinking of making spelter. He was already studying the chemistry of zinc and considering experimenting with furnaces. He would have liked to do precisely what Wetherill was trying to do, albeit for the company and not against it. Thus Wharton had a personal as well as the company's interest in mind in dealing with the partners. Understandably, his treatment of them was harsh.

Wharton sharply restricted Gilbert and Wetherill to the terms of their contract. He refused to allow them more than sixteen tons of ore daily, the amount needed to make four tons of oxide, and reminded them of their obligation to manufacture a product equal to the best made in Belgium. He called them to task for undertaking improvements without prior approval of the company, refused to pay for overcharges, and barred Wetherill from using company property for his private business. His long range plan involved removing the partners from the scene. He probably had little difficulty in convincing the directors of the need for this. Certainly in what followed he had their full cooperation.[19]

A first step was that of strengthening the legal position of the company. The reorganization of 1854 had been done under a newly enacted mining law, which permitted the owners or tenants of mineral lands to form a company by certifying their intent to the attorney general of the commonwealth, paying a small fee, and having the certificate recorded in the appropriate county and with the secretary of the commonwealth.[20] The process had been easy, but it created only a mining company. In order to become a manufacturing company the directors would have to have a bill passed by both houses of the legislature and signed by the governor. That would involve considerable effort. Opponents could be expected to fight against passage of the bill, and in those days, when the buying and selling of votes was common, the costs could be high.

Still, in the spring of 1855 the rechartering was accomplished through the political influence of some of the directors and their friends in Harrisburg. At a critical stage, when Governor Pollock seemed reluctant to approve the charter, Wharton traveled to Harrisburg and added his voice to that of others urging the governor to sign. The new charter gave the Pennsylvania and Lehigh Zinc Company the powers which the directors wished for it, although the charter also reaffirmed the contractual obligations of the company to Gilbert and Wetherill and James T. Lewis and Company.[21]

How, then, might Gilbert and Wetherill be removed? Wharton explored two possibilities. One was that of finding a flaw in Wetherill's patent. The other involved breaking the contract on the grounds that the oxide made was inferior. He explained both possibilities in a letter dated 7 February 1856 to William P. Tatham, who was in England and was a brother of the director Henry B. Tatham:

> Our Company is now bound by a contract with Gilbert and Wetherill to have made by them for our works a certain daily quantity of oxide of zinc, and on account of the unsatisfactory quality of their make and for other reasons we wish to erect new works and make a further quantity for ourselves. Gilbert and Wetherill claim that we cannot do this (on the plan we wish) without violating a patent taken out by Mr. Wetherill for the process of making oxide of zinc by burning a mixture of coal and zinc ore. We have ascertained however that Mr. De Gee had taken out a patent in Belgium for that process two years prior to Mr. Wetherill's application for a U.S. patent and we consequently believe that if any patent can be valid here for that process, it must belong to Mr. De Gee or his assignee and not to Mr. Wetherill. . . .
>
> What we now want is to get from Mr. De Gee an assignment of that patent for the United States. . . .
>
> Our Company's contract with Gilbert and Wetherill requires us to pay a certain price per pound for all oxide made by them for us which shall be made by dry process of catching and shall be of first quality made by such process, and a smaller price per pound for the No. 2 grade.
>
> Now, all the oxide they make for us is made by the dry process of catching, they get a high price for making it, and it is *very inferior* to the European first & second qualities which are nevertheless made by a dry process of catching.

When Wharton directly charged Gilbert and Wetherill with making oxide of substandard quality they replied by saying that the reason lay in the poor equipment with which the company supplied them. Wharton then gave the partners a free hand to make the changes they thought necessary and, after the alterations had been accomplished, wrote the following letter which shows as well as anything he ever wrote the clarity of his thinking and forcefulness of his expression:

You represented to us that certain alterations in our works would probably enable you to produce a better quality of Oxide of Zinc, and we thereupon consented to have those alterations made, at the expense of this Company.

In order that you might be unable to find fault with the alterations when completed, we intrusted them entirely to you agreeing to refund your expenses therein.

The job being thus undertaken and committed to you, you for your own gain and benefit in order that your profits derived from your manufacture for us, might be interrupted as short a time as possible employed a larger number of men on it than could work to the best advantage thereby making the job cost several hundred dollars more than it need have cost if done with ordinary economy of wages and without extraordinary dispatch.

Now, we were under no obligation to make the said alteration.

If we chose to make it, we were under no obligation to let you do it for us.

If we chose to let you do it for us, we were under no obligation to pay such extra expense as you incurred for your own gain.

Under these circumstances you feel hurt that your sight draft for the total amount of your expenses is not paid instanter before your bill is examined.

Your plea that your bill when examined proved nearly correct and was paid by us with a very small deduction, does not affect the question at all; I hope that all your future bills will be quite correct but they certainly will not be paid without examination.

In this instance I waived further scrutiny into how your men had been employed, solely on Mr. [Nathan] Bartlett's declaration that all who were charged to us had been employed on our work.

The contrast you draw between your own magnanimity and our infinitely small actions, is striking, but not once borne out by the facts.[22]

The dispute between the partners and the company reached a climax in the fall and winter of 1856–57. In September the company closed down the oxide works, probably in order to precipitate the legal action for which Wharton had been preparing. Gilbert and Wetherill countered by taking advantage of a clause in their contract permitting them under the circumstances to attach the property of the company and make zinc oxide on their own account. The company retaliated by seeking an injunction to stop the partners from using the works and followed this with a suit for damages.

These matters ended in compromise. The company bought out the interest of Gilbert and Wetherill, giving them promissory notes with a mortgage against the company for most of the sum. The partnership was broken up. Gilbert went to New Jersey where he continued for a time to be involved in various businesses dealing in zinc oxide and paint. The company was finally in full control of its property, with the exception of 30,424 shares of stock which were tied up with a suit involving the use of the Ueberroth farm.[23]

Wetherill stayed on in Bethlehem. He had possession of valuable ore lands in the Saucon Valley and was continuing his attempt to make spelter. Anticipating success, he had obtained a charter of incorporation for a firm to be known as the Wetherill Zinc Company "for the purpose of manufacturing metal zinc under a new patent process." The charter had been issued on 26 November 1856—a date occurring toward the middle of his litigation with the company.[24] Wetherill would be heard from again.

4

Into the void left by the departure of Gilbert and Wetherill stepped Joseph Wharton. That is not to say he immediately tried to use the company's resources as they had done. Wharton did not forget that as manager he had a first loyalty to his directors. Nevertheless, within a year of the dissolution of the partnership events were beginning to put that loyalty under strain. His success in ousting Gilbert and Wetherill gave him confidence in his ability; and, it seems, every time he had that feeling of self-confidence his ambition took another forward leap demanding satisfaction.

What happened in summary is this: He accepted a risk which the directors were unwilling to take, greatly profited therefrom in terms of money and power, and having reached a new plateau of accomplishment prepared for still greater heights, only to discover that now he could achieve these not by furthering the interests of his directors but by subverting them. From being their loyal servant he was subtly moving to become their competitor.

The big event which gave him his first opportunity for independent entrepreneurship was the Panic of 1857. On 24 August of that year the New York office of the Ohio Life Inusrance and Trust Company closed its doors. Other banks almost immediately halted payment in specie. Money became scarce; creditors began calling in their loans. Many businesses failed.

From the vantage point of the Pennsylvania and Lehigh Zinc Company the panic could scarcely have been more poorly timed. The company still owed money borrowed to open the mines and build the oxide works. Part of the company's stock was tied up in a trust against the possibility of a court ruling to satisfy the claim of one James R. Whiting against the lease of the Ueberroth farm. The settlement with Gilbert and Wetherill had been costly, and the sum promised the partners was still unpaid. The company even owed Wharton for part of his salary, then three thousand dollars a year. The total debt, according to Wharton's calculations, came to $253,176.35. Cash resources were almost exhausted, and the market for zinc white had drastically fallen off. Unless some unusual source of aid appeared, the company faced a real possibility of bankruptcy.[25]

Wharton provided that extraordinary source of aid. He did so by suggesting plans which would further his own fortune as well as that of the company. On 13 July he wrote to President Fisher offering to accept 3,500 pounds of number one oxide and the use of the company's paint mill in Bethlehem for the rest of the year in return for arrears in his salary.[26] This would have given Wharton a return far greater than the amount the company owed him, assuming that the paint could be sold. The directors did not accept the offer, and one can easily understand their position. Why should they permit Wharton to do for himself what he could do as well for the company? The property was theirs, and the conversion of oxide into paint and the sale of the paint involved no greater risk and outlay than were already present.

Another plan proposed by Wharton had greater appeal. He offered to lease all the properties of the company, thereby assuming financial control over the entire enterprise, in exchange for exclusive control over foreign sales during the life of the contract. He would pay the company eighty tons of oxide monthly as rent, a quantity which might be expected to satisfy the domestic market without depressing it by forced sales. James T. Lewis and Company would handle domestic sales as usual. Wharton would have all oxide which he could make above eighty tons per month, but he must sell it on the foreign market.

The attractive point of this plan, as the directors must have seen it, was that it assured them of an income sufficient to tide the company over many months of a poor market without sharing the grave risk which Wharton would take, that a new venture in foreign sales during a time of economic depression. The most they could lose was a manager, who was replaceable. If Wharton succeeded in opening a foreign market, they would have that as a bonus when the contract expired. The directors agreed to the plan, and the contract was signed. It was to run for six months, ending 13 April 1858.

Wharton immediately sent his brother Charles to England to establish the foreign market and selected Coates and Company, a firm with which the zinc company had previous communication, as his agent. Coates and Company was essentially a one-man operation, the person in question being an elderly gentleman named J. W. Coates who maintained an office at 13 Bread Street, Cheapside, London. Charles reported Coates to be "considered smart & active" and to be a "thorough worker."[27] Joseph gave Coates an exclusive right to market the oxide abroad and never regretted the choice. The relations between the two businessmen were cordial and lasted as long as Wharton remained in the zinc business.

Wharton stretched his modest resources to the limit in getting the new venture underway. He had to produce considerably more oxide per month than Gilbert and Wetherill had done. The works were capable of turning out the amount immediately needed, but the costs of operating them were also greater. He mortgaged everything he had, bought supplies on credit, paid his chief lieutenants partly in produce, and gave promissory notes to his workers for part of their wages. On 20 December he wrote to Charles that the expenses under the lease with the company had so far been sixteen thousand dollars, "that is to say I owe as much more than when I started it, and my share of the product would be worth $21,000 which if well sold will leave something after paying the expenses and say $3,000; but alas the expenses are certain and the sales are not." He offered to make zinc paint if that would sell abroad better than oxide; and he would ship ore abroad if that proved to be profitable. He worried about competition from the New Jersey Zinc Company, which was marketing paint in England, and heeded Coates's advice to keep shipments as secret as possible. He had oxide shipped in casks weighing variously from three hundred to five hundred pounds and marked only with a diamond containing the first letter of the last name of the person to whom the shipment was consigned. In December he tried unsuccessfully to establish a market for zinc oxide in Cuba.[28]

Yet by the end of the year the success of the venture was assured. Up to 1 January 1858 he manufactured a total of 1,048,932 pounds of oxide (about 470 long tons) of which 400,282 pounds (178 long tons) were due to the company. By that date, and in spite of his forebodings ten days earlier, he had realized a net profit of $8,606.25.[29] With this as a base he increased production to the limit. During the winter he built three new double furnaces for the company and stockpiled oxide which could not be immediately sold. He sent Charles to travel to various cities on the continent. "As for the French market for zinc oxide I don't have any faith in it because the folks there are accustomed to the best article and we have a heavy duty to contend against. Russia may do better; Germany may possibly do, or Belgium but neither very likely. The Southern European states however would be very likely to take zinc oxide if they can grind it there. . . . Constantinople is likely to resemble these latin markets. Still try and sell where you can."[30] Joseph sought and obtained from the United States Navy Department an endorsement of zinc oxide as preferable to white lead for naval purposes—important because ships could use paint made with the lower grades—and asked Coates if the English Admiralty might not be induced to purchase zinc oxide or zinc paint.[31]

In the euphoria of success he made mistakes which advertised his growing ambition to persons connected with the company. He was careless in observing the terms of the company's contract with James T. Lewis. This occasioned a remonstrance from that firm to which Wharton replied in an arrogant way:

Except for the arrangements which I made with the Zinc Co. I feel sure that it would have produced nothing this winter and might probably enough have become bankrupt. As it is, my only chance of coming out whole from the heavy burden of rent and expenses which I have assumed is in making a large amount of product (more than the American market can take) and in disposing of the surplus abroad in the cheapest possible manner. So long as my arrangement lasts you are sure of having the sale of as much zinc oxide as you can with all diligence dispose of in America, when it terminates no one can possibly predict what changes will take place.[32]

That clause, "when it terminates no one can possibly predict what changes will take place," effectively told James T. Lewis that Wharton would gladly dispense with his company's services. It brought forth a scorching letter from the firm's solicitor Samuel C. West, accusing Wharton of making "a shipment of oxide to Europe through another party in this city [undoubtedly Haydock] in direct opposition to our express wishes" and of being "chiefly instrumental in defeating our proposed contract with the Co. simply from prejudices you had imbibed against us. Certainly not to promote the interest of the Company, as I have reasons for knowing that it met the views and approval of a majority of the Board of Directors."[33] When the company failed to sell all of its oxide Wharton notified President Fisher that it was taking up too much space at Bethlehem and he would have to charge the company for storage.[34]

Wharton would naturally have liked to continue his lease of the company's works beyond the six months' limit. How could he convince the company that its best interests lay in doing this? One idea which he canvassed and rejected was that of buying Gilbert and Wetherill's mortgage notes and giving the company an extension of one year to pay them off in exchange for the option of continuing the lease for eighteen months. Again, he wrote Charles of the possibility of agreeing with the company to mine and sell abroad for three years twelve thousand tons of ore per annum in exchange for paying off all of the company's debts and assuring it of sufficient profit to declare a fifteen percent stock dividend at the end of the term. He speculated on ways of financing an enlarged operation if the lease should be continued and wrote Charles suggesting a three-way partnership between himself, Charles, and a third party which would supply capital.[35]

His ultimate proposal to the company was that of extricating it from debt in exchange for a lease of three and one half years on the mines and works with the privilege of taking from the mines during that time sixty thousand tons of ore. Would the company accept this offer?

It would not. With the effects of the panic wearing off, the directors could see another possibility of solving the immediate financial problem. They had also become wary of their manager. Complaints had been arriving to the effect that the oxide he was making for them and labeling as number one grade was less than that. This practice, if true, would hurt sales. Could

Wharton possibly be cleverly working to keep the company in a straightened financial position in order to force the directors into a hard bargain? They tabled Wharton's proposal and appealed to the stockholders for a loan of three hundred thousand dollars for five years at 6½ percent. Stockholders were to have the first chance to subscribe to this loan at 60 percent of the value of their stock. A circular prepared by a committee consisting of A. E. Borie, Charles Henry Fisher, Edward M. Hopkins, Charles Lennig, and James Markoe advertised the loan and the alternative of Wharton's proposal, observing that the profits from sixty thousand tons of ore converted into oxide would amount to at least three hundred thousand dollars.

In effect, the directors turned Wharton's proposal against him. They gave the stockholders to understand that he could do for the company anything he might do for himself, if he would. If he could clear three hundred thousand dollars in three and one half years by mining and selling oxide made from sixty thousands tons of ore, that would suffice to pay off the loan a year and a half ahead of schedule.[36]

The loan was successful, and Wharton was defeated. The prices paid for zinc oxide were increasing, and the market was again lively. At the expiration of his contract in April, Wharton again became general manager of the company, now at a salary of five thousand dollars.

He still had a large supply of oxide which he had manufactured for himself with the privilege of retaining the foreign market until it was sold. This involved him in a clear conflict of interest. He might delay sales abroad while waiting for higher prices and thereby postpone the time when the company could enjoy that lucrative market. Instead of doing this, he acted honorably for the company. He disposed of most of his oxide within twelve months after the end of the lease through Coates and Company, asking them to sell in large lots where it was possible to do so without loss, and relinquished the privilege of keeping the company out of the foreign market. He reported in May to Fisher that all equipment was operable and wrote to Coates, "The Vieille Montagne Co. [the principal manufacturer in Belgium] cannot make oxide so cheaply as we by a very large percentage; I know their process by drawings & descriptions both written and verbal."[37]

Yet Wharton must have smarted from his defeat. He had for a brief period been the chief executive of a highly prosperous undertaking. Now he was again an employee with no immediate prospect of securing control over the mining of ore and the manufacture of oxide. He had or could expect to obtain everything he needed to become the head of a successful zinc company except one thing, namely, an independent source of ore comparable in quality and location to that of the Saucon Valley. Perhaps at this point Wharton envied Wetherill his foresight in securing part of the Saucon Valley deposits. In any event, Wetherill's property was beyond the reach of Wharton, inasmuch as Wetherill was still trying to perfect a furnace for making spelter.

A possibility of obtaining a source of ore existed in the form of reputedly rich calamine deposits in East Tennessee, controlled by a man named Stephen Hills, Jr. Hills had before the outbreak of the panic tried to interest Wharton in them. Wharton had at the time treated the overture lightly yet had given Hills no definite reply. Then in March 1858, after the possibility of a renewal of Wharton's contract with the company had passed, he became seriously interested in the Tennessee deposits. Charles urged his brother to investigate, and Joseph traveled to Tennessee to study the situation. The result was disappointing. He wrote Hills that the quality of the ore was less, and the cost of mining was more, than he had first thought.[38]

No independent source of ore was available to serve his ambition. It might have been stifled, or he might have left the company for good if that had been the last of all possibilities for personal growth. In effect it was not. The way was now clear to concentrate on that matter of making spelter. If successful in this, he might introduce into the United States a new and highly profitable industry. He had little fear that Wetherill, for all his ingenuity as an inventor, would be able to outdo him in establishing a business. His chief competitor would most likely be the same as his principal source of support, namely, the Pennsylvania and Lehigh Zinc Company.

Wharton's thinking had evolved to a determination to be the chief person to profit from an industry in spelter. Why should he not enjoy the fruits of his initiative and skill? He and the company would surely work against each other to gain and keep the prize.

6

Venture in Zinc: Making Spelter

In America at midcentury an old order dominated by farm, individual enterprise, family, and revealed religion was giving way to a new regime emphasizing manufacturing, corporate enterprise, secular associations, and science. The industrial pioneers who were responsible for putting the new order into place had been born and reared in the old, and much of their thinking stayed there. They reasoned more in terms of personal responsibility, family, and church than of collective responsibility, class, and community. They did not correctly evaluate the social consequences of their labors, for they had left the well-traveled roads and were without guides. Theirs was an era of individualism, an individualism by default. As far as a suitable business and social ethic is concerned, they were moving in darkness, as in the words of Matthew Arnold in "Dover Beach,"

> Swept with confused alarms of struggle and flight
> Where ignorant armies clash by night.

The directors of the Pennsylvania and Lehigh Zinc Company were pioneer industrialists of this sort. They had, like Wharton, been reared in a culture dominated by aristocratic values and a family economy. Many of them had been partners in or heads of family firms. Ties of blood and religion weighed heavily in their thoughts. They brought prejudices concerning individual responsibility, familial obligation, social position, and religious affiliation to bear on their work for the zinc company. They had not yet developed a suitable ethic to guide them in an age of collective, capitalistic enterprise. No real sense of corporate or managerial responsibility conditioned their outlooks. Each took what he could from the joint undertaking and expected others to do the same. Not one of them but would put relatives on the payroll and concern himself with the details of daily work at mines and furnaces if he saw a personal advantage to be gained. The directors lined up according to interests and competed among themselves subject only to the general requirements of honesty and fair dealing demanded by the discipline of the Society of Friends.

This helps to explain their toleration of Wharton in his struggle to gain

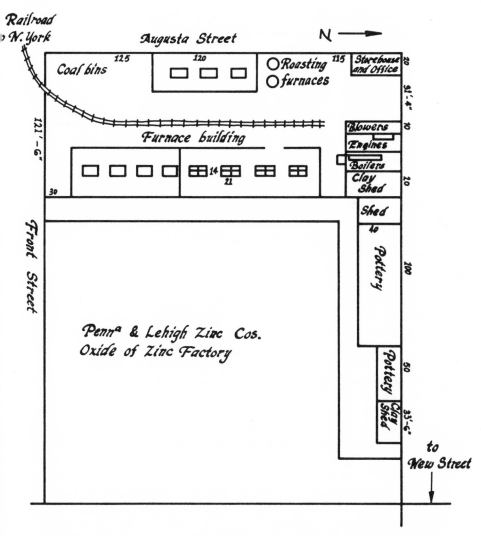

MAP 2. GROUND PLAN OF SPELTER WORKS. Joseph Wharton drew this sketch of his proposed spelter works (except for the lettering, which has been replaced) and sent it to Louis De Gee, a consultant, on 31 October 1859. The branch line labeled "Railroad to N.Y." connected with the main line of the Lehigh Valley Railroad. The spelter works, when built, became the first commercially successful plant in the United States for the manufacture of metallic zinc. *(Courtesy of the Friends Historical Library, Swarthmore College.)*

control of the company. He was only doing what they would have done in his place. As long as he made money for them they would support him, even raise his salary—as they did; and at the same time, they would watch and restrict him in order that he might not succeed in his designs against their wealth and power.

1

Wharton remorselessly maneuvered within this ethical void. He sensed rather than rationally appreciated the unsuitability of older values for the new age of business. He wrote to Anna, "The older I grow the more I perceive how we all exist in a sort of balanced condition—standing or progressing like a rope dancer with something like solidity immediately underfoot but with a charm all around into which a trifling inadvertency or accident may plunge us." "I *feel* the existence of justice and mercy of laws which govern and limit my existence."[1]

The "justice and mercy of laws" which he knew, as contrasted with the ones he felt, belonged to the old order which was passing away. Those ideals emphasized training and discipline for able-bodied persons and charity for the unfortunate. An obligation of a father to a son was that of rearing him for useful employment. Wharton found no difficulty in applying this precept to his conduct in the new order, however inappropriate it might be. He transferred the obligation of a father to that of an employer with capital to invest: The proper task was that of helping people to help themselves by creating jobs and stirring up initiative. He considered this to be, indeed, the best form of charity for a person like himself to practice. The other, more traditional, form involved aid to persons suffering afflictions beyond their control. This, too, as far as he was concerned, was a matter for individuals. Social action to improve the lot of the unfortunate was nothing more than individuals cooperating for charitable purposes, as with a committee of the Society engaged in doing something for Indians, blacks, women, and the deserving poor.

In preparing for a spelter works, Wharton once wrote to his mother:

We have different missions to fulfill in this world and I think it will be a real satisfaction to me to succeed in this enterprise as I believe I shall. It will be opening means of subsistence to many families . . . and perhaps doing something to forward the social harmony which ought to exist. I have always thought that a well managed factory was a better charitable institution, or rather a better and more useful philanthropic establishment than a hospital; provided it is so contrived as to be permanent, and is not pushed to such an extent as to provoke a sort of warfare involving the ruin of itself or competitors.[2]

Wharton regarded his responsibility for the welfare of others to be a personal debt he owed to his creator and not a social obligation for which he was answerable to any particular group of people. Again he wrote his mother:

Every person born into the world commences immediately to incur debt to all around him. Through infancy, childhood and youth he is a constant recipient of bounty and unrepaid service, and when finally he reaches maturity possessing more or less vigor and talent he resembles some great enterprise brought at great expense of capital and industry into a position to yield returns. He owes (to whom is immaterial) for all that he has, and is; in my opinion he must in honor discharge that debt, to whom, is immaterial to the present question. His debt is to the world, or perhaps I should say to his Creator; the world or his Creator is repaid and satisfied if equal or greater services are bestowed by him on any of his fellow creatures.[3]

What was missing from this philosophy was an appreciation of the disastrous effects which the new social and economic order sometimes had on people who were nevertheless able and willing to help themselves. Industrialists in the old order had never had to contend with cutthroat competition and periodic mass unemployment and the depressing effects of these on human dignity. Nor was there present in the old order any idea that everyone has a right to education and health irrespective of ability, income, or physical and mental state. As an employer Wharton considered that he must act honorably toward his employees: pay them just wages; provide safe working conditions and decent hours; protect them from external threats of physical and moral harm; reward good work and punish bad; know and treat the commonest of laborers as intrinsically equal with himself. He need not, he reasoned, be concerned with those "social services" which the family ought to supply: support of the unemployed; care of the sick, infirm, widows, orphans, and aged; education of children; and so forth.

Because he was certain concerning his social responsibilities, his conscience was clear. No feelings of guilt interfered with an enjoyment of life. He was still the person of gentle disposition and enjoyable company that he had been in his teens. He entered into the society of Bethlehem not always for business reasons but also to enjoy it: talked with people; learned from their experiences; attended outings, celebrations, lectures, concerts, funerals and other religious ceremonies; played billiards in the parlor of the Sun Hotel and maintained a boat on the Lehigh. He lived cleanly, avoiding affairs with women and petty social intrigues. He neither smoked nor drank strong liquors; had by his own admission not yet tasted lager beer; and rarely took a glass of wine. Clean shaven except for a moustache which he kept for several years and then removed, he dressed neatly and plainly in expensive clothes.

He wrote poetry and made sketches. His wit and sense of humor seemed always ready to serve him. With these he could even charm Anna away from brooding about his occasional disregard of her feelings. In the presence of Anna or by himself a boyish look or phrase might still escape him. Youth stayed with him as he matured beyond his years in the universe of scientific knowledge, manufacturing, and business.

Even so, the dangers of the new order stalked the vestiges of youth. His ambition, racing through hostile country, sometimes left him exhausted and feeling old. Only a residual strength allowed him to rediscover after every crisis a feeling of the springtime of life.

2

In 1871 Wharton wrote an article entitled "Memorandum Concerning the Introduction of the Manufacture of Spelter into the United States." The *American Journal of Science* published it in the same year. Professor Brush had since 1862 been urging Wharton to write such an article, but Wharton had always put it off.

The "Memorandum" is modest for the contribution which Wharton claimed for himself. It acknowledges the skill of the workmen and praises the quality of the spelter made by Wetherill. Also, it glosses over gloomier aspects of the struggle: fights with the company's directors; mistakes of judgment; differences with Anna; and the near disaster occasioned by a prospect of conflict between the North and the South.

When in the spring of 1858 Wharton prepared for making the production of spelter a primary aim, the greater part of his initial experimenting with furnaces and processes was concluded. He had started by reading everything he could find in English, French, and German on the subject of zinc and had, beginning in 1855, studied chemistry at Booth's laboratory. In September 1855 he consulted with the Swiss consul John Hitz concerning the feasibility of making spelter. Hitz had in 1838 made some from the red oxide found at Sterling Hill and used it at the U.S. arsenal in Washington to manufacture brass for a set of standard weights and measures. Hitz's estimates were optimistic, and on 25 October 1855, Wharton wrote to Illins, then president of the Pennsylvania and Lehigh Zinc Company, "He [Hitz] gives details adding up to $74 per ton meaning I suppose 2240 lbs."[4] That would be approximately three and one-third cents per pound for spelter which might sell on the market from between four and one-half and six cents.

During the same year Wharton began his experiments with furnaces. He maintained a spelter furnace in Philadelphia and in the winter of 1855–56 he caused a furnace to be built in South Bethlehem. Neither of these furnaces worked. Realizing his woeful lack of knowledge concerning the subject, he asked Roepper, who was going to Europe, "to get fuller information than we now possess relative to the best European processes of making spelter" and at the same time wrote of a desire to "import a few workmen skilled in the different branches of the business."[5] The following May he hired a man named Charles Hoofstetten to build a Silesian furnace of twenty muffles for the company. Hoofstetten's unsuccessful experiments demonstrated the problems involved in using silicate of zinc as the principal ore, anthracite as a fuel, and New Jersey clay for muffles. At the end of the year Wharton had another "small trial furnace" built, by whom and according to what plan are unknown. In April 1856, a man named E. J. Gerrand was experimenting with still another furnace, this one apparently near the mines.[6]

Upon the abrogation of the company's contract with Gilbert and Wetherill, Wharton employed Wetherill's former manager Nathan Bartlett to supervise the experiments in making spelter. Little is known of this highly competent man, who spent a lifetime in the zinc industry. Bartlett made the first important breakthrough shortly after Wharton had leased the oxide works and begun to develop a foreign market. Wrote Leibert to Wharton in December 1857, "Nathan is so well pleased with the successful working of the new furnace that he commenced dancing in the office for joy and said that he could not do justice to the subject in telling me how well they worked."[7] Under Bartlett's direction the experiments continued without pause.

Together Wharton and Bartlett settled on the Belgian furnace and undertook to adapt it to the peculiar ores, fuel, and clays of the Pennsylvania-New Jersey area. That is, they gave up hope of finding a revolutionary new process, being convinced that success could come in the easier way of improving on known methods. "It seems proper for me to add that I do not expect to introduce any startling novelties into the manufacture, nor to infringe in the least on any patent process, but merely to endeavor to bring the established European processes into practical use here with such modifications as circumstances or experience dictate," Wharton wrote to President Fisher.[8] In the "Memorandum" Wharton added the caution, "It is usually very bad economy to labor over the rudiments of an art which is to be transplanted, repeating perhaps, many futile unpublished experiments of its founders, when it is at all practicable for them to adopt the processes successfully used elsehwere."[9]

In August of 1858 Wharton asked Coates to send him "a complete set of the cylindrical vessels in which the charge is placed together with their appurtenances (the allonge, etc.) and the tools with which they are charged and cleaned" and also "1 dozen of each of the pieces of fire clay ware, and 1 or 2 of each of the iron tools with which they are worked", as well as "a crucible or pot with its cover and tube as the English spelter works use" provided they did not cost more than two or three pounds.

Probably about this time Wharton met Professor Brush, who visited Bethlehem and the zinc works at the end of August. Brush was several years younger than Wharton. He had studied under Silliman and become Professor of Metallurgy at the Yale Scientific School in 1855 after spending a year at the Royal Institute of Mines in London. For the next twelve years Wharton and Brush kept up a correspondence mostly on scientific subjects.

By November 1858 Wharton's initial experiments were nearing completion. Leibert wrote to him, "The metal furnace still continues to work successfully. Nathan took about 100 pounds from the retorts this morning. . . . Nathan has charged one of the retorts in a peculiar manner and expects an unusual quantity of metal from it."[10] Wharton was not complacent. He seriously considered going to Europe to learn more about the industry in spelter. The De Gee whom he knew by reputation to be an expert in the Belgian process was traveling in America. Wharton wrote him about the possibility of serving as a consultant and probably dropped the idea for the time being upon receiving from De Gee a reply to the effect that he would be available for one month at the exceedingly high figure of three hundred and forty pounds.[11]

By the end of the winter Wharton concluded that he had solved all major technical problems and was ready to begin making spelter on a large scale. He wrote to Coates, "It seems strange after a thing is once done that it was not done sooner, but the starting of a new manufacture is always difficult, and we have to contend here with want of knowledge as to the sorts of clay to be used, utter unskillfulness on the part of the workers, and the unfitness of our anthracite coal for the old forms of furnaces."[12]

Meanwhile, Wetherill had completed work on his spelter furnace and was preparing to begin production. Wetherill had not done as Wharton did by making adjustments to the Belgian furnace but had instead taken as a model an older European furnace no longer in use called the Carinthian and, according to Wharton, had closely followed "the patent of an Englishman named James Graham." The result was a furnace making excellent spelter. Roepper sent a superb pen and ink drawing of it to Brush. Wetherill obtained a patent for his invention in January 1859.

Wetherill made about fifty tons of spelter. He provided Alan Wood and Sons of Philadelphia with an ingot from which the first sheet zinc made in America was rolled. Then, almost as soon as Wetherill's venture was begun, it ended. His product was too expensive for the competition from European makers; his creditors were pressing him. Sometime during 1859 he abandoned the works altogether. Two years later the legislature amended the charter of his company to excuse it from paying certain bonuses and taxes which were due the commonwealth. In 1865 a local Bethlehem church weekly, *The Moravian*, contained a notice of intent to dissolve the Wetherill Zinc Company.[13]

3

On 1 March 1859 Wharton set down estimates of the cost of making spelter in his modified Belgian furnace. An oven containing forty-six muffles, he wrote, worked by five men should turn out six hundred pounds of spelter daily at a cost of $24.55. That was slightly more than four cents a pound. He was ready to approach the directors with a proposal.

Immediately, his ambition clouded his judgment. On 14 March he wrote President Fisher of the success of the furnace and went on to remark that since the company had not hired him to make spelter, he was free to patent his furnace and intended to do so. Wharton then offered to build for the company "for the sum of $10,000, realized from the sale of 10,000 reserved shares to the stockholders, and for 10,000 shares to be given to me, a complete spelter works capable of making 1000 tons of spelter per annum, and to contract with the Co. for 5 years to manufacture spelter for them in their works at 4 cts. per lb. I paying all expenses and cost of getting out and preparing ore."[14]

The directors could only regard this proposal as presumptuous. Wharton was their creature, not an independent manufacturer. What he did on company time and property belonged to them. The possibility that he might have paid the expenses of his experiments from his own pocket made no difference. Also, there was no way to check his estimates. And allowing him ten thousand shares of voting stock was out of the question.

Almost immediately after writing this letter to the company Wharton must have received counsel from someone, perhaps from his father-in-law Joseph Lovering or George T. Lewis, the director most friendly to him. The next day, and before receiving a reply from Fisher, Wharton presented Fisher with a more moderate proposal. He would not, he wrote, apply for a patent, in order to avoid any appearance of antagonism to the company; and instead of immediately building a spelter works he would entertain permission to erect a furnace to demonstrate the feasibility of the project. But, Wharton went on, if the company refused permission, he would build the furnace anyway. He gave the company a deadline of 1 May to reply.[15]

The directors surely needed no great amount of time in order to decide how to respond to this challenge. A week later Fisher replied to Wharton that the directors found his estimates of cost imperfect and for that reason refused a contract, "nor do I believe that a contract on the basis of your letter will ever be sanctioned by the directors, and possibly none on any terms."[16] The company would only agree to a demonstration furnace, and Wharton was to know that everything he did in preparing for the manufacture of spelter was the property of the company. The wording of Fisher's letter was such as to let Wharton know that if he chose to develop an industry in spelter for his own account he would be in deep trouble.

The directors had won. If he wanted to make spelter he had no realistic alternative to accepting their decisions. He wrote in a conciliatory tone agreeing to their terms "without reservation."[17] Privately he objected to what he regarded as their timidity in insisting on a demonstration furnace. As he saw it, his hope of success demanded that he assume that a complete spelter works was going to be built. He would in any event have to bring in skilled foreign laborers, and he could entice them to emigrate only by offering the prospect of permanent employment. The directors' hesitation was a source of vexation and delay rather than a cause for fearing a final veto.

Accordingly, Wharton bought land adjoining the oxide works and houses for laborers to live in and brought over several Belgians skilled in the business of making spelter.[18] In the summer he erected a demonstration furnace and by late September submitted a report to the directors proving that the cost of one thousand pounds of spelter was $40.71. Would they now agree to a full-scale spelter works?[19]

They hesitated, discussed the matter among themselves. Weeks passed. How Wharton must have chafed! He had proved he could make spelter at a little over four cents a pound which would sell for about six and one-half cents. New uses for metallic zinc were being found almost yearly, and a large market was developing in the telegraphic industry.

He prompted the directors with a proposal: He would build on their land and before 31 December 1861 a complete spelter works, which he would operate until then for his own benefit, paying the company $2.50 per ton for ore. After that date he would turn the works over to the company in exchange for eight thousand shares of stock.[20] He probably did not expect the company to accept this proposal, which would have given them little or no profit from the sale of ore and no real assurance that the factory would operate satisfactorily after 31 December 1861 and would have increased Wharton's equity in the company. Yet negotiations were at least underway, and he proceeded under an assumption that they would end in some sort of agreement. Using a Belgian workman named Lemal as an intermediary he again contacted De Gee, who had returned to Belgium, and offered to bring him back to the United States as a consultant for a reasonable fee. De Gee agreed to this, and Wharton immediately pressed him for other favors: samples of Belgian fire bricks and their molds; another potter; samples of Belgian zinc ore and Spanish carbonate ore. He arranged with De Gee to pay traveling expenses of a potter and the relatives of several of the workers who had previously emigrated.[21]

He finally signed a contract with the company on 11 December. He would build for the sum of thirty thousand dollars and by 1 July 1860 a spelter works of sixteen Belgian furnaces, each containing fifty-four muffles, suitably housed and serviced and capable of making three million pounds of spelter annually; would purchase from the company fifteen thousand tons of ore at an average price of $7.50 per ton; would rent the works from 1 July 1860, to 1 January 1863, at a sum of three thousand dollars per annum; and at the end of that period would turn it over to the company in good running order. The contract also required Wharton to hire the workmen imported from Europe at his own expense and to grant the company a free license to use any patents which he might take out. Disputes between him and the company were to be submitted to the arbitration of three referees, one each being appointed by Wharton and the company respectively and the third being chosen by the first two.[22]

Wharton would shortly call the contract a hard bargain. He was to receive nothing to increase his ownership in the company. He would have to assume all the risks of manufacture for a period of three years. He would receive only thirty thousand dollars in cash from the company while having to pay it at least $112,500 more for ore than the ore cost the company, the difference between $2.00 and $7.50 per ton for fifteen thousand tons. Actually, Wharton later claimed, the ore cost the company less than $2.00 per ton.

Wharton's letters in the fall and early winter of 1859–60 display gloom. He was risking his entire estate in a venture whose outcome was unforeseeable. He mortgaged all his real estate and used his negotiable securities as a means of raising cash. His first daughter, Joanna, had been born at Oak Hill on 16 December 1858, and since then Anna had rarely been with him in Bethlehem. Abandoning her earlier position, she now did not want to live in Bethlehem. Reluctantly he wrote her that they would have to rent rooms at the Sun Hotel and live there for the next few years. "My business is here and I have next to none in Philadelphia."[23] But the baby was sick a good deal of the time, so that Wharton faced a prospect of spending the winter in Bethlehem without his wife. He developed a carbuncle on an ankle and experienced headaches. About the time he wanted to begin building, the weather turned bad. He wrote to Anna:

> The weather had prevented even a beginning being made at the new spelter works, and I cannot feel very sanguine about that business, being left to my own resources to work out a difficult and comparatively untried manufacture and knowing perfectly well that human kind have no more mercy than wolves to any one who fails or even shows weakness. I feel in fact discouraged just now about my affairs generally, but will work on as well as I can, and suffer the consequences. . . . It probably seems impossible to thee that we could ever come to want, and in fact thee can have but vague notions of what that is, but in reality better people than we have found themselves unable to get clothing or food of the meanest kind, and I have a sort of abiding fear that we have had perhaps our share of good fortune in our youth, and must in some way atone for it before we die (if not after).[24]

He dickered with De Gee over a reasonable consulting fee. De Gee wanted a flat sum of four hundred pounds plus expenses for fifteen days. Wharton offered instead two hundred pounds plus expenses for a period of up to three months and a bonus of two hundred pounds if De Gee's advice proved valuable. Matters were not entirely settled when Wharton learned that De Gee planned to leave Belgium on the steamer *City of Baltimore* on 1 January.[25] Wharton wrote to Anna, "The further I go, the better I am satisfied that the enterprise of founding the new business can be accomplished successfully without the aid of De Gee, and though prudence dictates that I should not neglect any reasonable means of procuring his aid, yet my plans are now so well established and seem to me so satisfactory, that he will have to show good reason (if he should come) to induce me to change them."[26]

De Gee was already on the high seas, having received an advance of one thousand dollars from Wharton who knew that in the end he must pay what De Gee demanded. He wrote Anna, "I must try to get my $2000 worth out of him while he stays, and that may require strong pumping, to say nothing of the doubt whether I have buckets enough to hold all the water to be drawn from so capacious a well."[27]

De Gee arrived, cheerful, considerate, a model of professional competence, bringing with him two additional workers and the mother of another who had previously come to Bethlehem. Wharton found his French good enough to converse with De Gee and agreed with him for three hundred and fifty pounds plus expenses for a period of one month. "I like him better than I expected and think him a good bargain at the price. I think Father will like him, he is such a thoroughgoing chap."[28] The weather continued bad with storm after storm delaying construction and frost resulting from extremely cold temperatures ruining the foundation of the main chimney. Still, Wharton's spirits revived. De Gee added to assistance praise for his work.

Now, subtle flattery such as can be administered in the continental style was a new experience for Wharton. He fell hard and wrote to Anna:

De Gee does not spoil on acquaintance, and we agree together very well, helping each other forward with the work. . . . He thinks I must make a great deal of money by my contract, but does not yet put his estimate into figures. . . . While he stays . . . I learn what I can from him as to the business, as to talking French and as to habits, for he is remarkably temperate and robust, living at home on two meals a day, consisting of meat, bread, wine and coffee only. I fancy that he and I have had an effect on each other's state of mind or course of thought or magnetic condition, he becoming rather more subdued and tranquil—that is, less vehement and demonstrative; I on the other hand becoming a little more sprightly and less sluggish.[29]

During the next two weeks Wharton's admiration of Dee Gee increased. "I have some idea of trying to get De Gee to stay here another month to start the block of furnaces which is mostly finished, but it costs so high that I can hardly stand it." At Wharton's request De Gee agreed to remain for an additional month for three hundred and fifty pounds. "It is paying dear for instruction, but the school is perhaps not so dear as that of experience which we were told the fools insist on learning in. . . . A future partnership is thought of on both parts, by him I believe as favorably as by me, but naturally nothing can be arranged now as to that."[30]

The thought of a partnership by one as committed as was Wharton to the idea of single control indicates the extent to which De Gee captivated him. If

Wharton's enthusiasm outran his judgment—as it assuredly did—at least it helped him through a trying winter. Anna continued living in Philadelphia; the weather remained foul. Still, Wharton cheerfully worked at the factory during the day. He began training American workmen in the skills needed for operating a spelter works. He read or visited Roepper and others during the evening and even improved the manufacture of oxide, doing, as he put it, his bit "towards bringing Cosmos out of Chaos, and naturally feeling satisfaction therein."[31]

The financial picture of the company improved. The directors sought and obtained an amendment to the charter allowing them more control over the sale of stock, greater freedom in borrowing, and changing the corporate name to that of Lehigh Zinc Company.

Wharton pressed De Gee to remain in Bethlehem and manage the spelter works for three years. De Gee tentatively agreed to this provided that Wharton would pay him a fixed salary of six thousand dollars, give him half the difference between the cost of production and three and one-half cents a pound or one-fourth cent a pound bonus on all zinc made, whichever Wharton preferred, and allow him the free use of a house, a servant, a horse, heat, and light. Wharton replied that he was only willing to pay the six thousand dollars for a period of two and one-half years (from 1 July 1860 to 31 December 1862), provided that De Gee could make spelter for three and one-half cents a pound; but that he would split any additional saving with De Gee if he could reduce the cost below three and one-half cents.

De Gee hesitated and Wharton knew why. He wrote to Anna explaining that De Gee "has been examining afresh his calculations and finds a little mistake of about $100,000 to $150,000 which makes it quite impossible for him to produce zinc at or near the figure named . . . I shall probably have to work out my own salvation in this business, as nearly every body has to in nearly every serious affair, myself."[32] A few days later De Gee archly withdrew his original offer, informing Wharton he had no further offer to make.[33]

De Gee's error helped Wharton to modify his estimate of the man. Still, he acknowledged the assistance De Gee had given. De Gee had proposed several changes in the plan for the furnaces which Wharton not only accepted but allowed him to patent. Wharton had the petition for the patents drawn up a few days before De Gee was scheduled to leave for Europe. De Gee made a trip of several days to Philadelphia then returned to Bethlehem, where he had some final business to attend to before departing for New York.

In Bethlehem, De Gee dropped his urbane manner. Leibert wrote of it to Wharton:

> Mr. Fisher's two letters of today are received, also your letter containing bill of exchange and patent papers, and the packet received by De

Gee. The specification and two draughts of spelter furnace were duly executed this morning but the patent papers he preferred to take with him to New York to be executed there, as he could not read them. I suggested that if he desired I would ask Mr. Roepper to translate them for him as it would be better to have them executed in Pennsylvania and would give him more time to see his friends in New York. He then informed me that he had received a letter from Mr. Fisher stating that he would meet him in New York tomorrow and that he would have to leave with the morning 8 o'clock train, but desired me to fetch Roepper. When Roepper commenced reading the patent papers, he snatched them out of his hands and threw them on the floor and became much excited and quite angry and said that there was ample time to have had all these matters arranged before this and now at the last moment the Zinc Co. wanted to take advantage of him that he never said or agreed to grant a license for more than sixteen furnaces, that his contract was with him and you and not the Penna. & Lehigh Zinc Co., that he was no fool and not to be trifled with. I then picked up the patent papers and told him to hand them to Mr. Fisher at New York tomorrow and settle the matter with him. He did not pay me for the ticket and the divers sums of money you requested me to collect from him, but handed me the enclosed statement and letter for you. . . . There is something wrong somewhere and some foul play is going on.[34]

Wharton was stunned. A personality had emerged whose presence he had never suspected. Had Wharton unwittingly offended De Gee? Or was De Gee provoking a quarrel in order to cover up his mistakes? Clearly, the business about the patent papers was a pretext. Had De Gee expected something more than he got from Wharton or the company and in his disappointment fired this parting shot? Although Wharton thought that this was the best explanation, neither then nor later did De Gee's motives become clear. But the facts of his accusation against Wharton and angry departure could not be ignored.

Wharton wrote of the matter to Anna:

De Gee turns out to be a hog at last, which I am sorry for. I received this morning from Leibert a letter enclosing one from him with a trumped up bill against me for plans, etc., which were paid for with his services by the first £400. He also left a letter for me here claiming to have made me a present of £40 because when he asked £340 I offered £200, for another month's services, we compromised at £300. He failed to perform several things here which he had promised to do, failed to pay for his ticket to Europe or his board, but carried off my presents, which latter circumstance shows him to be less alive to what usually passes for honor than I had supposed him to be.[35]

Wharton understood his mistake and profited from it. Of De Gee he wrote, "What I learned from him was necessary to be learned, and though it cost dear, it could not be had cheaper." "I see continually plainer how great will be the difficulty of training, governing, and keeping in profitable work, 96 furnace men, all of whom must be made to work laboriously, honestly, and skillfully in a hard business new to the country, before profit begins to come to me."[36] His ultimate reaction took the course of downgrading De Gee's person and ability. In a letter to William Penn Tatham, Wharton congratulated himself on being rid of De Gee and for "not having made any closer association with the owner of a temper so incompatible with my phlegmatic one." In November Wharton wrote to President Fisher that Roepper had just returned from Europe "where he was commissioned to procure zinc information for me. He tells me (1) The Vieille Montaigne works are a dead ringer for ours; and that (2) De Gee is considered in Belgium, a charlatan."[37]

An immediate reaction of Wharton to De Gee's departure was that of taking steps to increase his force of skilled Belgian workers. He forwarded two hundred pounds to an agent, Ludwig Koch, to pay for their passage and sent one of the workers named Detrixhe to Europe to accompany them to Bethlehem. He prepared for their arrival by ordering pass books each of which would contain statements for the worker to sign. One was an agreement to stay with Wharton for a specified term; another was a promise to give at least a week's notice if the worker left after the first term of service was over. He also planned to hold back a tenth part of their wages "as security for their good behavior."[38]

Other problems beset him that spring. Heavy rains caused a flood in the streams coming down South Mountain. The water filled the ash pits of the completed block of furnaces and caused the blocks under construction to settle and crack. They would have to be rebuilt, and the loss would amount to two thousand dollars. President Fisher, urged on by a party of stockholders, pressed Wharton to resign from the board of directors on the grounds of conflict of interest. At first Wharton resisted, but then yielded. Detrixhe wrote from Belgium that he was having trouble getting workers because De Gee was discouraging them. Detrixhe wanted Wharton to sign a contract guaranteeing them two dollars per day and providing for other privileges which Wharton declared would leave them "very much their own masters." Trouble arose at the spelter works in the form of jealousy directed against Bartlett. An unnamed informer told Wharton that Bartlett was agitating against the spelter works behind his back. Wharton confronted Bartlett with the charges, writing that "My confidence in a man is not lost by trifles, but once forfeited, it is not renewed. I believe that nobody yet has thriven long after falling out with me. Between you and me there is no break now; how it will be in the future will depend on your conduct."[39] Bartlett denied the charges, and Wharton's faith in him was restored.

He had a tiff with Anna, who was still in Philadelphia. He criticized her for the care of Joanna (Joey), who was sick. "I thought a good deal about thee and the baby at bed time last night, but there seems to be no way but to let thee manage thy own way, since thee has the main charge and responsibility.

It is however well to remember that dry heat and confined air and dark rooms do not suit me at all, and that the baby probably partakes of my constitution as well as thine." He wanted Anna with him in Bethlehem: "Our housekeeping in Philadelphia is an expensive farce, and it is likely that I at least will settle here to reside." He commented on the danger of him and Anna growing accustomed to living apart.[40]

Anna joined him at the hotel for the early part of the summer. She did not especially trust the doctors in Bethlehem, and she was concerned about the health of her parents, especially her father. He suffered from neuralgia and with the passing of years had lost none of his possessiveness. His daughter Mary, together with the genial Charles, were often at Oak Hill. Joseph Lovering would have had Anna with him if he could have wheedled her into it. Wharton invited the Loverings to spend some time with them in June. Plans were made, but at the last minute Lovering canceled them, pleading a sore throat.[41]

Wrote Wharton, "A sort of callousness comes to my aid when things get very bad, so that I can go ahead for a good while through foul weather, and we all know that every storm has an end at last." In the midst of difficulties that spring he wrote to Coates, "I am now making but a trifling quantity of spelter with 2 furnaces, and do not expect to get the new works into full operation for some months; in the meantime my spelter is eagerly taken at $6\frac{1}{4}$ cts. per lb. while the best Silesian sells for 5 to $5\frac{1}{4}$, and something like this difference is expected to continue even after I turn out larger quantities."[42]

In June Anna and the baby came to the Sun Hotel. Their stay of several weeks coincided with a respite from troubles. But as spring turned into summer these were resumed. Progress on construction lagged behind schedule. The Belgian workers did not arrive at the time expected. He made a trip to Washington in an unsuccessful attempt to get support for an increase in the tariff on spelter from one-half cent to one cent a pound. Anna returned to Philadelphia and accompanied her parents on a vacation to Atlantic City.

Then came the disaster of Darlington.

Wharton needed a supervisor for the works. At one time he had thought of De Gee for the position, and after De Gee had left in a huff Wharton began looking for someone else. Men knowledgeable in making zinc did not exist in the United States. He wrote to several prospects in Europe and received no answers. Finally, on the basis of no strong recommendation from anyone, he engaged a man named George Darlington who had made spelter in Minna, England. Darlington was to come to Bethlehem on a trial basis at Wharton's expense. He arrived on 17 July, and almost immediately Wharton realized that he had made another error. Darlington, he wrote to Anna, was neither as energetic nor as experienced as he had hoped. "I am less pleased with him than I was with De Gee." Still, with Darlington on hand Wharton could leave for a few days and take a vacation with his wife at Atlantic City. "I do not mean to forswear walking, sailing, bathing, ten pins and riding, but I do mean to go to bed early every night."[43] On the twenty-fourth he returned to Bethlehem to find a heavy casting broken in the new block of furnaces, Darlington sick, and the workers close to rebellion.

Wharton tried to retrieve his mistake by educating the new manager, but Darlington had no aptitude for supervising people. The new lot of Belgian workers arrived on 1 August, thirteen in all, and soon joined the others in disliking Darlington. They would not work for a "Johnny Bull" they said. Before the end of the month discipline had almost disappeared. Wharton wrote to Anna, "Things have gone on very badly here since I last left—men in a meeting—no product from furnaces—Darlington going about with a pistol."[44] Darlington threatened to shoot one of the men, and Wharton fired him. Darlington left peaceably.

Again Wharton had made a mistake, and again he placed the blame elsewhere than on himself. He wrote to Brush, "These foreigners don't seem to do well in America. Their experience and prejudices and tempers are unsuitable to our climate."[45] The principal result of the affair was that Wharton had to manage the spelter works himself. He appointed Detrixhe as his assistant and resigned himself to a protracted stay in Bethlehem. Again he tried to interest Anna in living in the town. On 23 August she came with Joanna for a brief stay, then left for their Twelfth Street house complaining of the discomfort of the Sun's apartments. He tried without success to rent a suitable house, then asked Anna if she would prefer that they move to the Eagle Hotel. She gave a decided "no" to that and wrote, "It is no small trial for me to leave my own house and home, I can assure thee, although thee does not see any reason for it, but I go to Bethlehem especially for thy comfort, and let thee decide as thee may, I expect to abide by the conclusion with as good grace as I possibly can."[46]

He was overworked, and his Uncle Thomas Hollingsworth recommended that he resign the position of general manager of the company. Wharton hesitated. His salary was substantial, being $6,666.67 for 1860.[47] But the spelter works was demanding most of his time, and his troubles with the directors seemed to be increasing. He claimed that the company should make him an allowance of 6 percent in weight for the ore because of the moisture it contained. The company refused this, and the dispute went to arbitration. Then he and Fisher argued concerning the appointment of arbitrators.[48]

He waited until the spelter works was completed and operating for his own benefit. That was about three months after the stipulated date of 1 July 1860. Although the delay was for technical reasons allowable under the contract, it had meant a postponement of the time at which Wharton could expect to reap a profit. But on 15 October he sent a brief letter to President Fisher: "I desire to resign the position of General Manager of the Lehigh Zinc Company as soon as a suitable person can be found to take the place."

The company was prepared for this. A replacement, James Jenkins, was on hand. Thus ended Wharton's employment by Lehigh Zinc.

It did not mark the beginning of profit from the new spelter works. The deteriorating situation between North and South had further trials in store.

4

From the point of view of a refiner of metals the spelter works was a stunning success. Wharton was rightly proud of its product. He sought and received endorsements for the purity of his zinc from some of the country's leading chemists, namely, Brush, Booth, and the Massachusetts laboratory of Francis H. Storer and Charles W. Eliot. Brush suggested that Wharton make about one ton of pure spelter for use by chemists throughout the United States. Wharton was elated and made the zinc as promptly as possible. "I selected a quantity of the cleanest silicate of zinc, calcined it in a new roasting furnace, rejected, after roasting, all pieces which from discoloration or otherwise appeared suspicious, ground it in a clean mill, and then distilled it in a furnace which had never before been used, rejecting all the first and last products of distillation from each charge in each retort." He sent an ingot of the zinc to the Franklin Institute, which acknowledged the superiority of his accomplishment. A shipment of almost pure zinc ingots went to the Philadelphia and San Francisco mints "for reducing silver to the metallic state in separating it from gold (viz. mixing granulated zinc with Chloride of Silver)."[49]

But making the best zinc on the market would not necessarily pay the wages of the workers, as Wetherill had discovered. As soon as the spelter works was finished and operating, the market for zinc shrank and the price declined. The country was in the turmoil of a presidential election campaign with a threat that if Lincoln were victorious secession and possibly war would follow. Businessmen were cautious and cut back on orders; and at the same time the government seemed unconcerned about preparing for war. The election of Lincoln and the subsequent actions by southern states prolonged the depression. Not even the firing on Fort Sumter immediately relieved the situation. Normal trade with Europe and the Southern states was disrupted, and the country refused to believe in the possibility of a prolonged conflict. Zinc was essential for making cartridges. In the event of war it would become scarce and the price would leap upward. But why plan for a disaster which nobody wanted? For about nine months the trade in zinc products slowed almost to a halt and the manufacture of munitions did not significantly increase.

The depression occurred at a time when Wharton most needed money to repay the cost of building the works. He was heavily in debt, having borrowed from banks and individuals in Philadelphia and Bethlehem. Before the end of 1860 he floated a loan of ten thousand dollars from the Lehigh Zinc Company. Making spelter cost 3.47 cents per pound in 1861, not including selling costs, allowance for depreciation, and interest. At four cents he figured he might break even. Below that he would, if he sold at all, sell at a loss.

He toured the New England states seeking for customers who would be willing to pay a premium price for zinc of high quality. "I have been looking a little into the telegraphic zinc business, and have obtained Prof. Morse's promise to recommend the use of my zinc for all the batteries employed by the American Telegraph Co.," he wrote to Edward N. Trotter and Company, the Philadelphia firm which he had selected as agent for marketing spelter within the United States.[50] He sold small quantities abroad through the agency of Robert Haydock. He tried to cut shipping costs by using the canals, on which charges were lower than those imposed by the railroad companies; and he endeavored, apparently without success, to get a rebate on canal freight rates.[51]

The situation did not dissuade him from continuing full production. He knew that sooner or later, war or no war, the price would rise. The problem was to hold out, keeping his workers employed and happy, until it did. He paid the men partly in notes and supplies, as he had done in 1857. In late March 1861 he noted, "I have on hand here this morning 840,205 lbs. of common Spelter, which will be increased to about 880,000 by 4/1; also 57,914 lbs. Mint Ingots, and 5441 lbs. Pure Zinc."[52]

He sought from the company relief of a sort which he might have received from a member of the family. He was operating under a contract which required him to pay three thousand dollars a year rent and a high price for ore. He knew that if his contract were with Charles or Joseph Thurston it would be adjusted in view of the depression, especially as respected the price for ore. If the company would make allowances of this sort he would eventually provide everything the contract called for. But the directors of the Lehigh Zinc Company did not behave like members of his family. They acted as was customary in business. They held Wharton to the letter of his contract at every moment, granting him relief only when it was in their immediate financial interest to do so. He wrote to George T. Lewis objecting to this attitude. He pointed out that he had over fifty thousand dollars worth of spelter stockpiled; that spelter was selling at a loss; and that the company should grant him relief in the price he was paying for ore. He phrased his request so as to emphasize the company's dependence on him, warning that "when it comes to smashing, I will not be the only one hurt." He concluded, "That I am now solvent and in perfect credit and have strong family connections, is all true, but such times as these soon eat up margins and I will positively not accept aid from family connections."[53]

The Lehigh Zinc Company, to Wharton's indignation, offered instead to annul the contract entirely. This would have put Wharton out of the zinc business, led to temporary closing of the spelter works, and left the company in full possession of them. He refused, pointing out, "1st, It would I suppose entail on me the loss of outlay in establishing the business, and of tools & materials on hand; 2nd, it would throw 100 men out of work including a number of foreigners who are entirely dependent on me; 3rd, it seems unwise to break up a business so hard to establish for a cause which may pass away in a few months; and 4th, I should feel mortified to abandon the enterprise." He repeated a request that the contract be modified and not annulled.[54]

He tried another tack. He offered the company an opportunity to share the risk he was taking by buying two hundred thousand pounds of his spelter at four cents. He pointed out that the company would make a handsome profit by holding on to the spelter until the price rose to a normal six cents. Again the company refused, and Wharton turned elsewhere for relief. Nathan Trotter and Company had offered to advance him three and one-half cents per pound up to fifty thousand dollars. He accepted that and authorized Trotter to sell what he could at four cents.[55]

His next altercation with the zinc company concerned the quality of the ore. When Wharton was general manager he had seen to it that he received—and promptly—the best lump ore. Jenkins, the new manager, was not so generous. Wharton repeatedly claimed he was being insufficiently supplied, that production was therefore lagging, and that the ore sent was fine ore. The contract, he wrote, called for lump ore, and the calcining furnaces were only suitable for treating lump ore. At one point he refused to accept any further shipments of ore which he considered to be below standard. This dispute, like the one concerning moisture in the ore, went to arbitration. The company chose James C. Booth as its representative. Wharton opted for William Longstreth. These referees selected a Mr. Roberts (possibly the railroad engineer Solomon Roberts, whom Wharton knew and who was then frequently in the area) as the third arbitrator. When the company objected to this choice, and Booth considered withdrawing, Wharton blew up. He wrote scathingly to Booth:

"The Lehigh Zinc Co. has at its head a half-breed lawyer with some knowledge of business. That Co. made a bargain with me hard enough for the prosperous times on which it was predicated, held me strictly to the full performance of it in these times, sent me ore for several months notoriously below contract quality, (fine, not lump ore) and refused to allow me any deduction in price unless my claim was absolutely proved."[56]

The final decision was that of extending Wharton's lease of the factory from 1 January 1863 to 1 April 1863, "in order to compensate for certain deficient deliveries of ore."[57]

During the first four months of 1861 Joseph and Anna continued sparring about living in Bethlehem. Anna wrote from the Sun Hotel to her parents that the winter was dismal and Joey's health indifferent. "Bread, butter, molasses and molasses candy is about all she lives on."[58] She welcomed an occasional visit from Mary and Charles and baskets of freshly baked bread, butter, crackers, and fruits from the conservatory, which her mother sent once and sometimes twice a week. In late February she made an extended visit to Oak Hill. Joseph wrote her that he was keeping "Bachelor's Hall—all shutters & windows open, no fire in the room, played billiards with Jenkins and Luckenbach without feeling guilty, etc."[59] She returned to Bethlehem in late March and succeeded with Joseph in making Leibert promise to redecorate their apartment. The renovations occasioned another visit to Philadelphia, this time to stay with Charles and Mary.[60]

5

In the late spring of 1861 the depression in the zinc industry rapidly disappeared as Northern attitudes toward the South stiffened. President Lincoln called for volunteers. He and the Congress prepared to supply them with arms and ammunition. The stockpile at the Bethlehem Spelter Works— the name Wharton had given to his refinery—began to diminish. By the end of the year he was able to report that the average price he received for spelter sold in 1861 was 4.30 cents a pound. He paid the back wages of his workers and began coming out from under a mountain of debt.[61]

The war changed much else for him and persons with whom he had to deal. Patriotic sentiments provided relief from old tensions. A spirit of self-sacrifice and losses of loved ones helped people to forget their former petty squabbles and little acts of selfishness.

With the onset of hostilities a burst of patriotic fervor swept Bethlehem. Many young men answered the call for volunteers and earned the title, later treasured, of First Defenders. Anna's immediate reaction to the prowar sentiment was a concern for her husband. As a Quaker in a non-Quaker community he would be suspected of pacifism with consequent loss of respect from leaders of the community and the men at the spelter works. He might even be in some physical danger. An incident provided a test which she feared he might fail. Employees at the oxide works had demanded a flag be raised on company property. Jenkins had granted the request. Now, the men at the spelter works wanted the same thing. She knew her husband would not allow it.

She need not have been concerned. Wharton was not a pacifist, and he had the confidence of his workmen. Although his attitude toward slavery was the same as it had been almost a decade earlier, he believed that the South should not go unpunished for violating the nation's Constitution and laws. He wrote to his mother explaining the situation and justifying his position.

He had, he wrote, already given money to the committee which was supplying the volunteers and could not absolutely subscribe to a doctrine of non-
resistance,

> though I could to the propriety of less suffering, and of such conduct as
> will avoid giving offense to any. On the other side is a copy of a letter which
> I sent to the Committee having in charge the outfit of volunteers and the
> maintenance of their families. I gave that money because it appears to be
> rather mean to avoid having any part of the burdens of a community in
> which nearly all my possessions lie.
>
> My men at the Works determined to have a fine flag, and subscribed
> money to buy it, but I will not allow it to go on the works, because I choose
> to avoid being conspicuous if possible, and it will consequently be planted
> in a field just opposite the works—perhaps I will make a little speech on
> the occasion showing how necessary it is for all to be loyal to their
> government, and to their flag as the emblem of law & order, even if they do
> not go out and battle for it.
>
> I cannot find it in my heart to condemn the rest of our Northern people
> to meet the rebels in war. It seems to me that if they fail to do so, our
> civilization would be grievously if not fatally wounded, yet as there are
> numerous young fellows eager to fight, I am content to let them attend to
> that, which may be called the outdoor branch of the business, while I
> remain at home endeavoring, by keeping the factory at work to maintain a
> number of families in comfort.[62]

Although he did not say as much to his mother, he was in fact willing to
support the Northern war effort in everything but personally bearing arms.
He would make zinc for shells; use the profits to buy bonds; and contribute
money to the support of soldiers and their families. As for being drafted into
the army, he went to some pains in 1862 to be elected as a school director in
Philadelphia as a possible way of avoiding this, and after the passage of the
Enrollment Act of 1863 had little to fear.[63] Being married and over thirty-
five years of age, he fell into a class which was not to be called up until the
classes of all males between the ages of twenty and thirty-five years and of
unmarried men between thirty-five and forty-five were exhausted.

Wharton appears not to have been opposed to any war which in his opinion
was forced on the country as the only means of defending legitimate interests. He had, moreover, at this early stage of his career decided that the
principal threat to Americans came not from the South, whose people were,
after all, Americans, but from England, the rich and unscrupulous trading
nation whose policies he believed subverted the attempts of American industrialists to build a strong national economy. Wharton held a view concerning
the chief events of 1861 shared by a number of other Northern industrialists,
who later joined him in demanding high protective tariffs. He was willing, he
wrote Joseph Thurston, to allow the South to secede: "If Virginia, Maryland,

etc. stay in for a few months I think all will go tolerably well, even if the cotton people set up housekeeping permanently for themselves, which they are welcome to do so far as I am concerned. Then if we can buy out the darkies from what are now the Border Slave States, and annex Canada, we shall be stronger than ever."[64] The real danger to peace lay in the attitude of England, which by supporting the Southern states in secession would aggravate the government of the Union to a point of war. As late as May 1861 Wharton wrote Anna anticipating war with England in three months.

Probably the leading businessmen in Bethlehem knew of Wharton's attitude toward England and the South. At least some agreed with him. The majority of the people only saw him as doing his duty in helping fight the rebels. Already he had the cooperation of his workers. He went among them, talked with them, and defended them. On one occasion he took special pains to have jailed a bully who had fought with several. He attempted to get the supervisors of Saucon Township, in which South Bethlehem was then located, to build a road to the village of Friedensville where some of the workers lived. He wrote the legislature of the commonwealth asking that South Bethlehem be made a separate election district for the convenience of the workers, in order that they might not have to go to Hellertown, four miles distant, to vote.[65] All this and more, in addition to his success in manufacturing spelter and support of the war effort, made him almost universally popular. All doors were open to him. He entered many and by his wit, courtesy, consideration for others, and quiet dignity enhanced still further his standing in the community.

This popularity naturally worked to the benefit of Anna, who with the shifting opinions occasioned by war again changed her attitude toward living in Bethlehem. She now stayed most of the time with him in the Sun Hotel, wrote of enjoying life there, even encouraged him to begin a Friends' Meeting on fourth days in the "Methodist Meeting House." She made friends with the wives of Joseph's acquaintances and the townspeople. Her father and mother finally visited Bethlehem in what proved to be a triumphant occasion for all concerned. Other relatives made trips to stay with her and Joseph. Her sister Mary was a frequent guest, coming sometimes with her two children, Joseph Shallcross and Hannah, and often also accompanied by Charles. Cousins of both Anna and Joseph—Corbits, Hollingsworths, and Fishers—came from Philadelphia and Reading. The Thurstons and Haydocks visited from New York City. Philadelphia friends included the names of Dorsey, Shoemaker, Brown, Ogden, Fisher, and Tom Mott. Lucretia and James Mott signed the Sun Hotel register on 26 June 1862. Several nieces and nephews spent time in Bethlehem in addition to Charles's and Mary's children, namely, Hannah and Robert Haydock's children Samuel, Sarah, Mary, and Robert; Mary and Joseph Thurston's son William; and Sarah and Abraham Barker's son Wharton. Joseph hired young Samuel Haydock as an assistant at the spelter works. Anna's brother Joseph Shallcross Lovering visited on several occasions, as did Joseph's mother and sisters Anna and Hetty.

During the next eighteen months, when the price of spelter rose to six and one-fourth, then to seven and three-eights, and finally to fifteen cents a pound, Wharton made a modest fortune. He put forty thousand dollars of it into United States gold bonds and most of the rest into other investments. By the time he left the zinc business he was nominally worth approximately two hundred thousand dollars.[66]

He would have liked to continue in the business of making spelter, but knew he could not. On the first of April 1863 his contract would expire. He had cut ties with the directors of the Lehigh Zinc Company and could expect nothing more from them. He had tried and failed to discover an independent source of ore. He canvassed and gave up an idea of starting a rolling mill for turning out sheet zinc.[67]

He was not bitter. He had played with all the resources at his disposal and had lost the one thing on which success for him ultimately depended, control. But he had earned a substantial capital which was there to feed an ambition as yet far from being satisfied. He had gained friends, reputation, and self-confidence. His troubles with Anna seemed to be over. In late summer, 1862, she moved back to Oak Hill and on 27 September bore a second daughter, whom they named Mary. She did not thereafter return to Bethlehem except for short visits. He looked forward to joining her within several months at their Twelfth Street residence.

He had another consolation, one which he highly valued. He had made a major contribution to the development of an independent American economy. As he correctly wrote in the "Memorandum," "The entire spelter and sheet zinc manufacture of the United States, now a large and growing industry, may fairly be said to have sprung from this factory, for not only was it the pioneer in point of time by at least two years, but I believe that neither of the others succeeded until it availed itself of the services of men procured from this establishment." A growing sentiment of patriotism underlay this pride of accomplishment. He was sensing, as was many another Northern businessman of those times, a national unity which he was helping to bring about and which he considered ought to be highly regarded. Support of the Union cause and opposition to England strongly contributed to this patriotic spirit. It would continue to grow in him, becoming within a few years a prime source of motivation.

He began laying plans for leaving Bethlehem. Upon hearing of the birth of his daughter Mary he wrote to Anna, "I turn over in my mind many possibilities for the future, endeavoring to discern which of them will best conduce to the comfort and real welfare and development of all of us. . . . It is evident that next spring must witness a great if not almost total change in our course of life, and the new one must not be sluggish ease for either of us, for that is the beginning of death, which we are hardly ready for."[68]

Anna read him rightly and replied with characteristic sobriety, "Do not be hasty . . . about making any new investments. It is best as thee remarks to wait until the right path seems quite apparent. We have a snug and very comfortable home at present and I don't see any reason for making a change without mature deliberation."[69]

She could not, and did not really want to, put a stop to his ambition; yet she had unwittingly won a point. Wherever his future business interests might lie, never again would he consider any place but Philadelphia or its northern suburbs, where her parents lived, as a place of permanent residence.

7

Venture in Nickel

The Civil War brought prosperity to the North and hastened the growth of nationalism among industrialists, who promptly identified the welfare of America with themselves. They attempted to secure this identification by demanding gifts from those in control of America: suppression of the Indians by troops; grants of western lands; improvements in rivers and harbors; better banking and postal services; relief from taxes; protection by tariffs; and so forth. They saw themselves as "going places" and taking the country with them. They insisted that government should help build the roads along which they traveled, and having built the roads should do nothing to stop them from speeding along in whatever vehicles and at whatever pace they desired.

Yet even while making these demands Northern industrialists found that they wanted to travel along different roads, and that government could not build them all. Individual interests often clashed; and because this was so, the good of America could not be the same as that of any one party. It could indeed accommodate the interests of industrialists as a class only by admitting the existence of restraints on initiative such as would divert some activity from the pursuit of immediate financial gain to representation, discussion, and compromise. Northern industrialists saw that they must compete in politics as well as in the marketplace in order to determine which roads should be built; and then they must abide by the outcome.

Accordingly, their nationalism included two sentiments which cohabited more from necessity than love. One was an attraction to government as a source of favors; the other was a fear of it as a threat to liberty. They sustained the two sentiments by a devotion to constitutional forms and democratic processes, which they had fought the Civil War to preserve, and which they now intended to use to achieve some sort of working compromise between liberties to be supported and restraints to be imposed. They came to believe that a strong national economy depended on both the exercise of individual initiative and democracy, such as gave each a hope that he might benefit therefrom and a fear that he might not.

Wharton was one of the thousands of postwar industrialists who made

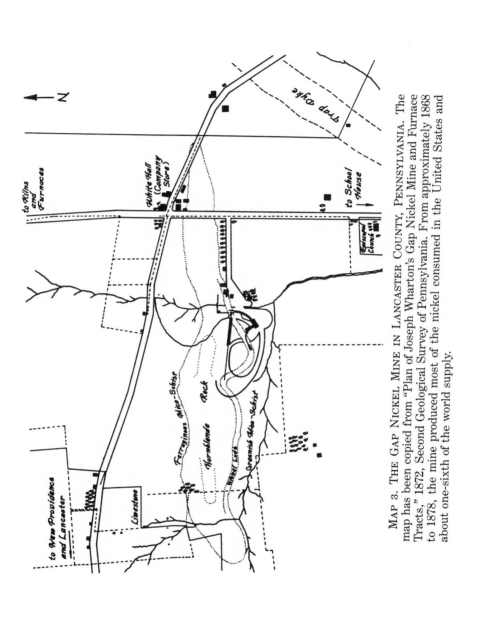

MAP 3. THE GAP NICKEL MINE IN LANCASTER COUNTY, PENNSYLVANIA. The map has been copied from "Plan of Joseph Wharton's Gap Nickel Mine and Furnace Tracts," 1872, Second Geological Survey of Pennsylvania. From approximately 1868 to 1878, the mine produced most of the nickel consumed in the United States and about one-sixth of the world supply.

America by an exercise of individual initiative up to that point beyond which any more threatened to wreck it—threatened, rather than accomplished the wrecking, because the precise location of the dividing line between freedom and restraint was never finally established and, given the diversity of interests and the continuing practice of democracy, could not be.

1

He was thirty-seven years of age when he left the zinc industry. His life up to that time seems to have been a preparation: He had concentrated on developing his powers, economizing his intellectual and physical strength in order to direct them with maximum force toward amassing a capital on which further growth depended. His life had moved through stages of which each was characterized by one thing only, first farming and then in succession bookkeeping, white lead, brickmaking, zinc oxide, and spelter. His future was not to know the same sort of progression from one enterprise to another. He would always be governed by personal interest and the availability of opportunities to promote it; but he would pursue these in the context of a larger view of his and the country's welfare and would not hesitate to undertake new projects before the ones in process were completed. He would simultaneously engage in the production of nickel, iron, and steel and add to these interests of lesser import such as sugar beets, fishing, railroads, and gold. While sustaining these industrial pursuits he would promote a plan of pure water for Philadelphia which would be both a public service and a source of private profit. Throughout the remainder of his life, whatever the range of other interests, he would carry the banner for high protective tariffs, engage in related political activities, and promote the cause of science through his own study and by contributions to education.

His later career was destined to be a model of the sort of thing happening to America. He was to make further landmark contributions that might be worthy of independent notice, for example, the founding of the nickel industry, the manufacture of pure malleable nickel, the establishment of the Wharton School at the University of Pennsylvania, and the gathering together of acreages in the pinelands of New Jersey to form what is known today as the Wharton Tract. Yet his true place as a pioneer industrialist was to depend not on any particular accomplishment but on the totality of activities through which he incidentally engaged in the collective work of nation building. His personality supplied the only logic which this empire of activities possessed.

He worked, as did other industrialists, without a comprehensive plan. He took advantage of opportunities as they appeared to him and for which he had resources. He followed each opportunity through a daily labor involving dealings with people of greater and lesser capacity, persisting in each through a multitude of petty frustrations and successes, animosities and friendships, profits and losses. His signal contributions emerged, it seemed at times, almost by chance from a routine of business, politics, and family life; yet behind each was the will and mind of a personage who, although less well known than many others, had few equals in perspicacity and power and in the general esteem of people who knew him best.

He began his industrial maturity with a venture into nickel. On 2 December 1862 he wrote to Brush, "I am projecting another dangerous voyage even before the present one is finished, wherein I am worse than Sinbad the Sailor, whose ardor for new adventures did not break forth until after a period of enjoyment of the fruits of the last." Ten days later Wharton confirmed that the new venture was nickel: "I have bought more than half of the Gap Nickel Mine in Lancaster Co., Pa., and taken the refusal of those at Litchfield, Conn., which I shall some day visit—probably early in January."[1]

Making nickel was not the only possibility available to him for the continuation of his career. He rejected several others for reasons which he did not always make clear. One such opportunity was that of refining sugar. He might have gone into the business with his father-in-law. Joseph Lovering's only son had neither interest nor aptitude for that line of work, whereas Wharton was interested and cooperative. When Joseph Lovering was experimenting with sorghum as a source of sugar Wharton grew the cane for him on the zinc company's Saucon Valley farm and had a sugar mill set up in South Bethlehem for extracting the juice.[2]

Another possibility for a career existed in the mining of coal. Fortunes were being made in the anthracite fields. While working for the Pennsylvania and Lehigh Zinc Company Wharton gained an entry into the business by buying into the William Penn Coal Company, which owned coal properties near Wilkes-Barre. He became a director and one of the largest stockholders of the company and had a major voice in its reorganization as the Sugar Notch Coal Company and in making decisions concerning the financing of operations and the mining. But about the time he opted for nickel he sold his assets in the Sugar Notch Coal Company and never again seriously entertained prospects of a career in anthracite.[3]

Wharton had scarcely begun the venture in nickel when chances for advancement opened for him in the field of making iron. In 1863 he twice refused offers to become president of the successful Thomas Iron Company, the principal pig iron producer of the Lehigh Valley, and on one occasion turned back an approach to take over the presidency of the Bethlehem Iron Company, a new venture located near the grounds of the Lehigh Zinc Company and in which he had bought stock.[4] He was shortly to become heavily involved in the business of manufacturing iron and steel, but not in the capacity of superintending operations.

Another possibility was that of copper. In 1863 Wharton bought into several companies with copper and timber lands on the Keweenaw Point of northern Michigan. He soon became the sole owner of these assets. He made several trips to inspect them at a time when mining there was in progress.

He even tested a scheme for detecting copper ores by means of electricity.[5] After mining was stopped, in the late sixties, he continued to hold ownership of these copper and timber lands.

But apart from any value which they might have had (and, as was eventually proved, the value was slight), engaging in copper mining and refining had a fatal weakness. It would have meant living away from Philadelphia, which he was determined henceforth not to do. His surrender to Anna's wish to live in the city represented the only long range plan for his life which directly affected his industrial and business concerns. The concession was important to the domestic tranquillity in which he found comfort and a renewal of strength.

He accompanied the decision to live in the Twelfth Street house with another which was also pleasing to Anna. This was the establishment of a summer house on a property which he had purchased many years earlier. The land lay off the Old York Road not far from Oak Hill and first appeared on his account books as "Milestone Lot." He added to and developed it as a farm, changed the reference to "Branchtown Property (Milestone Residence)," then named it Brookside. It was to become in later years the site of his mansion, Ontalauna.

The choice of the Twelfth Street house over others in Philadelphia was fortunate, for it proved to be centrally located with respect to his interests. The dwelling stood near Walnut and within a few blocks of the stations from which he caught trains bound for Bethlehem, New York, and Lancaster County. Barker Brothers and Company, the Farmers and Mechanics Bank, and other houses with which he did banking lay on or near Third Street between his home and the ferry to Camden. Since the death of her husband, Deborah had chosen Number 336 Spruce as a usual residence. All of these places, together with headquarters of the societies to which he belonged and the houses of many friends, were within walking distance for one as vigorous and fast as he. Also, schools and markets were close by. Anna and the children could take the train or ride by carriage to see her parents at Oak Hill or the large number of cousins and friends who inhabited the city and its northerly environs.

During those first years of residence on Twelfth Street he used an office in the nickel works as a headquarters. From here he supervised his various activities. Except for several trips to Europe, one each to Cuba and Mexico, and in old age travels to his gold mines in Nevada, he spent only occasional nights away from home on business. His family happily grew up in the Twelfth Street house. His third and last child, a daughter named Anna, was born there on 15 July 1868.

2

At the time Wharton bought the Gap Mine, nickel was less well known to science than was zinc. The Swedish scientist Axel Frederik Cronstedt first listed nickel among the metals in 1751 and three years later named it from *Kupfernikkel*, an alloy or impure grade of copper sometimes obtained from a species of ore called by the same name. *Nikkel* in *Kupfernikkel* was a pejorative term, which could be translated as meaning "false." The true characteristics of nickel remained unknown for a long time. The metal was first produced as a by-product of copper and cobalt, the latter being prized for the pure blue color it imparted to glass and to porcelain glazes.

For years after its discovery the only important industries using nickel were small concerns employing German silver, an alloy containing two parts copper and one part each of nickel and zinc, more or less; the actual composition varied considerably from one manufacturer to another, and it also contained the impurities of the ores from which it was produced. Because German silver was noncorrosible and looked like silver it was used for making cheap grades of cutlery. Later, another use was found for nickel as it might exist in a partially refined state. This was in the coining of small change. Several European countries experimented with token coins made partly with nickel. In the United States James Booth, melter at the Philadelphia Mint, in 1853 produced an experimental cent of 60 percent nickel and 40 percent copper. Two years later the Philadelphia Mint began regular coinage of a one cent piece of 12 percent nickel and 88 percent copper. This nickel cent became immediately popular. The mint could not keep up with the demand. When the Civil War broke out and the need for small money increased, Secretary of the Treasury Samuel P. Chase ordered issuance of three-cent bank notes, which people greatly disliked. They preferred metal coins and began hoarding them.[6]

Pure nickel still had no uses and was in fact almost completely unknown. "Commercial nickel is a very impure article, and bears no more relation to pure nickel than brass or bell-metal does to copper," wrote the scientist Lewis Thompson in 1863.[7] He went on to point out that the commercial nickel on the market was produced principally in England, France, and Prussia and contained from 76 to 86 percent nickel, the rest being cobalt, copper, iron, and arsenic, together with traces of zinc, manganese, sulphur, carbon, silica, and alumina. The principal reason for this ignorance concerning pure nickel lay in the difficulty in refining its ores. Nickel has an exceedingly high melting point (1453° C.) and possesses many of the properties of iron, from which it can be separated only with difficulty. The ores which had been discovered by that time were hard, resisted crushing, contained iron, other metals, and sulphur, and had only a few percent of nickel. European manufacturers began the refining process by roasting the ores, that is, burning then in kilns to eliminate much of the sulphur and waste material. The product of the kilns was called matte, a concentrate containing all of the metals and the remaining waste. The matte was subjected to several smeltings and then to a series of reactions with various reagents to selectively leach out the metals. The process was complicated and costly. Manufacturers closely guarded their secrets from competitors in order to preserve the small markets for themselves. No one had as yet found a way of ridding nickel of all impurities, much less of making pure nickel malleable so that it might be fashioned into any shape. The costs of refining were too great, and the prospects for a market too remote.

By the time of the Civil War various small deposits of nickel ores had been discovered in the United States. One of the oldest known deposits lay in Missouri, in a place originally exploited by the French and called by the gallicized name of Mine Lamotte. This deposit had been worked from time to time for cobalt. Other known deposits followed a line of ancient, crystalline rocks extending southward from Canada through New England and into northern New Jersey and southeastern Pennsylvania. The ores at Gap in Lancaster County belonged to them, as did smaller and poorer deposits in the Green Mountains; near Chatham, Torrington, and Litchfield, Connecticut; and at Lowell, Massachusetts. A few of these had been worked, albeit unprofitably.

The mineral deposits at Gap had been mined for well over one hundred years. Mineral springs containing copper sulphate first attracted the attention of German settlers, who called the flow *ziment wasser.* By 1730 the proprietaries of the province, anxious to profit from whatever mineral deposits they could find, had the two hundred and fifty acres containing the springs deeded one-sixth part each to Andrew Hamilton, James Logan, William Allen, Thomas Shute, Thomas Penn, and James Steel. In ensuing years the owners worked the deposits for copper. They dug shallow shafts, which in the wet hillside filled with water. Additional work was necessary to provide adequate drainage, and operations became unprofitable. The property was broken up and changed hands. Several later attempts, including an ambitious one begun in 1797, also failed. Eventually a shaft was sunk to a depth of sixty-five feet and a waterwheel was used to provide power for pumping. Miners dug many tunnels in the shallow places subject to natural drainage. Then for several decades all work stopped.

Sometime in 1849 or 1850 a group of Philadelphians, Henry Kinzer, Lewis Cooper, John Fausset, and E. F. Witmer, organized the Gap Mining Company. It was incorporated 8 April 1851, with a capital stock not to exceed one hundred and twenty thousand dollars "to mine and excavate for copper, lead, and other ores and metals; and the same to stamp, crush, and otherwise prepare for market."[8] The Gap ores contained no lead; but in the same year the director discovered from an analysis made by Genth that they had nickel in addition to copper, iron, and cobalt. Buoyed by this good news the directors pushed ahead. All of the stock was immediately subscribed for. The directors appointed a man named Joseph Rogers as superintendent but replaced him a month later with John Williams.

What followed has been repeated thousands of times in the history of mining and smelting in the United States. Great energy and determination and substantial capital proved unable to surmount hurdles in the form of lack of knowledge and skill, fluctuating costs and prices, and the vagaries of nature. The minutes of the board of directors, containing annual reports prepared by Williams, tell the story. The directors were enchanted with discoveries that the main vein consisted "chiefly of nickeliferous Pyrites mixed through the Copper Pyrites and Black Oxide of Copper" and that the nickel and copper content increased with depth. The principal vein began about sixty feet below the surface. No one could say how deep it might go. The supply of ore seemed, in the presumptuous language of the times, "inexhaustible."

The company sank several shafts and brought in steam engines for hoisting and crushing ores. Williams supervised the building of houses for workers, a modest mansion for himself, and a store. He purchased farm lands for supplying pasture and fodder for the horses and mules. In 1853 F. M. Buck, E. W. Coffin, and others built a small nickel refinery at Camden, which was operated under the firm name of Buck, Simonen, & Company and known as the Camden Nickel Works. From this time on nickel ore was the principal product of the Gap Mining Company. The workers dug 100 tons in 1852–53, 589 tons the following year, and 900 tons in 1855–56. Greenish crystals containing nickel oxide from the ores of Lancaster County were exhibited in the mineralogical department directed by Benjamin Silliman in the Crystal Palace of the New York Exhibition of 1854. By that time several scientific journals had published descriptions of the mine and its ores.

In May 1857 Williams noted, "The passage of the Bill authorizing the coinage of the Nickel Penny has greatly increased the consumption of nickel in this country." The directors then took steps to improve the efficiency of their operations by concentrating the ores into matte. The secretary of the Gap Mining Company, a man named Hoeckley, organized with others a company to build smelters. Possession of these fell to the Gap Mining Company in the Panic of 1857. Thereafter the Gap Mining Company was the sole owner of the properties surrounding the mine. From 1858 to 1860 the company had a brief period of prosperity; in the latter year the mines produced more than 2,948 tons of nickel ore and 155 tons of copper ore. By the beginning of 1860 the company was selling matte to not only the refinery at Camden but also several other domestic companies and the large firm of Evans and Askin in England.

The same war scare that troubled Wharton in making spelter ruined the Gap Mining Company. On 13 September 1860, William Coffin, president of the company, reported a monthly loss of nine hundred dollars and insufficient funds to purchase rights to a process for concentrating ore. The stockholders voted to advertise the works in Europe and America for lease or sale. Each stockholder deposited one-half of his shares with the secretary, to be taken up by anyone showing a disposition to work the mine "with energy." For the time being mining was continued. Early in 1861 the legislature authorized the company to increase its capital to five hundred thousand dollars and extended the life of its charter to twenty years. These moves came too late. When by the end of 1861 or early 1862 no one had bought or leased the property of the company, mining came to a halt. The shafts filled with water; the machinery rusted; furnaces and stacks began to decay and fall to the ground.

3

It is impossible to say exactly when Wharton became convinced that the ores at Gap were sufficient and suitable for an industry in nickel. He had probably learned of the presence of minerals at "Coppermine Ridge," as the site was called on some old maps, when he lived on the Walton farm about ten miles to the east. Possibly he knew of the presence of nickel in the ores at Gap before the directors of the Gap Mining Company did. Booth and Boyé had studied samples of iron pyrites from the Gap Mine as early as 1846 and found them to contain nickel.[10] Certainly Wharton had ample opportunity through his friendships with Booth, Boyé, and Brush to know intimately the ores and mines and the operations conducted at Gap and Camden.

The development that decided him to purchase the mines and refinery was the opening of a market through coinage at the mint. In a letter to the editor of *Lock and Bell* in June 1888 he wrote, "In the year 1862, after having established in this country the manufacture of spelter or metallic zinc, I was informed that the U.S. Mint was unable to procure nickel for making one cent coins, since the American attempts to produce that metal had broken down, and in no foreign country could an adequate supply be purchased. Inquiry at the Mint confirmed this."

Having decided to enter the nickel business, Wharton promptly acted to acquire complete control. He bought on 10 December 1862 a majority of the stock at one dollar and fifty cents a share and as of 1 January 1863 leased the properties of the Gap Mining Company and the refinery at Camden. He continued buying stock, but at lesser prices, and soon owned it all. Within three years of entering the nickel business he purchased outright the mining properties and the refinery. The Gap Mining Company ceased to exist. The refinery at Camden was renamed American Nickel Works.[11]

He made certain, too, that no one in the United States was going to compete with him. In May 1863 he investigated the known deposits of ore in New England and gained assurance that these were not economically feasible. The possibility that Mine Lamotte might provide competition was remote. The vast deposits of nickel ore in Canada were as yet undiscovered.

His immediate tasks on gaining control were pumping water out of the mines and putting the machinery and smelters into working order. He had ascertained that he could gain some income by selling matte to European refiners. In any event he would need a continuous supply before he could profitably refine his own nickel. He bought some new equipment; purchased information concerning the smelting of nickel ores from Thomas Macfarlane, a Scottish mining engineer living in Canada; and obtained other information from David Forbes of England. C. E. Benade, who had worked for Wharton at the spelter manufactory, became superintendent at the Gap Mine. Within a year Wharton replaced Benade with Charles Doble, an assistant to former superintendent Williams. Doble had been born in Devonshire, England, and had come to the United States in 1851 for the purpose of working for the Gap Mining Company. He had married a local resident, was raising a family, and proved to be exceptionally competent. Doble remained for the rest of a long life in charge of operations at Gap.[12]

The next job to be done was that of beginning the production of nickel from the matte. Wharton opened the refinery at Camden, put a former employee at the spelter works named Monnier in charge, gave him Samuel Haydock as an assistant—and immediately discovered that he could not profitably make even bad nickel by the means at his disposal. He tried various expedients; all failed. He closed the refinery and wrote to Brush in August of 1863 of having spent one hundred thousand dollars in the unsuccessful attempts.

He would have to develop a process of his own. "In the end I mean to make all the Nickel this country wants, and whatever Cobalt may come easily with it," he wrote Brush.[13] For this, Wharton needed expert help which was not readily available. He could not bring in workers en masse from Europe as he had done in distilling spelter. Few craftsmen existed for making nickel, and those few were disinclined to migrate to a country engaged in civil war. No one in America had the experience he needed, and he knew that his own knowledge of the art was inadequate. For a beginning he would need a metallurgical chemist who could experiment with applying the known processes, train the men, and in time help to supervise operations.

Wharton knew of one possibility. That was a young assistant to Brush named O. D. Allen. Wharton had been considering Allen before the first unsuccessful operation of the Camden refinery in 1863. In November of that year Wharton wrote to Brush, "If you have made up your mind to let him go, . . . I should be glad to take him."[14] Brush visited the mine and the refinery the following January. By February Allen was making assays for Wharton in New Haven under the direction of Benjamin Silliman.[15]

Allen arrived in Camden as Wharton's chemist in September of 1864. For a year he and Monnier worked trying to develop a commercially successful process. Lincoln was shot; the Civil War ended; President Johnson began his stormy interchanges with Congress. Still nickel proved to be intractable.

Wharton had no immediate financial problem. The mine was regularly producing. He wrote in his ledger for this period, "I have sold large quantities of nickel matte . . . to both England and Germany, enough in about two years to yield about 200,000 pounds of nickel, and I am now sending this matte to England to have the nickel extracted and returned to me, because the totally inadequate import duty upon nickel allows this to be done at a slight profit."[16]

In view of his overall design, he could only consider a dependence on foreign refiners as temporary. He needed someone with a more intimate acquaintance with the methods used in Europe than Allen possessed. Wharton asked Booth which manufacturer made the best nickel and received as reply the name of Dr. Theodor Fleitmann of Iserlohn, Prussia, member of the firm of Fleitmann and Witte. This was one of Wharton's customers for matte; Fleitmann could be expected to know the quality of the Gap ores as well as something concerning the enterprise of their owner. Wharton decided to send Allen to Europe to find out all he could about the metallurgy of nickel and its byproducts, the extent of its manufacture and use, and especially the reputation of Fleitmann.[17]

The expedition was successful. Fleitmann's knowledge and skill were extensive and his accomplishments were unquestionable. He was for a consideration willing to help modernize the American Nickel Works. Within a few months he and Wharton arrived at an agreement. Effective 1 May 1866, Wharton and Fleitmann would each contribute twenty-five thousand dollars of capital. They would lease the Camden refinery and obtain matte from the Gap Mine. Fleitmann would be in charge of the refinery, operating it through a chemist of his employ, and would spend at least four weeks a year at Camden. Wharton would continue managing financial and commercial aspects. Each partner would have free access to improvements patented by the other. Fleitmann would also advise concerning the operation of the Gap Mine. The partners would share in the profits in exact proportion to the capital contributed by each. Foreign sales would be handled exclusively by Theodor Fleitmann's brother Hermann of New York, who would receive a commission of 2.5 percent on nickel and 2 percent on matte. Fleitmann agreed to retain Allen "to superintend, manage and direct the chemical and manufacturing operations of said works."[18]

For a time the partnership worked well. Fleitmann came to Philadelphia in the summer of 1866 and personally took charge of renovating the American Nickel Works. When he returned to Prussia he sent over as his replacement a man named Frederick Voigt and charged him with beginning the manufacture of nickel and its by-products.

In a narrative sent to the family after Wharton's death Voigt recalled his early experience at Camden:

> My acquaintance with Mr. Wharton dates from my arrival in Camden early in October 1866. . . . When I first met him in Camden he was about forty years of age, tall and well proportioned, of commanding, quite attractive personality, unassuming in intercourse with his employees. I was a young fellow of twenty-four determined to acquit myself creditably,

and possessing the necessary training required to take hold of my duties as director. In a short time, before the close of the year, the home market was offered the first product of the Camden works, an Alloy containing both the Nickel and Copper as present in the ore, about 70% of the former and 30% of the latter, made by the shorter, "dry" method.[19]

The success of the process involved the loss of Allen. He was the key man in the laboratory and determined the specifications to be followed for each stage. His method was scholarly and his style, deliberate and systematic. Fleitmann was very much the caricature of the Prussian military figure, that is, gracious and delightful in society and imperious and brusque in the workshop. Before the year was out he offended Allen to a point of exasperation. Wharton wrote to Brush, "Allen will I fancy leave here next Spring, as Dr. Fleitmann has no patience with his dreamy undemonstrative ways, and expects from him more than I think reasonable. . . . Dr. F. chafes at home because his directions and expectations do not punctually fulfill themselves, and he charges too much to the debit of his manager and too little to the difficulties of the situation; and Allen feels that his honest endeavors are not appreciated by his employer Dr. F."[20]

Allen left early in 1867, to Wharton's regret. Subsequently Allen worked with several industrial and mining concerns and then accepted an invitation from Francis H. Storer at Boston to replace Charles W. Eliot as a collaborator in chemical work. Storer and Eliot, who had previously endorsed Wharton's spelter, had in 1865 become professors of chemistry at the newly opened Massachusetts Institute of Technology and two years later published *A Manual of Inorganic Chemistry.* Soon Eliot was turning to other pursuits. In 1869 he published "The New Education: Its Organization" in the *Atlantic Monthly* and was a few months later elected president of Harvard University. Storer removed to Harvard in 1871. Allen remained with Storer at MIT for only a short while and then returned to teach at Yale's Sheffield Scientific School. Among his pupils was one who was to play an important part in Wharton's life, Russell W. Davenport.

Wharton, too, soon became dissatisfied with Fleitmann. The Prussian had given Wharton what he needed for the time being; now, Wharton found Fleitmann an obstacle to further progress. American makers of German silver were refusing to take the mix of nickel and copper, even though it was easy to work with. They had become habituated to using nickel supplied by English and German makers. Wharton was left with the mint as his principal customer. He determined to install appliances for a wet process which would produce a much more acceptable nickel than was possible by the dry method. Fleitmann balked at this, and the partners quarreled. In June 1868 the refinery burned. It was insured, and they had it speedily rebuilt. But Wharton took the occasion to end the partnership. He bought out Fleitmann for $76,635.12 and for another $56,153.49 purchased the firms' assets.[21]

Wharton then enlarged the reconstructed plant to house apparatus for a wet method.

He wrote to Brush, "I found it necessary to part from Fleitmann, as the arrangement was too cumbersome and he had a troublesome brother. I bought him out at a heavy cost, keeping his foreman who is a brisk and competent fellow, and am rebuilding with certain improvements." The German silver makers, Wharton continued, had complained of the product. "Fleitmann went away at last like the devil in a thunderstorm because I refused to pay his brother Commission upon a sale of nickel which the customer not only refused to pay for but demanded heavy damages on."[22]

Wharton might have added another reason, which certainly must have been in his thinking. The firm of Fleitmann and Witte was a competitor; and as the American market for nickel grew, foreign firms were invading it. Wharton must meet the competition in part by improving methods and reducing costs. Fleitmann could not be relied upon to help with these improvements.

4

Even as Wharton labored to develop a wet process for refining nickel, he also worked to assure himself of a market. The German silver makers, such as the Connecticut firms of Coe Brass Manufacturing Company, Scovill Manufacturing Company, and Waterbury Brass Company, would take some. But at this early stage of his nickel business he looked upon the Philadelphia Mint, the only maker of small coins in the United States, as the buyer of the future. Nickel coins had been fashioned; people liked them, and the demand was bound to increase. A prejudice in favor of "buying American" was present and would help, although after the process of refining was perfected a higher protective tariff would also be desirable. The situation was such as to permit Wharton to dream of securing a monopoly over the supplying of nickel for the minting of American small coins.

He determined to achieve that monopoly. He knew this would take constant vigilance and work. His infrequent contacts with politicians in the past had acquainted him with the unpredictability of legislators and of executives who depended on legislators for position and powers. Government dispensed its gifts only to people who spent time and money to obtain them; and even then, fortune in the shape of competing interests and unfathomable personalities played a large part in determining the outcome of any proposal.

He was probably not at all surprised when in the year he began his nickel business the Congress, acting on advice from James Pollock, director of the mint, discontinued making the nickel cent, replacing it with a penny made of a bronze alloy. The reason, Wharton knew, was the lack of nickel, a reason which his business would soon remove. He also realized that a decision to resume the coining of nickel small change would not be automatic. Congress and the mint must be moved to act; and he, the only maker of nickel in the country, must be the mover.

There was another danger. Pollock in giving reasons why Congress should discontinue the nickel cent had not stopped by saying that nickel was in short supply. He had also made a case against ever using nickel, pointing out some indisputable disadvantages:

> Nickel derives its name from a certain unpleasant allusion [i.e., to "Old Nick"], indicating its character, and which, in a metallurgic sense, it honestly deserves. It is very obstinate in the melting pot, requiring the fieriest fire even when in alloy with copper. It commonly makes a hard mixture, very destructive to dies, and all the contiguous parts of the coining machinery. Perhaps as great an objection as any to the further use of this alloy is its limited use in the arts. With the addition of zinc it would make good German silver, and could be worked up into plated ware. Beyond this, and a few other applications, copper with 12 percent of nickel is of no more value to the artisan than copper alone; it is even a deterioration, as it is more difficult to melt.

Aluminum, wrote Pollock, was being experimented with and was held to have much promise for small coins, although it was still too costly for use.[23]

Wharton knew that reasoning such as this might lead to prejudices against nickel which, in the event other acceptable alloys were found, might forever bar its use. He immediately countered Pollock's arguments with a pamphlet bearing the date of 15 April 1864 and the cumbersome title of *Project for Reorganizing the Small Coinage of the United States of America, by the Establishment of A System of Coin Tokens, Made of Nickel and Copper Alloy.* He did not try to make a case for coins fashioned of pure nickel, as he would do a quarter of a century later, inasmuch as a means of making the pure malleable nickel necessary for rolling the blanks had not as yet been found. Instead, he argued that nickel-copper alloy was the best metal for small coins. Token coins, he reasoned, should be "cheap, handsome, not readily oxidable, capable of being readily worked by adequate means, durable in wear, and hard to counterfeit." One by one he pointed out deficiencies of other metals and alloys. Aluminum was untried. Cobalt was too scarce. Pure copper and bronze oxidized too easily, discolored, and had a disagreeable odor when handled; and coins made of them could be easily counterfeited. Silver was too valuable and soft. German silver was soft and, because of the volatility of zinc, unstable. The use of brass had not been proposed. Nickel had none of these disadvantages and met all the desired standards with some bonuses.

> The nickel and copper alloys (from 25 to 12 per cent nickel) are hard to melt, and hard to work and stamp, yet they can, by proper means and

skill, be perfectly worked into coins. They vary in whiteness, in hardness and in infusibility with the proportion of nickel, those richest in nickel excelling in all these particulars. They take sharp impressions from dies and have a great power of resisting both wear and oxidation. As the alloy of 25 to 75 is superior to it in all the requisites of coinage, (including that necessary one for token coins above the very lowest denomination) . . . it yields only to the best appliances, but it yields to them perfectly, making a very handsome coin, of a peculiar white color, different from silver, and possessing a clear and characteristic sonority or "ring."[24]

This pamphlet was the first of several which were soon to make Wharton one of the world's leading authorities concerning the manufacture and issuance of small coins. Its immediate effect on causing Congress to order a resumption of the use of nickel was probably small; and in fact, Wharton had surer tactics available. He could by means of the arrangements he had made with European refiners assure the mint of a sufficient and constant supply at a reasonable price. Booth and Pollock were favorably disposed toward Wharton and by no means really opposed the use of nickel-copper alloys, especially as their attempts to find more suitable metals had failed. Also, Wharton was becoming known among congressmen and senators from Pennsylvania. He used these contacts to make others. "Just now I am trying to persuade the Government to make nickel alloy coins up to 10 cts." he wrote Brush. "I saw the Assistant Sec'y of the Treasury today, and expect to go before a Com. of the House tomorrow about the coinage business," he wrote Anna.[25]

The results of Wharton's labors were two coins of 75 = 25 copper-nickel alloy. One was a three-cent piece authorized 3 March, 1865. The other was a five-cent piece legalized the following year, which quickly became generally known as the "nickel." In time the nickel entered the domain of things such as the silver dollar and Uncle Sam in defining American culture. Without Wharton's efforts it might never have existed; or, if it had eventually been coined, might have had a different composition, size, and design—might not have become, in short, a favorite coin and byword for Americans in making change.

The beginning made in coining the nickel coincided almost exactly with success in refining matte at Camden under the partnership of Wharton and Fleitmann. Wharton then opened a vigorous campaign for Congress to raise the duty on imported nickel from fifteen to forty cents a pound, which would have given nickel approximate parity with the duty on most other metals. Still, the principal danger from foreign competitors was several years away. For the period from 1865 to 1869 he almost completely realized his dream of being the unique supplier of nickel for American coins. During those years the Philadelphia mint consumed for coinage 253,111 pounds of nickel, of which 224,347 pounds came from the American Nickel Works. Prices ranged from approximately $1.80 to $2.00 a pound. Wharton's account books reveal income from these sales as being $31,595.13 in 1865; $63,996.97 for 1866; $139,372.52 for 1867; and $112,946.78 in 1868.[26]

He began to dream of increasing this market by giving the country a new and better system of small change. The nickel-copper alloy, he told himself, had proved its superiority. Why not make it the basis for all lesser coins? In 1868 he reissued his pamphlet on small coins, giving it the title, *Suggestions Concerning the Small Money of the U.S.A.* In it he argued that the existing coinage of bronze, nickel-copper, and silver pieces represented "no attempt at a system", was instead a "medley of small change, or counters," and should be replaced by token coins of ten, five, three, and one cent denominations, all composed of 75 = 25 copper-nickel alloy and weighing respectively ten, five, three, and one grams. His arguments emphasized the availability of nickel for such a coinage and the large profits which would accrue to the Treasury if his plan was adopted.[27]

Such reasoning represents one of many examples wherein Wharton identified the good of the country with his own industry. He had, he wrote here and in other places, put his imagination and drive to work to give Americans a better coinage. And, he added as a corollary, the country now owed him support for his enterprise. Over and over again he stated the principal sort of support which he expected, namely, an adequate protective tariff. His most lengthy exposition of this position is found in a pamphlet entitled *Statement Made January, 1866, Relative to Nickel, Cobalt-Oxide, Etc.* He added to and republished this pamphlet in both 1867 and 1868. The immediate purpose was that of convincing Congress to raise the tariff; and because Wharton faced some opposition to this from the German silver makers of New England, he phrased his arguments so as to identify their welfare as well as that of the country with his own.

He began the pamphlet by explaining in simple terms the chemistry of nickel and the history of its mining and manufacture in Europe and the United States. He briefly noted the beginning of nickel coinage but concentrated more on the use of the metal for making German silver. The whole of the industry, he remarked, depended absolutely on nickel. From this dependence Wharton drew a conclusion "that the country which intends to carry on the German silver manufacture largely, cannot afford to rely upon foreign nickel makers: to illustrate this point I will remark, that before my nickel operations were started, both the German-silver makers and the Mint of this country were at times embarrassed to procure adequate supplies of nickel, since all had to be brought from Europe, and Europe sometimes had very little to spare."[28]

Wharton then summarized the history of the Gap mine and the American Nickel Works to establish these in the minds of readers as legitimate industries, capable of supplying American needs, and affirmed that his nickel business deserved "not merely an even-handed equality of treatment with other manufacturers, but also favor, or exceptional protection and fostering by the Government." The current situation was unfair: "As things now stand, the American nickel ores must lie idle in the ground, or they must be carried across the ocean, and so much of their yield as the Europeans can spare, must be bought by American German-silver makers as their only means of continuing in business." A duty of fifteen cents would not suffice. "If my Government will now grant me equitable treatment, a valuable new resource will be given to the country; if I am to be discriminated against, as at present, by having less than the average protection, a considerable enterprise must be extinguished and destroyed." He demanded "as a right" a duty of fifty (and not forty!) cents per pound on nickel and comparably high duties on nickel and cobalt salts and ores and appealed "to the enlightened self-interest of the American consumers of nickel to aid and not to resist this long-deferred act of justice."

A duty of fity cents a pound on nickel would probably have prolonged the monopoly which Wharton desired over sales to the mint and possibly also have made him the only supplier for American German silver makers. But this prospect of creating a monopoly was a weakness. Americans idealized competition, not monopoly. Accordingly, in arguing his case he presented his present preeminence as being temporary. "My firm has a monopoly just as Columbus had a monopoly of discovering America. There will be plenty of people to share it with us whenever it becomes clear that the business of nickel-making yields profits proportionate to the capital, the patient toil, and the skill required for conducting it."

He convinced himself so thoroughly of the identity of interests between the American Nickel Works and the country that he could scarcely understand any opposing point of view. He was within a few years to have a partial success in cajoling Congress into raising the duty on nickel. The Schenck Tariff of 1870 set it at thirty cents a pound. But before that time, when the duty still stood at fifteen cents, the Treasury applied a free trade policy with respect to nickel. By 1868 control of the mint had passed out of Pollock's hands; and the following year George S. Boutwell of Massachusetts became secretary of the treasury. Under his supervision the Treasury Department followed congressional insistence that metals be purchased from the lowest bidder and ordered the mint not to give special preference to any domestic maker of nickel. Wharton was caught with a supply on hand which he had especially made for the mint. The manufacture of nickel took several months. He could not have been expected to foresee a shift in the direction of free trade, which in any event he considered harmful to the country. At the very least, he reasoned, the mint should purchase the lot he had made for it according to the previous policy. Wharton went to Washington, saw Boutwell, and received no satisfaction. The spirit of toleration left him. He wrote angrily, defensively, and arrogantly to Boutwell:

> Our interview this morning rather weakened my faith in plain truth telling and frank dealing, though I appreciated the courtesy of your conduct.

I have never been a whiskey thief nor a New York imposter nor a leech upon the Government in any way; but on the contrary, to serve the Government in its embarrassment arising from the inability to get nickel even at extreme prices, and upon what then seemed to me sufficient assurance of the mint's support, I voluntarily six years ago turned from a life of opulence and reputation to establish the production of nickel in this country. My pertinacious disposition has led me to do this in so thorough a manner that I now have almost the best nickel establishment in the world, and have over $400,000 invested in it. The result to the Government of this sacrifice on my part is partly shown by the enclosed letter from the late Director of the Mint.

At this moment I am more necessary to the Mint than the Mint is to me, and it is quite in my power to reduce that establishment to the same uncomfortable position from which I rescued it.

I was the only person in the nation possessing the necessary skill, means, and courage to build up this costly and troublesome establishment, of which I have borne all the burden while the Government has reaped the profit; if now my Government acknowledges no equity and sees no interest in keeping it alive, I had better abandon it and settle down to become an incubus upon the labor of others, though I revolt at the idea.[29]

For the next two years Wharton sold no nickel to the mint. Yet he made money, a profit of $36,882.05 in 1870 and $66,458.29 in 1871, as compared with less than half of the latter amount for 1869.[30] The tariff helped but little. More importantly, he had prepared for the worst by improving his processes of extracting metals from the Gap ores. Complacency was not now, nor was it ever to be, one of his failings. While ever hoping for monopoly, he was always preparing for competition. By the time he wrote the letter to Boutwell his brag of having "almost the best nickel establishment in the world" had substance.

5

He had become, he truthfully wrote, second only to Evans and Askin in England as a world supplier of nickel.

Several documents permit a description of his establishment as it was in the early 1870s. The most important of these is a manuscript by Doble which was extensively quoted in the industrial statistics section of the *Annual Report of the Secretary of Internal Affairs of the Commonwealth of Pennsylvania, 1874–1875*. A second source is the *History of Lancaster County, Pennsylvania*, by Franklin Ellis and Samuel Evans.[31] Various entries in Wharton's account books fill in some of the gaps in the description.

The mines, kilns, smelters, and farms lay in Bart and Paradise townships of Lancaster County. The landscape presented to the eye (and still presents) a wide sweep of gently rolling, partially wooded hills reminiscent of vistas in southern England or the Loire valley. Farms gave regularity of line and curve and added dashes of color to natural patterns without erasing anything of original beauty. Wharton's farms, which supplied the mining community with horses and mules, fodder, and food, were no different in appearance from others. They occupied several hundred acres of land adjoining mine and furnaces.

The mine was identifiable at the surface of the ground by piles of waste rock which accumulated over the years. As Doble described the mine, it "opened out on the vein, in length, by shafts and tunnels, about two thousand feet, and the deepest point attained is two hundred and thirty-five feet. There are six shafts, ranging from one hundred to two hundred and thirty-five feet in depth, and a few others from sixty to eighty feet in depth. All the shafts are perpendicular and the ore is rarely found in paying quantities nearer than from fifty to sixty feet to the surface."

The upper layer of ground around the mine was well drained. Nickel-Mine Run and Meeting House Run joined to form a fork of the west branch of the Octorara, a southerly flowing tributary of the Susquehanna. Pumps operated to remove water from the depths. A company town located near the mine was not much different in appearance from any other rural village. It contained houses for about two hundred and fifty employees and their families, Doble's two-story mansion, a store, an Episcopal Church, a school, and eventually cooper and wagon shops and a post office. Near the mine stood blacksmith and carpenter shops, sheds for housing the hoisting and pumping engines, and a brick yard.

Doble presided over the community like an ironmaster of a previous generation. His employees called him "Captain," a title of respect which had nothing to do with any military experience. There is on record a letter from Doble to Wharton, dated 8 June 1885, sent from the Nickel Mines Post Office, in which Doble requested that Wharton postpone a projected visit to the mine, the grounds being that on the original day selected for the visit "the nickel mines Band has made arrangements to hold a Festival (a little fair) on that evening, to try to raise some money towards paying for their uniforms, etc. To make this Fair a success our women folks has [sic] a great deal to do on that day in the way of baking cakes and making other preparations for it."

The village of Nickel Mines was fairly well protected from the smoke of kilns and smelters, which stood about three quarters of a mile to the north. There, fires burned day and night. Great clouds of sulphurous smoke spurted from tall stacks and were swept eastward by the prevailing winds. Wharton deliberately had the stacks built high in order to increase the draft and to give the smoke a chance to dissipate in the air before falling to the ground and ruining vegetation. This was only partially successful. Sometimes the fumes descended as much as two miles away and did damage.[32]

At the American Nickel Works in Camden smells of chlorine accompanied those of sulphur. There, too, Wharton had the stacks made high in hopes that as much of the smoke as possible would carry over the roofs of nearby dwellings and dissolve in the air. The works occupied several acres of ground between Cooper's Creek and Tenth Street and between York and State. The factory was, after the fire of 1868, one story high, built of concrete brick and covered with gravel roofing. Engine and boiler rooms stood at one end and at the other, two three-story dwellings for workers. In 1870 Wharton added a wharf, thus permitting direct delivery of the matte by ferry, and also a blacksmith's shop, a blue vitriol house, a shed for storing coke, and a building for working the matte to make sulphuric acid. Steam engines provided power.

The process of manufacture was lengthy and complicated. The principal steps can be reconstructed from several accounts. The steps taken in Lancaster County are described in Doble's manuscript and an article which appeared in the *Iron Age* for 1 January 1874. Wharton himself in that year wrote a lengthy description of the processes used at Camden. Joseph's document was coincident with a visit by Voigt to his parents in Germany and is sufficiently detailed to include the names of some of the workers on whose judgment success vitally depended: K. Heil in the furnace room; Louis Stang, a foreman also in charge of making some of the tests in the laboratory; Meehan, controlling the room for precipitating nickel; and Hermann Kiele, in charge of reducing the nickel oxide to pure grain nickel.

Two steam engines located near the mine assisted in the mining proper. One was a "low pressure" Cornish engine of one hundred horsepower for pumping water out of the shafts and tunnels, and the other was a twenty-five horsepower "high pressure" engine for hoisting out the ore. The ore was heavy, iron gray in color, and sometimes speckled with brightly hued copper ore. It was contained within a dark highly crystalline hornblende. Both the ore and the surrounding rock were hard and had to be loosened by blasting. This created much dust, none of which was wasted. It was too fine to be roasted as it was, and so was formed into square bricks using clay and flux as binders.

"The ore," wrote Doble, "after it is mined, is brought through the tunnels to the hoisting shaft in small railroad cars carrying about one ton each. It is then brought to the surface by hoisting in large buckets carrying about one thousand pounds each, or in square wooden boxes (skips) working in 'guides' carrying two thousand pounds each." From four to five hundred tons of ore, mixed with an additional tonnage of waste rock or gangue, were taken from the mine each month.

Having arrived at the surface, the ore was partially concentrated, that is, separated from the gangue. This was easily done because fractures naturally occurred at points where particles of ore touched the gangue. Later methods of concentration used machinery, but in the early years at the Gap Mine the work was done by hand. sledges shattered the mixed rock and ore. People then picked out and discarded the large lumps of worthless rock. The fine pieces of ore and rock were subjected to jigging, that is, separation in water depending on differences in specific gravity. The ore was then carted to the kilns and the larger pieces put through the jaws of a crusher, "Blake's Rock Breaker," which reduced them to lumps weighing about half a pound each, the size desired for roasting.

Then began the process of refining which, although complex, involved simple equipment and no great investment of capital.[33] The principal elements consisted of vats, tubs, filters, steam tubes, and carboys. Wheelbarrows provided the means for carrying solids from one place to another. Reagents were added to the solutions by pitcher or bucket. Filtering relied on gravity. At one point in the process, as Wharton described it, a worker determined when a solution had reached the proper temperature by dipping his fingers into the vat. Liquid wastes consisted largely of salts of hydrochloric and sulphuric acid and were dumped raw into Cooper's Creek.

In spite of the simplicity of equipment and seeming crudity of the procedures the process succeeded in turning out the pure nickel which Wharton desired. He also obtained marketable products in the form of cobalt oxide, blue vitriol, and copperas (hydrated ferrous sulphate). Blue vitriol was used as a fungicide. Copperas was employed in the arts of dyeing black and making black ink. In terms of weight and bulk, blue vitriol led the list, although pure nickel and nickel salts accounted for more than 90 percent of the income.

6

By the beginning of the first administration of President Ulysses S. Grant, Wharton was operating a lucrative business which excited him and absorbed his energy. For the second time in less than a decade he had established a new industry where others had failed to do so, and this time no one was there to turn him out of it. Making nickel was more difficult than the manufacture of spelter and for that reason provided more challenges to his versatile talents.

Nickel was still considered an unimportant metal, having no applications to the industries of construction or defense, and the high price of the metal discouraged its use for any purpose for which iron or steel might serve. The known deposits of ore seemed about right for the trade. News of the discovery of quantities of better and easily mined ore in New Caledonia were disturbing. Still, New Caledonia was half way around the globe and presented no immediate threat to European and American refiners. Wharton had the best deposit yet discovered in North America. The Gap Mine held out a promise of a supply of ore for decades to come; and he had developed a process of refining which was probably second to none.

Even without the protection of a tariff he would have made money. As events turned out, the tariff never greatly helped him to increase income. In the most profitable years of his nickel business the demand was so large, and the price so high, that the tariff was not needed and in any event could not have given him appreciable protection. What the tariff did provide was a hope of survival in the event of economic disaster. Even so, when he most needed a tariff, it was inadequate. In the long run his enterprise and the entire nickel industry of the United States depended on other considerations.

His addition to the metal industry of the United States went almost unnoticed for at least a decade. Before the coming of nickel steel, the world industry in nickel was minuscule by comparison with ventures in iron, steel, lead, copper, gold, silver, even zinc. *The Iron Age,* which generally and usually accurately gave news of the metals industries of the country, paid no attention to Wharton's enterprises at Gap and Camden until 1874, when electroplating with nickel began being of importance and a world shortage of nickel was being experienced. But while reporters were catching up with Wharton's accomplishments, the work in nickel was greatly developing his character. It helped increase his knowledge concerning the vagaries of mining, the properties of ores of metals, and the metallurgy of their extraction. His blooming as a scientist, known and respected by the leading chemists of America and England, dates from this period. The fight for a high protective tariff brought him into the mainstream of lobbying in the nation's capital. He became an expert in the issuance of small coins and extended his knowledge of the methods of banking and commerce. The demands which the nickel business made on his mental and physical resources led him to further economies of thought and movement. Voigt's narrative contains a description of Wharton's style in managing the American Nickel Works:

In all these years Mr. Wharton personally managed and attended to the financial and commercial part of the business, including all office work, bookkeeping and correspondence, without assistance, except that which I could give, in taking charge of the minor office affairs, and acting as his attendant during his presence in Camden, for a number of years. Our little office, with laboratory adjoining, remained his headquarters for a long period, not only for the transaction of all business relating to the mines and the Camden plant, but also his vast and ever increasing correspondence relating to public and private activities and engagements.

His morning hours were usually occupied in Philadelphia in the offices of corporations, institutions, banks and bankers that he was connected with. About noon or shortly thereafter, unless prevented by visits at the mines or other outside localities, he would come to Camden and frequently remain until quite late in the evening, receiving my report of everything relating to the routine work, while eating a frugal lunch picked up on the way from the ferry to the works. He would then transact his private affairs and attend to his correspondence, and finally, whenever time permitted, make a trip through the works with me for observation, explanation and discussion of its operations. In this way he would thoroughly familiarize himself, and keep himself in touch with all details of manufacture without loss of time. His increasing financial success spurred him on to greater personal effort until his burden seemed too much for even a man of his phenomenal activity to carry, and he was forced to look for means to economize in time.

He began by using a horse and carriage in his race to and from the works, and to keep his driver in attendance while engaged in his work. This worked well in some respects, but L. his driver, . . . a former german cavalry man, was of little use in office work, although he saved Mr. Wharton considerable time by his reckless driving. The horse was rather fast, and the carriage ancient and none too strong for two large persons, and the way that outfit dashed over the streets and lots of Camden, and at times along the river front from one ferry to the other trying to catch the first boat out, was an amusing sight, and many a time a serious accident was only averted by the keen sight and quick action of Mr. Wharton, in grabbing the reins at the right moment. . . .

How Mr. Wharton managed to get the utmost amount of work done in a given time is shown by his habit of putting his watch in front of him on the desk, while at work in the Camden office, and to mark on its face the last moment to which he could remain. In his earlier years he would limit himself to ten minutes in his walk between ferry and works, a distance of fully a mile, and the unfortunate fellow who, like myself at times, had to accompany him, was kept on a continuous trot, while Mr. Wharton marched steadily on, enjoying the exercise.

Members of the family stood in awe of Wharton's energy. Hannah Haydock, who probably learned more about the nickel business than most, as her son Samuel was employed there, was especially respectful. Samuel remained with Wharton, living in Deborah's home at 336 Spruce, until about 1869, when he returned to New York to assist his father in the auction business.

Sometimes Wharton took his daughters to see the nickel works. Joanna wrote of being fascinated by the pungent odors and the sight of mysterious appearing vats. Their excitement must have pleased him, for it was something of the same sensation which he felt. He never tired of his nickel works. In the postwar years he gave it most of his attention and undertook experiments well beyond the necessities of business. His aim became more than that of making money; he would be a leader in the metallurgy of nickel. He would produce not only all the nickel America needed, but also the best nickel in the world.

Who can doubt that the aim was in the best interests of the country, that insofar as the nickel business was concerned, he served the good of the nation while serving himself? The challenging question is, did he in fact well serve himself?

Only Anna could have answered that question. Given the respect in which she held his work and the warm good humor which he bestowed on his family, she did not deny it.

8

Iron and Steel

When Wharton began his nickel business the iron industry of the United States was over one hundred years old. With it contributing, the American colonies had won independence from Britain. Without a strong iron industry, the Southerners were losing their war against the North. A necessity to military strength, iron appeared in postwar years, when military spending dropped to nothing, as the vital metal upon which a prosperous domestic economy depended. The housewife, the farmer, the artisan witnessed the advance of an iron age every time she or he went to market.

And yet, the things they purchased represented a small part of the product of the industry. The Great Customer was the Railroad. It needed iron for engines, cars, bridges, and especially rails. The tracks, which were finding entry into every county and city and crossing rivers, mountains, and prairies, formed a network of iron catching up local economies into a single web of manufacturing, banking, and commerce.

The technology and industry of making iron developed in response to the demand. The iron plantation of colonial days disappeared. Furnaces were larger and used a heated blast. Along the eastern seaboard anthracite became the normal fuel, although west of the Alleghenies ironmasters were experimenting with coke, following patterns traced in Europe. The black-smith's bellows gave way to forges and rolling mills operated by water power or steam. Ironmasters and railroad engineers went to Europe to learn about the latest improvements in metallurgy and engineering and returned to put the results of their education into practice.

In the years before the depression beginning in 1873, mining, smelting, and manufacturing enterprises were small. Many were individually owned or governed by partnerships, although the corporate form was gaining adherents. It had an advantage of raising large amounts of capital while tying the allegiance of investors to the prospects of iron and railroads. A fierce competition existed, from which many companies profited in times of prosperity and many fatally suffered in years of a slowing down or shrinking demand.

When Wharton was making spelter for the Pennsylvania and Lehigh Zinc

Company, southeastern Pennsylvania was the industrial heart of the nation's iron making. Excellent ores and limestone for flux lay in the valleys crossed by railroads bringing anthracite to market. Hundreds of small pockets of easily mined hematite dotted the Lehigh, Schuylkill, and Susquehanna river valleys and their nearby hills. Across the Delaware in the ridges of north central New Jersey were further deposits of an ore called magnetite. Many of the Jersey ores were initially worked as open pits, although the best of them went deeply into the ground and required elaborate tunneling in order to be fully productive. The choicest iron came from mixing the magnetite of Jersey with the hematite of Pennsylvania.

Many furnaces and rolling mills appeared in the Lehigh Valley. Farmers found a secondary source of income in the deposits located on their lands— the "winter crop," they called it. Heavily loaded wagons carrying ore to blast furnaces destroyed the roads. Branch railroad lines and even small independent companies laid track to accommodate the industry. Capital poured in from Philadelphia, New York, and Boston. Foreign-born workers, especially Irish, supplied manpower.

The lower Lehigh Valley centering on Bethlehem and Allentown had for a time leadership in making iron over other parts of southeastern Pennsylvania. "I have some acquaintance with most parts of our state, and have visited many Iron Works, but I have never been able to see a region equal to the Lehigh Valley for making Iron," wrote Wharton in 1860.[1]

1

He entered the business of making iron without that zest for adventure which had accompanied the work in spelter and was driving him to make nickel. He was not doing something original in iron. He had not, he told Luckenbach on refusing the presidency of the Thomas Iron Company, the background for making iron. Yet he had more preparation for that than he had for turning out nickel. The metallurgy of nickel was in its infancy, whereas that of iron had grown to adolescence and Wharton had studied it. Nor did he lack opportunity for gaining complete control. He did not have to work for the Thomas or Bethlehem Iron companies in order to make iron. He could—and did—start a company of his own. But he did not pursue that venture with the imagination and energy which might have made it into a major enterprise. It was never more than a source of income, and when it stopped making money for him, he let it go. He was some twenty years later to feel the lure and mystery of iron such as inspired John and George Fritz, Holley, Firmstone, Hewitt, Kelly, Mushet, and Siemens and other great masters in making iron and steel. A love affair with iron accompanied his purchase of the magnetite beds in New Jersey. He was, too, to feel the attraction of steel at a time when steel became a sine qua non for American power. But not at present. Perhaps he sensed a limit to his own powers in neglecting iron in favor of nickel. Possibly, too, the timing of opportunities in iron did not exactly coincide with the periods of his search for new ventures. The reasons are not entirely clear, but the fact is. Even as he began his nickel business he directed some of the profits from making spelter, temporarily held in the form of government gold bonds, into two ventures in iron which provided income, securities for the loans needed to bring the American Nickel Works into production, and a modest voice in iron making and railroading.

Wharton's small, independent venture in iron began when he was prospecting for zinc ore in the Saucon Valley. He purchased a deposit of iron which he developed as the Hartman Mine. Shortly thereafter he bought another iron property in collaboration with Joseph Diehl, manager of the zinc company's Saucon Valley farm. This was opened under the name of Mory Mine. In 1865 Wharton purchased Diehl's share of the Mory.[2]

In August 1866, Wharton and other Philadelphians named Jacob Riegel, J. Gillingham Fell, Joseph R. Whitaker, and George W. Whitaker, organized a concern called the Saucon Iron Company for the purpose of mining, smelting, and selling pig iron to rolling mills and other users. Wharton took three hundred of the original two thousand shares and thereby became the largest stockholder, a preeminence which he held for the life of the company. Although he chose not to serve as president, he nevertheless supervised operations in a general way. He sold the company the Hartman and Mory mines and saw to it that a branch railroad was built to connect the mines with a blast furnace in Hellertown. John M. Hartman, the first engineer in America to make designing of blast furnaces a specialty, built it and also a second furnace erected four years later. These were reputedly among the first blast furnaces in the country to be constructed with sheet iron shells resting on cast iron columns. Wharton led the directors in increasing the capitalization from an original two hundred thousand to six hundred thousand dollars and in buying or leasing other ore lands in the Saucon Valley and north central New Jersey. From the time the first blast furnace went into operation until the depression of 1873 the company made large profits and regularly paid annual dividends of from 10 percent to 12 percent.[3]

Possibly in those years Wharton spent more time with the Saucon Iron Company than he did with Bethlehem Iron, although he did not give great attention to either. He first bought stock in the Bethlehem Iron Company—two hundred shares—on 31 December 1862; almost immediately became a director; and within eighteen months acquired an additional six hundred shares and emerged as the largest stockholder, a position he held as with Saucon Iron for the life of the company.[4] Still, by contrast with Saucon Iron, his directorship in the Bethlehem company initially allowed him a small voice in making policy. The majority of directors of Bethlehem Iron were employees or stockholders of the Lehigh Valley Railroad and operated under the watchful eye of Asa Packer, controller of that road. Although Wharton's contributions to the fortunes of the Bethlehem Iron Company were much appreciated by the other directors, he could be effective only as long as he followed their lead, which took the company in the direction of specializing in making rails.

Yet even while Wharton put most of his energy to work elsewhere, a situation was in the making with Bethlehem Iron which would profoundly affect his future. It involved the company, the Lehigh Valley Railroad, and especially some fairly young men who were to be his colleagues in iron and steel making for almost forty years. Two of these were Robert H. Sayre, Jr., and John Fritz.

Bethlehem Iron was the brain child of a Moravian businessman of Bethlehem named Augustus Wolle, who planned a smelting operation for south Bethlehem using local ores. This was two years after Packer had completed the main line of the Lehigh Valley Railroad from the coal mining terminus of Mauch Chunk to Easton. Here the Lehigh Valley made a connection with the Central Railroad of New Jersey, which carried the trains to New York City. The year preceding the beginning of Wolle's venture the North Pennsylvania Railroad had finished its line into South Bethlehem, thus affording the Lehigh Valley a route for its coal cars into Philadelphia. Wolle's property was located near the junction of the North Penn and the Lehigh roads and was ideally suited for supplying them with iron. Packer wanted an independent source of iron, especially for rails, and consequently supplied the money, men, and ideas for making Wolle's undertaking a success. From the time of the incorporation of the venture as the Bethlehem Iron Company in the spring of 1860 Packer's men were in control. They planned a rolling mill, a forge, and a blast furnace for supplying at least part of the iron needed for rails and other shapes.

After the company was organized, Packer personally gave it little attention. His principal effort went into developing the railroad, an enterprise in which he was wonderfully successful. In succeeding years he pushed the line northward into New York state, bought or built railroads into all the adjoining coal fields, and planned for an independent route to New York City. He became one of the richest and most prominent industrialists of the commonwealth. He left control of the Bethlehem Iron Company to lieutenants who, when the period of shortages occasioned by Civil War came to an end, kept it in a constant state of expansion and improvement to meet the needs of Packer's railroad empire.

Chief among these lieutenants was Robert Heysham Sayre, Jr., a handsome man of commanding stature, powerful build, and keen intellect. Sayre was slightly less than two years older than Wharton and had superintended construction of the main line of the Lehigh Valley road. Railroading had long since moved from being Sayre's second nature to having first place in governing his outlook on the world of men and work. He was to remain general superintendent of the Lehigh Valley system until after the death of Packer and to be dominant in the affairs of railroads in one capacity or another for the remainder of his life. A native of the coal regions, he was a son of William Sayre, an accountant for the Lehigh Coal and Navigation Company and in former years a land agent in the neighborhood of Mauch Chunk for the elder William Wharton. Young Robert had completed the local school and then continued his education by self direction as he went from one job to another, working as a surveyor, foreman, and engineer for coal and canal companies. Sayre had assisted in surveying for and building the back track portion of the gravity Switchback Railroad of the Lehigh Coal and Navigation Company. Packer had known the Sayres for years and in 1852 made Robert chief engineer for planning and constructing the Lehigh Valley road.

Sayre's outstanding qualities as an industrialist were an understanding of railroad operations, an ability to command the work and allegiance of men, and a loyalty to Packer. Although sometimes criticizing Packer even to a point of questioning the older man's judgment, Sayre always, obediently and fully, carried out orders. He accepted Packer's standards of living as his own with the exception of political allegiance. Packer, an industrialist of the prewar era with Southern sympathies, was a Democrat, whereas Sayre, a northern industrialist of the postwar period became, as did most of his contemporaries, a Republican. But otherwise Packer defined the goals. Sayre fairly anticipated Packer's desires for the railroad and fulfilled them. Although unable to suppress an eye for the female figure, he curbed his impulses and followed Packer into a life of puritanized Episcopalianism. Sayre became a father of marriageable daughters, a pillar of the church, a promoter of hospitals and education, and a student of iron making—all following patterns established by his master.

Packer responded by entrusting Sayre with positions of responsibility and discretion in all major projects outside, as well as central to, the business of railroading. Sayre dominated others of the Lehigh Valley system and local concerns in establishing the Episcopal Church of the Nativity in South Bethlehem and subsequently in directing its affairs. When Packer donated land and money for founding an institution of practical higher education, to be called the Lehigh University, he left Sayre with the work of coordinating the project and directing, subject to Packer's frequent personal interventions, the building of the campus and the physical plant. Packer saw to it that Sayre was made not only a director of the Bethlehem Iron Company but also, with John Knecht and Wharton, a member of the finance committee, which in the early years served the board as an executive committee. Sayre himself had only a small financial interest in the company. Sayre and Knecht, another friend of the railroad, would always be able to guide the work of Wharton, the finance committee's unofficial chairman.

Sayre, the better to fulfill his obligations toward Packer, built a large house for himself and family on an eminence called Fountain Hill, directly opposite the Church of the Nativity and overlooking the junction of the Lehigh Valley and North Penn railroads, the station, the university, and the iron company. There, or wherever Sayre happened to be at the end of a day, he wrote in a clear hand and with great economy of words his impressions of the people and events in his life. He did this for fifty-six years, almost until the time of his death. The accomplishment displays the precision of his mind and the persistence and thoroughness with which he accomplished his duties. The series of diaries comprises the sort of record against which the completeness and accuracy of other accounts of the events recorded therein are to be measured.

Part of Packer's success as an industrialist lay in his insistence on having the best for whatever was vital to his operations. If he could not afford the best he would forfeit the operation. No worry such as this confronted him in beginning the manufacture of iron. He needed an excellent ironmaster. One was potentially available. Packer gave Sayre the task of persuading that ironmaster to leave a lucrative position and come to Bethlehem in spite of the untried nature of the enterprise and the unsettled conditions of the economy preceding the Civil War.

The man in question was John Fritz, who with an equally talented brother named George had recently developed for the Cambria Iron Company at Johnstown, Pennsylvania, a three-high rolling mill for making rails. Until then, a two-high mill had been standard. Red hot iron had been passed between rollers, then returned to the point of origin and passed again. This took time, so that the iron cooled too much between the first and second rollings for best results. John and George built the three-high rolls in order to eliminate the time consumed in sending the rails back to the point of origin. With the three-high set, the iron passed first between the bottom and middle rollers and then was instantly passed, going in a return direction, between the middle and top rollers. The saving in time and expense and the improvement in the quality of the rails thus made was enormous.[5]

John Fritz was three years older than Wharton. John and George had been born and reared in the Great Valley of Chester County and had followed opportunity into towns and villages having blast furnaces and rolling mills. By means of hard work, observation, and general likeableness of personality they had learned the secrets of iron making and, adding imagination to accumulated knowledge, had successfully innovated and become known as superior engineers and iron makers. That was before the founding of engineering schools such as the Massachusetts Institute of Technology, the Stevens Institute of Technology, and the Lehigh University, which were to make of engineering a systematic, scientific study. John Fritz, wrote Frederick W. Taylor, was "one of the greatest and one of the last" of the "school of empirical engineers. When I was a boy and first saw Mr. Fritz, most of the drawings which he made for his new machinery were done with a piece of chalk on the floor of the pattern room, or with a stick on the floor of the blacksmith shop, and in many cases the verbal description of the parts of the machines which he wished to have made were more important than his drawings. Time and again he himself did not know just what he wanted until after the pattern or model was made and he had an opportunity of seeing the shape of the piece which he was designing. One of his favorite sayings whenever a new machine was finished was, 'Now, boys, we have got her done, let's start her up and see why she doesn't work.'"[6]

Sayre went to Johnstown to observe what the Fritzes had accomplished. "Very much pleased with what I saw," he wrote in his diary for 3 September 1860. Sayre explained the opportunity to John: the financial soundness of the undertaking; the growing reputation of Packer; the prospects for wealth; the large discretion Fritz would be allowed in doing his work. Sayre was good at such encounters. His manner was forthright and reassuring and his flattery had a ring of genuine admiration. Fritz listened closely. He knew from a previous experience at Catasauqua about the advantages of making iron in the Lehigh Valley. He was sensitive concerning the people he might have to answer to. Like many great artists, he was something of a prima donna where outsiders were concerned. He felt his lack of formal education. Others had to write important letters for him. All his efforts had gone into becoming an engineer and were going into being a better engineer. He had small patience for the work needed to acquire proficiency in the domain of letters. What mattered to him was a chance to build, improve, supervise what he had built, and plan for more; and to have the resources and the permission to build the best of all establishments for making iron. Sayre knew all this, or perhaps he sensed it as he began talking with Fritz. In any event, Fritz's doubts vanished. He agreed to come to Bethlehem and build the plant of the Bethlehem Iron Company at a salary of five thousand dollars a year.[7]

He arrived anticipating that he could not meet the deadlines which the directors were setting. He had experienced economic depressions before. The directors wanted a rolling mill completed by the end of 1860; he got it under roof by the following summer. Then came the shortages occasioned by war. This he knew the directors would understand; and he had full confidence in his ability. But some of the other stockholders might panic. After his retirement he composed an autobiography in which he wrote of the winter of 1861–62, "It became almost impossible to raise money for any new enterprise and taking into consideration the whole outlook it was most extremely discouraging and for a time I was fearful the stockholders would stampede as it was difficult for some of them to raise the amount they had already agreed to."[8] Yet by the middle of the summer almost all of the stock had been subscribed, and the work was progressing. Fritz put the first furnace into blast on 4 January 1863 and had puddling furnaces and the rolling mill operating by late summer of that year. He began planning for other furnaces. In 1865 he opened the original machine shop and three years later, the foundry.[9]

He fulfilled the expectations of Packer, Sayre, Wharton, and the others directing the fortunes of the company. In the first partial year of operations (1863) the profit was 7 percent of the stock subscribed.[10] For the next ten years the directors declared dividends ranging annually from 6 percent to 20 percent.

2

Five years after the Bethlehem Iron Company had begun making iron the directors voted to build a Bessemer Steel plant. Wharton put the motion which the directors accepted: "That this Company should proceed immediately to the production of Bessemer Steel, and that the Manager of this Company be and hereby is instructed to prepare without delay for the said manufacture at these works."[11]

Behind the motion lay a rapid series of developments in the metallurgy of iron and steel. This time Americans were only a little behind the British, although America had as yet an insufficient plant for fully profiting from the inventions.

On 11 August 1856, Henry Bessemer of England described to a skeptical audience a new process, that of introducing a blast of air into molten pig iron in a converter. In explaining what happened he said that the oxygen in the air decarburized the pig iron, that is, removed the carbon, turning it into a soft, malleable product. About a year later another Englishman, David Mushet, showed how the introduction of a mineral called spiegeleisen into the converter at an appropriate stage hardened the product so that it might be used for rails and many other things. The spiegeleisen which he used consisted approximately of 86.25 percent iron, 8.50 percent manganese, and 5.25 percent free carbon. He concluded that the manganese combined with the oxygen which was locked into the iron and passed off with the slag while the product was recarburized to the point at which it became hard steel.

Several more years passed before the Bessemer-Mushet process became commercially feasible. A special necessity was that the ores used to make the pig iron be low in sulphur and contain no more than 0.02 percent phosphorus. By 1862 Bessemer's plant in Sheffield was on the way to becoming profitable. That same year an American mechanical engineer, Alexander Lyman Holley, studied the process at Sheffield. A year later, he obtained American patent rights for it and began building an experimental converter at Troy, New York. He succeeded and was immediately in demand as a supervisor or consultant in building Bessemer converters elsewhere.

Somewhat before Bessemer read his paper in England an American, William Kelly, discovered and used the same process at his iron works in Eddysville, Kentucky. The resulting controversy concerning who was first and hence who was entitled to patent rights had important consequences for

American steel producers. The Cambria Iron Works chose to operate using the Kelly patents. George Fritz, the general manager, installed a converter and patented improvements of his own. As far as production was concerned, both processes used essentially the same technology. Most of the first American ironmasters who went into the business of making steel by the Bessemer or Kelly method used the improvements made by Holley, George Fritz, and others.

The Bessemer-Kelly method could turn out steel in quantity at a lower cost than the older processes could do. This opened up possibilities for using steel for railroads. Iron rails cost much less, but they were not as serviceable as those made of steel. Iron rails sometimes broke, causing accidents. They lasted only five or six years and then had to be taken up and rerolled. Rails made of steel were more reliable and could last many times longer. A railroad which could afford the initial expense would in the long run greatly profit from switching from iron to Bessemer steel.

Packer and his lieutenants well understood the advantage of using steel for rails. They saw, too, the trackage of a rival railroad, the Lehigh and Susquehanna, being laid with steel rails imported from England. They scarcely hesitated in beginning the work of tearing up the iron tracks and putting down steel. Like their rival, the Lehigh Coal and Navigation Company, they ordered the rails from England. The results were not entirely satisfactory. The Lehigh Railroad Company paid a high price for the imported product, and some of the rails broke. When analyzed, they were found to contain 0.06 percent phosphorus, well above the limit of 0.02 percent.

That was when the railroad men on the board of the Bethlehem Iron Company raised the question, could Fritz turn out a better product? Timid souls might hesitate. Only two companies in the United States had as yet begun production, the works of William F. Durfee at Wyandotte, Michigan, and those of John F. Winslow, John A. Griswold, and Holley at Troy, New York. The directors had tests made of Lake Superior ores, which were found to be too high in phosphorous. Although they found some local ores within tolerance limits, these were too low in iron content to be profitably mined and smelted. But neither Packer nor Wharton was fearful. Both had done before what others had held back from doing. The prospect seemed to them good for making steel and steel rails at least as strong as those imported from England and at a far lower cost. Besides, they had faith in Fritz, who had been at Cambria when his brother George was experimenting with the Kelly process.

Fritz was among those who hesitated before plunging into the new venture. He held back not from timidity. His willingness to undertake new projects considerably exceeded that of directors such as Sayre, whose tendency to caution was one of the qualities which had endeared him to Packer. Fritz was troubled about the availability of suitable ores, a subject which was to be a special concern of his for many years. He took pains to let the directors know that if the Bessemer plant he built did not work, they would have to blame the ores. Then he set about erecting the best plant he could. He called in consultants. Sayre wrote in his diary for 26 October 1867, "Spent the afternoon with Wm. Reed, Mr. Belden, Prof. Seymour & J. Fritz examining process for manufacture of steel from ore." Fritz went to Europe to study steel works there. In the following several years Holley made occasional trips to Bethlehem to advise Fritz, who took his time in designing, fashioning, and installing machinery. When Holley once suggested that Fritz had probably made some of the machinery unnecessarily strong, he is reported to have laughed and said, "Well, if I have, it will never be found out."[12]

Fritz built a Bessemer steel plant which not only worked but also called forth the admiration of other engineers. Robert W. Hunt wrote of Fritz's innovations, "He arranged his melting-house, engine-room, converting-room, blooming and rail mills, all in one grand building, under one roof, and without any partition walls. He placed his cupolas on the ground and hoisted the melted iron on a hydraulic lift, and then poured it into the converters. The spiegel is melted in a Siemens furnace, also on the ground floor, and the melted spiegel is also hoisted and poured into the vessels. . . . Instead of depending upon friction to drive the rollers of the tables, Mr. Fritz put in a pair of small reversing engines."[13] The appreciative directors raised Fritz's salary to ten thousand dollars in 1872. But they did not put him up for membership on the board.

The Bethlehem Iron Company became the eleventh American concern turning out Bessemer steel. It made the first blow amid considerable fanfare on 4 October 1873, and it was a success. The directors almost immediately announced that the company had received orders for two thousand tons of steel rails respectively from the Jersey Central and the Lehigh Valley roads. Low-phosphorus ores were brought in from the Hibernia mine near Port Oram, New Jersey, and for a time were imported from Algiers. The furnace for making spiegeleisen used the residues of zinc ores procured from the New Jersey Zinc Company.[14]

As the plant was readied for production the directors increased the stock of the company by 25 percent, having already declared a stock dividend of 10 percent. They began talking about going into the business of making steel tubing and other steel products.[15]

3

During the first ten years of the life of the Bethlehem Iron Company the business of making iron and steel brought Wharton to Bethlehem about once a month to attend meetings of the boards of the Bethlehem and the Saucon iron companies. One board would meet in the morning and the other in the afternoon. Usually he caught an early morning train from Philadelphia and returned to the city in late afternoon of the same day. Occasionally he came to Bethlehem the previous night to talk over matters with Knecht, Sayre, and others. When he did this he stayed at the Sun Hotel.

He worked harmoniously with the other directors, who were six in number in addition to himself. He had known Alfred Hunt, the president, several years before buying stock in the company. When Wharton was commuting from Philadelphia in the closing years of his spelter business he sometimes traveled to Bethlehem with Hunt, a Philadelphian of Quaker origin. Hunt was a reliable manager who followed rather than led in making key decisions concerning new projects. He was a bachelor, maintained an apartment in the Sun Hotel, and remained as president of the company until he died. Wharton respected Sayre, the principal spokesman on the board for Packer; and he worked well with Ario Pardee, coal baron and sometime collaborator with Packer in various business deals, as well as with Knecht, Wolle, and the men who filled the seventh directorship for short periods.

These directors behaved much as had those of the Pennsylvania and Lehigh Zinc Company, with the important exception that the men of the zinc company had not been subject to the overriding voice of a railroad monarch. The directors of Bethlehem Iron were during the lifetime of Packer constrained to do his will. Aside from this, they used the company pretty much as they pleased, and in ways which showed a poor sense of corporate responsibility. Relatives and friends went on the payroll. In the midsixties Sayre, Knecht, and several of their friends had a blast furnace built on property adjoining that of the company. The enterprise was incorporated as the Northampton Iron Company. In 1868, before the furnace was put into blast, Sayre and his colleagues sold the property to Bethlehem Iron.[16] Sayre recorded in his diary for 24 December 1868 that he had made a profit of about eighty thousand dollars on the transaction.

Although Wharton in these early years did not engage in such practices, he did not oppose them. He voted with the majority to purchase the Northampton Iron Company's property. After the death of Packer, he handsomely profited from some operations involving the company with projects of his own. But during these early years with the company he realized the weakness of his position. He was an outsider, a Philadelphian, nonresident in Bethlehem, and in no way dependent for his livelihood on the prosperity of the Lehigh Valley Railroad. The other directors respected his ability, and they could not overlook his status as principal stockholder. But they did not feel obliged to him and refused his few requests for special consideration, namely, a proposal to sell the company the Hartman and the Mory mines and another for the company to buy several Bethlehem houses which remained to him from the days of his spelter business.[17]

Wharton's best work for the company during those years did not appear on its yearly balance sheets of profit and loss. It had to do with the building of a reputation as a lobbyist in Washington. He did not do this as a paid representative of the Bethlehem Iron Company, but for protection of his own interests. He had begun by asking Congress for a duty of a cent a pound on spelter and had progressed from this to a fight for protection of his nickel business.[18] While the battle for higher tariffs on nickel, cobalt, and their products was going on, he undertook the added task of fighting for higher duties on iron ore and iron and steel and their products. In this way he quickly found himself defending an entire industry whose mines, furnaces, and rolling mills were to be found in every state of the union. His commitment to the general cause of protecting all of American industry grew. He came to believe that effective lobbying for any one industry depended on a rational, consistent plan, arrived at by the representatives of all industries, before Congress was approached. No means of achieving such a plan then existed. When in 1868 the tariff came up for revision he saw a scurrying to and fro of self-serving lobbyists whose activities as likely as not put them into conflict with one another. Such confusion, he reasoned, weakened support for the cause of protection and reduced the chances for any lobbyist to be successful. Only in union was there strength. The idea that Wharton came up with for achieving this, and which he put into effect and carried out in practice, was the Industrial League. There existed in 1868 a dying organization called the American Industrial League, which had branches in several states including Pennsylvania, the most important industrial state of the union. Wharton's idea was that of taking over the Pennsylvania branch and transforming it into a sort of holding company for lobbyists representing industries across the country. And this is what he, Daniel J. Morrell, Morton McMichael, William Sellers, and Henry C. Lea did.[19]

These cofounders became lifelong friends of Wharton. Morrell and a partner, C. S. Wood, had taken over the Cambria Iron Company and transformed it from a financially insecure to a stable enterprise. Morrell was from 1867 to 1871 a congressman and chairman of the House Committee on Manufactures. McMichael, born of immigrant Irish parents, was a journalist and sometime editor and publisher who had been sheriff of Philadelphia at the time of the anti-Catholic riots of 1844 and was from 1866 to 1869 mayor of Philadelphia. Sellers was an inventor of machine tools of all sorts, such as steam injectors, rifling machines, riveters, hydraulic machinery, steam hammers, and turntables. He had organized his own concern in Philadelphia, known as William Sellers and Company, and was soon to become one of the founders of the Midvale Steel Company. Lea, a nephew of the economist Henry C. Carey, was born into the publishing business. At an early age he entered the firm of his father, but spent most of his middle and later life writing on various aspects of religious history. When he was about forty years of age he became active in protesting against corruption in Philadelphia politics and in 1870 organized the Municipal Reform Association.

Almost as soon as the League was founded Morrell brought in another gentleman who became as closely associated with it as were these others. This was Cyrus Elder, a young lawyer practicing in Johnstown, who served as solicitor and general agent of the Cambria Iron Company and was later to be one of the organizers of the Bessemer Steel Company.

All five of these men were Republicans. Lea and McMichael were among the founders of the Union League of Philadelphia. Morrell, Sellers, and Elder were in the business of making iron. McMichael and Lea were journalists. Morrell and McMichael held important public office. All were writers.

The decision to organize was made in McMichael's office and was followed by a public meeting attended by Pennsylvania industrialists and merchants. Morrell became the first president. Elder was secretary and continued to hold that post for many years. An executive committee, whose most active members over the years were Wharton (chairman), Lea, and Sellers, advised the president and supervised most of the work of the league. A representative council included persons from each branch of industry, for example: Stephen Colwell, iron workers from the East; James Park, Jr., iron workers from the West; J. Gillingham Fell, coal; Charles Lennig, chemicals; Richard Garsed, woolen fabrics; Wharton, metals; Lea, books.

The league took a bipartisan position. General Robert Patterson, a Democrat, became the second president. Still, the membership was overwhelmingly Republican.

Wharton, Lea, and Sellers informed the Committee on Ways and Means of the House of Representatives of the birth of the league. All bills for raising revenue must originate in the House; and the Committee on Ways and Means is primarily responsible for taking care of such matters. General Robert C. Schenck was then chairman of the committee. His views on the tariff were the same as those of the league. He invited Wharton and his associates to prepare a tariff bill. Wharton went to work and with the aid of Lorin Blodget, assistant secretary of the treasury, produced the text which with slight modifications became the Schenck Tariff Act of 1870.[20]

Wharton and other leaders of the Industrial League thereafter continued to write tariff proposals. They often worked with the American Iron and Steel Association, opposing such nonconformists in the iron industry as Abram Hewitt, a moderate free trader and a Democrat.

The league had great success during the administrations of President Grant, who supported protective legislation. It published and distributed free a large edition of the *Industrial Bulletin,* a monthly journal edited by its secretary; annually printed and sent out many thousands of copies of a protectionist almanac; purchased and distributed speeches of leading protectionist members of Congress; supplied college libraries with textbooks teaching American economics according to protectionist views; hired lecturers; sustained friendly newspapers; and promoted in every possible way the study of protectionist economic ideas. The league called on its members for donations to defray expenses and maintained a slush fund to finance its dealings with Congress.

Most of the contributions of Wharton to the work of the league are lost in the anonymity which its leaders usually adopted. According to Lea, the league was "virtually Mr. Wharton."[21] Certainly, Wharton was continually speaking and writing for it and interceding with others on its behalf. In 1872 he prodded the boards of the Saucon and the Bethlehem iron companies to contribute to the work of the league. The minutes of the Saucon Iron company read: "Mr. Wharton stated that other Iron Companies were contributing to the fund to sustain the 'Industrial League' an organization formed to work against the machinations of the Free Traders and that it was the interest of this Co. as well as others that this organization should not fail in its good work for want of funds. Therefore it was Resolved that the Treasurer be and is hereby authorized to subscribe to said Industrial League the sum of one thousand dollars."[22]

The directors of the Bethlehem Iron Company voted a sum "not to exceed $2500."[23] This was one request from Wharton which they did not ignore. The league had been highly successful in its efforts to have Congress impose a high tariff on steel rails. Packer, who rarely spoke or wrote about his business affairs—or about anything at all, for that matter—was obviously pleased. McMichael was, incidentally, a personal friend of Packer, who asked him to respond to the laudatory speeches made on the occasion of a dinner in Packer's honor at the time of the founding of the Lehigh University. Henry C. Carey, in a way the ideological father of the league, was one of the speakers at that dinner. J. Gillingham Fell, who represented coal on the council of the league, was a director and had been president of the Lehigh Valley Railroad. Packer saw that Wharton was faithfully supporting the Lehigh Valley system and its iron and steel supplier and was doing this not from sycophancy but from a conviction that the best interests of the country lay in promoting the strength of its railroads, iron works, and other industries.

In 1872 Wharton became a member of the board of the Lehigh Valley Railroad. He had previously owned no stock in the company, but in the year of joining the board he purchased five hundred shares and doubled that amount in 1873. Packer, it seems, had decided that Wharton's counsel could be useful even though he was not a railroad man. In any event, as far as Packer was concerned, Wharton was always on trial.

4

One contribution of Wharton to the Bethlehem Iron Company in those years went almost unnoticed at the time. This was William Thurston, only son of Wharton's sister Mary and her husband Joseph. That "gift" was prompted more by family feelings than any concern for improving the making of iron and steel.

Upon the death of the elder William Wharton in 1854 the family economy disappeared. William made provisions in his last will and testament for Deborah and the children, specifying that the children were to share equally in his estate. Deborah continued to maintain unity among members of the family by the force of her personal qualities and her status as a minister in the Society to which all her children belonged. The reverence given her by the children was spontaneous and deeply felt. "She is so purely innocent, and so truly noble," wrote Hannah.[24] On Deborah's seventy-sixth birthday Joseph sent her this letter:

"Many times when I have considered that we must at last be separated by death, and that the younger might probably be the survivor, I have thought of Elisha's request, 'Elijah said unto Elisha, ask what I shall do for thee before I be taken away from thee. And Elisha said I pray thee let a double portion of thy spirit be upon me.' If such requests could be granted, and if I by cleaving to thee and passing over Jordan with thee had become worthy of such a blessing, this is what I should crave."[25]

Charles, who as the eldest surviving son might normally have expected to inherit some of the paternal mantle, forfeited the right by choosing to retire from business and live off his inheritance. In doing so he followed his nature. He hated the pressures of business which Joseph welcomed as a channel for his vigor. Charles remained his former genial self, devoted to his wife and children and a welcome guest for all members of the family.

Esther (Hetty) Fisher, Joseph's youngest sister, had in 1859 married Benjamin R. Smith of Newport and gone to live there. This enhanced a trend, begun several years earlier, of members of the family making Newport the site of their annual summer vacations.

No one really took the elder William Wharton's place. Joseph was the person to whom the other members of the family looked in time of financial need. He was successful, rich, lived among them, and was usually willing to help. Although they gave him none of the paternal respect which they might have shown Rodman or Charles, they maintained with him sound brotherly and sisterly affections.

One who did not need financial help in those postwar years was Abraham Barker, Sarah's husband. Abraham, although not a Quaker, was as much a member of the family as the others. He used the plain language when addressing them and undertook many projects of interest to members of the Society. During the war he was a member of the Freedman's Relief Association, of which Stephen Colwell was president and which included as members among others Thomas Mott, William Sellers, William Biddle, Henry C. Carey, William Dorsey, and a host of Parrishes. In 1865 Abraham vigorously and successfully cooperated with other members of the association in fighting for the removal of a ban on blacks riding the street railways of the city. His banking house had become one of the largest and most respected in Philadelphia. He was during those years Joseph's principal banker. All of the Whartons and their spouses and children used his offices on Third Street as a meeting place and a clearing house for messages. The death of Sarah in 1866 and the subsequent remarriage of Abraham did not disturb these relations. Sarah left behind four children, Wharton, Sigourney, Deborah Wharton, and Anna, who grew up in an atmosphere thickened by the conversation of Wharton aunts, uncles, and cousins.[26]

The ablest of these children was Wharton Barker, born in 1846 and destined to become variously a supporter, collaborator, and opponent of his illustrious uncle, albeit even in opposition never going to an extreme of destroying the mutual respect which each had for the other. Although raised a Quaker by his mother, Wharton Barker did not share the pacifistic, antipolitical bent of the majority of the Society. While still only eighteen years of age he helped to raise a regiment of black troops to fight for the Union. In 1866 he received a baccalaureate degree from the University of Pennsylvania and the following year, upon attaining the age of twenty-one, entered politics, joined the banking house of his father, and married Margaret Corliss Baker of New York City. He was soon on his way to becoming a junior partner in his father's establishment. In politics Wharton Barker worked within the Republican Party and supported the Industrial League.

He was handsome, good-natured, supremely self-confident, and ambitious. After receiving an A.M. degree from the University in 1869 he helped to organize a magazine entitled *The Penn Monthly* This journal advertised itself as "A popular magazine devoted to literature, science and political economy conducted by Graduates of the University of Pennsylvania under the Editorial Charge of Otis H. Kendall and Robert Ellis Thompson." *The Penn Monthly* had a life of ten years and during that time published a miscellany of essays, articles, and reviews of a scholarly and semischolarly nature by such writers as Thompson; Henry Coppée, president of the Lehigh University; Henry C. Carey; William Elder; Henry C. Lea; J. G. Rosengarten of the Industrial League; and Joseph Wharton. The journal was frankly protectionist. Wharton Barker probably wrote many of the editorials, which were unsigned. Barker Brothers and Company financed the publication. Barker Brothers and the Wharton Railroad Switch Company were regularly found among the journal's few advertisers.

Joseph's brother William was one of those who heavily depended on Joseph. William had experimented with railroad switches and related devices for moving cars about the yards and in 1865 invented an unbroken main line switch which greatly improved the ease and safety of moving cars from a main line to a siding. He followed this with improvements on switches and frogs, that is, joints for allowing one set of tracks to cross another, and organized the Wharton Railroad Switch Company with office and factory in

Philadelphia. Barker Brothers financed the company and promoted its products in America and abroad. Joseph also supplied timely financial aid and supported the younger brother's enterprise with large purchases of stock. William's company marked the beginning of an undertaking which in the twentieth century became part of the Taylor-Wharton Company.[27]

The children of Susanna and Rodman and of Hannah and Robert Haydock also benefited from Joseph's largesse. Susanna did not remarry, and her finances were slender. Joseph helped finance the education at Yale College of her son Rodman, or "Roddy" as she called him; and several years after Rodman's graduation Joseph briefly employed him as a supervisor for several of his iron properties in New Jersey. Joseph had hired Samuel Haydock first for the spelter and then for the nickel works at a time when the Haydocks were financially distressed. Samuel had returned to New York City and in 1870 died. A few years later Joseph took the Haydock's second son, Roger, into his employ.

The Thurston children, Hetty and William, were in a different situation from these others, because they became orphans. Mary Thurston's death came unexpectedly after a short illness in 1856, leaving her husband to care for Hetty, aged six, and William, who was four. Even then the dreaded germs of tuberculosis were working in Joseph Thurston. He had sufficient means to provide for his children, but he could not buy health. He died on 3 June 1861, leaving Joseph Wharton and Deborah as guardians of the children. These were already living with Deborah on Spruce Street. She supervised their education and accepted with a resignation born of religious devotion the early appearance of consumption in Hetty. Deborah had seen the disease gnaw away the life of too many other people, including her own daughter Anna, to hope for Hetty's recovery. Hetty slipped into the life of a semi-invalid, heavily under the influence of religion. She died at the age of twenty-five.

Her brother William for the time being escaped the family malady. He was alert, spirited, and ambitious, like his cousin Wharton Barker, whom he frequently saw. But unlike the elder cousin, William Thurston found intellectual activities boring. He entered the University of Pennsylvania and dropped out. He wanted a life of action such as that of Uncle Joe, who had not needed a university education in order to become powerful and rich. Joseph Wharton understood the special genius of his ward and had him placed as a laborer in the machine shop of the Bethlehem Iron Company, knowing that if young William proved able he might rapidly advance. Joseph was probably not at all surprised to receive a letter from William in less than a year from the time of his first employment pressing his advantage:

> My own interest in the shop has flagged because I do not think it possible for the Bethlehem Iron Co. as at present conduction to turn out a thorough first class machinist, jobs are hurried through and often patched up

so that they will do, but without being finished as machinery ought to be. Independent however of this it was not my intention nor I think thine that I should remain in the shop until I had learned the trade, which would take anybody at the least calculation three years in a perfectly regulated shop. In fact I am beginning to feel that I would be of more use to the company and myself in some different position where I could be learning something about business and finance. I am also tired of being an associate in a shop with walking animals whose main occupation is cursing, swearing and conversing in filthy language.[28]

The plea was effective. Uncle Joe used his influence and young William was moved out of the shop and into the office, where he worked in close proximity to the general manager. He was not yet twenty-one, but had already acquired the art of pleasing his supervisors. Robert Sayre and other leaders of the company and the community were soon inviting William Thurston into their homes. He copied their way of life and gained a taste for expensive things. An allowance from the proceeds of his inheritance enabled him to indulge himself more than most men of his age. He lived to the limit of his means and scorned to save, yet acquired none of the expensive vices which might interfere with his advancement.

He had good reason to dream of one day becoming president of the company of which his uncle was the chief stockholder.

9

The Great Years of the Nickel Business

During the years of the 1870s, nickel was the principal source of Wharton's wealth from the time the furnaces at Gap began producing matte until the onset of competition depending on ores from New Caledonia and Canada. He used the money from nickel to increase his leverage in Bethlehem Iron. Smaller projects in glass and sugar beets were begun and ended. In all of these he combined an acute sense of business with an intellectual interest in the advancement of science and technology. Then, in a contrasting mood, he indulged a fancy by putting surplus funds into thousands of acres of Jersey pinelands, which cost little but whose value seemed destined to remain small.

He advanced along the economic front in spite of one of the worst depressions of the century. In the summer of 1873 rumblings of financial distress shook banking houses in Europe. A few months later Jay Cooke and Company closed its doors, ushering in six years of distress for Americans. Prices and wages tumbled. (At the Saucon Iron Company wages were cut approximately in half.) Many firms went bankrupt; unemployment was widespread. A trend toward consolidation of enterprises in industry, banking, and transportation gained momentum accompanied by loud cries against monopolies, trusts, plutocracy in general.

The depression did not touch the nickel industry. A series of political happenings in Europe gave it a boost which it had never previously known and possibly has not seen since. Bismarck united Germany over the opposition of Austria and France, then decided on a uniform coinage for the Empire. Some of the coins were to be made of a 75 = 25 copper-nickel alloy. This meant a sudden, enormous demand for nickel. Prices soared, with payments being made in gold.

What could not Wharton do with an influx of gold, when tempting opportunities were going begging for want of buyers?

1

A few months before the failure of Jay Cooke and Company Wharton made a trip to Europe. The occasion was the International Exhibition in Vienna, at which were featured the latest developments in science and technology. Wharton had arranged for a small exhibit of the products of the Gap Mine and the American Nickel Works. It was his first attempt at a public display in which he might call widespread attention to his accomplishments. His hopes were not fulfilled, for the products of Gap and Camden went almost unnoticed. His weakness lay in failing to recognize that a well organized display is not enough. It has to be explained to the judges for its full importance to be realized and suitably rewarded.

The trip itself had no such shortcomings. The means by which Wharton traveled represented an acknowledgement of his status among American manufacturers and men of business. Congress had voted to send to Vienna at its own expense one hundred honorary commissioners, men "eminent for their patriotism and for scientific or professional attainments." Wharton was asked to be one of these. He used the opportunity to meet scientists and industrialists in England, Prussia, and Austria, to gain valuable information concerning nickel and sugar beets, and to widen his understanding of Europe and its peoples.

He began the trip reluctantly, being finally persuaded to go as a companion to his friend Henry C. Lea. Upon embarking aboard the *Pennsylvania*, the first steamship of the first American line to cross the Atlantic, Wharton wrote to Anna that he found "the pain of parting . . . quite too much like the final parting to suit my feelings" and besought her to tell the children "that they must learn to consider for themselves what is right, and not to act as Poll [Mary] sometimes does in a rash and headlong manner. Joey is old enough to help thee in many ways and to help Poll along too. Little Nan [Anna] can comfort thee if she can do little else. They are all dear little girls and will all in time learn to 'mind the light' as George Fox says." He kept a diary for the three months he was in Europe and wrote long letters home.[1]

In London, his first stop, he obtained various bits of information from his rivals, Evans and Askin and Vivian and Wiggins. The information was sufficient for him to estimate the world production of nickel, which he set down in his diary as follows:

1873 Nickel Made	Minimum	Maximum
Evans & Askin	200,000	300,000
Vivian	130,000	150,000
Fleitmann	100,000	150,000
Wharton	170,000	200,000
Sachsichn blau farben work	40,000	60,000
Klefa ⎫ London Victoria ⎭	20,000	30,000
Schoeller & Co. Vienna	100,000	120,000
Other English makers	50,000	50,000
	810,000	1,060,000

Wharton found everybody in the nickel business in London anticipating the Prussian coinage. Before leaving London for Germany he obtained through the influence of General Schenck a letter of introduction to the U.S.

minister in Berlin "to be used as a means of access to the mint people of the German Empire."[2] En route to Berlin he stopped at Unna and visited Voigt's father, mother, sister, and brother-in-law and then proceeded to Fleitmann's home in Iserlohn. Wharton was uncertain of the reception he might receive from Fleitmann, as the two had corresponded but little since their disagreement and separation. He was relieved to find Fleitmann "friendly and amiable . . . frank and communicative." The two makers of nickel talked until late into the night and all the next day of the prospects of nickel, iron, and steel; of the possibilities of making malleable nickel; and especially of the forthcoming Prussian coinage. Fleitmann expected to make all or most of the blanks for the German mint. Wrote Wharton, "He thinks it well for me to see the German authorities at Berlin, but not to offer to sell to them: rather to offer to aid the German nickel makers. If nickel should be needed from me he would take it and allow me the same price his firm gets." A talk a few days later with the director of the mint in Berlin confirmed Fleitmann's expectations.[3]

At Vienna Wharton met another German maker of nickel of some renown. This was Hermann Krupp, brother "of the famous Krupp steel cannon maker etc. of Essen." Hermann took Wharton to see his works (Schoeller & Co.) at Barnsdorf. Thus began another friendship, which lasted for many years.[4]

When Wharton arrived back in the States he geared his mine and refinery to maximum production. For the next ten years he annually produced about two hundred thousand pounds of nickel. This was as nearly as can be determined between one-sixth and one-third of the world supply in each of these years.[5]

At the time he was preparing for the Prussian coinage, he developed a means for making pure malleable nickel. He did not do this to meet the needs of the mints or the makers of German silver, who could use an impure product. Another industry had appeared, which must have something better. This was the electroplating of iron with nickel. Cast anodes made from ordinary nickel tended to crumble and break in solution. As yet the electroplating industry was small, but it would probably grow. In any event, pure malleable nickel conceivably had other uses which would be discovered as soon as it became available. Because nickel could substitute for iron for many purposes and was noncorrosible, it might be used for a variety of shapes if made as malleable and strong as good wrought iron. And as always, behind a desire to make money lay a curiosity that incidentally promoted the science of metallurgy.

Doubtless, Fleitmann inspired him. The two manufacturers thought closely along the same lines where nickel was concerned. Each knew and respected the other's ability. Their industrial pursuits, although going separate ways since 1868, were soon again to touch. Wharton was the first to make malleable nickel, but Fleitmann followed with a better process for commercial production and ideas for plated ware which Wharton felt he needed.

Wharton's papers contain no description of the process he himself developed. Possibly he took a cue from Bessemer's discovery that the addition of spiegeleisen to pig iron in a converter can make the metal malleable; that the manganese in the spiegel removes gases which make the iron brittle. This is speculation. At a later date Wiggin of England was supposed to have made nickel malleable by adding from 2 percent to 5 percent manganese.[6] All that is known for sure is that Wharton successfully achieved his metallurgical triumph. He retrospectively wrote of his accomplishment:

> In the years 1874 and 1875 I made a number of articles of malleable nickel. . . . The hammered rods, rolled sheets, knives, lightning rod tips, bridle bits, cups, etc. which I made of pure nickel were the first objects ever made of wrought nickel. . . . In the years 1875 and 1876 I made a number of pure nickel magnets of horseshoe and bar shapes, thus entering upon an almost unexplored field, though it had long been known that both nickel and cobalt were attracted by steel magnets. Some of these were mounted as magnetic needles, and I also had made several complete ship compasses, the needles of which were of pure nickel.

He sent one each of the compasses to the governments of the United States, Britain, France, and Russia, hoping that they might compare it with ordinary steel needle compasses, and reported the sequel. "No notice of them was taken except by France and Russia; probably the nickel compass was never sent to sea by either of these, nor in any way tested in practical working in comparison with a steel-needle compass."[7]

With the exception of a few scientists, people who might have profited from his achievement were indifferent to it. When he exhibited the results of his work at the Centennial celebration in Philadelphia the judges damned the display with faint praise as being "worthy of an award." Greater recognition was forthcoming at the Paris Exposition of 1878 because of the efforts of a few friends. A writer for *The Iron Age* described Wharton's exhibit there in these terms:

> Philadelphia makes a very interesting exhibit of nickel and cobalt ores from the celebrated Gap mines . . . together with their products. The exhibit is contained in an upright desk showcase. In the desk part is shown ordinary nickel ore and Millerite, with some samples of copper pyrites and nickel matte. . . . In the upright part of the case the products of these ores are shown and the manufactures from the same, consisting of pure nickel and cobalt in cubes and grains, nickel and cobalt oxide, sulphate and ammonia, sulphate of both metals and pure cast nickel and cobalt in plates, bars and rods, and also rolled and wrought. Two horseshoe magnets of wrought nickel and a magnetic compass of nickel are also shown, together with articles plated with nickel and others colored with cobalt oxides. On top of the case are three clusters of beautiful vitriol crystals under glass shades. The exhibit is not only a very fine one, but very interesting as well.[8]

Professor W. P. Blake and Daniel J. Morrell, U.S. commissioner representing Philadelphia at the Paris Exposition, were responsible for calling the
attention of the judges to the special value of Wharton's exhibit. Other
displays had greater sparkle, such as that of the Vivians of England, "large
cases filled with beautiful objects of hollow and solid ware made of nickel-
silver," as Blake explained it. None of these represented the scientific
advance of Wharton's less glamorous contribution. Wrote Blake, Wharton's
objects were "very different from *alloys* of nickel. In fact, very few chemists
had ever seen *nickel*. Pure nickel was a rarity, a curiosity, just as samples of
indium or thallium are to-day. It was not strange, therefore, that the expert
chemists and metallurgists of Europe on the international jury showed some
incredulity and surprise when whole ingots and forged bars of metal and
numerous finished articles of pure wrought nickel, without alloy, were offered for their inspection." Blake suggested that the jury have Wharton's
articles of wrought nickel analyzed. This was done, and as a result Wharton's
exhibit received a gold medal.[9]

Shortly thereafter the industrial and scientific world was made aware that
Fleitmann had found a way of cheaply manufacturing malleable nickel on a
large scale. Fleitmann patented his discovery, thereby making his method
known. The *Iron Age* commented on it thus: "Fleitmann's process for making nickel malleable consists in adding a very small trace, only one-twentieth
of a per cent of magnesium, which is introduced in the form of a bar into the
liquid nickel while in the crucible. This small percentage of metallic magnesium renders this brittle metal perfectly malleable, and it can even be
welded. Magnesium is well known to oxidize very easily (at high temperatures) and hence serves to remove these injurious gases."[10]

Fletimann's discovery sparked Wharton to undertake a major overhaul of
the works at Gap and Camden. He briefly closed down mine and works in
1879, modernized them, and resumed operations. He purchased American
rights to Fleitmann's process, patented a process for rolling nickel anodes,
and in 1880 built a rolling mill at the American Nickel Works. The mill
contained two trains of 40-inch rolls eighteen inches in diameter, with an-
nealing ovens and their adjuncts, and a ninety horsepower engine.[11] Here
Wharton could roll pure nickel into sheets up to seventy-two inches long by
twenty-four inches wide.

Fleitmann then developed a process for plating iron with nickel. He had
discovered that pure malleable nickel could be welded onto iron or steel and
rolled with it to any desired thickness. As one source described the process,

The quantity preferred by weight is 8/10 iron and 2/10 nickel, one-tenth of
nickel being placed on each surface. To secure union, the iron or steel must
be perfectly flat and clean. A pile is made with outer facings of sheet iron
to protect the nickel from scaling. When the whole is heated to the proper
degree, it is passed through the rolls. The two metals become so firmly

united that they may afterwards be rolled down two or three together, or separately, to the thinness desired. . . . The physical properties of the two metals, iron and nickel, are so nearly the same that they work well together and they adhere tenaciously. . . . Dr. Fleitmann claims to have produced steel wire similarly coated, and proposes to make nickeled boiler plates.[12]

Wharton acquired American rights to Fleitmann's process and arranged for Fleitmann's son to spend a year at Camden putting it into operation. Soon the American Nickel Works was offering to the public saucepans, kettles, and other cooking utensils of a quality and beauty superior to anything of comparable price which had yet been put on the market.

2

They did not sell well. Voigt later reported the situation: "The Fleitmann products, principally stamped and drawn Cooking Utensils made of Wrought Iron or Steel covered with Sheet Nickel by welding and rolling, unfortunately did not meet with favor in the American market, where the cheaper Enamel-Ware was in general use, and the cheaper electro-plated metals found very extensive application. In addition to this there arose a distinctly hostile feeling against the new invention among the German Silver makers, which threatened to end our friendly business relations. Again the business engagement with Dr. Fleitmann came to an untimely end in 1884."[13]

The failure of the attempt to create a large market for products made of malleable nickel was a passing cloud over Wharton's nickel business. Genuine thunderheads appeared in the discovery and exploitation of better ores elsewhere at a time when the world demand for nickel was not significantly increasing.

The first black cloud appeared in the form of ores in Noumea, or New Caledonia, a French penal colony located approximately eight hundred miles east of Australia. A civil engineer named Jules Garnier had discovered silicate ores of nickel there about 1863. The ores were much richer in nickel than were those mined around the North Atlantic basin. They contained oxides, not sulfides, and so were less costly to refine; and they were also relatively free of arsenic and other impurities. They were, moreover, located near the coast and could be mined by open pit methods. These deposits fell into the hands of the Rothschild banking interests and became the source of ore for a monopoly known as Le Nickel. By the beginning of the 1880s ores from New Caledonia were flooding the market. According to the *Iron Age*, world production from 1882 to 1884 reached one thousand tons yearly, whereas the market could absorb only from seven to eight hundred tons. Prices for nickel fell. They had topped three dollars a pound in gold during

1874, 1875, and 1876, the years of the Prussian coinage; had dropped to a little over a dollar currency in 1879; and now slipped to under a dollar. European nickel makers either ceased production or came to terms with Le Nickel.[14]

Wharton looked to the tariff for protection. Fleitmann might survive the crisis caused by Le Nickel because of superior skill. "Germany is the place where nickel was first separated as a separate metal," Wharton told the House Committee on Ways and Mean. "Germany is the home of chemistry. It is full of skilled chemists and skilled workmen, and has all the advantages for the business. Germany is a country that has free trade in nickel." America was not so fortunate, he argued. He, Wharton, was alone in the business and needed at least the same level of protection that was extended to iron and steel and most other metals.[15]

Congressmen patiently listened, then turned away. Politically, iron and steel were a world apart from nickel. Iron and steel had strong support in every part of the country. Nickel was the monopoly of one man, who had no effective means of proceeding against people who opposed him. Wharton fought in every Congress for retention of the thirty cent duty imposed in 1870 only to lose the battle in 1883, when the Congress lowered the duty to fifteen cents a pound. That still gave him protection at a rate of 25 percent of the market price, the same rate as had been established in 1870. Twenty-five percent had been unacceptable to him then. It was even less able to give him protection in the depressed markets of the 1880s.

In Germany, Fleitmann, who Wharton thought might ride out the Noumean flood on his wits, only remained in business by concluding an agreement with Le Nickel. This was an alternative available to Wharton. He considered it. He had before 1874 obtained samples of the Noumean ores and worked out a process for refining them at Camden. Now, he drafted a plan whereby he might purchase both refined and crude nickel from Le Nickel over and above a stipulated minimum of output from Gap and Camden in exchange for Le Nickel staying out of the American market.[16]

Was he serious? The draft is in Wharton's handwriting but is unaccompanied by correspondence or other papers which might prove that he formally proposed the plan to Le Nickel or even discussed it with representatives of the company. The inference is that he could not abandon an ideal of independence; that he continued to have faith in his ability to sustain the American Nickel Works at least as long as the ores at Gap held out. Le Nickel might capture much of the mass market for cheap grades. He would retain customers desiring the best quality. He continued to improve his plant and equipment and to expand production, although his profits registered a general sharp decline.

A second thundercloud appeared from Canada. Nickel and copper had as early as 1848 been known to exist in the neighborhood of Sudbury, Ontario. Wharton was aware of the deposits when he bought the Gap Mine. He had then discounted their importance. His papers contain no reference to the commencement in 1878 of mining by the Orford Nickel and Copper Company, of that firm's purchase of land for a refinery near Constable Hook, New Jersey, in 1881, or of the organization of the Canadian Copper Company and its early work near Sudbury. The reason is that these early ventures did not seriously involve nickel. Copper was the metal sought. After 1883 the situation began to change. Excavation of a cut for the Canadian Pacific Railroad disclosed immense deposits of ore containing not only copper but also about the same percentage and quality of nickel as were in the ores at Gap. The Orford company discovered the substantial existence of nickel when attempts to extract copper by the usual methods failed. At first the people at Orford were discouraged. Competition from copper interests in the western states was already about as keen as they could stand. Then, on considering the higher price of nickel, their dismay vanished. Nickel was the metal on which to concentrate. A single process for refining both metals existed and had only to be learned and applied. Sales of copper could be used to cover most of the costs of the refining. In spite of the difficulties involved with sulfide ores and the relatively high costs of labor, the Orford company might undersell Le Nickel! A pattern of enterprise quickly developed which remained in existence until the formation of the International Nickel Company in 1902. The Canadian Copper Company obtained control of the best deposits in the Sudbury region and worked the mines. The Orford Nickel and Copper Company, renamed the Orford Copper Company, took care of the refining.[17]

Obviously, the Orford company could also undersell Wharton if it chose to do so. But Wharton saw advantages as well as dangers in the new situation. Sudbury was close by and open to prospecting for additional sources of ore. The Orford Company was American, not French, and needed help such as Wharton could give. And markets for nickel were improving. As matters turned out, Orford successfully stood off Le Nickel's attempt to invade the American market. Wharton cooperated with Orford and substantially benefited. What finally precipitated his retirement from the nickel business was neither Orford nor Le Nickel but the exhaustion of the deposits at Gap.

3

Wharton made several million dollars from his nickel business during the 1870s. He used some of the profit to increase his influence in the Bethlehem Iron Company. His voice there was still strictly limited. As long as Packer lived, Wharton could not take full advantage of his position as the largest stockholder. He patiently served the company, as did others on the board. None dared to cross the old man, who could by the scratch of a pen eliminate their hopes for power and wealth.

The Lehigh Valley Railroad had its best year to date in 1874, the first full year of the depression.[18] Other railroads were not so fortunate; and all suffered in the following half decade. The market for steel rails and other steel products fell to almost nothing; that for iron was greatly reduced. Leadership of the nation's iron industry passed out of the Lehigh Valley never to return as furnaces went out of blast and rolling mills went to the block. Bethlehem Iron survived and expanded, not because of owning a steel plant, for the idle mill was a heavy charge, nor yet only because of the economy practiced by stopping the payment of dividends and cutting down on wages and salaries, for all companies did these things, but because of owning special assets. Bethlehem Iron could call on the money and talent possessed by Wharton and by others deriving profit from the Lehigh Valley Railroad.

"Our contracts . . . were either repudiated or virtually cancelled," President Hunt told the stockholders at the June, 1874, meeting. The directors voted and sold one million dollars worth of 6 percent twenty-year coupon bonds in order to consolidate debts and raise capital.[19] Wharton bought two hundred thousand dollars worth. Other directors and several banks subject to Packer's influence purchased substantial amounts.

This was the first time the Bethlehem Iron Company had borrowed heavily. Railroad money was now more than ever subsidizing iron and steel operations. The membership of the board of Bethlehem Iron correspondingly was changed to admit Packer's righthand man on finance, a nephew named Elisha Packer Wilbur.

Wilbur was seven years younger than Wharton and fully as loyal to Packer as was Sayre. Wilbur had been educated at the public schools in Mauch Chunk and at the age of fourteen had gone to the coal mining town of Nesquehoning to work in one of his uncle's stores. He had briefly been a rodman surveying for the railroad and had then entered the countinghouse. By the time Wilbur was twenty-three years of age Packer had given him charge of the company's accounts and of his Philadelphia office. Wilbur served as Packer's private secretary for the remainder of the railroad king's life. He moved to Bethlehem, where the headquarters of the Lehigh Valley road were located, built a mansion close to that of Sayre, and founded one of the community's largest banks, the E. P. Wilbur Trust Company. His personal interests in the Bethlehem Iron Company antedated his election to the board. He had been one of Sayre's partners in forming the Northampton Iron Company and disposing of its assets to Bethlehem Iron. Immediately upon taking his seat on the board Wilbur became a member of the finance committee, which was still the principal executive body.

John Fritz was another valuable asset. Although temperamental and annoying to the directors, largely because of the poor spirit in which he took orders, he served the company well by showing imagination and skill in improving operations. One of his innovations involved increasing the output of anthracite furnaces. In western Pennsylvania ironmasters had proved the greater efficiency of coke. They could, according to Fritz, "make nearly double the amount of iron in the same sized furnaces that we could with anthracite as a fuel." Fritz countered this advantage by strengthening furnaces number three and four, then under construction, and by increasing the pressure of the blast. This resulted in making "as much iron in a given time with anthracite as they could with coke."[20]

Fritz was especially important to the board during the depression years because of a decision to take advantage of low prices to modernize and expand. He persuaded the directors to install the Martin-Siemens, or open-hearth, process for making steel, then impressively accomplished the installation. The process had developed from an invention by the Siemens brothers of a regenerative gas furnace of great power and economy. One of the brothers, William by name, found that by passing a stream of air heated by the furnace over an open hearth containing pig iron to which, when melted, iron ore or scrap was added, he could get the same product that Bessemer had obtained in his converter. This could be changed into a hard, malleable steel by adding spiegeleisen at an appropriate moment. In France Emile Martin and his son Pierre improved this process in part by adding wrought iron and steel scrap to the melted pig to produce steel of excellent quality. Both William Siemens and the Martins received gold medals for their inventions at the Paris Exhibition of 1867.

The Siemens-Martin or open-hearth process had several advantages over the Bessemer. The initial expense of installation was much lower; less fuel was consumed; a larger quantity of steel could be made in a single operation; and scrap iron and steel which otherwise might be wasted could be saved. In addition, the open-hearth process produced a steel which had more uses than Bessemer steel. The open hearth was slower than the Bessemer; and before the coming into use of silica brick the high heat of the air sometimes melted the furnace itself. Still, the open hearth was a serious rival to the Bessemer converter. Many, including Holley, thought the open hearth would eventually replace the Bessemer. By 1875 Holley had become thoroughly acquainted with the process and was urging American steelmakers to introduce it.[21]

Fritz was fairly well acquainted with open-hearth technology by the time the company decided to install it. He had put in seven Siemens regenerative gas furnaces at the time the steel mill had been built and had probably met William Siemens at the Centennial Exposition in Philadelphia, at which both men served as judges. On 24 July 1878, Fritz left for Europe to study the mechanices of the Martin-Siemens furnaces and while there decided in favor of the Pernot furnace, a recent improvement on open-hearth technology made by Charles Pernot of St. Chamoud, France. The Pernot furnace used a revolving hearth on which red hot pig iron covered with scrap was placed. In October Holley was retained as consulting engineer for one year beginning 1

January 1879, at a salary of one thousand dollars. Later that year the head of the steel mill, William Stubblebine, invented another sort of gas-heated regenerative furnace, whose operation was prominently displayed in the *Iron Age*.[22]

In order to help finance the installation of the open-hearth process the directors authorized the issuance of five hundred thousand dollars worth of second mortgage bonds. As with the million dollar issue, this was largely subscribed to by Wharton and persons and banks depending upon the Lehigh Valley Railroad.[23]

The increased steel-making capacity necessitated additional sources of pig iron. Accordingly, the Bethlehem Iron Company bought the furnace of the North Penn Iron Company at nearby Bingen on the North Pennsylvania Railroad. This, together with the furnace of the Northampton Iron Company, five regular furnaces and the one for making spiegeleisen, gave the company eight stacks with an annual output of one hundred thousand tons, making it equal in the production of pig iron with the Thomas Iron Company, previously the largest producer in the valley. On motion of Wharton the board voted to build two additional blast furnaces.[24]

This burgeoning of capital investment and steel-making capacity was accompanied by the appearance on the board in 1876 of the son-in-law of Packer, Dr. Garrett B. Linderman, an imperious, hard-working executive three years younger than Wharton. Linderman had been educated to the profession of medicine and had practiced it in early life. He had relinquished it after marrying Packer's only daughter, Lucy, preferring the employ and support of his father-in-law. Linderman had rapidly advanced in Packer's service, organized and become president of banks in Bethlehem and Mauch Chunk, and acquired a sufficient interest in Bethlehem Iron to become the second largest stockholder. Linderman was brusque of manner and efficient. "Just the man to hold the line on Fritz," Packer might have said.

That apparently was the reason Linderman came to the iron company at this time. Fritz was indispensable but costly. He was inclined to undertake projects and incur expenses without previously consulting all the memnbers of the board; and he paid less attention to daily production than to his inventions. The sloppy workmanship which William Thurston had noted in beseeching his uncle for a transfer to office work had continued and needed correction. The year after Linderman became a member of the board he assumed the position of general manager and became Fritz's superior. Fritz was given a new designation, that of chief engineer. He would have charge of designing and erecting all new works and making all modifications of existing works, buildings, and machinery. Linderman would supervise manufacturing. Revisions in the structure of the board accompanied this change. Linderman succeeded Sayre on the finance committee. Sayre, Wharton, and Wilbur revised the bylaws to create an advisory committee, which after 1876 served as an executive committee in place of the finance committee. But for the next two years the composition of the two committees was the same, namely, Wharton, Wilbur, and Dr. Linderman.[25]

Wharton agreed with all of these developments. Fritz clearly needed supervision in the interests of keeping expenses down. Opposition to the men of the Lehigh Valley Railroad was not to be thought of, at least as long as Packer lived. Linderman as second largest stockholder had a leverage in his own right which could not be ignored. Still, the appearance of Linderman constituted a danger such as Wharton had not met in Wilbur or Sayre. Wilbur especially worked well with Wharton in financial matters. In addition, the two shared much the same vision concerning future operations. Perhaps that was another reason for Linderman appearing when he did—to check the younger Wilbur and the Philadelphian who seemed to be influencing him. For Dr. Linderman strictly held the company to the specialty of making rails and other products used by railroads and opposed ventures pointing in other directions.

An incident illustrating this appeared in the fate of a proposal to begin the manufacture of armor plate. The controversy over armor plate has to be pieced together from scattered evidence; it never reached the point of eliciting a decision by the board. Yet the board talked over the issue, as an entry in Sayre's diary for 27 November 1878 indicates: "Board discussing the propriety of getting ready to make armour plate for Russian ships. Wharton full of it." What had happened was this: Wharton Barker, acting as a junior partner in Barker Brothers and Company, had established relations with Russian officials at a time when their government was anxious to restrain commercial vessels of other nations from cruising in her waters. Through Grand Duke Constantine, general-admiral of the Russian navy, Czar Alexander II ordered four cruisers from Wharton Barker, who arranged for them to be built by Cramp and Sons of Philadelphia. The first of these vessels slid down the ways in June 1878, with a ceremony attended by Russians and local dignitaries, including Joseph and Anna Wharton and daughter (probably Joanna). Two more cruisers were launched later in the year. Their immediate destination was Holland, there to be outfitted with guns made by Krupp.[26] Joseph Wharton had analyzed the sequence of events and spotted an opportunity. European countries were expanding their navies with vessels equipped with armor plate to withstand the improved firepower of big guns. Voices were beginning to be heard in the United States demanding a navy suitable for protecting American shores. A market was present, and it accorded with a need to protect American interests. Why, then, should the Bethlehem Iron Company not consider entering the field of making armor plate and perhaps other heavy forgings? The issue struck a positive response from Fritz. In his *Autobiography* he insisted that for years he had been urging a strong navy for the country, and that he took the lead in asking the directors to begin the manufacture of armor plate.[27]

Linderman, according to Fritz, put a stop to such talk. Fritz wrote out his version of the sequel in a paragraph not included in the published version of his *Autobiography:*

> In talking with one of the directors who was a large stockholder I found him formally inclined towards the project so much so that I concluded to get up a complete set of drawings of a mill and a general plan for the lay out, but in some way the general manager learned what I was doing and came to me like a mad bull dog, and wanted to know where I got authority to build a plate mill. I told him I had none, but plates were in demand and the demand was sure to increase, and there was great money in the business, and had talked with one of the directors and he was so favorably impressed with the project that I thought it would be well to have a set of drawings and ground plans made. He asked who the Director was that I had talked with. I told him who he was, and calling him by name saying damn him, I will let him know that he is not going to run the Bethlehem Iron Company's plant. This brought the plate mill scheme for the time to a very abrupt end.

The "director who was a large stockholder" was undoubtedly Wharton, who owned in 1879 eight thousand shares as compared with 1,356 possessed by Sayre and 395 by Wilbur. The director who allegedly aroused the ire of Dr. Linderman might have been either Wharton or Wilbur; for Wilbur actively pushed the project several years after the death of Packer.

Linderman seriously irritated Wharton, an irritation undoubtedly made worse by the board's refusal in 1875, 1876, and 1877 to purchase the Saucon Iron Company. Certainly a dislike of Linderman surfaced during the May 1878 meeting of the board. At that time Wharton alone among the directors refused to accept all of Linderman's first annual report. A crisis impended. If Wharton had persisted in his stand, Linderman would probably have been forced to resign. But Wharton's anger was premeditated. Before the board could take action, he left the meeting, thereby providing time for conciliation. What was at stake for Wharton was an interest in the career of his nephew William Thurston. This determined and headstrong relative had anticipated the need for controls which had brought Linderman on the scene as general manager. Thurston had thereby earned the hostility of Fritz and the warm support of the board. He had also married Ellen Coppée, daughter of President Coppée of Lehigh University, a good friend of Packer, Sayre, and Wilbur, and had by her sired two sons, Edward Coppée (1874) and Joseph Wharton (1876), with a third child momentarily expected (William Wharton, born 27 May 1878). Thurston had become a respected member of the community of South Bethlehem. Quite possibly Wharton wanted his nephew for the position of general manager. In any event, Wharton appears to have used Linderman's weakness as a newcomer to the business of making steel as a level for advancing the career of young Thurston. Immediately following Linderman's report Sayre acted as conciliator. At the annual stockholder's meeting held a few days later Thurston gave a report on the mines and furnaces; and on 25 June the board elected him to a newly created post of vice-president and reelected Linderman as general manager.[28]

During the next few years Wharton bought additional stock in the company, as though to protect himself against competition from Linderman for the position of largest stockholder. By 1882 Wharton owned eight thousand five hundred shares, or 21 percent of the total, as compared with six thousand shares possessed by Dr. Linderman.[29] The rivalry between Linderman and Wharton appears to have been the only major rift in amicable relations among directors during the period of financial hardship. Even this clash of personalities was not of sufficient strength to break into public view. Yet it was there, a foreshadowing of more serious disputes among members of the directorial family in later years of high prosperity. Linderman had Packer's ear and may have had something to do with Wharton's resignation from the board of the Lehigh Valley Railroad several months after the events of May 1878. Sayre briefly reported the resignation in his diary: "Tues. Nov. 12. All passed off pleasantly until at the dinner table when the Judge and Longstreth expressed their views as to Wharton's attempt to get Bridge across at the Beth^m Iron Works, he left angry." "Tues. Dec. 10. Accepted the resignation of Joseph Wharton. Elected Jas. T. Blakeslee [brother-in-law of Packer] in his place."

From 1874 to 1878 inclusive the Bethlehem Iron Company paid no dividends. Yet the company prospered by comparison with most other iron and steel works. In 1877 the directors refused to enter a pooling agreement with the other ten American producers of steel rails. This was an attempt by the industry to stabilize conditions by controlling prices and limiting production. The directors of the Bethlehem company rejected the arrangement on the grounds that it would be contrary to the best interests of the company; or, in other words, the company was getting customers where its competitors were not.[30] Wharton contributed much to the company's welfare. Between 1877 and 1880 he bought rails of it at times when orders were slack and prices were low. He later resold the rails at a profit, but by means of the operation he helped the company to keep its mills operating and its work force intact. And he secured for the company the custom of his younger brother's firm, the Wharton Railroad Switch Company.

In 1878 Wharton began a long tenure as principal representative of Bethlehem Iron to an organization known as the Bessemer Steel Company, Limited. A year earlier the Bethlehem Iron Company had become an equal stockholder with the other ten Bessemer steel producers of the country in this concern, which had been organized for the express purpose of acquiring all the patents of Bessemer, Kelly, and others pertaining to the Bessemer process. The new organization helped extricate the companies from the legal tangle which had stemmed from the rival claims of Bessemer and Kelly.[31]

It also had a potential for helping to stabilize conditions among steel producers by a monopolistic practice of acquiring sole rights to other patents involving the making of steel. Soon the directors were taking this road and exposing themselves to severe criticism from antitrust agitators.

4

When in 1875 the American Nickel Works was at the height of its prosperity, Wharton purchased an adjoining property which he developed as a glass factory, specializing in fashioning mason jars. He named it the Camden Glass Works. It was small, having in 1882 a valuation on his books of $86,867.05. Thereafter the value declined. He was sued for an infringement of patent rights, and he chose to leave the business. After 1884 he allowed the glass works to remain idle most of the time and dismantled them in 1892.[32]

No less unsuccessful was an attempt at the commercial production of sugar beets in the sandy soils of southern New Jersey. This venture, however, was more important to him than that of manufacturing glass. The cultivation of sugar beets had a greater scientific aspect; and if successful, the venture would have meant introducing into the United States yet another industry. Entrepreneurs from California to Massachusetts had been discussing the potential of sugar beets. Most of the sugar consumed in the country came from cane grown in Cuba, then under the control of Spain. Why could not an American industry be developed, one not dependent upon foreign sources nor even on the distant sugarcane plantations of Louisiana? Europe provided examples of what might be done. France, Prussia, Austria-Hungary, and Russia had reacted against a high price for sugar being shipped from British and Spanish possessions in the West Indies. Agriculturalists in these countries had experimented with beets and successfully developed home industries which their governments dutifully protected.[33]

Already one attempt at raising sugar beets in New Jersey had been planned and abandoned. In the late 1860s a Philadelphian named Colonel William C. Patterson had laid out a development near the pinelands town of Atsion which he called the Fruitland Improvement Company. Patterson had planned a community based on farming, and one of the crops he wanted to grow was a French type of sugar beet. But Patterson overextended himself, and the plan fell through.[34]

Joseph S. Lovering was probably a motivating force behind Wharton's decision to make another attempt. Although an old man, Lovering was still refining sugar in Philadelphia. Wharton had cooperated with him in the earlier unsuccessful attempts at making sugar from sorghum. Lovering was able to offer Wharton substantial help with the refining, provided the beets could be grown nearby at a reasonably low cost. Possibly, too, Wharton received advice and encouragement from old Jacob Barker, recently removed from New Orleans to live with his son Abraham, and who had considerable experience in raising sugarcane in Louisiana.

The first step in the venture was that of acquiring suitable land. Wharton took this step in 1873 by purchases in southern Jersey. In doing so he bought far more land than he needed, and most of what he obtained was unsuitable for farming. In January he received from his friend Charles Lennig the mortgage on about fifteen thousand acres lying between the Batsto and the Wading rivers and touching the village of Batsto on the east. About the same time, he acquired from another friend, S. R. Colwell, a mortgage on about twenty-three thousand acres surrounding the village of Atsion and extending from there northeastward to include some of the headwaters of the Batsto River. A few months later he bought approximately twelve thousand acres from the City Bank of Philadelphia. This purchase included land lying west of the Mullica or Atsion River and also touching Batsto on the west.[35]

In sum, shortly before the onset of the great depression of 1873 Wharton bought about fifty thousand acres of land in what is known as the pinelands of southern New Jersey, a mysterious country of pitch pine and white cedar with a thick underbrush of scrub oak, holly, laurel, and assorted brambles and veined with sluggish, winding streams and swamps. These pinelands occupy an area about eighty miles long, measured from north to south, and from twenty to forty miles wide. Geologists have reasoned that the region was in ancient times an island, around which land rose to fill in the rest of what is now southern and central New Jersey. Only a few isolated points lie more than eighty feet above sea level. The generally sandy soil gives way in swampy areas to deep masses of mould and mosses interspersed by fallen logs and covered with dense growth.[36]

The land which Wharton bought lies within the watersheds of three rivers, which come together near tidewater and empty into the Great Bay, an inlet dotted with islands lying a few miles north of Brigantine and Atlantic City. The rivers are called the Wading, Batsto, and Atsion or Mullica. The Wading flows down from the north; the other two run parallel from the northwest. To call these streams rivers does injustice to giant watercourses such as the Hudson and the Mississippi. These of the pinelands are little more than rivulets. Their upper and middle reaches have places in which two canoes cannot pass each other. In the uplands, branches of trees overarch the streams and in summer blot out the sun. Occasionally the forest recedes, showing a pencil line of beach from which a sandy bluff arises, the lower strata an orange yellow and the upper, a dull gunmetal gray. The sands are coarse and filled with small waterworn pebbles. In the swamps the forest gives way to rushes and marsh grasses and the rivers sometimes widen into long ponds formed by beaver dams. In such places there is no bank, but only ooze. Here and there small water lilies grow. The water of the streams and ponds is fresh and sweet, but unclear. On a cloudy day it looks black and lifeless. When the sun is bright the water has a color of cedar, imparted by decaying organic matter and intensified by the existence of bog iron ore lying on the stream bed.

When Wharton first made purchases in the pinelands they were experiencing the end of a romantic past and facing a dreary future. European settlers had begun wresting the land from the Indians in the early 1700s. The first were woodcutters, who built sawmills and cut off the best timber, especially the cedars, which were prized for shingles. The lumbermen never left the pinelands, although their activity diminished as time passed. They were prepared to serve as makers of charcoal when ironmasters arrived to exploit the bog ores of streams, lakes, and swamps. These ores originated when the rivers and their tributaries carried particles of limonite from the headwaters and deposited them further downstream. Ironmasters built furnaces and forges at Batsto and other places in the 1760s. On the eve of the Revolution a company erected an iron furnace at Atsion, about eight miles upstream from Batsto as the crow flies. This and other furnaces supplied cannonballs for Washington's army and for three-quarters of a century filled much of the need for iron to people in the surrounding countryside and even in further away places such as Camden, Philadelphia, and lower New York state. Villages came into being: Quaker Bridge, Pleasant Mills, Washington, McCartyville, and others. A true regional economy developed around the iron industry.

Then, in the 1840s, iron making among the pines became unprofitable. The readily accessible bog ores were gone. Canals and railroads opened up other parts of the country to the manufacture of iron. The industry in southern New Jersey died. People began leaving the villages. Attempts were made to save industry. Glass works were built in Batsto and elsewhere in the midforties. Atsion got a paper mill. None of these attempts succeeded for long. Villages became ghost towns. Roads reverted to trails overgrown with brush. Batsto, once the largest town with almost a thousand people, had fewer than two hundred by the time of the Civil War and was still declining. In February 1874, before Wharton began his work of cultivating sugar beets, a fire burned down a large part of what remained of the town. An unidentified writer chronicled the aftermath for a Camden newspaper: "The long roofs of the glass factories curve in, and a pool of water has rotted holes through them. The walls are crumbling. The foundry, with its foundation of a century ago, is decaying; the old spring of sweet water, where the men have slaked their thirst for a hundred years, is filling up; the old mansion [former residence of the ironmasters] is growing musty; the long lines of stables are falling, and the stiff, stark chimneys add to the spectacle of desolation."[37]

Why did Wharton suddenly and without obvious reason buy thousands of acres of such waste land? The various uses to which he later put or intended to put it are not mentioned in his correspondence or business papers of 1873 nor indeed in those of the succeeding several years. To be sure, most successful businessmen bought land, but they bought good land, not property such as this, which was going at sheriff's sale for several dollars an acre because no one wanted it. Did Wharton give credence to talk, current about that time, of the possibility of digging a canal across the country suitable for oceangoing ships to enter the port of Philadelphia? Nothing in his papers suggests this; and Wharton was not inclined to base his investments on rumor.

The answer seems to be that ownership of these wastes of pine and cedar swamp satisfied something deep within him, which he perhaps could not have explained to himself. Occasional remarks in his early correspondence suggest that the wilderness of southern Jersey had always attracted him.[38] Now, without risk to his other enterprises, he could satisfy a dream.

In any event, he planned to put small parcels of land into the cultivation of sugar beets. He had this in mind when he traveled to Europe in 1873. He recorded in detail in his diary visits to the Rothamsted experimental farm in England, at which trials of the culture of sugar beets had been made, and the agricultural complexes of Knauer and the Zimmermann brothers in Prussia, which included refineries and large fields of beets. He scribbled notes concerning the culture of beets, for example, "Barnyard manure gave good results. Mineral manures alone very bad. Mineral manures and nitrates much better. Mineral manures and rape cake very good. It is highly probable that with Marl, . . . guano, and the manure of cattle fed on beet refuse very excellent beets could be grown in New Jersey." He took down the names of several people who might serve as managers of a sugar beet operation in New Jersey and worked out a timetable: "In 1874 make bricks & build farm buildings; in 1875 begin to cultivate beets; in 1876 build factory."[39]

He missed keeping to this schedule by several years. His first major accomplishment on returning to the states was that of finding someone to take charge of all his lands in southern New Jersey. The person whom he hired was Elias Wright, a former Union general who had commanded black troops during the Civil War. Wright served Wharton as a real estate agent and surveyor for over a quarter of a century, although the managing of Wharton's farms soon passed to others.

Wharton planted his first large crop of beets in 1877 and in the same year renovated a grist mill at Batsto for extracting the juice and boiling it down to crude sugar so that it could be shipped to Philadelphia, possibly to Lovering's refinery. An account in the Hammonton *Item* for 17 November 1877 contained a description of the process:

> The beets are pulled and stacked in the field without trimming; they are then hauled to the factory and weighed; the tops are then cut off, the beets washed, weighed and then put in the grinding machine, which grinds them into a fine pulp, the machine grinding them as fast as man can shovel them in. The pulp is then taken up, weighed again and put into a large cylinder (making 2,500 revolutions per minute) which extracts all the

juice; the pulp is then taken out, weighed again, salted and packed away to feed the cattle during the winter. The juice is pumped into tanks through filters, then into large iron kettles, where it is boiled; then through the filters again, passing from the first to the third floor three times; then in the boiling kettles again, the chemist testing it in its various stages. When it is boiled down to the consistency of good molasses, it is drawn off to barrels and hogsheads and sent to the city for refining. The establishment gives employment to about twenty-five hands, and runs day and night.[40]

In January 1878 Wharton advertised for beets from other farmers. A circular which he had printed and distributed to them describes what he had in mind: "In order to test more fully the fitness of Jersey soil for sugar beet culture, I propose to contract with land owners in the vicinity of Batsto, Hammonton, Elwood, and Egg Harbor, for the purchase in 1878, of as many sugar beets as can be worked up at my Batsto mill, beyond my own crop; say about 1000 tons." He stipulated that farmers must buy their seed from him in order to be sure of obtaining the best quality. He promised them, "My agent [Wright] will endeavor to visit the plantation of each contractor several times during the season, in order to look after the crop and to give any information in his power." He advised farmers concerning the cultivation of beets:

Sugar beets thrive best in loamy soils which have been well worked and well manured for the last preceding crop. It is thought best to plough the land the Fall before planting in beets, and to apply the manure at that time, in order that it may be thoroughly rotted and incorporated with the soil, and the soil itself be subjected to the action of the winter frosts. . . . In Europe experienced beet growers get, upon suitable soils, when in good condition, 12 to 20 tons per acre of beet roots, containing 9 to 15 per cent of sugar; these highest figures being exceptional; it does not seem extravagant to hope here for 10 tons to the acre, and for 10 per cent of sugar. Though my experimental crop at Batsto, last year, was planted too late (May 23rd to June 10th), upon an old and very poor field which had not been cultivated for many years, the best patches in the field had about 10 tons to the acre, and the percentage of sugar was about 8.[41]

The experiment did not succeed. The silence which so often accompanies failures gives no hint concerning the reasons or how long the experiment lasted. The account books contain no information after 1878, when a single entry, for 28 March, appears: "rec'd. from S. & F. Field proceeds of beet syrup of 1877. $66.75." The venture in sugar beets was certainly over by 1881, the year in which Joseph Lovering died, as by then his sugar refinery had ceased operating, a victim of depression and Lovering's advancing years.

But the purchase of property in the pinelands continued. In 1874 and 1875 he had Wright buy approximately five hundred acres in small parcels from various people, and in 1876 he acquired 33,500 acres from Martin B. Gray at sheriff's sales. These acquisitions gave Wharton almost complete ownership of Batsto and resulted in a consolidation of his properties into a single large tract, still interspersed, however, with numerous plots of land owned by others. Over the next twelve years he bought many of these and some adjoining tracts, all told about 3,500 acres.

Although the experiments with sugar beets failed, other minor farming and forestry ventures succeeded, or at least continued, thereby ending the region's economic blight and establishing a modest prosperity for families that remained. He planted maple trees, began at Batsto and Atsion the cultivation of cranberries and sweet potatoes, and purchased a herd of beef cattle. He drew freely from his farms at Gap to supply these infant enterprises in the pinelands. He revived the industry in timber by going into the business of logging and by building a sawmill to serve himself and others. A letterhead from 1882 bears the heading "Joseph Wharton's Batsto Farm" with E. Wright, Manager, and lists the items offered for sale to the public: "Wood; Charcoal; Cedar Posts; Cedar Rails; Cedar Knees; Cedar Siding; Cedar Shingles; Cedar Hop Poles; Cedar Bean Poles; Cedar Hoop Poles; Cedar Tank Stuff; Cedar Boat Boards; Jersey Pine Lumber; Plows and other Agricultural Implements; Country Store Goods."

Quite possibly during these years Wharton envisaged considerable development of the higher ground within his domain into farms, homes, and factories. On a map of New Jersey dated 1877 he shaded his southern Jersey holdings in pink and drew a red line through them, from Atsion to the Great Bay at the mouth of Egg Harbor River and on to Beach Haven. He wrote at the bottom of the map an explanation of the line: "shows probably best line for railroad."

At Batsto Wharton repaired and enlarged the manor house of the early ironmasters. He soon had a building containing thirty-six rooms and a tower 116 feet high. Towers were prominent features of Victorian houses, and Wharton liked them. He had suggested one for Bellevue immediately following the death of his father. Ontalauna and Marbella were in time to have them. At Batsto the purpose of a tower was more than ornamental. The scrubby timber lands with their thickets of underbrush sometimes caught fire in dry seasons. He intended the tower as a lookout for spotting fires, hopefully in time for men to contain and extinguish them.[42]

The mansion was finished and furnished by May 1880, in time to serve as a place of convalescence for his daughter Mary, who had suffered a nervous breakdown. There under the care of a housekeeper named Mrs. McClure, whom Wharton referred to as "the duenna," Mary found the clean air, quiet, and restful surroundings which other members of the family felt that she needed. Wharton once wrote her concerning short trips from Batsto to nearby places: "Gen'l Wright says you want to ride upon new roads, and I have advised him to direct you to Egg Harbor, where you can visit one or more of the wine making establishments, see how wine is made, and buy a dozen bottles. It is so far (9 miles) that you will perhaps want to rest a little when there. . . . . Hammonton is an interesting place 9 miles off and the road is good. Atsion is 8 miles, road mostly sandy and brushy."[43]

Pleasant as the mansion and its surroundings were, Wharton and his family spent little time there. Anna did not especially like the house and seldom visited it. The building of Marbella on Narragansett Bay several years later gave the family a summer home for enjoying water sports. Still, Wharton kept the Batsto mansion in repair and sometimes used it.

The country round about remained quiet, secluded, and sparsely populated. Atsion was served by a railroad which passed through the northwestern portions of Wharton's property. The line Wharton had drawn on the map of 1877, which might have opened up Batsto to the outside world, never came.

10

"A Monstrous War"

Wharton's business interests led him to espouse the cause of protection of American industry. He plied it with the thoroughness which he gave to every major project. It made of him a politician in all but name. No Quakers ever dedicated themselves more completely, unselfishly, and passionately to their various humanitarian endeavors than Wharton did in his dedication to the advancement of protection. He undertook the business with a belligerency akin to that which had possessed the Quaker abolitionists of his parents' day. Indeed, he went beyond the abolitionists in daring. They had been willing to risk war; he viewed the cause itself as war, justified because of the greatness of the end. True, Wharton's conflict was commercial, not military—America against Europe, especially Britain, for economic independence—but he recollected the military phase of 1812 and faced the prospect of another. His obstinacy on the subject of protection was most unWharton-like. Samuel Rowland Fisher might have understood, but would not have approved. The grandson's fight for his particular truth threatened to end the peace on which Samuel Rowland Fisher's truth was predicated. Joseph was soon to argue that the needs of protection of American industry justified rearmament, a position which he eventually took to the dismay of pacifists who wished to believe in him without compromising their ideals.

Possibly Wharton saved himself from criticism in his years of middle age by refusing to become an officeholder who had to make decisions concerning war and peace. In 1872 he was tendered a Republican Party nomination for a seat in the national House of Representatives. The nomination would have been tantamount to election. Should he accept? A number of his industrialist acquaintances had served in the House, for example, Asa Packer, Abram Hewitt, and Daniel J. Morrell. Wharton refused and explained to his mother, "I wrote yesterday declining the nomination and felt a little as if I had done something selfish. Anna and her father are both strongly opposed to my going to Congress."[1] Never in later years did he seriously consider running for a major office. Elected politicians, he knew, had duties other than that of fighting for the protection of American industry. Wharton had carefully established his priorities. He could fight for his country more effectively as a lobbyist and support it more positively by making nickel, iron, and steel than by performing the varied duties of a politician. The rhetoric he might use as a lobbyist and industrialist would not have the same impact as it would have coming from the mouth of a senator or a cabinet member.[2]

1

Protectionists in those years found a congenial environment in Philadelphia. Most of the city's educators, politicians, and businessmen, whether Democratic or Republican, favored protection. Chief among them and in a sense their intellectual father was Henry Charles Carey, one of the few Americans in the immediate post-Civil War years deserving the appellation "economist."

Carey had been born in Philadelphia in 1793, son of a famous post-Revolutionary War printer, pamphleteer, editor, and publisher who had emigrated to the United States from Ireland. Carey spent his early years in his father's shop and then entered the publishing business with Isaac Lea, father of Henry Charles Lea, and married Isaac's sister, Frances Ann. Carey became for a time the American publisher of Thomas Carlyle, Washington Irving, and Sir Walter Scott. He had his father's taste for journalism and in 1835, with his fortune assured, left business and devoted the remainder of a long life to writing.

Carey began his career as an economist by closely following the ideas of English writers on the subject, especially John Stuart Mill, whose text on economics was standard for several generations. Mill was a free trader who shared the outlook of other English economists concerning the inevitability of poverty among the working classes and the ultimate inability of an expanding population to feed itself. Carey's first major work, *Principles of Political Economy*, published in three volumes between 1837 and 1840, reflects these pessimistic ideas. But in the 1840s he had second thoughts concerning them. He read and absorbed the ideas of Auguste Comte, French "father of sociology," and soon shared that philosopher's faith in the ability of a new, social, science to solve the problems which the English economists thought to be unsolvable. Carey concluded that science, applied to agriculture, could increase the productivity of land, thereby supplying food for an expanding population; and a judicious use of political power, rather than an insensate hostility to government, could alleviate hardships among the workers.

Carey also shared the optimism of other Americans who liked to contrast the young spirit of the nation and its abundant resources with the allegedly tired and worn out lands and peoples of Europe. The result of these prejudices and reflections appeared in his *The Principles of Social Science*, published in three volumes in 1858 and 1859. In effect he reworked the

English economic and the Comtian social thought to fit the dominant American predilections of his times. His influence was great, especially among Republicans starting to reconstruct a country recovering from civil war and determined to build at all costs a strong nation. Horace Greeley printed his articles. Many leaders in politics, business, and education paid him homage.

Carey's central economic idea was that of a self-sufficient community in which farmers and manufacturers maximized production through competition and exchanged goods without interference from middlemen. These "traders," as he called the middlemen, produced nothing yet demanded payment for services. They were, in other words, freeloaders; the wealth which they claimed ought in justice to go to those who made it. Hence, middlemen should be eliminated; and to the extent that practical circumstances made them necessary, they should be prevented from gaining monopolistic positions from which they might exploit farmers, manufacturers, and laborers.

Translated to the national level, Carey's idea of a self-sufficing community meant a diversified, independent economy based on freedom of competition capable of supplying its own needs. Where necessary, government should interfere in economic activity to promote this. Free trade among nations of unequal industrial power, he said, led to a wasteful specialization; the more advanced industrial countries undersold the less advanced and, because of their stronger position, charged the costs to the less advanced. If the United States had free trade, its farmers would receive low prices for the food they exported and all of the people would pay high prices for imported manufactures. In addition, he declared, Americans would pay the traders for the long supply lines needed to send raw materials and food to the industrial centers of Europe and to bring back finished goods. Carey pointed to the antebellum South as a prime example of a country which had been impoverished by free trade. The South's low standards of living, lack of self-reliance, and poverty of culture were effects of an overspecialization in cotton at the expense of a well-rounded economy. Britain and her prewar free trade policy, he said, had been the chief culprit. Carey was strongly anti-British. English manufacturers, he argued, cut the price of labor at home in order to undersell American competitors. This produced the large, abysmally poor working class which characterized the British Isles. Protective tariffs aimed against Britain, he asserted, would allow American entrepreneurs to pay labor a decent wage while earning reasonable profits. Tariffs would "buy time" for Americans in the sense of allowing them to remain in business while catching up with the British in scientific and technical know-how. Eventually, a free trade on a world scale might be allowed, when all nations had achieved the same level of progress, in order to facilitate an exchange of surplus goods; but that was a possibility for the future, not a present concern.

Carey's social science contained much else besides arguments for protecting home industries. He broached and gave answers to most of the leading questions of public life. Almost always the position he took agreed with the dominant opinion of his audience. He upheld the sanctity of marriage and the family; accepted the puritan virtues of honesty, hard work, and saving; appealed to God as the Creator; equally praised farming and manufacturing; extolled education; passed as a friend of the downtrodden; and above all displayed an exuberant faith in science, material progress, and the future of America.

At the height of his popularity Carey held weekly discussions in his Philadelphia home, usually on Sunday afternoons. Carey called them vespers. He had a large house and one of the best private collections of paintings in the city. Handsome and dignified, he seated his guests at a round table in the dining room, served them the best of Rhine wines, and let them enjoy animated conversation on whatever topics appealed to them. "We discuss everything and decide nothing," he once said of these sessions. Wrote Robert Ellis Thompson in *The Penn Monthly*, "Whatever visitor of notable worth or name was to be found in our city, was sure to be carried thither, to meet not only Mr. Carey, but one of the most remarkable assemblages of character and intelligence to be found in any American city."[3]

Wharton frequently formed one of the group. "It must have been before 1870 that my father commenced attending the informal Sunday afternoon receptions called 'vespers' at the house of Mr. Henry C. Carey," wrote Joanna.[4] How often Wharton participated in the vespers and how long he continued coming are unknown. He certainly did not attend every Sunday, for he maintained a custom of taking Anna and the children to Oak Hill for Sunday dinner. He probably met Carey at other times. Carey's house was at 1102 Walnut, close to Wharton's. Joseph came to know the economist sufficiently well that Carey felt at ease in calling on him for an occasional favor. "Come over here at 5 tomorrow afternoon [Monday]," he once wrote Wharton, "and take a glass of wine with a very clever Englishman of whom you have heard us speak, to wit—Mr. Stanley, of Aldersley. He wishes some instruction on the protection question, and you can help to give it to him."[5] On another occasion Carey sent Wharton the proof sheets of an article to be read and corrected. Wharton made minor emendations and returned the sheets with a letter redolent of the spirit of Carey's Anglophobia, writing in part, "John Fritz, the manager of our Bethlehem Iron Co., has just returned from a trip to Europe. He gave me yesterday a full account of his experience among the English iron masters, of their undisguised hostility to our nation and their bitter chafing at our tariff fortifications which they hope to see overthrown next winter."[6]

Wharton's association with Carey and his circle provided him with a treasury of ideas to use in fighting for favorable action concerning tariffs. Yet he did not slavishly imitate the economist. Wharton had his own style. He took up arguments which Carey had dropped and developed them further, supporting them with examples from his wide reading of history and literature. The term "national self-protection," wrote Thomas Macfarlane, was an invention of Wharton.[7]

During the years of his association with Carey, Wharton published two articles on the subject of national self-protection. One was first delivered as an address at a general meeting of the American Social Science Association held at the University of Pennsylvania on 27 October 1870 and later published as a two-part serial in *The Penn Monthly* under the title, "International Industrial Competition."[8] The other article was entitled "National Self-Protection" and appeared in the *Atlantic Monthly* for September 1875.

The leading ideas of these two articles are the same, although some of the examples and points of emphasis differ. Wharton's starting point was the idea that unrestricted trade is a "modern and highly civilized style of warfare" in which "improved machinery takes the place of improved artillery; the enemy's forces—his industrial population—are driven from their guns by missiles of textiles and metal wares, and are destroyed in their homes by starvation rather than by bullets in the field."[9] Only regulation could end the warfare. Nations, wrote Wharton, are natural communities—actually, families—acknowledging no superior power. They stand in the same relation to one another as do persons in society, except for the fact that nations have no government over them. Because of this, each has to protect its citizens from the bad effects of international trade. Tariffs are a necessary means of doing so.

In "National Self-Protection" Wharton organized his material by first stating the arguments of free traders and then refuting them. Free traders, he claimed, regard free exchange of commodities as a natural right and hence immune from governmental interference. Also, Wharton wrote, according to free traders, unrestrained competition among nations results in specialization such that each produces what it can at the least cost and exchanges the surplus with other nations for what it needs. Maximum productivity on a world scale, the argument ran, results from this exchange. Wharton further contended that free traders believed tariffs artificially raise prices, thus causing misery to the poor; that they are unjust because they represent subsidies to domestic manufacturers, that is, by means of tariffs governments take money from some and give it to others; that as a result inefficient and costly operations are encouraged at national expense; that the farmers and wage earners ultimately pay the bill; and that "general stagnation, destruction of industry, corruption of morals, and ruin must end the scene in all protected countries."[10]

Wharton began his refutation of these points by asserting that property and trade are conventional, not natural rights. Governments must exist before possessions can be secure enough for trade to result. In "International Industrial Competition" he specifically denied the doctrine of laissez-faire, or governmental noninterference in the economy, which he attributed to free traders, and argued that the regulation of property and trade and the protection of the country from invasion are among the primary purposes of any government. He used the example of patents and a wealth of historical material to support his position. Fundamentally, his argument came to this: In a situation of unrestricted competition between the strong and the weak, the weak always suffer; yet the strong never gain as much as the weak lose because the weak become too poor to be good customers. A just government equalizes the conditions of competition, he wrote. Only depraved nations submit to the indignity of exploitation. "A small, weak, or timid nation yields to foreigners in such matters, and patiently buys from them at high prices such meagre supplies as it can afford. A great nation, aiming to be self-centered and independent, carefully examines its own resources and develops them through struggle and sacrifices if necessary, undeterred by the obstacle raised by those foreigners whose profits are threatened."[11]

Wharton went on to say that when tariffs are present the foreigner always pays the duty, and any rise in prices of dutiable goods is temporary, inasmuch as native industries develop and compete to drive prices down. In "National Self-Protection" he illustrated this by explaining the steady drop in prices of steel rails from $165 in gold per ton in 1864, when all had to be imported from England, to $80 in gold per ton five years later, when under the protection of a tariff a domestic steel industry had been born sufficient to supply American needs for steel rails. With the aid of a protective policy, he maintained, American labor could enjoy a higher standard of living than workers in Europe possessed; and farmers, whatever they might lack of the luxuries of city dwellers, over the years would receive a steadier income than would otherwise be possible.

In both articles Wharton criticized traders for taking an unearned increment. In both he also briefly warned against a misuse of tariffs. "In nothing is it easier to show stupidity than in the framing of a tariff law." He ended "International Industrial Competition" by calling for the formation of a commission of customs, consisting of three tariff experts, which would hear the arguments of interested parties and prepare bills for introduction into the House of Representatives. His conclusion in "National Self-Protection" was a clenched fist raised against England: "We shall take for ourselves, without asking her leave, the same privilege of consulting our own interests and doing our own thinking. We shall grow in strength and national completeness and independence, despite the groans of the Cobden Club [free traders], after England shall have distinctly failed at grasping at universal domination through trade. We decline to be her victim or her imitator."

2

Wharton took one thing more from Carey. This was a conviction that the arguments favoring protection were scientific conclusions. They were not, for either man, armchair speculations depending uniquely on logic, but were truths demonstrable through the histories of nations. Hence Wharton moved to the attack with a conviction born not only of private interest and patriotic fervor but also of a love of science, which was giving men the means of exploring nature and controlling their destinies. Although Carey died in 1879 at an early stage in the battle for protection, he had lighted fires in people such as Wharton which continued burning on their own fuel, similar to the exothermal reactions of nickel ore in the kilns at Gap.

Working for a protective tariff modified Wharton's thoughts and acts as much as anything he ever undertook. It enlarged his vocabulary, circle of friends, and range of experiences; tested his temper and powers of endurance; helped to determine his investments, manner of living, and conduct of enterprises; and led him far into the political world which his father and grandfathers had despised. The work conditioned his appreciation of public morality. He maintained his integrity to the extent of never consciously telling a lie; but at the same time he teetered on the edge of the abyss by withholding relevant information, hiding behind a veil of ignorance, and lashing out at opponents with stinging invective. He saved himself from engaging in sordid political practices by concentrating on the battle of ideas, where he was a natural leader, and of helping to raise funds rather than determining how they should be spent. He had no patronage to dispense, although he often tried to influence those who had. His position as a lobbyist depended not at all on the manipulation of issues and money to which elected and appointed officers frequently had to resort. He was not a professional who sold influence for a fee; he had no paying clients. He gave rather than received money concerning the cause.

During the 1870s Wharton extended his lobbying activities to include the American Iron and Steel Association. This trade organization had begun an existence under the name of American Iron Association in 1855. Its major purpose was "to procure, regularly, the statistics of the trade both at home and abroad; to provide for the mutual interchange of information and experience, both scientific and practical; to collect and preserve all works relating to iron and steel, . . . and, generally, to take all proper measures for advancing the interests of the trade in all its branches." The secretary, J. P. Lesley, in 1859 published under the auspices of the association *The Iron Manufacturers' Guide to the Iron Works and Iron Ore Mines of The United States*. From 1873, when James M. Swank began his long and remarkably effective career as secretary, the association published at intervals of several years a *Directory to the Iron and Steel Works of the United States*. It also put out an *Annual Statistical Report* and a *Bulletin* and provided its members with a large technical library. Swank himself wrote several books on the history of the iron and steel industry.

The association became active in tariff matters at an early period of existence. Swank and the officers were largely responsible for maintaining continuity of policies. The officers usually retained their positions until they resigned, died, or took a higher post. Thus, Abram S. Hewitt was a vice-president from 1864 until his death in 1903. Morrell became president in 1879 and resigned in 1884, a year before he died. B. F. Jones, steelmaker from Pittsburgh, succeeded him and remained in office until his demise in 1903. Wharton, elected a vice-president in 1875, continued as such until he became president in 1904 following the death of Jones.[12]

It was as a representative of the American Iron and Steel Association that Wharton had his longest and most edifying period of service as a lobbyist. He worked for it with the rhythmic regularity of congressional sessions. Every two years a slightly different set of legislators went to work to change something in the tariff laws. Wharton met the ablest of these in appearances before the House Committee on Ways and Means and the Senate Committee on Finance. He went before one or both of these committees in every Congress between 1862 and 1902, a period of forty years. He outlasted all but a few in the struggle, including senators, representatives, presidents, cabinet members, and lobbyists. If he did not win every argument from his opponents, at least he and the American Iron and Steel Association rarely lost.

There is no better way to judge his performance than to see him in action through the printed hearings of these committees. An especially revealing session was that of 5 February 1884. The Democrats had gained control of the House in 1882 and were bent on lowering tariff walls. William R. Morrison of Illinois had replaced Wharton's good friend William D. Kelley of Pennsylvania as chairman of the Committee on Ways and Means. Other democrats who were ready and willing to tear the nickel manufacturer apart on the subject of protection were Roger Q. Mills of Texas, Hilary A. Herbert of Alabama, and especially Abram S. Hewitt of New York. Hewitt knew as much as Wharton about the business of iron and steel and more than he concerning its technology. Hewitt had long been associated with Peter and Edward Cooper in the Trenton Iron Company and the New Jersey Steel and Iron Company. He was in fact one of America's great ironmasters. And he was a capable politician. He had managed Samuel J. Tilden's presidential campaign in 1876 and had opposed the Tammany machine in New York City. In questioning witnesses he always went directly to the point. He was short-tempered and blunt to the point of rudeness.[13]

The subject for investigation was the high duty on steel rails. Hewitt had stated his position on the subject in the previous Congress:

Last year the production of steel rails in this country was in round numbers a million of tons. Inasmuch as the demand exceeded the supply, the whole, or nearly the whole duty, $28 per ton, was added to the price. I think I am justified in saying from my knowledge of the business that the profits of last year were between fifteen and twenty millions of dollars, on an original investment of not more than the same amount. Now, if this vast profit had been divided between the owners of the works and the labor employed in operating them, the community at large, though still paying an extravagant price for the steel rails which they require, might perhaps look with some complacency upon the exactions to which they have been subjected by the operation of the law. [14]

Hewitt was primed, in short, to catch Wharton in the act of attempting to defend the indefensible. Moreover, the issue of the duty on steel rails had a fellow traveler on that February day of 1884, which favored the opponents of protection. This involved the Bessemer Steel Company, Ltd., on whose board Wharton sat for Bethlehem Iron. The charge was to be that the Bessemer Company had a monopoly over steel patents, made possible by the high tariff, and was using its power to stifle the development of an iron industry in the South.

The background was this: In 1881 Wharton, assisted by Linderman, Wilbur, Fritz, and Sayre had urged the Bessemer Steel Company to purchase what became known as the Thomas-Gilchrist patents for a basic process in making Bessemer steel. These patents provided a solution to the problem of phosphorus in ores. Phosphorus remained in an acid form because nothing was present to remove it. Sidney Gilchrist Thomas and a cousin, Percy Gilchrist, both of England, had succeeded in eliminating it by changing the lining of the Bessemer converter. The lining had been of acid brick; they contrived to use instead a basic brick. The phosphoric acid then combined with the lining and passed out with the slag.

Hewitt had acquired the Thomas-Gilchrist patents for the United States at a time when their commercial feasibility was still in doubt. The process was being used successfully in Europe, but the costs were high. In the ordinary Bessemer manufacture the converter linings needed infrequent changing. With the basic process the linings were decomposed by chemical action and had to be changed often. As a result fewer charges could be made in a given period of time. No less a person than Holley had pointed this out. The entire industry knew the problem. Wharton and his friends from Bethlehem Iron had to use pressure in order to convince the Bessemer Steel Company to purchase the patents. [15]

But, once the purchase was made, a potential for discrimination existed. Hewitt, Wharton, and the industry knew that the South stood to benefit from the Thomas-Gilchrist process if it should prove to be an even moderate commercial success. Large and easily mined deposits of iron ore existed in several states, especially Alabama and Tennessee. These ores were by and large much higher in phosphorus than were those mined in Northern states. Any difference in costs of manufacture between the acid and basic processes might be made up by the lower costs of labor in the South. In sum, the Thomas-Gilchrist process might be the one thing a Southern steel industry needed in order to become strong.

Against this background, the Bessemer Steel Company had refused to grant a license for the Thomas-Gilchrist patents to the Roane Iron Company of Chattanooga, Tennessee. The reasons for the refusal were unclear but suspicious. Was the Bessemer Steel Company, which represented the eleven Northern steel makers, deliberately suppressing competition? That was the charge; and the Democratic members of the Committee on Ways and Means were intent on proving that the duty on steel rails promoted such monopolistic practices.

Hewitt was not present when the Committee began its session on the morning of February 5.[16] Morrison recognized Wharton, who had anticipated that the attack would aim at the interdependence of profits and monopoly and so devoted most of his remarks to a defense of bigness in the steel industry. It was, he maintained, natural and necessary to prosperity. Only large corporations in the manufacture of steel could take advantage of improvements in technology, which ultimately reduced prices for consumers. He used as an illustration the differential between iron and steel rails: The Pennsylvania Railroad had been able to reduce rates from ten mills per ton mile to four mills because of the change. "They [steel rails] now carry 50,000 pounds to the car, where formerly (when they had iron rails) they could carry only 20,000 pounds. They have now better tracks, better ballast, harder and stronger rails."

Wharton tied the need for bigness in the steel industry to the requirements for success in competing with foreign manufacturers. Steelmakers in Europe, he said, had become big and were reaping the advantages of large size: "They are all making improvements just as fast as we are, and we can no more keep pace with their immense progress, without having equally large establishments, than a red man in a canoe can run a race against a Mississippi steamboat."

Finally, Wharton extended the argument for size in the nation's steel industry to include all manufacturing. He supported large-scale industry in principle on the grounds that it increased stability. This was a point on which he felt deeply and had previously written and spoken much. He became eloquent:

When a manufacturer in this country amasses a large sum of money (which, of course sometimes happens) he does not, by so doing weaken the resources of the country; he does not rob his neighbor; he does not take money from any one to whom it belongs. But in gathering up from out of the earth, or from the surface of the earth, wealth which would otherwise go to waste, he brings into existence that which otherwise would not exist. It is not liable to be brought into hostile array against us as British capital is liable to be. It is part of the possessions of the country. That wealth, when the man dies, he does not carry off with him. It remains here as part of our resources. I am sorry to say that the instances in which an American manufacturer leaves one of those great estates are very rare. When that point is impressed on the minds of the committee, as I believe it will be, the committee will see that the persons who do amass fortunes are not the enemies, but the best friends of the country; and that their capital so amassed is not used to the injury or oppression of others, but is used mainly for the further extension of the machinery which is already existing; that the very possession of those means is probably the only way by which we can keep pace with other countries.

One may imagine that the members of the committee impassively listened to this rhetoric. Certainly a number of them were unwilling to accept as true the propositions that bigness strengthened the resources of the country and was "not used to the injury or oppression of others." They were prepared to prove the opposite.

Mills began the questioning by probing to establish differences in costs of manufacture between American and foreign makers of steel rails. This was old ground, which the Democrats had gone over *ad nauseam* in the previous Congress. Herbert continued the debate by introducing the subject of the Bessemer Steel Company. Was this company using the Thomas-Gilchrist process, he asked? Wharton replied that the Carnegie establishment at Pittsburgh and the Pennsylvania Steel Company were experimenting with it. Asked whether the Pennsylvania Steel Company had found the process successful, Wharton declared it had not. "They have expended a large amount of money in it, and are working it successfully, so far as technical success is concerned; but in an economical point of view they have not been able to obtain success so far."

Herbert then by lengthy and adroit questioning brought out the potentiality of the Thomas-Gilchrist process for developing a Southern iron industry.

"Do you know why it is that the process has not been tried in the South, where the ores are so well adapted to the process?" Herbert asked.

Wharton sidestepped. "When the Thomas-Gilchrist patents were brought over here, and there was some talk among Southern men of obtaining the use of those patents, we said to them, 'It isn't time yet; we do not know what those patents are worth. They have not been tried here.'" Wharton then explained the Bessemer Steel Company to the assembled congressmen, arguing that it performed a service to the public as well as to its members by discriminating between good and bad patents.

Was then, asked Herbert, the Bessemer Steel Company in business to educate the public? Wharton was not to be enticed into taking such a ridiculous position. "Philanthropy is not the principal motive of any business association," he replied. But he took the opening given by Herbert to add, "For my own part, I confess that a motive of that sort of public comity does, sometimes weigh with me almost in advance of mere money advantages. Wherever, in other words, a concern gets so large as the iron and steel interests of this country, it cannot, if it would, ignore what is to the public advantage. It has to be managed in a way conformably to the public interest or it breaks down; and I think that the higher people get in the world, the more that class of consideration weighs."

At this point Hewitt entered the room and took the lead in asking questions. He had been well briefed concerning the point at which the interrogation had arrived and wasted no time repeating what had gone before. "Have you established a rate by which the Thomas-Gilchrist patent can be used?" he asked.

"All our patents, including the Thomas-Gilchrist patent, are thrown open to the public on the same terms as the owners enjoy," replied Wharton.

Hewitt wanted to know more specifically what these terms were. Wharton hedged, averring that he did not know. Hewitt expressed no surprise at this. He retorted that he had been the agent for selling the Thomas-Gilchrist patent to the Bessemer Steel Company, "and as soon as it was perfected I applied for a license for the Rowan [*sic*] Iron Works in Tennessee, and I received as an answer that the Bessemer Steel Association was not prepared to make any terms. And up to this time . . . I have never been able to get the terms on which we could use the process."

Hewitt had made his point: The Bessemer Steel Company had been guilty of restraining trade. He followed this victory with questions concerning fees charged by the company to determine if restraining trade was a regular practice. Wharton squirmed. Fifty thousand dollars was the standard price for using patents possessed by the Bessemer company. Established companies could easily afford this. Small, newly organized concerns could not. Again Hewitt scored: The very size of the fees made the Bessemer Steel Company's position monopolistic.

Herbert then introduced the issue of the tariff on steel rails. He insisted that this had enabled the members of the Bessemer Steel Company to make huge profits. He persisted:

Mr. HERBERT. Your association has had for the last ten years practically a monopoly of the steel manufacture in the United States?

Mr. WHARTON. Of steel rails, practically.

Mr. HERBERT. And you paid how much for this Thomas-Gilchrist process?

Mr. HEWITT. The Bessemer Association paid $225,000 for it.

Mr. WHARTON. I believe that is correct.

Mr. HEWITT. I received the money, and I know it.

Mr. WHARTON. (To Mr. Hewitt.) Was not that the final payment; and was there not a payment in advance?

Mr. HEWITT. The purchase was made for $275,000, but one of the members of your association [in fact, Carnegie], being a little smarter than the rest, got a bonus of $50,000 for making the sale, and you got him to divide that bonus among the other associates, so that the whole cost to your association was $225,000.

Mr. WHARTON. I think that we paid $275,000 and then that there was some bonus.

Mr. HEWITT. There was a bonus of $50,000, so that you paid for the Thomas-Gilchrist process $225,000.

Mr. HERBERT. That high tariff of $28 a ton which you enjoyed enabled you to buy that patent at $225,000, and to withhold it, so far as it has been withheld, from the people in the South and Southwest. Was it not the tariff that enabled you to do this?

Wharton was caught. On the basis of his own reasoning concerning the necessity of the tariff on steel rails Herbert was absolutely correct. The press and the country in general would probably not notice the important qualifying phrase which made the statement correct, namely, "So far as it has been withheld." Even if the Bessemer Steel Company had purchased the patent rights without the aid of the tariff, the country would not forgive a practice of monopoly.

Wharton's immediate response was a flight into eloquence:

There is an old saying that every man likes to be the father of his own children, and I much prefer to make my own statement rather than to have it made for me. You did not state accurately what I said. I want to lift this thing, if I can, out of this small way of looking at it. There is a monstrous war going on between the industries of this country and the industries of other countries. We who are engaged in that war have to be constantly watching the strategy of our enemies, and have to be constantly providing beforehand against what our enemies are going to do, and have to make sacrifices for the future exigencies of business. You may say that that is a selfish consideration. To a certain extent that is true; just as an army in the field is actuated by the motive of self-preservation when it fortifies its own position. The army when it does so is not merely preserving its own life but is preserving that of the country and of the cause for which it is fighting. Now if we were to neglect taking these precautions we would be simply defeated, and if we (the fighting army) should do so, the country which we are serving is also defeated. I wish that gentlemen could look at the thing in this large way, and not imagine that everybody who is carrying on business in this country is plundering his neighbor. I feel warmly on this subject, because I have given up a life of ease to go into a life of industry, and I feel when I come here that I am almost looked upon as a criminal before his judges. We are here very much in the condition of innocent men who are allowed by the judge to give a reason why sentence of death should not be pronounced upon them.

He had overreached himself, but not badly.

"My dear sir, you come here at the instance of your own people, not at our request," Mills reminded him.

"That is a very good peroration, Mr. Wharton," observed Morrison. Herbert persisted:

I ask you this simple question: If you had not had a very high tariff on Bessemer steel of the manufacture of which your association had practically, as you say, a monopoly, would you have been able to pay $225,000 for this Thomas-Gilchrist invention and thereby to stop it and prevent it from going down South (as Mr. Hewitt says it would have gone) where the ores abound that are suited to the manufacture of this kind of steel which is cheaper and better than the Bessemer steel? Would you, I say, have been able to do that if it had not been for the very high tariff which you enjoyed for many years? I want to get at the operation of the tariff. That is what we are discussing.

Herbert, too, had overreached himself. Wharton had not meant to say that the Bessemer Steel Company had a monopoly on the manufacture of steel rails, only that the member companies were the only ones in the business; and the inference that steel made by the basic process was cheaper than that manufactured by the acid process had not been established and was in fact untrue.

Wharton kept his presence of mind. He knew better than to question the accuracy of the details in Herbert's question, especially since Herbert had by wanting to "get at the operation of the tariff" pointed a way in which Wharton could escape from the snare.

Mr. WHARTON. Bless you, we are not keeping it away from the people of the South. The operation of the thing is this: The English people and the German people are determined to possess this market, which is worth more to them than all the other markets of the world. We have to defend this market in the best way we can and in doing that to give employment to our own capital and our own labor. You in the South desire to have your capital and labor employed. You think you have in your mines ore suitable to the Thomas-Gilchrist process, and if you want the Thomas-Gilchrist patent you can have it.
Mr. HERBERT. I would like to know on what terms.
Mr. WHARTON. Your people already know that.
Mr. HERBERT. I would like the public to know it.
Mr. WHARTON. If the Thomas-Gilchrist patent is not controlled in this country, and if we have no foothold for it here, it is employed in the other countries of Europe where all the materials for the manufacture of steel are nearer together, where labor is cheaper, and where ores and coal are easier of access. . . .

At this point, the battle was a standoff. The committee could not of course know that the Thomas-Gilchrist process was destined not to be widely used in the United States because of the simultaneous discovery of a basic process for the manufacture of open-hearth steel.[17]

3

Wharton's work for the Industrial League lasted into the 1880s, when the league went out of existence. Much of its lobbying was taken over by the American Iron and Steel Association. Appearances before congressional committees were only dramatic high points. Here the battle of words took place. Of greater practical importance was the mass of daily detail by which he cultivated the acquaintance of influential people on behalf of the industry, for upon such ties control over appointments, nominations, and elections depended; and these decided the outcome of the power struggle. That was what really mattered. Words were less important than the position one took when the vote was called for. Always his choice of arguments had to take into account the strength and alignment of forces in the contest for power. He must not compromise with the enemy; and he must not offend allies.

Wharton chose the Republican Party for partisan political activities. It agreed with his prewar Whiggism and made him current with the tide. Most men of affairs in Philadelphia entered the party of Grant, Hayes, and Blaine. Like them, Wharton saw it as a nation builder fighting against forces of reaction represented by the Democrats. Most protectionists were Republicans, and Wharton did what he could to promote that identity. He once wrote to William E. Chandler, who was doing preliminary work on the Republican Party platform for the campaign of 1872, "The Republican Party cannot afford to be anything but distinctly Protectionist. Republicans who are shaky on Protection are shaky all over and most of them are all ready to drop into the Democratic camp. . . . Our party *cannot afford any doubt or equivocation* as to its undeviating adherence to the American policy on Industrial questions and it will perish when people lose faith in it on that head."[18] When liberal Republicans split with the mainstream on questions of protection, big business, and sound money, Wharton privately read them out of the party.[19]

He contributed money to the presidential campaigns of Grant, Hayes, and Garfield; hosted President Hayes at the Twelfth Street residence; collaborated with Simon Cameron and Matthew Quay in support of candidates; and stirred Sayre and others at Bethlehem Iron to give money and appear at rallies. George H. Boker, U.S. ambassador to Russia, expressed a mutual sentiment when he wrote to Wharton on 5 January 1877, "I noted with pleasure what you say about the election of Governor Hayes. I hope that our party will show no sign of wavering before the empty bluster of the Democrats. . . . If the Democrats get cross, we should get crosser. If they wish to shed our blood, we should thirst for theirs. At all events, we should not weaken before them. Quakers as we both are by blood, friend Joseph, 'thee' and I both know that there are some things better than even peace, and worth purchasing by a breach of it."[20]

Wharton campaigned extensively for Garfield in 1880 and gave a rousing speech at the Academy of Music for him and other Republican candidates. Surely no one ever waved the bloody shirt with more colorful language than he used on that occasion. He equated the Democratic Party with a South tainted by treason and repression.

A future of surpassing prosperity seems to be within our reach, when the baleful spectre of Southern labor-degradation appears again upon the scene. . . . The South, which by passing laws that convicts shall be hired out to forced labor, and by then convicting tens of thousands of black men upon any show of evidence, true of false, for any slight offense, has virtually re-established slavery, with its chained gangs of laborers, its whips and bloodhounds; the South, which by her atrocious murders of Republicans, her suppression of Republican votes and her infamous ballot box stuffing, is solidly Democratic; which, by her insufferable cruelties to innocent laboring people, has begun to drive away from her borders the class of working people that has been her dependence, undertakes to say to us of the North that she only is fit to govern, and that the country wants a change.

The South, he alleged, had compounded her iniquity by allying with "that ghastly humbug, British philanthropic Free Trade," which she would if given a chance use to destroy the industry and prosperity of the working classes of the North. Are our industries, he asked, "to be overthrown and our homes high and low brought to want because a tyrannical minority of Southerners prefer degraded labor, and because English labor starvers count upon their people's willingness to stand more misery than ours?" The issue for intelligent voters, he declared, was clear: "The Republican party has never failed to stand by the working people who built it up and have kept it in power. With hands outstretched to welcome the new South, the real South that shall soon, when freed from its domestic tyrants spring to our side, the Republican party stands as a strong champion of the rights of man and the dignity of intelligent labor. Long may its benignant rule endure."[21]

Wharton's campaigning for Garfield was in part an expression of loyalty to his nephew, Wharton Barker, who had been largely responsible for the nomination. Barker had become a member of the Industrial League and spent almost as much time as his uncle on tariff matters. That is not to say that either depended much on the other. Barker Brothers and Company had become one of the top banking houses of the country. As a junior partner in that concern Wharton Barker found doors opening to him without assistance from his uncle. He built four cruisers for the Russian government, which honored him with the Order of St. Stanislaus and followed with a contract to develop the coal and iron resources of southern Russia. Only the assassination of Czar Alexander II, and a decision by Alexander III to use Russian personnel, prevented the realization of this ambitious project.

Wharton Barker had been largely responsible for founding *The Penn*

Monthly, which his father's bank financed. In 1875 he worked with others to organize the Penn Club for the purpose of holding dinners in honor of distinguished visitors to Philadelphia and for eminent Philadelphians. The Penn Club was in a way an extension of Carey's vespers to a larger audience and on a grander scale. In 1880 he allowed *The Penn Monthly* to die, replacing it with a weekly journal, *The American,* which was more narrowly political, in fact an organ for promoting the career of Wharton Barker. The Barker Publishing Company took care of finances. Barker wrote most of the editorials and W. Ralston Balch, the managing editor, wrote about Barker. Together they projected to the public an image of Wharton Barker as a hard-working man of principle; knowledgeable in finance, economics, and politics; a formidable competitor; yet honest, warm, and generous; patriotic; prescient; self-confident.[22]

Wharton Barker possessed all of these qualities in moderation and was in addition self-confident to a superlative degree. Overconfidence blinded him at times to his true strength and made the older leaders of the party uneasy concerning the soundness of some of his projects. Joseph Wharton delicately phrased the shortcoming in a letter to Blaine in 1881, "Should Mr. Barker join your little band you will find in him force, firmness, quiet intelligence which will justify the choice and a sweet temper which will make his presence among you constantly pleasant—but he will need the support which your greater experience can give and must be [sometimes] checked from too lavish expenditure of his vitality."[23] Barker had at the time this letter was written been bypassed in favor of Wayne MacVeagh in the allocation of a cabinet post among Garfield's supporters from Pennsylvania. The oversight was portentous. Barker gracefully accepted it, but nevertheless found it easy to sympathize with reformers (such as MacVeagh) who were basically critical of the administrations of Garfield and Arthur. Barker was a member of the Republican League, in which Independent Republicans, as they called themselves, opposed party regulars. Wharton Barker's turn to the left in Republican politics partially alienated him from his uncle, who in 1882 wrote to Congressman Kelley, "I think you know that I have from the first refused to take any part in the Independent Republican movement, yet you also know that I am so situated as to hear much of their view. . . . I am persuaded that the Independents have the power to destroy the Republican ascendency if unable themselves to take the reins, and that as things now stand there is every prospect of them doing so."[24]

In the years 1880–81 a break between nephew and uncle was still in the future, and the two collaborated on several projects which they urged on Republican administrations. One was the idea of a commercial union *(Zollverein)* of the United States, Canada, and Mexico. According to this idea the countries would enjoy free trade among themselves and establish common tariff barriers with respect to the rest of the world, especially Britain. A companion to this idea, privately discussed but not made part of the proposal, was that such a continental agreement might be a prelude to political unification. Certainly Joseph Wharton looked favorably upon the possibility of a union with Canada, an idea which he had entertained from the time of the Civil War. The Industrial League went so far as to ask Garfield, then running for the presidency, to endorse the idea of a continental customs union; but that sensible gentleman declined with thanks.[25]

The other plan which Joseph Wharton and Wharton Barker promoted was that of establishing a commission of experts to propose revisions in the tariff laws. The idea had appeared in Joseph Wharton's article, "International Industrial Competition." Demand for a tariff commission grew out of disgust at the primitive quality of congressional action. Poorly drafted bills created loopholes by means of which foreign manufacturers could subvert the intent of the laws. Joseph Wharton and his nephew had more success with this idea than with that of a customs union. The 47th Congress (1881–83) established a tariff commission, which drafted reforms meeting the approval of scholars on the subject. But the work of the tariff commission still had to pass the political hurdles of congressional process, with a result that the final product was disappointing. The experiment with a tariff commission was not repeated.[26]

4

In the opening years of the first Cleveland administration Joseph Wharton established a political friendship which was as happy as any he ever made—and with a Democrat. The person in question was Francis Wharton, son of Thomas Isaac Wharton, one of Philadelphia's most respected lawyers and legal scholars, and a grandson of Isaac, brother to Charles, Joseph Wharton's grandfather. That made Joseph and Francis second cousins. Francis had recently returned to his native Philadelphia to lead a scholar's life in semiretirement. During the course of a long career he had served as assistant attorney-general for the commonwealth; had taught English history and literature at Kenyon College in Ohio, theology at the Episcopal Theological School in Cambridge, Massachusetts, and law at the new school associated with Boston University; had occupied for a time the pulpit of St. Paul's in Brookline, Massachusetts; and had written on criminal law, medical jurisprudence, private international law, contracts, and evidence. Now, having spent a year traveling in Europe, he looked forward to completing a work on the international law of the United States and of doing research and writing on some other subjects both historical and jurisprudential. Distinguished, sociable, kindly, hard-working, he easily mingled with other educators and scientists whose accomplishments gave Philadelphia a justifiable claim to fame, yet whose lives were largely hidden from public view by the shams and frivolities of the rich and powerful who set fashions and captured headlines during Philadelphia's gilded age.

Joseph probably met Francis at the Penn Club, the University, the Science and Art Club, and in various drawing rooms and saw what others also found obvious: Francis Wharton had all the necessary requirements for distinguished service in the Cleveland administration. Although not a protectionist, he favored the idea of a continental customs union and could be counted on to defend the interests of the United States against attempts by ill-advised people to compromise them by inaction or to barter them away by treaty. The proper place for him would be the Department of State. A position was vacant, that of examiner of claims and solicitor. Joseph interested Francis in it and then worked through friends to secure the assent of Secretary Thomas F. Bayard, nomination by the president, and confirmation by the Senate. By the end of 1885 he had succeeded and as reward had a voice in some of the policy-making activities of the Department of State.[27]

Almost immediately an issue drew Joseph and Francis together. The Canadian government, headed by Prime Minister Sir John A. Macdonald, was threatening the fishing interests of citizens of the United States contrary to provisions of the Treaty of Washington (1818). By terms of that treaty the United States, the original proprietor of the disputed waters, ceded to Britain rights for American fishermen to fish within the three-mile limit in some parts of the eastern coast of Canada, Newfoundland, and Labrador but retained the right in other waters, together with a right for American fishing boats to enter Canadian ports for repairs and supplies. Inhabitants in the Maritime Provinces complained of inequity: American boats could fish off their shores but Canadians shipping fish to the United States had to pay a high duty. The Canadian Parliament under prompting of the Government took up the cause and upheld residents of the Maritime Provinces in closing their ports to American fishing vessels. The Government furthermore threatened to deny Americans any right to fish in Canadian waters unless the United States entered into a reciprocal trade treaty with Canada. As Wharton Barker put the issue, "The fisheries question is used by the Canadians merely as a means to an end; they mean to force us to grant reciprocity by it."[28]

That was the situation which disturbed Joseph. A reciprocal trade agreement was different from a customs union, which implied a separation of Canada from Britain. A reciprocal trade agreement would by contrast "turn Canada into another Gibraltar—a depot for the smuggling of British goods across the line."[29] Cleveland, Joseph reasoned, was the sort of president who would wink at such blackmail if he believed in the justice of the Canadian position. He was known to favor a broad commercial treaty with Canada.

A good deal of correspondence passed between Francis and Joseph concerning the fisheries question. Francis sought out Joseph for advice and in turn provided information concerning the progress of negotiations. The two men agreed on the desirability of the United States taking a hard line to defend the interests of American fishermen, although they had somewhat different views concerning the means. When Joseph suggested using the navy to protect American vessels Francis answered, what navy? "We may not duly estimate the difficulty of getting a navy off (unless with 'Quaker' guns), when we have none ready. When we came into power there was no navy, & the Fisheries were given away. What shall we do?" The Canadian Pacific Railroad was then under construction. John Macdonald and the directors of the road planned that the transcontinental line should cross over Maine to an eastern terminus in Halifax, Nova Scotia. Both Francis and Joseph advocated that the American government retaliate by withholding permission. Francis believed that such a move would mean war but nevertheless favored it as a last resort. "The great object is peace *with* honor, *without* honor, war."[30]

Francis introduced Joseph to George Baden-Powell, a member of the British Parliament, and to Joseph Chamberlain, also an M.P. and recently president of the Board of Trade. Both men were concerned with the fisheries issue from the British point of view. Francis sent Joseph a manuscript on the subject of fisheries intended for publication in the third volume of his *Digest of the International Law of The United States*, asking for corrections. Joseph complied. When the volume was published, Francis sent Joseph a copy. Joseph offered to pay for it, but Francis refused the money, writing, "Of course the book was a present to you. A strange thing it wd. be if you had to pay for it when you are one of its authors. The fishing chapter in Vol. III, owes some of its most potent touches to you."[31]

In the same letter Francis lamented the absence of Joseph in the Senate. A vacancy from Pennsylvania had been filled by Quay whom Joseph had supported. Wrote Francis, "How I wish I could . . . see you in the Senate, with your strong brain & kind will. I am sickened at Quay coming here from Pennsylvania. It means, not statesmanship, but low party dickering. The administration has no personal cause to complain of Cameron and his lot. On the contrary, they keep clear of any factious opposition to opportunists, & make things generally easy. But our foreign relations require strong men in the Senate, & here comes from Pennsylvania another representative of the 'boodle' school."

Francis wrote confidentially to Joseph concerning the success of the commissioners in settling the fisheries controversy. "Of course I can say nothing until the Senate removes its injunction of secrecy. I may say that a week ago (though this is confidential) the negotiation was near a break, Canada refusing to submit to our demand. But we did not break. This is better than war, though I shd. like to have seen the Pres't., by way of retaliation, stop the Canada Pacific."[32] A treaty was signed in Washington on 15 February

1888, between the United States and Great Britain, which essentially re-affirmed American fishing rights under the treaty of 1818.

Francis Wharton died the following year while putting the finishing touches on the first volume of his *Diplomatic Correspondence and the Revolution*. Almost twenty years later Joseph, recollecting the friendship with Francis, wrote, "He in fact did a great deal of Secretary Bayard's work in the way of preparing important documents which Bayard signed. He was . . . a man of the first rank in international law. . . . He frequently sent to me public papers for my scrutiny and criticism, so that I became intimate with him and much attached to him as I became better acquainted with his intellectual superiority and his sweetness of temper."[33]

Deborah Fisher Wharton

Joseph Wharton as a young man

The Whartons on the porch at Ontalauna, *(left to right)* Anna Lovering Wharton, daughters Anna and Joanna, Joseph, daughter Mary Lovering Wharton

Ontalauna

Marbella

The Whartons at the Batsto Mansion, *(left to right)* daughter Anna, Joseph (with his wife behind), daughters Mary Lovering and Joanna (on the horse)

Joseph Wharton at Marbella

Anna Lovering and Joseph Wharton on their golden wedding anniversary, 1906

Joseph Wharton at Marbella, July 1908

11

Science and Education

In the late spring of 1881 Wharton faced a crisis within the extended family, namely, the apostasy of his nephew William Thurston. Two years earlier the signs of tuberculosis had appeared in Thurston. He had taken a leave of absence from the iron company and gone to Europe for a rest. There he regained his strength. His wife Ellen and the children joined him; and in Paris Ellen died of malaria contracted in Rome. Thurston, physically improved but emotionally emptied, returned to Bethlehem with the children and sought forgetfulness in work and religion. Bethlehem had no community of Quakers. The men with whom he worked at the iron company belonged to the Episcopal Church of the Nativity, as had Ellen and the other Coppées. Thurston was baptized an Episcopalian.

Although a switch from the Quaker to the Episcopal religion was fairly common (for example, Abraham Barker), this was the first instance of it among the descendants of Deborah and William Wharton. Thurston wrote of the conversion to his uncle. How would Joseph receive the news?

His reply to Thurston is an exemplary expression of toleration:

> The announcement did not surprise me, though I confess the step does not please me, for the drawing away from us of those we love cannot be a pleasant thing. Still, in these matters each one must think and act for himself. As Paul says, "Let every man be fully persuaded in his own mind."
>
> For my part, when I see the domination of priest and parson, and compare it with the absolute and dearly bought freedom of our society which its members so often fail to appreciate, I think of Paul's remark to the captain who with a great sum had bought his freedom. "But I was free born."

This letter is dated 19 June 1881. Three days letter there appeared over Joseph Wharton's signature an almost equally perfect example of intolerance. The document was the indenture by which the Wharton School of Finance and Economy was to be established. Wharton wrote that the school was to have a

Professor or Instructor upon Industry, Commerce, and Transportation to teach how industries advance in excellence or decline, and shift from place to place; how by intelligent industry nations or communities thrive; how by superior skill and diligence some nations grow rich and powerful, and how by idleness or ill-directed industry others become rude and poor; how a great nation should be as far as possible self-sufficient, maintaining a proper balance between agriculture, mining and manufactures, and supplying its own wants—

The message was that of national self-protection as contained in Carey's *Principles of Social Science*, supplemented by Wharton's conclusions concerning the desirability of big business and combinations of business to protect property. No allowance was made for the professor to disagree with the message, which was treated as a scientific truth to be imparted to young minds with the same assurance as were the truths of natural science.

The contrast between the letter to William Thurston and the wording of the indenture has a relationship to a controversy then raging among intellectuals concerning the proper domains of religion and science. This was the era of Darwin, Huxley, and other biologists whose studies of evolution challenged orthodox views concerning the nature of life. The controversy called into question the foundations of religious belief. "Here are the proofs of evolution and the natural order of the world," the challengers declared. "What are the proofs of Christianity? Of any religion?" Theologians, pushed to the defensive, responded with the ancient argument that no form of reason can disprove religion, which depends on faith; for faith is superior to reason in all that pertains to the supernatural. Came the rebuttal, what then pertains to the natural and what to the supernatural? To the things of Caesar and the things of God? If indeed a supernatural order exists (and many scientists and philosophers denied its existence), where is the line to be drawn, and how, and by whom?

Wharton's responses are typically Hicksite: Where there is no theology, no line needs to be drawn. The inward light is not limited by science or any other form of reason or nonreason; it shines in each individual as it will. In a manner of speaking, its truth is personal and inviolable. Each decides for himself. Because of this, toleration is the proper attitude to take toward the objects of its illumination. But it is otherwise with science. Wherever the inward light does not shine, the reason is free to roam. The disciplined reason which is science can operate without opposition, for no other form of cognition is worthy of contesting it. And science is by nature tolerant only at the frontiers of knowledge. A person must accept and learn what has been proved beyond question if he would intelligently engage in the theorizing and experimenting for achieving the next step forward in understanding nature and her laws. Wharton, believing as he did that his philosophy of protectionism and big business was scientifically established, acted consistently in wanting to be unquestioned in a school which might depend for its very life on the epistemological value of social science.

1

Many people in Wharton's time saw that this positivistic attitude toward science, when applied to the nascent social sciences, was unwarranted, even ridiculous. Wharton also soon came to realize it, although he never became fully reconciled to the idea that historians, economists, or political scientists might validly disagree with him on the subject of protection and others resulting from his research and analysis. The pedestal on which he put the "truths" of social science in these early years suggests indeed the presence of lingering doubts concerning their certainty—doubts later translated into certitude by emotional attachment rather than reason. In effect, the lack of modesty which presided over his adherence to social science in the 1870s and early 1880s strongly contrasts with his attitude toward the natural and physicial sciences. Here, the taint of dogmatism is absent; Wharton was intolerant in an approved scholarly way but respectful, even humble.[1]

He enjoyed the company of physicists, chemists, metallurgists, and other scientists. His collected papers contain no disparaging remarks concerning them. From the time he began the study of chemistry he cultivated their friendship. In his youth he knew the Philadelphia scientists Booth, Boyé, and Genth and somewhat later expanded his acquaintance to include the Yale contingent of Silliman and Brush and the Boston team of Eliot and Storer. He heavily depended in his work on Roepper, Allen, and Macfarlane. On his trip to Europe in 1873 he made special mention to Anna of having attended a banquet at the Chemist Club in London and of having met there the "great scientists" Owen, Huxley, Tyndall, and Galton. In middle age he extended his friendships to include Wolcott Gibbs of Harvard (whom he probably first met at Booth's laboratory in Philadelphia in the 1840s) and Joseph Leidy of the University of Pennsylvania, and he had a speaking acquaintance with most of the nationally known analytical chemists and metallurgists in the major colleges, universities, and institutes of the United States and a scattering of those in England, Germany, and Austria. The autarchic spirit which assailed his politics never touched his attitudes toward natural science and scientists. Here, he was completely cosmopolitan.

He differed from academic scientists by being primarily an industrialist, and he was self-conscious about the difference. His important discoveries had come in making zinc and nickel. He could not publish some of the scientific aspects of these discoveries without revealing trade secrets. More-over, he was aware of the limited knowledge needed for what he had done. He once wrote to Brush, "Here am I, with so little pretension to scientific knowledge that I have to wonder at your patience with me, who yet find means to make that little knowledge avail."[2] Such modesty was genuine and persisted into old age. In 1895 Charles Loring Jackson of Harvard asked Wharton to be chairman of the Committee of the Overseers to Visit the Chemical Laboratory. Wharton at first declined. The department then had a small but illustrious faculty, including among others Jackson, Gibbs, and the future Nobel prize winner, Theodore W. Richards. The offer, Wharton wrote Jackson, "grows apparently out of an unduly high estimation of my attainments or ability, which in my judgment are not adequate to qualify me for the proper discharge of the duties of the post in question." When Jackson refused to fill the position with anyone else, Wharton again expressed reluctance on the grounds of inadequacy: "On several occasions the really scientific men of both this country and England have shown to me a consideration beyond my deserts, and this I must not abuse." Eventually, Wharton took the position. He immediately convened the committee and with its help drafted a report recommending emphasis on practical technical instruction.[3]

In general, scientists who knew Wharton accepted him and valued his work. Most of them were also part-time industrialists. The divergence of pure science from its applications, which was to create tensions between university and industry, was only beginning. Scientists of the stature of Gibbs, Jackson, and Richards understood Wharton's position. His emphasis on practical applications did not disturb them. As far as they were concerned, he admired and supported scientists, could talk intelligently on a wide variety of subjects, was not competing for place, and had proven ability. That he might be an amateur in everything except zinc and nickel made no difference.

That was, indeed, his position. A description of his other activities in the domain of natural science helps to illustrate the catholicity of his interests. An order of fifteen book titles, taken from his business papers and dated 22 November 1872, includes seven in fields as varied as chemistry, physics, archaeology, and medicine and shows sufficiently well the scope of his curiosity: *Ten Laws of Health; Slow Horses Made Fast; Froude's Eng.* (probably James Anthony Froude, *History of England from the Fall of Wolsey to the Death of Elizabeth*, twelve volumes); *Bits of Travel; Through the Looking Glass; Light and Electricity; Forms of Water; Household Taste; Ancient Stone Implements; Molecular Physics; Off the Skelligs; Electric Affinities; Spectrum Analysis; Martin Chuzzlewit; Oliver Twist*. Wharton was a reasonably active member of the Academy of Natural Science, the American Philosophical Society, and the Franklin Institute. In 1896 he gave a lecture on the subject of volcanoes to members of the Geographical Society of Philadelphia. He became one of the mainstays of a Science and Art Club, whose members met in various homes and discoursed on their favorite activities. Wharton's papers contain extensive notes for two lectures which he probably gave before this group. One dealt with the metallurgy of iron and its manufacture; the other is a superb survey of the field of semiprecious stones.

The interest in gems began in the early days of his work for the Pennsylvania and Lehigh Zinc Company. He collected such stones as agates, garnets, and turquoises and even a few of the more precious sort such as rubies. Some of these he had cut and set in pins and brooches. He did not do the work himself. He admired their chemistry and beauty and intently studied and read about them. He became an expert gemologist.

From time to time he published short papers in scientific journals. Two early papers appeared in the *American Journal of Science*. One was entitled "Speculations Upon a Possible Method of Determining the Distance of Certain Variably Colored Stars" (September 1865). He had acquainted himself with an "undulatory theory of light" and reasoned that the color of light emitted by an object must vary with the distance from the viewer. Because this seemed true, the phenomenon might be useful in measuring the distance of some differently colored stars. The other article had the heading, "Observations upon Autumnal Foliage" (March, 1869). This contained a theory concerning the changing color of autumn leaves. He reasoned that the circulation of sap kept the alkalinity-acidity content of chlorophyll in balance. When a sudden frost killed the flow of sap, the "blue" in the leaves (green being a mixture of blue and yellow) was exposed to the acidifying effect of oxygen in the air, with a result that they took on their characteristic reddish color.

His only published scientific paper on nickel is in no way connected with the processes which he used at Camden. It was entitled "On Two Peculiar Products in the Nickel Manufacture" and appeared in the same journal, now renamed the *American Journal of Science and the Arts* (January–May 1870). One of the "peculiar products" was a deposit of tough and highly magnetic crystals inside of cavities in the slag of the smelters. The other consisted of hollow globules of nickel-copper alloy filled with water, formed by tempering the molten metal. He explained the phenomenon by saying that the molten metal, when plunged into water, was giving off carbonic oxide gas; for a time as the metal began to cool the gas continued to form and expand, thus causing the hollow; and the pressure produced pores invisible to the naked eye as the gas sought to escape. The cooling of the metal caused the remaining gas to contract, leaving a near vacuum which sucked in water through the pores.

Wharton seems to have placed somewhat more importance on a paper which he delivered for the 150th anniversary of the American Philosophical Society in 1884, "Dust from the Krakatoa Eruption of 1883." Krakatoa was a volcano in the East Indies, approximately ten thousand miles from Philadelphia, which had exploded with tremendous force. He wrote, "The splendid roseate glows which in the winter of 1883–84 were visible in the winter sky after sunset and in the eastern sky before sunrise" led him to surmise that Philadelphians were seeing light reflected from volcanic particles suspended at a great height in the atmosphere.[4] He tested the theory by collecting clean snow from a field in open country far from urban areas, melting it, burning away organic material, and examining the residue under a microscope. He discovered that the particles recovered from the snow were identical with pumice from Krakatoa which he had obtained from sailors. He then compared the particles taken from the snow with dust collected from the smoke of blast furnaces, which are themselves artificial volcanoes. He found these to be similar, but sufficiently different to leave no doubt that the particles he had collected were not a result of local air pollution.

In later life Wharton responded to an invitation to describe the extraction and manufacture of nickel and cobalt for the 1896 *Annual Report* of the U.S. Geological Survey. His last scientific publication was a study of palladium, a little-known noble metal, traces of which occurred along with silver, gold, and platinum in some of the Sudbury nickel and copper ores. He read the paper before the American Philosophical Society on 7 April 1904, after which it was printed in an extended form in the society's *Proceedings*. Dr. Alois Weiskopf, whom Wharton had met during the year at the St. Louis Exposition, translated the article into German.[5]

These occasional papers have far less importance for the development of science that they have for an understanding of Wharton's character. Perhaps as important as anything in a survey of his scientific activities is the absence of evidence displaying a similar interest in mechanics. Not that he lacked knowledge in the field, as his work in developing a spelter furnace indicates. He even sent Brush a model of the furnace which he had made, scale $1'' = 1'$. Various incidents in his life show that he was quick to appreciate innovations in engineering. From time to time he suggested improvements in machinery, and he reverenced talent in engineering as readily as he did in science. His regard for Fritz as an engineer was deep, genuine, and lasting. Wharton showed no one else at Bethlehem Iron the respect which he accorded Fritz; his appreciation was sufficiently great to make him tolerant of Fritz's many shortcomings as a businessman and a leader of men. But Wharton did not enjoy tinkering. Throughout life he thought as a chemist and metallurgist, from the time of his experiments with cottonseed oil to his final work refining gold.

2

Wharton's two major ventures in education exactly reflect his tolerant/intolerant glance toward matters religious and scientific. He helped raise Swarthmore College from infancy to adulthood in a way that was discontinuous but effective and not the less loyal for being unemotional and detached. He unconditionally gave of time and money; made no undue attempt to determine what should and should not be taught; and avoided any temptation to advertise his work. His frequent deferring to others in the Society of Friends was not indifference, for he had definite opinions on most educational issues. He saw himself in the position of a mechanic helping to service an engine built and driven by others. It was otherwise with the Wharton School.

Other Friends had gone a long distance toward establishing Swarthmore College before he became involved. He had no taste for causes such as attracted many members of the Society. He came to Swarthmore almost with reluctance. But Swarthmore was a "cause" of a rather special sort. It represented a reversal of an opinion held by early Hicksites toward higher education. They had looked on the prevailing classical course of study as useless and on sectarian colleges as promoters of doctrines which interfered with a true practice of religion. They agreed with Orthodox Friends in insisting that education be useful, meaning capable of preparing the mind for immediate practical work, but the early Hicksites differed somewhat from the Orthodox in appreciating what was useful and practical. The emphasis of Hicksites on the simple life turned them away from artistic and most professional pursuits in favor of farming, manufacturing, merchandising, and the trades. No higher education was needed for these. So, Hicksites were indifferent if not openly hostile to it. Presbyterians, Roman Catholics, and members of other religious groups worked to establish academies and colleges, as did Orthodox Friends. Haverford, founded as a school in 1833, soon attained the status of a full-fledged college. A few years later Earlham in Richmond, Indiana, received a collegiate charter. The work of the Hicksites in establishing a comparable institution of higher education lagged behind those others by about a generation.

A few farsighted Hicksites were uneasy about the attitude of their society toward learning. Consciences of youth had to be nurtured. Who outside the home was to do this? At least one profession seemed necessary, that of schoolteacher. But the Hicksite community contained few qualified teachers and no means of training more.

Rumblings of discontent with this situation were heard in all of the yearly meetings. In Baltimore Mrs. Martha Tyson expressed her concern and called for greater educational opportunities for youth. In 1854 a committee of the Baltimore Yearly Meeting, which included her and Benjamin Hallowell, issued a report defining a need for *"an institution*, where our children can receive an education *in its true sense*, by the simultaneous cultivation of their intellectual and moral powers."[6] The report was published and circulated. Tyson and Hallowell continued to promote the idea through the medium of committees, reports, and visits to other meetings. Within a few years committees of the Yearly Meetings of New York and Philadelphia became involved. By the end of 1860 the three had agreed that a school or college should be established and that it should be coeducational, strongly oriented toward education in the natural sciences, and should embody friendly discipline.

The Civil War delayed completion of the project. Still, by the end of 1862 a Friends Educational Association had been organized. It sold stock at twenty-five dollars a share to members of the Society. In this way the Society could finance and control the school in much the same way that any group can do with a business enterprise. The stockholders elected a board of thirty-two managers, half men and half women. The question of site was answered by selecting an eminence in the country several miles west of Philadelphia. A charter was obtained, and the name, Friends Educational Association, was changed to that of the Corporation. Largely as a result of the war the interest of the Baltimore Yearly Meeting declined, leaving the Yearly Meetings of Philadelphia and New York with most of the burden of launching the venture. Finally the opening was set. At an inauguration ceremony on 10 November 1869 Lucretia Mott, assisted by her son Tom, planted two young oaks on an elevation east of the as yet unfinished building. The president outlined the college course: "Mathematics, Natural and Physical Sciences, Language, History and Geography, Literature, Intellectual and Moral Philosophy."[7]

Deborah and William Wharton were instrumental in working within the Philadelphia Yearly Meeting for the establishment of the college. Deborah continued the activity after William died and was joined in it by her daughter, Hannah Haydock. Both became charter members of the board of managers and remained as members until such time as they voluntarily retired. Hannah served on several of the important committees; Deborah contributed much money and later endowed a scholarship. In 1868 she owned two hundred and twenty shares of stock.[8]

Only Susanna, Rodman's widow, of the members of the immediate family did as much as Deborah and Hannah in the opening years of the college. The board selected Susanna's brother, Edward Parrish, as the first president. Parrish was a practicing chemist. He had been graduated from the Philadelphia College of Pharmacy and had later taught there. As president he was especially concerned with the collegiate course, whereas a preparatory course of study was given into the superintendency of Edward H. Magill, a dynamic young graduate of Brown University who had fallen under the spell of Wayland Brown and his "New College System," which advocated elective as well as practical offerings in the arts and sciences.[9] Susanna's two children, William Rodman and Susan, became first-year students in the preparatory course. They participated in the closing ceremonies of 1871, grandly called "commencement exercises" even though no students were as yet eligible for graduation. Rodman delivered a declamation by Robert Browning, "How They Brought the Good News from Ghent to Aix," and Susan recited an essay by Wendell Phillips, "Woman's Rights."[10]

Although Deborah and Hannah urged Joseph to greater effort on behalf of the college, he did little before the formal opening. The Swarthmore *Alumni Review* of 1940 indicates that he was before 1869 on a committee which solicited subscriptions, although he certainly was not a member of the committee appointed in 1867, which included his mother and thirteen others.[11] He took no recorded part in the meetings and committees which made decisions. He was, probably at his mother's urging, one of the incorporators named in the charter of 1864, which indicates that he was a stockholder. This put him on record as being one of the co-founders. That was by virtue of his gender. Women who had done much more, such as his mother and sister, were not permitted to sign as "charter members" and so missed the dignity of being formally "co-founders."

Wharton became a member of the board of managers in 1870, replacing his mother. He still exercised only a modest influence, not only because of his immersion in business and public affairs, but also because the bylaws of the college commanded an extreme decentralization of control. The president of the college had little power, being completely subject to a board whose members insisted on concerning themselves with daily details. But the bylaws also refused power to the board as a unifying body, vesting it instead in its committees, each of which ruled like a monarch. Originally the only officer of the board was a clerk. When this was changed, and a presidency was created, the president of the board was also accorded little authority. He represented the board at official functions and could preside over meetings, held four or five times a year. The business of presiding over a Quaker meeting, which is what sessions of the board amounted to, is scarcely a position of power.

The largest of the committees was an executive committee, consisting of sixteen persons who were entrusted with "the general supervision of the College." This meant essentially control over discipline, the appointment of professors, and surveillance of daily life on the campus. Each week the executive committee designated several of its members to form a visiting committee whose members were expected to participate in affairs involving students and faculty. Other committees dealt respectively with building and property; the museum; the library; the Anson Lapham Repository, soon to be renamed Friends Historical Library. A finance committee controlled expenditures. A committee of instruction had oversight of the curriculum. A committee on trusts, endowments, and scholarships solicited for funds, managed financial resources, and eventually became the principal body for controlling the budget and planning. A special nominating committee, at one time composed in such a way as to represent the three yearly meetings, appointed members to the committees. In addition to these standing committees the board created special committees to which it often delegated a right of final decision in its name.

In sum, Quaker democracy prevailed. The situation was saved from chaos by the existence of a broad area of agreement among students, faculty, and administrators and by a continuity of personnel. Although all appointments to committees were annual, members were reappointed year after year until such time as they died, resigned, or went to some other (usually higher) assignment. The situation also favored the formation of factions operating as power centers behind the scenes, sometimes in the best interests of the college but occasionally otherwise.

Wharton's first prominent activity after becoming a member of the board was part of the aftermath of a painful situation involving President Parrish and the principal of the preparatory course, Edward Magill. Differences of opinion arose between the two men within a year of the opening of the college. Their disagreement quickly became entangled with disputes between Parrish and the board, such that the board felt a necessity to choose between the two men and opted in favor of Magill. Parrish was bitterly disappointed. He returned to lecturing at the College of Pharmacy. Magill became president. Within the year Parrish's wife died, and he accepted an appointment from President Grant to help settle some difficulties among Indians in Oklahoma Territory. There Parrish contracted malaria and died on 9 September 1872.[12]

Parrish's many relatives, including Susanna Wharton, were incensed at allegations staining Edward's reputation. Susanna and her surviving brothers Samuel and Joseph wrote to the board requesting a release of information concerning the firing of President Parrish. By coincidence Joseph Wharton was serving a term as clerk and had to handle the correspondence. Setting aside any personal feelings in the matter, he acknowledged on behalf of the board the great contributions of Edward Parrish toward establishing the college and the high personal regard in which the managers held him, but declined to release the information on the grounds that it "would be w/o benefit to the living, and unjust to the dead. . . . It could do no good at this late date to review the various steps by which their conclusion was reached."[13]

Wharton never put his personal feelings in this matter into any writing which has survived. He clearly sympathized with Susanna, did nothing to offend her, acquiesced in the enrollment of Susan at Vassar, and helped to defray the cost of Rodman to continue his education at Yale. At the same time, both he and Hannah loyally supported President Magill. Hannah had a high regard for Magill's ability as a teacher. Wharton applauded his strong support of education in science. The two men got on well together and respected each other's position and accomplishments.

Still, a cold undercurrent existed. Wharton did not include Magill on the list of friends to whom he sometimes sent copies of his publications. Magill in his autobiography mentioned Wharton only twice, once in connection with a donation for the first science building and again for endowing a professorial chair. Magill did not include Wharton in naming members of the board with whom he took counsel; and in making a roster of fifteen of the most active managers he put down the name of Hannah Haydock but not that of Joseph Wharton.[14]

Hannah was throughout these early years of the college urging her brother to greater involvement. She belonged to the executive committee and the committee on instruction and sacrificed much by way of personal comfort to travel from New York City to attend to college business. Her letters to Joseph concerning Swarthmore were sometimes critical, at other times supplicating. "The College is so infantile, its managers so uneducated," she once complained. Again, she wrote, "I beg of thee to stand by the college and interest thyself more in its affairs. Thy presence is important when differences arise. Thee sees things clearly and is not afraid to speak."[15]

Wharton responded favorably to her pleas, although without any show of emotional involvement or ambition. He dutifully and variously served on the executive committee, the committee on instruction, the committee on trusts, endowments, and scholarships, and many special committees. A partial listing of these includes committees to "take into consideration the propriety of rearranging the price of tuition, also charges for the use of books"; to consider an appropriate title for the principal of the college; "to take into consideration the actual requirements of the College and take such steps as will tend to procure the means to meet them"; "to solicit subscriptions to purchase the West Farm"; "to make such use of the college buildings for the entertainment of guests during the summer vacation of 1876, as they may think proper, care being taken that no improper use be made of the property in any way"; to provide for the relocation of a road; to see to it that "a proper deed to the West Chester and Philadelphia R.R. Co. was prepared for the ground on which the new station house was erected"; to consider the proper salaries of officials of the college; to prepare an appeal for raising funds "to establish the College on proper footing"; "for the purchase of all Books for the Library as well as for the use of the College"; and to seek a new matron (the predecessor of the dean) to replace Caroline S. Wood.[16]

In 1878 the board of managers voted to have a meeting house.[17] Deborah suggested to her son that he build it, and he promptly complied. Arthur Beardsley, the college's professor of engineering, drew the plans. Joseph chose the site on a hillock above the college building, supervised the construction, and paid the bill, in all $4,200.

Other friends of the college looked to Wharton for contributions for another purpose. Swarthmore with its emphasis on the practical had easily responded to the drift favoring education in science and engineering. The Manager's Report for 1879, well written but not in Wharton's style, emphasized a need for strengthening scientific studies and demanded a new science building.[18] Who would supply the money? Eyes were turned toward the few members of the Society who were wealthy and involved in industrial and scientific pursuits. Wharton and Samuel Willetts, a merchant from New York who was president of the board of managers, responded. Each contributed fifty thousand dollars toward the erection and furnishing of a building especially designed to take care of the needs of Professor Beardsley, who was teaching in a section of a wooden gymnasium.[19]

The task of overseeing the project fell to Wharton. In those days most private colleges and universities did not have departments equipped to take charge of building projects. The donors undertook the work of construction. They built as they pleased, then turned the completed structures over to the institution. As a result, the buildings were often not well suited to educational needs. But with the science building (as with the meeting house) Wharton did not insist on his own ideas. He had Beardsley draw the plans. Here as elsewhere Wharton deferred to scientists whose judgment he trusted and resisted any temptation to an undue exercise of power in a project associated with the Society of Friends.

Then, as the science building was completed, Willetts died, and the position of president of the board of managers was vacant. The contribution of Wharton and his work in education at Swarthmore and in establishing the Wharton School were in the minds of many. Would he accept the presidency? He was sounded out, but demurred. For several years business and politics had made unusually heavy demands on him. He had the previous year complained of carbuncles, neuralgia, and other ailments. Friends and relatives had noted a decline in his usual good humor and patience. Henry C. Lea had invited him to a short vacation in his yacht, and when Wharton refused, had lectured him. "Men like you & me, I take it, have no fear of death, further than the mere animal instinct of self-preservation; but what is to be dreaded is, as Swift said, to die atop like a tree. You have one of those rugged physiques, that will not give out suddenly . . . but unless you take more care of yourself you run the risk of living on indefinitely after becoming incapable of usefulness, & this to a man like you would be the most galling of fates."[20]

Accordingly, Wharton had to be persuaded. Edward H. Ogden, of the committee entrusted with the task of selecting a president, wrote to him, "thee can go off of all the active committees & really have less to do in actual work that heretofore—thee knows thee has a *national* reputation & I always think the 'office should seek the individual' & here is a case."[21]

Reluctantly Wharton accepted. Hannah was overjoyed and treated his election almost as a personal victory. At the same time, she permanently retired from the board, citing age and home duties as making it "proper for me to give place to a younger woman."[22] As for Joseph, he made no attempt to use his considerable leverage in business and politics to increase the power of the presidency of the board. He absented himself from meetings whenever more important matters of business or public affairs interfered, although he dutifully represented the college at ceremonies, entertained its faculty, students, and friends, helped it with legal and other matters, and gave the commencement address which had become a traditional function of the board's president. He also retained his membership on the committee on trusts, scholarships, and endowments, which gave him considerable influence in managing the finances of the college.

His important accomplishments as president of the board were, indeed, few and unexciting. On most projects he worked with Isaac Clothier, the merchant, who became a close friend and sometime business associate. They promoted the idea of a general endowment fund and the establishment of a Stock Trust Association "for the purpose of aiding in keeping Swarthmore College under the control and management of persons in sympathy with the objects of its founders."[23] Both men also responded, as did others, to President Magill's call for endowed professorships—although they might have done as much if they had not been members of the board. The members agreed to put together a number of contributions to found a Magill Professorship in Mathematics and Astronomy. Clothier arranged to provide two thousand dollars each year for a Professorship of Latin Language and Literature. J. V. Williamson gave forty thousand dollars, the income to be used to finance a chair in Civil and Mechanical Engineering. Wharton provided forty thousand dollars worth (par value) of 6 percent first mortgage bonds of the San Antonio and Aransas Pass Railroad Company, the income of which was to be used to pay the salary of a Professor in History and Political Economy.[24]

The choice of Wharton for endowing a chair in social rather than natural science or engineering is indicative of the esteem in which members of the Society held him for founding the Wharton School. But whereas he insisted on supervising the course of studies of that school, he desisted from attempts to control the teaching of the Swarthmore Professor in History and Political Economy. In later life Wharton declared he had not even been consulted concerning the title to be given the endowed chair.[25] Yet he supported it in a time of financial distress. In the early nineties the San Antonio and Aransas Pass Railroad defaulted on its bonds. Officials at the college looked to Wharton to supply the money for the professor's salary. At first Wharton refused on the grounds that in endowing the chair his responsibility for the position had ended. Then, having made his point, he supplied the money anyway.[26]

Wharton never changed his attitude toward Swarthmore. Later he placidly deferred to Clothier and others when they decided without his knowledge on replacing Charles De Gormo, the fourth president of the college, with a sterner disciplinarian.[27] Wharton fully cooperated with the effort of Joseph Swain, the sixth president, in increasing the endowment. Although Wharton sometimes arranged for a guest speaker, such as Cyrus Elder, to bring the message of protectionism to the students, he repulsed purely on the grounds of expense an idea for a major addition of courses in business and social science, such as were taught at the Wharton School. To be sure, Wharton freely used his prerogative in giving the commencement address to express his personal views on a variety of subjects. But he made only one serious attempt to influence the curriculum. That concerned the teaching of religion. Old-time Hicksites opposed this on grounds that it contravened the emphasis of the Society on behavior. Wharton, supported by his daughter Joanna (who became a member of the board in 1894), argued to the effect that religion could and should be taught as part of the history of civilization, that is, as a social science. This view agreed with an emerging sentiment among national leaders in higher education and eventually prevailed at Swarthmore.[28]

3

Wharton's regard for Swarthmore was altogether different from his attitude toward the school at the University of Pennsylvania which bore his name. The difference in a way expressed two sorts of dependency. Swarthmore would have survived without him, although perhaps less well. The Wharton School would not have existed; and the University of Pennsylvania would probably not have been able to boast of pioneering in the field of business education. Accordingly, Wharton might be expected to have been more defensive and demanding vis-à-vis the Wharton School than Swarthmore.

But the contrasting attitudes have causes deeper than that represented only by ego involvement. The ideas of others conditioned Wharton's stance toward the two institutions. The Society of Friends sustained the ideals permeating Swarthmore. The Wharton School had no comparable body of supporters. In establishing it Wharton was promoting ideals which as yet lacked general acceptance. Part of his task was that of creating a favorable public. Validation of his ideals, as well as the success of the school, depended on this.

The country, he reasoned, needed a well-educated leadership such as businessmen might provide. Protective tariffs were not enough. The other pillar for supporting a strong nation was good management. No one, it seemed to him, was attending to this. Industrialists such as Andrew Carnegie considered a college education as unnecessary, even harmful, to success in business. Educators looked on businessmen as money grubbers. The latter attitude especially disturbed Wharton. He wrote in 1870 to Brush, "There is something very sad to my mind in the spectacle of New England colleges which do so very much on the one hand to fit our Youth for higher places of thought and action, teaching on the other hand that the nation owes nothing to that class alone, of her numerous classes of pioneers, who break the ground for new industries which are to afford direct sustenance to many of her future citizens and greater facilities and independence to all the rest."[29] Wharton wrote in the indenture for the school that, as a result of this neglect, an inheritance of young men possessing "wealth, keenness of intellect, and latent power of command or organization" was unused. "No country can afford to have this inherited wealth and capacity wasted for want of that fundamental knowledge which would enable the possessors to employ them with advantage to themselves and to the community. . . . Nor can any country long afford to have its laws made and its government administered by men who lack such training as would suffice to rid their minds of fallacies and qualify them for the solution of the social problems incident to our civilization."

Wharton's reasoning continued: Even if educational leaders changed their attitudes toward businessmen, the problem was still not solved. The country also needed an educational package different from anything which had as yet existed. Training by apprenticeship was slow, incomplete, and inefficient. Formal education in the classics was unsuitable. The leaders of tomorrow would need a knowledge of the sciences of society, such as were being promoted by Carey and his friends; of business law; and of advanced techniques of banking, bookkeeping, and related skills. And so, he wrote in the indenture, there should be a dean and professors variously specialized in accounting; money and currency; taxation; industry, commerce, and transportation; and elementary and mercantile law. In addition, students should learn Latin, German, French, mathematics, geography, history, "and other branches of an ordinary good education."

Who might teach and administer? Because higher education had few or no teachers for many of the subjects, they would have to come from outside the traditional fields. This was as true for courses in public affairs, economics, and American history as for those in law and accounting. The social sciences, like the natural sciences, had been born and nurtured beyond the ivy-covered walls. The great names in social science were not those of professors but of journalists or free-lance scholar-writers subsisting on incomes from other sorts of occupation, men such as J. S. Mill, Auguste Comte, and Herbert Spencer. Even in Philadelphia, where support for the social sciences was strong, the professorial class enjoyed a minority representation within Carey's circle. The most prominent and prolific scholars, men like Carey himself and Lea, were not academicians.

In sum, Wharton found no one within the academic community on whom to rely in carrying out his plan. This explains why in the indenture he not only described in detail the principles for guiding the course of study but also dealt with matters of instruction and administration which ordinarily would be left to the faculty or the trustees. The dean, he wrote, "should, besides taking such part as may be found expedient in the routine instruction of the various classes, give stated and formal lectures, constituting a part of the instruction of the graduating class, and should in each year produce for publication a treatise upon some topic of current public interest connected with the lines of study pursued in the School, which treatises should be of such nature as to bring reputation to the School and to possess permanent value as a series." Wharton prescribed that professors were not to use the lecture method, which prevailed in Germany, for this encouraged lazy habits of thought. The course of study was to occupy the last three years of the normal four-year period. "Athletic exercises within moderate limits should be encouraged, as tending to vigor, self-reliance, and freedom of gesture." Each student should have to write a thesis "upon some topic germane to the instruction of the school" as a requirement for graduation. This thesis should be "lucid, terse, and sincere, showing mastery of the subject, with appropriate conclusions reached." As an incentive to students to write good theses he added, "For the best thesis, and also for the best general proficiency in the studies taught in the School, should be given annually a gold medal weighing about one ounce, to be called respectively 'Founder's Thesis Medal,' and 'Founder's Proficiency Medal,' the same to be awarded by the Dean and instructors in council." All professors, Wharton indicated, were to teach business ethics. He emphasized the puritan virtues of honesty, industry, thrift, and legality and a traditional Quaker concern for solvency.

He asked that the new school be called the Wharton School of Finance and Economy "to commemorate a family name which has been honorably borne in this community since the foundation of the city."

The plan was elitist. The democratic sentiment which pervaded Swarthmore and Wharton's participation in Swarthmore's affairs was entirely lacking. He regarded science as a discipline capable of mastery by a few; and he concluded, possibly by way of generalizing from his own situation and that of many of his friends, that a person who had the intelligence to succeed in business could also master the discipline of science. Thus, he reasoned, his plan was realistic: The school would take from society the talented few with ambition for business and provide them with the education necessary to become leaders in public as well as private affairs. A strong technocratic spirit, associated in Europe with the thought of the radical French utopian Saint-Simon, animated Wharton's educational philosophy.

And the plan *was* radical, whether for America or Europe. The institution which came the closest to what Wharton had in mind was that of the German commercial school. Apart from this, the nearest counterparts were the relatively new scientific schools at Harvard, Yale, and the University of Pennsylvania and, perhaps, a school of political science which was emerging from the planning stage at Columbia University.

Wharton laid his plan before the trustees of the University of Pennsylvania in the summer of 1880. He probably thought of no other place as a home for the new school. Several members of the staff of *The Penn Monthly* taught there. His friend John Welsh, wealthy manufacturer and fellow

Careyite, was influential in university affairs. Wharton Barker had recently become one of the trustees. Early in 1881 a dynamic new provost named William Pepper took control. A scientist and professor in the medical school, Pepper was eager to improve standards and bring higher education into closer alignment with societal needs. He liked and accepted the plan. Wharton gave one hundred thousand dollars in the form of securities as was his custom: five hundred shares of Delaware and Bound Brook Railroad Company stock valued at $110 and five hundred shares of Schuylkill Navigation Company mortgage bonds (1907) at $90. He established these as a trust for the uses elaborated in the indenture and reserved a right to revoke the gift in the event that the school departed from the scheme for the support of which the grant was made.[30]

The Wharton School opened that fall with thirteen students. A man was hired to teach mercantile practice (basic accounting and business law). Various university professors supplied other instruction. Robert Ellis Thompson provided the heart of the curriculum with a course in economics.

Wharton's work in establishing the school did not stop when he turned control over to the university. He actively publicized the school and received several commendations which undoubtedly immensely gratified him. Wayne MacVeagh, the attorney general of the United States, responded with congratulations and an observation that he was sure Wharton would supplement the gift from time to time. Rowland Hazard, Philadelphia manufacturer who was a fellow of Brown University, enthusiastically sent congratulations.[31] But the response of greatest interest came from W. Stanley Jevons, logician, philosopher of science, and one of Britain's most noted economists. Jevons had recently resigned as professor of political economy at the University of London. He praised Wharton's deed and portentously signaled several weaknesses in the plan arising from Wharton's inexperience with educational matters:

> I have repeatedly read the prospectus of your proposed Economic School with much interest and admiration of the wisdom & liberality which prompts it. I can easily imagine that it is only the beginning of a movement which in another generation or at the most another century will be as well recognized a necessity as railroads & blast furnaces. I have often regretted, if not wondered at the small attention which can in this country be given to the *viva voce* teaching of economics & social philosophy. In the London University College my professional work never consisted in giving more than 40 lectures in the year to one class of at most 30 young men and women. My predecessors Cairnes, Courtney, & others, gave fewer lectures. There is hardly any college or university in the United Kingdom where economic studies are more flourishing, with the possible exception of Edinburgh.
>
> It is with great pleasure then that I hear of the rise in Philadelphia of a different state of things. I do not think I have any critical remarks of

importance to make in your scheme. If anything I should say it is rather too complete & full; & insufficient prominence is given to the general principles of economics. I fancy it is rather hard on the Dean or Principal to require him to produce an original work *every year* & submit it for approval, etc.! The Whately professors at Oxford such as Senior, Rickards, etc. were required by the terms of endowment to publish lectures every year, but the result is a series of rather scrappy pamphlets. I should prefer to see it put on some such footing as this—"The Dean shall be appointed for a period of (say 3 or 5 or 7 years) and shall not be reappointed unless he shall in the opinion of the electors have published original and important contributions to the literature of political economy."[32]

Jevons was right. The position of dean remained vacant and the qualifications desired for the head of the school were never enforced. The observation that the plan was "too complete and full" was proved correct when, a few years later, the school obtained the energetic and capable leadership for which Wharton was seeking. The new leaders inevitably had some ideas which differed from his and possessed an experience with faculty and students which he lacked.

The changes began in 1883 when Pepper hired Alfred S. Bolles, Philadelphia lawyer, judge, author, and sometime editor of *Banker's Magazine* as professor of mercantile law and head of the school. Bolles in turn secured John Bach McMaster as professor of American history and Edmund J. James for a chair in public finance and administration. McMaster had been teaching mathematics at Princeton. He wrote history in his spare time and had just published the first volume of *History of the People of the United States*. James had been educated at Northwestern and Harvard and had then gone to Halle, Germany, where he studied social science under Johannes Conrad. Thompson, whose approach was also historical, was promoted to the endowed John Welsh Professorship of History and English Literature.

McMaster and James quickly became mainstays of the school. McMaster's course in American history was at the time a questionable innovation, but it rapidly became popular with the students. It was a two year course and vied with economics for the position of being the core of the curriculum. James introduced the German Ph.D. degree, the lecture, and the seminar into the institutional structure of the university. With Wharton's support he traveled to Germany to study commercial education there. Upon his return he became the effective head of the school. He hired Simon Patten to teach economics and Joseph French Johnson to instruct in journalism and to conduct a research program for seniors. Both men were Americans who had studied at Halle. As time went on James added several others to the staff to teach methods, political administration, and transportation. In 1886 he published *Schools of Political and Social Science*. He was socially inclined and did much to publicize the Wharton School among leaders in business and industry. His speech before the American Bankers Association in 1890 became a classic statement of the aims, course of study, and history of the school.[33]

Wharton reluctantly accepted these departures from his plan: the two-year course of study instead of three; the refusal to appoint a dean; the emphasis on American history in addition to economics; the use of the lecture method; and the teaching of journalism, a subject for which he had little respect. He was too closely associated with the struggling new school to harm its chances for success by fighting with its leaders. It needed all the support he could give, and he faithfully responded. He entertained faculty and students in his home and defended the school against charges that it accepted an indifferent quality of student and provided a substandard course of instruction. He wrote on one occasion to the editor of *The Evening Post*, "That school aims to teach branches which are not included in the curriculum of other institutions of learning, and it therefore could not possibly find, as ordinary schools can, ready-made teachers and text-books, nor instantly convince a considerable number of young men and their parents that knowledge of accounting, banking, the care of property, national economy, and so on, are important parts of a reasonable modern education."[34]

The early success of the school was largely the work of James, who mediated between the dogmatism of Wharton and educational realities. He gained the confidence of Wharton and, having that, he and the faculty conducted the school pretty much as they pleased. James remained the leading figure in the Wharton School until 1896, when he left to take a position at the University of Chicago. Shortly thereafter he became president of Northwestern University and after a brief sojourn at Northwestern accepted the presidency of the University of Illinois. Patten became the head man at Wharton. Patten was an excellent administrator and developed into a distinguished economist. Although he never won the confidence of Wharton as James had done, their relationship was cordial. Patten and the faculty substantially improved the quality of the students and instruction. Faculty and students courteously listened to Wharton's advice, included him in various activities, and flattered him by requests to speak, by displaying his portrait, and by putting his image on the medals given to the top students.

Wharton accepted these little attentions with pleasure, although they did not swerve him from his views on educational matters. In old age he was still complaining of certain practices, such as a tendency of the faculty to over-emphasize courses in the liberal arts and to depreciate the more "practical" courses in "the science of accounting and the art of bookkeeping." He recommended that the school train persons for the consular and diplomatic services and complained when he found out that "this has not yet been done nor even commenced." On several occasions he reminded the administration of the stipulation in his grants that, if the university failed to spend the proceeds for the purposes therein defined, the principal would revert to himself or his heirs. "I have been led to doubt by several occurrences whether it is expedient for the connection between the University and the Wharton School of Finance and Economy to continue," he wrote in 1902. "This school is apparently not favored by at least some of the controlling powers of the University, and I am inclined to refer to that feature of the deed of gift, which looks towards the severance of that connection in certain contingencies."[35]

Such threats were not idly made. Wharton was not the sort of person to bluster. He was angry when he made them and probably had some vague idea of carrying them out. Possibly he was checked by his pride, which had insisted on the name "Wharton" for the project. This was, after all, the *Wharton* School! He could not easily repudiate anything bearing the name. He stemmed his anger and temporized. When the faculty departed from the strict commitment to protectionism he allowed himself to be persuaded by an argument that teachers could not be blatantly partisan and wrote to Swank that the students were being presented with both sides of the tariff question "in order that they may not be deceived by the shallow arguments of the free traders."[36] Appeals for money immediately elicited resistance accompanied by a recollection of grievances; but both disappeared with the passage of time. On one occasion the provost sent him information that the expenses of the school were exceeding its income and asked for "advice." Wharton understood the veiled appeal for money and curtly replied that under the circumstances the administration had but two choices. It could cut expenses or make up the deficit from university funds. Both, he admitted, were unpleasant prospects, but "such is life." Yet on another occasion he paid a deficit of $2,581.82.[37]

Wharton continued to provide money for expansion. In 1893 he donated seventy-five thousand dollars worth of San Antonio and Aransas Pass Railroad Company 4 percent first mortgage bonds. Nine years later he gave $261,575 worth of securities to bring the total endowment of the school up to five hundred thousand dollars. By means of this gift he accomplished a change in name from Wharton School of Finance and Economy to Wharton School of Finance and Commerce and extracted a promise from the trustees that, as soon as the school should have a separate building, they would provide it with a dean as they did for the schools of law and medicine. He then began planning for the building, but encountered labor troubles and postponed the project indefinitely.[38]

The hoped-for reorganization of the school came about anyway. In 1904 the Wharton School attained a semi-independent status within the university with a director and faculty of its own. The increasing popularity of education in business was carrying it forward. The school became a model for similar departments in other universities and colleges. By 1908 the Wharton School had four hundred and twenty students and was still growing.[39] It had by then long since passed the stage at which the founder could help it with educational advice.

In effect, Wharton had stopped giving it. Although the indenture of 1902, accompanying his last major gift, restated ideas elaborated in the original deed, including the charge of teaching protectionism, he did not follow this with anything resembling censorship of the course of study. His work as an educator in the domain of business and social science had dwindled to almost nothing.

Still, the spirit of a teacher remained and at times burst forth. One such eruption belongs to the year 1896. A student named Bernheimer, recipient of one of the medals for excellence, had written Wharton complaining that his name had been misspelled on the engraving. Wharton replied:

> Your note of the 29th acknowledging receipt of the Wharton School medal which you had won by superior diligence is received, and I was annoyed to find that the name engraved on the medal is not correctly your name.
>
> As it stands on the medal it is exactly that which Mr. [George S.] Fullerton [the vice provost] furnished to me: It seemed rather unusual but, as he had taken care to make it perfectly distinct, nothing could be done but follow his directions.
>
> Byron said that military glory consisted in being killed in battle and having your name wrongly spelled in the Gazette. The civic eminence which you are on the way to attain appears to entail upon you only one of those penalties.[40]

The matter came to the attention of Fullerton, who discreetly inquired of Wharton the reason for his acerbity. Wharton replied that he was irked that "the most eminent scholar of the Finance School could send out so careless a note as the one in question," and then lectured the vice provost, "Among the many signs by which men are judged is the style of their casual writings such as every day letters or notes, and no one who aims to become useful or important in his community can at all afford to appear slovenly in this respect.

"You have perhaps observed that Harvard University has lately taken a decided stand in requiring good command of the English language as a condition of admission: a condition which all universities and colleges must shortly insist on."[41]

On another occasion, in 1905, Wharton discovered a saying of Confucius which he thought should have more general circulation. He wrote to the person in the Chinese Legation in Washington who had supplied it, "The copy you kindly had made for me of that motto of Confucius, which signifies that 'The Scholar (or Student) who consults his ease, is not worthy to be called Scholar (or Student),' was duly received by Prof. Rowe and has now been carefully framed. . . . It will now be hung in a conspicuous place in the Wharton School, and I hope will prove useful to the students there."[42]

12

The Whartons in the Gilded Age

By the beginning of the 1880s Wharton had entered the dream world of ambitious American youth, the land of millionaires. It was a country of denser habitation than had existed before the depression years of the seventies. Its most opulent citizens included men of genius such as Carnegie, Rockefeller, Vanderbilt, and Morgan. These and a few others were within the next ten years to rule gigantic empires and amass truly colossal fortunes, such as would screen from public view the smaller principalities and the fewer millions of Wharton and many others. But whatever the size of the estate, the citizens of this materialistic Beulah Land shared opinions concerning individualism, private property, big business, protective tariffs, sound money, labor unions, and the right of the rich to rule. True, they inconsistently called these ideals into question by supporting a democratic and constitutional government which permitted the rise and progress of an opposition. Government was still a necessary adjunct to the competition which sometimes divided them. Joseph Wharton saw the cleavage in the tendency of Wharton Barker, Lea, and other Independent Republicans to pull away from the organization controlled by Simon Cameron, Matt Quay, and Boies Penrose. He experienced it too in the vanishing of Carey's influence from among the aristocracy of Philadelphia. Wharton had tried and failed to raise money for a statue to commemorate the recently deceased economist.[1] Carey's opposition to monopoly and his championing of justice for farmer and worker had made him by 1880 more acceptable to a nascent Populism than to big business. Lines for the great economic and political battles of the Cleveland, McKinley, and Roosevelt administrations were swiftly being drawn.

The great fortunes rested upon impressive industrial foundations. The last of the Indian wars was fought in the eighties; the entire country was now available for settlement. Immigrants from northern Europe augmented the ranks of settlers. Railroads provided the means of travel. The New York Central, Pennsylvania, Baltimore and Ohio, Northern Pacific, and Southern Pacific were only a few among literally dozens of great lines whose tracks and equipment united the country and made possible the founding of cities and factories and the opening of lands for farming, grazing, and lumbering. Telephone, telegraph, electric light, the bicycle, photography, the phonograph, the linotype, Portland cement, steam boilers, and dozens of other things were invented or improved and quickly put to use. Mines and quarries supplied material in superabundance. Money and talent—still partly from Europe, although Europe's contribution was less important now than formerly—provided the means.

It was too much too soon for aristocratic tastes to absorb. The excess spilled over into useless products, artificial manners, unnatural styles, political waste. Middle classes aped the rich; the poor looked on in envy. The phrase *gilded age* began to be heard to describe the manner of life of the times. The simplicity of Puritan and Quaker discipline became anachronistic. Hannah Haydock rejoiced to see the world advancing in "mental and spiritual atmosphere." That was a reflection of her happiness more than a sober judgment. It was in fact a world whose heart had become a dollar sign, whose ambition was to get rich, and whose outward appearance betrayed the moral aridity associated with greed.

Wharton could not help but be affected by the caricatures of good living which pervaded work and play in the land of millionaires. With progress and prosperity came a democratic demand for conformity. Gone were the days when a John Price Wetherill might, as cousin Sydney George Fisher had suggested, live as a gentleman and a pig. Part of what had once been private was now exposed to public view and censure. A millionaire had to live as his neighbors expected him to do, thereby becoming respectable, as a condition for doing business. A son of Deborah and William Wharton could not hope for special treatment from a society which had largely forgotten the difference between Hicksite and Orthodox and was indeed far more interested in reading about Quakers than willing to practice their ideals.

How did he adjust?

1

In part adjustment came easily and naturally. Quakers were not hostile to wealth and could readily agree with Russell H. Conwell (then living in Philadelphia) in his *Acres of Diamonds* lectures that "the love of money and not money is the root of all evil." Their rich eighteenth-century merchant forebears in Philadelphia, Newport, the West Indies, and London had lived according to their station while insisting on plainness in speech and fashion. Among them, the Fishers and the Whartons had maintained Cliffs and Bellevue as country estates in addition to large and comfortable town houses. Wealthy Quakers had always regarded carriages, servants, summer vacations, libraries, medical care, well-made clothes, and good food as necessaries for those upon whom rested obligations to educate or direct the work and play of the multitude. This was the heritage of Joseph and Anna, and it matched them as perfectly as a somber but finely stitched suit of brown cloth had fitted "Crazy Billy" Wharton.

Nor did Joseph and Anna depart from the Quaker injunction to use their aristocratic privileges selflessly and without ostentation. Their natures as well as their tradition supported preferences for simplicity of adornment and economy in the expenditure of energy. Anna, in spite of the greater liberality of her parents by comparison with the Whartons, became more reserved in these respects than did Joseph. Ever since the winds of business had destroyed her marital illusions she had regarded life as a series of daily duties to be cheerfully performed without afterthought or much concern for the future. Planning was for her husband to do. She would be as Penelope to Ulysses. She filled her days with managing the household and the domestic servants; caring for children and, in time, grandchildren; visiting with or writing letters to aunts, uncles, cousins, and other members of the extended families; and practicing private charities. A strong constitution gave her an endurance easily equal to the vigor which her husband wanted her to have, and which she lacked. She was also fairly capable in business, as management of properties inherited from her parents demonstrated; but mostly she gladly put the responsibility for business matters on Joseph. She preferred the quietness of home and the company of friends and relatives. She dressed neatly and plainly, choosing black over bright colors except for weddings and other festive occasions, when a cheeful maroon might be allowed. Although she held back from some of the luxuries on which Joseph insisted, she had a few of her own, such as a carriage when vacationing in Newport. She never opposed Joseph to a point of rebellion in anything except the eating of onions—and this had nothing to do with being either rich or Hicksite.

She had no particular reason to disagree with Joseph when he proposed giving up the Twelfth Street home and building a splendid mansion on the site of their summer place, Brookside. She liked Twelfth Street, had reared the children there, and found it in almost all ways satisfactory. President Hayes had consented to visit her husband at Twelfth Street. Why could not Blaine, Professor James, Drexel, Carnegie, and the rest be satisfied with being entertained in a modest domicile? She accepted on faith Joseph's assertion of a need for a more luxurious establishment to match his national stature in business and politics. He knew best in these things, and the children were following—indeed, going beyond—him in eagerness to accept new styles and fashions. If change there must be, no better place existed than Brookside. It was within the orbit of the Hicksite communities of both Germantown and Philadelphia. Oak Hill was less than a mile away. Charles and Mary lived within walking distance on the Old York Road in an eighteenth-century house once inhabited by the painter Russell Smith and now named Birdwood. Charles's and Mary's son, J. S. Lovering Wharton, had built a dwelling between, and adjoining, Charles's and Joseph's properties.[2]

At Brookside Anna would be close to her sister and father, who needed care. Ever since her mother had died in 1876, Joseph S. Lovering, now over eighty years of age, had been living alone in Oak Hill, crippled by rheumatism and almost completely deaf.

In building the new home Wharton kept to a plan combining luxury with architectural simplicity. The more than sixty-three acres of rolling ground were left in a natural state, excepting what was necessary for walks, drive, gardens, a lodge for the coachman and his family, and several other outbuildings. A stream was diverted to fill a large pond for swimming in summer and skating in winter. The house was built of sandstone quarried on the property. At ground level were a porte cochere and a piazza. Above these the house rose solidly for four stories and ended in a tower, Wharton's only major concession to architectural extravagance. From the top of the tower a person could look over trees, hills, and river into New Jersey. The first floor contained a large and imposing front entrance, hallway, staircase, parlor, and dining room, all exhibiting much marble and polished woodwork and intended almost exclusively for the use of guests, as were many of the bedrooms on the second and third floors. The family normally inhabited quarters which were more modest, albeit luxurious by Twelfth Street standards. They ate most of their meals in a breakfast room adjoining the kitchen and gathered for evenings in a well-stocked library. Here and there were touches reflecting the special interests of Joseph. A bust of Garfield adorned his study. The fourth floor contained a gymnasium with chest machines, rings, a trapeze, Indian clubs, and other instruments of exercise. Pure malleable nickel was the material of which hinges, door knobs, ornamental parts of locks, and some other hardware were made.[3]

Wharton named the dwelling Ontalauna, an Indian word meaning "Little Branch." The house was sufficiently completed for family and servants to move by early June 1881. His daughter Mary was then staying at the Batsto mansion for her health with Mrs. McClure. Wharton wrote describing the transfer:

> Dear Polly Dolly Adelina Amelia Anna Malone,
> We moved out yesterday to the new house at Branchtown, which Joey still wants to have called Ravenstonedale, and we are not particularly comfortable. . . . Mother had done what she could toward getting a little order in a few places, but there was no bedding for our room—only a bedstead with two slats in the bottom. Joey [age 22] sat on a sofa in the hall singing a few remarkably clear notes. Ann [age 12] poked her nose into things generally, showing concern for the common welfare at all points. Letty [a servant] was practical & busy, Grace solemn and staid, Eliza rather bewildered but full of good will.
> As for the black cat, that "pure animal" as Ann expressed it, was in a miserable state of uneasiness, and wandered into the various rooms quite lost and dazed under and over the furniture. This morning it was on the

breakfast table, and I think tried to eat the canary bird, but in vain.

Well, the girls [that is the servants] were put by Mamma into one of the frescoed rooms on the third floor where, between the unaccustomed grandeur and the constant roar of the water pumped into the great iron tank, they slept but little all night. Joey and Ann got along very well and so did Mamma, but for my part I felt as if the spongy mattress, high in the middle, was constantly watching for a chance to toss me out on the floor. Still we all survived and had an appetite for breakfast.[4]

Wharton employed a small community of servants to care for the new house and grounds. The domestic staff included at least four women over whom Anna had complete control. Wharton's books for 1890 show regular monthly payments ranging from $30 to $50.28 respectively for seven men. One of these, Patrick Clarke, was for decades a coachman and personal attendant to Wharton.

Ontalauna well served the purpose of providing hospitality for Wharton's business and political associates. His daughter Joanna wrote in retrospect:

My father's interesting guests have been numerous and of many different shades of color and belief, from our American Statesmen and titled Englishmen to the dark-skinned Brahmin, the gentlemanly Parsee, a follower of Zoroaster, and the stately Chinese. . . . There is tall, white-haired, dignified Senator Morrill; Mr. Andrew Carnegie, differing greatly from the former, being rather short of stature and with sharp businesslike ways and ever ready conversation; James G. Blaine; Benjamin Harrison; Sir Lothian Bell; Professor Langley, too, the great astronomer, and President of the Smithsonian Institution, his courtly manners and elegant appearance suggesting a past generation.[5]

The eclipse of Brookside by Ontalauna spurred thought concerning a summer home on a scale to match the elegance of the new mansion. Where was it to be? In the country or at the shore? Anna preferred sea breezes and the expanse of ocean. Joseph, too, liked these as well as swimming and boating, water sports at which he had excelled during his youthful days at Bellevue, with the Schuylkill nearby. Sometimes he and Anna spent a few weeks during the summer at Atlantic City or Cape May or visiting Hetty and Ben Smith and other relatives at Newport. As early as 1863 he had bid for a property at Newport, which he regarded as an investment as well as a site for a summer home, only to see it knocked down to Governor Sprague of Rhode Island and his brothers.[6]

By 1881 Joseph was not regretting this loss. Deficiencies had appeared in the fashionable beachside resorts of both New Jersey and Rhode Island, and especially at Newport. There, a noisy crowd of newly rich from New York and Boston was moving in, buying up choice lots, and encouraging precisely the sort of social life he and Anna sought to avoid. New Jersey was as bad, although in a different way. In 1880, following a vacation at Cape May, he wrote to his mother, "The monotonous Jersey land, the wooden caravansaries [sic], the flat and paltry back country, the greater warmth and dampness all contrast most unfavorably with the clear sea green breaking upon the rocks, the lovely outline of promontories and bays, the rich interior and refreshing climate of Newport. Besides there are so many vulgar looking people in Jersey, and so few that we know or care to know; the fat man in tight clothes with a belt around his paunch, and the lean undesirable female in baggy dress are seen bathing on all the beaches."[7]

He had for years been inquiring concerning another place, which might possibly be ideal. This was an island some seven miles long in the middle of Narragansett Bay west of Newport called Conanicut. It was almost two islands, a large one joined by means of a short neck of sand and gravel to a narrow strip of land resembling a tail, which caused residents to refer to it as Beaver Tail. Facing Newport was the village of Jamestown, incorporated in 1678, and south of that along the shore a line of rocks called The Dumplings. An article in *Harper's* for August 1874 described these: "The Dumplings, on Conanicut Island, furnish an excellent panoramic view of Newport. . . . They lie not far from the entrance of the harbor; are diademed with the ruins of an old fort [Fort Browne], or martello tower; are not only picturesque in themselves, but reveal the picturesque wherever the eye can reach. Not to visit the Dumplings is like going to Naples without climbing Vesuvius, or doing Switzerland and avoiding Zermatt."

Narragansett Indians had sold Conanicut to the whites in 1656 for one hundred English pounds in wampum and peage. Followers of Roger Williams and William Coddington had settled there. They and their descendants had farmed part of the island. A road ran from Jamestown across the neck and south over Beaver Tail to a lighthouse.[8] No roads as yet penetrated the wilderness of the Dumplings at the southern tip of the main part of the island.

Wharton had become interested in the rocky terrain of the Dumplings as early as 1875. A map of the island shows several tracts marked and scribbled over with his handwriting and accompanied by the draft of a letter to Daniel Watson, agent, dated 17 August 1875. The tracts which Wharton marked included High Hill on West Cove, opposite Fort Browne, and Cliffs on the southern tip of the main island. Still, he made no purchase. He had Brookside. By the time Ontalauna was completed several other Friends were seriously considering building on Conanicut. Among them were Charles Wharton and Isaac Clothier. The Quaker painter of seascapes, William T. Richards (father of the future Harvard scientist), had just erected a house called Gray Cliff near the Dumplings. If Wharton would take an initiative, other Friends might follow; a regular Hicksite community could come into being, a haven of loveliness, protected by sea and legal land titles against invasion from Newport socialites and tourists.

That is what happened. Toward the end of 1881 Wharton negotiated with the Ocean Highlands Company for thirty acres including the southern headland. He paid the company twenty-five thousand dollars for the property.[9] He called the new possession Marbella, meaning "beautiful sea." Others sometimes referred to it as Horsehead, from a peculiar rock formation along the shore. Almost immediately he began building. When the mansion was completed it had a tower and thirty-six rooms, including fourteen bedrooms and eight baths. Like Ontalauna, it had elegance but little of the gingerbread so characteristic of the times. A motto, "Pax Vobiscum," adorned the main entrance. A set of sixty-three steps led down the cliff to a cove for swimming and launching boats. Servants' quarters, stables, and so forth, occupied a separate structure from which a path led to another cove reserved for their enjoyment.[10]

Marbella was several years a-building, but by the summer of 1884 it was sufficiently completed to be occupied. It immediately became a rallying point for many members of the extended family. A caretaker—in 1890 and later Charles Soule—lived there the year round. In May and June he prepared the place for occupancy, making such repairs and alterations as Anna and Joseph wanted. About the first of July, when the waters of the bay had warmed and a blanket of summer air lay across the land, the family would arrive with servants and baggage for a stay of three months. Swimming, fishing, sailing, and lawn tennis were the principal sports. Visitors would come and go, including friends, relatives, and a parade of scientists, steel magnates, and businessmen and their wives.

From then until the end of his life Wharton rarely missed spending most of July, August, and September at Marbella. He would break up his vacation there with several trips to Philadelphia, New York, or other places on business. The assistant in his Philadelphia office, Wenner, wrote almost daily concerning important matters. Only absolutely necessary affairs had priority. This was a time for fun, for enjoying the vigor which he carried with him from youth through middle into old age. First days saw the family and other Friends gathered in the house of Isaac Clothier, who led the meeting. Or Wharton led it when Clothier was absent. Newport, with assorted relatives, tennis tournaments, regattas, and other amusements, was a short ferry ride away. Wharton could readily agree with the words of Clothier, "Because we have good reason to believe in the life here, our interest even our affections cling around this—our enchanted—island and we leave it each season with more and more regret."[11]

In building Marbella Wharton accomplished more than he knew. He had thought of a permanent vacation spot for the family to which he could also bring associates in business and public affairs. In addition he helped to restore his family to their Newport roots in the Fishers, Redwoods, and Rodmans. Marbella became a bridge to a renewing of ties with the first Quaker capital of the New World. The land on which it stood emerged as a homeland for members of the family and their descendants. Marbella and several other properties on Conanicut Island remained standing long after urban developments had swallowed and destroyed Ontalauna, Oak Hill, and other of the old homes in and near Germantown.

2

Anna and Joseph steered between Hicksite simplicity and worldy ambition in raising their three daughters. The girls were early taught proper behavior and became acquainted with Quaker literature, as a diary begun by Anna in her seventeenth year amply records. They visited within a circle of aunts, uncles, and cousins, most of whom were members of the Society, and were not allowed to attend the dinners and parties given by their parents for business associates and celebrities until they had gained their majority. All were physically strong and highly intelligent and developed a good head for business. Joanna and Anna showed talent in art, music, and literature. Private schools and tutors provided the girls with the best available education. Their mother saw to it that they attended dancing school and learned the principles of good manners and good taste in dress and conduct.

The family lived as a unit. This was an age in which wealthy and respectable parents might without censure leave much of the upbringing of children to governesses. A father might seldom see his children. That was not Joseph's way. He spent much time with his daughters, helped with their education, taught them games, shared in their play and sports. As they grew older he made companions of them. Joanna and Anna especially adored him. Mary, the intermediate in age, was also irresistibly drawn to him but emotionally leaned more toward her mother—a "mother girl," Anna called her.[12]

Joanna became twenty-three later in the year in which the family moved to Ontalauna. She easily entered upon the round of social duties and delights which her family's status opened to her. "Joey," Anna wrote in her diary, "is the smallest of the daughters, and very good looking. She tries to make herself agreeable to almost everyone she knows, and she is very fond of company. She is very energetic, and likes to see others so likewise. She approves of sociability highly." Joanna liked stylish clothes and good jewelry. She preferred intellectual pleasures, might be frequently seen at the opera or the Academy of Fine Arts, and sought out intelligent male and female companions.[13] She was in no hurry to get married. When the time came, she chose a member of the Society, J. Bertram Lippincott, youngest son of one of her father's close friends, Joshua Lippincott. The Lippincotts lived fashionably on Rittenhouse Square. Joshua had founded, nurtured, and sustained the firm of J. B. Lippincott and Company as one of the foremost publishing houses of America. He had been associated with Wharton in many ventures such as the Saucon Iron Company, the Bethlehem Iron Company, the Philadelphia and Reading Railroad, the Farmers and Mechanics Bank, and Swarthmore College and was also a trustee of the University of Pennsylvania. Bertram spent a year at the university, then entered his father's publishing house and by the time of the engagement was a partner in the company.

After an engagement of a year, for the times a normal period of waiting, the wedding of Joanna and Bertram took place in May of 1887 at Ontalauna. It was a gala affair, not at all resembling the simple meeting at which Deborah Fisher and William Wharton had pledged themselves to one another. But Joanna insisted on a fashionable wedding, and Anna and Joseph approved. Even the traditionalist Hannah Haydock accepted the transformation of a Hicksite ceremony into a social event. "The sunlight on the lawn and moonlight through the trees were so beautiful," she wrote. "We shall all of us remember how the bride and groom drove off with the full moon lighting their way."[14]

Joseph Lovering had died shortly after the move into Ontalauna, and Joseph Wharton had purchased Oak Hill from his estate. He now gave the property to Joanna as a wedding present.[15] It became the home of Bertram and Joanna for many years. Twenty-one months after the marriage Joseph and Anna became grandparents. Their grandchild was a boy, appropriately named Joseph Wharton Lippincott. The Lippincotts were never far from Joseph and Anna, whether at Oak Hill or on Conanicut Island. There Bertram built a house called Meeresblick on Beaver Tail, within sight of the tower of Marbella.

Mary found the decade of the eighties painful. As a baby she had been restless—hence the nickname which Joseph gave her: Poll, an abbreviation of pollywog. At the age of nineteen Mary suffered a nervous breakdown which impaired her health. Wharton took her to Batsto, and in the quiet and fresh air of the pinelands she began to recover. The next year she vacationed at Nantucket. On one occasion Wharton wrote concerning his favorite theme of vigorous activity as the best medicine: "It is time for thee to quit dosing. As Shakespeare makes one of his characters say, 'Throw physic to the dogs.'" There followed a lecture on the danger of taking pills.[16] In fact, Mary liked sports and being out of doors possibly more than did his other two daughters. Wrote Anna, "She approves highly of bathing, fresh air, and exercise, and sits out of doors almost every single day, in rain, wind or fog. She has decided opinions on duty, and expects to carry them out, even if they are against the ways of the world, and the opinions of her friends. She is broad and strong, and has charming brown hair and a good face."[17]

Mary never completely recovered from the effects of the breakdown. She remained unmarried and lived with her parents, although after the birth of the Lippincotts' second child, Marianna, in 1890, she spent considerable time at Oak Hill. In later years she became a beloved Aunt Polly to nieces and nephews.

Anna fell short of her sisters in prettiness and regularity of features and was conscious of being less attractive. At the beginning of her diary she wrote:

> I was seventeen years old the 15th last July. I am five feet & ten inches in height . . . and I weigh about 131 pounds. I am thin, and feel awkward sometimes among girls who are short and plump. My ideal is a large and strong woman, with fine proportions, and kindness and love for everyone beaming from her face. A woman who is above nonsense and trashiness, but is *not* above helping her meanest sister, and who is not prejudiced, but does not scorn those who are. Who is running over with sympathy, and who neither puts herself forward nor holds herself back, but does the right thing at the right time. Who cannot be offended, and does not brood over her own troubles, but is always cheerful.[18]

The description closely fitted her grandmother, Deborah Fisher Wharton, although Anna did not seem to see the resemblance. Like Joanna, Anna looked not inward and backward for her ideals but outward into a non-Hicksite world. She enjoyed secular intellectual pursuits. She played guitar and piano and as she grew older began writing and selling short stories. Frequently as a young lady she accompanied her father to public appearances and once wrote of a lecture which he gave at the New Century Club: "Father spoke so clearly, naturally, & interestingly! & the people clapped so! I was *very* proud of him, & yet I did not feel so *proud* of him as I did, *fond* of him; he is so *sweet*, so much more lovable than most men whom one hears speak in a hall; & then he looked so young, & strong, & *fresh*, while the others were white, or bald, or *stout*, or uninteresting."[19]

Anna, again like her sister Joanna, waited a number of years before getting married. She probably met Harrison S. Morris, her husband-to-be, in 1892. Their association over the next two years ripened into love. Morris was beginning a career as manager of Philadelphia's Academy of Fine Arts, having previously served for nineteen years in the treasurer's office of the Philadelphia and Reading Coal and Iron Company. He had always been interested in art and letters and while working for the coal company had co-authored a book of verse, *A Duet in Lyrics*, and made many friends in the worlds of art and literature. Talented though of little private fortune, he was a businessman who also followed a career in creative writing and had exceptional competence as an art critic. The wedding was held on 2 June 1896, at Ontalauna, with about, according to Anna, two thousand persons attending.[20]

Three years later Anna bore her only child, Catharine, familiarly known as Kit. On his seventy-seventh birthday anniversary Joseph gave Anna a valuable business property at Fourth and George streets in Philadelphia. It stood six stories high and, according to Joseph, contained engines, boilers, dynamos, steam heat, elevators, and electric appliances.[21] Wrote Anna, "This is really as a sort of balance to Oak Hill which he gave to Joey soon after her marriage." Anna's immediate thanks to her father were more a test of her endurance than his: Father and I "danced the length of the parlor, pirouetting up and down, singing at the same time. (Dunderbeck). My breath gave out before his."[22] In 1899 Harrison Morris took on the job of editing *Lippincott's Magazine* in addition to his position as manager of the Academy of Fine Arts.

3

Wharton allowed few of the trappings of the Gilded Age to enter his private life. Although a millionaire, he was not of the *nouveau riche*; he had been reared in an atmosphere of Hicksite simplicity; and the combination did its work. He was a cultural aristocrat and unselfconscious about it.

He dressed comfortably and soberly. No diamond stickpin kept his tie in place. A silk hat was for ceremonial use. He chose indeed to go about bareheaded, a preference with which nature cooperated; for his hair remained bushy even as it began to gray. He compromised with the coming fashion in chin whiskers by cultivating an appendage halfway between a goatee and a beard, unlike his brother Charles, who allowed a full bush to cover his face from ear to ear. A deep vertical crease furrowed the space between Joseph's eyes, a sign of intelligence, according to popular mystique, although the most visible effect was that of imparting dignity to his expression when he chose to pose, straight-faced, before a camera. He had no tendency to put on weight and retained an erect posture and briskness of movement. When smiling he had especially a youthful mien, as Anna had noted, and preserved a suggestion of adolescence into old age. The economist Scott Nearing, describing him as an occasional lecturer at the Wharton School, underestimated his age by about ten years.[23]

Wharton was normally vain about his robust constitution and ability to look younger than he was. He never wore glasses for photographs or portraits. Yet his vanity had a foundation in a conscious and loyal adherence to Hicksite ideals dating from the 1830s. Looking young was a function of being by habit a traditionalist.

He had no desire to escape that tradition, which found expression in relations with people rather than with buildings. As a young man he had been too closely involved in constructing property to feel much sentiment for things made of brick or stone. Bellevue was gone, the land divided among the heirs, the portion containing the manor house condemned by the city for a reservoir which was never built, and the mansion itself boarded up and crumbling. He felt no regrets, only a smoldering anger at the presumption of the city in condemning some of his property.[24] Number 336 Spruce Street remained—Deborah still lived there—but when it entered his possession after she died he allowed it to become a boardinghouse.[25]

True, Wharton was an indulgent parent according to the standards of the times. But as far as his own conduct was concerned he retained the discipline he had learned in childhood. He did not smoke, made wine his only alcoholic drink, and sparingly partook of that. At a time when fraternal orders were becoming fashionable he repulsed all overtures for membership. He enjoyed the company of beautiful and intelligent women; but nothing in the voluminous correspondence of the female members of the Wharton clan, filled as it is with family chatter, suggests any irregularity. Hours saved from work and public affairs were spent with the family. First day meant attendance at meeting, followed by dinner with the family, ending perhaps with preparation in his study for work the following day.

Yet his life was not Spartan. He relaxed easily between business engagements, and when he did so he amused himself by walking, riding, reading, writing, or participating in informative and witty conversation. On a trip to Cuba with a small party of Bethlehem Iron people to inspect the company's mines, Sayre noted in his diary, "Wharton quite a boy, singing love songs, etc."; and in another entry, "Mr. Wharton and Mrs. Shatler entertained us with singing and piano."[26] He found time during his first trip to Europe to climb part way up Mont Blanc, the highest peak in the Alps, and wrote an article about the adventure which appeared in *The Penn Monthly*. On a second trip to Europe, this time to examine armored plate works for the Bethlehem Iron Company, he took the family on a grand tour of England, France, Germany, and Switzerland, again climbed part way up Mont Blanc, and wrote of it to his mother, "At home my wife is rather timid about horses," but on this occasion she rode a mule "with her gloves on, a veil over her face, and her feet hanging over the precipice."[27] J. Bertram Lippincott accompanied Wharton on a trip to Mexico, made for the purpose of examining various mineral deposits. The men took the opportunity to entertain themselves. Wharton wrote: "B. and I of course enjoy our freedom from the conjugal yoke. He smokes pipes and cigars, and drinks coffee without let or hindrance. My dissipation is perhaps not quite so wild, consisting as it does in eating boiled Onions on several occasions: how innocent they are after Mexican garlic which we tasted unordered many times."[28]

Some of his best poems, which were published, came from trips such as this. The journey to Europe in 1873 produced "Stewardson's Yarn." The voyage to Cuba resulted in "The Royal Palm" and "The 'Sweet Reasonableness' of a Yankee Philistine in Cuba." The trip to Mexico inspired the poem "Mexico." On a trip to his gold mines in Nevada he wrote "The Buttes of the Canyon."

Letters, some written in times of stress, contain humor and economy of expression coupled with great descriptive power. Once when passing the night with the Fritzes in Bethlehem he had a sore throat, received from his hostess a mustard plaster as a remedy, and the next day felt much better. He wrote of the cure: "How was that mustard plaster applied? Mrs. Merrick may believe it or not, but that mustard plaster was applied dry to the top of the mantel piece, about two feet from the foot of the bed. Does not that beat all the homeopathy? I do not wish Dr. Karsner to put this in the medical journals, for I do not wish to have to answer a lot of questions as to the material of that mantel, the points of the compass, etc."[29] He wrote in a lighthearted style concerning an accident arising from his preoccupation with affairs:

At New Haven I found that a train left in about 20 minutes for Ansonia, one of the places I wished to visit, so there was time enough for lunch. After it I walked leisurely, depending on my watch, to the depot, but just before reaching it, saw a train running off at an accelerating rate. It required but a moment to run after the train, to overtake it in a breathless condition, to sling my baggage upon the platform, to seize the rail in an attempt to get on board, and to be thrown violently to the ground with bleeding face and a cracked knee pan. I say it required but a moment to do all this, but I thought the moment could be better spent, so in a little perturbation I walked placidly on to the depot, where I found my train waiting.[30]

The handwriting in these letters displays an immunity from the excesses of the Gilded Age. There are no flourishes, not even in the signature. Also, the writing is rarely marred by emendations. Each motion of Wharton's pen deviates from an arc or a straight, slightly slanted line only to the extent necessary to make a letter distinguishable from those immediately preceding and following it. The script rises and falls across the page like the wavelets on a lake or treetops in a pine forest. The overall effect is that of rapid, unbroken, efficient thought.

4

Wharton's respect for tradition is evident in his treatment of relatives and friends of long standing. Thus, his attitude toward Hannah is reminiscent of the days in which she had washed his face and seen to it that he got to meals on time and did not play in the street. He acceded to her not only in becoming more concerned with the affairs of Swarthmore but also in requests to donate money to causes in which she was interested. He helped her and Robert with money in the period of their financial distress and took first Samuel and then Roger into his employ. He also hired for several years Susanna's son, William Rodman, as manager of the New Jersey iron properties, until that young graduate of Yale switched to begin what became a lifetime of service in the enterprises of his uncle William Wharton. Wharton's affection for Abraham Barker outlasted the death of Sarah and went far deeper than can be explained by a harmony of financial interests. When Barker Brothers and Company smashed in the depression of the early nineties Wharton voluntarily assumed an obligation of Abraham of fifty thousand dollars toward the University of Pennsylvania and was subsequently hurt when Abraham, fast becoming a partial recluse, avoided meeting him. The political differences which soon separated Joseph from Wharton Barker never destroyed the amity of their personal relationships. Joseph also aided his younger brother William, who expanded his enterprises to include the manufacture of equipment for street railways and the building and operating of trolley routes in Philadelphia. In this William also received applause from Wharton Barker, who editorially supported him in *The American*. Joseph helped William along rough financial passages, reminiscent of the days in which the elder William Wharton had used a family fortune to ease the burden of the sons. The strong friendship of Joseph for William Thurston continued, eventually to be succeeded by an assumption of legal paternity over his sons.

The special closeness of Joseph to his elder brother Charles never diminished. That affection appears in a letter written by Joseph to Charles following the death from consumption of Charles's and Mary's only daughter Hannah at Asheville, North Carolina, in 1887. Joseph wrote in part: "When thee left us all at Mother's dinner table the day of thy last departure, I felt a sadness which has clung to me since—a foreboding of one of the events that break up old associations and habits and that change the course of human lives. You were to be at Asheville in your hour of anxiety and pain—you to spend the winter and perhaps next summer there—you might wander to California, to Europe—you might never quite resume the old familiar closeness of intimacy. A leaf of the great book was turned, and who could tell what the next one might reveal."[31] Such foreboding on Joseph's part was groundless. Charles and Mary were as much homebodies as he. They traveled for amusement, in one year to Europe, but usually to nearby resorts such as Brown's Mill-in-the-Pines in New Jersey. They always returned to Birdwood or Braeclough and were seldom far from Joseph and Anna.

Debts of gratitude to friends, incurred many years earlier, were not forgotten. Joseph attended the funeral of Joseph S. Walton in 1876, although it meant losing the better part of a day from work. He remembered the Walton's daughter Margaretta, who became a minister and presiding clerk of the women's side of the Philadelphia Yearly Meeting. During the busiest years of his life he would take Margaretta for a ride through Fairmount Park. Anna might have to delay dinner; Robert Sayre, calling at the Philadelphia office without an appointment, might find Joseph out; but Margaretta would have her drive. On one occasion Joseph recommended Charles

McGinley, a nephew of the housekeeper of boyhood days, for employment with the Central Railroad of New Jersey, knowing nothing of the youth but noting that, because of his relationship to Margaret McGinley, there must be something good in him.[32]

The special role in Wharton's life filled by his mother persisted to and after her death. One of his most beautiful poems was a composition presented to her on the occasion of her eightieth birthday anniversary. Deborah visited infrequently at Ontalauna, preferring the simplicity and familiarity of surroundings on Spruce Street. Joseph's daughter Anna wrote, "I had never been much with this beautiful character, after I was grown up, but I felt how deeply my father reverenced her."[33] Deborah died on 16 August 1888, at the Newport home of Hetty and Ben Smith at the age of ninety-three. Wharton wrote an obituary, which reads in part:

> Her mental activity was that of the intellectual nonagenarian. Old persons, whose minds are interested in the present and whose sympathies are in constant activity, seldom "die at the top," as the selfish Dean of St. Patrick's [Swift] dreaded. The receipt for a long life, given a sturdy constitution, would seem to be a useful one; only those old folks whose interests center in themselves are liable to stagnation and mental torpor. Mrs. Wharton was to the last keenly interested in modern literature, in addition to the seasoned favorite books and classics of her younger days. She was a woman who held by old ways strongly. Witness the unmodernized house in which she spent her winters for long over half a century, and the deliberate choice of simplicity in living, with ample means at her disposal for all modern lavishness of luxury. Perhaps this adherence to quiet and simplicity may have had considerable to do with her vigorous length of days.

The lack of sentimentality in the obituary is deliberate. Wharton instinctively backed away from this Victorian trait, which accompanied the Gilded Age. "Stale sentiment is worse than stale eggs and they are not pleasant," he had written Anna in the times of budding romance. Sentimentality he considered to be a weakness of a rude people unpracticed in the arts of expression.

Another reason also accounts for his not mourning his mother with mawkish phrases. Hicksite discipline viewed death as a translation to a higher life. Art and literature should not demean it with unbecoming emotional display. Sentiment, such as he had shown in the letter to Charles, might be tolerated. But sentimentality—never!

13

Industrialist of the Eighties

On 1 January 1883, Wharton set down the value of his assets at over four million dollars: to be exact, $4,315,987.04. The nickel business represented less than a million of this figure ($757,435.71).[1] In the ensuing years it was to decline in value even though he mightily worked to modernize and expand it. Yet he could not be comfortable with only one or two projects. As the profitability of nickel decreased, he cast about for other work to fill his days and his pockets. In a sense, in the 1880s he began a third career, even more diversified than that which had centered on nickel. He increased his activity in the Bethlehem Iron Company; expanded farming and forestry in the pinelands; undertook activities in commercial fishing for the menhaden; began mining and smelting the iron ores of northern New Jersey; bought stock in a gold mining company; heavily invested in railroads; and became involved in the financing and managing of several railroad companies. The only undertakings which he ended were those of raising sugar beets (which had probably terminated in 1878), the manufacturing of glass, and the Saucon Iron Company, whose sale to the Thomas Iron Company he engineered in 1885.[2]

Not all of the new concerns returned a profit. During the next fifteen years the value of Wharton's assets increased by about eight hundred and fifty thousand dollars, far less than might be expected of an astute businessman who already had a base of over four million on which to build. Much of what he did in the years from 1883 to 1898 went to establish a foundation which, about the turn of the century and later, proved to be immensely profitable.

1

In the pinelands Wharton sold small parcels of land to individuals and from 1880 to 1889 bought about six thousand acres. Some of the new properties were cranberry bogs, for he planned to add the culture of cranberries to the products of the farms at Batsto and Atsion. George Wright took charge of the store and farm at Batsto. Wharton bought cattle for the farms and for several years sent steers to Gap to be fattened. He cut young trees for mine timbers, ran the sawmill, and made charcoal.[3]

None of these operations provided enough income to justify the time spent on correspondence and negotiations. They represented an attempt to use the meager resources of water and the scrabbly land to pay expenses. He made a few hundred dollars here, a few thousand dollars there, enough for taxes and not much more. In the long run he probably lost money. He faced legal expenses almost constantly, and forest fires swept over parts of the land in the dry seasons. Perhaps he gained some amusement from this farming and forestry. He had General Wright send crates of cranberries and sweet potatoes to friends and relatives during the holiday season. He wasted nothing and chafed at the thought that the natives were trespassing on his land to pick the wild huckleberries which grew there. This represented no loss of income, as he had never made of them a commercial crop. But it violated the principle of the sanctity of private property and was no more to be tolerated than was the condemnation of part of Bellevue by the city for a public purpose.

Tangential to his interests in the pinelands was the business of catching and processing the commercial fish known as menhaden or, more popularly, mossbunkers. These were valued for their oil, which was used for such purposes as softening leather. The residue remaining after the oil had been squeezed out was sold for fertilizer and called fish scrap. In 1881 Wharton bought for twelve hundred dollars a small boat from a man named Austin Mathis and later that year realized a sum of twenty-seven hundred dollars for the sale of the scrap alone. The profitability of the venture attracted him. He could always use some of the scrap on his farms in the event of a poor market. Two years later he bought the steamer *Ospray* and hired Mathis to take charge. Within a few years he had the beginning of a small fleet.

He bought islands in the Great Bay into which the waters of the Mullica, Atsion, and Wading rivers flowed. On one of them, Crab Island, he established a factory for rendering oil and making scrap. In his accounts for 1885 he listed the assets of the venture as follows:

For estimated value of my menhaden fishing establishment on Great Bay, N.J. near Tuckerton comprising the island called Foxburrows containing about 2000 acres (excepting a few strips belonging to others), and the group of islands called the Seven Islands (excepting Cariless & Sooy's fishing which has right of occupancy of a part of one of those islands) with bars etc. . . . . Improvements on one of the Seven Islands, viz. a complete steam fish oil & scrap factory, with dwelling house, divers buildings, etc. . . . Steamer 'Ospray' and purse boats etc. . . . Sloop 'Restless' . . . Sail boat 'Gen'l. Wright', divers nets, apparatus and supplies of all sorts . . . Fish scrap on hand at fishing and Batsto . . . $20,000.[4]

He was in time to expand this small beginning into a million-dollar venture. Yet over the years it appears to have taken more from him in work and worry than it returned in profits. Schools of menhaden followed ocean currents whose course was unpredictable. When the fish were found in numbers, profits could be huge. But then came the lean years; and always, there was repair and upkeep of boats and factory to be provided for. Also, ship captains who had a knack of locating the mossbunkers were not always the best businessmen.

2

Wharton's strangest investment during this period of great activity was that of mines of gold and silver in El Dorado Canyon near the Colorado River in Nevada Territory. In 1879 and 1880 he paid through Barker Brothers and Company over sixty thousand dollars for twenty-eight thousand shares of stock in a mining company and advanced the operators an additional ten thousand dollars.

He was by no means the only businessman taking a risk of this sort without visiting the site or receiving reliable data concerning it. Many eastern and European capitalists of otherwise sound business sense swallowed the bait represented by gold or took the lesser lures of Western silver and copper. By contrast, he never made a decision concerning an iron or nickel property which he was considering as an investment without having it investigated as thoroughly as he knew how.

Probably Abraham or Wharton Barker gave him whatever information he had concerning the Southwestern Mining Company, as this enterprise was called. They, together with Joseph and two other men, controlled a majority of the stock. For upwards of five years the venture appeared on Wharton's books under the heading "Nevada Silver Mine"—although gold was the principal metal sought. He never received a dividend from the venture. In December 1880 he listed the value of his holdings as one cent a share. In 1891 the company made a profit, and he revalued his holdings at twenty-eight thousand dollars, only to drop the valuation a year later to seven thousand dollars and to put it down in 1894 at one hundred dollars.[5]

Yet this venture was to become in his old age one of his principal interests.

3

In the same year in which he first purchased stock in the Southwestern Mining Company he began another business which also endured for the rest of his life. This was the mining and refining of northern New Jersey magnetite ores. The venture appeared in prospect to be exactly suited to his talents as a manager. If he could integrate mines, furnaces, and mills into a single operation he might conceivably dominate the production of pig iron in the East. Certain properties in Warren and Morris counties had come on the market. He purchased these and leased others and found a man to manage the lot.

The first of the properties was the Hackettstown Furnace, which Wharton bought in December 1879. Local businessmen had built it and failed to make it a success. Wood Brothers of Philadelphia took it off their hands and quickly resold it to Wharton. He renamed it the Warren Furnace, put it into good working condition, and leased several nearby ore properties, specifically, the Redell, Brown, and Thomas mines.[6]

A second property, which he acquired by lease, was the Boonton Rolling Mill. It took much of the pig iron made at the Warren Furnace. After Wharton took control of it he sent large shipments of iron from Boonton to his brother for the Wharton Railroad Switch Company.

A third property was a furnace at Port Oram in Morris County. Port Oram was strategically located for iron mining, being close to the Hibernia range containing excellent Bessemer ores. Port Oram began as a depot built by the Delaware, Lackawanna and Western Railroad Company and lay along the Morris Canal. The name came from Robert P. Oram, resident manager for a company operating several nearby mines. In 1868 a group of businessmen, some of whom owned interests in the Boonton Mill, organized the Port Oram Iron Company. The venture was ambitious and for a time, profitable. Ario Pardee leased the works in 1872 and successfully ran them for four years. But in January 1877 bankruptcy overtook the company. The bondholders bought it, reorganized it as the Port Oram Furnace Company, and for a short time ran it. Then the furnace was allowed to go out of blast. Wharton purchased it in 1881, leased two other ore properties, the Doland and King mines, put the furnace into good order, and refired it.[7]

The first man whom Wharton chose as manager of this iron-making venture was his nephew, William Rodman Wharton. William Rodman held the post for two years, then passed into the employ of his other paternal uncle, William Wharton. His replacement was a local man named Tooke Straker, who continued as manager of the northern New Jersey iron business until his death in 1891. Edward Kelly succeeded him.[8]

Wharton began this venture when the future for Jersey iron was promising. Following the depression years of the seventies the production of iron in New Jersey rapidly increased, reaching a high of 932,762 tons in 1882. Then, almost as soon as Wharton became established in the business, the boom ended. Rich and low-cost ores from other sources, especially upper Michigan, flooded the market. Most of the Jersey mines closed down. By 1885 the tonnage mined within the state had sunk to little more than a third of its level in 1882. In the following five years production somewhat recovered, but only to a little more than half of the 1882 high.[9]

Wharton survived this reversal by large outlays of money to streamline and modernize his holdings. He gave up the lease on the Boonton Rolling Mill, sold the Warren Furnace, and got rid of several unproductive ore properties. This left the furnace at Port Oram, which became the center of operations. In 1885 he bought the Baker Mine and three years later the Willis, also sometimes known as the Wharton or Hibernia Mine. These purchases gave him sources of ore near the furnace. The most important of them was the Hibernia, which had for years been one of the largest iron mines in the state and was estimated to contain immense reserves of ore. In 1889 Cooper Hewitt and Company helped to modernize the furnace. The following year Wharton purchased a controlling interest in the Morris County Railroad. This road, together with a branch line called the Hibernia, serviced mines and furnaces and connected with the Central Railroad of New Jersey.

His strategy was simple. He planned on offsetting the lower cost of mining and refining of Michigan ores by savings on production (because of his managerial skill) and freight charges (by proximity to Eastern customers). For a time the strategy worked. In 1890 he listed Hibernia ore on hand as being worth three dollars a ton and Lake Superior ore, $6.75 a ton.

In that year also he valued his iron business at $357,819.50 and his holdings in the Morris County Railroad at $243,900.[10]

4

He would scarcely have been representative of his times if he had not entered the market in railroads. That was where the greatest power and money lay. They were the industrial heart of America. When they prospered, the whole economy was warm and comfortable. When they failed, it shivered. They made possible great industrial empires and quickened the pace of life. Especially, they gave the common man an assurance that the country was strong and the future outlook, bright. A first generation, that in control when Wharton was a boy, had regarded "the cars" with suspicion. Subsequent generations loved them. The sight of a line of smoke coming up from a canyon or fading across a plain became as familiar as flocks of birds against a morning sky. The sound of a steam whistle assured farmers and villagers that the five-thirty was on time; that God was indeed in his heaven and all was right with the world.

When Wharton retired from the board of the Lehigh Valley road he retained his stock in the company and in the succeeding years acquired and held for varying periods of time stocks, bonds, or scrip in the Delaware and Bound Brook; the Manchester and Keene; the Allegheny Valley; the Oregon Pacific; the New York, West Shore, and Buffalo; the San Antonio and Aransas Pass; and the Philadelphia and Reading.[11] None of these excepting the Lehigh Valley and the Reading had any direct relationship with his industrial enterprises. Yet they provided him with income, credit, and standing in financial circles.

Three of these ventures in railroads, those with the Philadelphia and Reading, the Oregon Pacific, and the San Antonio and Aransas Pass, deserve special mention.

Over the years Wharton invested more money in the Philadelphia and Reading than in any other railroad company. The Philadelphia and Reading was the oldest of the great anthracite coal roads. The main line extended up the Schuylkill from Philadelphia to Pottsville. By the 1880s the Reading had absorbed many small routes and had over twenty-five hundred miles of track not including sidings. It had leased the Central Railroad of New Jersey, owned and operated its own express and telegraph services, and possessed immense holdings in coal lands and other real estate.

The Philadelphia and Reading, like the Lehigh Valley, successfully weathered the depression years of the seventies. Then, as most of the rest of the economy chugged ahead, the Reading was derailed. An able, energetic, and irascible man named Franklin B. Gowan served as president and pushed the company to the verge of bankruptcy. A fight developed between him and the bondholders, the chief of whom belonged to a syndicate headed by J. Pierpont Morgan and A. J. Drexel. Gowan had protectd himself by buying the stock of the Vanderbilts and could not easily be dislodged. The Morgan-Drexel interests, ably represented by John Lowber Welsh, Austin Corbin, and others, charged Gowan with mismanagement.

Wharton had begun his venture into Reading railroad bonds in the midst of the controversy. He purchased one million five hundred thousand dollars worth of scrip and bonds on favorable terms in 1882 and added two hundred thousand dollars worth of bonds to these holdings during the next two years. Barker Brothers and Drexel were his agents for these transactions. When the Reading defaulted, the Jersey Central was also involved, since the Reading had leased the road several years earlier. On this occasion Wharton and Barker Brothers provided $175,000 to pay the interest on the Jersey Central's first mortgage bonds. Wharton supplied one hundred thousand dollars of the amount.[12]

As a bondholder Wharton was on the side of Drexel and Morgan in the dispute over the Reading's management. Wharton Barker urged his uncle to become a member of the board, if for no other reason than to protect his interests. Wharton refused; he was at the time suing its lessee, the Central Railroad of New Jersey, for setting fire to his forests in the pinelands. In 1885, when the case had been settled (Wharton lost), he briefly came on the board. There he served with J. B. Lippincott and A. V. Williamson as a committee for drafting a plan of financial reorganization. Gowan disliked the plan, and Wharton resigned, anticipating opposition from Gowan at the next annual election.

The economy was working against Gowan. Receipts in 1885 were still too low to satisfy the company's financial needs. The Morgan-Drexel syndicate threatened foreclosure and finally forced his resignation and a reorganization of management. For five years the road was to be under the control of five trustees. Four of these were to be Morgan, Welsh, Henry Lewis, and John Wanamaker. They were to choose the fifth, and they asked Wharton to be that person.

He considered the offer, then refused. The job would take too much time, and he would never be his own master. Wise investment in railroads could be profitable and provide leverage for promoting his other ventures. But as far as control of the Reading was concerned, he could never be more than a servant of J. Pierpont Morgan.[13]

5

He would have done as well if he had refused to have anything to do with the Oregon Pacific. He was accustomed to success in business. Here, he failed. He never entirely outlived the humiliation he felt as a result of the failure.

In its time the building of the Oregon Pacific raised enough unanswered questions to merit the label of "affair." Leslie M. Scott ably wrote about it in the *Oregon Historical Quarterly* of 1915 without, however, showing much knowledge of or sympathy for the part played by Eastern financiers. In fact, that role was creditable if somewhat unwise. Wharton, Barker Brothers and Company, and others acted honorably, although in their own interests, to support a project which was geographically speaking unrealistic. No one, indeed, appears to have been intentionally deceived. Inhabitants of Corvallis, seat of Benton County on which the scheme of the Oregon Pacific centered, believed in the project, invested, and also lost.

According to the census of 1880, Corvallis was a town of 1,128 persons. It lay along the Willamette River eighty miles south of Portland. Corvallis was also situated forty-five miles east of Yaquina Bay, a rather small body of water opening directly on the Pacific Ocean. Although the densely forested Coast Range separated Yaquina Bay from Corvallis, a pass through the mountains made travel between the two places relatively easy. Twenty-five miles to the east of Corvallis rose the higher and more rugged Cascades with occasional snowcapped peaks. Like the Coast Range, they contained a pass by means of which trains might move out of the Willamette Valley. Beyond the Cascades the lava plains of central and eastern Oregon stretched for several hundred miles to the Snake River in Idaho.

The plan of the directors of the Oregon Pacific was that of establishing a railroad from Yaquina Bay to Corvallis and from there eastward to the Snake River, where connections might be made with other lines. Corvallis would then become the western terminus of a great transcontinental railroad, diverting traffic from the upper Columbia River basin away from Portland, a town listed in the 1880 census as having 17,577 persons. The directors of the Oregon Pacific also reasoned that Yaquina Bay would be the major port for ships sailing up the coast from San Francisco. The ships would dock in the bay and send their cargoes overland to Corvallis and from there to other cities in the valley both north and south. This would save almost two hundred miles of travel over the old route along the coast to the Columbia River and up that river to Portland near the mouth of the Willamette. Corvallis would thus snatch from Portland the centrality of an immense economic region. It might indeed become the great metropolis lying between Seattle and San Francisco.

The plan was taken up by Colonel T. Egerton Hogg in 1871–72. Building began at Corvallis in 1877 at a time when other entrepreneurs were pushing railroads through the region. The name Oregon Pacific was adopted in 1880 when Hogg went east seeking fifteen million dollars in bonds to finance his project. The prospectus which he circulated mentioned a land grant of over nine hundred thousand acres and estimated earnings of over one million dollars annually in freight and passenger traffic, this being nearly six times the annual interest on the bonds.[14]

Barker Brothers and Company invested; and in August 1888 Joseph Wharton exchanged Reading bonds for notes of the Oregon Pacific, probably on the basis of information received from Barker Brothers. The following spring he purchased $500,000 worth of Oregon Pacific bonds and $125,000 of its stock.[15] That was the spring in which he and J. Bertram Lippincott traveled to Mexico. On their return they headed northward through San Francisco to Corvallis. There they stopped for a day. Wharton surveyed the project and liked what he saw. A line between Corvallis and Yaquina Bay had been completed; ships were entering the bay and sending cargoes overland to Corvallis; the company was operating several steamboats on the Willamette River; and construction had been begun eastward toward the Cascades. On returning to Philadelphia he claimed to be sufficiently impressed to want to take another $500,000 worth of bonds and to consider confirming a purchase of forty thousand tons of steel rails from the Bethlehem Iron Company, to be paid for with bonds worth $1,350,000 at 82½. He wrote glowingly of the project. Barker Brothers and Company was then trying to put together a syndicate for buying another $4 million worth of bonds. Wharton Barker included his uncle's letter in a promotional pamphlet.[16]

This optimism cannot be excused in businessmen who were supposed to be closely attuned to fundamentals of politics and geography as well as of finance. Congress had not granted land to the Oregon Pacific and never did. By 1889 Portland had already outdistanced Corvallis as a hub for railroads serving a large economic region. The Northern Pacific had completed a line connecting Portland with Chicago. Another road, the Central Pacific, led southward from Portland into California. Several other railroads traversed the Willamette Valley from north to south. Corvallis since 1880 had grown hardly at all, whereas the population of Portland had more than doubled. Also, Yaquina Bay could not compare with Portland as a harbor. Much of the bay was shallow. It was directly exposed to winter storms coming off the open ocean. Portland had a large, deep, quiet, fresh water port and was already receiving most of the ships entering Oregon from San Francisco.

Fortunately for Wharton the Oregon Pacific became bankrupt before he could buy more bonds or the Bethlehem Iron Company could complete the sale of rails. The mortgage held by the bondholders stipulated that the bonded debt should not exceed twenty-five thousand dollars a mile. With almost all of the $15 million bond issue placed and only about 143 miles of road built the debt was already greater than one hundred thousand dollars per mile. The beginning of worldwide depression in 1890 made further raising of capital impossible. The company went into receivership. The court appointed Hogg, the president, as receiver in charge of operating the bankrupt road.[17]

At this point a protracted series of legal battles began involving Hogg, various factions among the bondholders, and others with financial stakes in the Oregon Pacific. At first the issue was the priority of reimbursement among the creditors. After much negotiation the bondholders reached an agreement: Hogg would purchase the road at sheriff's sale for a sum sufficient to pay off the floating debt and refinance the company without depriving the old bondholders of their equity. He accordingly put together a syndicate and arranged for it to buy the property for $1 million. But Wharton and some other Eastern bondholders were suspicious of Hogg, whom they believed had been less than honest in dealing with them, and brought suit to prevent the sale. They alleged that the sum was too low and that some of the provisions being made for refinancing would in fact subordinate the interests of the bondholders to the claims of other mortgagees. Wharton and his group lost their case but obtained their objective when the sale fell through because of disagreement among members of the syndicate.

Wharton and other bondholders continued to attack Hogg and demanded his removal as receiver. They argued that he had grossly mismanaged the affairs of the company, alleging among other things an unreasonably large operating deficit. The court agreed and appointed Everest W. Hadley to replace Hogg. Deficits continued under Hadley's management but in greatly reduced amounts. As a token of confidence in the new receiver Wharton and several other bondholders advanced a total of forty thousand dollars to pay the back wages of workers.

Again the court ordered the property sold. This time the purchasing syndicate included Joseph Wharton, James Blair, J. J. Belden, Henry Martin, F. K. Pendleton, and S. S. Hollingsworth. The amount of the sale, which was held 15 December 1893, was two hundred thousand dollars, of which Wharton put in twenty thousand.[18]

Then, with victory almost in sight for Wharton and his group of bond-holders, the court refused to confirm the sale. It held that the purchase price was far too low. Hadley agreed, pointing out that even if the property were sold as scrap it would bring four hundred thousand dollars. Suddenly Wharton and his associates found themselves accused of trying to engineer a "steal." The Oregon press soundly abused them. In fact, two hundred thousand dollars was more than any other purchaser was willing to pay for a property which, by now, was little more than the remains of a blasted dream. The sheriff repeatedly put the property out for bids but found no one willing to pay a price satisfactory to the court.

At last, on 22 December 1894, A. B. Hammond and E. L. Bonner bought the road for one hundred thousand dollars. The state's circuit and supreme courts confirmed the sale, although the sum was sufficient to pay only token amounts of the accumulated taxes, court costs, salaries, and the claims of other creditors. Wharton and his friends who had advanced the forty thousand dollars to pay the wages of the workers received ten cents on the dollar. Stockholders and bondholders lost everything.

Wharton was furious. In addition to having been attacked for what he considered to be a straightforward business transaction, the road had been sold for half of what he and his companions would have paid. He suspected the court of conspiracy without having any evidence to support a legal charge. In the course of subsequent court battles he wrote of the Oregon Pacific affair as "the greatest swindle I have ever suffered from, and out of which I see no prospect for the bondholders to get anything. . . . I never saw such a complicated and unmitigated swindle."[19]

About the time of the aborted two hundred thousand dollar sale Wharton was approached with a request to acquire large quantities of nickel ore existing near Riddle, a mountain in southwestern Oregon. These deposits were in the second half of the twentieth century to become the only working mines of nickel in the United States. Wharton had several years earlier sent Voigt to investigate the deposits and had decided that the ore was "too widely diffused and too thin or poor to be inviting." Now Wharton found another reason for refusing to invest in the deposits. He wrote to one William Jacks: "My experience in Oregon with a quantity of railroad bonds that I hold has filled me with utter distrust of the Courts of that State. Public opinion seems to hold that any foreigner is simply prey for the inhabitants to feed upon and the Courts seem to take that view. As at present advised I should not venture to put money into Oregon on any terms, but also as at present advised I would not take Riddell Mount [*sic*] for a gift if compelled to work it."[20]

6

In sharp contrast to Wharton's experience with the Oregon Pacific was that with the San Antonio and Aransas Pass Railroad in Texas. Its directors were in the mideighties preparing to build the main line from Aransas Pass on the Gulf Coast inland to San Antonio. Here, as with the Oregon Pacific, Wharton received his information from other investors in Philadelphia. The difference was that the Aransas Pass project was geographically feasible; the company could survive financial difficulties.

In the several years leading up to 1889 Wharton sold about three quarters of his holdings in the Reading and used the proceeds to buy over one million dollars worth of first mortgage bonds of the San Antonio and Aransas Pass.[21]

A transaction which he and E. P. Wilbur entered into with this railroad illustrates one of the advantages which he hoped to gain from these investments with railroads. The Bethlehem Iron Company was facing stiff competition in the manufacture and sale of steel rails. The price had dropped to a level at which the company could scarcely afford to continue the manufacture. Wharton planned to use his leverage with the iron company and the railroads to make money from the situation. He would buy rails from Bethlehem Iron and sell them at a higher figure to the railroads in which he had a heavy investment. Payment would be made in whole or in part with railroad securities. This was a risky sort of payment, one which an iron company with a need for cash disliked to assume. Wharton had probably contemplated a transaction of this sort with the Oregon Pacific. That in which he and Wilbur engaged with respect to the Aransas Pass appears on his books in the following terms: "First we bought from Beth[m] Iron Co. the debt due to it by M. Kennedy of $589,102.04 agreeing to pay it in full. Second we bought from B. Iron Co. 15,030 tons steel rails @ $27 per ton. Third, we sold to M. Kennedy 15,030 tons steel rails @ $40 per ton. Fourth we bought from M. Kennedy 1800 First Mortgage Bonds and 400 Second Mortgage bonds all of $1000 each of San Antonio & Aransas Pass RR Co., buying them by the above 15,030 tons rails, by cancelling Kennedy's above named debt of $589,102.04, by cancelling the due bills held by us for about $23,000 each, and by $215,630.14 to be paid to him in cash." In sum, Wharton and Wilbur purchased $2,200,000 worth of bonds valued at 90 ($1,980,000) for approximately $1,452,000 and in addition planned on making a profit of $195,390 on the steel rails. Wilbur was to receive ⅜ths and Wharton, ⅝ths of the proceeds.[22]

This transaction was successfully consummated. The San Antonio and Aransas Pass, badly managed as were the Oregon Pacific and the Reading (and a great many other railroads), went into receivership in 1889. But the San Antonio and Aransas Pass was successfully reorganized and refinanced. The old 6 percent bonds were exchanged for new ones bearing a rate of 4 percent guaranteed by the Southern Pacific. The San Antonio and Aransas Pass resumed paying interest on its bonds in 1894. Also, as a result of the reorganization the par value of Wharton's bonds was doubled. He and E. P. Wilbur received full payment for the rails they sold to the company. Eventually this investment returned Wharton far more than he lost through the Oregon Pacific.[23]

14

Armor Plate and Guns

Asa Packer died in 1879. He attempted in a last will and testament to keep his properties, especially the Lehigh Valley Railroad, under control of the men he had trained. To accomplish this he had set up a trust to be managed by his two sons, Robert A. and Harry E., together with Sayre, Wilbur, and whoever should be president of the Lehigh Valley road. The trust came to be called the Asa Packer Estate. It was the operator of the Lehigh Valley system from 1879 until 1897, when it lost control to the Morgan-Drexel interests.[1]

The scope of the Asa Packer Estate did not include the Bethlehem Iron Company, inasmuch as Packer's pecuniary interest in the iron company had been small. The directors no longer had to follow his lead and hold to a specialization in making rails. They could and did change direction, and in doing so they made the Bethlehem Iron Company rich. The Asa Packer Estate bought its stock; and a time arrived when the estate's holdings in the company enabled the trustees to forestall for several years relinquishing control over the railroad. They could avoid this because the Bethlehem Iron Company had become financially sounder than the railroad: The iron company, which had been the tail to Packer's pet interest, became the dog. The switch in financial importance was largely a result of the imaginative leadership and effort of Joseph Wharton.

1

Wharton's interest and activity in Bethlehem Iron rose as soon as Packer died. He was not alone in this respect. Sayre and Wilbur relished their freedom from Packer's restraining presence. The railroad king had been in his grave only a few months when Wharton led a willing board to a decision to build two additional blast furnaces. In 1880 Wharton brought his brother-in-law, Joseph S. Lovering, Jr, onto the board in place of Jacob Riegel, a Packer man who had sat during the depression years. When two years later Lovering resigned, shortly before he died, Wharton succeeded in having the post filled by Vice-President Thurston. In 1882 the company began buying iron mines in Cuba in cooperation with the Pennsylvania Steel Company and a man named Alfred Eamshaw. The following year these partners organized the Juragua Iron Company, Ltd., to own and operate the Cuban mines. Thurston was made president of this company.[2]

Two years later the iron company became involved in the controversy concerning rearmament. In Europe the unification of Germany under Bismarck marked the beginning of an arms race involving especially Britain, France, Germany, and Russia. This meant, for offensive strategy, bigger and better guns; and, for defensive, armor plate for naval vessels. Each advance in the power of weaponry sparked a search for more protective armor.

The United States at first stood aside from the arms race. Since the Civil War, Congress and the president had largely neglected the nation's defences. But soon voices were heard insisting that an America capable of enforcing the Monroe Doctrine needed a large and modern navy. Editors of the *Iron Age* were among those taking up the cause for rearmament and kept readers informed of the country's weakness in face of Europe's growing might. England had sixty-eight ironclads bearing 725 guns, whereas the United States had twenty-four armed with 28 guns, wrote one commentator.[3] Congressmen began raising the issue of naval rearmament, and in the early 1880s President Arthur and his secretary of the navy, William E. Chandler, agreed that it should be done.

The issue became bipartisan. On 3 March 1885, Congress appropriated $1,895,000 for the building of two cruisers and two gunboats. The Cleveland administration, which took office the following day, continued the work. Cleveland appointed one of the nation's most promising industrialists, William C. Whitney, as secretary of the navy. Whitney was zealous for the project. "The American Navy has been the butt of satire at home and the subject of no very complimentary opinions abroad," he declared when interviewed by a correspondent of the *Iron Age*. "We want to start with first class steel cruisers. We should have about 20 of that class right away. We have the money to make a beginning, and I hope Congress will keep up the good work, now that it has made a start."[4] The "start" to which he referred was an act dated 8 August 1886, appropriating $2,500,000 for nine vessels, three of which were the Maine (armored cruiser), the Texas (armored battleship), and the Amphitrite (monitor). Whitney also obtained authorization from Congress to give preference to American manufacturers in supplying these ships with guns and armor plate. He saw this as necessary in order to develop a reliable domestic source of supply.[5]

Who was to do the work? European countries had large steel plants especially fitted for the purpose and directly or indirectly subsidized by their respective governments. England had the firm of Sir Joseph Whitworth, one of the world's great steelmen. At the time of the Crimean War Whitworth had experimented with producing better rifles and was soon leading the field of small arms makers. He then gave attention to heavy ordnance. France benefited from Schneider and Company, more commonly referred to as Le Creusot from the place in the department of Saône-et-Loire in which the principal works were located. Le Creusot had been in operation since the thirteenth century and had been turning out ordnance since 1782. The works represented a massive enterprise of furnaces and mills for making steel and fashioning it into locomotives, rails, ships, bridges, and many other products. In Germany the principal firm making armaments and armor plate was that of Krupp in Essen. Krupp was leading continental Europe in the manufacture of large guns. The works had come under the sole management of Alfred Krupp in 1848 and were devised after his death in 1887 to his son, Friedrich-Alfred. They were, like Le Creusot, a family enterprise and had by the last third of the nineteenth century grown to become a huge and varied undertaking. The German government officially supported the Krupp works.[6]

America had nothing which could even remotely compare with Whitworth, Le Creusot, or Krupp. A government-built and operated armor plate mill was always possible—but where would the experts come from to make it successful? Reliance on existing companies seemed best, if their management could be interested in the project. Midvale Steel under the direction of Sellers and Clarke had made important advances in the manufacture of guns, although it was too small to be seriously considered for heavy forgings such as armor plate. The Delamater Iron Works of New York had pioneered in developing a semisubmersible torpedo boat and could conceivably be expanded and renovated for larger work; but the proprietor, Mr. Delamater, was old and uninterested in the business. Among several other possibilities the most likely seemed to be the establishment of the energetic Mr. Andrew Carnegie of Pittsburgh, Pennsylvania. Already in possession of the Edgar Thomson Steel Works at Braddock, Carnegie had in 1883 purchased the Homestead Works and begun modernizing them. Secretary Whitney contacted Carnegie concerning the possibility of bidding on government contracts for making heavy ordnance and armor plate and found him sufficiently interested to send a rising young employee, Charles M. Schwab, to Europe to study the processes used there, especially at Krupp and Le Creusot. Schwab's report was discouraging: Technical difficulties in the manufacture would make compliance with naval specifications impossible, especially as concerned uniformity of product. Carnegie backed off. He made Schwab general superintendent of the Homestead Works but ordered a halt to plans for establishing an armor plate mill.

The Bethlehem Iron Company was another possibility. The person who brought the matter to its attention was Lt. William H. Jaques of the naval Bureau of Ordnance and a friend of Chandler, whose son-in-law he eventually became. Jaques had canvassed developments in Europe, especially at the works of Joseph Whitworth and Le Creusot. He knew Fritz, who needed little urging to take the matter up with the directors.[7]

Bethlehem Iron was in several respects ready for a proposal of the sort presented by Jaques. Storm clouds were beginning to gather around its specialization as a supplier of railroads. Sayre had written in his diary at the end of 1884, "Steel rails sold as low as $25 per ton. Reading stock down to $9. NY Central to 85. N.J. Co. to $35. All railroad earnings have fallen off. Anthracite coal traffic less than last year by 1,000,000 tons and prices . . . of iron and steel lower than ever before." The situation was so bad that the next year the company entered a pool with other leading producers of steel rails to divide the market, Bethlehem's share being 12 percent.[8] Also, in 1885 the board lost by death the man most likely to oppose diversification, Dr. Linderman, who had previously put a stop to Fritz's plan for making heavy forgings. ("Congestion of the brain," wrote a biographer. "Drink ruined him," noted Sayre.) Dr. Linderman's post was temporarily vacant. Wharton, Wilbur, and Sayre comprised the advisory (executive) committee. The other directors—Thurston, the aging President Hunt, and John Knecht—could be expected to follow their lead.

The proposal implied grave risks. It meant a fresh exploring for talent, an acquiring of patents, and a multimillion-dollar outlay for a project of unique use to a patron that was notoriously temperamental. A contract with government was not a normal agreement between equals, because Congress could at any time alter the conditions for doing business. Future legislators might change existing programs, even repudiate contracts. Carnegie had weighed these uncertainties along with Schwab's report concerning technological problems. Managers of other steel companies were also unimpressed with the prospects of reaping large profit from specializing in making heavy forgings for government ships.

By contrast, the directors of the Bethlehem Iron Company scarcely hesitated before deciding to undertake the venture. Sayre's diary and the minutes of the board contain evidence of the sequence of events. On 7 October 1885, Sayre, Fritz, Wilbur, Thurston, and Wharton met in Philadelphia to hear Jaques's report concerning his visit to Whitworth and Company and the propriety of Bethlehem Iron undertaking the manufacture of shafting and other large forgings. A month later a congressional delegation consisting of Senators Joseph R. Hawley (Conn.) and Nelson W. Aldrich (R.I.) and their secretaries made a site visit to the Bethlehem plant. The decision had been made by 25 November 1885, when the iron company's board appointed Wharton, Sayre, and Wilbur as a committee to draw up a contract with Sir Joseph Whitworth for the constructing and building "in this country of certain steel forging presses and appurtenant plant." Sayre recorded on the same day that the company "have about resolved to erect large hydraulic presses for forging shafts, guns, etc." A contract with Whitworth and Company was executed the following 18 January.

Who was primarily responsible for this precipitous decision? Fritz in his autobiography, written after all the directors were dead, claimed the initiative for himself and named Wilbur as his champion in convincing the board of the soundness of the project. Fritz also implied that Wharton opposed it, writing that "some of the directors belonged to a sect that was opposed to fighting in any way or manner."[9] The "sect" in his statement could only be that of the Quakers; many Quakers were indeed becoming vocal in opposing a modern navy; and the only Quakers on the board were Wharton and Hunt.

But Fritz's comment is the only recorded denial of the leadership role played by Wharton. Sayre's diary contains nothing on the subject. Certainly Sayre was not responsible. Although he was no more bound by the dead hand of Packer than was Wilbur, he was conservative in his approach to the iron and steel business. Wharton and Wilbur were the entrepreneurs willing to risk much for large gains. Of the two, Wharton was the better placed to obtain the information on which a wise decision should be based. He had contacts in Washington and in the steel industry through his membership in the Bessemer Steel Company and his work with the American Iron and Steel Association. He probably knew as soon as anyone that Carnegie did not intend to build an armor plate mill. Wharton had not objected to his nephew Wharton Barker's negotiations with Russia for ships of war; and he believed that a modern navy might eventually be necessary to protect American industry against the free trade policies of Britain. In 1907 he wrote to the then secretary of the navy, "I may mention that, as the largest stockholder in the Bethlehem Steel Works, I was the person most influential in establishing in this country the manufacture of armor plates, gun forgings, etc." His daughter Joanna supported this assertion, as did James M. Swank: "The conception of the project to establish the Bethlehem armor plant, the pioneer plant, originated with Joseph Wharton."[10]

Still, Wharton had misgivings apart from a principle of rearmament. He preferred projects over which he was complete master. His influence with Bethlehem Iron was far from that. After the death of Packer he still could not persuade the other directors that Bethlehem Iron should purchase the Saucon Iron Works. Also, at the time the decision to manufacture armor plate was made, the positions of one board member and the general managership were vacant, and shortly thereafter he lost in the competition to fill them. He proposed for the board Thomas McKean, Philadelphia Quaker and manufacturer connected with the Drexel interests. The stockholders chose instead Dr. Linderman's only son, Robert P. who had inherited his father's large holdings. Robert was twenty-two years of age, having been graduated from Lehigh University two years previously. He had gone to work for his father's firm of Linderman and Skeer, miners and shippers of coal, becoming president of the firm upon the death of his father; and he had married Sayre's daughter Ruth. Also, a few months after the election of Robert, the board upon a proposal from Wilbur selected Sayre as general manager over opposition from Wharton and Thurston. This was the first serious conflict among the directors since Wharton's opposition to the continuation of Dr. Linderman as general manager. Thurston tendered his resignation from the position of vice-president. Wharton threatened to sell his stock in the company. He did not carry out the threat; and Thurston's resignation was not accepted. "It is quite evident Uncle Joe & he do not intend to sever their connections," wrote Sayre.[11] Wharton had probably discerned that young Linderman was talented and teachable. Besides, dividends were large and negotiations with the government were proceeding smoothly.

2

The decision to stay having been made, Wharton put his best effort into making the venture a success. In late May he went to Europe to inspect steel works. That was the trip on which he took his wife and daughters. While they looked at historic monuments and museums in London and Paris he met Jaques and Fritz, who had sailed separately, and visited Whitworth and Company, the Woolwich Arsenal, and the Le Creusot Works. During the next ten months he supervised the preparation of contracts with Schneider and Company and the Department of the Navy.

On 22 May 1887, he, Fritz, Sayre, Jaques, and several others gathered in Washington and presented bids to Secretary Whitney. They involved $3,610,707.50 for armor plate for the Puritan, Amphitrite, and other armored vessels "at least equal to the highest grade forged steel armor plates hitherto produced in Europe"; and $902,730.79 for gun forgings for six-, eight-, ten-, and twelve-inch breech-loading rifles.[12]

The department accepted the bids. As expected, Carnegie had taken no action. Midvale Steel had sent in a bid for guns. The Cleveland Rolling Mill had submitted one for armor. But Secretary Whitney had indicated in advance that priority would be given to a company bidding on both armor plate and guns, and Bethlehem Iron was the only company to do so. The directors who were large stockholders provided money for the bond, viz., Wharton ($150,000); Wilbur ($130,000); Linderman ($106,000); Sayre ($105,000); and Knecht ($50,000).[13]

By the time the contracts were signed Fritz and the directors were already working on preliminaries for making guns and armor plate. They had two and one-half years in which to build forging presses and all other machinery needed to fulfill the terms of the contracts. The work included an extensive renovation of, and a large addition to, existing facilities. Fritz had recently completed a mill for rolling rails of forty-five feet in length which did not work well. The directors voted aid to Fritz to put it in good working order.[14] He chose to give his time to the new project, and the rail mill remained idle.

For a time Fritz had some uncertain help from Jaques, who in 1890 entered the employ of the company as ordnance engineer. Jaques had more talent in public relations than in engineering. He remained with the company for four years, then left under circumstances which were not disclosed but were clearly unpleasant. He became an opponent of Bethlehem Iron and later through his influence with Chandler, who had become a senator, helped to blacken its reputation with Congress.

Of immense help to Fritz and the directors was the acquisition of Russell W. Davenport, who in 1888 resigned from Midvale Steel to head the armor plate department of Bethehem Iron. Davenport was a graduate of the Sheffield Scientific School at Yale, where he had been a student of O. D. Allen, Wharton's former chemist at the American Nickel Works, and served as an assistant to Brush. Davenport had studied at the Royal School of Mines of the University of Berlin and then joined the staff at Midvale as a chemist. At Midvale he had successfully made gunmetal according to the stringent specifications demanded by the Department of the Navy. In 1882 Sellers and Clarke had made him general manager.[15]

Almost a year before the contracts were signed the board had voted to float an issue of one million five hundred thousand dollars of first-mortgage bonds to finance a plant for making heavy forgings. They raised additional funds by increasing the capitalization of the company in 1889 from two to three million dollars and the following year, to five million. In 1893 another large bond issue was floated, bringing the total bonded debt to four million dollars.

The entire iron and steel industry of the United States looked in on what was happening at South Bethlehem. They watched as Fritz installed larger basic open-hearth furnaces and diligently worked to construct a new machine shop. The company without effort on its part enjoyed excellent relations with the press. At the Maritime Exhibition held in Boston in 1889, Bethlehem Iron exhibited a hollow crankshaft made of open-hearth fluid compressed steel for the Calumet and Hecla Mining Company and ten- and twenty-inch breech-loading rifles. Commented the *Boston Herald*, "What is so well known in the foreign world as Whitworth fluid-compressed steel has already been replaced in this country by Bethlehem fluid-compressed steel, and Bethlehem steel is now the standard for heavy shafting, gun forgings, and armor-plate."[16] In 1891 the *Iron Age* described Fritz's new machine shop as "the largest building of its kind under one roof in the country, and possibly in the world."[17] This was the Number Two machine shop, later to become a scene of Frederick J. Taylor's experiments in scientific management.

The work of making heavy ordnance progressed smoothly. Fritz ordered for the purpose two large hydraulic presses from Whitworth. They arrived late, but the tardy arrival did not seriously delay fulfilling the contracts with the government. Bethlehem Iron was soon receiving other contracts for manufacturing heavy guns for the army and the navy.

Progress in the manufacture of armor plate was much slower, being broken by false starts and disagreements among Fritz and the directors. He originally had to choose between several methods for making armor plate and selected that being used by Schneider at Le Creusot. Schneider had the plates cast as a single piece and gave them the required hardness and toughness by pounding them with a hammer. He had built for the purpose a hammer of one hundred tons, the largest of its kind in the world. Such treatment gave the plates a close grain and was, Fritz believed, much superior to the method then used in Britain. There, manufacturers forged several plates and welded them together. The outer plate was made hard, in order to resist penetration by a missile, whereas the inner plate was tough, designed to absorb the shock.

Fritz built a 125-ton hammer on the banks of the Lehigh River. This took time; and he had trouble in the construction. The heavy blows unsettled the foundations, which had to be strengthened.[18] He was almost constantly at odds with Thurston and Sayre concerning methods of work, the quality of ores being received, and other matters. Each side blamed the other for the tardy progress. On several occasions Wharton had to intervene to soothe the injured pride of the temperamental Fritz, who never worked well under supervision.[19] By the end of the two and one-half years specified in the contract, the armor plate plant was still unfinished. Secretary B. F. Tracy, who had replaced Whitney as head of the Navy Department with the advent of the Harrison administration, granted an extension of six months, then allowed another period of grace from twelve to fifteen months.

And still the plant was unfinished. The hammer, which was essential to making the plates, became operative only in August 1892. By then it was obsolete. Although the press hailed it as a triumph of engineering and gave it much publicity, the company used it briefly. It delivered a quick stroke, whereas a heavy pressure constantly applied, such as was given by improved hydraulic presses, turned out a more uniform product. Fritz designed a fourteen thousand ton forging press to replace the hammer, and that press served the company up to the time of the Second World War.

The slowness of Bethlehem Iron in delivering armor plate inadvertently worked to the advantage of the navy. During the period of the delay Tracy had opportunity to investigate the potentiality of nickel steel, to have the contract of 1887 revised to require Bethlehem to use nickel steel, and to have Congress authorize the expenditure of one million dollars for purchasing the nickel. If the company had delivered the plates on schedule the vessels for which they were intended would have been made of ordinary steel and consequently out of date by the time they hit the water.

Another consequence of the delay was not so fortunate for the Bethlehem

Iron Company. Tracy, disgusted with the slow progress being made by Bethlehem, asked Carnegie to reconsider his earlier decision not to enter the field. At first Carnegie refused, but gave in when pressed by President Harrison and received a contract for making five thousand tons of plates.[20] Carnegie established a plant at the Homestead works, which was ably operated by William Ellis Corey and his assistant, W. A. Cline, under the supervision of Schwab. Sayre reported in his diary for 1 November 1894, "Hemphill, Owen & I went to Homestead & met manager Schwab who showed us through every part of the Works, shops, etc. They have as good an armor plate plant & shops as we have, and the very best plate mill, beam mill angles & shapes I have ever seen. All modern and complete and kept in excellent order."

Carnegie's entry into the business of making armor plate brought him and Wharton together more often. Controversy arose concerning patents for making nickel steel which involved Schneider and Company, the Harvey Steel Company, Carnegie, and Bethlehem. Other points of contact were competition among the makers of armor plate in the international market and conditions for doing business on the domestic scene. On one occasion when a business conference was scheduled at Carnegie's home in New York City he wrote inviting Wharton and Anna to come and stay with him and Mrs. Carnegie over Sunday. "I should so much like to have a season of communion with you. You are about the only one of the old set left in Philadelphia. Townsend, Drexel, Childs, all vanished."[21]

The close cooperation between the Carnegie and Bethlehem companies on a number of points later led to charges made in the press and in Congress of collusion between them in submitting bids, especially for making armor plate. In fact they were keen competitors in this as in other fields. As they were the only two American companies then making armor plate they frequently faced each other in seeking orders from the government and such firms as William Cramp and Sons, which built vessels for the governments of other countries and for private concerns. "Of course C[arnegie] will try to get ahead of us in any future work by grabbing the whole of it if he can, as he tried to take all of the last contract," Wharton informed Linderman. On another occasion Wharton wrote, "From what Meigs tells me, Cramp has got the Department fixed for buying ships complete with the armor, and this means that he will give all the armor to Carnegie to make I think. If you or Mr. Sayre or Mr. Davenport can stop this I guess there is no time to lose." Wharton was quick to scotch rumors that Carnegie might be making better steel plates than Bethlehem was doing. "Without rather numerous trials it would seem imprudent to assume . . . that a plate reduced in thickness by rolling [as Carnegie was doing] would be better than a plate reduced in thickness by hydraulic forging [the method used by Bethlehem Iron]. And should it prove true that a plain straight plate is improved by rolling after case-hardening, how can a tapering plate or even a curved plate be so rolled?"[22]

3

Through his connection with Bethlehem Iron, Wharton by 1893 found himself a leader in a project receiving more national attention than anything he had ever undertaken. The Bethlehem Iron Company, which had once been a modest manufacturer of rails, had become a major maker of armaments for the nation and a principal supplier of armor plate for warships. For the remainder of its existence as an independent company Bethlehem Iron retained this position, notwithstanding competition from Carnegie and other firms. Wharton's reputation, influence, and fortune correspondingly grew. The directors of Bethlehem Iron met with increasing frequency in his office in Philadelphia. In 1893 the company rented a suite of rooms in the same building and put Roger Haydock in charge with the title of sales agent. Nephew and uncle worked well together, and Wharton was also soon using young Haydock for commissions not directly connected with the business of the Bethlehem Iron Company.

Wharton's greatest loss during the conversion of the company to defense contracting was personal rather than monetary, namely, the death of William Thurston.

Thurston, following his recovery from tuberculosis, the death of Ellen, and his conversion to Episcopalianism, devoted himself to work. He turned over part of the responsibility for raising his four sons to Ellen's parents, Professor and Mrs. Coppée. The youngest son, Henry Coppée Thurston, died in 1883 at the age of four. Thurston gave some time to the welfare of the employees of the Bethlehem Iron Company and their dependents. He took in charge the establishment of a chapel for workingmen and their families, called St. Joseph's. It was located near the furnaces on land supplied by Joseph Wharton. Smallpox visited the Bethlehems in 1882 and left many orphans. Thurston decided to found a home for them. He rented a house, hired a matron, and for four years bore most of the expense himself. The project was incorporated in 1886 and two years later moved into quarters built on a lot which he provided.[23]

Then he gave other members of the family occasion for comment by marrying again. The new wife was Louise Mitchell, a relative of Ellen and the daughter of Mr. and Mrs. Edward Coppée Mitchell of Philadelphia. The couple was married on 25 April 1887, at a time when signs of tuberculosis were reappearing in Thurston. Other members of the family could see the effects and guess his future. Thurston, buoyed by his love of Louise, refused all such thoughts. He surrounded her with luxury well beyond his means. A disgusted Hannah Haydock wrote to Wharton following a visit with Thurston and "his handsome boys" imploring him to talk with Thurston about his style of living: "Will is so confidentially in your employ that we naturally still cleave to him as a part almost of the days that were."[24] But William Thurston had matured beyond the point at which Wharton could give him personal advice unasked. Ambition drove Thurston on, sometimes to the embarrassment of his uncle.

Thurston with some justice had distrusted Dr. Linderman, who at one point had indicated he would have liked to replace Thurston in the vice-presidency with Sayre's son, Robert, Jr.[25] The death of Dr. Linderman, followed by the abortive attempt of Wharton and Thurston to prevent the appointment of Sayre as superintendent, did nothing to relieve Thurston's anxiety. He and Sayre clashed, this at a time when Fritz was proclaiming an inability to work under either person. In truth, Thurston was seeking a way of protecting himself against both men.

A revision in the bylaws, engineered by Wharton in 1882, provided a possible means. The bylaws stipulated that the vice-president should exercise the powers and duties of a chief executive in the absence of the president. This advertised to all interested parties that under normal circumstances the vice-president would be next in line for the presidency. Thurston then attempted to maneuver Hunt out of the presidency and in 1886 wrote to his uncle, "I want thee to have a plain talk with Mr. Wilbur about Bethlehem matters. I cannot stay there subject to petty annoyances and taking the responsibility of the business not being compensated. Mr. Hunt, this is in confidence will resign, if I am made President with $10,000 a year and matters clearly understood between Sayre & myself which we can arrange when together."[26] Wharton faithfully responded to this invitation, only to encounter strong objections from Wilbur, who pointed out that if Hunt resigned in favor of Thurston, Sayre would probably have to leave the superintendency and even retire from the board. Writing to Sayre, Wilbur commented, "I further told him [Wharton] that I would not remain with the Company if it required constant contest, and that we all had too much to occupy and annoy us, and life was too short for it. I advised him to talk freely with Beth. people and then make up his mind whether he could afford to risk it." Wharton did as Wilbur suggested and as a result withdrew his support from Thurston, thereby extending the status quo for two more years.[27]

In the spring of 1888 Hunt died and Thurston became president, too late to benefit from the promotion. Consumption was eating his life away. In June 1888 he received a leave of absence for six months. It was extended for three successive periods of six months each. Wilbur briefly exercised the duties of the president, then relinquished them to young Robert Linderman, who succeeded to the vice-presidency. Thurston never again saw Bethlehem. He and Louise, leaving behind the boys and a daughter, Mary, who had been born to Louise, went to Cuba, then to Egypt, hoping that rest and a warm climate might restore strength. To no avail. May of 1890 found William and Louise in London, to which they had traveled from the Near East. Wharton Barker, on a business trip, saw them and wrote, "There was never a man so thin and so destroyed as Bill." Wharton Barker was on hand the night Thurston died. "Louise was quiet and while a child in many ways is more of a woman than I had thought."[28]

Thurston left a small estate, sufficient to support Louise in modest style. The inheritance from his sister Hetty had been placed in trust for the children. The will named Louise and J. S. Lovering Wharton as guardians; but Lovering declined to serve and asked Joseph to take his place. For a time Wharton was undecided. Louise's mother wrote asking him for help in finding a place to live in Germantown. He declined. "The marriage of your daughter and my nephew always seemed to me a grievous error for all concerned. If he had given me opportunity I should have tried to dissuade him, but he gave no opportunity . . . took his own way, as he had legal right to do, but hardly moral right in view of his physical condition and his duty to his boys. . . . As for the guardianship, particularly as far as it relates to the boys, I may feel bound to act but have not yet decided—perhaps I must first see them. I wrote to Coppée last month inviting all three to spend some part of their vacation with us on Conanicut."[29]

The boys arrived at Marbella: Edward Coppée ("Coppée"), age fifteen; Joseph Wharton ("Joe"), age thirteen; and William Wharton ("Wharton"), age twelve. They captured the hearts of all the family. "We have an abundance of jokes, & laugh morning, noon, & evening," wrote Joseph's daughter Anna. The boys "have taken to playing crambo & writing poetical descriptions of things we do, so that we are fairly swimming in poetry. . . . Coppée wrote me a long, good poem, which I value. . . . Wharton T. was too sweet for anything! He would spread a shawl for me on the rock, & sit in Thoughtful Gully with me nearly the whole afternoon, while I read him poetry. . . . On the 16th Joe went afoot from our front door to the Beaver tail light house in 43½ min., & we followed him in the carriage, with whiskey, water, etc., in case of need. . . . Bertram had agreed to give him $10 if he did it in ¾ of an hour."[30]

Thurston's daughter Mary went to live with her mother; the boys, with the Coppées near the Lehigh University campus. Joseph Wharton became guardian to a third generation of Thurston males.

15

Industrialist of the Nineties: And the End of the Nickel Business

In the autumn of 1890 Barker Brothers and Company failed, one of the first in a chain reaction which within a few years reached into all sections of the country. The principal trouble lay with the railroads. They were mismanaged and overcapitalized. European bankers had become uneasy and began withdrawing capital, with the result that many railroads failed. Barker Brothers and Company had heavily invested in some of these bankrupt roads, including the Oregon Pacific; the Ohio and Northwestern; the Charleston, Cincinnati, and Chicago; and the San Antonio and Aransas Pass. The final blow had come when Baring Brothers, one of England's most respected firms, closed its doors. Baring was the London agent for the Barkers. Creditors began calling on Barker Brothers for payment, and the company could not meet the demand. As one Philadelphia paper summed up the situation, Barker Brothers and Company "had ventured their argosies upon so long voyages that they could not get back to port when the sudden storm overtook them."[1]

The failure was a personal disaster for Abraham Barker. He was one of the oldest and most respected members of the Philadelphia stock exchange. His fortune was gone, his reputation shattered. Wharton Barker, too, suffered. He had obtained the prestigious positions of president of the Pennsylvania Finance Company and a directorship in the Investment Company of Philadelphia. He gave them up and concentrated on saving what could be salvaged with the aid of friends. Early in 1891 the firm reopened under the name of Barker and Company with Abraham and Wharton Barker now joined with J. C. W. Baker.[2] But it was not the same. The old firm, one of Philadelphia's financial landmarks, was gone.

The Barker failure was more than a disaster for Abraham and his son. It was also a portent. An old order of banking was dying. Big finance was entering the scene along with big industry, transportation, and communications. Little firms would have a hard time competing against giants protected by the financial resources of men such as John Pierpont Morgan. The ensuing quarter of a century was to witness a radical transformation of American economic life.

Joseph Wharton avoided the disasters which overcame many other businessmen. His success contrasted to the loss suffered by his brother-in-law. When Barker Brothers failed, Wharton was able and willing to assume some of its obligations to members of the family. For example, he took from it the burden of financing the Wharton Railroad Switch Company and helped brother William through many troubles; and when in 1898 bankruptcy became inevitable, Wharton purchased the property and had it reorganized with William still in control.[3] Wharton did this without sacrificing anything of importance to his own undertakings. Throughout the decade his fortune modestly increased and his influence grew. He bowed to bigness and supported it and saw himself as one of the captains of industry upon whom the welfare of the country depended.

The anomaly of the situation was that his eminence depended not at all on bigness. As size was becoming measured in that decade of industrial revolution, his fortune and renown came from his management of a rabbit's nest of little or medium-sized ventures, not one of which was, if left to itself, likely to have survived the trend of the times.

1

He retained a general good health. "I suppose that next fall we should be hearing of your joining the University foot-ball team and distinguishing yourself in the scrimmages with Princeton and Yale," wrote Henry C. Lea in 1891.[4] To be sure, constant activity occasionally wore him down. He once wrote to his wife, "I am tired of business and would gladly be out of it all to have a little leisure before I die, but it is hard to get out of business," and to MacVeagh, "This would be a lovely time to be out of business, and, as Blaine once said to me, to be off for Europe with no fixed time for returning and with a sufficient letter of credit."[5] Such complaints were few and are unconvincing. He liked action, of both business and play. Philosophizing in quiet moments was good for relaxation, but it always ended by leaving him vexed. He would think deeply concerning the cosmos, but not for long. And play, however, enjoyable it might be, was like brandy: a little was good medicine, a steady diet was ruinous. In any event business provided a *joie de vivre*, and the opportunities for it in a maturing America had rewarded him. He had sought fulfillment and found it together with power. As ruler of an industrial empire he was exacting, kindly, energetic, and happy.

His empire must have appeared fantastic to a casual observer, for it had no organic unity. Wharton had not built it around a major thrust, as had Packer with railroads and Carnegie with steel. The parts of Wharton's empire—the mining and refining of nickel; the manufacture of steel; the Jersey mining and smelting business; farming and forestry in the pinelands; fishing for the menhaden; and mining for gold, to mention the most lasting and time-consuming—had no essential interdependence. Each part was complete in itself. Furthermore, with the exception of the Bethlehem Iron Company he completely owned each enterprise. When wisdom dictated a joint stock venture, as happened with his north Jersey railroads, he kept all but a few shares for himself and took care that the remainder went to trusted friends, relatives, or employees. He appointed the manager of each enterprise; and each manager answered to neither partners, directors, nor stockholders, but only to Wharton.

An assistant, Henry C. Wenner, entered Wharton's employ as an office boy at the age of nineteen and in time became a valued secretary and an aide in administering the American Nickel Works. Wharton never gave Wenner authority over the managers. Nor did Wharton have any other full- or part-time assistants who might control them through legal, financial, or real estate operations. He employed lawyers and other specialists as the need arose and personally took care of financial ties with banks and major transactions involving property. He also kept each enterprise free of debt and met a deficit in one with profits from others.[6] The nature of his operations was such that he frequently had to borrow large sums. He did this without mortgaging any part of his independently owned enterprises. Instead, he kept a large portfolio of stocks and bonds, which he offered as security for loans. In the nineties most of this paper was in iron companies and railroads. It is not too much to say that his principal reason for keeping railroad securities was that of safeguarding the financial independence of his industrial empire; and that one reason for his ability to weather successfully the economic crisis which sank Barker Brothers and Company was the growing prosperity of the Bethlehem Iron Company and a perspicacity in selling and buying railroad securities at times favorable to himself.

In terms of profit-making capacity Wharton's industrial empire was unrelievedly lopsided. Steel and nickel made money, as at times did Jersey iron, although the latter experienced many lean years. (Carnegie at one time told Wharton that the Jersey iron undertaking was "foolish.")[7] But farming, forestry, fishing, and gold mining nowhere nearly repaid in profits the attention that Wharton gave them.

The explanation for this unlikely assortment of enterprises is found in Wharton himself. He was the focus, the source, the dynamo, the preserver of each. All but a few were concerned with the mining and refining of metals; and those few exceptions were the result of personal interests of other sorts. Furthermore, in managing them he effectively reproduced the family economy of his ancestors. What fell to his control he keenly felt responsible for and treated as a father would a son. He demanded obedience from his managers and allowed them a large measure of freedom. It was understood that, as sons should magnify the father, so should his enterprises establish the dimensions of the talent of Joseph Wharton.

The rudimentary nature of office work in the nineteenth century facilitated this paternal approach, for it placed a premium on personal relationships. Whenever possible, Wharton conducted business on a face-to-face basis. His first office—if it can be called that—was a corner in the American Nickel Works, although he often used the facilities of Barker Brothers and Company on Third Street as a meeting place and clearinghouse for information. Later, probably in 1883, when he hired Wenner, he opened a central office in downtown Philadelphia at 401 Chestnut Street and a few years later moved into the Philadelphia Bank Building. From these several headquarters he wrote letters in longhand and posted copies in letterbooks, made handwritten entries in ledgers and kept small and unsophisticated files. He had neither receptionists nor other office specialists. Even after he began using typewriter and telephone, about the turn of the century, he often preferred the older methods of communication. He would correspond almost daily with his managers by letter or telegram. He might write as many as four letters in an afternoon on as many different subjects to Edward Kelly or one of the others. Occasionally he would ask a manager to come to Philadelphia for a discussion. More frequently, he visited a manager at his place of business.

A letter to Anna written in 1895 contains a typical itinerary. He had started from Marbella, where he was vacationing. "Going down to Milford, Dr. Wm Pepper was with me and we had much conversation. At New Haven G. Willits met me and I visited the pipe factory with him, then on to Bridgeport to see owner of steamer I want, then to New York, then to Port Oram where after inspecting furnaces I went to Kenil for supper and lodging. This morning to Hibernia mine, thence to Mount Hope mine, thence again to furnace, thence via High Bridge to this office [206 Philadelphia Bank Building], where I have been overhauling divers things, and am now about to start for Ontalauna. Tomorrow I mean to take 6 a.m. train for Bethlehem, leave there 12:30 and spend afternoon here. Thursday morning here till 12:55 or 3:30 then to New York for several business affairs, and at 6:30 leave for Newport."[8]

On trips such as this he carried no briefcase. He committed information beyond that which he could easily remember to scraps of paper. Wrote Wenner, "It was not an unusual sight to see him pull out a large envelope from his inside coat pocket—which envelope contained memoranda, which gave as much satisfaction as our present auditors are able to collect in several week's time."[9]

The pattern of Wharton's activity as overseer of an industrial empire is sometimes as puzzling as was the nature of the empire itself. In addition to making major decisions he occasionally became concerned over minor matters, for example, a return of several carboys of no great value, negotiation for the sale of a few crates of cranberries, and a transfer of mules from Gap to Batsto. His managers were accustomed to his whims, which rarely if ever disrupted normal operations. They could predict the wishes of their employer and were content. His interferences were in fact less frequent and more trivial than those which he had experienced in his youth from the directors of the Pennsylvania and Lehigh Zinc Company.

Certainly any annoyance which the managers might have felt at Wharton's interference was more than compensated for by his practices of consulting them in connection with important decisions and impartially adjudicating complaints. Voigt wrote of him, "His kindly and absolutely fair treatment of every one, and at all times, invited the confidence and insured him the respect of his employees, and their good will."[10] Following the custom of the times, he maintained no programs of social insurance. Also, he did not pay his managers high salaries or give bonuses, although on at least one occasion he allowed a manager (Gracey) a share in the profits. Still, the managers could enjoy normal upper-middle-class luxury; and they knew that Wharton would not desert them in time of need. His books show that during a number of years he paid occasional sums of fifty or one hundred dollars to C. E. Benade and Mrs. Benade of Bethlehem. Benade had briefly preceded Captain Doble as manager of the Gap Mine. The payments suggest that Benade had met with an industrial accident for which Wharton felt some responsibility. And when Captain Doble retired, Wharton made certain that he was provided for.

Wharton's paternal concern nowhere appears better than in words of advice which he gave to young Andrew Etheridge, who in the late nineties became manager of the farm at Atsion: "As for your handwriting it was not my intention to discourage you, but to encourage you. You have good sense and diligence which fit you to perform your duties faithfully, and it is a pity that you must appear to disadvantage for want of a little schooling which you could acquire in the winter evenings. This letter of yours that I am now answering is better written than your previous letters, and shows that you can improve yourself even without a teacher, if you will get a copy book for writing, and a spelling book."[11]

Wharton left labor relations to his managers, with the result that his correspondence and account books contain little on the subject. He followed prevailing practices, which provided workers with no job security or what today are sometimes called fringe benefits. He was especially annoyed when an employee tried to force him to pay compensation for an injury incurred as a result of his own carelessness. Attempts of this sort increased after the depression of 1893 and sometimes resulted in litigation. "I cannot afford to run a hospital and charity group," he wrote on one such occasion.[12] Yet he rarely experienced serious problems with labor. He paid standard wages and tried in other ways to retain the loyalty of his workers, realizing that in the mining and refining of metals the loss of a key employee might also mean a loss of trade secrets.

Like most employers of his times, he disapproved of the militant activities of labor unions. In the rare event of a strike, as happened for example at the spelter works when the employees revolted against Darlington, he sought out the trouble and tried to correct it. On only one occasion did he have to deal with a strike organized to force unionization. Then, he supported Kelly, who roughly put it down, and wrote of the event to William Whitwell, Chairman of the North England Board of Conciliation:

> I have in fact just suffered the annoyance and loss of a strike at my principal iron furnaces, which though lasting only a week, cut down the output of pig iron about 5000 tons. The demand made by my people was particularly unreasonable, because they were already receiving as high wages as were paid by any of my competitors, and in some instances still higher. This strike was by the furnace men, engine drivers, etc., only (not extending to the much larger number working in the mines), but was intended to start a movement that should prevail not only among my own people wherever employed, to the number of about 2000, but also throughout the furnace and mine industries of my part of the country.[13]

Inevitably, perhaps, his roles as a real and a virtual father overlapped. He practiced nepotism as readily as his ancestors had done, and he forgave much to an employee whom he especially valued (for example, George W. Miles, who before his death in 1901 ineptly managed the menhaden fishing business in New York and New England waters). His relations with Anna and the girls were subtly conditioned by business practices. In some ways he seemed to treat family as another enterprise. He kept no separate family financial records. Familial and business expenses were entered in chronological order in the same ledgers. When the girls were young, he looked on his wife as their "manager" and made her a regular and none too generous allowance for household expenses. When Joanna and Anna grew up, married, and thereby became parts of separate households, he still tended to treat their economic affairs, insofar as they depended on him, as business enterprises. An unforeseen but happy consequence of this was that the girls' husbands, J. Bertram Lippincott and Harrison S. Morris, became "managers" in a special sense and were of much help to Joseph in his last years.

As had been true with his father and grandfathers, the lack of feeling associated with business did not mar the affection he felt for kin. Nor did he seek out business in order to escape the family. "The difficulty is not in keeping him at home when once he arrives but in knowing when to expect him," wrote Joanna.[14] He enjoyed play at home as much as he liked working at the office. He once wrote to his wife, "If I come by the first train, arriving at Chelt[enham] 5:10 there would be time for a sleigh ride before dinner. Let Patrick bring my fur coat and cap." Anna would accompany him on the ride. Again, he wrote to his daughter Anna, "As there is a time for everything surely there is a time for innocent youthful hilarity and for that deep enjoyment of unsophistocated nature which has a basis of seriousness or even of solemnity. The great pageant is constantly spread before men's eyes, if only they would look up and see the glory of it."[15]

After Joanna and Anna were married, Joseph and his wife lived alone in the big house with Mary sometimes present. No one felt lonesome. Mary came and went as she pleased. Managing the servants took much of Anna's time. She had private charities to attend to as well as a farm on the Lime Kiln Pike, a legacy from her father. Letter writing, visits with relatives, and shopping had to be fitted in. Anna, like Joseph, could never be bored, for neither was ever idle.

2

No other enterprise was as dear to Wharton as was his nickel business. He personally kept the accounts of the American Nickel Works. Although in time Wenner took over many details of office management at Camden, Wharton maintained contact with customers, suppliers, competitors, and the government and personally organized and controlled his mining ventures in Canada. Yet when a time arrived that the nickel business could no longer be profitable as an independent concern, he relinquished it to become part of an International Nickel Company with as much ease and good will as he had shown in giving Joanna to J. Bertram Lippincott and Anna to Harrison S. Morris.

An event of major importance earned Wharton a reprieve in ending the nickel business. This was the discovery of nickel steel, a breakthrough of a sort for which the international nickel industry had been waiting to take up the surplus product coming from the mines of New Caledonia and Canada.

The leading armament makers of Europe had begun experimenting with nickel in the 1880s. In 1889 James Riley, manager of the Steel Works of Scotland, publicized the advantages of nickel steel. In the United States the transition from his report to industrial applications came about when Samuel J. Ritchie, an enterprising director of the Canadian Copper Company, brought it to the attention of Secretary of Navy Tracy, who immediately obtained information concerning the progress which had been made in producing nickel steel. Tracy discovered among other things that a few months earlier an American inventor and steelmaker, Hayward August Harvey, had found a means of cementing nickel to steel in such a way as to increase the hardness of the surface. Tracy employed Harvey to experiment with applying his discovery to the problem of armor plate. The result was that Harvey successfully developed a heat-treating process for face hardening armor. Tracy tested the results by authorizing a trial of three armor plates, representing the best sorts of simple, nickel, and compound welded steel. The trial was held in September 1890 and produced a triumph for the makers of nickel steel. Congress authorized the purchase of one million pounds of nickel to continue the experiments, which were uniformly successful. The navy adopted nickel steel for armor plate and, wherever possible, for guns. Within a few years the Harvey process became almost universally employed not only for armor plate but also for products of many other sorts such as guns, marine shafting, axles, structural forms, shear knives, bicycle spokes, and gears.[16]

The advantage of using nickel steel to make armor plate having been established, the next question was, who would refine the nickel? Secretary Tracy talked with Robert M. Thompson of the Orford Copper Company and Wharton, both of whom at first anticipated that Wharton would do the work, as he still owned the only modern refinery in the country. But Thompson, an exceptionally shrewd and hard-working entrepreneur, outmaneuvered Wharton. He did what Wharton might have done in the years of youth when he was more daring and had little to lose. In an informal memorandum to Tracy, Thompson indicated that Wharton's price was too high and mentioned a lower price for which he could make the nickel. Thompson did not at the time have a process for doing this. Perhaps Tracy knew this; in any event, he decided to give the younger man a chance. Tracy would rather do this than bargain with Wharton, who was an annoying defender of the Bethlehem Iron Company in the matter of delinquency in meeting contract dates. When Thompson admitted that he still had to find a low-cost process, Tracy told him to go ahead, that time remained. The Bethlehem Company was behind in filling its contracts; and the Navy Department was continuing experiments with the Harvey process. Thompson agreed to make the attempt.[17]

He succeeded. In 1893 Thompson described the work:

The first process employed was the use of dilute sulphuric acid on the raw or uncalcined matte, thus dissolving out the nickel and iron sulphides, and leaving the copper behind. The nickel and iron were then crystallized from the solution as sulphates, and these sulphates were calcined, producing an oxide of nickel and iron quite free from copper. The objection to this process was the very large plant required, its slowness, and the difficulty of making a complete separation of the matte, as a large portion of the nickel was always left behind, and the matte soon got into such condition that the operation could not be continued.[18]

The superintendent of the works, John L. Thomson, and his assistant, Charles Bartlett, then experimented along a different line. They inadvertently rediscovered a process which had been used as early as 1776 by the Swedish chemist Gustavus von Engestrom and then neglected, and which had been again discovered and patented by an American, William B. Tatro, in 1877 but again neglected.[19] This soon became popularly known as the "tops and bottoms process."

Wharton in his essay, "The Production of Nickel and Cobalt in 1896," described the tops and bottoms process thus:

Matte of first fusion . . . is practically freed from iron by subsequent roasting and smelting, and then smelted in a cupola furnace with sodic sulphate and coke. The product of this fusion drawn off into suitable vessels divides by gravity while fluid into two portions, a lighter and a heavier, easily separable when cold, the lighter called tops, containing nearly all the soda, copper, and iron, while the heavier, called bottoms, contains nearly all the nickel. As the separation of nickel and copper is not quite complete, the bottoms are again or more than once retreated in substantially the same manner until nickel sulphide of satisfactory purity is obtained. From the tops metallic copper is ultimately produced. The very small quantity of cobalt present goes with the nickel and there remains. The nickel sulphide just named becomes, when dead roasted, nickel oxide, which is considered good enough for use in producing nickel steel. When this nickel oxide is reduced, melted, and poured into water "shot nickel" is produced, which looks well, but is not approved for nice uses.

Wharton further explained that nickel steel for armor and ordnance was usually made by mixing nickel oxide "with a carbonaceous substance" and throwing the mixture "into the bath of melted steel before pouring it into molds."[20] Several years later he elaborated on this topic in a letter to William W. Whitney of the Cambria Iron Company: "The Bethlehem Iron Co. mix nickel oxide with powdered coke and fine lime, moist enough to hold together, then form the mass into small bricks which are dried and thrown into the bath of fluid steel, where the oxide is reduced and thoroughly blended with the steel. . . . The Carnegie Co. prefer to use nickel in the metallic form, but as their waste of nickel is much larger than ours, and their product no better, no good reason appears for paying the higher price that nickel metal costs over nickel in oxide."[21]

Having discovered (or rediscovered) the process he needed, Thompson bought Tatro's patent, secured his own patents in the United States and many other countries, and negotiated with the Canadian Copper Company for the entire output of its mines. He was then in a position to compete with Le Nickel, even within its home territory of continental Europe. According to the historians of the International Nickel Company, John F. Thompson and Norman Beasley, he became his own salesman and crossed the Atlantic thirteen times in one year. "He had learned it was a mistake to make a quotation on nickel to a prospective European customer. The prospect was able to save money by taking the quotation to Le Nickel. It always shaded the price. Thompson learned quickly. Thereafter, when invited to submit a bid, he jumped on the first steamship, appeared in person, asked for an offer and, almost always, made the sale."[22]

Wharton applauded Thompson's success in thwarting Le Nickel. Before the sudden enlarging of the market, when competition with Le Nickel had appeared impossible for small firms, Wharton had seriously considered coming to terms with the Canadian and the Orford companies, perhaps even selling out to them. Voigt later wrote that interests located in Cleveland, Ohio, which controlled these companies, took an initiative in seeking cooperation: "The Canadian Copper Co. being the first to erect a smelting plant, shipped its matte to the Orford Copper Co. at Bayonne for treatment, but as the plant of this establishment was not [yet] adapted for the separation of nickel from copper, the result was disappointing, and Mr. Wharton was appealed to, by the Cleveland Co. offering him all the interest he wished in their concern, to induce him to take up the refining of their nickel."[23]

Certainly Wharton had considered some sort of coordination of interests as a means of meeting the competition presented by Le Nickel. Wharton's papers contain an agreement in his handwriting, drafted sometime in 1887 or 1888, and never ratified. The principal articles of the proposed agreement were: (1) Wharton would advise the Canadian Copper Company concerning the reduction of ore to matte; (2) he would have an option to purchase the four thousand unissued shares of the company's stock, this being 8 percent of the total; (3) if he took up the option the company would in turn purchase the American Nickel Works; and (4) if he did not take up the option he would for twenty years be the exclusive agent of the company for selling its nickel products.

Voigt wrote that Wharton ultimately refused to cooperate with the Canadian Copper Company because of a dislike for one of its directors, who was "publicly charged with having 'stolen a railroad.'"[24] The director might have been Ritchie, who had large interests in the Central Ontario road.[25] But the board voted Ritchie's ouster in 1891; and the event elicited no especial comment from, or change in attitude, by Wharton. The more likely explanation is that Wharton saw in the revolution being made by the Harvey process an opportunity for continued independence of, and profit for, the American Nickel Works.

In sum, even after the discovery of the tops and bottoms process, Wharton for a time regarded the situation as providing custom for himself and the Orford Company. He could continue making nickel salts and pure grain nickel of high grade, which his regular customers desired. "My nickel is made in a better and more costly way than [that of] any of its rivals, and it commands a preference, or even a higher price, where nice results are desired," he wrote in 1895.[26] He could, moreover, share with Orford the new market in making the lower grades used for nickel steel. He could control purchases by the Bethlehem Iron Company, and he could use some of Orford's nickel oxide at Camden. He once wrote, in 1897, "I have bought from Orford Copper Co. 100,000 lbs. nickel in oxide at 24 cts. per lb. . . . and I have sold of this 60,000 lbs. nickel in oxide to Bethlehem Iron Co. at 26¼ cts. per lb." The remaining forty thousand pounds he sent to Camden "for reduction to metal for those of my customers whom it will suit."[27]

As though in exchange for consideration from Thompson, Wharton sometimes put the Orford company in touch with customers for copper and nickel oxide beyond the capacity of the American Nickel Works. And in 1896 Wharton readily agreed to participate in a pool arranged by Thompson with Le Nickel for raising prices and dividing the market. The pool promised stability and profit to all concerned. Wharton wrote of it on 13 January 1896, to C. P. Goss of the Scovill company:

> Robert M. Thompson of Orford Copper Co. has returned from Europe, where he made a contract with "Le Nickel" that looks to a steadier market with a higher price for nickel. The immediate effects are the establishing of a common selling agent in Europe for "Le Nickel" and the Orford-Cleveland-Canadian people, the raising of price in Europe by three pence per lb., and the withdrawal in the near future of "Le Nickel" from the American market. No price has definitely been fixed for nickel in America. Mr. Langbeth [?] of the American Metal Co. is to reach this country about a week hence, and a conference is then to be held between him, Thompson, and me. The price seems likely to be fixed at 33 cts. for a few large favored buyers and to range upward for the smaller ones, perhaps to 40 cts. for single kegs.[28]

3

The division of the North American market between the American Nickel Works and the Orford Copper Company might have lasted indefinitely if Wharton could have been assured of a steady and cheap supply of good ore. No one knew better than he the importance of this to success. He had learned the lesson when working for the Pennsylvania and Lehigh Zinc Company. His failure to find an independent source of zinc ore had forced him to give up hope of becoming a leader in the spelter business. He had made an American monopoly of the nickel industry by controlling the only commercially profitable nickel mine on the continent. He had for years protected that monopoly by systematicaly investigating reports of discoveries of nickel ore elsewhere, being prepared if necessary to buy them. He had lost his monopoly when deposits of nickel were discovered which he could not control, first in New Caledonia, then in the Sudbury district of Ontario. Now he had to face the realities of the Gap Mine playing out and of being unable to find a reliable substitute.

Mining at Gap had for years been increasingly expensive as the richer ore bodies near the surface became exhausted. He had closed the mine for almost two years in the early eighties, when nickel from the New Caledonia deposits had come on the market, and operated the American Nickel Works on accumulated supplies of matte. In 1884 he reopened the mine and recorded profits from it for that year and for 1885 but lost money on it every year thereafter. The American Nickel Works provided the profits for his nickel business. He continued to renovate and enlarge them until by 1898 they had an annual capacity of one million pounds or five times that of 1873, the year immediately preceding the Prussian coinage.[29]

Inevitably, as he enlarged the refinery, a time arrived when the Gap Mine could no longer supply it with all the ore it needed. He began in the late 1880s buying matte from the Canadian Copper Company and several other firms which were attempting to establish themselves in the Sudbury district. Finally, at the end of 1893, the richer ores at Gap gave out altogether. "With great regret, I say stop," he wrote to Doble on 31 January 1894, and five days later wrote again, "I presume that our old Gap Mine is in the hands of the undertakers by this time. . . . It makes me sad to give up the mine, but though the ore is there somewhere I can't throw away all my means in looking for it." He cautioned Doble to keep the pumps in good condition "for any one who may desire to open up again."

He now depended entirely on ores from Canada and began a search for a reliable supply. He made four major attempts to secure good Canadian mining properties. The first was the purchase with E. K. Davis of the Beatrice Mine, which provided some ore but soon proved to be unprofitable. A second venture involved acquiring a half interest in ore lands including the Blézard Mine, which a firm called the Dominion Mineral Company had owned. For a time the prospect looked good. Wharton contemplated receiving more matte than he could use and wrote to his friend Arthur Krupp at Berndorf, Austria, suggesting an alliance. But the mine failed to yield paying quantities.

A third attempt to locate a commercially viable source of ore involved acquiring control of the Murray Mine from H. H. Vivian. This was one of the original mines in the Sudbury district. Vivian also wanted Wharton to take the Violet Mine, but he settled for the Murray and in 1897 bought control. Although ores already above ground supplied him with matte for several years, attempts to locate more were unsuccessful. "The Murray Mine has been disastrous to me, and will apparently result in a net loss of $10,000 or more."[30]

The fourth venture was that of purchasing shares in the Trill Mining and Manufacturing Company. This concern had acquired the ore properties of the Drury Mining Company, which had become bankrupt. Again he considered an alliance with Krupp of Berndorf and again was disappointed in the mine. Although he received some matte from the Trill, the management was poor, the machinery was in disrepair, and the creditors were impatient.

These Canadian ventures having ended in failure, he considered the possibility of using the low grade ores at Gap. Might these not be profitably used with the aid of concentrators? Captain Doble had died in 1897 and was succeeded in the managership of the Gap property by his son, Charles A. Doble. Wharton wrote to him, "You probably remember hearing your father say that there is a great mass of low grade ore in Gap Mine, carrying about one per cent of nickel, that could be got out cheaply. Do you know where that ore is, can you form an idea of the quantity and of the cost of mining it? And can you estimate the cost of getting the mine and machinery into condition to start mining that ore?"[31] He had Doble send a keg of poor ore to the Wetherill Separating Company, a firm producing an improved concentrator invented by John Price Wetherill, son of Wharton's former competitor in the zinc business, Samuel Wetherill. When Wharton received the report of the company he immediately ordered Doble to sink a shaft in search of a sufficient quantity of ore. For six months in 1899–1900 Doble worked, then reported discovery of a large deposit and requested permission to equip the mine. Almost immediately the vein petered out. Wharton ordered all work on the new shaft stopped.[32]

That was Wharton's last attempt to explore the remaining potential of the Gap Mine. He remained convinced that much good ore remained in the ground. He wrote in "The Production of Nickel and Cobalt in 1896": "Three great masses of nickeliferous pyrrhotite were successively exhausted, and search for other masses was discontinued because of the moderate prices and abundant supplies of nickel matte from Canada. As this mine was worked only to the depth of less than 300 feet, and much ore of about 1 per cent is known to exist above that depth, it is reasonably certain that large resources of ore remain there untouched, awaiting discovery by the diamond drill followed by modern methods of mining and smelting."[33]

4

Principally because of nickel steel, the American nickel industry prospered as much in the nineties as it had suffered in the eighties. Political and legal difficulties were removed. In response to intensive lobbying, especially by the Canadian Copper Company, the Congress in the McKinley Act of 1890 reduced the tariff on nickel and copper ores and through the Wilson-Gorman Act of 1894 entirely removed it. A subsequent threat from the Canadian government to keep the business of refining the ores in Canada by means of an export duty was met and removed. Although the pooling arrangement engineered by Thompson briefly existed, the price remained sufficiently high for both Orford and the American Nickel Works to register profits.

Yet Wharton was uneasy. He wrote to Doble of feeling himself "exposed to some danger of being concerned by the Canadian Copper Co. and the French Co." He kept a generous supply of matte on hand. In October 1895 he received an invitation from Hilary A. Herbert, who had succeeded Tracy as secretary of the navy, to bid on 805,000 pounds of nickel oxide for armor plate. Wharton began preparing the bid, then stopped. He discovered that the Orford Company had put in a lower bid than he could afford to submit.[34]

The signal could not have been clearer. Unless he could find a way of making nickel oxide more cheaply than that turned out by the tops and bottoms process, he would sooner or later be completely squeezed out of the new markets opened by the coming of nickel steel. He examined and rejected methods being developed by N. V. Hybinette and Ludwig Mond and experimented with making nickeliferous pig iron.[35] Nothing succeeded.

Could he, possibly, remain in business by expanding the market for the "nicer grades" of nickel, such as his wet process made? He turned once more to the mint, which had originally inspired him to enter the nickel business. Many years earlier the mint had ceased buying nickel directly from refiners. It purchased blanks; refiners sold nickel to the concerns which made them. Wharton had been indirectly supplying nickel to the mint largely through the intermediary of the Scovill Manufacturing Company of Connecticut. The market was not large, but the prices paid were satisfactory. Suppose, instead of making coins with a 25 percent nickel content, the mint decided to use pure nickel? This would mean a new coinage and a sudden large demand followed by a steady and more expanded market for top grade nickel than had existed when nickel coins had been made mostly of copper.

The possibility was worth pursuing. Sometime around 1892 the director of the mint, E. C. Leech, had complained to Wharton that the 25–75 nickel-copper alloy was too soft and asked him to recommend a better. Wharton had replied that pure nickel was best, such as was used in Switzerland and Austria. No action had immediately followed this exchange; but in 1896 Congress became interested and Wharton gave the issue priority. He wrote to friends in diplomatic posts for information concerning the use of pure nickel for coins by other countries, obtained sample blanks from Krupp of Berndorf, who had furnished blanks for pure nickel coins made in Austria and Switzerland, and wrote Dr. Fleitmann for the latest refinements on the process of making pure malleable nickel. He prepared a memorandum for Leech showing that the use of pure nickel for coins would be highly profitable for the mint, albeit somewhat more costly than the use of nickel-copper alloy, and wrote Charles W. Stone, chairman of the House Committee on Coinage, that pure nickel coins "would last in good condition much longer, and being strongly attracted by the magnet would be far less liable to counterfeiting."[36]

Wharton wrote to Fleitmann: "It is not decided that the United States will use pure nickel coins. Our Congress, at its last session, ordered sample coins to be made of diverse metals and alloys including pure nickel. Those samples will be presented by the Director of the Mint, together with his Report, to the *next session* of Congress which begins on Monday, December 7th. No one can foresee how soon a decision will be reached—perhaps not until some time after the meeting of *next Congress* which will begin in December 1897—and no one can tell whether pure nickel coins will be adopted or not."[37]

Wharton appeared before Stone's committee and noted that the members seemed "indifferent to the project."[38] Congress did not act, and the strategic moment passed. The McKinley administration which took office in March brought changes in personnel, including a new secretary of the treasury and director of the mint. These people had little knowledge of nickel, and the issue died.

At the turn of the century the demand for nickel was excellent. Wharton's profits for the three years from 1899 to 1901 were respectively $9,486.77, $35,689.17, and $65,424.75.[39] But he knew he was beaten. The Bethlehem Steel Company was up for sale and soon could no longer be relied on to buy Wharton's nickel. A significant number of his former customers were finding the Orford product satisfactory for their purposes. He wrote to Voigt concerning the hiring of an assistant capable of taking Voigt's place in an emergency, "The apprehension that such a subordinate might carry off to a rival the processes we employ has now very little weight, because Orford Co. has cheaper processes that seem to satisfy customers."[40]

An opportunity to sell out was at hand. The trend of consolidation within the industry was moving fast. In Europe Le Nickel was concluding agreements with customers, especially in the steel industry. The leading steel companies of Britain in 1901 from the Steel Manufacturers Nickel Syndicate with the aim of receiving adequate supplies of the metal from Le Nickel at reasonable prices and with preferential treatment. "The British firms which formed the syndicate benefited by getting all their supplies from the only existing source on a sliding scale rebate based on the total purchases of the whole group," wrote J. D. Scott in *Vickers, a History.*[41] The only reasonable answer of Thompson and the Orford company to this challenge was a consolidation of North American nickel makers into a rival combination sufficiently strong and appropriately backed to counter the initiatives of Le Nickel. The groundwork for this had been prepared. Canadian and American governments had arrived at workable policies on the subject of duties. This and the collaboration among American and Canadian manufacturers had established an identity of interests among most of the nickel makers in the two countries. Thompson had acquired control of the Nickel Corporation, Limited, of England and the Société Minière Calédonienne, both of which possessed acreages in New Caledonia.

Thompson needed money to bring these and several other companies together. He unsuccessfully tried to obtain it from the Rockefellers, then turned to the newly organized United States Steel Corporation, which provided the backing he needed.

Schwab, the president of U.S. Steel, worked with Thompson to put the new corporation together. The International Nickel Company (INCo) was formed 29 March 1902, with an authorized capital of $24 million and a privilege of floating $10 million worth of thirty-year 5 percent bonds. Announcement of the new company was made the following day. International Nickel immediately issued almost $9 million each of common and preferred stock in order to purchase outright or to obtain a controlling interest in the Canadian Copper Company, Anglo-American Iron Company, Vermillion Manufacturing Company, Orford Copper Company, Nickel Corporation of London, La Société Minière Calédonienne, and the American Nickel Works. Ambrose Monell, formerly assistant to the president of the Carnegie Company, became president. Thompson was chairman of the board. Wharton became one of twelve directors.[42]

Wharton gave up every part of his nickel business to INCo in exchange for shares of its stock. The properties included the Drury of Trill and a one-half interest in the Blézard mines; the Gap Mine and all adjoining property except the farms; the works in Camden; and all chattels, inventories, and stuff in process. He estimated the total value of these properties to be $294,814.37.[43]

The manufactory at Camden and the Gap Mine were reorganized within the new corporate structure as The American Nickel Works Company. Wharton became president with largely titular duties. Most of the work of directing fell to A. W. Johnston, the vice-president. Voigt continued as general manager until his retirement in 1903.[44] In that year, too, Wharton resigned as president in favor of Johnston. In 1905 the American Nickel Works Company was consolidated with the Orford Copper Company.[45]

Thus ended the nickel business, begun forty years earlier, the second great pillar of the industrial personality of Joseph Wharton. The first had been the making of zinc oxide, culminating in Wharton's becoming the first person to engage in the successful commercial manufacture of spelter in the United States. Following that, the nickel business had become his principal means of expression and a source of money for starting other enterprises. Even in retirement from making nickel he retained an active interest in the metal. He served from time to time as an agent for the Scovill company and continued to promote the cause of using pure nickel instead of copper-nickel alloy for the five cent piece. As late as 1905 he produced a memorandum for George E. Roberts, director of the mint, entitled "Brief History of the Introduction of Pure Nickel for Coins."[46] The memorandum displayed the same comprehensive coverage, attention to detail, and powers of exposition as had his earlier pamphlets concerning small money. He kept abreast of developments in the science and processes of refining nickel and highly approved of those used by INCo.

Importantly, during the course of his nickel business Wharton had developed such a multiplicity of other interests that handing it over to INCo left no gap—no feeling of loss, no additional leisure time. Nothing else in his industrial empire in any way depended on his nickel business. His life as an industrialist and businessman continued in other fields as fully satisfying and profitable as ever. Indeed, his holdings in the International Nickel Company provided income and additional security for his other ventures.

16
Scientific Management and the Sale of Bethlehem Steel

In the same year that Wharton gave up his nickel business he severed every connection with Bethlehem Iron, which had become the Bethlehem Steel Company. The end came following almost three years of work on the part of Frederick W. Taylor to improve the efficiency of its operations. Taylor has been called by his principal biographer, Frank B. Copley, the Father of Scientific Management. Although Taylor's success in establishing scientific management at Bethlehem is disputable, this had less to do with his leaving the company than might be supposed. Taylor, Wharton, and the other directors were preoccupied with somewhat different problems, which temporarily and coincidentally overlapped. The experience of Taylor at Bethlehem Steel is of concern to a biography of Wharton largely because of the fame which later came to Taylor and his methods. He proved that he could save money for an employer who was sufficiently strong and willing to discard traditional ways of doing things in favor of practices based on a careful analysis of operations from the unique viewpoint of maximum efficiency, by which is meant performing specified work with the least expenditure of time and money. He demonstrated at Bethlehem what could be accomplished and wrote of his experiences in prose which, although lacking in the economy he insisted upon for shop management, nevertheless captured the imagination of a large audience. In later years disciples steadily came to visit him at Boxly, his estate in Germantown.

The story of Taylor's sojourn at Bethlehem has often been told, and Wharton's small part has been generally appreciated. However, some aspects of the telling have lacked a precision of detail and refinement of context which two important and hitherto unavailable sources of information can give, namely, the diary of Robert Heysham Sayre and the Wharton papers. These also add somewhat to previous knowledge concerning the sale of Bethlehem Steel as told by careful researchers such as Robert Hessen, the biographer of Schwab. The story which emerges from all sources is that of strong-willed and talented people brought together by a concern for efficiency yet sometimes fighting each other because of differences of opinion as to the objects at which efficiency should be aimed.

1

About the time that the Bethlehem Iron Company filled its initial contract for making armor plate, the directors made several decisions of considerable importance for the future of the company. They ordered the building of a new mill for rolling armor plate; and they planned to help pay for it by getting the custom of governments other than that of the United States. These decisions set in motion a train of events which soon had the directors facing the problem of cutting costs below levels necessitated by normal competition with Carnegie.

Behind the developing trouble was a change in the way in which the press, the public, and Congress regarded the country's steel mills. In the eighties the steel companies had been hailed as leaders in industrial progress. Now they projected an ambivalent image. They were still celebrated for building up the nation's defenses; but at the same time they and all big companies were portrayed as villains robbing the workingman, the farmer, and the small businessman of a just return for his labor. Widespread sentiment for labor unions, cheap money, and the prevention of trusts and monopolies, had done much to effect the change of opinion.

The Carnegie Company was the first of the two makers of armor plate to experience the popular wrath. It rolled the plates, which it could do at lower cost than Bethlehem incurred in forging them, but at the expense of turning out a product of uneven quality. When personnel at the Department of the Navy discovered that some plates did not meet the standards claimed for them by the Carnegie people, the company was fined and publicly accused of endangering the lives of American seamen for private profit.[1] The directors at Bethlehem did not enter the controversy over the Carnegie plates. They could easily sympathize with Carnegie, whose practice of rolling plates they were about to copy.

Bethlehem's trouble began when the depression almost eliminated the railroads as customers. Although in March 1893 the iron company received another large order for armor plate, the directors became uneasy at the prospect of relying solely on the United States government, especially as the flight of gold out of the country was removing a treasury surplus which had been built up in more prosperous times. This and the competition from Carnegie (and from Midvale, for ordnance) persuaded the directors to seek markets abroad for armor plate. In 1894 they got from Russia a contract for twelve hundred tons of armor at two hundred and fifty dollars per ton in a competition with other leading armament makers of the world, including Carnegie.[2]

Later, the directors of Bethlehem Iron claimed that two hundred and fifty dollars was below costs of manufacture, and that they had submitted the ruinously low bid as part of a strategy to enter the world market. This sort of defense in no way helped them with Congress or the public. The directors found themselves accused of using money supplied by Congress to assist in arming the potential enemies of America. This and related charges of misconduct quickly created an image of a powerful and unscrupulous maker of munitions, at one and the same time an enemy of peace, social justice, and common decency.

Public relations officers were as yet unheard of. Directors and managers were expected to respond to such accusations if they thought it worth their while to do so. Wharton took the initiative in defending the company, principally by letters to the editors of newspapers. He wrote to the Philadelphia *Public Ledger* on one occasion to refute an allegation that the American government had created the Bethlehem Iron Company for the purpose of making the nation's armor plate, and that the company had acted treasonably in selling to Russia. Wharton declared that the United States government "'created' the Bethlehem Iron Company very much as John Milton's publisher 'created' the 'Paradise Lost' by paying him £5 for that poem after it was finished. . . . If the large body of trained workmen required in armor plate making should be scattered by reason of having no work, they could not promptly be gathered again when needed. It is therefore an important service to our government to keep those men employed on other orders until it again requires them. Every armor plate maker in the world thus seeks and takes orders out of his own country: every nation that is fortunate enough to have armor plate works within its own territory gives all its orders to those domestic works, but is perfectly content to let them also make armor plates for the ships of other nations."[3]

Nevertheless, the country was aroused against Bethlehem and Carnegie. Various persons in the press and public office took note that Bethlehem Iron and Carnegie charged the government of the United States between five hundred and fifty and six hundred dollars per ton for plate which the Bethlehem Iron Company had agreed to supply to Russia for two hundred and fifty dollars. Secretary Herbert had already told representatives of the two companies that prices for armor plate would have to be greatly reduced, that they had now made sufficient profits to cover the initial cost of plant and equipment. He had asked for figures concerning costs and been refused. Now, with the disclosure of the price Bethlehem was receiving from Russia, several powerful members of Congress began listening to Herbert.[4] In 1895 the House passed an appropriations bill for three new battleships. The Senate, on receiving the bill, amended it so that the price to be paid for the armor plate should not exceed three hundred and fifty dollars a ton. At the same time the Senate authorized Herbert to ascertain the actual costs of making plate and instructed its own Naval Committee to conduct a similar investigation.

Foremost among the senators who were incensed at the "extortionate" profits of the steelmakers were Eugene Hale, Republican of Maine, "Pitchfork" Benjamin R. Tillman of South Carolina, and William E. Chandler,

Republican from New Hampshire, chairman of the Naval Committee and former secretary of the navy. They led the controversy over the price of armor plate, which raged for almost half a decade. It was most intense during the final fifteen months of the second Cleveland administration. Secretary Herbert urged Congress to consider having the government build and operate an armor plate plant if the Bethlehem and Carnegie companies refused to lower their prices. The companies responded to this by offering to sell their mills to the government. They did so from different perspectives. Carnegie made armor plate as a minor part of his total operations and could well afford to give it up. Bethlehem had by contrast chosen to specialize in the business. For Bethlehem, relinquishing the armor plate operation might possibly have meant bowing out of the ranks of the major producers of steel. Not surprisingly, then, Wharton was not serious in making the offer to sell the plant, but did it as part of a strategy to demonstrate in dramatic fashion the costs and problems of fashioning armor plate. He wrote to Sayre, "It will not lead to a sale of the Bethlehem works, but will tend to discourage the Govt. from erecting works for themselves."[5]

As to the price of armor plate, Wharton, Wilbur, Sayre, and Linderman for Bethlehem and Schwab, Frick, Lt. C. A. Stone, George Lauder, and John G. A. Leishman for Carnegie variously met and discussed strategy. Competitive under normal business conditions, the two firms readily collaborated when facing a threat to the stability of conditions under which they operated.[6] They could attempt to bargain in an effort to get Chandler and his group to raise the minimum price to a more realistic figure. They could refuse to bid and thereby bring the shipbuilding program of the government to a halt.

The steelmakers knew they could count on the support of the senators from Pennsylvania, especially Quay and later Penrose. They also knew that Herbert was in a difficult position. He had started a fire which was getting out of hand. Chandler and other members of Congress were in a mood to spread the blaze in such manner as to engulf the whole shipbuilding program for which Herbert was responsible. Herbert was prepared to negotiate between the steelmakers and Congress. The representatives of the Bethlehem and Carnegie companies took advantage of his position. Wharton suggested to Herbert "that instead of having to appeal to Congress at every session, authority should be given to contract for say 6 battle ships leaving it to the Navy department to contract for all at once or from time to time."[7] Shortly thereafter Wharton wrote to Carnegie, "The situation of the six battle ship question at Washington I judge to be hopeful. Herbert tries to get us to break price without making a contract; we make known our willingness to consider something on an absolute order for 6 ships (besides the 2 already contracted for all but the armor), which would give us some continuous work for say three years. We declined any fresh concession on the 2 ships, but would yield say $25 per ton on the new 6 ships, though we have not named that or any other figure. Your people and ours are working in full harmony I understand."[8]

At the end of 1896 Herbert reported to Congress that the price paid for armor plate should be not more than $391 per ton. This was probably close to the minimum price for which Bethlehem and Carnegie were then willing to settle. But the Senate committee still thought the price was too high. When the naval bill for 1897 reached the Senate, Chandler obtained an amendment fixing the price at $300 and renewed a threat to have the government build its own plant if the companies did not accept the figure. The House agreed to the maximum of $300.[9]

In effect, Congress had opted for a confrontation. On 13 March Linderman, Wharton, and Henry S. Drinker, counsel for the Bethlehem Iron Company, met and decided not to bid on armor at the statutory low price of $300. Frick, acting for Carnegie, still held out for a strategy of bargaining and, according to Sayre in his diary for 2 April, advised bidding "a fair price for the armor notwithstanding the limit on it placed by Congress." His suggestion did not prevail. The next day representatives of the two companies met together and decided not to put in a bid for armor plate.[10] In a manner of speaking, they went on strike.

A year of stalemate followed. Cleveland and Herbert went out of office. McKinley and a new secretary of the navy, John D. Long, came in. The Republicans still controlled Congress and Chandler remained chairman of the Naval Committee. Congress created an Armor Factory Board and authorized it to investigate the existing armor plants and report to the secretary of the navy concerning the desirability of having the United States build and run a plant. Again the directors of the Bethlehem Iron Company made a gesture of offering their works for sale to the government.[11] Dickering for a higher price continued with at one point Linderman discussing the prospect of getting $425 per ton.[12] The press kept the issue before the public.

In 1897 the Bethlehem Iron Company purchased from the continental Harvey Steel Company an interest in the Krupp process for making armor plates on terms equal to those enjoyed by others.[13] Bethlehem used the Krupp process when filling orders for foreign governments. In 1900 Wharton wrote Penrose extolling the superiority of Krupp armor and added, "Not only Japan, but all the great naval powers are using these plates, and every armor plate establishment in the world except the two in this country is crowded with orders to make them. Ours are kept idle, and our Navy is stunted because of the failure of misguided Congressmen to bully the American works into selling armor for half the market price of the world."[14]

Such essentially was the situation during the months leading up to the arrival of Taylor in Bethlehem and the beginning of his work there. Although the company was expanding and making large profits, the prospect of losing the battle with the United States government over the price of armor plate forced a greater consideration of economy than might otherwise have prevailed. Even if the company eventually won, it would have to contend with competition from Carnegie; but that, for the time being, was of lesser concern.

2

Steelmaking at the Bethlehem Iron Company was anything but efficient. The fault lay not so much with the processes used, which thanks largely to Fritz were of the most advanced design, but with management. At every level, from the shop to the board, a spirit of self-interest prevailed over a corporate interest in producing the best steel at the least cost. Workers clung to outmoded practices. Foremen resisted interference with their prerogatives in dealing with men and machines. Personal considerations often prevailed over merit. An atomistic organization of shops and mills meant little systematic coordination. Especially, the forging press could turn out work faster than machine shop number two could handle it. Wharton, ever concerned with efficiency, in 1895 wrote Linderman to the effect that the company was going to lose much money "if we are behind times on delivery, as we surely shall be if we go on in the old fashioned way. You have got to put some life into our people, and put this work through in advance of the stipulated time, for lots of adverse things may happen to delay, and if we really get done ahead of time we shall be all ready for Uncle Sam or some other customer."[15]

Neither Wharton nor anyone else seemed to appreciate that before work at the lower levels could be much improved, management at the top level would have to be changed. Directors would have to stop interfering with jobs and stop putting friends and relatives on the payroll. In addition, managers everywhere would have to give up the idea that the battle for efficiency was won when the best men were hired and given full authority to work out their problems. The fault lay less with the men than with the system within which they had to operate. The old feudal arrangements would have to give way to a highly centralized, scientifically established managerial system.

In the presidency was the young Robert Linderman, who had inherited his father's large holdings of stock but had no experience with management. The other men who made key decisions—Fritz, Wilbur, Wharton, and Sayre—were old and still following rules which had prevailed in the sixties. Two of them, Wilbur and Wharton, were heavily involved with other affairs and had no time to watch over daily operations in mills and yards. Wilbur was the financial workhorse of the Asa Packer Estate, which until 1897 had controlled the Lehigh Valley Railroad, and had many other interests. Wharton, while leading the fight for the company on the political and legal fronts, spent most of his time in Philadelphia.

The remaining two, Fritz and Sayre, were constantly at work in the yards and mills and sparred with one another as they had done in the past. The directors had recognized Fritz's lack of managerial skill when in the early 1870s they had relieved him of control of daily operations and placed them under Dr. Linderman. As superintendent of new construction, Fritz took orders in a poor spirit, opposing in turn the appointment of every person placed over him, first Dr. Linderman, then Thurston, Sayre, and Robert Linderman. The directors recognized his genius as essential to the success of designing the processes and machines for making armor plate and guns and in 1890 used their influence to have him elected to the board in place of the deceased Thurston. That somewhat mollified Fritz, but it in no way improved the management of the company or stopped the intermittent disputes between Fritz and Sayre. This old railroad man was an excellent ruler of men but still believed that the personal qualities of excellence could solve all problems of management.

In 1892 Fritz decided to retire from active work. He had completed most of the machinery for making armor plate and guns and could supervise what remained from a less demanding position. He was seventy years of age and clearly slowing down. The announcement of his retirement was sent out, and the entire iron and steel industry came forth to honor him. *The Iron Age* paid him the unusual honor of a full-page picture. Representatives of the international iron and steel community held a testimonial dinner. The board voted him an unprecedented gift of twenty-five thousand dollars.[16]

Immediately, Fritz made trouble for Sayre. Fritz's actions recall the futile impetuosity of the retiring King Lear but with results more comic than tragic. Fritz tried to dictate the choice of his successor. He wanted this to be Davenport, the able head of the armor plate department. Davenport expected the promotion. Sayre had other plans. He privately offered the position of superintendent to his friend Owen Leibert, a career steelman, and the board respected his decision. Davenport received the honorific post of second vice-president (Sayre was first vice-president) at an elevated salary of ten thousand dollars a year. Then Leibert committed what for Fritz was the unforgivable sin of appointing Sayre's son Robert to the position of assistant general superintendent. Fritz took the appointment as a personal insult and for years refused to speak to or shake hands with Sayre. Fritz reluctantly accepted the position of consulting engineer which the board offered him, but resigned it after working for three months under the new management. The following year he left the board.[17]

Sayre was finally fairly well in control of operations. His position was for a time buttressed by the election to the board of E. B. Leisenring of the Lehigh Valley Railroad to succeed Fritz. Sayre had an opportunity to show what he could—and could not—do. The board agreed to his request to put in a mill for rolling armor plate, allowing him two years in which to complete it. Less than two years later it was finished and operating. "No Fritz about this work," he boasted.[18] Other contracts for armor plate and guns were obtained, including the ill-fated one with Russia. Tests made of Bethlehem armor plates were almost always successful, and the press was lavish in its praise of the results. Still, in many ways work in the yards and mills limped along.

Wharton had been strengthening his position on the board. In 1891 a Philadelphia businessman named Beauveau Borie had been elected in place of Knecht. Borie was an associate of Wharton in a number of business affairs. Leisenring, after a year on the board, retired and was replaced by J. Bertram Lippincott, who obtained the stock needed to qualify for membership only with the aid of his father-in-law.[19] Thus strengthened, at the annual reorganization meeting in 1896, Wharton demanded that Sayre be replaced as general manager. The move was unsuccessful, but it shook up the aging Sayre, who wrote of it in his diary:

> Tues. June 23. . . . Mr. Wharton made fight on my reappointment to Gen'l. Managership. Mr. Wilbur stood by me like a man and defeated Wharton Fritz & Co. scheme. A curious phase of human nature. Wharton a fourth owner of the Stock of the Co. which was prosperous and paying large dividends attempting to disorganize whole working force of the Co. Damn him.
>
> Wed. June 24. I am not in very good shape phisically [sic] nor have I been for two or three weeks past, and Wharton's devilish attempt to degrade me yesterday has unnerved me. The thought that 34 years as a Director of the BI Co and 10 years as Gen'l Manager should have brought forth the attempted action of Mr. Wharton has humiliated me and given me a worse opinion of human or rather inhuman nature than I imagined could exist.

Wharton did not relent and renewed the fight the following year. By this time his position had been strengthened through his leadership in the struggle with the government over the price of armor plate; and that of Sayre and Wilbur had been weakened as a result of difficulties attending the financial plight of the Lehigh Valley Railroad. Also, George H. Myers, one of Sayre's supporters on the board, had become insane, leaving the Sayre and anti-Sayre forces evenly balanced. Sayre wrote out his resignation. "If they can stand it, I can," he recorded on 23 May 1897, and four days later wrote, "My resignation as Vice Pres't and Gen'l Manager was accepted by the Board of the Beth^m Iron Co. yesterday without note or comment. A shabby low down lot."

Sayre did not brood over his loss of power or try to exercise an authority he no longer had. At the same time, he did not hesitate to make a full use of the lesser position to which he had been relegated. He was still a member of the board of directors and of its executive committee; and a month after his resignation the board reappointed him vice-president without compensation.[20] He possessed furthermore the allegiance of his son and Leibert, owned a home within walking distance of the works, and had a wealth of valuable experience which he was willing to make available to employees who sought it. Nor had he given up the old habit, possessed by all of the aging directors, of personally interfering with operations when he thought he could do so to his credit.

Still, from Sayre's vantage point, Wharton was now principally in control. From 1888 Wharton had missed on the average one board meeting a year. From 1896 until the time the company was sold his record of attendance was perfect. Wharton was pressing for increased efficiency of operations. And in 1898 Davenport came on the board in place of Myers, the same Davenport who at Midvale had known and admired the reforms being made there by Frederick W. Taylor.

3

Frederick Winslow Taylor was at midpoint in his career in 1897. He had been born in Germantown in 1856 to parents belonging to old Philadelphia Orthodox Quaker families. Originally intended for the study of law, he turned to mechanics when his eyes temporarily gave out. He entered the machine shop of the Midvale Steel Company and soon became a subforeman working with Davenport. While at Midvale Taylor conceived the basic ideas for a system of scientific management. He put some of them into operation there, but left the company when it changed hands. He then spent several years as a sort of efficiency expert working for other companies and as a consulting engineer.

Taylor was a humanitarian at heart who believed that science, applied to management, could enhance the happiness of all concerned. He maintained that with proper reorganization of shop practices workers would not need to form unions and engage in strikes, with their disastrous effects on wages and profits. They did so now, he said, because of a system which rewarded jobs and not men: A laborer who was well fitted for a particular task received the same wage as did another who worked much more slowly. As a result, the capable worker had no incentive to hustle but "soldiered on the job." The situation was general throughout industry. Men worked to half of capacity or less with correspondingly low production, profits, and wages. What was necessary to avoid this, he claimed, was a systematic and minute analysis of jobs to determine the optimum time needed to perform each, followed by the establishment of a "differential piece rate" for rewarding workers according to their performance. Then, he said, the better laborers would have an incentive to work to capacity. An ancillary concern of Taylor was that of rationalizing jobs and improving machinery so as to eliminate useless, time-consuming, and otherwise inefficient operations which impeded a maximum performance by highly motivated workmen.[21]

After years of trying out various of his ideas, Taylor made his first attempt at a systematic and public statement of them in an address given in 1895 before the American Society of Mechanical Engineers. The paper, entitled "A Piece-Rate System," was published the same year. He identified three elements of his plan: a "rate-fixing"—that is, time study—department; a differential rate system of piece work; and a policy of paying men rather than positions. In connection with "rate-fixing" he mentioned a need for correcting the defects in the design of machines and systematizing the small details in the running of a shop: "These details, which are usually regarded as of comparatively small importance, and many of which are left to the individual judgment of the foreman and workman, are shown by the rate-fixing department to be of paramount importance in obtaining the maximum output, and to require the most careful and systematic study and attention in order to insure uniformity and a fair and equal chance for each workman." Especially, he insisted that payment for an industrious worker should be significantly higher than the ordinary day wage. "MEN WILL NOT DO AN EXTRAORDINARY DAY'S WORK FOR AN ORDINARY DAY'S PAY."[22]

The paper received considerable attention. Employers were less attracted to the humanitarian aspects than to the possibility of cutting labor costs. Among these employers was Wharton, who on 26 April 1895 wrote to Taylor, "I have read with care your treatise in 'A Piece-rate system,' and find it interesting. There ought to be opportunity at Bethlehem for the introduction of such a plan, and I am forwarding your treatise to our people there that they may consider it. But I fancy that much must depend upon the skill with which the system is applied, for the workmen must be satisfied that the rate fixed is both competent and fair."

Taylor's reply to this letter is unknown. In any event, no action immediately followed. Sayre was still general manager at Bethlehem, and as events later showed, was unsympathetic to ideas as disruptive of ongoing practices as those presented by Taylor. The next overture to Taylor came from Davenport and was made after Sayre had resigned the general managership and Davenport had been elected to the board.[23] Consultations followed between Taylor, Davenport, Wharton, and Linderman with a result that in the spring of 1898 Taylor began a period of almost three years as an employee of the company.

Frank B. Copley in his excellent account of Taylor's experiences at Bethlehem makes the point that Linderman understood not at all what was involved in introducing piece work into the machine shops.[24] Wharton, too, could not have guessed what some of the important implications were, for all that he had read "A Piece-Rate System" "with care." Taylor hints at this in his report to Davenport concerning an interview with Wharton: "When I told him, however, that it involved paying from 33 to 50% higher wages in order to get out properly really hustling piece work he said at first that this was out of the question. After talking with him for some time, however, and explaining that men would not work extraordinarily hard for ordinary wages he seemed convinced on this point."[25] Linderman assuredly represented Wharton as well as the other directors when he wrote Taylor in June 1898, expressing concern that piece work should be established "as soon as possible, by which accurate promises as to the date of delivery of orders can be made, and the delivery at the times promised insured."

Taylor began his work in Bethlehem surrounded with optimism and well wishing. The directors were behind him, including Sayre, who was not the sort of man to sabotage a decision of the board. Heads of departments assured Taylor of their support. "I find the Superintendents and men in the works with whom I come in contact here very agreeable and a progressive set of men," he wrote. Taylor was especially impressed with the attitude of a young department head named Archibald Johnston, whom he declared to seem "very much interested in the scheme. I have not the slightest doubt whatever as to the genuineness of the interest there."[26]

Taylor established himself at Bethlehem by taking action of two sorts. One was to put together a staff of assistants upon whom he could rely. He brought to Bethlehem such former colleagues or admirers as Henry L. Gantt and Carl G. Barth. Taylor's second action was to establish his authority within the company by securing the appointment of a top manager with power to give orders to heads of departments. Specifically, he recommended creating a superintendency of manufacture in charge of "the piece work rate fixing, the wages of the workmen in the manfacturing departments, the direction of the laying out of the departments, the estimate of the cost of new work, and the making of promises for dates of delivery, together with the cost keeping." Taylor suggested Davenport for the position.[27]

This proposal met with opposition. Taylor had been hired especially to reorganize practices in machine shop number two. Now, he wanted a change in top management, and of a sort which must inevitably interfere with the authority of others. Following Robert Sayre, Sr.'s resignation as general manager, the post had been vacant. Its duties had largely passed to Leibert and the younger Sayre. These now protested Taylor's proposal, arguing that Davenport was unfitted for the position.[28]

But Taylor for the time being got his way. On 31 August 1898 the board created the office of superintendent of manufacture, appointed Davenport to fill it, and authorized construction of a new office building to house his and Taylor's operations.[29] This allowed Taylor to extend his influence into various parts of the sprawling Bethlehem Iron Works. Backed by Davenport and the board he began the task of reorganizing and standardizing which he considered a necessary prelude to the introduction of piece work. Harry Leibert, Owen's brother and head of machine shop number two, resigned rather than see his authority dispersed among others.[30]

The results were from Taylor's point of view a triumph for scientific management. As Daniel Nelson summarized the accomplishments in *Fred-*

erick W. Taylor and the Rise of Scientific Mangement, "By 1901 Machine Shop No. 2 was the world's most modern factory and potentially a prototype for manufacturers and engineers in other industries."[31] Involved in the triumph was Taylor's most impressive technological discovery, that of high speed tool steel. He worked with Maunsel White, the company's metallurgist, at the task of standardizing cutting tools. After a great many expensive tests the two men discovered that by heating a cutting tool much above the point at which it was supposed to work well they could operate it at speeds twice as fast as formerly and with better results. The discovery was exciting and in various ways promised additional income to the company. Taylor promptly recommended the many changes needed to accommodate production to the discovery, to which the board, after receiving estimates from Leibert, assented. Robert Sayre, Sr., was impressed and recorded in his diary, "I went down to the Mill to see Taylor's Experiment with new shaped cutting tools new tool steel and increased speed. Wharton came later. The Experiment showed that great improvement could be made in the output of the Machine Shops."[32]

The discovery enhanced Bethlehem's reputation as one of the nation's top steelmakers. Still, opposition to Taylor remained. The changes he had made had been expensive; the anticipated return in the form of lower costs had not yet been realized. Also, he had irritated many persons of responsibility within the company besides Leibert and the Sayres. He was by nature imperious and often tactless. Linderman became more cautious in granting Taylor's requests.

Taylor then turned to a project which promised dramatic evidence of the value of his work. He applied a form of wage incentive related to piece work (but not identical with it) to the unskilled pig iron handlers in the yard. These were ordinarily paid $1.15 per day and loaded on the average of thirteen tons of pig iron per man. Taylor had the ten best men timed when working at maximum speed and found that each of them handled an equivalent of seventy-five tons a day. He arbitrarily deducted 40 percent for rest, delays, and so forth and arrived at a figure of forty-five tons a day as the amount which a first class man ought to handle. This was more than three times the actual output. He then adopted a "piece rate" of 3¾ cents per ton, such as would enable a man loading forty-five tons to earn $1.68 per day—a 46 percent wage increase over the base of $1.15. At the same time, he set no minimum daily wage, with the result that slower workers would be penalized. A man who only doubled the average tonnage would earn ninety-one cents per day. Now, a true piece rate system according to Taylor would have a wage base to protect the slower workers; and the piece rate would be determined on the basis of time studies far more elaborate and objective than those used here.

Naturally, Taylor's first attempt to apply this scheme met with resistance. On 16 March the ten best men were assigned to piece work and promptly objected. Under Taylor's orders they were immediately fired. There ensued a clash with the Sayre-Leibert team which has heretofore been incompletely reported. The principal source of information has been a paper by Taylor's assistants entitled, "Report on the Establishment of Piecework," which carries this account: On the way to the time office the men "were met by Mr. Robert Sayre, Jr. Ass't. Gen'l. Supt., who having inquired what the trouble was, told the men to wait at the Scale House until he had looked into the matter. He stated . . . that he feared a strike would follow the discharge of these men and that he wished to consult the General Superintendent, Mr. Owen Leibert (Mr. Davenport being absent) before taking any further action."[33] Thus, the men were temporarily allowed to continue working for a daily wage.

Robert Sayre, Jr., was less than candid in giving out this reason. Davenport was not "absent," although he perhaps was out of the office. What young Sayre did was to go to Leibert, who went to Linderman; or perhaps Sayre himself went directly to Linderman. Linderman went straight to Robert Sayre, Sr., who gave the order that the ten men be kept and allowed to work by the day. An irate Taylor immediately sought out Davenport and threatened to resign unless the order of the assistant general superintendent were disobeyed, whereupon Davenport ordered the men discharged. Later in the evening, when Robert Sayre, Sr., heard of this he upheld Davenport. The next evening when Taylor came to see Sayre, Sr., about the matter, the old man reassured him.

The relevant entries in Sayre's diary, which disclose these developments, are as follows:

"Thurs. Mar. 16. Some of the Beth^m Iron Co.'s men refused to load pig iron by the ton. Rob [Linderman] came to see me about it and I told him to let them work by the day, in the eve Rob came in to say that Mr. Taylor said unless the men were discharged in the morning he would leave and Mr. Davenport ordered the men discharged. Told Rob to discharge."

"Fri. Mar. 17. Taylor in to see me about the trouble among the loaders. I told him the men had been discharged and he went off satisfied."

Following this incident the experiment with the pig iron handlers proceeded to a successful conclusion as far as Taylor was concerned. Out of it came the story of Schmidt, the "first class man" who increased his income by more than 50 percent through piece work, thereby becoming a model for others. The story is probably the most dramatic that Taylor ever wrote.

Did Taylor really intend to resign if Davenport followed Robert Sayre, Jr.'s order to keep the ten pig iron handlers on day wages? This is doubtful. He was either bluffing or Linderman misunderstood him. Such impulsive conduct was contrary to the advice which Taylor gave to others. And he had every reason to remain with the company. The reorganization of the machine shops was proceeding well; his triumph with self-hardening tool steel was fresh. At this time, too, negotiations were under way to increase the capitalization of the company through formation of a Bethlehem Steel Company. Rumors that this was about to happen sent prices for Bethlehem Iron Company stock skyrocketing. Taylor, having advance information concerning the pending transaction, hoped to profit from it. Three days after the incident with the pig iron handlers he went to Philadelphia to see Wharton about acquiring Bethlehem Iron Company stock. Finding Wharton out, he wrote to him, averring an intent within the next two years "to make that stock valuable," expressing faith in the future of the company, and ending, "Can you not put me in the way of subscribing to as large an amount of the new common stock and as close to the ground floor as possible?"[34]

Taylor, Davenport, and Wharton had for the time being won out over the opposition of the Sayres, Leibert, and some of the department heads. Davenport was named general manager of the newly organized Bethlehem Steel Company, which gave him increased authority vis-à-vis Leibert. Sayre, Sr., submitted his resignation from the executive committee and the board, but the resignations were not accepted. Later in 1899 Robert Sayre, Jr., was shunted aside. Sayre, Sr., recorded on December 28, "Archie Johnston was by Genl. Supt. Davenport appointed his assistant, leaving Robt. Sayre [Jr.] in rather an anomalous position."[35]

4

Time and events worked against Taylor. Under the McKinley administration prosperity returned to the country. A war with Spain was fought and won. Acquisition of the Hawaiian Islands and the Philippines and the growing power of Japan brought home to Congress the realization of a desirability to continue building up the navy. The Congress, largely as a result of negotiations engineereed by Schwab, relented from its insistence on a three hundred dollar maximum per ton on the price of armor plate and gave up the idea of a government-owned and -operated plant. The contract signed with Carnegie Steel in 1899 was for four hundred and sixty dollars. Soon Bethlehem Steel was again making armor for the American government and in addition had large contracts to supply armor to Japan and Russia.[36]

All of these events relieved the pressure on the company to reduce costs. Then, in the midst of prosperity, a new danger arose in the form of United States Steel, the nation's first billion-dollar corporation. Schwab, drawing upon the industry of Carnegie and the financial resources of Morgan, was primarily responsible for assembling the huge combination and became its first president. Bethlehem was not included in the new corporation. It "would have provided nothing but duplication," Schwab explained toward the close of his life.[37] That left Bethlehem vulnerable, facing competition from a giant whose resources Bethlehem could not match. The directors decided to sell, if they could, before a decline in the demand for steel might reduce the value of their equity.

Taylor was a casualty of the sale. The opposition to him had been muted but not destroyed. Sayre, Sr., wrote in his diary for 12 March 1901: "Went through No. 2 and No. 3 shops with Archie Johnston & Owen Leibert. Do not see where the $1,100,000 dollars went to in the last two years. Think the bringing of Taylor here and placing all the manufacturing under Davenport was and is a failure." Wharton continued to support Taylor, who in turn sometimes went to Wharton over the heads of Linderman and Davenport. Linderman could scarcely have been happy with the situation.

That was the state of affairs in March 1901, when Taylor decided on a push for greater control. He visited Wharton in Philadelphia twice that month.[38] On the second visit (27 March) E. T. Stotesbury was present. Stotesbury had succeeded Lippincott on the board and was closely associated with the Morgan-Drexel interests. Taylor then decided to write to Linderman. Possibly Taylor did this on advice from Wharton or Stotesbury, for after drafting the letter Taylor sent it to Wharton for "criticisms." It read in part: "There are many minor details of your plant which must be modified in order to successfully introduce my system of management, and it is obviously necessary that I be given the requisite authority to see that these details are arranged in harmony with the new system. . . . I do not want any authority in any matters except those immediately affecting my system of management and accounting, but I respectfully request that the various *officers* [italics added] of the Company be instructed to carry out all orders which may be given them by me in relation to those subjects."

That is, the officers as well as department heads were to obey Taylor in all that concerned the establishment of a piece-rate system.

Taylor's letter bore a date of 4 April 1901, a Thursday, and was probably mailed on the fifth. It arrived in Philadelphia on Saturday the sixth, after Wharton had left for Rhode Island.[39] The next week, when Wharton returned to Philadelphia, he made some corrections on the draft and returned it to Taylor. Taylor made a few more corrections, including among others the insertion of a "1" before the "4" in the date, thus thinking to change the date of the final letter from 4 April to 14 April. He then gave the corrected draft to a typist, who produced a perfect copy *except for the date.*. The typist apparently failed to see the "1" before the "4" and left the date as incorrectly reading "April 4," a mistake which later misled researchers into thinking that Linderman received the letter ten days or so before he actually got it.[40]

The fourteenth was a Sunday. The letter therefore could not have been posted (possibly not even typed) before 15 April. Linderman could not have received it before the sixteenth.

That was the day Linderman notified Taylor he was fired.

Linderman's brief letter, "I beg to advise you that your services will not be required by this Company after May 1st, 1901," bears a date of 17 April. But Sayre in his diary recorded this for 16 April: "Cleaver [A. N. Cleaver, Sayre's son-in-law and assistant to the president] in, told me R. P. Linderman had given Mr. Taylor notice that his services would not be needed after May 1."

This comment and the timing of events suggest that the decision to fire Taylor was unaffected by Taylor's letter, which was probably received after the decision had been made. Linderman would not have fired Taylor without the backing of Sayre and also, probably, Wilbur. Wilbur, Sayre, and Linderman saw each other almost daily. The decision to fire could have been made much earlier than 16 April.

Wharton backed Taylor to the end. Although Copley, citing a remark made by one of Taylor's associates, throws some doubt on this, the circumstances of the case and Wharton's character allow no other conclusion. Wharton did not deal hypocritically with people. He would not have collaborated with Taylor in revising a letter to Linderman if he had previously agreed with Linderman that Taylor was to be fired. If Wharton had changed his mind on the subject between the time he made the revisions and 14 April he would have telegraphed or telephoned Taylor to let him know and so save him the chagrin of sending a useless letter.

What actually occurred can be easily reconstructed. With the sale of the Bethlehem company pending, Wharton's power over Linderman and the other directors had evaporated. "Power deserts a dying king," Wharton had once written to Brush. From Linderman's point of view Taylor had successfully reorganized the machine shops and was now a nuisance. Linderman could easily and conscientiously give in to local voices of opposition, loud by comparison with possible dissent from Wharton in Philadelphia. So Taylor went.

The paths of Wharton and Taylor did not again cross. Following his departure from Bethlehem, Taylor retired to his Germantown estate of Boxly, where among other pursuits he did missionary work for his ideas concerning scientific management. Wharton was not among the many people who came to Boxly; and Taylor did not visit nearby Ontalauna. Belonging as they did to different societies within Quakerdom, the families never socially intermingled.

Also, the two men had less in common with their ideas of science than might be supposed. Taylor's scientific management grew out of his experience as a mechanical engineer and was primarily concerned with the organization of production in the shop. Wharton's interest in the application of science to business methods came largely from his experience in establishing enterprises in an environment affected by domestic and foreign competition. Unlike Taylor, Wharton was concerned with the larger field of organization at a national level and the status of the businessman in national esteem.

That both men were more systematic than scientific in their approach to management was to be expected. Taylor never did find a means of objectively determining how long any particular job ought to take. To do this he would have needed masses of physiological, psychological, and sociological data which were not then (and are not now) available. Wharton surely knew this. He probably from the time of his first long talk with Taylor realized the dreamy quality of the ultimate goal; and he was probably not surprised when, after the purchase of Bethlehem Steel, Schwab swept away the Taylor system. What captured Wharton's attention was the systematic aspect of Taylor's methods, which promised greater efficiency along with fewer labor problems. Wharton disbelieved in the existence of sure blueprints for success; but he nevertheless believed in the desirability of having good blueprints for more limited goals.

5

As Bethlehem's largest stockholder, Wharton took the lead in negotiating for the sale of the company. He was not sorry to sell. In 1900 he was seventy-four years old, and members of the family were urging him to slow down. He knew that was unlikely to happen, but selling the works would provide more time for attending to enterprises in which he had a greater interest.

The works might not have been sold at all if United States Steel had not been formed. Before that event, the directors had taken steps for possible expansion. The formation of United States Steel made those steps obsolete.

The initial plan of reorganization was a cooperative effort of the four largest stockholders, namely, Wharton, Linderman, Wilbur, and Sayre. They had for years kept the company grossly undercapitalized, with the result that dividends were exceptionally high and very little of the stock changed hands on the open market. As late as 1899 the capitalization was still only $5 million and the bonded indebtedness, $1,351,000. The company was worth much more. Wharton wrote in March 1899 that "the old Co. has $5,000,000 capital, and between 5 and 6 million surplus, besides having charged off sundry millions in depreciation."[41]

One part of the plan, put into effect in the spring of 1899, was that of increasing the capitalization. The directors declared a scrip dividend of 50 percent out of accumulated earnings to shareholders of record as of the previous 29 March. The scrip was convertible into stock certificates on the following 15 May. This increased the capitalization to $7,500,000.[42]

Another part of the plan, carried out at the same time, was that of creating a holding company, such as would provide immediate profits and flexibility for growth. This was the Bethlehem Steel Company, formed with a capital of three hundred thousand shares valued at $15 million. The Bethlehem Steel Company was to lease the property of Bethlehem Iron for 999 years, guarantee stockholders of the iron company dividends of 6 percent yearly in gold, and spend not less than $3 million in improvements within the next ten years.[43] Holders of the one hundred and fifty thousand shares of iron company stock were given an option to buy two shares of steel for every one that they owned. The options, moreover, could be sold on the open market. They could be converted into stock certificates by a down payment of one dollar per share. Other, unspecified installments, would be payable later.

These actions led to considerable speculation in Bethlehem securities. Public faith in the soundness of the iron company pushed up prices of its stock and of options to buy into the holding company. Wharton noted on 28 March 1899, sales of iron company stock at $150.00 and of rights to Bethlehem Steel Company stock at $21.50. In April Sayre paid $25.00 per unit for three thousand of Bethlehem Steel rights.[44] Prices later receded from these figures but remained high.

The real unearned profit to the old stockholders at the time of these transactions was obscure to all but an inner circle. Holders of iron company stock had to make a down payment of one dollar per share to realize their rights to steel company stock. They could anticipate having to pay later installments to a total sum of fifty dollars, the par value. Indeed, a possible second installment of one dollar, payable about 1 October 1899, was publicized.[45] But no later payments were called for. Owners of Bethlehem Iron Company stock who took up their options to buy into the steel company had the new stock for a dollar per share. The difference between one dollar and whatever they could sell the stock for on the open market, for example, twenty-four dollars per share in 1901, represented a gift. In addition, they could expect at least 6 percent annually on their iron company stock and probably a dividend on steel company stock (which was paid).

Thus in the spring of 1899 a new holding company, called Bethlehem Steel, seemed ready for a great future. Then came the formation of United States Steel, with Bethlehem left out, thereby changing the outlook. The directors decided to sell. The rich Bethlehem Steel Company suddenly became as available as an American heiress in search of a European title of nobility.

Who would buy and take the chances which the directors of Bethlehem Steel were unwilling to assume? No other steelmaking facility in the country had anywhere near the power of United States Steel, backed as it was by Morgan. Several potential customers showed an interest, then turned away. Precisely who these were is unknown, as such matters were kept confidential. Only one of the early inquiries led to a serious proposal. That came from a company which conceivably might have been able to stand up to the power of United States Steel, namely, Vickers Sons and Maxim of Britain.

Consolidation within the steel and armaments industries in Britain had occurred at least as fast as in the United States. The company of Sir Joseph Whitworth had been sold to, and then consolidated with, the works of Sir W. G. Armstrong; and Armstrong found a strong competitor in Vickers, which built ships of war and supplied them with armor and guns from its own plants. This ability to turn out a complete warship in its yards made Vickers the envy of shipbuilders in countries that had to rely on independent firms for armor plate and guns. Vickers had the support of the Admiralty Board, which was expanding the Royal Navy to counter the increasing strength of the German fleet. The Admiralty was unlikely to put barriers in the way of allowing Vickers to build warships in America for either Britain or her potential allies. Expansion of the Vickers shipbuilding capacity through an American combination of shipyards and steel works seemed very possible.[46]

Wharton conducted the negotiations with Vickers. Before the formation of United States Steel, Wharton acknowledged that Vickers was showing an interest in the Bethlehem company. Eighteen months later, in early May 1901, talks became serious concerning the purchase of Bethlehem by a syndicate including Vickers, the Cramp shipyards, and perhaps other parties. Wharton wrote to Linderman on 18 May that the syndicate would probably buy if the directors could guarantee to deliver one hundred and sixty thousand shares of stock. The directors would have had no trouble doing this, as Wharton, Sayre, Linderman, and Wilbur controlled much more than that.

From that time on, events moved fast. Within two weeks Bethlehem Steel was sold—not to the Vickers syndicate, but to Schwab. Sayre's diary records the highlights:

May 21. "Linderman is in New York trying to close up the sale of Bethlehem Steel Co."

May 24. "Home by the 12:30 p.m. train to meet Wharton and Linderman and hear their report on the sale of the Beth^m Steel Co. to the Vickers, Cramp Syndicate, a conditional sale made at 22.50 per share."

May 28. "Bethlehem Steel Co. turned down the offer of the Vickers Cramp Co.'s of $22.50 per share because the V. C. Combination wanted the time given for examination of the works extended. Damn foolishness."

May 31. "Rob Linderman came in on his arrival from New York last Eve to say he had completed a sale of Beth^m Steel Co.'s Stock to Schwab at $24 per share, thus dropping out the Vickers Cramp deal. . . . Linderman wired me he had seen Wharton who had agreed to the trade with Schwab."

June 1. Cleaver had informed Sayre that Linderman "had concluded his deal with Schwab but included the sale of the Beth^m Iron Co. by agreeing to take 6% bonds for the Bethlehem Stock, each at par and cancel the lease to the Beth^m Steel Co. This is not satisfactory to me and I doubt its being so to others."

In fact, on 30 May Schwab conditionally contracted for one hundred and sixty thousand shares of Bethlehem Steel Company stock at twenty-four dollars per share. The stipulation made by Schwab, to which Sayre referred, was that the holders of the Bethlehem Iron Company stock should exchange it for steel company bonds. Bethlehem Steel would float a bond issue of

$7,500,000. Iron company stockholders would receive a one thousand dollar bond for each twenty shares of iron company stock. According to Schwab's plan—soon carried out—when this financial arrangement was complete, the steel company would cancel the lease with the iron company, which would then cease to exist. Bethlehem Steel would be transformed into an operating company capitalized at $15 million with a bonded indebtedness of $8,851,000.

The stockholders of the Bethlehem Iron Company had to ratify the agreement between Linderman and Schwab before it could become binding. Sayre, a reluctant partner in the deal, noted considerable controversy concerning the wisdom of the sale and doubted that it would be approved. But on 15 August the stockholders overwhelmingly accepted the transaction and on the same day the directors met and gave effect to their decision. Wharton presided over this final meeting of the board of the Bethlehem Iron Company. A meeting of the Bethlehem Steel Company's board in Philadelphia the following day ratified the decisions of the iron company.[47]

The newspapers speculated concerning Schwab's motives for buying Bethlehem Steel. They looked on the transaction as especially puzzling because Schwab was president of United States Steel. Most thought that he had bought the Bethlehem company for the "Steel Trust," as United States Steel was being called. Some considered the possibility that he was acting as an agent for E. H. Harriman, the railroad magnate who had recently concluded an agreement with Morgan concerning control of the Northern Pacific. But, given the circumstances of the sale, the most compelling motive seems to have been that of preventing the Vickers syndicate from getting Bethlehem Steel and thereby acquiring a strong base from which to invade the steel and shipbuilding industries of the United States.

Schwab almost immediately resold the company to a syndicate controlled by the Morgan interests. Somewhat later he repurchased it and put it into a combination called the U.S. Shipbuilding Company. From this venture, after considerable financial turmoil, came a reorganization known as the Bethlehem Steel Corporation with Schwab, now retired from United States Steel, as head.

Wharton had nothing to do with these later events. With the initial sale of Bethlehem Steel to Schwab his connection with the management of the company was ended. He and the other directors retired in favor of a board handpicked by Schwab. Neither Wharton, Wilbur, Sayre, nor Linderman was ever again called upon for service to the company.

Also, the sale of Bethlehem Steel ended Wharton's ties with the boroughs of Bethlehem and South Bethlehem. He had no further business interests there. His wards, the Thurston boys, had left college and were living elsewhere. Yet he sometimes met in Philadelphia his former colleagues with the iron company; and he included them on the lists of persons to whom he sent copies of his speeches and other publications. The Wharton papers contain several letters giving evidence of these continuing ties. One is a copy of a communication sent to Fritz, for whom Wharton retained an affectionate regard. Wharton wrote of receiving a letter from Fritz dated 19 March 1904, "which is very clearly written . . . but I am sorry to hear that though you can write a little you are unable to read writing, and I suppose at your age it is hardly to be hoped that you will ever learn. You remind me of a man who had received a note from John G. Johnson, who is supposed to be the worst writer in America. He could not read a word of it, but remembered that a friend of his who is a druggist was good at deciphering cramped chirography, so he handed the letter to him to read. The druggist looked at it, retired to his back room, came out directly with a bottle which he handed to the other man and said there is your prescription, fifty cents please."

At Christmas time, 1902, Wharton had his poem "Mexico" illustrated, printed, bound, and sent to eighty-eight persons, many of whom responded with words of appreciation. Two of these were Linderman and Sayre. Linderman's acknowledgment was nostalgic: "It seemed a little strange but at the same time most familiar to find on my desk this morning an envelope addressed in your handwriting. It at once took me back to the 'old times' when epistles between us were a matter of almost daily occurrance [sic]— and I have yet to recall one that I would not be glad to receive again or read over again. No one ever gave me heartier support or more encouragement in my sixteen years work for the 'Bethlehem Company' than you did, and I thank you for it."

Sayre, now in the seventy-eighth year of his age, had clearly put all thoughts of the previous differences between himself and Wharton behind: "Thank you for your 'Xmas Greetings,' greetings conveyed in the guise of a descriptive poem on Mexico, handsomely executed on good paper and profusely & artistically illustrated. . . . I must congratulate you as a book maker, from contents to cover it could not be better, and I am especially glad to find we still have a 'Quaker Poet' with us. The 'Sweet Reasonableness of a Yankee Philistine in Cuba' and 'Mexico' will surely entitle you to sign J.W. and who shall, with the difference of a single letter, discern between J.G.W. of the past and J.W. of the present?"[48]

17

The Jersey Ventures

Three parts of Wharton's industrial empire were centered on the state of New Jersey. These were his farms in the pinelands, his north Jersey iron business, and fishing for the menhaden in coastal waters. He began these ventures in the 1870s and 1880s while still involved with the American Nickel Works and the Bethlehem Iron Company. When after the turn of the century the nickel and steel enterprises passed into other hands, the Jersey businesses remained and grew in size and complexity. They provided him with much occupation, however questionable they sometimes might have been as sources of income.

1

At a time when John Dewey was beginning to develop the pragmatic proposition that the unanticipated consequences of actions are more lasting than those anticipated, Wharton's property in the pinelands was proving the point. None of the purposes which he had in mind for the land was of any great national impact, neither the raising of sugar beets or other crops; grazing; timbering and lumbering; nor supplying cities with pure water, to mention the best known. Yet in pursuing each goal he added to the conservation of a vast, compact, and unique wilderness area known to later generations as the Wharton Tract or Wharton State Forest, destined to become a place of study for ecologists and of delectation for the public.

After the accession of Theodore Roosevelt to the presidency, conservation of natural resources became a major issue in national politics. Wharton supported Roosevelt because he was a Republican; but Wharton differed from Roosevelt in almost every other way. Once, when Roosevelt made a fiery denunciation of trusts on the occasion of the dedication of the new capitol building at Harrisburg, Wharton, who was on the platform with him, was heard to remark that President Johnson had been impeached for less treasonable utterances.[1] Conservation through public ownership was one of the ideas which Wharton opposed. He strongly believed that government

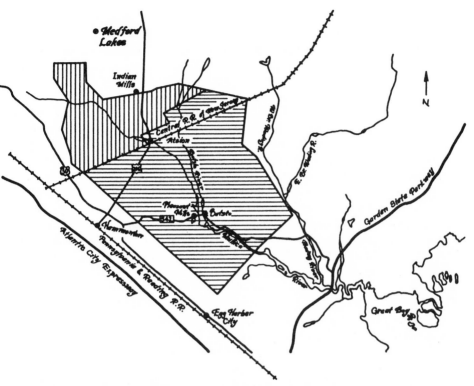

MAP 4. THE WHARTON TRACT IN THE PINELANDS OF NEW JERSEY. Drawn from various sources, the map shows the general location and extent of the properties acquired by Joseph Wharton. He began buying land along the lower reaches of the Mullica and Batsto rivers in 1873, when he conceived of an idea of raising sugar beets. In 1892 he proposed using the waters of the pinelands to supply Camden and Philadelphia. From that time on, most of his purchases were along the upper reaches of the Mullica and the Batsto. At the time of its greatest extent, the tract encompassed approximately 150 square miles. The area of most purchases 1873–1891 is shown by horizontal lines. That of most purchases 1892–1909 is shown by vertical lines.

should dispose of the public lands, that economic growth and national strength could come about only by private development for profit. This goal of profit motivated him in everything he did with his south Jersey lands, this and the subjective, undefinable urge which had led him to ownership of those lands in the first place and later compelled him to keep them intact.

That is to say, Wharton did not oppose conservation of natural resources, but insisted that this must be done through private and not public ownership. His plan for using the streams and marshes of the pinelands to supply Philadelphia and Camden with pure water perfectly illustrates this position. The idea apparently came to him in the early nineties from a businessman of Haddonfield, New Jersey, named Isaac A. Braddock, who owned tracts in the area and, like Wharton, raised cranberries.[2] Braddock had for many years done business with Wharton and Elias Wright, Wharton's agent, buying and selling land for them and arranging for the disposition of the products of bogs, farms, and forests. Wharton had helped to finance Braddock in some of his local dealings. He took Braddock's idea and with aid from C. C. Vermeule, a consulting engineer from New York City who had made the first topographic survey of New Jersey, developed it into a program whereby the owners of the Jersey lands might make a goodly profit while Philadelphia and Camden solved a pressing problem of public health and people at large enjoyed a recreational facility.

The problem of obtaining a supply of pure water was especially acute for Philadelphia, which during the nineties had one of the highest death rates from typhoid fever of any city in America. Research proceeding from Louis Pasteur's pioneering work concerning the germ theory of disease left no doubt as to the cause. Raw sewage was dumped into the Schuylkill and the Delaware near the spots from which Philadelphia took its drinking water. Prompt action to correct the situation seemed essential, yet was not forthcoming because of a divided opinion concerning a solution. Some persons favored finding new sources of supply, either in artesian wells or uncontaminated streams flowing many miles distant from the city. A more modern, scientific idea was that of using filtration beds. This had an advantage of allowing the city to retain its existing sources but the disadvantage of being new, not yet completely proved in practice, and therefore suspect. The forces favoring various plans were sufficiently balanced to prevent positive action. During the years that city councilmen argued the merits of the plans, people kept dying of typhoid and other waterborne diseases. More than a decade elapsed before the council finally put an end to the issue by opting in favor of filtration.

No sooner had the idea of using Jersey water to solve Philadelphia's health problem surfaced than Wharton set Vermeule to work ascertaining the volume of water in the rivers draining the swamps of the pinelands. Vermeule estimated that the daily flow was almost 900 million gallons or nearly six times the amount daily used by Philadelphia and Camden. He later wrote in the *Annual Report of the State Geologist, 1892,* "These southern New Jersey streams will be found valuable potable waters when the time comes to utilize them. The popular idea has been that we must go to the hills for pure waters, but there is little doubt that a systematic comparison at all seasons would result favorably to such of these streams as have forested water-sheds at least, if not to all of them."[3]

With his ideas thus made respectable by science, Wharton began buying land in the western part of the pine barrens. Most of his earlier purchases had been along the lower reaches of the Batsto and Mullica rivers, between Atsion and tidewater. Now he bought at the headwaters as well. (See map p. 305.) His largest single purchase was that of the Raleigh tract, consisting of over twenty-three thousand acres. This was, like several of his earlier acquisitions, a bankrupt development project, part of which he allowed to return to its pristine condition. He had by 1892 approximately one hundred and fifty square miles of land containing a runoff equal to double the daily water needs of Philadelphia and Camden. He pointed out that property adjacent to his contained as much available fresh water.[4]

Using the engineering sevices of Vermeule, Wharton drafted a plan for bringing this water to the cities and had it printed in a pamphlet dated March 1892, entitled "The Best Water for Philadelphia." The plan read in part:

Approximately parallel with, and about 10 to 20 miles eastward from the Delaware River opposite Philadelphia is the broad region, mostly flat and in parts swampy, in which rise streams flowing westward to the Delaware and also streams flowing eastward into the Atlantic. The lowest part of this divide is where the headwaters of Cooper's Creek approach those of Atsion River, and is about 95 feet above mean tide at the lowest point.

The projected ship canal which has occasionally been brought to public notice, to run from the Delaware River at Philadelphia across New Jersey to Great Bay on the Atlantic coast, would naturally follow the valleys of Cooper's Creek and of Atsion and Mullica Rivers. . . .

Between those shallow valleys the land is undulating, though flat, and is mostly poor and sandy, covered more or less thickly with scrub oak and pine forests, and, except near the railroads, is very sparsely populated, though settlements of small-fruit growers are creeping inward constantly from the thrifty railroad towns of Hammonton, Elwood, and Egg Harbor. A number of small interior towns, such as Batsto, Crowleytown, Washington, and Herrmann, are now nearly or quite extinct.

The whole of this large region is remarkable for its absolute freedom from malaria and for its general healthfulness. . . .

All this water, falling upon sand and gravel in a region of extremely small population, is of the highest purity. . . . By a system of dams, forming lakes, and by connecting those lakes by means of canals through the forest, all the affluents of Mullica River can be gathered at three different levels; the most easterly at an elevation of 30 feet, the middle at 50 feet, the highest, near the divide, at 70 feet, above the sea.

The water of the 30-foot level, backed up to the foot of a dam of the 50-foot level, can be readily lifted into the chief lake of that level; similar backing up and lifting will deliver from the 50-foot level to a lake of the 70-foot level.

A canal about five miles long, cutting through the sandy divide, will carry all the water thus collected at the 70-foot level into the valley of the North branch of Cooper's Creek, in which valley the waters of several small westward-flowing streams will also be collected into a considerable lake, which may be called Haddon Lake, near Haddonfield, at an elevation of 61 feet, whence it will flow by gravity to Camden and to Philadelphia, crossing under the Delaware River through several large steel pipes or through a tunnel.

Wharton announced an intention of forming a company

to be called "The South Jersey Water Company," to which I should convey all my lands and waters above mentioned, except such as are below the 30-foot level (particularly near Batsto, where I have a residence), and except some smaller parcels of ground outside the needful territory.

It is intended that this company should acquire by purchase or condemnation such additional lands and waters as may seem desirable, and should construct and operate water-works under contracts with the two cities for selling water delivered at a suitable point within the limits of each at a fixed price per million gallons. Also that the company should carry out such policy as may prove expedient for utilizing the land as parks, game preserves, fishing stations, and residence sites; probably for one or more great hotel establishments, which latter can be admirably suited for both health and pleasure in this region of deliciously wholesome air, with drives about the lakes and forests, and with attractive opportunities for boating and bathing.

The South Jersey Water Company was never formed. Before it stood any chance of success the cities of Camden and Philadelphia had to accept Wharton's plan or something similiar to it, and the officials of neither city showed the slightest interest. Wharton's agents in the pinelands spent the next several years raising and selling cranberries and other crops, experimenting with new plants (for example, sperry grass), and cutting timber for mine props. The aging General Wright reduced his activity to that of taking care of real estate transactions and of clearing titles. George Wright retired as manager of the farm at Batsto and was replaced by Alonzo Norton. Andrew Etheridge took charge of the general store and farm at Atsion.[5] The costs of buying land and paying of legal fees added to Wharton's general financial burden as the depression of the nineties deepened. In August 1893 a fire swept over approximately forty thousand acres, destroying the value of the timber thereon.

Wharton became gloomy about the prospects of receiving any appreciable monetary return from his holdings in the Pinelands. "I . . . have very little appetite for Jersey land & have in fact much more of it than money," he wrote Wright on 26 February 1894, and a month later, "I spent yesterday about the Jersey property and have seldom felt so discouraged about it. . . . I intend to buy no more land, and to cut down expenses. Your work in clearing up lines and titles is valuable if the land it relates to has value—otherwise not. The water scheme has no sign of life in it—no more than anything in Jersey."[6]

Yet he would not sell land which might compromise the water scheme, and in fact continued his purchases. As long as the Philadelphia city council had not acted, he had hope. He temporarily gained the ear of Boies Penrose during that politician's abortive attempt to become mayor of Philadelphia; spoke before the Science and Art Club of Germantown, the New Century Club, and the student body of the Wharton School; invited members of the Geographical Club of Philadelphia to visit his Jersey lands and let it be known among the doctors of the city that he was ready and willing to answer their questions; gained more financial engineering data from Vermeule; and in 1895 revised and reprinted his pamphlet.[7]

The council discussed the problem of water supply again in the spring of 1895. Wharton was pessimistic concerning the chances for success in having his plan adopted. He expected, he wrote to F. P. Stearns, that only a "civil and perfunctory attention will be paid by our city officials to my scheme. Indeed, I am rather wary of putting it before successive committees."[8] His fears were justified. On 13 May, when he was called on to explain his plan, the council narrowly defeated a motion to defer hearing from him until the vacancy at the head of the city's bureau of water had been filled. He gave his talk, answering questions as they arose. When he broached the topic of financing the project by means of a private company he made the point that such a procedure would "lift the entire matter out of politics." The reporter for the *Public Ledger and Transcript* gave the sequel:

Whether this statement detracted from the committeemen's interest in the scheme or not is not known, but just at this point they began to slip out of the chamber, some alleging other committees and other business as an excuse for their going. Chairman Byram had an engagement with one of the Directors, and he, too excused himself, Mr. Clay taking his place. Mr. Wharton continued to explain his scheme, despite the interruptions caused by the departing members until Mr. Deany rose to a point of order, and called the Chairman's attention to the fact that there was not a quorum present, and Mr. Clay, after a count of heads, assured himself of this fact and declared the meeting adjourned.[9]

The municipal government at Camden eventually became mildly interested in Wharton's plan. Although the council in May voted to erect an experimental filtration plant for one distribution district, the idea of bringing in water from the headwaters of the Rancocas, Mullica, and Batsto rivers had some support. The council's water committee together with the mayor and other officials visited the area in June. But when Wharton was asked to submit a bid, he declined to do so. He explained his refusal: "The scheme is perhaps possible as for Camden alone, but I would not wish to join in it. . . . The larger scheme that I have felt interested in—namely gathering all the available waters for the use of both cities, Philadelphia and Camden—could hardly fail to be injured by the taking of a part of the needful waters for the use of Camden alone."[10]

Wharton wrote on 9 October 1895 to the editor of the New York World, "It is perhaps exactly because I am quite alone in this enterprise that it excites so little attention. Probably after the problem has become difficult through the dispersion of my land by reason of sale or because of the accidents of life and death, it may become necessary to do . . . what is now rather easy for those in authority."

On several later occasions Wharton pressed his plan on city council and the public. Once was in 1896, when a new chief of the water bureau, William C. Trautwine, showed an interest in the project. Another occasion was June 1898, when the Philadelphia city council voted down by fifty-two to fifty a proposal to erect a filtration plant.[11] A year later, when Wharton's plan seemed to be gaining some support, opponents suggested legal difficulties. They quoted a statement of Governor Leon Abbett of New Jersey to the effect that the state would not permit its water to be withdrawn or used in another state. Writing about this, Wharton commented, "This led me to inquire of Mr. Griggs [Hon. John W. Griggs, attorney general of the U.S. and counsel for the East Jersey Water Co.] what the law of New Jersey was on this question: his reply was emphatic that there was no law to prevent the taking of water over the line." The city solicitor then gave an opinion that the New Jersey legislature would have to give explicit permission before water could be withdrawn from the state.[12] Wharton countered this objection by obtaining a statement from Vermeule concerning the history of water being sent from New Jersey to other states and containing an opinion that the water on Jersey lands could be delivered "at the State line, to the City of Philadelphia or a Water Company incorporated in Pennsylvania, without effective objection by any one."[13]

The issue came to a head early in 1900, when the Philadelphia city council asked the people to vote by way of a referendum on a filtration system. Wharton's supporters urged him to help in organizing a Pure Water League with branches throughout the city in order to defeat the measure, but he declined, saying the project "strikes me as being too elaborate and involving too much toil. I am too old and busy. . . . Yesterday's Phila. Times had an article by Isaac A. Braddock, and today's Public Ledger has one from me on the Jersey water project, both aiming to educate public opinion."[14] Still, he drafted and had printed and distributed a handbill asking voters to consider the alternative of pure water from New Jersey and to defeat the referendum. In the handbill he recanvassed the legal issue, assuring the voters that it contained no substance.[15]

Clearly, he was tired of the subject. Two months later he wrote with uncharacteristic bitterness: "I do not mean to bother them [the councilmen of Philadelphia] or any one with my better and cheaper plan for supplying good water. We have good authority for not casting pearls before swine and the same authority tells us that 'The dog returns to his vomit again, and the sow that is washed to her wallowing in the mire.'"[16]

Thus chances for Wharton's scheme being adopted disappeared, not because of adverse action on the part of the legislature of New Jersey, which came later, but because of indifference shown by the officials and councilmen of Philadelphia. Yet the dream remained. Wharton was convinced that his plan was sound, better than any other which had been proposed. Although Philadelphia got a filtration system, he never ceased regarding this as a temporary measure and kept on perfecting his lands in southern Jersey, buying over twenty-six hundred acres between 1898 and 1902. In this year he sent a copy of his pamphlet on pure water to a Mr. Randal Morgan, noting that the initial filtration plant did not seem to be giving satisfaction, and adding, "It is probable that Philadelphia will ultimately need to take naturally pure water from the most available source, and that source is to be found in the streams of New Jersey which I own."[17] Wharton continued to buy land among the pines until the time of his death.

2

He had put together, like pieces of a giant jigsaw puzzle, an immense tract mostly consisting of forests and swamps. He was proud of the accomplishment and had General Wright collect into books the briefs of title and other documents defining the property, a project to which Frank Middleton succeeded upon the death of Wright.[18]

But what should Wharton do with the tract? He seems to have been caught between the romantic streak which initially led him to buy in the pinelands and his business sense. While awaiting a time when officials in Philadelphia might agree with him concerning pure water, he said that he would like to sell the land. Uses other than that involving pure water soon appeared. When he learned in June 1902 that the state of New Jersey wanted to establish a refuge for persons suffering from tuberculosis, he suggested his south Jersey lands for the purpose. Two years later a firm of realtors in New York City informed him that the U.S. government might buy the tract as a "site for Army and National Guard manoeuvres." Representatives from the War Department of the Army made a site visit.[19]

Other possibilities existed in the form of organizing matters along the Jersey coast in such a way as to make the property attractive to developers. Isaac Braddock told him early in 1902 of a plan for establishing an electric trolley from Philadelphia to the resorts of Atlantic City, Sea Haven, and Beach Haven. The line would bisect Wharton's tract. Would he be willing to grant right of way? The idea was not new. Wharton had long ago entertained it. He replied on 1 February that he would grant a right of way "in exchange for an equitable number of lots on the Beach Haven or Sea Haven Beach."[20] Shortly thereafter Braddock had another plan. This was a proposal to make Atlantic City into a major seaport. He would close both the Atlantic City and Brigantine inlets and dig a ship canal behind the city to connect the inlet to the north with Great Egg Harbor Bay. This, said Braddock, would facilitate the growth of a Greater Atlantic City. Lands reclaimed by closing the present inlets would add to tourist beach facilities. A fast trolley line passing through Wharton's (and Braddock's) land would complete the scheme. Wharton thought sufficiently well of the plan to have a consulting engineer in 1904 verify the feasibility of deepening the entrance to Great Bay sufficiently to allow for the passage of oceangoing vessels.[21]

None of these plans materialized and indeed Wharton had no real enthusiasm for them. Possibly he thought them too unrealistic to bother with. Yet that would not explain his failure to explore them more fully or excuse the obstacles he set before potential purchasers. He absolutely refused to subdivide the tract. He asked an unrealistically high price of $2 million from the U.S. government and at the same time wrote the firm of New York realtors that they could expect only a 1 percent commission if the sale went through. He did nothing by way of creating an opportunity for disposing of the tract at a profit, as he was to do with the Bethlehem Iron Company and the nickel works. His dream of pure water compounded by a mysterious attraction of the land itself seems to have held him fast.

What he effectively did was to continue using the land as before, realizing a very small income from a multiplicity of uses centering around farming, grazing, and forestry. He sold among other products cranberries, sweet potatoes, cattle, hogs, hay, corn, mine timbers, lumber, and charcoal. In 1901 Etheridge experimented with peanuts. Five years later Wharton's lands produced one hundred bushels of peanuts, and he planned to increase the acreage devoted to them. He established a farm of about five hundred and forty acres on Well's Island in Great Bay and another farm on Wharton's Island.[22]

Fires were a constant hazard. They were especially prevalent in the drier weeks of late winter and spring and occurred with such frequency that the local inhabitants accepted them as part of the natural order of things. "The smoke is so thick here you can not hardly see," wrote Etheridge on one occasion.[23] Wharton was not so willing to bow down before nature. He insisted, and with good reason, that the blame was about equally divided between careless people and sparks from engines on the South Jersey Railroad. He fumed at the losses fires gave him and once wrote to an acquaintance:

> As for observing fires and quenching them, I built at my Batsto house a tower overlooking all tree tops and furnished with pointers to the various points of the compass, in order to be able to locate fires. A force of men and horses was held ready to move on short notice towards the flame by night or the smoke by day. . . . I am not sanguine as to the success of your attempts to put a stop to this wretched waste. It almost seems as if the Jerseymen must be born again or replaced by a more civilized creature, and as if the railroad companies must be conquered before any ameliora-tion can be expected. I shall hardly live to see the Leopard and the Ethiopian thus change their spots and their skins.[24]

In 1902, when the water scheme was dead, at least insofar as concerned the immediate future, Wharton began experimenting with scientific forest management. He did so cautiously, as one who has to be convinced of its soundness, and not with the easy confidence with which he applied scientific method to the refining of metals. He came into contact with a professional forester named F. R. Meier and asked him to supply information concerning the advantages of tree farming and good forest management. Meier re-sponded with a report which among other things recommended the planting of a nursery for raising trees. Wharton hesitated; he had many years earlier planted seedlings of chestnut and pine. Why did he need a nursery? Meier responded by pointing out that it was a part of good forest management and argued for his science: "We cannot regard forestry any more from a senti-mental standpoint; or as an interesting experiment. Forestry is too well established even in the U.S. for any doubt that it is a paying business. . . . It is true as you say that the nature of your tract in South Jersey differs greatly from that of Northern New Jersey . . . but the principles underlying those methods must be the same all the world over; that is to cut so that a second crop—a valuable second crop—can be raised in the shortest time. In other words do not cut so that scrub oak or scrub pine follows the first cutting, as is generally the case in ordinary lumbering. Fires have not done it all." Meier went on to say that nursery-grown seedlings were best for planting when one or two years old. He ended, "Like all reformers the forester is little understood in the beginning. . . . Why not give the matter a trial?"[25]

Wharton agreed to this and employed Meier as a consultant and super-visor for a stipend of one hundred dollars a month for three or four months of the year. Meier selected a site for the nursery near Atsion and prepared the ground. "I have no doubt that we [Norton, Etheridge, and himself] will work together with advantage and the prejudice of the men against some of the work will die away as the work goes on and as they see the practical side of it."[26] In the spring of 1903 Meier planted ten thousand seedlings each of white pine and cottonwood and seeds of Scotch pine, yellow pine, Austrian pine, European larch, Norway and Douglas spruce, western Catalpa, black locust, and black walnut. He also asked Wharton to consider the possibility of growing basket willows, since some land near Atsion was suitable for the culture. "It would be very profitable to work the willows into baskets at the place."[27]

The trees in the nursery flourished and the following year Meier made another suggestion, namely, that Wharton "set aside a certain area of your tract, say 1000 acres, as a demonstration forest. On this area I would demonstrate how a forest should be treated according to practical forestry methods, adapted to suit local conditions. . . . You possess over ⅛ of the 'pineries' of the State and work as the above recommended would be a permanent object lesson."[28] Wharton invited Meier to draw up a plan specifying in detail what must be done. Meier did so and submitted it to Wharton, who found it reasonable. He had confidence in Meier and once described him as "a careful man having European as well as American experience in forestry, who I think is entirely honest as well as capable."[29] A site was selected near Atsion and suitably protected against fires by streams and fire lanes. Two years later Meier with Wharton's permission entertained a state forestry commission which visited the site in order to find out what was being done.[30]

In sum, during the last years of his life Wharton began a rational forest program on his property in the pinelands. He became, quite unconsciously, a conservationist in practice. Fifty and more years later, men of the United States Forest Service and in the more responsible private lumber companies were following in the direction pointed out by such pioneers.

3

In contrast to the wilderness unintentionally left by Wharton as a precious legacy to future generations, little remains of his iron-mining and smelting operation in northern New Jersey: a name; hills riddled with tunnels, closed and forgotten; slag heaps visible under a forest matting only to a practiced eye; a few railroad tracks; abandoned roadbeds. He would have liked the iron business to be the start of a major undertaking in the making of steel. It was in fact the largest and most ambitious enterprise of his later years.

The management of the business belonged to Edward Kelly, who succeeded to the position upon the death of Tooke Straker. Kelly had been born in 1858 at Oxford, New Jersey, of Irish immigrant parents. At the age of fifteen he had begun work for the Oxford Iron and Nail Company. Five years later he entered the employ of the Boonton Rolling Mills, where he became a timekeeper. Straker noticed him, moved him to Port Oram, and made him assistant superintendent.[31]

Another person associated with Wharton in his iron business in 1897 and later was Benjamin Nicoll, president of the Mount Pleasant Mining Company. Nicoll served as general sales agent for Philadelphia and New York.[32] Roger Haydock also helped with sales after being released from the Bethlehem Steel Company following its purchase by Schwab.

Wharton's iron business centered on the Hibernia Range, a mountain not over twenty miles long and less than 1,400 feet high. The business in 1890 consisted essentially of the Hibernia, Baker, and Willis mines, the Wharton Furnace in Port Oram, and the Morris County Railroad with its Hibernia branch. The early nineties were years of depression for the eastern industry in pig iron, as the richer and most available deposits had been exhausted and an influx of ore from Alabama and northern Michigan flooded the market. By the middle of the decade only a handful of mining operations was to be found in New Jersey: the New Jersey Iron Mining Company, working the Hurd and New Sterling Slope mines; the Andover Iron Company, operating mines along the Hibernia Range; the Thomas Iron Company of Hokendauqua, Pennsylvania, which took its magnetite ores from the Richard Mine; the Hurd Mining Company, digging from the Hurdtown Mine; Wharton's mines near Port Oram; and the New Jersey and Pennsylvania Concentrating Company, which worked deposits at a place called Edison near Ogdensburg, somewhat to the north and west of the Hibernia Range.[33]

The company with which Wharton had the closest ties in addition to his own was that of the New Jersey and Pennsylvania Concentrating Company. This was the property of Thomas Alva Edison, who directed it in much the same fashion as Wharton had done in developing the nickel business. Edison financed the undertaking from the profits of his other enterprises and acted as his own engineer and manager. He had begun the venture in iron at a time when prices were depressed but not disastrously so. He reasoned that success depended on a large operation, which in turn necessitated new and better machinery, for example, giant cranes; heavy crushing rollers, driers, and conveyors; more efficient means of concentrating ore. With his customary energy and imagination he had set about inventing the machinery. Over a period of approximately eight years he spent about two million dollars in the undertaking. "For five years," wrote Frank L. Dyer and Thomas C. Martin in *Edison, His Life and Inventions* he "lived and worked steadily at Edison, leaving there only on Saturday night to spend Sunday at his home in Orange, and returning to the plant by an early train on Monday morning."[34]

Wharton quickly realized that Edison was a man from whom one might learn much. Apparently Edison had the same opinion concerning Wharton, for the two men became friends. Their several plants were less than twenty miles apart. Wharton helped where he could with Edison's experiments.

Edison used trackage of the Morris County Railroad for some of his needs for transportation and probably hoped for the Bethlehem Iron Company as one of his customers.[35]

"We are in need of a Chief Engineer (steam)," Edison wrote Wharton on one occasion, "who is both theoretical and practical, and one who is capable of taking entire charge of our steam plant here—and who is active, careful and ambitious, and has had a great deal of experience and is quick to see possible future trouble and correct it—also one well up in economics of fuel etc. We will pay $2000 to $2500 per year. Can you recommend anyone to us? Please do not reply and say that there was once such a man described above, but that he was crucified about 1900 years ago. Send me the address of the man in your opinion who comes nearest to conditions as stated."

"I have yours of 9th," Wharton replied, "and have started an inquiry at Bethlehem for the kind of man you want. To this I should have an answer tomorrow or next day: it is of course much more important to get *the right* man than to get some kind of man instantly. But why don't you invent one, or fix up some kind of Kinetoscope that will work so exactly like a bang up engineer that your boilers and engines won't know the difference? Or again why not take some stupid honest fellow and hypnotize him as Trilby was hypnotized! There is work ahead for you. I will write you again as soon as I have anything definite to say. Just now I don't know the man you want."[36]

Three days later Wharton wrote to the effect that people at the Bethlehem Iron Company had not been able to suggest anyone for the position, but that Major Brooks of William Sellers and Company knew of a possible candidate. More than seven months later Wharton returned to the subject, suggesting one John van Gestel, "the man who wrote the really astonishing account of the Krakatoa eruption in 'The Cosmopolitan' for April," and the sort of person for whom Edison had been looking "several months ago."[37]

An invention of Edison's of especial interest to Wharton was that of a magnetic separator. Edison's work with this and Wharton's ultimate reaction to it explains in part why Wharton succeeded with a venture in the mining and smelting of Jersey ores, whereas Edison failed.

The concentration of ores at the minehead was standard practice in most mining operations. Originally this had been done by hand, using women and boys. Sometimes operators took advantage of differences in specific gravity and separated ore from the gangue by jigging the output of the mines in water. Then came experiments with chemicals and machines of various sorts. The machines which were tried in the iron industry of New Jersey were based on a realization that the ores were slightly magnetic. If raw ore was crushed to a desired degree of fineness and passed by a magnet the oxides would move close to it and the gangue would go into the tailings. The discovery had inspired inventors for over forty years. By 1893 many magnetic separators were in use. Some allowed crushed ore to fall close to magnets. Others employed a revolving drum with a magnetic center. A number used a system of belts passing under or over magnets or magnetic drums.

These separators were small. Edison conceived of a large machine which would make an almost complete separation of the oxides of iron from the useless rock. He devised a system of rollers capable of reducing blocks of ore weighing several tons to a powder. This was then passed along a series of magnets. Dyer and Martin described the process:

> At the start the weakest magnet at the top frees the purest particles, and the second takes care of others; but the third catches those to which rock adheres, and will extract particles of which only one-eighth is iron. This batch of material goes back for another crushing, so that everything is subjected to an equality of refining. We are now in sight of the real "concentrates" which are conveyed to dryer No. 2 for drying again, and are then delivered to the fifty-mesh screens. Whatever is fine enough goes through to the eight-inch magnets, and the remainder goes back for recrushing. Below the eight-inch magnets the dust [containing phosphorus] is blown out of the particles mechanically, and they then go to the four-inch magnets for final cleansing and separation. . . . Obviously, at each step the percentage of felspar and phosphorus is less and less until in the final concentrates the percentage of iron oxide is 91 to 93 percent.[38]

Wharton was skeptical of this process. He spotted a difficulty of which Edison was already aware. The concentrates did not reduce well in the blast furnace. The magnetites of New Jersey had always been difficult to refine. When they were ground to a powder they also tended to clog the furnace. Wharton, who was experimenting using Edison concentrates mixed with other ores, suggested that they be solidified using lime. He wrote to Kelly, "The Edison concentrate might perhaps work well if mixed with lime in a mortar bed, and allowed to dry so as to break easily into lumps like rough mortar. This would not do as treatment of ore for transportation but might answer well at the furnace to hold the ore together down to the melting zone, where it should melt rapidly and start the other ores. Try it." A few days later Wharton again wrote, "Edison suggests that his fine concentrates should work well, mixed in the barrow with . . . Lake ore. It would work better mixed thoroughly in a mortar box with fine wet Lake ore, but even then not so well perhaps as if mixed with lime."[39]

Edison's answer to the difficulty was that of inventing a briquetting machine. "Briefly described," wrote Dyer and Martin, "the process consisted in mixing the concentrates with the special binding material in machines of an entirely new type, and in passing the resultant pasty mass into the briquetting machines, where it was pressed into cylindrical cakes three inches in diameter and one and a half inches thick, under successive pressures of 7800, 14,000, and 60,000 pounds. Each machine made these briquettes at the rate of sixty per minute, and dropped them into bucket conveyors by which they were carried into drying furnaces, through which they made five loops, and were then delivered to cross-conveyors which carried them into the stock-house."[40]

The briquetting of the concentrates solved the difficulty of refining them. Five hundred tons of briquettes went to the Crane Iron Company at Catasauqua, Pennsylvania, for testing.[41] The tests proved that use of the concentrates increased the output of iron with less use of fuel and flux and at the same time reduced the percentage of silica and phosphorous to a point that at least some of the ores could be used in a Besemer converter.[42]

Edison was now ready to expand his plant so as to deliver briquettes on a large scale. He needed more capital in order to do this and asked Wharton for support from the Bethlehem Iron Company in the form of a letter of intent to purchase the concentrates. Wharton complied and wrote on 21 May 1895, as follows: "Yours of 17th reached here when I was in New York. I observe with interest that the attainment of your aims in producing concentrated magnetite seems near. You already know that the adverse view of your enterprise which I held after seeing your original plant gave place to the contrary opinion after I looked over your new plant. Though my examination was not thorough, I came to the belief that you could produce good ore cheaply enough to have a very satisfactory profit for yourself while selling it low enough to enable buyers to make Bessemer pig iron at or under ten dollars per ton. And this in large quantity. When this is done you will have rendered an important service to the steel makers of the Eastern States."

The Bethlehem Iron Company ordered one hundred thousand tons of briquettes. Wharton gave an opinion to Kelly that a steady use of them "would change many conditions: among other things might greatly change the style of furnace construction and blowing engines. Low furnace stack and light pressure of blast might then be the requisites."[43]

The Eastern iron industry had no real chance to experiment with these and other innovations. Ores from the newly opened Mesabi range came on the market. These in addition to concentrates from Alabama and Michigan resulted in a still further reduction of prices. Ores which would have brought six dollars a ton in 1890 sold in 1898 for two dollars, and the prices received for pig iron correspondingly declined.[44] Edison could not meet the competition. His separator necessitated the additional operation of briquetting, the cost of which was largely responsible for making the difference between his hoped-for financial success and his ultimate failure. Also, apparently, by no means all of his product was suitable for the Bessemer converter. E. G. Spilsbury in the *Iron Age* for 25 February 1897 wrote, "Even under the present conditions of low prices, if resulting concentrates were low enough in phosphorus to bring them within the Bessemer limits the operation could be carried on to financial success, but unfortunately such is not the case, and therefore until the price of foundry pig shall advance to a figure at which it will be profitable to purchase a 68 per cent iron ore at 6 cents a unit it is not probable that the Edison works can be run continuously at a profit. It stands, nevertheless, a monument of perseverance in original research which certainly deserves our admiration."

Edison had made his separator maximally efficient, but as a result had also made the process geared to its use too expensive. Wharton did not employ Edison's separator, but chose machines of lesser efficiency. One was invented by Clinton M. Ball of Rockaway, New York. Ball's machine produced an imperfect separation of iron from gangue and therefore occasioned a greater waste of iron but left the concentrates in a sufficiently coarse state that briquetting was unnecessary.[45]

In 1899 Edison abandoned his enterprise. His plant was dismantled; the town of Edison disappeared. He shifted some of the heavy machinery to a new venture in the mining of cement rock and the manufacture of Portland cement. This left Wharton as the undisputed largest miner of iron ore in New Jersey.

4

Until Wharton in 1908 created the Wharton Steel Company his mining and smelting operations in New Jersey had no common name. They comprised, colloquially, his "iron business." He systematically expanded the business in response to conditions of the market, buying properties and renovating plant and equipment when prices were low, pushing production to the maximum when prices were high. Like most businessmen, he complained of costs when the market was bad and was silent on the subject when it was good.

During the prewar depression, which had been the immediate cause of Edison's failure, Wharton shut down operations at Port Oram. On 12 April, 1897 he wrote to Kelly, "It is clear that 1898 will show a heavy excess of cash outlay over cash receipts, and I think the Jan. 1 inventory is likely to show also a large diminution of loose assets, so that the year's business will be disastrous. Such improvements as have been made are only what every iron business must constantly be making and charging to cost of iron. They are any way no more than enough—probably not enough—to pay royalty on ore taken out. The business will of course finish if it can't do much better in the near future."

It did much better following the outbreak of war with Spain. Wharton lost $30,757.54 in his pig iron operations in 1898, but estimated a profit of seventy-five thousand dollars on the fifty thousand tons which he planned to turn out in 1899.[46] The recovery in the pig iron industry was, indeed, spectacular. In the middle of it he briefly considered joining forces with Nicoll, his sales agent and an independent operator of mines. The idea was to form a corporation to be known as the Wharton Iron Company with a capital of two million dollars. Nothing came of this hypothetical venture. Two years later Wharton bought outright the properties controlled by Nicoll.[47]

At the end of 1900 the market in pig iron collapsed, revived the following year, and fell again in 1902. Each boom saw small operations come into existence, and each decline witnessed their demise. By the end of 1902 all independent mines were closed; only those connected with blast furnaces remained in operation.[48] During these and subsequent years Wharton continued to expand his North Jersey mining and smelting enterprises, frequently by buying out competitors. Early in January 1900 he purchased the Standard Coke Company in Fayette County, Pennsylvania (the Connellsville Region). This small operation included about eighty acres of coal lands and was the first expansion of his iron business outside the state of New Jersey. He renamed the company the Wharton Coke Works. Other major acquisitions betwen 1900 and 1905 included properties of the Glendon Iron Works, the Andover Iron Company, and the New Jersey Iron Mining Company; hematite mines in St. Lawrence County, New York; and about five thousand acres of coal lands in Indiana County, Pennsylvania. The mines in New York were held by the Rossie Iron Ore Company, of which Wharton acquired all the stock. On his Indiana County coal lands he built a large coke works and established a small town named Coral.[49]

The name of Port Oram was changed to that of Wharton in 1902. By that time almost all of the people there and in the immediately surrounding area depended on him for employment. Indeed, by the time he acquired the property of the New Jersey Iron Mining Company he was producing at least 50 percent of all iron ore mined in the state. After the death of Abram S. Hewitt in 1903 Wharton was, according to the *Iron Age*, the nation's largest manufacturer of pig iron and the foremost authority concerning its production and marketing.[50]

In 1905 Wharton produced two memorandums describing his Jersey iron business. One was addressed to Judge Elbert H. Gary, chairman of the board of the United States Steel Corporation, and was intended to interest that concern in buying the properties. The other anticipated a reorganization of the holdings into a firm to be known as the Wharton Steel Company.[51] The memorandums are long, yet they only summarize the properties defining the iron business. These are the essentials:

(1) "Two large new blast furnaces, and one smaller furnace at Wharton, New Jersey, having a normal productive capacity on ore mixture of 56% of 800 to 900 tons daily."

(2) The Morris County Railroad Company, "which is about to be rechartered [as the Wharton and Northern Railroad] so as to take in the following roads, viz. (1) the principal Morris County Railroad, which runs southward from the N.Y. Susq[uehanna] & Erie R.R. near Charlottesburg to junction

one mile west of Wharton with the Del[aware] Lack[awanna] and West[ern] R.R. and Central R.R. of N.J. (2) The Hibernia branch R.R. reaching from Morris Co. R.R. to the top of Hibernia Hill. (3) The Morris County Connecting R.R. reaching from Morris Co. R.R. direct into the furnace yard, and (4) the Port Oram R.R. a small branch forming connection between the Central R.R. of N.J. and the furnace yard railroads. . . . Total length of roads including yard roads about 81 miles."

(3) The Andover Iron Company, "which represents the (1) Andover Iron furnace at Phillipsburg, New Jersey, lately rebuilt and modernized. . . . This property having a frontage on the Delaware River, and a canal at its back, is abundantly supplied with water. A large limestone quarry upon this furnace property is about ¼ mile from the furnace; a large dwelling house suitable for a manager's residence is on this property."

(4) Iron ore mines. The Jersey mines were located in Morris and Sussex counties. "My mines now working are those on Hibernia Hill, the nearest of them about eight miles, the furthest about twelve miles by rail from my furnaces at Wharton, and the Hurd Mine about one-third mile from those furnaces—all magnetites—also the Rossie Mine in St. Lawrence County, N.Y., which is compact hematite.

"The vein of ore in Hibernia Hill is opened for over 6400 feet in length and is known to extend on my land 3000 feet further to the southwest, with a certain extension of unknown length, also on my land which runs more than a mile further to the northeast. I have gradually acquired all this Hibernia vein from eight different parties each of whom thought his or their share a fortune. . . . There is an underground railroad running into Hibernia Hill about 1¼ miles long, and about 320 feet below hilltop, by which much of the ore, and all the water are taken from the mines. . . .

"The Hurd Mine is now working a vein of 60% ore 16 feet thick at north east and where my land adjoins that of the Lord estate, and 20 feet thick at southwest end of present work. . . . It extends through a tract, not mine nor known to be good ore land, to my Baker, Dell and Byram mines, all good but not now working.

"My Allen and Teabo mines occupy all the ground between the Richard mine [of the Thomas Iron Company] to the southwest, and the Mount Hope mine [of the Empire Steel and Iron Company] to the northeast, about 5000 lineal feet. . . .

"It seems safe to estimate 30,000,000 tons in all my magnetite mines, not all of which are here mentioned. I own 4830 acres of land in the iron mine region about Wharton, etc, including mining lands, furnace tract, Wharton town lots, site for steel works etc. On these lands are dwellings for 247 families.

"The Rossie mine tract including what I own outright and that of my mineral rights, contains about 230 acres, with 32 dwellings.

"The Rossie ore is hematite, red and brown of 45 to 50% near the surface;

but blue, of 55 to 60%, in depth. It lies in two beds about 8000 feet long, 4000 feet wide, together 15 feet to 20 feet thick, incline about 25° from the horizontal. The quantity of this ore is obviously great, if continuous (as it appears to be) and of 10 ft. total thickness, and reckoning 9 cubic feet per ton, the total is over 35,000,000 tons. . . .

"The normal daily output of all my mines, magnetic and hematite, the former being 8/10 of the whole, is bout 1,800 tons, or per month of 26 working days, about 46,000 tons."

(5) Coal and coke. "In Indiana County, Pa., I own nearly 5,400 acres of coal carrying three veins, only one of which, a very regular vein 6 feet thick is worked; the others are 4½ feet and 4 feet thick. . . . Here I have 296 first class new beehive ovens. . . . Normal monthly output of coke about 12,000 tons. . . . I built here fronting on the railroad a small town with 85 good new dwellings, a large country department store and some other buildings. The town is named Coral, and all belongs to me, including the stock of store goods.

"In Fayette County, Pa., I own a small but good coke plant with 86 beehive ovens, but only coal enough to run them about five years."

"All of these properties," Wharton informed Gary, "belong exclusively to myself and are free of debt except $16,700 not matured on Rossie Mine, and ordinary current expenses of the business as a going concern."

Such was the small empire which he put together over a period of a little more than twenty years: territories over which he had almost sovereign control, dispersed among three states. His lands supported mines, smelters, roads, railroads, houses, meadows, farms, woodland, and several towns with assorted small businesses. In the several years following the writing of the memorandums he substantially added to his business. He described some of the important acquisitions in a letter to Frick, dated 2 May 1906:

"Since we last met I have increaed my coal ownership in Indiana County, Pa. to about 8000 acres, and have also bought over 30,000 acres of the best coal in West Virginia. Besides this I have bought at Wharton, N.J. a tract of land adjoining on the North East my Hurd Mine, where I am working to within a few feet of this purchase a solid vein of Magnetite, 18 to 20 feet thick, and averaging about 62% iron. I now have one and one half miles of this continuous vein, the shafts in which are about one quarter mile from my furnace."

He would have liked to sell his iron business. He wrote in 1904, "If I were 20 years younger, or if I had some capable son, I should certainly not sell this establishment, but as it is I would sell." He insisted that if the business were to be sold, it must go as a unit. Given this requirement and in spite of the prosperity of the times no one was interested. The United States Steel Corporation twice turned him down, and so did Bethlehem Steel under the control of Schwab.[52]

As the iron business grew in complexity, managing it became more and more complicated. Wharton was soon dealing with several subordinates in addition to Kelly. For this and other reasons a corporate form of organization was highly desirable. Wharton scouted the possibility in 1901, yet year after year postponed action. When finally ill health forced him to turn part of the management over to others, he organized a company with "steel" in the title to indicate his intention for further progress; and he kept control closely within the family. The Wharton Steel Company had a capital stock of ten million dollars. Only five thousand of the one hundred thousand shares were issued. Of these five thousand, Wharton, the president, owned all but twenty-two, which were distributed among J. Bertram Lippincott, vice-president; Harrison S. Morris, treasurer; Harry C. Wenner, secretary; Edward Kelly, general manager; and August Munson, superintendent under Kelly.[53] As long as Wharton lived, these others were in no position to exericse power beyond what he allowed them.

5

Wharton's third major economic involvement with New Jersey was fishing for the menhaden in coastal waters and processing the catch at the factory on Crab Island in the Great Bay. This is the most uncharacteristic of all his ventures. It bears no relation to the mining and refining of metals; has no connection with any scientific or educational project; is different in kind from his interest in railroads and in the pinelands. Catching the menhaden had not even any emotional involvement with a love of the sea. Wharton's papers give no indication that he made a voyage on one of his fishing boats or even visited the factories in which oil was refined and fish scrap prepared (and he must have done both). Other members of his family ignored the business and probably could not have described the difference between a mossbunker and a cod. Yet in its formative years Wharton gave the business a great deal of detailed attention and only relaxed in this when it became too big, and he too involved with other things. Then he put Roger Haydock in charge.

He set a value of $20,787.59 on the business as of 21 December 1894.[54] James E. Otis was then manager of the fertilizer factory on Crab Island and the steamers *Alert* and *Active*, which comprised the fishing fleet. That was the year, too, in which Wharton enlarged the business by employing George W. Miles to fish in New England waters. Miles owned a fish fertilizer plant at Welsh Point, Milford, Connecticut. Wharton chartered for him an ancient steamer of 188 tons called the *Acushnet*, which had been used during the Civil War to catch blockade runners and had later been rebuilt as a passenger boat and had run between New York and New Bedford, Massachusetts.[55]

For the remainder of the nineties Wharton did little by way of expanding the fishing business. He purchased Miles's factory, bought and remodeled the *Acushnet*, and bought and sold another boat, the *Albert Brown*. In years when the fish were running he made money and took a renewed interest in the business. In off years he talked of selling.

Toward the beginning of the Spanish-American War the menhaden industry began to experience some consolidation. A syndicate was formed for the purpose in 1898, headed by Captain N. B. Church. At first Wharton offered to sell the syndicate his various interests for thirty thousand dollars. When the syndicate failed to respond, he tried to sell the *Acushnet* to the federal government for a price of twenty-five thousand dollars, this being more than twice its actual value. The government was not interested.[56]

Wharton's change in attitude toward the menhaden venture coincided with his departure from active work in making steel and nickel. In 1901 he bought another steamer, the *Olive Branch*, whose name he petitioned to have changed to *Adroit*. Captain C. W. Mathis replaced Otis as manager of the fish works. Church's syndicate had by now been organized under the name, The Fisheries Company. Wharton put his fishing properties into another combination, called the Newport Fertilizer Company, in which he bought a controlling interest. From that point consolidation within the industry rapidly went ahead. The Newport company became the Wharton Fisheries Company. Wharton also acquired control over the Cape Fear Fisheries Company of South Carolina and finally in 1906 purchased Church's firm. The combination of the three companies was capitalized at three million dollars. Its properties included forty-one steamships and eight plants for making fish oil and fertilizer and employed about 2,600 people. Its yearly product was estimated to be worth approximately one million dollars.[57]

These transactions effectively gave Wharton a monopoly over the menhaden fishing and fertilizer industry of the Atlantic coast. He was president of the enlarged Wharton Fisheries Company and Haydock was vice-president. According to an article in the Philadelphia *Bulletin* for 4 June 1906, "The deal has accrued to the advantage of Philadelphia, for the New York office has been closed and a handsome new suite of offices opened in the Drexel building."

In a sense all of his Jersey ventures were "to the advantage of Philadelphia." He had not planned it that way, but such was a result. It was, from his point of view, natural. That the city council rejected the water project, which would have been of greatest benefit, was not surprising. Politicians, he believed, frequently did things against the best interests of the people. Industrialists did better. The work which they undertook for their own profit formed a woof into which were woven the strands of interests of family, city, state, nation, and humanity to form a seamless and attractive cloth.

18
Far Western Gold

El Dorado! The Spaniards gave the place its name for the flecks of gold they saw in the sun-baked hills. El Dorado is one of many canyons which before the filling of Lake Mohave extended right and left of the Colorado River slightly below the site of the present Hoover Dam. According to legend (probably apocryphal), Jesuit priests first worked surface deposits there. The rediscovery of gold in the canyon by Americans several centuries later, about 1859, is supposed to have occurred with the help of an old Spanish map. Two years after the rediscovery the official name of El Dorado Canyon Mining District was applied. For more than three-quarters of a century thereafter men worked hundreds of mines in its seventy-five miles of barren hills and washes. "There is absolutely no doubt that countless millions in gold lie hidden among the mountains on both sides of the Colorado river," wrote Wharton in 1904.[1] The El Dorado District in the course of its active mining life gave up close to four million dollars worth. The Techatticup was the richest mine, and the most productive periods were before 1891 and during the years 1915 and 1919 and from 1937 to 1940.[2]

Although wealth came both before and after, but not during, Wharton's presence on the Colorado, it might not have come later without his work from 1899 to 1909 in organizing mines and mill into an efficient operation.

1

By 1880, when Wharton first invested, the Southwestern Mining Company had taken over most of the claims in El Dorado and sunk shafts into many. Wharton Barker was treasurer of the company and W. S. Mills was resident manager.[3] Although the small knot of Eastern capitalists who financed the undertaking on several occasions experienced the thrill of a rich strike, most of the time they put more gold into the venture than Mills took out. At the time of the Barker failure, the mines were unproductive and for lack of funds soon became inoperative. An ordinary mining venture might at that point have been abandoned, but this undertaking involved proven

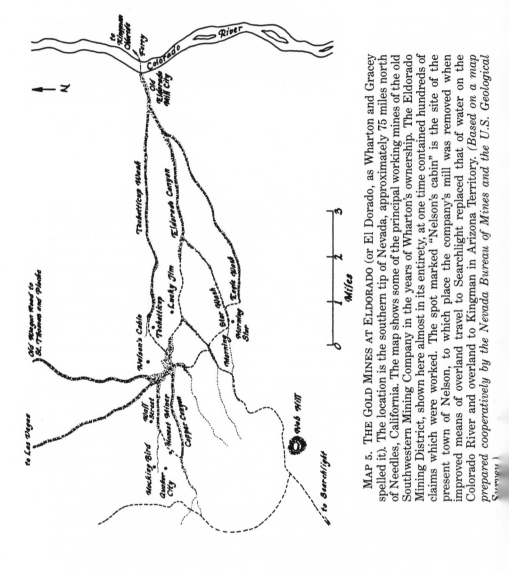

MAP 5. THE GOLD MINES AT ELDORADO (or El Dorado, as Wharton and Gracey
spelled it). The location is the southern tip of Nevada, approximately 75 miles north
of Needles, California. The map shows some of the principal working mines of the old
Southwestern Mining Company in the years of Wharton's ownership. The Eldorado
Mining District, shown here almost in its entirety, at one time contained hundreds of
claims which were worked. The spot marked "Nelson's cabin" is the site of the
present town of Nelson, to which place the company's mill was removed when
improved means of overland travel to Searchlight replaced that of water on the
Colorado River and overland to Kingman in Arizona Territory. (Based on a map
prepared cooperatively by the Nevada Bureau of Mines and the U.S. Geological
Survey.)

resources. Experienced miners had discovered that beneath the occasional rich surface veins lay millions of tons of low-grade gold ore, scantily interspersed with small rich lodes and in places containing silver, copper, and other metals. With the use of quicksilver and the cyanide process the refining of gold could pay. Capital, good management, and patience ought to make the Southwestern Mining Company again profitable.

From the time that the reorganized Barker and Company appeared willing to relinquish its almost valueless stock in the company, Wharton was seriously considering adding the mining of gold in El Dorado Canyon to his other enterprises. He wrote in 1894 to Mills, "As gold is about the only thing in the world that has not depreciated it is a pity we can't dig out a few hundred millions to relieve the existing stringency, or even if we could dig out a much smaller sum to relieve individual stringency it would be gratifying. As things stand we all seem to agree that we have a good manager but we are in doubt as to all other points." Early in 1896 Wharton sent his mining engineer in Canada, Ian Cameron, to El Dorado to investigate the deposits. After receiving Cameron's report Wharton wrote to Mills, "It seems to me fairly probable that with improved process the lean ores of our region may pay to work on a considerable scale, for ores of no higher grade certainly do pay well in other localities. The enclosed slip concerning a modification of the cyanide process may be of interest."[4]

Mills died a few months later. His assistant Charles Gracey took over the position of resident manager. Gracey journeyed to Philadelphia to talk with George Burnham, Jr., who was president of the company, Wharton Barker, and Joseph Wharton. The following year Joseph wrote to Gracey, "The prospect of getting our money back is not very promising, but I guess you will fetch it out if it is there (and I think it must be that you will run against a streak of good luck some day)." Wharton asked Gracey for estimates of costs to put the mines back into operation.[5]

Investing in Western mines was fashionable, an acceptable form of gambling. Most of Wharton's friends did as he had done sixteen years earlier and bought stock in gold, silver, or copper mines of the Rockies and beyond. But now Wharton was not planning to gamble in this random, un-Quakerish fashion. If he went into gold mining it would be with the same expenditure of energy as he had applied to his other enterprises. He would completely own the business; appoint and train the manager, introduce the latest technology, and reap the profits.

Several years later he declined to participate in an iron venture in Alabama, giving as a reason, "The region is entirely too distant for me to operate in."[6] The distance from Nevada to Philadelphia did not bother him. He had caught the gold fever.

Still, in 1896 he was not quite ready for another heavy burden of business. During the preceding five years he had put as much time as he could spare into political matters, and these were still commanding his attention. Populists and other reformers were arousing demands for cheap money by means of a free and unlimited coinage of silver. He opposed this in the name of the gold standard. The election of Cleveland had endangered the country's tariff structure, and worse: Cleveland had proposed to substitute a personal income tax for the tariff as the principal source of revenue. Wharton and fellow Republicans had fought this with everything at their disposal. A Democratic Congress had passed the measure; the Republicans, returned in a majority by the elections of 1894, had taken pains to see that the tax was not levied.

These and related issues had found foci in the presidential campaign of 1896, which became the bitterest since Lincoln had run for office in 1860. William Jennings Bryan for the Democrats and the Populists was advocating almost everything which Wharton opposed. William McKinley, the Republican candidate, was according to Wharton somewhat soft on the issue of trusts but otherwise the hope of the nation for financial sanity and economic progress.

Wharton was actively working for the election of McKinley. He and Swank volunteered to raise one hundred thousand dollars from the iron and steel industry for the Republican campaign fund. Wharton gave speeches on behalf of several Republican congressional candidates and contributed to their expenses. His name was on the ballot that year along with the name of John Fritz as one of the Republican presidential electoral candidates from Pennsylvania. He was proud of the honor. When he learned that some people frowned on directors of national banks being presidential electors, he resigned his directorship in the Farmers and Mechanics Bank, which he had held for many years. He headed the ticket for the Republicans and was chosen chairman of the Pennsylvania delegation. (He was not the only Wharton to be a candidate for presidential elector that year. His nephew William Rodman Wharton was on the Prohibition ticket pledged to Joshua Levering.)[7]

Immediately following the election campaign came the scramble to enjoy the fruits of victory. The Pennsylvania legislature had to fill a vacancy in the U.S. Senate. Wharton vigorously campaigned for Boies Penrose, a strong McKinley man, against John Wanamaker and was gratified when Penrose won.[8] Wharton recommended his friend Charlemagne Tower, a Philadelphia railroad and iron company executive with scholarly interests, for a major diplomatic post, and was again successful.[9] Tower received the ambassadorship to Austria-Hungary and, after spending a year in the post, became U.S. ambassador to Russia.

By the middle of 1897 the main political battles were over, well fought and won, according to Wharton's way of thinking. He had time once more for the gold-mining project. He had done his preliminary thinking and made his investigation and was ready to act. The plan was simple. He had effectively followed it before. He would buy the stock of the Southwestern Mining

Company, force the company into bankruptcy, and purchase the property at a U.S. marshal's sale. He wrote of the plan to Gracey, adding, "This as I understand it makes it desireable that you should have some sort of interest in the working—not as a stockholder, for I see no use in forming a company, but as a percentage of profit realized."[10] Owners of a majority of the stock were ready to sell. Wharton bought their holdings and continued buying, with the intention of purchasing it all in order that no former owner might on some legal technicality challenge him. He collected deeds and in February 1898 wrote to the Nevada law firm of Torreyson and Summerfeld that he now had them for the following properties: mining claims, including Wall Street, East Extension of Wall Street, Lucky Jim, Tough Nut, Jubilee, Mocking Bird, "and sundry others"; the Wall Street, Powers Spring, and Lincoln Silver Mining Company's mill sites and buildings; and four salt lands on the Virgin River, namely, the Colorado, Belding, Moapa, and Recluse.[11]

The foreclosure took place as planned, and the property was ordered to be sold. Wharton anticipated being the only bidder and, consequently, the buyer who would succeed to the Southwestern Mining Company as owner of its properties. The actual sale was not scheduled to take place until late in 1898. Pending the event, Wharton was reluctant to recommence mining in the canyon. But he had no need to await the sale in order to begin negotiating with Gracey. The first step was to see the property and become better acquainted with its manager. Wharton scheduled a trip for late winter, before the torrid heat of the Southwest made travel inadvisable. He left Ontalauna on 1 March 1898 for Chicago, planning from there to board the Atchison, Topeka, and Santa Fe Railroad for the frontier town of Kingman in western Arizona Territory. Gracey would meet him at Kingman and drive him by horse and wagon the remaining sixty-five miles through the desert to El Dorado.

Thus began a venture which was also adventure. Before he died it had involved seven trips under primitive conditions to America's last frontier. As a business operation it was small by comparison with the nickel and pig iron enterprises. It provided frustrations but also an immense satisfaction. A big strike was always possible, and the work was sufficiently successful to keep the prospect alive.

The greatest gain for later generations was a series of letters unequaled in descriptive power by anything else in Wharton's correspondence. They comprise a travelogue through a land in the process of coming for the first time under the reign of law and order and include vignettes of prospecting, mining, the desert, and above all of people.

2

El Dorado Canyon lies on the western side of the Colorado River in that part of Nevada which narrows to a tip at the common border between

California and Arizona. This is part of the Great American Desert. In Wharton's time adobe formed the principal building material. Fuel came from driftwood carried down the river with the spring freshets. Supplies were hauled overland from railheads at Kingman or up the river from Needles, California, about eighty miles distant. A hamlet called Chloride was thirty miles north of Kingman and forty east from El Dorado.

The only natural feature for the support of human life was the Colorado River, cold and swiftly flowing on its way from the mountains of Colorado and the canyons of Arizona to the Gulf of California. Narrow strips of cottonwoods and other vegetation lined the banks. Piute and Mojave Indians divided these lowlands and used the river for travel. A hundred miles to the east lay the uplands of Arizona. There in 1887 Geronimo and the last of the Apaches had surrendered to U.S. troops and been evacuated to Florida. Minor trouble with the Indians still remained. Although friendly to whites they formed a majority of the population. Two years before Wharton first came to the country a Piute named Avote had murdered several people at El Dorado. Gracey had administered a frontier justice against Avote by having friendly Indians follow and kill him. By the time Wharton arrived on the scene peace prevailed, although recollections of recent violence remained.[12]

The train ride from Chicago to Kingman took three days and nights. He read novels, talked with other passengers, and when the jolting of the cars eased, wrote letters to Anna. Kansas with its "immense dull plains" bored him. New Mexico he found more interesting. The dryness shown by arroyos, patches of alkali, treeless mountains, and adobe villages was awesomely oppressive; the people, mostly Indians, whether behind a plow, carrying a pottery vase on the head, or selling souvenirs, were fascinating.

At Kingman he left the train. He wrote to Anna of the wagon ride to El Dorado, using stationery of the Kingman and Arizona Sampling Works— "assaying promptly done":

> The train brought me to this place on the 5th, a little before dawn, and the place looked rather desolate, but just before the cars started a figure loomed up in the darkness and responded to my hail of "Hullo, Gracey." So there I was, cut off from civilization like a man left on a strange shore, with the ship sailing away on her voyage. By the time the sun rose we had gone to the little hotel, to the stable yard where the buck board stood and to the store where Gracey deals; thence to get what Gracey called China hash—a middling fair breakfast. The sun was more than an hour high when the ramshackle team started out of the one street little hamlet on a smart loose going trot that soon brought us to the first ascent, past a half acre garden where a spring kept some peach and fig trees in good heart, over lava fragments that made a pretty good road, and then, mounting always, past a great level topped hill of columnar basalt with other masses of similar basalt around us. Still mounting we gained a great pass between high lava hills until the road opened a wide spread view over the Sacra-

mento Valley lying broad and dim below us. Into that valley we descended finding it a dry desolation of arid desert with no vegetation but thorny crawly things that stood ready to wound with every spine. Over this monstrous and nearly level desert, bounded like the Mexican valleys by great barren mountains entirely destitute of verdure we rode until about 1 o'clk when we stopped for lunch at a slight one story wooden house kept by an old German who formerly lived in Philadelphia. The desert there had at least one road and one house. After lunch and over the same sandy desert we rode for a couple of hours or more toward the mountains on our left and entered into a pass that after a few miles of gentle ascent dropped steeply down into the upper end of a long gulch or canyon. Still there was a very passable road not excessively steep, and leading always between mountains of a savage roughness that can hardly be conceived by one who knows only the verdurous smooth mountains of our State.

Two or three hours of this, and we saw below us the bright ribbon of the Colorado River, but did not go on down to it; our camp was to be on a nearly level spot by the side of the main canyon, and here we stopped, unharnessed the horses and took off the baggage, preparatory to spending the night on the ground there. But as it was still broad day we went afoot up a trail to a prospector's camp and then by a similar foot trail to the tent where Gracey's man Rosenberger was to be found. This trip, call it a mile, occupied an hour, and by that time the sun was quite gone and the moon was shining. After some consultation and some supper we concluded to spend the night in Rosenberger's tent and he was sent back to bring up a cot bed stead for me with some other matters. While he was gone, Gracey and I climbed the mountain in the moonlight to inspect the general situation of the new mineral ledge that he invites me to join him in. A most silent absolutely still night in a landscape as dead as that of the moon.

(While marking time awaiting the resumption of work by the Southwestern Mining Company, Gracey had examined some outcroppings on the eastern side of the Colorado and staked two claims, called the Alabama and the Klondike. One of them was the ledge which Gracey and Wharton examined that night. Gracey had insufficient capital for working the claims and wished Wharton to join him on some suitable share basis.)

Rugged uncompromising peaks and ridges, shadowy valleys with dark recesses, a distance of endless rude shapes mellowed in the softening moonlight, a sky clear as ether set with sparks of stars—and down in a near valley, the one sign of humanity, a little white tent in a crevice.

Rosenberger came back with his load, and after some little chat we turned in, I lying in state on the cot bed stead, the other two men on a huddle of stuff on the ground. I slept well enough.

Next morning we all worked over the ground [of the claim] making as careful examination as our knowledge and appliances permitted, and here I first saw the mystery of horning for gold [probably meaning testing for gold with a horn spoon] which can be explained when we meet; the gold was made to appear plainly in the crushed rock that, in the mountain side, looked as hopeless as my stone quarry.

At noon we descended to the camp, harnessed the team, piled on the baggage and started again, Rosenberger now with us, up the dreary canyon, out upon the desert and reached at sunset the tip of another canyon leading down to Colorado River, nearly opposite to El Dorado Canyon on the other side. This canyon, about 12 miles long, occupied three hours in the descent of 3,000 feet and we then drove a mile or two along the sandy river bank to our ferry, where after a short interval our hail was answered and a row boat brought over to us. The horses were left on this side and in a few minutes we had passed the gleaming, swift flowing Colorado and were in our own dominions.[13]

Wharton continued the account of his first trip to Eldorado and the inspection of the mines and mills there in a letter written on stationery of the Palace Hotel, San Francisco:

A recent letter ran to the point of my arrival at El Dorado Canyon after crossing the Colorado River on a row boat in the moonlight.

A picturesque transit over the swift river to an unknown place where anything might happen. The call across the river, the waiting for a response, the tardy appearance of lights, the sound of oars and the sight of a struggling boat which brought up against a large leaky flat boat moored to the shore—all this and much more rise to mind as I write.

Next morning after breakfast at the Chinaman's house and looking through the Company's store, where I found some remarkably good apples, we started to visit some of the mines riding upon the same buck board which had brought us so far in the last two days. The road ran right up El Dorado Canyon, a broad cut through the hills and mountains with a quite uniform upward slope of about 320 feet to the mile, its bottom being the rocks, gravel and sand brought down by the stream that covers it in times of rain. For this channel discharges the volumes of rain water that fall over the whole region (perhaps 50 square miles) that the Canyon, with all its tributary valleys, drains, the violence of which may be guessed from the fact that the torrent is sometimes several feet deep and in places as wide as from our house to the annex. A few years ago two of our great ore wagons weighing about 3 tons each were swept away by such a flood into the Colorado River and there lost.

But on this occasion the sky was clear and sharply blue, and the sunshine was hot on our backs as we ascended the long tortuous gravelly slope. We passed the narrow pass where our two teamsters were shot dead by Avote, the cabin of John Heuss and the spring which he tries to claim as his property, the cabin and arastra mill [a rock-lined pit in the ground containing stones which are dragged over the ore to crush it] where a Scotchman toils for months to get out gold enough for an animal spree in San Francisco, the Lucky Jim mine which we shall visit another day and at last arrive at the Wall Street Mine.

Here are large openings from which thousands of tons of ore have been taken, some of it rich enough to pay a good profit though none such has lately been found, most of it capable I think of yielding profit if properly worked with modern appliances, though not a particle of gold can be seen with a lens.

Here we took lunch and afterwards examined the ground more carefully, with the impression fixed on my mind that with dililgent skilful working this mine is a good property that may yield steady gains for many years, though as hitherto worked nothing but steady loss can be expected.

Next we went on higher and higher to the Quaker City Mine about 3,000 ft. above the Colorado River.

This also is a large deposit of moderately rich ore that must yield profit if worked as it should be.

The wild solitude of these places is striking, as is the absolute bare sterilty of the rocks; this bareness being a great advantage to the geological observer, for whatever comes to the surface is clearly visible.

A long ride back down the Canyon for about ten miles brought us again to our settlement at the river; after supper and an hour or two sitting out doors in the moonlight we went to bed.

I did not sleep well, being disturbed by diarrhea, which lasted through next morning and kept me abed, though in the afternoon I was able to walk to the mill and to examine it. It needs considerable expense to make it efficient, for, as it is, no profit can be expected from it even if the mines were well worked.

Next morning March 9th we visited others of the Company's mines, all that are counted good for much besides those visited on the 7th. Of those now inspected the Lucky Jim seems most reliable, though the Techatticup and the Savage have yielded richer ores in bygone years. Having started out at 7:30, we returned in time for dinner and after dinner I again inspected the mill and examined some accounts.

In the evening clouds gathered, which next morning were thicker. When we crossed the river, on a rickety boat that rocked and leaked in a very unpleasant manner, a little rain was beginning and it grew more and more decided as we climbed the nameless canyon that brought us out on the desert. Colder and colder it grew till snow might be expected but snow did not arrive. After more than three hours and a half we emerged upon the bleak upland desert and set out at a smart trot for Desert Station which though but a mean little cabin that cost perhaps ten dollars gave a most welcome shelter from the winter weather outside during the half hour while the horses had hay and water.

Again we started and I found overcoat, mackintosh, fur cap and arctic overshoes none too much for comfort. So it lasted till we reached Cross Station where I was able to telephone to Kingman, and then we drove back to old John Tillman's for the night. After a wild dash of rain the clouds thinned so as to show a bit of blue sky at sunset.

A couple of hours later the stars were shining and a fierce North wind was blowing as we sat after supper by the stove and listened to old John's stories of his Indian fighting. He gloried in having scalped seven Indians in one day, but all that is gone by.

The night was wretchedly cold so that I slept but little, and next day we drove on into Kingman as has been already told, taking train afterward for Los Angeles.

From Los Angeles Wharton traveled to San Francisco, where he visited with various people, including Mrs. Henry Coppée, who following the death of the professor had gone to live with a married daughter, Eugenia Griffiths, near San Rafael. "She asked many questions about all of us, and sent the usual messages to thee and to all the family.

"After a good plain dinner composed mainly of corned beef, cabbage and onions, Onions, ONIONS, I sat down to write this, and shall now go to bed." Wharton ended two days of business in San Francisco with "a dip in the waters of the Pacific Ocean."[14]

When the Southwestern Mining Company had begun operating it had located the mill, store, and houses of the manager and the workers at the confluence of the canyon and the river. The location was chosen because of the proximity of the river and the overland route to Kingman as means of transportation. As yet no easy entrance into the region existed from the west. Wharton on his early trips to inspect the mines began and ended at the little settlement. The mines lay well back from the river, none being closer than two miles. The principal paying veins—the Techatticup, Savage, Wall Street, Lucky Jim, Quaker City, etc.—were located about seven miles up the canyon near a spot at which it merged into a westward directed wash known as Copper Canyon. The place was the site of a cabin formerly inhabited by a man named Nelson, who had been one of Avote's victims.

In 1907 Wharton described a descent into the Techatticup:

After scrambling along the tunnel into the mountain side I got into an iron basket just large enough to hold me when crouching down as much as possible and was lowered 250 feet to the top of an incline, walked along it 120 feet to the top of a wooden ladder, then down it to the bottom of the mine, then this way and that along muddy galleries looking from time to time at the spots where the broken rock showed little pin head sparkles of ore—not by any means pure gold, but pyrite carrying a tiny percentage of gold. All this moving about from the mouth of tunnel to bottom of mine in absolute black darkness except for the candles we carried.[15]

The vastness and desolation of the desert haunted Wharton:

The absolute stillness is remarkable—no sound whatever beyond whatever rustling the wind may produce if it should happen to blow.

There are no moving creatures that make any sound except at night the howling of the coyotes, cowardly little wolves that never disturb a living man but will devour a dead one as to leave nothing but the polished bones.

Jack rabbits, lizards, walla-wallas, horned toads, chipmunks and desert rats move as silently as the hawks and buzzards that are occasionally seen sailing around in search of food. What they find is a mystery to me, for, though they are few, their prey is apparently scarcer.

Around and overlooking from the distance all this vast expanse of flat or undulating desert with its hostile prickly plants that bear a sharp stinging prickle at every point—cactuses of various sorts, choyos, nopals and what not—loom up the bare and ancient mountains. In the distance when the sunlight of morning or evening sends its level rays across them they have a grim austere beauty fitting to their task of guarding well the treasures they enfold.

All over them, through their canyons and defiles, tramp the prospectors, with humble outfit of tools, blanket and grub borne upon their tough little ponies or patient burros, scrutinizing the rocks every where for signs of the gold bearing ledges. Usually they wear out their slender means in vain, yet now and then make a strike—many are the stories of the lucky or unlucky chances, among them—tales of selling for a trifle claims that developed into great paying mines.[16]

3

The trip to El Dorado in the spring of '98 convinced Wharton of what he had earlier suspected. The mines and mill needed the touch of an expert such as himself. He would begin the renovation of the mill and have Gracey reopen the mines as soon as the sale of the property was completed. Until then he intended to move quietly so as not to call attention to what was being done. He sensed the greed of gold-hungry people in gold-bearing territory. If a rumor should start and spread to the effect that the El Dorado Canyon was not as played out as people thought, he might have bidders against him at the sale who would run the price of the property sky-high. Talk was already spreading about the Wall Street Mine, which had produced well in the past, probably because he had especially chosen to visit it. He wrote to Gracey, "The excitement you mention about Wall Street and the country generally is injurious to us for it will make a lot of buzzards being around watching a chance to snatch some of the Southwestern property either by jumping claims or by violence or by bidding at the sale."[17]

While waiting for the sale he could safely begin work with Gracey on the Alabama and Klondike sites. Before Wharton had left the canyon he had agreed to supply the capital needed to open these ledges. When he reached San Francisco he sent Gracey a first installment of cash and asked him to set up a small stamp mill and build a road to the river. Gracey complied, moving a five-stamp mill from El Dorado to the Klondike and beginning to work the ledge. Soon he ran out of money and asked for more. Prices of everything were high, and the content of precious metal was much less than had been anticipated. Wharton grudgingly supplied another installment of working capital. He appreciated the problem: He and Gracey had done as many another prospector did in having assays made. They had chosen the best appearing samples. One assay had showed 15.76 ounces of gold and 81.88 ounces of silver per ton of two thousand pounds. If this had been representative of the entire lode the mine would have been a bonanza. As Wharton remarked, "A few sparks of metal in the sample would run up the assay."[18]

Also while waiting for the sale to take place, Wharton had a complete inventory made of claims on the property of the Southwestern Mining Company and had Gracey buy all the gravel bars near El Dorado and all the bottom lands between the mines and the opposite side of the river in order that he might have "solid ownership of everything on both sides of the river in that region. In that way there would be a foundation for a large establishment if the gold is there, and if the management is good."[19]

The sale finally took place and was without annoying incident. Wharton then bought for a few cents each all the shares which he could find of the now defunct company.[20] He ordered the mines reopened, and when he visited the canyon the next spring he arranged for the repair and purchase of equipment. He bought a cyanide plant and put it to work on the tailings, purchased a ten-stamp mill with capacity for increasing the number of stamps to thirty-five, and arranged for acquiring a traction engine capable of hauling fifty tons of ore daily from the Wall Street Mine to the mill. Wharton later recalled to Gracey other thoughts of that new beginning: "Remember I told you my intention was to develop the property on a large scale. I pointed out site for 100 stamp mill. We talked about railroad, trolley road, traction engines for bringing down the ore. The time that has been allowed to pass since then has not been lost. . . . The ore fairly in sight can be reckoned by millions of tons and it will average I presume $7 per ton without reckoning the pay streaks of $25 to $50 per ton."[21]

Unforeseen developments in the ten years of Wharton's presence in El Dorado prevented fulfillment of much of this ambitious project. A recount of all of them is unnecessary, as they present nothing that was disastrously upsetting to his plans or of unusual occurrence in the trials and tribulations of Western frontier mining. The high prices which prevailed in the mining districts of Nevada were a problem. Wrote Wharton to another claim holder, "Cheap mining, cheap hauling and cheap milling are needed to work low grade ores to any profit, but to fix things for such cheap working costs a big lot of money for the plant."[22] Ores of gold showed as many local variations as did those of zinc and nickel with a result that processes of refining which worked well in one place needed subtle adjustments in order that they might succeed in another. Thus Wharton wrote concerning gold ores containing tellurium, that he had been informed that "to treat telluride ores successfully they must be roasted (with great care) to free the gold so that the cyanide can attack it but so as not to volatilize the gold with the tellurium. The ore may first be stamped and amalgamated, and the tailings then roasted and cyanided. But it takes skill and careful manipulation to save the gold."[23]

He had trouble with claim jumpers, not only for the gold mines but also for the claims containing salt, which he had not worked. "My idea was to hold those lands undeveloped until the country is opened by railroad, and I am still of this mind," he wrote.[24] Thievery was a constant headache. Machinery broke down and was idled until parts could be obtained from Kingman or Needles. In 1904 a cloudburst wiped out many houses and much equipment in El Dorado Canyon and brought all mining to a halt for eighteen months.[25]

Wharton recognized the difficulty of managing as complicated a property as that of the mines and mills at El Dorado and other places on the Colorado from a distance. He necessarily had to rely on Gracey and accorded him a large discretion in managing affairs. Gracey excelled in an ability to get along with the Indians, Mexicans, Chinese, and Americans upon whom success depended, whether they were skilled or unskilled workers, prospectors, teamsters, ranchers, or lawmen. He was not as skillful in the use of machinery and had to be educated concerning improvements which might be suitable for the El Dorado mines. Correspondence between Wharton and Gracey is voluminous, being exceeded during these years only by that between Wharton and Kelly. Wharton could spare no more time than three weeks a year to visit El Dorado. Roadbeds in the Southwest were poor and train schedules were unreliable, so that he was sometimes cheated in the amount of time he expected to pass on the Colorado River.

Even so, as the country became more settled the conditions of travel rapidly improved. In 1900 a newly installed branch line from Kingman to Chloride shortened the wagon route through the desert by about thirty miles. A few years later an entrance from the west became possible. On his last two trips Wharton continued on the main line of the Santa Fe past Kingman to a station called Barnwell. From there a branch line ran to the mining town of Searchlight, which lay about forty-five miles southwest of El Dorado. Wharton took the train to Searchlight (which did not run every day) and rode by wagon over the desert to the head of El Dorado Canyon and inspected his mines as he followed the road down to the Colorado. On his last trip west he wrote concerning Searchlight, "There we heard of a slight occurrence the night before in which a man lost his life—that is he was shot in a street altercation which grew out of doings of a drunken man going about town naked with a knife in his hand. But I am told that such things are not frequent."[26]

When Wharton first took possession of his gold-bearing properties he principally concentrated on the Klondike ledge and the Wall Street Mine. The Klondike paid its way for a number of years, but not the Wall Street. The ore there became poorer as the shafts went deeper into the ground. In the summer of 1903 Wharton ordered the Wall Street closed. The next year came the destroying cloudburst. He thought of selling but took no real action toward achieving that end, and when people asked him to set a price on the properties he asked too much to interest serious buyers. He bought the equity of Gracey in the Klondike and Alabama claims and on various occasions repeated his faith in the potential of the region. A rich strike at the Quartette Mine in Searchlight buoyed his hopes.[27]

In 1905 Wharton and Gracey consulted together and decided to renew mining at two of the most likely places, the Savage and the Techatticup. Almost immediately they struck a small, rich vein in the Techatticup. By the time Wharton made the trip to El Dorado in the spring the best assays showed around two hundred dollars per ton of gold and silver. His account of arrival at El Dorado that year gives some detail. He took the new branch line to Barnwell and came in via Searchlight. He wrote Anna that Gracey drove him in the buckboard

> to the Quartette Mine about 30 miles arriving just as the officers were going to dinner about 6:30 p.m., and were made welcome. . . . Next morning we started off again on the buck board wagon to the head of El Dorado Canyon, about 30 miles and down that Canyon about 12 miles to the Colorado river, stopping to inspect my several mining properties and to glance at those of the new comers who have lately been flocking in to seize whatever they could. They have tried to seize some of mine which they fancied were merely held by mining claims, but as I had during the last year taken out United States patents which give absolute title they found themselves thwarted. The region doubtless contains much precious metal and as I own about all of the most promising spots, this new excitement seems likely to do me good rather than harm, for, if some of the locations which Gracey thought unpromising turn out good when opened by the new comers, that merely goes to demonstrate the value of the region in which I hold what are apparently the best parts. Without undertaking to describe my property in detail I may mention that a shaft which has been sunk in one of my mines within the last half year [Techatticup] beyond the barren ground through which it passed for a year, has now reached very good ore which Gracey estimates to average about $50 per ton, while he finds the choice bits to contain over $400 per ton. This good ore was but 2 inches thick when first reached, is now 18 inches thick still increasing in thickness as we sink further in it, so that Gracey is confident of having a really profitable mine before this year ends. He is now having set a fine, strong new gasoline hoisting engine which I found nearly ready to run, and is in several other ways doing what I had directed in the way of improvements at other places.[28]

The width of the vein in Techatticup increased to three feet and then dwindled to three inches but did not completely disappear. Several years later it was still producing well. The Savage was also proving to be profitable. In 1906 Wharton wrote to Gracey, "I think you know that the Savage and Techatticup veins come together somewhere near where you are working, perhaps a little further to the west, and you know that such a junction of veins is very apt to indicate strengthening of the lode and higher values."[29]

Commented Wharton, "I hear of so many rich gold deposits being found in different locations that my little Techatticup vein looks very small in comparison, yet it may be that it will out-live some of these other things which are now so much bragged about."[30] He was right: The Techatticup produced gold as late as the 1930s. But for the more immediate future its continuing productivity must be attributed to the good management of Wharton and his decision to make the poor ores pay a profit. He did this especially by using new technology to cut costs. For example, in 1907 he had Gracey purchase two concentrators of a type called New Standard. "The new concentrators seem to make a good separation, and I think they are what is needed for this kind of ore," wrote Gracey.[31] The journal *Mining Science* of Denver reported, "Experimental tests on the ores of the Wharton property by Mgr. Chas. Gracey prove them to be amenable to concentration. This is the first actual experiment test of any value that has been made on the ore."[32]

Wharton also moved the smelter to the junction of El Dorado and Copper canyons near the old Nelson cabin. This reduced the cost of hauling ore from mine to mill. Within a few years the spot acquired a post office, called Nelson, and became the principal settlement of the mining district.

4

Wharton accomplished a few special missions on his round trips from Philadelphia to El Dorado. He visited other mines, gave a talk to students at Stanford University, went through the plant of the Union Iron Company at San Francisco (a customer of the Bethlehem Iron Company), and on the way home stopped at Coral to inspect coke works. Although he always took the Sante Fe route from Chicago west, he varied the return trip. He sometimes went to San Francisco and from there swung north to Portland and then east. At other times he headed directly east from San Francisco. On his last trip he omitted San Francisco and stopped for a tourist's view of Salt Lake City.

On the return trips in 1904, 1905, and 1907 he included Boise, Idaho, in order to see another venture in gold which he had undertaken. In 1906, a year in which he omitted a trip to El Dorado, he nevertheless made a journey in May to inspect this other property.

Boise Basin had long been one of the largest and most profitable gold-producing areas of Idaho. The initial boom had occurred in the years after the Civil War. Although some prospectors dug into the quartz veins of the mountains, most of them sought their fortunes in the extensive deposits of gravel forming the present and former beds of streams. Some of the deposits were as much as forty feet deep. Entrepreneurs put together companies engaged in hydraulic mining, which soon stripped the beds of the easily available and rich deposits. Then came a lull. Exploitation of the poorer sands and deeper beds had to await the invention of dredges capable of daily moving vast quantities of material. By the turn of the century they appeared, many operated by electricity. The Boise Basin again became a scene of speculation and extensive mining operations.

Wharton's venture lay near Centerville and included about two thousand acres of lands along the south fork of the Payette River and its tributaries near the divide separating the river from Grimes Creek, a tributary of the Boise. He became interested in it through contact with several men of the International Nickel Company who had investments in other parts of the Boise Basin. A firm called the Union Gold Dredging Company had prepared to begin work, found problems greater and costs higher than anticipated, and defaulted on its bonds. Wharton saw what he thought was an opportunity to apply the formula he had used to gain control of the property of the Southwestern Mining Company. He invested in the company and acquired its mortgage. He purchased its almost worthless stock until he had a majority of the shares. This put him in a position, he believed, to force the company into bankruptcy. He wrote anticipating this result to his lawyer in Boise in the spring of 1904, "I shall have title to all the property which belonged to the Union Gold Dredging Co."[33]

The plan went awry. One Herman Hoopes, a stockholder of the Union Gold Dredging Company, in collaboration with his employer, the Westinghouse Company, an Idaho corporation, objected. Wharton controlled 74,037 shares of stock and Hoopes and Westinghouse had power over 10,410 shares. They applied to the court to halt the bankruptcy, thus beginning a series of lawsuits which lasted for several years. Wharton fumed at failing to get the full control he desired. Still, the court had not enjoined operations. The company could continue work in preparation for recovering alluvial gold from Idaho streams. Wharton appointed Norman Gratz, president of the company, as manager and gave him much the same authority as he had bestowed on Gracey. Wharton had Gratz patent the company's claims, for example, the Gorden Gulch Bar, in order to obtain for the company a secure legal possession of its property.

In addition to his trouble with Hoopes and Westinghouse Wharton inherited the problems which had earlier stymied the company. He found himself in 1906 and 1907 engaged in an expensive project of building a dam and a power station on the Payette and of establishing access roads. He refused to pay the General Electric Company for a shipment of equipment which arrived later than the stipulated date and thereby missed the season for building and caused a delay of a year. This led to further lawsuits. Wharton wrote rather wistfully in 1908 that if the dam could be completed by the end of the summer and the machinery installed "the whole establishment will be immediately productive."[34]

Idaho gold was Wharton's last business venture, and he pursued it with increasing vigor to the end of his life, costly though it was. He was determined that the gold at the end of this far western rainbow should not elude him. Yet in the few years that he had left to live, it provided little more than hope and frustration.

19

The Vigor of Old Age

Joseph Wharton did not mellow with age. Quite the contrary. The furrowed brow of his later portraits expresses the energy, determination, and powers of concentration that he gave to a final sharpening of traits formed in his youth. His mood was changeable. He could be sweet and reasonable; and he could be acid and dogmatic. A shift from one to the other mood might occur in the course of a letter. He knew that his best years were behind, that he had struck pay dirt long ago and was now mining lesser ore. But he also believed that in doing so he was serving the thousands of people who depended on him for jobs and the millions who used the products of their industry.

His wife and daughters urged him to reduce his load of business and politics. Carnegie had done this, they argued. Why could he not do the same? Wharton refused. Carnegie was following his conscience in retiring and giving away his millions. Wharton woul also follow conscience and vigorously continue to mine and manufacture. His ultimate fate, whether "dying atop like a tree" or rotting at the trunk, was in the hands of the Almighty.

1

Six loves held him fast. The first was business of the sort that he had made his own. It did not include trading in stocks and bonds. At a time when the men of largest fortunes were making millions by manipulating securities, he emphatically disclaimed this for a vocation. He once wrote to the editor of the *New York Times*, "A friend hands me the enclosed slip from your yesterday's paper, stating that I 'can be seen bustling around the Stock Exchange whenever the market is active' etc. This grotesquely absurd statement displeases me. I cannot remember to have ever been in the Stock Exchange, nor do I have any transactions in stocks or bonds except on the rare occasions when a real purchase or sale seems necessary."[1]

Yet he would not condemn the activities of multimillionaire bankers such

as Morgan, George F. Baker, James Stillman, or Jacob H. Schiff, any more
than he would repudiate the financial manipulations of industrialists like
Carnegie, Vanderbilt, the Rockefellers, Schwab, Frick, Gary, and Andrew
Mellon. He strongly believed that by consolidating firms through the formation of holding companies these people were serving the country, that the
combinations they made brought stability to an economy which always
seemed to be on the brink of chaos. The millions which they took in,
Wharton believed, accurately reflected the importance of their work. He,
too, had helped himself to the savings of investors when he and others had
organized the holding companies of Bethlehem Steel, International Nickel,
and the Wharton Fisheries.

Still, the securities of these firms had little water when compared with
that of giant corporations such as United States Steel. And he refused to
make paper profits from his enterprises in iron and gold and in the
pinelands.

His special love remained, as it had always been, that of mining and
refining metals. Zinc, nickel, and iron had occupied most of his adult life. He
had worked little in making articles for sale across the counter. The emphasis was on the products of the earth, not the objects of consumer use: spelter,
not zinc paint; pure grain nickel, malleable nickel, and nickel salts rather
than cutlery or coin blanks; pig iron instead of castings and forgings. The
business of making steel rails, guns, and armor plate was not uniquely his, as
work with the other metals was. When he left the business of refining nickel
he turned to gold. Probably only his advanced age and the distance of his
office from the mines and gravel bars stopped him from success in gold
similar to that achieved with zinc, nickel, and iron.

A second love was that of farming, "the most honorable employment of
all," as William Rotch had told Deborah Fisher Wharton. Joseph had left the
Waltons, not because of disliking farming, for he did not, but because it did
not by itself satisfy his ambition. Although he had never again attempted
dirt farming, he had discovered substitutes for personally tilling the soil. He
had explored the possibilities of raising sugar beets; cultivated farms in the
pinelands; retained those at Gap when the rest of the nickel business was
sold; maintained a farm on the Milestone lot until the building of Ontalauna;
helped his wife to manage her farm on the Lime Kiln Pike; and after the
establishment of Marbella had purchased a farm, christened Beaver Tail, on
Conanicut Island. There he raised turkeys among other things and sent
them, as well as cranberries and sweet potatoes from Batsto and Atsion, as
gifts to friends and relatives during the holiday season.

Family, a third love, included the enlarged circle of brothers, sisters,
nephews, nieces, and their spouses and children. To be sure, members of his
generation were thinning out. Joseph, William, and Esther were by 1907 all
who remained of the ten children of Deborah and William Wharton; and
William had but one more year to live. Hannah Haydock and her husband

had died in 1893 and 1894 respectively, and Charles in 1902, after surviving his wife by five years. Abraham Barker fell victim to a street car accident in 1906. Benjamin Smith was also gone. But members of the younger generations were plentiful. Joseph and Anna welcomed them at Ontalauna and Marbella. The young people variously loved him, admired him for his success, and drew upon him for inspiration or financial support. He was not exactly a patriarch—the days of patriarchy were gone, probably forever. But he was certainly head of the extended family, its master. That, of necessity, made Anna its mistress. As usual she lived in her husband's shadow, at least as far as everyone else was concerned. Her health was as good as his; and the pace of her daily life was better suited to old age. No lover of vigor, she would nevertheless shortly begin to fill a void left by his declining powers.

Wharton was especially fond of the Thurston boys. He had been their guardian, as he also had been for their father. They had lived with grandparents, Professor and Mrs. Coppée, in a house on Fountain Hill immediately adjacent to the borough of South Bethlehem, had attended the school of William Ulrich in Bethlehem, which prepared boys for entry into the Lehigh University, and had in due time entered Lehigh. He had been a critical paternal presence for them during those college years. He had disapproved of their decisions to join a fraternity and to spend time on many extracurricular activities which—suddenly and uselessly, it seemed to him—had appeared as part of college life. Yet he also sagely counseled them; provided money for them to attend dances, buy football uniforms, visit friends, and enjoy other small luxuries; and helped them to begin life in the outside world.

He watched their careers develop. Coppée Thurston, the eldest, had specialized in metallurgy. After graduation he studied for two years at the Freiburg School of Mines in Germany and then took employment with the Robinson Deep Mining Company of Johannesburg, South Africa. The Boer War interfered with that enterprise, and by 1900 he was back in the States working as a mining engineer for himself and for various companies. Joseph Wharton employed him on several occasions to investigate matters at the mines in El Dorado Canyon.

Joseph Wharton Thurston, the second in age, had majored in classics and pursued an exemplary undergraduate career in scholarship, sports, and journalism. After he received his degree, Wharton obtained employment for him with the Bethlehem Iron Company. Joseph Wharton Thurston was working his way up to an executive position when Schwab took control and fired all of the relatives of the former directors. Thereafter, for the remainder of his uncle's life, young Joseph lived precariously. He married an heiress and moved from one job to another. His ambition, talents, and inherited style of living constantly outdistanced his means. He borrowed five thousand dollars from his uncle, wasted it, and broke off communications, so that Wharton learned of his activities only from Coppée.

William Wharton Thurston, the youngest, studied mechanical engineering, but not very hard, and dropped from school to avoid being asked to leave. Uncle Joseph issued dire words of warning concerning the fate which awaits idlers, then let the boy fend for himself as he apparently wanted to do. William Wharton Thurston went to San Francisco and after holding a number of jobs entered into a partnership to sell iron, steel, and related products on commission. He had the beginning of a promising business when the earthquake and fire of 1906 destroyed it. Wharton loaned William five thousand dollars to restore the plant.[2]

Neither Joseph Wharton Thurston nor William Wharton Thurston repaid the loans from their uncle. He had not really expected them to do so. He regarded the loans as advances on his estate, in much the same manner as his own father might have done. In his will Joseph Wharton provided for the forgiveness of these "loans."

He drafted his last will and testament in such a way as to keep the family together. At the time he did this, in 1905, he had about fourteen million dollars in assets of which a little over six million was in negotiable securities. He directed that approximately three million dollars were to be divided among various members of the family. Most of this was to go to his wife, daughters, and grandchildren. Legacies of five thousand dollars each were specified for J. Bertram Lippincott, Harrison S. Morris, Hetty Smith, Coppée Thurston, Joseph Wharton Thurston, William Wharton Thurston, Abraham Barker, Wharton Barker, a cousin of his wife named Annie Perot, Edward Kelly, and Frederick Voigt. Roger Haydock was to receive eight thousand dollars. Most of the remainder of his estate, including his ongoing enterprises, was to be held for the heirs in trust by the Girard Trust Company. The executors, his wife and sons-in-law, were to manage the enterprises, buying and selling as business conditions indicated to be wise. In this way Wharton also meant to provide for the thousands of employees who depended on his business for their livelihood. The properties held in trust were not to be distributed until after the death of the last surviving child.

The only large legacy which Wharton specified for going outside the extended family was that of a sum of one hundred thousand dollars to Swarthmore College for the completion of a Wharton Hall dormitory. He had earlier pledged part of the money for the project and desired that his estate should continue to support it. The original will had also provided five hundred thousand dollars for the Wharton School, part of which was to be used for a building; but Wharton added a codicil canceling the grant. The reason, as his daughter Anna later explained, was that he disapproved of the conduct of Charles C. Harrison, provost of the University of Pennsylvania, in a controversy concerning the reappointment of Harrison S. Morris as manager of the Academy of Fine Arts.[3] In 1905 a conservative faction of the board of the academy had blocked the reappointment, and Morris had removed to New York City to become art editor for the *Ladies Home Journal.*

Wharton's fourth love was politics, which was an acquired taste. He had first entered politics as a promoter of high tariffs on zinc and nickel and had later expanded the subjects of his lobbying to include iron and steel. Lobbying was a necessity which became pleasant. In 1869 he wrote to Anna, "It is a curious life, and when you have to wait the pleasure of the dignitaries it is highly disgusting, but when they willingly come to you and seem glad to exchange views, it is sometimes very satisfactory."[4] Shortly thereafter he was thoroughly enjoying himself in promoting the cause of national self-protection. Politics continued to grow on him as he mingled with Republican party leaders at state and national levels. He actively campaigned for every Republican presidential candidate from 1876 to 1900, as well as for many Republicans who were seeking senatorial or congressional seats or state or municipal office.

Long before he was an old man he was taking an immense satisfaction in influencing national leaders. "This morning I conversed with President McKinley concerning the Hawaiian Islands, which are to be annexed to this country," he wrote in 1897 to Shiro Sheba, member of the Japanese parliament and one of the first graduates of the Wharton School, and to Penrose the same year, "I am strongly convinced that we ought to annex the Islands without delay."[5] Wharton heard grievances from Cuban sugar planters who were caught between the Spanish government and guerrilla insurgents; advised Roosevelt as assistant secretary of the navy against establishing a government armor plate plant at Newport News; gave Senator W. B. Allison information which he requested concerning the denominations of bonds to be issued in connection with financing the war with Spain; interceded with President Roosevelt on behalf of Charlemagne Tower and assisted in having Tower transferred from the ambassadorship at St. Petersburg to that in Berlin; and interceded with President Roosevelt on behalf of John Fritz to obtain a pardon for a South Bethlehem postmaster who had been convicted of misappropriating government funds.[6]

When Ida M. Tarbell, a writer for *McClure's* who became famous for her exposure of the Standard Oil Trust, came to interview Wharton for an article concerning the tariff, his daughter Anna recorded that "he talked all the evening. He told of how Roosevelt gave him the sheets of his Message to Congress, when the Reciprocity people wanted the tariff revised their way. Father told the President that his Message *would not do,* explaining that if we tied ourselves up by promises to other countries, not to exceed a certain tariff,—then in case of a horrible war, which used up money like dirt, *how* should we get the necessary sums? The President was convinced enough to make changes in his Message."[7]

The tariff question governed almost every aspect of Wharton's politics. More than anything else it accounts for his sometime militancy in promoting a strong United States of America. The tariff was not an issue in the war with Spain. Wharton had no quarrel with Spain and accordingly was equivocal in judging of the rectitude of the conflict. He wrote to Thomas Macfarlane, "Our war with Spain is to me a source of apprehension rather than of satisfaction. Not because I would have my nation flinch from doing a man's work in the world, but because I could wish our undertaking of the momentous task to have been more absolutely and indisputably right. No doubt this war is more righteous than most wars, but the old judgment, 'They that take the sword shall perish by the sword' rises up before me as a barrier not lightly to [be] stepped over."[8] By contrast, where Britain was concerned, the tariff was always an issue, and Wharton's anglophobia remained. It found partial expression in a desire for union between the United States and Canada, even at the price of war. He wrote in the same letter to Macfarlane in 1898, "I dread the prospect of war in the future between this nation and Canada. It seems to me that union between these two is as natural and mutually advantageous as between man and woman—for my part I have a strong and sincere regard for the Canadian people whom I perceive to be fully the equals of our own. But Canada will find it difficult to leave the parental roof." Wharton never ceased regarding Britain as a greater threat to the United States and, by the same token, to world peace, than Germany, a country for which he had great sentiment. Wharton saw Germany as the land of the Krupps, Dr. Fleitmann, and other leading industrialist-scientists—the "home of chemistry" as he once put it.

Science was Wharton's fifth love. It fascinated him. As a small boy he had listened to the chattering of his uncle, Thomas Fisher, concerning telescopes and microscopes and what they could do. As a man of middle age he had experimented making pure malleable nickel well beyond the exigencies of success in business. He had become friendly with famous chemists and metallurgists, published articles, and promoted science through founding the Wharton School and at Swarthmore. Harvard had recognized his accomplishments by making him chairman of the visiting committee for the chemical laboratory. The University of Pennsylvania and Swarthmore awarded him honorary degrees. From Mexico came an honorary membership in the Société scientifique "Antonio Alzate."[9]

Wharton's love of science amountd to a passion which governed his attitude toward not only business but also life in general. Science was for him the highest form of reason, the unique way to truth. He explained to an audience at Swarthmore at the commencement exercises of 1891 his position, in words reminiscent of Henry C. Carey, that science means "accurate and uncompromising knowledge . . . against which nothing can contend, which gives to man not only increasing mastery over nature, but also increasing power to attain still further mastery both over externals and over himself, for the intellectual touch of a mind so trained to accurate observation and deduction is like the touch of Ithuriel's spear. The false shrinks away, disguises drop, and truth stands revealed."[10]

In connection with a study of society and culture, Wharton understood science to mean the historical method. When applied to religion, the historical method gave him a substitute for the dogmatic theology which Hicksites disdained. Wharton insisted that the scientific reason of the historical method should set the boundaries within which faith should move. He told a Swarthmore audience in the commencement address for 1888, "You observe that faith is not to supplant reason and assume to act as guide, for that is not its function. Reason must decide to what faith which binds so firmly shall be attached. You are not to allow your faith to fasten to any imposter or humbug that may claim it."[11]

Wharton was heavily influenced by the writings of the French philosopher Ernest Renan, whose *Life of Jesus* was an historical critique of many commonly accepted theological ideas. A passion for the historical approach underlay most of Wharton's latter-day forays into the domain of religious controversy, for example, his argument for including the study of religion within the curriculum at Swarthmore; a detailed investigation of the meaning of a paradox announced by the third-century father of the church Tertullian, *Credo quia impossibile est* (I believe because it is impossible); and an opposition to a passage in the Book of Discipline of the Philadelphia Yearly Meeting.[12]

The last example illustrates the intolerance to which Wharton's passion for science could sometimes lead. The Philadelphia Yearly Meeting (Hicksite) had decided in 1892 to reexamine its Book of Discipline with a view to possibly revising parts. Wharton maintained that the existing version contained a passage which violated absolute freedom of conscience and ought to be expunged. The passage implied a necessity for believing in the Trinitarian doctrine that the godhead consists of three persons, the Father, the Son, and the Holy Spirit. He hunted the libraries and private collections of Friends for information concerning the wording of earlier books of discipline and then wrote a pamphlet, "The Creed in the Discipline" (1892). He sent the pamphlet in draft to several friends for criticism, received their comments, had the text set in type, submitted the proof to other friends for their reaction, and had it printed. The result was an excellent historical essay à la Renan proving that a tenet concerning the Trinity was for Friends a relatively recent introduction into the discipline, therefore spurious.

The reaction of Quaker ministers and elders to Wharton's pamphlet can be easily imagined. They neither regarded him as one of the lights to whom people should look for spiritual guidance nor valued as necessarily binding the precedents which he so accurately set forth. They took pains to make sure that his influence would be minimal.

Wharton's sister Hetty Smith saw the weakness of her brother's position:

Intolerance as a means can never successfully defend tolerance as an end. She wrote to him:

> We have just returned from Atlantic City, where we went for a short change, & where we saw Isaac Clothier. He gave me to read thy pamphlet, "The Creed in discipline" and for the relief of my mind I send thee a few suggestions, which, if thee chooses to act upon, will make me glad. In the first place let me say that when calling others intolerant we should be very careful not to fall into the pit ourselves, and thy zeal, it seems to me, places thee somewhat in that position. In the next place the dignity of thy article, to my mind, is much lessened by some expressions or words which thee has used, & lastly by the personal allusions. Being no student of the Bible, I cannot contradict the statement thee makes on page 4, where thee says, "several important texts or passages in the Bible, each of which however when examined proves to be flagrantly false," but could not a more moderate term be used rather than flagrantly false, as the translation is not only time honored, but believed in by most readers I suppose.

She continued in the same vein, selecting for comment the purplest passages, for example, "butchers working for the devil in the name of God" and "this insanity reaching its climax," and concluded, "Now I have said my say, which I fear may have no effect, but I will be best satisfied to send it to thee, after saying that Isaac asked me to make any suggestions I might like. Where there is love there is freedom & so no harm can be done by thy affectionate sister Esther F. W. Smith sending this to thee."[13]

The sisterly advice had little effect. After repeated failures to influence the Yearly Meeting Wharton wrote in 1895 to a friend, "The bigots and the formalists have nearly killed the Society which for a time led the van in religious progress. It is doubtful whether the old root has life enough in it to endure the abrasion of another century."[14]

The dogmatism of "The Creed in the Discipline" strongly contrasts with Wharton's usual benignity in religious matters, as expressed, for example, in the letter to William Thurston on the occasion of Thurston's conversion to Episcopalianism. The difference in tone between the two documents can be essentially traced to Wharton's intolerance in supporting what he believed to be scientific truth.

Wharton's sixth love was for the sea. As he loved the land for itself and its treasures, so too he embraced water. "I can swim almost as well as I can walk," he had long ago written his fiancée. Almost fifty years later he boasted to Fleitmann that he could still swim in the deep sea at Marbella.[15] Respect for the sea as a highway of commerce was in the family from the first Joseph Wharton, the Fishers, Rodmans, and Redwoods. He scorned the urban pomp of Newport and established Marbella—"beautiful sea"—where its dwellers could overlook the bay on three sides. There a government chained to a policy of sea power lashed out at him and demanded some of his land for a coastal fort. He angrily opposed the demand, tried to bargain with the Navy, and lost. The government took part of his estate and the property of the Shoemakers, Braeclough of Charles and Mary Wharton, and Gray Cliff of William T. Richards. On the site overlooking a choice part of The Dumplings the government commenced building in 1896 a fortress which was finished four years later and named Fort Wetherell after Captain Alexander Wetherell who had lost his life in the Spanish-American War. [16] But Wharton gave no thought to moving his summer home away from Conanicut: If he should lose Marbella to the government he would still have Beaver Tail. He was wedded to the island and its rocky coast: sails out on the bay on a clear day; storms coming in from the ocean; combers breaking on the rocks at the southern tip. His spirit had the restlessness of the open sea as surely as it possessed the hardness of minerals embedded in the land. Much of his best poetry concerns oceans. In a passage of the poem "Looking toward the Sunset," he expressed himself while telling of the sea:

> . . . the unstable, infinite deep,
> Inscrutable, indifferent as fate,
> But yet caressing him with subtle charm.

2

The last great adventure of Wharton's life, in 1907, concerned the sea. Charlemagne Tower, the ambassador to Germany, invited him to *Kieler Woche* (Kiel Week), the splendid regatta and display of naval strength annually staged by Kaiser Wilhelm II. Tower wrote, "If you were to sail by the 'Kaiser Wilhelm II,' from New York on the 11th of June, you would reach Berlin by the 18th or 19th, and we could go from there to Kiel together. I shall have arranged beforehand for your presentation to the Emperor."[17]

In a retrospect accented by two world wars the Kiel Regatta appears as a lavish and impudent show of strength staged by a vain and ambitious emperor who, urged on by his ministers, was attempting to outdo the English in building a modern navy. Prince von Bülow, the German chancellor, later wrote of it: "How lovely Kiel Bay looked, sparkling in the June sunshine! Everything there, Kiel Week, all the gay doings in Kiel, were William II's creation. Nowhere did he feel more at his ease. For him it was a kind of equivalent to the growling of cannon, the gallop of neighing steeds for Napoleon, the parade ground of Krasnoie Selo for Nicholas I, chamois hunting for the Emperor Maximilian I, museums and picture galleries for the Medici." In the races "His Majesty would be eaten up with the urge to take the helm himself, but he knew that the skippers would not approve. . . . [He] would then do his best to cajole them and win them over with friendly words. He became hail-fellow-well-met with them, slapped them on the shoulder, offered them cigarettes. Usually he managed to win them over."[18]

Wharton did not divine the imperial pettiness and spirit of aggression which underpinned Kiel Week. He saw only a triumph of statesmanship by a country for which he had a high regard. He considered the invitation to attend as a fitting tribute to his eminence in politics and industry and became excited at the thought of seeing the greatest naval regatta of its kind and of talking with the monarch who made it possible. The races, he knew, would be thrilling. Also, princes, statesmen, and *haute bourgeoisie* from most of Europe would attend.

Wharton's daughter Anna wrote that her father was undecided whether or not to go.[19] That stance only expressed the propriety which he maintained with members of the family. He regularly wrote to his wife when he traveled far from home to inform her that reasons of business prompted him, that he was stoically putting up with the hardships of journeying, and that she should not think he was enjoying himself too much. He was not undecided about going to Kiel. He would be available for the trip as soon as he returned from his annual visit to El Dorado Canyon and Boise Basin. He immediately accepted the invitation and wrote to Carnegie:

> Our Ambassador to Berlin, Mr. Charlemagne Tower, and his wife, have invited me with much urgency to visit them about the middle of June, and to go with them from to the celebrations at Kiel which are to begin I think on June 20. Mr. Tower has for several years been inviting me to come to Berlin to be presented to the Kaiser, in order that I might have the opportunity of some familiar talk with him, and he says that this occasion at Kiel will afford much better opportunity for such intercourse with the Kaiser (including a dinner with him on his great yacht), than could be expected when he is overwhelmed with official duties in Berlin.[20]

Carnegie replied by sending an invitation to visit Skibo, his castle in Scotland. Carnegie had been urging this on Wharton at least since 1901. Wharton accepted the invitation and also arranged to meet Monell, the head of the International Nickel Company, in Paris. The stage was becoming set for an exciting and hectic two weeks.

He embarked on the *Kaiser Wilhelm II* the evening of 10 June following a last minute rush around New York City to wind up business affairs. His daughter Anna was there to see him off. She took him to dinner and watched in amazement as he ordered ox-tail soup and sardines—a meal which Wharton characterized to his wife as "a poor soup and a box of sardines." Anna had not come but was at Oak Hill, where she intended to stay with Joanna for the first few days of Joseph's absence. The invitation sent by the Towers had not included her, and she felt the slight. Joanna, alarmed at the idea of her eighty-one-year-old father traveling alone, had at the last minute insisted that her son Joseph Wharton Lippincott, then twenty years old and a student in college, accompany him.[21]

On board the *Kaiser Wilhelm II* that evening while still in port Joseph wrote to Anna: "So far I have had no such uncomfortable feelings of something akin to homesickness as troubled me on other departures from home, but I do not cease to wonder at my having really broken off from all the cares of business and the comforts of home to make an apparently useless journey over sea. Probably the change of habits and scenes and persons may be of advantage, but I am not expecting very much pleasure or gratification."[22] At 5:30 the next morning the ship left harbor for Bremen.

The voyage was uneventful. The Wanamakers were aboard. Wharton made peace with John and played dominoes with them. "We must be on visiting terms with them," he wrote Anna. He praised a concert, commented on several friends that young Joe had made, and speculated on travels after leaving Kiel. "If we must miss Skibo we may go to Norway, or to the Scotch Highlands and the English Lakes and London, or to Paris and the Chateau region." From Ontalauna Anna sent her husband clippings from newspapers with a comment, "They will inform thee that thee is not [the] only favored guest of the Towers but that Mr. and *Mrs.* Carnegie are to share the honors at Kiel." The underlining of "*Mrs.* Carnegie" was heavy. Anna added, with an irony of which she was perfectly capable, that Isaac Clothier had spoken at Swarthmore, "I understand, almost entirely a eulogy on thy character."[23]

Kiel was everything Wharton had anticipated. "The Kiel Week of 1907 was especially brilliant," wrote von Bülow.[24] Wharton sent an account of the opening of the regatta to Clothier:

> Joe Lippincott is with me, and we have already seen Bremen, Hamburg and this place [Kiel] with such thoroughness as good carriages and good legs and eyes would permit. And yet we did not reach Bremen until late in the afternoon of the day before yesterday.
>
> This morning Mr. Tower took us two and Mr. Carnegie to the Imperial yacht Hohenzollern to leave our cards and see the vessel. When all was done and we were about to go back to Mr. Tower's launch, suddenly the Emperor appeared and said: "Hullo, Tower, what are you doing here?" We were all presented, the whole crowd of gold laced officers fell back, leaving us four alone with Wilhelm II, so that we talked with complete freedom, no formality at all, but a sort of almost jolly sincerity that was most gratifying. His handshake at parting was also honest, and so we parted. Mr. Tower says that an invitation to dinner on the Hohenzollern is likely to follow soon.[25]

In a letter to his wife Wharton added, "The conversation was absolutely informal and at times almost jocular, Carnegie talking most, the Emperor next, Tower and I about equal and Joe saying nothing but enjoying much."

The hotel at which they were staying, wrote Wharton, "was built by the same Krupp who dined with us in 1877, and was a sort of compliment to the Emperor to help make Kiel more agreeable to the naval officers who must congregate here. Kiel is a superior Newport without the few over-costly residences there and the pet-monkey society that have almost destroyed the old hightoned and comparatively simple life that formerly prevailed there."[26]

Wharton dined with the Kaiser and again wrote to Anna.

This regatta . . . was the fitting climax of our remarkable visit here during which I have twice seen and spoken with the Emperor and once dined with him (though no opportunity existed for a real conversation), have been all over Kiel on foot and in carriages, have sailed up and down the harbor from side to side and end to end, have entered the great Kiel Canal at this end, have taken lunch on Mrs. Gocht's fine 2400 ton yacht where a German countess (whose husband is a great coal and iron mine owner) invited us to visit their domain in upper Silesia, have visited upon his yacht the owner of Monte Carlo who is Prince of Monaco, examined with him his varied scientific apparatus and have been invited by him to visit him at Monaco, have attended a great garden party given by the admiral of the Port, have twice dined with Mr. & Mrs. Carnegie and arranged with them for our visit to Skibo Castle between July 5 and 11.[27]

From Kiel Wharton and his grandson went to Copenhagen, then directly to Paris. Wharton kept his appointment with Monell and saw several other friends. The pair visited the chateau country and on 1 July arrived in London in a cold rain for a short stay before going to Skibo.

Stateside, Anna and her daughter Mary went to Conanicut with the Lippincotts to begin the summer vacation. Mary wrote to her father complaining of Carnegie "scattering his millions," commenting that it made her "feel kind of sick, as I am fond of simplicity and justice all round." Anna wrote to her husband from Meeresblick, the Lippincott estate on Beaver Tail, "It is particularly quiet on the island, too much so for Joey's gay taste, but it is congenial with my feelings. I really enjoy seeing Bertram pottering around in his own place, and in his own house unmolested, and taking a week's holiday."[28]

The next news from London was a cable from one Dr. Sinclair, "Threatened paralysis. No immediate danger. Someone come."[29]

The tree which had seemed sound was starting to fall.

3

Joanna and Bertram immediately went to New York and the next day sailed for England aboard the *Majestic.*

Anna recorded her father's illness as told to her by Joe Lippincott: "It appears that Father went to bed all right on July 2nd, and woke up on July 3rd with disordered mind. . . . Joe found him in the bathroom, cold as ice, pulling a chair about. Joe saw him reel, and rushed up, to be crushed down by him. Joe got him to bed, and put his own warm things on him, and sent for a doctor Sinclair. . . . The next day he appears to have been worse, weak as a baby, and raving about going to theatre."[30]

In sending news of his grandfather's attack to Tower and Carnegie Joe Lippincott was reserved. Neither at first realized the seriousness of Joseph Wharton's illness, although Carnegie soon found out and frequently telegraphed to London to discover the state of health of his friend.[31] Wharton also made light of the catastrophe and wrote to his wife:

We have taken passage on the Baltic which is to leave Southampton on the 24th of July and is expected to arrive at New York on the afternoon of Aug. 2. The whole Lippincott party are to be on the Baltic also.

My present intention is to invite Annie Perot to go with me from N.Y. to Fall River and Newport the night of 8/2. She will come to Marbella if desired, or if not will go to Meeresblick where Joanna says she will be ready to take her in. Let William have the carriage at Rail Road station in Newport at 8:15 on 8/3. He must be informed to which house Annie is to go. I shall send trunks from Jamestown by baggage express.

Joe and I expect to leave here for Skibo Castle tomorrow morning and to arrive at Skibo shortly after noon next day. I expect to consume every day while there whisky onions and cheese. Joe looks forward to unlimited oat meal mush. . . .

Now for the first time I am partaking of a pastime or [undecipherable] which Americans in Europe seem to consider a part of the game. That is, I am spending the time in bed under the care of three doctors and two nurses. When we arrived here the evening of 6/30 Joe thought I needed a doctor and said so to the hotel people who called in a Dr. Sinclair whom they habitually call in such cases. He promptly brought in the nurses and also a Dr. Ferrier. Next, Sir Lauder Brunton was called in. He is a famous specialist in heart and lung troubles and is also Physician-in-ordinary to King Edward. He finds my ailments to be gout, disturbed digestion with constipation and too great heart tension, joined to old age weakness of the arterial walls. Of course abnormal pressure within the arteries (140 against the normal 20) makes a rupture somewhere not impossible. Should some little artery in the brain give way some blood exudes, a clot is formed and an apoplectic stroke follows, but this is not expected in my case. . . .

Sir Lauder talks frankly about the King and this [is] the nearest approach we can muster to the royal family for the King seems no ways inclined to make the most of his present opportunity to draw closer the hands between the two great nations. For instance—none of us was invited to the great Court Ball last Friday, nor has either of us been invited to go in the royal yacht to Cowes to see the regatta there. On the other hand every shop keeper or cabby whom we have met has shown a gratification which we think sincere.[32]

The handwriting was jerky and the letter was unsigned. Anna and her daughters needed no medical opinions to inform them of what lay between the lines of this letter. The man of vigor had become a physical wreck. The stroke had weakened his mind but not to an extent completely to deprive him of the power of reason. He would in coming months be silent, withdrawn, moody, incoherent, irascible, yet on occasion perfectly rational and seemingly responsible. The spirit of vigor was still there along with the habit of giving orders, calculating, and taking risks. The combination would change his personality in such ways that his family would not know what sort of conduct to expect from him.

Anna described the homecoming. The Lippincotts, Joseph, and two nurses, Mrs. Figgins and Miss Letitia Adams, returned on the *Baltic*. Harrison Morris and Roger Haydock went aboard the ship in quarantine in New York harbor. Harrison entered Wharton's stateroom.

> He found Father sitting eating, clothed in pajamas. He put his hand on him, saying 'Here's Harrison,' and Father made no sign of knowing that anyone had come into the room, much less spoken. . . . But when they were all on the special car, he improved wonderfully, exchanging stories with the others. At Wickford Junction were two automobiles. Into Lippincotts' got Father, Mrs. Figgins, Dr. McClellan and Joey. Into Theo's got Harrison and Roger. The latter arrived at Marbella first, to prepare Mother. Soon the other came around the circle, father looking toward the house. One seldom experiences so intense a moment as that. I have never seen anything so beautiful, so exquisite as Mother's behaviour! . . . She walked out the path alone, to the automobile, *smiling!* Before the machine stopped, Father made a joke about onions to her, and she answered it in the same vein. Then he got out and stood on his feet, with no further idea of what to do, everybody breathless. Mother kissed him. Still, he had no idea what to do. Here was Mother, used to having him lead in every way, obliged to take the initiative. And she did it nobly, courageously. With the air of a young girl, she said gaily, "Will thee take my arm?" He immediately put out *his* arm, saying "The gentleman usually gives the lady his arm," and turning to the doctor, "That's more like it, isn't it doctor?" Then Father and Mother walked slowly, arm in arm, up to the doorway and in. Mary and I kissed him, but he said nothing. In the hall stood Kit, and he cried, "Why, there's little Kitty!" He looked pleased as a child, while walking in, and Mother's face was flushed and beautiful as a bride's.[33]

In the relaxed atmosphere of familiar faces and the panoramas of rocks, sky, and sea Wharton regained strength. The two nurses stayed with him. A doctor was either in residence or nearby. For a few weeks he used a wheelchair but soon abandoned it and walked about slowly with a cane. He relied completely on his wife for the first time in his life. At the end of the summer the family moved back to Ontalauna. He was still weak and occasionally had fits of vomiting. Yet he insisted on resuming work at the office. Members of the family objected—Wenner, Roger Haydock, and the two sons-in-law were able to take care of things. He persisted in wanting to resume full control, and no one could make a sufficiently good case to keep him at home. His daughter Anna conceded, "As a rule, childlike, gentle, unconscious of time and conditions, while at home, or else apathetic, immovable—his mind making its best effort while in his office."[34]

He knew he had not much time left. He wrote to Gracey, "I observe your final remark that you think my venture in El Dorado Canyon is a success, and that if I will just live on for awhile you will prove it. I have no objection whatever to doing this, but have little expectation or hope that I shall live so long."[35] Wharton believed that no one was prepared to replace him at the head of his enterprises, and at the time he was right. Bertram was engaged full time with his publishing house; Harrison was working for the *Ladies Home Journal* in New York. So Wharton made the decisions. Business associates may have detected no great change in him other than a slowing down of movement and some hesitancy of speech. But the old sagacity was gone. He made mistakes. In October of 1907 the Wharton Fisheries Company failed. In his prime Wharton would have found a way to save it. Now he could not; he let it go, doing nothing.

A greater crisis was in the offing. The bankruptcy of the fisheries company weakened the confidence of some creditors in Wharton and was followed in the same month by a bank panic. Money became scarce; banks were reluctant to lend it even at 20 percent; and creditors hastened to call in loans. A situation developed in which Wharton's bank, the Farmers and Mechanics National Bank of Philadelphia, refused to stand by him.

The events leading to the refusal represented nothing unusual in Wharton's business life. Always a large borrower from banks and trust companies, he owed about two million dollars, mostly payable to the lenders on demand. The sums were covered by securities which, however, if disposed of at forced sales in a tight money market would bring only a fraction of their true worth. Wharton had his checking account at Farmers and Mechanics and also borrowed money from the bank when he needed cash. At times he had to write checks for very large sums, so that a danger of being overdrawn was always present. He covered the possibility by having a special arrangement with the bank. He deposited about two hundred thousand dollars worth of bonds with it as security, in return for which the bank treated any overdraft as a loan. This gave him time to raise the cash.

At the end of October 1907, Wharton needed large sums to pay the furnace bills of his iron works. The bank had already discounted $261,000 worth of his notes and advanced him $128,650. The officials decided that the limit of his credit had almost been reached; they would allow him an additional fifty thousand dollars and no more. When he exceeded that figure they informed him of his standing and warned him to prepare against any uncashed checks. On 6 November the bank received additional checks of his, and the president, Howard Lewis, sent him the following letter:

"Your checks have come in against your account again to-day, which would further increase your overdraft, and I regret to say that I am instructed by the Executive Committee to return the checks if not made good at the usual time, say half past one o'clock, in order to reach the Banks sending the checks by two o'clock, which is the Clearing House Exchange rule."[36]

Disaster threatened. If even one check had gone back all of Wharton's creditors would have demanded immediate payment. His financial standing and reputation as a business man would have been irreparably damaged, and he would have lost a great deal of money. He went to the bank and talked with Lewis, who advised him to have his wife's account transferred to his name. Wharton angrily refused this, and Lewis sent a message to Anna with a check for her to sign. She complied, thus buying time for Wharton to raise the necessary cash to cover all charges against his account.

The crisis precipitated a relapse. Before it began Wharton was under orders from doctors to give up business entirely and had perversely responded by increasing his work. The day after his interview with Lewis he had, according to daughter Anna, "'a stroke and a fit' on the way home in the close carriage with Mrs. Figgins. He was got home, and to bed, and the next day he did not remember having any attack."[37] On Thanksgiving Day he fainted and fell down the steps leading to the cellar. Although no bones were broken he was badly hurt and was confined to bed for weeks.

From this time on, Bertram and Harrison took a more active part in Wharton's business. They volunteered to raise the money needed to keep him solvent and unsuccessfully tried every likely source of funds in Philadelphia. Then they went to Carnegie in New York who, according to Anna, responded instantly, "Help Joe Wharton? I should think I would help Joe Wharton! Everything I have is his. *I* don't want any collateral, or any note. I'll make him a present of the hundred thousand!"[38] Bertram and Harrison accepted a loan. The crisis was over, but nothing was solved. "We are sitting on a slanting roof, not knowing what minute we'll slip off into something unexpected or fatal," wrote his daughter Anna.[39]

Still Wharton refused to give up the direction of his enterprises. In the middle of January 1908 he again began going to the office on his "good" days and at other times having Wenner come to Ontalauna to take dictation. The two sons-in-law assisted where they could and otherwise stood ready to take over. Harrison, the obvious choice as director of Wharton's businesses in the event of total incapacity, left the *Ladies Home Journal* and became chairman of the Finance Committee of the National Academy of Design in New York. The family as a whole marked time. Anna wrote on 3 March, "This is Father's eighty-second birthday, and I did not see him. He has been particularly unmanageable lately, so that Dr. Betts has kept away, and both nurses have violent headaches, and Mother is very nervous. We are all

waiting for a disaster. Yesterday he planned to go to New York and fright-
ened everybody to death by persisting until the last minute. He went to
Philadelphia instead in a freezing drizzle. He plans to buy two houses, to
build a row of houses, to build a railroad, to give a large dinner-party to the
President and other big men, and so on, nearly every week a new plan. The
old brain-power forging ahead, without its rudder." The day after his birthday he had another attack which again resulted in confinement to bed. "Poor
Father has been very frail and weak ever since," wrote Anna, "though
getting downstairs each day about 2:30, eating dinner slowly, then dozing."[40]

Six weeks later Wharton was writing Gracey of a possibility of traveling to
El Dorado, asking if it would be easy to stop en route to see Yellowstone
National Park.[41]

4

He received few visitors during the final eighteen months. William Wharton Thurston and Coppée Thurston called at different times; the family
gladly receiving them. Old friends sent letters of encouragement. The family
went to Marbella as usual that summer. Wharton was weaker and his spells
came more frequently. Daughter Anna recorded, "7/5/1908. The night of the
29th, he had a convulsion, and another the next morning, which have left
him terribly weak. . . . It is like seeing a great wounded lion." Wharton sent
Gracey a recent photograph of himself with the comment, "It does not look
so old as I do, but the doctor today declared me much improved. I myself do
not feel much better except that my pains are less severe. My legs are very
weak and appetite bad. I am holding out a pretty good fight yet."[42]

A streak of generosity appeared, such as he had never before shown. He
planned to endow a chemical research laboratory at Harvard Univeristy and
vigorously pursued the project with Professor Richards and President
Eliot.[43] The project came to nothing, for reasons still unexplained. He began
giving gems from his collection to the ladies and sent gold coins as keepsakes
to the doctors in London who had helped during the days of his first
seizure.[44] Shortly before Christmas, 1908, he gave to the city of Philadelphia
twenty-five acres of woodland "where the North Pennsylvania Railroad
crosses Green Lane" for use as a park, ordaining that the city was to call it
Fisher Park in honor of his mother.[45] (Half a dozen years later his heirs had
to defend the memorial designation against a false report that Fisher park
had been named for William Logan Fisher.)

The sudden appearance of generosity contrasted with a new-found crank-
iness. He frequently complained of the treatment he received and occasionally insulted people as he had never before done. He peremptorily asked De
Lamar of the executive committee of the International Nickel Company why
he had not been informed concerning the market price of certain bonds and

for some unrecorded and alleged misdoing unmercifully flailed his nephew Joseph S. Lovering Wharton.[46] He laid his difficulties in commencing the dredging for gold in the Boise Basin at the doors of Gratz and the lawyer, a young man named William E. Borah, who in 1906 was elected to the U.S. Senate. Wharton once wrote to Gratz, "This entire Idaho business is the worst defeat I have ever suffered, and the worst part of it is that which has occurred since I intrusted [sic] it to your hands. The only bit of comfort is that you get a snug little fortune out of it."[47]

In calling the Idaho business "the worst defeat I have every suffered" Wharton was apparently forgetting his failure to control the spelter business and his losses in the Oregon Pacific affiar. Gratz was probably as competent as Wharton's other managers. Certainly Wharton never fired him. Concerning Borah, Wharton had more reason for complaint. Borah had failed to prevent issuance of the injunction which barred Wharton from having the Union Gold Dredging Company declared insolvent and so had caused him delay in getting possession of its properties. Wharton wrote to Gratz, "I had intended, if Borah carried through my business properly, to write to two or three important Senators in such manner as to put him on a better footing in the Senate than he would likely get otherwise, but as the result of his management was so highly stupid and unsatisfactory, I thought fit to take the other course and give warning to at least one man in the Senate as to what kind of a man Borah is. . . . Borah seems to have thought that I was a stupid old Quaker without any influence, whom he could injure without any harm to himself."[48]

Christmast 1908 came and went. Wharton was in bed most of the time. On the last day of the year he received a letter from Swank. Wharton started to dictate a reply and got as far as, "Yours of 31st inst. received. I have read carefully all you say," then decided to finish the letter in long hand. He continued in a shaky script, "and approve your suggestion as to your letter of resignation and my reply to it. There is I believe cash in hand to pay all debts including your salary. It seems odd for another big tariff fight to be on and you and I not in it. The play of Hamlet with Hamlet left out."

It was the last letter he wrote with his own hand, although he dictated several others. On 3 January the doctor reported him to be sinking fast, that his heart was giving out. Tuesday, 5 January, Harrison wrote to Swank, "I regret to inform you that Mr. Wharton had a very serious turn on Sunday afternoon and was in bed yesterday when I saw him for a few moments only." Yet in the afternoon Wenner arrived at the house and Wharton dictated a two-page letter to Gratz which showed little sign of failing mental powers or a changed personality, except for a little uncharacteristic sarcasm:

Although my ventures mainly through your means have turned out failures, there is one asset that may have particular value and that is the road to the Payette River and across the Dam to the Public Road. So far as

I know no communication exists betwen the two roads and connection with Centerville must now be established. I understand also no road or projected road runs across the mountains and joining with what roads are there.

As I have made at my own expense a road to Payette River, a public road can be established between the two sides of Payette River, most convenient to the County of Basic [read: Boise] or State of Idaho—as to which some suitable lawyer may indicate the best course for me to take. I wish to have the project before the lawyer and would be prepared to convey my rights for the consideration of $100,000, payable in Bonds of the City or County of Boise or State of Idaho. . . . I regret my feeling toward Senator Borah is not the same as formerly and I cannot advise you to consult with him. . . . So far as I understand there is no public road into the timber country except the road up Grimes Creek—the most essential part is the crossing of Payette River by building of one or two courses of logs on top of the work [that is, the dam] I have already built, being a continuation by means of two or three logs firmly fastened by anchor bolts and railing on each side to prevent accident of wagon or person dropping in the river.

There is very little chance I shall ever see you again for I narrowly escaped total wreck from paralysis and since then a very serious accident by falling in to the cellar at my house, so that at present the Doctors have me confined in bed, though they give out hopes that I will gradually improve, as to which they are more sanguine than I. When you are answering I wish you to tell me frankly about the road and bridge plan. I hope you and your interesting family have started the New Year with every prospect of prosperity.

Wharton signed the letter after Wenner typed it. "Good night, Harry," he said as Wenner left. The next day Wharton lapsed into a coma. Lippincott, knowing the end was near, took care of the few business letters which had to be sent, only informing correspondents that his father-in-law's state of health was "alarming." The nurses and members of the family took turns watching at the bedside.

Within a few days the failures, insults, slights, and other hurts of the last eighteen months would be forgotten in a wave of eulogies. Wenner would write, "The maxim he had inscribed on his medals for the Wharton School of Finance and Commerce show the fine as well as the staunch principles in the man. 'Suum Cuique'—'Let each have his own' was the inherent principle in dealing with those in his employ."

Kelly would offer, "He was to all an able leader, a wise counsellor, and an Employer who will always be remembered for his Kindliness of manner, and fair and just treatment."

To Anna Wharton Morris eighteen months later would come a letter from Skibo:

I do not believe there was any man who exerted such influence in Washington as your father did. He kept to the point and imprest Commitee after Committee, until, under the mantle of temporary protection, the steel industry was able to stand alone, as it is today.

In all business matters, your father's word was all that any one required, and in trying times his decision was sought as one of ripe judgment. In cases of dispute, there was no man more frequently appealed to as arbiter than your father.

A man of few words in counsel, but those always to the point. His speech "yea, yea," or "Nay, nay," as became a Quaker. He could dispatch business with expedition, but with his natural modesty, he concealed his poetic gift until the very last. . . . After my retirement from business, we drew closer than we ever did before, and our meeting at the Hague [read: Kiel] was a source of great joy to Mrs. Carnegie and myself. As you know, it was arranged that he was to come to us at Skibo, but was stricken in London en route and I saw him no more, altho many sweet messages passed between us.[49]

The night of 10 January was overcast and raw. Inside Ontalauna the watchers took their last turns. Wharton spoke no memorable words. His last message was the business letter to Gratz. In the early hours of the morning all gathered at his bedside and at 6:30 A.M. Monday, 11 January, he died.

Or, as his mother would have said, using words which by 1909 had become old-fashioned, was translated.

Appendix
The Dry and Wet Processes of Making Nickel

The processes used by Fleitmann and Wharton in making nickel are most intelligible if several characteristics of the metallurgy of nickel and its ores are kept in mind.

The first is that the metals in the Gap ores, the nickel, copper, cobalt, and iron, occurred in the form of sulfides. If they had been held as oxides, the refining would have been cut in half, so to speak, as the initial steps in the refining involved changing sulfides into oxides. But, in distant geologic time, sulphur had been incorporated in these ores; and there it was.

A second characteristic is that nickel and iron are chemically similar. This makes their separation difficult. Essentially, all but the final stages in the refining of the Gap ores gravitated around measures designed to eliminate iron. Once that was done, separation of nickel from the remaining copper and cobalt was relatively easy.

A third characteristic is that when air or some other source of oxygen is introduced into the heated ore, the iron begins to oxidize sooner than the other metals do. The oxide is, furthermore, lighter than the sulfides, so that gravity can be used to separate it out. In a smelter iron oxide will be carried off with the slag, whereas the sulfides will sink to the bottom and can be separately drawn.

A fourth characteristic, however, is that as the flow of air continues, oxidation of nickel, cobalt, and copper begins before that of iron ends. Because of this, if a single smelting is used to remove all of the iron, then nickel, cobalt, and copper sulfides of great purity can be obtained, but at the same time a great deal of these metals will go as oxides with the iron into the slag. A series of smeltings and roastings is needed, each carried on under suitable but differing conditions so as to remove the iron by stages without losing any of the other metals until a point is reached at which the remaining small amount of iron can be leached out.

All of the steps involved in removing the bulk of the iron constitute a "dry" process. Before it began, however, the ore was concentrated into matte near the mine. After Blake's Rock Breaker had reduced the ore into pieces of suitable small size, men shoveled it into kilns, which looked much like old-fashioned lime kilns. Each held eighty or ninety tons. Here, the ore was roasted. In roasting the only escape for impurities is through a stack, unlike smelting, in which a flux is used to carry away impurities in the form of slag. The purpose of this first roasting was to remove excess sulphur. A wood fire was lighted in the kiln to start the process. When the ore reached a certain temperature an exothermal reaction took place. That is, the mixture generated its own heat so as to continue the roasting to a normal conclusion. The mass of ore burned for five or six weeks.

The roasting being finished, the product was taken from the kilns, cooled, and carted to the nearby blast furnaces. There were three of these, two being in operation day and night. They were capable of smelting approximately six hundred tons of ore a month. Layers of ore were alternated with layers of coke and a flux consisting of powdered flint mixed with some limestone. Three draws were normally made every twenty-four hours. A large part of the remaining worthless matter passed out with the slag. The residue was matte.

"The matte," wrote Doble, "comes out of the furnace in a liquid state, and is run into 'pigs' in sand moulds similar to the pig-iron from an iron furnace. This pig-matte is next put through the 'rock breakers' and then through a powerful Cornish crusher by which it is reduced to a coarse powder, in which condition it is inclosed in barrels and shipped to the refinery in Camden, New Jersey."

Wharton's matte contained varying amounts of nickel. One shipment to Van Wart & McCoy of England assayed from 6.5 percent to 10.5 percent "or thereabouts" of nickel. A shipment of 85,841 pounds of matte to Fleitmann and Witte contained 10.43 percent nickel.[1]

Fleitmann's Dry Method.

At Camden the refining of the matte took place. A description of the dry method used by Fleitmann has survived.[2] It is written in bad German and is poorly organized and incomplete. Still, the principal steps in the process are clear. Matte was smelted three times to remove the remaining useless material. Cobalt and iron passed out with the slag and presumably could be recovered by other processes. The product of the third smelting consisted principally of oxides of nickel, copper, and some impurities. It was then roasted three times, being ground to a coarse powder before each roasting. For the last roasting, soda was added. The product was again ground, washed to remove the last traces of soda, formed into cubes by means of a bonding agent (starch), and subjected to a final burning. This gave a mixture of nickel and copper salts which was marketable. Nickel hyperoxide could then be separated from the copper salts by dissolving the product in hydrocholoric acid to which 2 percent or iron had been added and then precipitating the iron and copper with lime. Additional lime and chlorinated lime were used to precipitate the nickel hyperoxide, which was formed into cubes. If desired, metallic nickel could be recovered by grinding these and roasting the powder with a reducing agent such as charcoal.

At each stage of the process Fleitmann had laboratory samples taken and tested to determine the completeness of the previous reaction, the composition of the product, and the precise mix, etc., to be used for the next state. At each smelting mechanical details such as force of blast and composition and structure of furnace or crucible were as important as timing, temperature, and chemical composition of the product.

Wharton's Dry and Wet Methods.

Wharton added some important details in his description of the dry method of refining nickel. He specified that at Camden the smelting took place in a reverberatory furnace. This differs from a blast furnace in having the fuel separated from the charge of ore and flux. In a reverberatory furnace a column of heated air accomplishes the melt. Spouts separately draw off the concentrated matte and slag.

The three roastings which followed the three smeltings, wrote Wharton, aimed at producing a "dead roasted matte," that is, one in which the last traces of sulphur had been eliminated. He explained the roastings thus: "Thorough roasting is most important, for if the oxidation of the metals is imperfect, subchlorides are formed in the dissolving process and cannot be properly separated by the subsequent precipitations. Roasting No. 1 drives off some sulphur, imparts some oxygen, and makes the matte tender so as to grind easily and finely. Roasting No. 2 is very important and if not well done makes a good result impossible in the final roasting; it requires a high heat and honest working by furnace tender, nearly all the sulphur must be driven off at this time. Roasting No. 3 must be continued until the charge has a uniform dark blue color, which indicates that no suboxides are left. A reddish brown or leather color even in spots shows that the process is incomplete."

Upon conclusion of the third roasting the wet process began. The matte now consisted almost entirely of oxides of cooper, cobalt, and nickel, with some iron tenaciously remaining. The aim now was to separate out and recover all four metals. The first step involved a removal of some of the copper. The matte was heated with dilute sulphuric acid, which dissolved the oxides and precipitated copper sulphate. This was suitably washed and taken to the blue vitriol house for drying. The wash water was added to the remaining liquor. In all later steps wash waters were added to the remaining liquor and residues were returned to be reworked with later charges of matte.

Wharton might have chosen arsenic as a means of separating nickel from the remaining metals, as nickel has an affinity for arsenic. Many nickel ores contain traces of arsenic which in any event has to be removed. Wharton attributed use of this method to Evans and Askin, whom he believed produced nickel of 97 percent purity.[3] He rejected this way for the American Nickel Works. The Gap ores contained no arsenic; and the process was detrimental to the health of the workers.

In a subsequent and involved series of leachings Wharton used milk of lime (a suspension of $Ca(OH)_2$ in water) to precipitate iron; hydrogen sulphide gas to remove the remaining copper; and chloride of lime to separate out cobalt salts. Finally, nickel oxide was the only compound left. This was precipitated by a dilute solution of milk of lime, filtered, dried, and pressed into plates which were calcined in a reverberatory furnace, ground, washed, mixed with sal soda, dried, again calcined, and again washed with a very weak solution of hydrochloric acid. Pure nickel was made by placing alternate layers of ground oxide with charcoal in crucibles containing sixteen to nineteen pounds of oxide and heated in a reducing furnace. The product of the furnace was dumped into water, and the nickel settled in the form of grains, which were put through a polishing apparatus and packed in five-hundred-pound kegs for shipment.

Abbreviations

AIME	The American Institute of Mining Engineers
ALW	Anna Lovering Wharton (Joseph Wharton's wife)
ASME	The American Society of Mechanical Engineers
BICo	Bethlehem Iron Company
DFW	Deborah Fisher Wharton (Joseph Wharton's mother)
FHL	Friends Historical Library, Swarthmore College
FWT	Frederick Winslow Taylor
HSP	The Historical Society of Pennsylvania
JFI	*Journal of the Franklin Institute*
JW	Joseph Wharton
PMHB	*Pennsylvania Magazine of History and Biography*
SIT	Stevens Institute of Technology
WB	Wharton Barker
WP	Wharton Papers in the Friends Historical Library

Notes

Chapter 1. The Beginning of a Family

1. Genealogical information concerning the Fishers and the Whartons is best found in Anna Hollingsworth Wharton, *Genealogy of the Wharton Family of Philadelphia, 1664 to 1880* (privately printed, 1880), copy in FHL; Anna Wharton Smith, *Genealogy of the Fisher Family, 1682 to 1896* (privately printed, 1896), copy in FHL; Nicholas B. Wainwright, ed., "Memoir of William Logan Fisher (1781–1862) For His Grandchildren," *PMHB* 99, no. 1 (Jan. 1975): 92–103; Anna Wharton Morris, "The Romance of the Two Hannahs," *Bulletin of the Newport Historical Society* 46 (Oct. 1923): 1–33; Sydney L. & Catharine Morris Wright, *The Good Old Summertime* (privately printed and distributed, 1963), copy in FHL.

2. In early life Joseph Wharton professed indifference and confusion concerning his antecedents. JW to DFW, 31 July 1864, WP. In later life Wharton became more interested and had a copy made of Sir Anthony Van Dyck's portrait of Philip, Lord Wharton, which had been painted in 1632 and was hanging in The Hermitage, St. Petersburg. Lord Philip Wharton had championed Roger Williams against the Puritan rulers of Boston in a fight to obtain a charter for the colony of Rhode Island. Charlemagne Tower to JW, 21 March, 19 April 1900, WP; and see *Burke's Peerage: Baronetage and Knightage* (any ed.) for an account of Lord Philip Wharton and his descendants. No one has established a familial connection between the noble Whartons of England and the Whartons of America.

3. Abraham Ritter, *Philadelphia and Her Merchants* (Philadelphia: privately printed, 1860), 181–82; Anna W. Morris, "The Romance of the Two Hannahs," 6. Various bills of lading, invoices, etc., illustrating the nature of Charles Wharton's business are to be found in WP; the Family Papers (1732–1826) of Sarah A. Smith, HSP; the Family Papers (1728–1846) of Edward Wanton Smith, HSP.

4. Unsigned memoir by DFW concerning William Wharton, n.d., WP.

5. Robert F. Oaks, "Philadelphians in Exile: The Problem of Loyalty During the American Revolution," *PMHB* 96, no. 3 (July 1972): 298–375; Sarah Fisher, "A Diary of Trifling Occurrences, Philadelphia, 1776–1778," reprinted in *PMHB* 82, no. 4 (October 1958): 412, 462.

6. Samuel Rowland Fisher diary 1779–1881, WP.

7. Samuel Rowland Fisher diaries, HSP; MS by Samuel Rowland Fisher (15 Feb. 1785), FHL; *Journal of Samuel Rowland Fisher,* entries for 15 May 1819, 3 Nov. 1820, FHL; Anna W. Morris, "The Romance of the Two Hannahs," 16; JW, Memorial to DFW, n.d., WP.

8. JW, Memorial to DFW, n.d., WP.

9. Eliza Cope, ed., *Philadelphia Merchant: The Diary of Thomas P. Cope, 1800–1851* (Gateway Edition: South Bend, Ind., 1978), 410–11.

10. JW, Memorial to DFW, n.d., WP.

11. The correspondence involving Scattergood and William Wharton concerning this trip is in WP.

12. Joanna Wharton Lippincott, "Deborah Fisher Wharton," in Gertrude B. Biddle and Sarah D. Lowrie, *Notable Women of Pennsylvania* (Philadelphia: University of Pennsylvania Press, 1942), 126.

13. All material concerning this phase of William and Deborah's courtship comes from copies of letters which William wrote to Charity Rotch, 11 Mar., 11 July 1813, 10 Oct. 1814, 15 Dec. 1815, paperback memorandum book entitled "William Wharton 1809," WP.

14. Harold D. Eberlein & Cortlandt Van Dyke Hubbard, *Portrait of a Colonial City: Philadelphia, 1670–1838* (Philadelphia: J. B. Lippincott Co., 1939), 460.

Chapter 2. From School to Farm

1. For sociological aspects of the Hicksite Separation see Robert W. Doherty, *The Hicksite Separation* (New Brunswick, N.J.: Rutgers University Press, 1967); for a historical account,

see Rufus M. Jones, *The Later Periods of Quakerism* (London: Macmillan & Co., 1929), 1:435–87.

2. JW to Talcott Williams, 10 May 1900, WP.

3. The Hicksite Separation was largely confined to the states of New Jersey, Pennsylvania, New York, Maryland, Delaware, Ohio, and Indiana. In New England the Orthodox had swiftly dealt with a New Light Movement which began in 1815 by disavowing many who might later have been leaders in a separation. The weak meetings in the South also remained within the Orthodox fold, as Friends with Hicksite leanings had earlier left and resettled on free soil in the West. English Quakers, too, avoided separation. Jones, *Later Periods of Quakerism*, 1:435–87.

4. Walt Whitman wrote one of the best descriptions of Elias Hicks's magnetic personality. See Jones, *Later Periods of Quakerism*, 1:441.

5. JW to Andrew Carnegie, 10 July 1906, WP.

6. Elias Hicks to William and Deborah Wharton and Sarah and Thomas Fisher, 14 Feb. 1825, WP. The WP contain several letters written by Hicks.

7. For the lives and labors of these two Hicksite leaders see John Comly, *Journal of the Life and Religious Labours of John Comly, Late of Byberry, Pennsylvania* (Philadelphia: T. Ellwood Chapman, 1853); Jesse Kersey, *A Narrative of the Early Life, Travels, and Gospel Labors of Jesse Kersey, Late of Chester County, Pennsylvania* (Philadelphia: T. Ellwood Chapman, 1851); copies in FHL.

8. William Wharton, draft of speech at closing session of Yearly Meeting, 1827, WP.

9. J. Comly, *Journal*, 320.

10. Minutes of the Philadelphia Monthly, Quarterly, and Yearly Meetings (microfilm), FHL.

11. Minutes of the Men's Yearly Meeting of Philadelphia (microfilm), FHL.

12. Eberlein and Hubbard, *Portrait of a Colonial City*, 461.

13. DFW diary, 4 June 1876, WP.

14. Of the numerous references to Bellevue, the following are of especial importance: Brief of the Title to the Estate Late of William Wharton Situated in the Twenty-Eighth Ward of the City of Philadelphia Known as 'Bellevue,' WP; Hannah Price to Charles Wharton, 9 Aug. 1824; JW to DFW, 1 Aug. 1855, 17 July 1856, WP; Sarah A. Smith Family Papers, 1732–1826, HSP; *Bellevue for the Children* (privately printed, n.d.), copy in library of Catharine M. Wright, Fox Hill Farm, Jamestown, R.I.

15. Esther Wharton Smith to Mrs. Harrison S. Morris, 22 Apr. 1909, WP.

16. JW to Hetty Thurston, 13 Jan. 1862, WP.

17. "Jacob Barker," *Penn Monthly* (Dec. 1872, 638–48, copies in libraries of Lehigh University and University of Pennsylvania.

18. Minutes of the Spruce Street Monthly Meeting (microfilm), FHL.

19. "Anna is a delightful creature, admirable in character and very beautiful, one of the most beautiful women I ever saw. Her face combines regularity of features with expression. She has glorious dark hazel eyes, a sweet smile, a fine complexion, dark hair, a true Grecian contour of head, nose, mouth, and chin exquisitely chiselled. If she had more roundness to her graceful figure she would be perfect." Sidney George Fisher, in Nicholas Wainwright, ed., "The Diary of Sidney George Fisher, 1863," *PMHB*, 88, no. 4 (Oct. 1964): 478.

20. Principal sources of information concerning JW's schooling to the age of sixteen are a Memorandum Book given to him at the age of five by his Uncle Thomas and presently in the possession of the family; letters to his parents and a "Book of Character" of JW kept by Thomas Conard, WP. The school operated by Henry Pike is described in Joseph C. Martindale, *A History of the Townships of Byberry and Moreland* (Philadelphia: T. Ellwood Zell, 1867), 100–124.

21. JW to Brush, 4, 20 Oct. 1862, Brush Family Papers, Yale University Library (hereafter Brush Papers).

22. JW to "Dear Mrs. Wister," 4 Feb. 1897, WP.

23. Ibid. See also Joanna Lippincott, *Biographical Memoranda Concerning Joseph Wharton, 1826–1909* (Philadelphia: privately printed & circulated by J. B. Lippincott Co., 1909), 22, copy in FHL.

24. William Wharton to JW, 30 Sept. 1844, DFW to JW, 29 Sept. 1844, WP.

25. DFW to JW, 7 July, 1 Sept. 1842, Charles W. Wharton to JW, 20 Aug. 1842, WP.

26. Record of Births, Fallowfield Meeting (microfilm), FHL; Rodman Wharton to JW, 23 May 1844, WP.

27. Letters by Joseph S. and Abigail Walton, Walton Papers, FHL; Minutes of Fallowfield Men's Monthly Meeting, 1835–44 (microfilm), FHL; Photograph Album of Walton Family,

Chester Co. Historical Society, West Chester, Pa.; George A. Walton and J. Barnard Walton, eds., *Diaries and Correspondence: Margaretta Walton, 1829–1904* (1962), Chester Co. Historical Society; T. Chalkley Matlack, *Brief Historical Sketches Concerning Friends' Meetings of the Past and Present with Special Reference to Philadelphia Yearly Meeting* (Moorestown, N.J., 1938), 3:754–55; Minutes of the Fallowfield Men's Monthly Meeting, FHL; R. C. Smedley, *History of the Underground Railroad in Chester and the Neighboring Counties of Pennsylvania* (New York: Negro Universities Press, 1968), 30, 32, 34, 134–35.

28. JW's notes for a speech praising the Pennsylvania RR, WP.
29. JW to Hannah Wharton (later Hannah Haydock), 28 June 1842, WP.
30. Ibid.
31. JW to his parents, 3 July 1842; JW to DFW, 10 July 1842, WP.
32. JW to DFW, n.d., 1 Sept., 23, 30 Oct., 13, 20, 27 Nov. 1842, WP.
33. JW to DFW, 23 Oct., 13 Nov. 1842, WP.
34. JW to DFW, 27 Nov. 1842, WP.
35. DFW to JW, 1 Sept. 1842, WP.
36. Margaret Mann to DFW, 2 Apr. 1842, WP.
37. DFW to JW, 21 June, 7 July, 2, 14, 25 Aug., 11 Sept., 23 Oct. 1842, 2 Apr., 27 Nov. 1843, 19 Apr. 1844, WP.
38. JW to DFW, 2 Apr. 1843; DFW to JW, 13 June 1844, WP.
39. JW to DFW, 7 May, 4 June, 18 Aug., 22 Sept., 1843, WP.
40. DFW to JW, 18 June 1843, WP.
41. JW to DFW, 12 Nov. 1843, WP.
42. JW to DFW, 23 June 1844, WP.
43. DFW to JW, 13 June 1844, Charles W. Wharton to JW, 22 June 1844, Rodman Wharton to JW, 13 June 1844, WP.
44. JW to Mary Wharton, 25 Aug. 1844, WP.
45. JW to DFW, 27 Apr., 18 Aug., 22 Sept. 1844, WP.
46. JW to DFW, 18 Aug. 1844, WP.
47. Rodman Wharton to JW, 20 Sept. 1844, WP.
48. William Wharton to JW, 30 Sept. 1844, WP.

Chapter 3. A New Beginning

1. Joanna Lippincott, *Biographical Memoranda*, 25; biographical sketch prepared for publication in the *Iron Trade Review* and corrected by JW and attached to letter, JW to Mr. B. S. Stephenson, 20 Mar. 1907, WP.
2. Material concerning the Wharton family economy is taken mostly from William Wharton's financial records for the decade of the 1840s, WP, and includes: (1) Cash Book #1 for the years 1842–44; (2) Cash Book #2 for the years 1845, 1846, and the first few months of 1847; (3) a Ledger covering the years 1841–47; (4) a Petty Cash Book for the years 1849–54. The cash books record receipts and expenditures in chronological order. The Ledger deals with much of the same material organized by subject. The Petty Cash Book is narrower in scope than the others and is of little value for understanding the family finances. The entries in all of these books are confusing. Those of Cash Book #1 especially seem to follow no logical plan. Those of Cash Book #2 are more orderly, the debit column being organized into separate categories of household expenses; real estate; and the business concerns of the children. The improvement of Cash Book #2 over that of #1 is probably a result of the increasing work of Rodman in managing his father's property.
3. Deborah had received from the estate of Samuel Rowland Fisher stock in the Schuylkill Navigation Company, the Belmont & Eastern Turnpike Road, and the Conshecton & Great Bend Turnpike Road. In 1829 William Wharton purchased three shares of the Falls Bridge Company and in 1845 bought a little of the stock of the Chesapeake & Delaware Canal Company. Ledger 1841–47, WP.
4. JW Account Books, 1855–57, WP.
5. JW to DFW, 5 June 1856, WP.
6. DFW to JW, 16 Nov. 1859, WP.
7. Ledger 1841–47; JW to sister Mary, 10 July 1854, to Anna Lovering, 11 July 1850, WP.

8. Rodman Wharton to Ed. Shoemaker, 15 Sept., 25 Oct., 12 Dec. 1845, 22 June, 11 Sept. 1846, 8 Feb., 16 Nov. 1847, WP.

9. Rodman Wharton to S. L. Carpenter, 6 May 1847, WP.

10. JW to DFW, 29 Oct. 1845, WP.

11. Concerning chemistry and chemists in Philadelphia see Edgar Fahs Smith, *Chemistry in America* (New York and London: D. Appleton & Co., 1914), esp. 236–37, 245–47, 261–63.

12. Articles of Agreement in Box 42, JW Ledger to 1853, Rodman Wharton to JW, 17, 23 July 1847, JW to Anna Lovering, 17 Oct. 1849, WP.

13. Leebert Lloyd Lamborn, *Cottonseed Products* (New York: Van Nostrand Co., 1904), 17–19.

14. A separate folder in Box 42, WP, contains all memorandums, notes, etc. concerning the venture of refining cottonseed oil.

15. Jacob Barker to JW, 15 Oct. 1849, WP.

16. JW Ledger to 1853; Folder on cottonseed oil, WP.

17. Erwin W. Thompson, "The Manufacture of Cottonseed Oil," *Transactions ASME* 6 (Nov. 1884–May 1885): 414–28, 436.

Chapter 4. The Vigor of Youth

1. Hannah Haydock to JW, 22 Aug. 1852, WP.

2. U.S. Patent #4,521, May 16, 1846.

3. JW to sister Mary, 6 Mar. 1850, to Robert Haydock, 21 Oct. 1849, to Anna Lovering, 6 July 1850, WP.

4. JW to sister Mary, 12 May 1850, WP.

5. JW to Anna Lovering, 2 Aug. 1850, WP.

6. JW to sister Mary, 11 Sept. 1850, WP.

7. JW to Anna Lovering, 11 July and esp. 2 Sept. 1850, WP.

8. JW to his uncle Thomas Fisher, 6 Oct. 1851, WP.

9. During the southern trip JW wrote almost daily, and sometimes twice daily, to Anna Lovering giving details of his movements. WP.

10. JW to Anna Lovering, 30 Jan. 1853, to sisters Anna and Hetty, 5 Feb. 1853, WP.

11. JW to his father, 28 Jan. 1853, WP.

12. JW to DFW, 13 Feb. 1853, WP.

13. JW to Anna Lovering and DFW (separate letters), 13 Feb. 1853, WP.

14. Charles W. Wharton to JW, 11 Feb. 1852, WP.

15. Charles W. Wharton to JW, 7 Aug., 17 Nov. 1843; William Wharton's Cash book #2, entries of 28 Oct. 1842 and 30 Apr. 1848, JW to sister Mary, 20 Dec. 1846, WP; Minutes, Spruce Street Monthly Meeting, Record of Marriages, and of Cherry Street Monthly Meeting (microfilm), FHL.

16. Several entries in William Wharton's Cash Book #2 concern the insane asylum. One for 17 July 1845 reads, "comm. for Insane Asylum. Paid P. W. Call Mayor $245." A similar entry for 10 Oct. 1845 indicates payment of "balance, $25." On 16 Oct. 1845 the entry reads, "D. L. Dix (for Insane Asylum) Paid her $220."

17. JW to Joseph Thurston, 29 Aug. 1849, to sister Mary, 25 July 1850, WP. The Sarah A. Smith Family Papers in HSP contain a copy of the marriage certificate of William Wharton and Anna Walter. The Minutes, Spruce Street Meeting, 24 Dec. 1852, FHL, record that "there was no break of our testimonies in the accomplishment" of William's marriage, and that he was on his request continued as a member.

18. JW to Anna Lovering, 11 Aug. 1853, WP.

19. Anna Lovering weighed 104 pounds in the summer of 1850. Anna Lovering to JW, 2 July 1850, WP.

20. A picture of Joseph Lovering's sugar house appears in *Philadelphia as It Is in 1852* (Philadelphia: Lindsay & Blakiston, 1852), 138. A penciled MS in the Joseph S. Lovering Collection, HSP, contains a description of Oak Hill. Joseph S. Lovering described his career at some length in a letter to JW, 20 June 1860, WP.

21. Joseph Lovering to Anna Lovering, 5 Jan. 1848, to DFW, 26 Mar. 1842, to his sister Sarah, 17 May 1844, WP. The WP contain a great deal of correspondence by and concerning the

Loverings from which the characters of the several members of the family and their manners of living can be ascertained.

22. JW to Anna Lovering, 14 Sept. 1849, WP.
23. JW to Anna Lovering, 9 Feb. 1850, WP.
24. JW to Anna Lovering, 3 July 1850, WP.
25. JW to Anna Lovering, 10 Sept. 1850, WP.
26. JW to Anna Lovering, 14 Aug. 1853, WP.
27. JW to Anna Lovering, 19 Mar., 18 May, 24 June 1850, WP.
28. Anna Lovering to JW, 7 May 1863, WP.
29. Anna Lovering to JW, 3, 5, 7, 9, 11, 12 July 1850, WP.
30. JW to DFW, 17 July 1850, WP.
31. Anna Lovering to JW, 27 Jan. 1853, WP.
32. Charles W. Wharton to JW, 19 Mar. 1853, WP.
33. JW to Anna Lovering, 11 Aug. 1853, WP.
34. JW to Anna Lovering, 26 Jan. 1854, WP.
35. Cherry Street Monthly Meeting, Marriages (microfilm), FHL.
36. JW to Hetty Smith, 10 June 1859, WP.

Chapter 5. Venture in Zinc: Making Oxide

1. JW to Coates & Co., 18 Dec. 1857, WP.
2. C.T. Jackson, "On the Manufacture of Zinc and Zinc White," *Proceedings of the American Association for the Advancement of Science* (Washington, D.C., 1850), 4:35–37; JW, Statement on Manufacturing Zinc and Spelter in the United States, 1860, WP: JW, "Memoranda Concerning the Introduction of Spelter into the United States," *The American Journal of Arts and Sciences* (July–Dec. 1871) 102:168; Walter R. Ingalls, *Production and Properties of Zinc* (New York & London: The Engineering and Mining Journal, 1902): 13; New Jersey Zinc Co., *The First Hundred Years of the New Jersey Zinc Company* (New York, 1948), 11–15.
3. JW to Brush, 19 Mar. 1860, Brush Papers.
4. The best source of information concerning Bethlehem up to the time of the founding of the zinc industry is Joseph M. Levering, *A History of Bethlehem, Pennsylvania* (Bethlehem: Bethlehem Times Publishing Co., 1903).
5. JW to ALW, 21 Apr. 1859, WP.
6. Benjamin L. Miller, *Lehigh County, Pennsylvania: Geology and Geography* (Harrisburg: Dept. of Internal Affairs, 1941), 327.
7. M. I. Wilbert, "Early Chemical Manufactures—A Contribution to the History of the Rise and Development of Chemical Industries in America," reprinted in *JFI* 157 (May 1904): 7–8, 12; Miriam Hussey, *From Merchants to "Colour Men"—Five Generations of Samuel Wetherill's White Lead business* (Philadelphia: University of Pennsylvania Press, 1956), 34.
8. Charles P. Williams, "Notes on the Method of Preparation of Zinc Oxide," *Transactions AIME* 5 (May 1876–Feb. 1877): 45; W. J. Taylor, "Manufacture of the Oxide of Zinc near Lancaster, Pennsylvania," *JFI* 67 (1859): 279–80. Jones received his patent 24 Feb. 1852. Wetherill applied for a patent in that year but his claim was contested so that he did not receive it until November 1855. He also patented an improvement on the tower process and, later, several improvements on his own invention. *JFI* 40 (1855): 385; 42 (1856): 315; 43 (1857): 110; *The Mining Magazine* (New York) 2, no. 4 (April 1854): 521–23.
9. Richmond E. Myers, "The Story of the Zinc Industry in the Saucon Valley," *Rocks and Minerals* 10, no. 2 (Feb. 1935): 19.
10. The most reliable and useful sources concerning the founding and first few years of the Pennsylvania and Lehigh Zinc Co. are: Peter Fritts, *History of Northampton County, Pennsylvania* (Philadelphia; 1877), 211–12; Matthew S. Henry, *History of the Lehigh Valley* (Easton, Pa.: Bixler & Corwin, 1860), 237; William C. Reichel, *The Crown Inn Near Bethlehem, Penn.* (Philadelphia; 1872), 143–44; *New American Cyclopaedia* (New York: D. Appleton & Co., 1863), s.v. "Zinc"; Myers, "Story of the Zinc Industry," 18–21; Levering, *History of Bethlehem*, 720–21; JW, "Memoranda Concerning the Introduction of the Manufacture of Spelter into the U.S."
11. Herman LeRoy Collins and Wilfred Jordan, *Philadelphia: A Story of Progress* (New York, Philadelphia and Chicago: Lewis Historical Publishing Co., 1941), 4:83.

12. *The Mining Magazine*, 2 no. 3 (Mar. 1854): 289; no. 4 (Apr. 1854): 410; no. 6 (June 1854): 643–44.

13. The value of the stock of the Pennsylvania & Lehigh Zinc Co. declined from 2⅝ in January 1854, to 1½ in August 1854. *The Mining Magazine*, 2 no. 2 (Feb. 1854) 172; 3 no. 3 (Sept. 1854): 292.

14. JW to ALW, 7, 10 Sept. 1854, WP.

15. The register of the Sun Hotel is in the Moravian Archives, Bethlehem, Pa., and contains a record of all persons staying at the hotel, together with the dates of their arrivals and room assignments, and of persons dining there, with dates.

16. JW to ALW, 4, 18 Jan., 8 Feb. 1855, WP.

17. ALW to JW, 22 Feb. 1855; see also ALW to JW, 12, 19, 26 Sept. 1854, WP.

18. JW to Daniel Hanna, 8 Mar. 1856, to ALW, 7 Aug. 1855, Day Book 1857, p. 24, WP.

19. JW to Richard Pascoe, 26 Oct. 1855, to Gilbert and Wetherill, 30 Nov. 1855, to Leibert, 11 Sept. 1855, to ALW, 11 Mar. 1855, WP.

20. E. Cooper Shapley, Jr., *Legal Guide for Oil Companies and Stockholders; Including a Digest of the Mining Laws of Pennsylvania* (Philadelphia: Fowler & Moon, 1865), 4.

21. Correspondence in the WP concerning this transaction at Harrisburg includes: JW to ALW, 8 Feb., 25, 26, 27 Apr. 1855; Charles W. Wharton to JW, 25 Apr. 1855; JW to Charles W. Wharton, 26 Apr. 1855.

22. JW to Samuel Wetherill, 22 Feb. 1856, WP.

23. News items, *Easton Daily Express*, 22, 26, 30 Sept. 1856; JW to Pascoe, 28 Jan. 1857, to Illins, 1 Sept. 1855, 24 Mar. 1857, to Leibert, 11 Apr. 1857, to James T. Lewis & Co., 9 Dec. 1857, Leibert to JW, 30 Oct. 1857, WP.

24. *Laws of the Commonwealth of Pennsylvania*, Session of 1861, 610.

25. JW to President and Directors, Pennsylvania & Lehigh Zinc Co., 12 Jan. 1858, WP.

26. JW Ledger 1855–57, entry for 30 Oct. 1857, shows that JW received as salary from 1 Jan. to 1 Oct. 1857, $2,250.

27. Charles W. Wharton to JW, 4, 20 Nov. 1857, WP.

28. JW to Charles W. Wharton, 20 Dec. 1857, to Coates, 5, 30 Oct. 1857, to Leibert, 27 Nov. 1858, to Morison & Co., 4 Dec. 1857, WP.

29. JW to S.F. Fisher, 9 Jan. 1858; JW Ledger 1855–57, WP.

30. JW to Charles W. Wharton, 5 Mar. 1858, WP.

31. JW to Coates, 2 Mar. 1858, WP.

32. JW to James T. Lewis, 22 Dec. 1857, WP.

33. Samuel C. West to JW, 26 Dec. 1857, WP.

34. JW to Pres. Fisher, 9 Jan. 1858, WP.

35. JW to Charles W. Wharton, 11 Nov. 1857, 5, 8 Jan. 1858, WP.

36. Circular, 2 Mar. 1858, WP.

37. JW to Coates, 23 June 1858; and see JW to Coates, 11 May, 20 Sept, 27 Dec. 1858, 18 Jan. 1859, to James T. Lewis & Co., 31 Dec. 1858, Leibert to JW, 24 June 1858, JW Acct. Bk. 1858–62, WP.

38. Hills to JW, 11 Feb. 1857; JW to Hills, 13 Feb. 1857, 29 Mar. 1858, to Charles W. Wharton, 20 Dec. 1857, Charles W. Wharton to JW, 5, 20 Jan. 1858, WP.

Chapter 6. Venture in Zinc: Making Spelter

1. JW to ALW, 19 Oct. 1856, 18 Oct. 1854, WP.

2. JW to DFW, 30 Oct. 1859, WP.

3. JW to DFW, 18 Nov. 1857, WP.

4. JW to Illins, 29 Sept., 24 Aug. 1855, WP.

5. JW to Roepper, 18 Apr. 1856, to Leibert, 28 Feb. 1856, WP.

6. JW to Joseph Thurston, 15 May 1856, to Hoofstetten, 22 May 1856, to Pascoe, 2 June 1856, to James Hodge, 4 Jan. 1861, to ALW, 3 Dec. 1856, WP.

7. Leibert to JW, 26 Dec. 1857, WP.

8. JW to Pres. Fisher, 6 July 1858, WP.

9. JW, "Memoranda concerning the Introduction of the Manufacture of Spelter into the U.S.," 168–69.

10. Leibert to JW, 20 Nov. 1858, WP.

11. De Gee to JW, 14 Mar. 1859, WP.

12. JW to Coates, 15 Feb. 1859, WP.

13. JW to Hodge, 4 Jan. 1861, to Leibert, 31 Dec. 1858, WP: Roepper to Brush, n.d., Brush Papers; *JFI* 60 (1859): 252; *Laws of the Commonwealth of Pennsylvania*, Session of 1861, 609–10; *The Moravian* (23 Feb. 1865), p. 4.

14. JW to Pres. Fisher, 14 Mar. 1859, WP.

15. JW to Pres. Fisher, 15 Mar. 1859, WP.

16. Fisher to JW, 22 Mar. 1859, WP.

17. JW to Fisher, 2 May 1859, WP.

18. JW to ALW, 3 Mar., 21 Apr. 1859, to De Gee, 15 Oct. 1859, WP.

19. JW, "Memoranda Concerning the Introduction of the Manufacture of Spelter into the U.S.," 170–71.

20. JW to President and Directors, Pennsylvania & Lehigh Zinc Co., 5 Sept. 1859, WP.

21. JW to De Gee, 15, 25, 31 Oct., 7, 14 Nov. 1859, WP.

22. JW, "Memoranda Concerning the Introduction of the Manufacture of Spelter into the U.S.," 170.

23. JW to ALW, 14 Sept. 1859, WP.

24. JW to ALW, 8 Dec. 1859, WP.

25. JW to Coates, 22 Nov. 1859, De Gee to JW, 20 Dec. 1859, JW to De Gee, 20 Dec. 1859, WP.

26. JW to ALW, 22 Dec. 1859, WP.

27. JW to ALW, 18 Jan. 1860, WP.

28. JW to ALW, 27 Jan. 1860, WP.

29. JW to ALW, 31 Jan. 1860, WP.

30. JW to ALW, 16, 21 Feb. 1860, WP.

31. JW to ALW, 7 Mar. 1860, WP.

32. JW to ALW, 21 Mar. 1860; see also De Gee to JW, 11 Mar. 1860, JW to De Gee, 17 Mar. 1860, WP.

33. De Gee to JW, 25 Mar. 1860, WP.

34. Leibert to JW, 26 Mar. 1860, WP.

35. JW to ALW, 28 Mar. 1860, WP.

36. JW to ALW, 29 Mar. 1860, WP.

37. JW to William Penn Tatham, 3 Apr. 1860, to Fisher, 17 Nov. 1860, WP.

38. JW to ALW, 15 May 1860; see also JW to Koch, 10 Apr. 1860, to William Christy, 23 June 1860, WP.

39. JW to ALW, 15 May 1860; see also JW to ALW, 2 May 1860, to S.F. Fisher, 24 Apr. 1860, to Joseph Thurston, 2 May 1860, WP.

40. JW to ALW, 2, 23 May 1860, WP.

41. Joseph Lovering to ALW, 29 June 1860, WP.

42. JW to ALW, 13 May, to Coates, 14 May 1860, WP.

43. JW to ALW, 18 July 1860; see also JW to Joseph Thurston, 2 May 1860, to Darlington, 20 May 1860, to ALW, 23 May 1860, to Coates, 21 May, 2 July 1860, to G.T. Lewis, 18 July 1860, WP; JW to Brush, 2 July 1860, Brush Papers.

44. JW to ALW, 9 Aug. 1860; see also JW to ALW, 24 July, 14 Aug. 1860, to Coates, 17 Aug. 1860, WP.

45. JW to Brush, 23 Aug. 1860, Brush Papers.

46. ALW to JW, 19 Sept. 1860; see also JW to ALW, 14 Aug., 18, 19 Sept. 1860, WP.

47. T. G. Hollingsworth to JW, 25, 26 Sept. 1860, JW Ledger 1858–63, WP.

48. JW to Trotter, 29 Aug., 11 Oct. 1860, to S. F. Fisher, 20 Nov. 1860, to "Dear William" Longstreth, 12 July 1861, WP.

49. JW, "Memoranda Concerning the Introduction of the Manufacture of Spelter into the U.S.," 176; JW to Brush, 23, 27 Sept., 2, 9 Oct., 7 Nov. 1860, Brush Papers; JW to Frazer, 18 Oct. 1860, to Coates, 20 Dec. 1859, to Booth, 20 Nov. 1860, WP; *JFI* 70 (Dec. 1860): 422.

50. JW to Trotter, 2 Feb. 1861, WP.

51. JW to C. H. Lanning, 31 May 1861, to Sec'y Del. Div. Canal Co., 25 June 1861, WP.

52. JW to Trotter, 27 Mar. 1861, WP.

53. JW to G. T. Lewis, 23 Apr. 1861, WP.

54. JW to S. F. Fisher, 21 May 1861, WP.

55. JW to S. F. Fisher, 10, 11 June 1861, to Trotter, 19 June 1861, WP.

56. JW to Booth, 17 July 1861; see also JW to G. T. Lewis, 23 Apr. 1861, to James Jenkins, 28 June 1861, to S. F. Fisher, 2, 3 July 1861, WP.

57. JW, "Memoranda Concerning the Introduction of the Manufacture of Spelter into the U.S.," 173–74.

58. ALW to parents, 19 Feb. 1861, WP.

59. JW to ALW, 27 Feb. 1861, WP.

60. JW to ALW, 15, 22 May 1861, WP.

61. JW to ALW, 15 Aug. 1861, WP; JW, "Memoranda Concerning the Introduction of the Manufacture of Spelter into the U.S.," 172.

62. JW to DFW, 26 Apr. 1861; see also ALW to her mother, 24 Apr. 1861, WP.

63. JW to F. M. Etting, 3 Apr. 1861, to ALW, 5 Sept. 1862, WP.

64. JW to Joseph Thurston, 3 Feb. 1861, WP.

65. JW to Reeder, 17 Nov. 1860, Leibert to JW, 18 Mar. 1859. WP.

66. JW Journal, 1863–68, WP. The methods which Wharton used to evaluate his estate are unknown, but he was surely inconsistent in this matter. The valuation he placed on his estate as of 31 Dec. 1862 was $204,764.51 (loose sheet in Ledger 1858–63), and exactly a year later he put his net worth at the lower figure of $174,329.88 (Ledger 1863–68, s.v. "Estate," p. 1). There is no reason to believe that he lost money in the intervening twelve months. On the contrary, given the appreciation of values as a result of war, his real net worth was probably much higher at the end of 1863 than it was at the close of 1862.

67. JW to ALW, 17 Oct. 1861; Indenture between JW and Henry Ueberroth, 6 Apr. 1860, JW to George, 20 June 1861, WP.

68. JW to ALW, 28 Oct. 1862, WP.

69. ALW to JW, 29 Oct. 1862, WP.

Chapter 7. Venture in Nickel

1. JW to Brush, 12 Dec. 1861, Brush Papers.

2. JW to Coates, 1 Feb. 1858, to Charles W. Wharton, 20 Dec. 1857, to Leibert, 21 Dec. 1857, 23 Oct. 1858, WP.

3. The WP contain an extensive correspondence of JW concerning his connections with the William Penn and the Sugar Notch Coal companies.

4. JW to Brush, 1 Aug. 1863, 16 Apr. 1864, Brush Papers.

5. JW to ALW, 2 Sept. 1866, to Edwin Kenwood, 20 Jan. 1899, JW Private Accounts, 1869–75, entry of 9 Apr. 1869, WP; JW to Brush, 17 Dec. 1868, Brush Papers.

6. Lewis Feuchtwanger, "Nickel and Its Uses in the Arts," *JFI* 96 (1873): 204–13; JW, *Memorandum Concerning Small Money and Nickel Alloy Coinage: With Illustrations and Descriptions of Existing Nickel Alloy Coins* (Washington, D.C., 1877), 37–39; James R. Showden, *A Description of Ancient and Modern Coins in the Cabinet Collection of the Mint of the United States* (Philadelphia: J. B. Lippincott & Co., 1860), 119–20; R. S. Yeoman, *A Guide Book of United States Coins*, 27th rev. ed. (Racine, Wis.: Whitman Publishing Co., 1974), 10. See Lewis Feuchtwanger, "Nickel and Its uses in the Arts," 204, for a contrary judgment concerning the popularity of the "nickel cent."

7. Lewis Thompson, "On the Manufacture of Nickel," *JFI* 74 (1863): 355. See also A. R.Roessler, "Nickel Linnaeite," *JFI* 89 (Jan.–June 1870): 85; J. D. Whitney, *The Metallic Wealth of the United States* (Philadelphia: Lippincott, Grambo & Co., 1854), 496; Frederick Overman, *A Treatise on Metallurgy*, 6th ed. (New York: D. Appleton & Co., 1868), 624–30.

8. *Laws of the General Assembly of the Commonwealth of Pennsylvania*, Session of 1851, 369–71. The Minutes of the Board of Directors of the Gap Mining Co. are in HSP. The history and description of the Gap Mine can be found in these articles in the *Journal of the Lancaster County Historical Society*: R. G. Houston, "The Gap Copper Mines," 1 (1897): 283–98; Jean M. Lichty, "Digging and Devotion at the Gap Nickel Mines Since 1857," 68 (1964): 121–26; H. Luther Willig, "Two Notable Mining Industries of Lancaster County," 28, no. 1 (1924): 73–78; John D. Long, "The Nickel Mines of Lancaster County," 80 (1976): 157–77; and also Franklin Ellis and Samuel Evans, *History of Lancaster County, Pennsylvania* (Philadelphia: Everts & Peck, 1883), 664–66, 669; "A Visit to the Gap Mine of Lancaster County, Pennsylvania" (reprint

from *JFI*), *Mining Magazine* (New York) 2 (Jan.–June 1854), 321–22; Persifor Frazer, Jr., *The Geology of Lancaster County, Second Geological Survey of Pennsylvania: Report of Progress in 1877* (Harrisburg, 1880), 78–80.

9. "Notice of the Mineralogical Collection in the Crystal Palace," *Mining Magazine*, 2 no. 4 (June 1854): 591, 603.

10. *Dictionary of American Biography*, s.v. "Boyé, Hans Martin"; W. P. Blake, "Nickel," in Albert Williams, Jr., ed., *Mineral Resources of the United States, 1882*, a Report of the Dept. of the Interior, U.S. Geological Survey (Washington, D.C., 1883), 417.

11. These transactions occupy a large number of entries in JW's financial ledgers, WP. There are three sets of ledgers: (1) separate ledgers for the Gap Mining Company and the refinery at Camden (the ledgers for the mining company are variously entitled "Gap Journal" and "Gap Establishment"; those for the refinery are entitled "Camden Ledger" or "American Nickel Works"); (2) a set of ledgers combining much of the information in those listed above and entitled from 1863 to 1868 "Joseph Wharton Journal" and after that, "Nickel Business"; (3) an account of income, expenditures, etc., for all of his enterprises, called "Private Accounts" for 1869 to 1875 and "Ledger, Private Accounts" for 1876 to 1898.

12. *Biographical Annals of Lancaster County, Pennsylvania* (J. H. Beers & Co., 1903), 971–72.

13. JW to Brush, 1 Aug. 1863, Brush Papers; JW, *Suggestions Concerning Small Money*, 16.

14. JW to Brush, 18 Nov. 1863, Brush Papers.

15. JW to Brush, 5 Feb. 1864; see also JW to Brush, 23 Feb., 6 Apr., 17 Aug. 1864, Brush Papers.

16. "Camden Ledger," 1863–67; "Gap Journal" 1863–67, gives details of sales of matte to European buyers.

17. JW, *Statement Made January 1866, Relative to Nickel, Cobalt-Oxide, etc.* (Philadelphia: privately printed), 11–12, WP; Frederick Voigt, MS untitled sent to ALW following the death of JW, probably written in spring 1909, 1 (hereafter cited as Voigt MS), WP.

18. Statement signed by Oscar D. Allen, 20 Oct. 1865, WP. There are several memorandums in the folder "Iron & Minerals 1859–1908" in Box 42, WP, concerning the agreement between Wharton and Fleitmann and between the firm of Wharton and Fleitmann and Hermann Fleitmann of N.Y.

19. For a description of the dry method see Appendix.

20. JW to Brush, 4 Jan. 1867, Brush Papers.

21. JW Journal 1863–68, entry of 12 Aug. 1868, WP.

22. JW to Brush, 30 Sept. 1868, Brush Papers.

23. *Annual Report of the Director of the Mint for the Fiscal Year Ending June 30, 1863* (Washington, D.C.), 9–11.

24. JW, *Project for Reorganizing the Small Coinage of the United States of America, by the Establishment of a System of Coin Tokens Made of Nickel and Copper Alloy* (privately printed, 15 Apr. 1864), 4, 10–11, copy in WP.

25. JW to Brush, 11 Mar. 1864, Brush Papers; JW to ALW, 26 Jan. 1865, WP.

26. JW, *Suggestions Concerning Small Money*, 26; JW Journal 1863–68, entries of 14, 22 Mar. 1864; JW, *MS note*, "Acct. of Sales of Nickel to U.S. Mint," WP.

27. JW, *Suggestions Concerning Small Money*, 2, 24–25, 28.

28. JW, *Statement Made January 1866, Relative to Nickel, etc.*, 4–5.

29. JW to Boutwell, 23 June 1869, WP.

30. JW, "Acct. of Sales of Nickel to U.S. Mint," JW Private Accts., 1869–75, s.v. "Nickel Business," pp. 131–33.

31. Ellis and Evans, *History of Lancaster County*, 664–66.

32. JW to Kraemer, 13 June 1904, WP.

33. For a description of Wharton's process of refining nickel, see the Appendix. The original MS is in Box 42, WP.

Chapter 8. Iron and Steel

1. JW to Johnson, 11 June 1860, WP.

2. JW Journal 1863–68, entry of 31 Dec. 1865 et al., WP.

3. Minute Book, Saucon Iron Co., Bethlehem Steel Corporation, Bethlehem, Pa.; JW Journal 1863–68, entry of 27 Aug. 1866, WP.

4. JW Account Bk. 1858–63; Journal 1863–68, many entries. J. T. Johnston was the second largest share holder during these years with 660 shares. Asa Packer owned three hundred. BICo, List of Stockholders, 1864–82, Bethlehem Steel Corporation, Bethlehem, Pa.

5. Much of the information concerning John Fritz's life comes from his *Autobiography* (New York: John Wiley & Sons, 1912). Fritz, however, was barely literate. He wrote a draft with trembling hand in pencil on rough paper. Natt Emery, vice-president of Lehigh University, prepared the MS for publication. This information does not appear in the published version, but comes to the author through conversation with personnel of Lehigh University. Emery freely rearranged Fritz's material, rewrote some of it, and omitted some. There is no reason to believe that Fritz disapproved of any of Emery's editorial work. About one-third of the original MS remains in the archives of the Linderman Library, Lehigh University, and contains some unpublished material, hereafter referred to as "Fritz autobiographical MS."

6. Quoted in Frank B. Copley, *Frederick W. Taylor, Father of Scientific Management*, 2 vols. (New York and London: Harper & Bros., 1923), 1:101.

7. BICo Minutes of Bd., 20 June 1860.

8. Fritz, autobiographical MS.

9. BICo Minutes of Bd., 7 May, 9 July 1861; Sayre diary, 26 Sept. 1863; Levering, *History of Bethlehem*, 725.

10. BICo Minutes of Bd., 27 Jan. 1864.

11. BICo Minutes of Bd., 12 Dec. 1866.

12. Jeanne McHugh, *Alexander Holley and the Makers of Steel* (Baltimore and London: Johns Hopkins University Press, 1980), 241, also 21, 151, 190–91; Robert W. Hunt, "A History of the Bessemer Manufacture in America," *Transactions AIME* 5 (May 1876–Feb. 1877): 202–4.

13. Hunt, "History of the Bessemer Manufacture in America," 212–13.

14. *Iron Age*, 31 July 1873, p. 9, 13 Nov. 1873, p. 20; BICo Minutes of Annual Meeting, 1873.

15. BICo Minutes of Bd., 12 Nov., 13 Aug. 1873; Sayre diary, 4, 17 Apr., 9 Aug. 1873.

16. Levering, *History of Bethlehem*, 725; BICo Minutes of Bd., 8 Apr., 23 Sept. 1868; "John Knecht & Son," *Daily Times* (Bethlehem, Pa.: Sesquicentennial Industrial Edition, June 1892), 21, copy in Linderman Library, Lehigh University.

17. BICo Minutes of Bd: (for Hartman Mine) 2 Feb. 1863; (for Mory Mine) 9 Aug., 8 Nov. 1864; (for Bethlehem houses) 6 Apr., 12 Aug., 13 July 1864.

18. For some of JW's efforts to obtain a higher tariff on spelter see JW to E. J. Morris, 6 Jan. 1860, to Thaddeus Stevens, 13 June 1860, to William Bigler, 13 June 1860, to ALW, 23 June 1860, to J. P. Veree, 15 Feb. 1861, WP. In December, 1860, JW wrote on the subject of a tariff on spelter to W. Morris Davis, E. J. Morris, Thaddeus Stevens, Henry C. Longenecker, Justin S. Morrill, William Bigler, Simon Cameron, and others, WP. For some of his attempts to get a higher tariff on nickel, cobalt, etc., see JW to Brush, 4 Jan. 1867, Brush Papers, and JW, *Statement Made January, 1866, Relative to Nickel. etc.*

19. JW to Cyrus Elder, 26 June 1903, WP; A. W. Morris journal, 13 Feb. 1907; Joanna Lippincott, *Biographical Memoranda*, 45–48; The Industrial League, *Tariff Tract No. 1, 1855*, WP. Box 42, WP, contains a folder, "Industrial League," which has considerable material on the league.

20. Henry C. Lea to Joanna Lippincott, 4 June 1900, WP; JW, *The Duty on Nickel* (Philadelphia: privately printed, 3 Feb. 1883), 3, 11, copy in WP.

21. Lea to Joanna Lippincott, 4 June 1900, WP.

22. Minute Book, Saucon Iron Co., Bd. Meeting of 15 Apr. 1872.

23. BICo Minutes of Bd., 10 July 1872.

24. Hannah Haydock to JW, n.d., WP.

25. JW to DFW, 24 Oct. 1871, WP.

26. "Jacob Barker," *Penn Monthly*, Dec. 1872, 647–48; Scrapbook, Box 26, WB Papers, Manuscript Division, Library of Congress (hereafter referred to as WB Scrapbook); Abraham Barker to ALW, 12 Jan. 1869, WP.

27. William Wharton, Jr., *Company Catalog*, 1915 copy in library of the Franklin Institute, Phila.; Abraham Barker to JW, 26 June 1873, JW Private Accts. 1869–75, many entries, WP.

28. Wm. Thurston to JW, n.d., WP.

Chapter 9. The Great Years of the Nickel Business

1. JW to ALW, 21 May 1873, WP; see also Joseph Lovering to JW, 24 June 1873, WP.

2. JW to ALW, 22 June 1873, WP.

3. JW to ALW, 28 June 1873, JW diary of a trip to Europe 1873, 24, 25 June, 1, 2 July, WP.

4. JW to ALW, 11 July 1873, WP.

5. For estimates of the production of nickel in the world and in the U.S. see Blake, "Nickel," 410.

6. "Metallurgy of Nickel," *Iron Age*, 29 Sept. 1881, 15.

7. JW, "The Production of Nickel and Cobalt in 1896," extract from Dept. of the Interior, U.S. Geological Survey, *18th Annual Report of the Survey 1896–1897. Part V—Mineral Resources of the U.S. Calendar Year 1896* (Washington, D.C.: Govt. Printing Office, 1897), 15.

8. *Iron Age*, 11 July 1878, 18.

9. Blake, "Nickel," 418.

10. "Metallurgy of Nickel," 15.

11. Blake, "Nickel," 419.

12. Blake, "Nickel," 419–20.

13. Voigt, MS, 5–6.

14. *Iron Age*, 11 Feb. 1886, 11; E. D. Peters, Jr., "The Sudbury Ore-Deposits," *Transactions AIME* 18 (May 1889–Feb. 1890): 289; "A Nickel Syndicate," *Mining Journal* (London) 58 (25 Feb. 1888): 210; JW, Letter to editor, *Lock and Bell*, June 1888, 2.

15. *The Tariff: Metals and Metal Ores*, extracts of a hearing before the House Committee on Ways and Means, 5 Feb. 1884 (Washington, D.C.: privately printed), 92–93, copy in WP.

16. The MS, untitled, is in the WP.

17. John F. Thompson and Norman Beasley, *For the Years to Come: A Story of International Nickel of Canada* (New York: G. P. Putnam's Sons, 1960), 22–36, 53.

18. R.H. Sayre, summary in back of diary for 1874.

19. BICo Minutes of Bd., 10 June, 9 Sept., 11 Nov., 9 Dec. 1874.

20. Fritz, autobiographical MS.

21. McHugh, *Alexander Holley*, 278–83, 294–97.

22. *Iron Age*, 6 Apr. 1876, 24, 1 Apr. 1880, 1; Sayre diary, 24 July 1878; BICo Minutes of Annual Meeting, 1879; BICo Minutes of Bd., 31 Oct. 1878.

23. BICo Minutes of Bd., 18 Dec. 1877.

24. BICo Minutes of Bd., 26 Mar., 26 Nov. 1879; *Iron Age*, 25 Dec. 1879, 15.

25. BICo Minutes of Bd., 27 June, 25 Oct. 1876.

26. WB Scrapbook.

27. The editors of *Iron Age* were strong supporters of naval rearmament. See for example issues of 17 Apr. 1874, p. 37, 18 June 1874, p. 19, 3 Dec. 1874, p. 7, 28 June 1877, p. 4, 12 July 1877, p. 14, 19 Aug. 1886, p. 25.

28. Sayre diary, 29 May, 11 June 1878; BICo Minutes of Bd., 25 June 1878.

29. List of Stockholders, Bethlehem Iron Co., 1864 to 1882.

30. BICo Minutes of Bd., 31 Oct. 1877; Report of the President, BICo Minutes of Annual Meeting, 1878.

31. Report of the President, BICo Minutes of Annual Meeting, 1877; BICo Minutes of Bd., 29 May 1878.

32. JW Private Accts. 1869–75, entries of 6, 15 April 1875, JW Private Accts. 1876–84 and 1885–98, many entries, Voigt MS, 4–5.

33. W. R. Aykroyd, *The Story of Sugar* (Chicago: Quadrangle Books, 1967), 96–101.

34. Sarah W. R. Ewing, *Atsion, a Town of Four Faces* (Batsto, N.J.: Batsto Citizens Committee, 1979), 15.

35. JW Private Accts. 1869–76, entries of 20 Jan., 25 Apr. 1873. After the onset of the depression of 1873 he continued buying land. The entry for 24 Nov. 1873 reads, "For my promissory notes given to Maurice Raleigh in part payment for 4083½ acres of land lying South of New Jersey & Vineland Railroads adjoining Atsion village viz. dated 11 mo. 20." The purchase price was $5 per acre or $20,417.50 for the tract.

36. Arthur D. Pierce, *Iron in the Pines* (New Brunswick, N.J.: Rutgers University Press, 1957), 4–5.

37. From the *New Republic* (Camden, N.J.), 18 Apr. 1874, reprinted in *Batsto Citizens Gazette* (Spring/Summer 1968), 4.

38. For example, in a letter to his sister Mary on 29 March 1854 JW wrote, "Tell Joe [Thurston] I was strongly reminded yesterday of our tour to Arthurboro by a trip I made to one Cedar Swamp 25 miles down Jersey and wished he was along. The country was wild and barren, houses scarce and my compass useful and the sight of the close thrifty young cedars very pleasant." WP.

39. JW diary of a trip to Europe 1873, 21, 22 June, 5 July. JW to ALW, 1, 11 July 1873, to Joseph Lovering, 19 June 1873, WP

40. Quoted in the *Batsto Citizens Gazette* (Spring/Summer 1978).

41. A copy of the circular is in the folder, "Misc. Notes & Documents," Box 42, WP.

42. Bertram Lippincott, *An Historical Sketch of Batsto, New Jersey* (Philadelphia: privately printed, 1933).

43. JW to daughter Mary, 25 June 1881, WP.

Chapter 10. "A Monstrous War"

1. JW to DFW, 27 Feb. 1872, WP.

2. In 1884 JW was informed that he had been "unanimously" elected president of the 22d Ward Republican Club of Philadelphia and was urged to accept (C. Wetherill to JW, 19 Aug. 1884, WP), but there is no indication that he did so.

3. Robert Ellis Thompson, "Henry Charles Carey," *The Penn Monthly*, Nov. 1876, 831–32.

4. Joanna Lippincott, *Biographical Memoranda*, 74.

5. Carey to JW, 6 Mar. 1873, WP.

6. JW to Carey, Edward Carey Gardiner Collection, HSP.

7. Macfarlane to Joanna Lippincott, in Joanna Lippincott, *Biographical Memoranda*, 50.

8. *Penn Monthly*, Dec. 1870, 476–93; Jan. 1871, 28–43. The paper was also separately published by Henry Carey Baird in 1870, copy in WP.

9. JW, "National Self Protection," 298.

10. Ibid., 301.

11. Ibid., 302.

12. "History of the American Iron & Steel Association," *Bulletin of the AISA* 46, no. 15 (31 Dec. 1912): 1; James M. Swank, Address to the AISA in Philadelphia, 12 Dec. 1909, copies in WP.

13. Allan Nevins, *Abram S. Hewitt* (New York and London: Harper & Bros., 1935), 400–431.

14. Quoted in ibid., 423.

15. McHugh, *Alexander Holley*, 317–20, 347–55; *Iron Age*, 12 July 1883, 28; BICo Minutes of Bd., 26 Feb., 26 Nov. 1879, 22 Feb. 1882.

16. These hearings before the House Committee on Ways and Means of 5 Feb. 1884 were separately printed under the title *The Tariff: Metals and Metal Ores* (Washington, D.C., n.d.), probably by the American Iron and Steel Association. Copy in WP.

17. McHugh, *Alexander Holley*, 360.

18. Quoted in L. B. Richardson, *William E. Chandler, Republican* (New York: Dodd, Mead & Co., 1940), 130.

19. See for example JW to Kelley, 29 May 1882, Wm. D. Kelley Papers, HSP.

20. Geo. H. Boker to JW, 28 Dec. 1876, 5 Jan. 1877, WP.

21. A draft of JW's speech for Garfield at the Academy of Music is in WP.

22. WB Scrapbook.

23. JW to Blaine, 22 Feb. 1881, WP.

24. JW to Kelley, 29 May 1882, Wm. D. Kelley Papers, HSP.

25. Smith to JW, 25 Apr. 1879, WP; see also *Letter of Wharton Barker to Hon. James A. Garfield, House of Reps., Washington, D.C., Apr. 27, 1880* (Philadelphia: privately printed, n.d.), 4, 6, copy in WB Papers, Library of Congress; *The Industrial League to Its Constituents, Mar. 3, 1879* (Philadelphia: privately printed by the Industrial League), 12, copy in WP.

26. JW, *Brief Statement of the Action in Behalf of the Eaton Bill for a Tariff Commission, and the Reasons for Renewing the Movement, June 6, 1881* (Philadelphia: privately printed by

the Industrial League, n.d.), 6–7, JW, "Shall the Tariff be Revised by a Commission" (reprint of an address before the N.Y. Tariff Convention, 30 Nov. 1881) (Philadelphia: Industrial League, n.d.), WP; JW to Kelley, 1, 19 June, 18 Dec. 1882, Wm. D. Kelley Papers, HSP; Edward Stanwood, *American Tariff Controversies in the Nineteenth Century*, 2 vols. (New York: Russell & Russell, 1903), 2:203–4; Richardson, *William E. Chandler*, 337.

27. Francis Wharton to JW, 22 Mar. 1, 10, 18 Dec. 1885, 28 Nov. 1888, WP.

28. WB Scrapbook. For a description of the Canadian Fisheries controversy see Francis Wharton, *A Digest of the International Law of the United States*, 3 vols. (Washington, D.C.: Government Printing Office, 1886), 3:46–47.

29. WB Scrapbook.

30. Francis Wharton to JW, 2 Apr. 1886, 7 Feb. 1888, WP.

31. Francis Wharton to JW, 11 Jan. 1887, WP.

32. Francis Wharton to JW, 17 Feb. 1888, WP.

33. JW to J. B. Lippincott, 12 Feb. 1907, WP.

Chapter 11. Science and Education

1. The best sources of JW's philosophy of life are the annual commencement addresses which he gave as president of the Board of Managers of Swarthmore College. Several of these are included in Joanna Lippincott, *Biographical Memoranda*. Others were summarized or printed in whole or in part in the *Friends Intelligencer*.

2. JW to Brush, 6 Apr. 1864, Brush Papers.

3. JW to Alexander McKenzie, 11 Jan. 1895, to Jackson, 10 Apr. 1895; see also JW to E. A. (undecipherable), 2 Oct. 1895, to Jackson, 8 Oct. 1895, to Gibbs, 19 Apr. 1895, WP; Harvard University, Announcement of the Dept. of Chemistry 1895–96.

4. JW, "Dust from the Krakatoa Eruption of 1883," *Proceedings Commemorative of the One Hundred and Fiftieth Anniversary of the American Philosophical Society* (Philadelphia, 20–26 May 1893). Copies of all of JW's scientific writings are in the WP.

5. JW to Weiskopf, 12 Jan. 1905, WP.

6. Quoted in Homer D. Babbidge, Jr., *Swarthmore College in the Nineteenth Century: A Quaker Experience in Education* (Ph.D. diss., Yale University, 1953), 48, copy in FHL.

7. Inauguration Ceremony of Swarthmore College, 7–9, FHL.

8. Swarthmore College, Stockholders Assn. Minutes (microfilm) (hereafter cited as Swarthmore, Stockholders Min.), 1 Dec. 1868, FHL.

9. Edward H. Magill, *Sixty-Five Years in the Life of a Teacher 1841–1906* (Boston and New York: Houghton Mifflin & Co., 1907), 40–52, 139–42.

10. *Friends Intelligencer*, 15 July 1871, 315.

11. *Swarthmore Alumni Review*, 1940, 18–19; Swarthmore, Stockholders Min., 3 Dec. 1867.

12. Magill, *Sixty-Five Years in the Life of a Teacher*, 152; Babbidge, *Swarthmore College*, 98–108.

13. Swarthmore College, Board of Managers Minutes (microfilm) (hereafter cited as Swarthmore, Board of Mgrs. Min.), 11 Feb. 1873, FHL. Cf. Babbidge, *Swarthmore College*, 109.

14. Magill, *Sixty-Five Years in the Life of a Teacher*, 210.

15. Hannah Haydock to JW, 18 Feb. 1874, 26 Mar. 1876; see also Hannah Haydock to JW, 15 Jan., 7 May 1873, WP.

16. Swarthmore, Board of Mgrs. Min., 14 Feb., 5 Sept. 1871, 11 Feb. 1873, 5 May 1874, 14 Sept. 1875, 3 Dec. 1877, 5 Apr. 1878, 12 July, 27 Sept. 1881, 14 Mar., 19 June 1882.

17. Swarthmore College, Exec. Comm. Min. (microfilm), 5 Apr. 1878, FHL.

18. Swarthmore, Stockholders Min., 2 Dec. 1879.

19. Swarthmore, Board of Mgrs. Min., 13 Sept., 25 Oct. 1881; JW Private Accts., 1876–84, entries of 12 Mar. 1881, 8 Feb. 1882, WP.

20. Lea to JW, 31 Mar. 1882, WP.

21. E. H. Ogden to JW, 20 Nov. 1883, WP.

22. Hannah Haydock to JW, 6 Dec. 1883, WP.

23. Swarthmore, Board of Mgrs. Min., 5 Dec. 1887, 30 Nov. 1885, 16 June 1886.

24. Swarthmore, Board of Mgrs. Min., 18 June, 3 Dec. 1888.

25. JW to Swain, 12 Nov. 1904, WP.

26. JW Business Papers; JW Private Accts., 1885–98, entries for 14 Jan., 11 Mar., 30 Nov. 1891, WP.

27. JW to Clothier, 1 Dec. 1897, WP.

28. Swarthmore, Board of Mgrs. Min., 15 Sept. 1896, Stockholders Min., 6 Dec. 1897.

29. JW to Brush, 20 Sept. 1870, Brush Papers.

30. Indenture dated 22 June 1881, copy in WP; JW Private Accts., 1876–84, entry of 22 June 1881. See also Sellers to JW, 7 Feb. 1881, WP; "Weekly notes," *The American*, 26 Feb. 1881, 312, copy in Van Pelt Library, University of Pennsylvania.

31. MacVeagh to JW, 14 Apr. 1881, Hazard to JW, 22 Apr. 1881, WP.

32. Jevons to JW, 19 May 1881, WP. Jevons was drowned in 1882.

33. E. J. James, Speech before the American Bankers' Assn., 8 Mar. 1890, in *Proceedings of the Convention of the American Bankers' Association* (New York, 1890), 20–33. See also Steven A. Sass, *Pragmatic Imagination: A History of the Wharton School 1881–1981* (Phila.: University of Pennsylvania Press, 1982), 20–52; JW to De Gormo, 19 Apr. 1894, WP.

34. JW, draft of letter to editor, the *Evening Post*, dated 8 Sept. 1888 and printed 11 Sept. 1888, WP.

35. JW to C. C. Harrison, 4 Feb. 1902; see also JW to Joseph P. Johnson, 11 Dec. 1893, to Dr. R. G. Harlan, 30 Apr. 1907, Indenture, 15 Nov. 1893, WP.

36. JW to Swank, 17 Nov. 1903, WP.

37. JW to Harrison, 11 Nov. 1898, JW Private Accts., 1885–98, entry of 1 Feb. 1893, WP.

38. Indentures 15 Nov. 1893, 17 June 1902, JW to Harrison, 19 Jan., 22 May 1903, Jesse Y. Burke to JW, 19 Feb. 1903, WP.

39. "The Wharton School," *Old Penn*, 25 Jan. 1908.

40. JW to Bernheimer, 30 Oct. 1896, WP.

41. JW to Fullerton, 12 Nov. 1896, WP.

42. JW to Sir Chengtung Liang Chang, 7 Mar. 1905, WP.

Chapter 12. The Whartons in the Gilded Age

1. JW to Swank, 17 Oct. 1898, WP.

2. "The Man on the Corner—Homes of the Members of the Wharton Family," *Independent Gazette*, 19 Mar. 1925, clipping in WP.

3. The most complete description of Ontalauna is to be found in A. W. Morris journal, 4 Jan. 1886, but see also JW to Charlemagne Tower, 12 Jan. 1895, to DFW, 22 July 1881, JW Private Accts., 1876–84, entry of 31 Dec. 1880, WP.

4. JW to daughter Mary, 2 June 1881, WP.

5. Joanna Lippincott, *Biographical Memoranda*, 90–91.

6. JW to ALW, 3 Sept. 1863, WP.

7. JW to DFW, 20 July 1880, WP.

8. S. L. Wright and C. M. Wright, *The Good Old Summertime*; W. L. Watson, *History of Jamestown on Conanicut Island in the State of Rhode Island* (Providence, 1949), 6–10, 60.

9. Copy of the deed, which was recorded 16 June 1882, is in the possession of Catharine M. Wright; JW Private Accts., 1876–84, entries of 14, 27 Dec. 1881, 14 June 1882; Harrison S. Morris, *Masterpieces of the Sea: William T. Richards* (Philadelphia and London: J. B. Lippincott Co., 1912), 39.

10. The best description of Marbella is to be found in Wright and Wright, *The Good Old Summertime*.

11. J. Clothier to JW, 15 Oct. 1902, WP.

12. ALW to JW, 19 June 1873. WP. For Joanna's description of JW as a father see Joanna Lippincott, *Biographical Memoranda*, 35–37.

13. A. W. Morris journal, 4 Jan. 1886.

14. Hannah Haydock to ALW, 29 May 1887, WP.

15. JW Private Accts., 1885–98, p. 6.

16. JW to daughter Mary, 27 July 1882, WP.

17. A. W. Morris journal, 4 Jan. 1886.

18. Ibid., 6 Jan. 1886.

19. Ibid., 18 Mar. 1892.

20. Ibid., 23 June 1895, 13 Apr. 11 Aug. 1896.

21. JW to Harrison S. Morris, 5 Mar. 1903, WP.

22. A. W. Morris journal, 5 Mar. 1903.

23. Scott Nearing, *The Making of a Radical: A Political Autobiography* (New York: Harper & Row, 1972), 52.

24. JW to H. M. Levering, 20 Mar. 1894, WP. For a description of Bellevue in 1913 see "Tales of the Town," *Philadelphia Record*, 16 Mar. 1913, clipping in WP.

25. JW to Craig Biddle, 28 Mar. 1898, WP.

26. Sayre diary, 8, 12 Mar. 1888.

27. JW to DFW, 16, 21 June 1886, WP.

28. JW to ALW, 10 Apr. 1889, WP.

29. JW to daugher Anna, 18 July 1888, WP.

30. JW to DFW, 2 Aug. 1880, WP.

31. JW to Charles W. Wharton, 25 Feb. 1887, WP.

32. Geo. A. Walton and Bernard Walton, eds., *Diaries and Correspondence, Margaretta Walton*, 12, 14, 88, 95; JW to Peter Wycoff, 8 Feb. 1894, WP.

33. A. W. Morris journal, 21 August 1888.

Chapter 13. Industrialist of the Eighties

1. Loose sheet in front of JW Private Accts., 1876–84, WP.

2. Saucon Iron Co., Minute Book; *Iron Age*, 18 Dec. 1884, 22 Jan. 1885.

3. The FHL has an extensive and detailed file of JW's real estate transactions in the pinelands, including blueprints; and his correspondence in the WP concerning his interests there is extensive.

4. JW Private Accts., 1885–98, item "Final Month 1st 1885," p. 3 in back of book; also JW Private Accts., 1876–84, entries of 10 May, 29 Nov. 1881, WP.

5. JW Private Accts., 1876–84, entries of 3, 15 Jan., 15 Aug. 1879, 10 Mar., 19 Apr. 3 Dec. 1880, 3 Dec. 1884, JW Private Accts., 1885–98, entries of 3 Dec. 1891, 3 Dec. 1892, 31 Oct. 1894.

6. JW Private Accts., 1876–84, entries of 18 Dec. 1879, 28 May, 6 Aug. 1880. Kenneth R. Hanson, "Joseph Wharton in New Jersey," *New Jersey History* 86, no. 1 (Spring 1968): 9; Geological survey of New Jersey, *Annual Report of the State Geologist*, 1880, pp. 116, 120.

7. Hanson, "Joseph Wharton in New Jersey," 9; Geological Survey of New Jersey, *Annual Report of the State Geologist*, 1884, p. 85; *A History of Morris County, New Jersey*, 2 vols. New York and Chicago: Lewis Historical Publishing Co., 1914), 1: 213; J. Wesley Pullman, "The Product of the Hibernia Iron-Mine, N.J.," *Transactions AIME* 14 (June 1885–May 1886): 909.

8. Hanson, "Joseph Wharton in New Jersey," 9; JW Private Accts., 1876–84, s.v. "Port Oram Furnace," "Boonton Mill," "Warren Furnace."

9. William S. Bayley, *Iron Mines and Mining in New Jersey*, vol. 7 of Final Report Series of the State Geologist (Trenton: Geological Survey of New Jersey, 1910), 18.

10. JW Private Accts., 1885–1898, many entries.

11. JW Private Accts., 1876–1884, 1885–1898, many entries.

12. WB to Mr. Twombly, 31 Jan. 1885, Letterbrook #17, WB Papers.

13. WB to JW, 13 Sept. 1884, WP; Joanna Lippincott, *Biographical Memoranda*, 143–44; JW, draft letter to ed., "The Reading Question," *Press* (Philadelphia), 10 May 1893, WP; clippings from the *Press* loose in Sayre diary for 1886.

14. Leslie M. Scott, "The Yaquina Railroad," *Oregon Historical Quarterly* 16 (1915): 228–45.

15. Pamphlet on Oregon Pacific Railroad, WB Papers, Misc. Papers, Box 25; JW Private Accts., 1885–98, entries of 1 Aug. 1888, 1 Apr. 1889.

16. WB Scrapbook; Sayre diary, 12, 15, 25 Apr. 1889.

17. These and subsequent facts are taken from Scott, "The Yaquina Railroad, 228–45, supplemented by a large correspondence of JW and the following articles from the *New York Times:* "The Oregon Pacific," 9 July 1891, p. 2, "Oregon Pacific Troubles," 19 May 1892, p. 2, "Oregon Pacific," 15 Dec. 1892, p. 3.

18. JW Private Accts., 1885–98, entries of 11 Dec. 1893, 23 Jan. 1895.

19. JW to "Mr. Ch," 9 Feb. 1894, WP.

20. JW to Wm. Jacks, 16 Mar. 1894; and see JW to Thomas Prosser, 28, 30 Oct. 1895, WP.

21. JW Private Accts., 1885–98, many entries.

22. JW Private Accts., 1885–89, s.v., "San Antonio Venture."

23. JW Private Accts., 1885–98, esp. entries of 30 May, 19 July 1893, JW to Heidelbach, 3 June 1898, WP: *New York Times*, 5 Aug. 1889, p. 5.

Chapter 14. Armor Plate and Guns

1. Minute Book & accts. of the Asa Packer Estate are in the Linderman Library, Lehigh University, Bethlehem, Pa.

2. BICo Minutes of Bd., 1880–82.

3. *Iron Age*, 28 June 1877, 14. See also issues of 18 June 1874, p. 29, 3 Dec. 1874, p. 7, 17 Apr. 1874, p. 37.

4. *Iron Age*, 19 Aug. 1886, 25.

5. *Iron Age*, 15 Aug. 1889; Robert Hessen, *Steel Titan: The Life of Charles M. Schwab* (New York: Oxford University Press, 1975), 42–43.

6. "The Career of Sir Joseph Whitworth," *Iron Age*, 24 Dec. 1884, 7, 9; Fritz, *Autobiography*, 191–93; *La grande Encyclopédie* (ed. 1886–1902), s.vv. "Creusot," "Krupp."

7. H.F.J. Porter, "How Bethlehem Became Armament Maker," *Iron Age*, 23 Nov. 1922, 1340; Hessen, *Steel Titan*, 42–44.

8. BICo Minutes of Bd., 30 Oct. 1885.

9. Fritz, *Autobiography*, 183, 188.

10. JW to Hon. C. J. Bonaparte, 14 Apr. 1907, WP; Joanna Lippincott, *Biographical Memoranda*, 58; James M. Swank, *Progressive Pennsylvania* (Philadelphia: J. B. Lippincott Co., 1908), 241

11. Sayre diary, 28 Apr. 1886, and see entries for 10, 13 Nov. 1885, 16, 17, 22, 23 Apr. 1886; BICo Minutes of Bd., 30 Dec. 1885.

12. BICo Minutes of Bd., 6 Apr. 1887; Sayre diary, 21, 22 Mar. 1887; Whitney to JW, n.d., WP.

13. Sayre diary, 10 Aug. 1887; BICo Minutes of Bd., 12 Aug., 30 Nov. 1887.

14. Sayre diary, 26 Oct. 1887.

15. Typed obit of Davenport (probably written by F.W. Taylor), Taylor Papers, file 57C, SIT.

16. Quoted in "Bethlehem at the Maritime Exhibition," *Iron Age*, 19 Dec. 1889, p. 952.

17. "The Bethlehem Armor and Gun Plant," *Iron Age*, 26 Mar. 1891, p. 577.

18. MS biography of JW, attached to letter, JW to B. S. Stephenson, 20 Mar. 1907, WP.

19. Sayre diary, 1 May, 20, 26 June, 28 Oct. 1888.

20. Hessen, *Steel Titan*, 44. Sayre wrote in the back of his diary for 1890, "We have done moderately well at the iron works but should have done better. Sec'y of Navy had sat down on us pretty hard and given 5000 tons of plates to Carnegie."

21. Carnegie to JW, 6 Nov. 1894, WP.

22. JW to Linderman, 29 Dec. 1893, 31 Jan. 1895, to Commodore W. T. Sampson, 16 Apr. 1895, WP.

23. W. R. Yates ed., *Bethlehem of Pennsylvania: The Golden Years, 1841–1920* (Bethlehem, Pa., 1976), 98–100.

24. Hannah Haydock to JW, 1 Sept. 1887, WP.

25. Thurston to JW, 9 May 1880, WP; Sayre diary, 8 May 1883.

26. Thurston to JW, 16 Dec. 1886, WP.

27. Letter of Wilbur to Sayre is in back of Sayre diary for 1887.

28. WB to JW, 10, 14 May 1890, WP.

29. JW to E. S. Mitchell, 11 June 1890, WP.

30. A. W. Morris journal, 22 July 1890.

Chapter 15. Industrialist of the Nineties: And the End of the Nickel Business

1. "The Barker Failure," *Times* (Philadelphia), 21 Nov. 1890, in WB Scrapbook, and see "Help for the Barings," *New York Times*, 17 Nov. 1890, p. 1; "As the Big Firm Fails," *New York Times*, 21 Nov. 1890, p. 1; Sayre diary, 12, 15, 25 Apr. 1889.

2. "The Barker Failure," *Daily Evening Telegraph* (Philadelphia), 1 Dec. 1890, and other items in WB Scrapbook.

3. JW Private Accts., 1885–98, many entries; JW to S. A. Baylor, 12 Feb. 1896, to secretary of William Wharton Switch Co., 11 June 1896, to W. B. Cooke, 3 June 1898, Joseph T. Buntin to W. B. Cooke, 8 June 1898, WP.

4. Lea to JW, 2 Jan. 1891, WP.

5. JW to ALW, Mar. 1890, to MacVeagh, 19 Feb. 1897, WP.

6. He once bragged of this in a note accompanying a letter to Drexel & Co., 25 Feb. 1902, WP: "I do not pretend to be a financier. The margin shows my principal affairs: in none of them have I any partner or debt."

7. "Mr. Carnegie, with whom I talked for 2½ hours last Friday, said that my operations at Port Oram are foolish." JW to Nicoll, 4 Mar. 1901, WP.

8. JW to ALW, 30 July 1895, WP.

9. Wenner to Anna W. Morris (n.d., but probably Feb. 1909), WP.

10. Voigt, MS, 7.

11. JW to Etheridge, 24 Jan. 1895, WP.

12. JW to Pitney, 7 Apr. 1894, WP.

13. JW to Whitwell, 12 Dec. 1904, WP.

14. Joanna Lippincott, *Biographical Memoranda*, 148–49.

15. JW to ALW, 14 Feb. 1894, to daughter Anna, 18 Aug. 1897, WP.

16. Francis L. Sperry, "Nickel and Nickel-Steel," *Transactions AIME* 25 (1896): 56.

17. Thompson and Beasley, *For the Years to come*, 68–70.

18. Robert M. Thompson, "the Orford Nickel Process," in R. P. Rothwell, ed., *The Mineral Industry, Its Statistics, Technology and Trade in the United States and Other Countries*, (New York: Scientific Publishing Co., 1893), 1:357.

19. Thompson and Beasley, *For the Years to Come*, 90–91.

20. JW, "The Production of Nickel and Cobalt in 1896," 8, 14.

21. JW to Whitney, 20 Apr. 1897, WP.

22. Thompson and Beasley, *For the Years to Come*, 93.

23. Voigt, MS, 6.

24. Ibid.

25. Thompson and Beasley, *For the Years to Come*, 73.

26. JW to Franklyn S. House, 18 Jan. 1895, WP.

27. JW to (undecipherable), 5 May 1897, to Sayre, 17 April 1897, WP.

28. JW to Goss, 13 Jan. 1896, WP.

29. JW to Thompson, 8 Nov. 1898, WP.

30. JW to R. P. Travers, 7 Feb. 1898; and see JW to Vivian & Co., 14 May 1897, 4 Jan. 1898, and other JW correspondence from 1893 to 1898, WP.

31. JW to Doble, 20 May 1897, WP.

32. JW to Doble, 2, 8 Mar., 5 Apr., 12 Dec. 1899, 23 Apr. 1900, to D. M. Wright, 7 Oct. 1899, to Kelly, 14 Feb. 1900, WP.

33. JW, "The Production of Nickel and Cobalt in 1896," 3: and see JW to James P. Hall, 21 July 1893, to Doble 18 Dec. 1893, WP.

34. JW to Herbert, 31 Oct. 1895, to Fleitmann, 26 Nov. 1895, WP.

35. JW to Cameron, 1, 11 Nov. 1895, to Mond, 14 Nov. 1895, 3 June 1896, to F. L. V. Skiff, 19 May 1893, Albert Colby to Linderman, 18 Nov. 1893, WP; JW, "The Production of Nickel and Cobalt in 1896," 8.

36. JW to Leech, 3 Apr. 1896, to Stone, 3 Apr. 1896, WP; and see JW to MacVeagh, 22 Jan. 1897, to Krupp, 6 Oct., 2 Nov. 1896, to Fleitmann, 21 Oct., 30 Nov. 1896, Tower to JW, 31 Dec. 1897, JW to M. I. Carter, 14 Mar. 1894, WP.

37. JW to Fleitmann, 30 Nov. 1896, WP.

38. JW to (undecipherable), 3 Feb. 1897, WP.

39. JW Nickel Business 1899–1902, s.v. "Profit and Loss," p. 32.

40. JW to Voigt, 18 Apr. 1901, WP.

41. J. D. Scott, *Vickers, a History* (London: Weidenfeld & Nicolson, 1962), 87.

42. Thompson and Beasley, *For the Years to Come*, 139–44, "International Nickel," *New York Times* 30 Mar. 1902, p. 1, 2 Apr. 1902, p. 10, *Iron Age*, 3 Apr. 1902, p. 45.

43. JW Nickel Business 1899–1902; JW to Monell, 12 May 1902, Gap Farms Inventory, 30 Apr. 1902, WP.

44. JW to John Maddock & Sons, 8 Nov. 1902, to Richard Fleitmann, 11 May 1903, to Theodor Fleitmann, 3 July 1903, to Max Pam, 23 Dec. 1902, WP.

45. Thompson and Beasley, *For the Years to Come*, 166.

46. Contained in letter JW to Roberts, 11 Feb. 1905, WP.

Chapter 16. Scientific Management and the Sale of Bethlehem Steel

1. Hessen, *Steel Titan*, 45–58.

2. JW to Quay, 22 Feb. 1895, WP; BICo Minutes of Annual Meeting, 1896.

3. JW, draft of letter dated 14 Jan. 1896 to ed. of *Public Ledger*, WP.

4. Hessen, *Steel Titan*, 91–92.

5. JW to R. H. Sayre, 10 Feb. 1896, WP.

6. The Sayre diary records meetings between personnel of the Bethlehem and Carnegie companies on these dates: 26 March, 19 June 1896, 3, 14, 19 April, 1 May 1897, in addition to other meetings not specifically dated and telephone conversations.

7. JW to Sayre, 18 Feb. 1896, WP.

8. JW to Carnegie, 7 Mar. 1896, WP.

9. Richardson, *William E. Chandler*, 503–4.

10. Sayre diary, 13 Mar., 2, 3 Apr. 1897.

11. *Daily Globe* (Bethlehem, Pa.), 20 Oct. 1897, 1.

12. Sayre diary, 23 May 1897.

13. Sayre diary, 14 Jan., 20 June, 2 Nov. 1898; BICo Minutes of Bd., 26 May 1897.

14. JW to Penrose, 3 Jan. 1900, WP.

15. JW to Linderman, 31 Jan. 1895, WP.

16. *Iron Age*, 6 Oct. 1892, 626–27; BICo Minutes of Bd., 28 Dec. 1892, 27 June 1893.

17. BICo Minutes of Bd., 28 Dec. 1892, 22 Feb., 25 Oct. 1893; Sayre diary, 11 Dec. 1892, 25 Oct. 1893, Copley, *Frederick W. Taylor*, 2:6.

18. Sayre diary, 15 June 1896.

19. JW to Linderman, 3 Jan. 1895, WP.

20. Sayre diary, 22 June 1897.

21. Daniel Nelson, *Frederick W. Taylor and the Rise of Scientific Management* (Madison: University of Wisconsin Press, 1980), 33–46; Judhir Kakar, *Frederick Taylor: A Study in Personality and Innovation* (Cambridge: MIT Press, 1970), 124.

22. Quoted in Copley, *Frederick Taylor*, 2:408.

23. Davenport to FWT, 22 Nov. 1897, Taylor Papers, SIT. See also Biographical Note, "Frederick Winslow Taylor," *Transactions ASME* 28 (1906): 29.

24. Copley, *Frederick W. Taylor*, 2:14.

25. FWT to Davenport, 4 Jan. 1898, Taylor Papers, SIT.

26. FWT to J. H. Griffiths, 10 June 1898, to Gantt, 2 June 1898, Taylor Papers, SIT.

27. Quoted in Copley, *Frederick W. Taylor*, 2:18, and see pp. 22–25.

28. Copley, *Frederick W. Taylor*, 2:18, Nelson, *Frederick W. Taylor*, 83.

29. BICo Minutes of Bd., 31 Aug. 1898.

30. Nelson, *Frederick W. Taylor*, 83.

31. Ibid., 85; BICo Minutes of Annual Meeting, 1899.

32. Sayre diary, 30 Nov. 1898.

33. Quoted in D. Nelson, *Frederick W. Taylor*, 93.

34. FWT to JW, 20 Mar. 1899, Taylor Papers, SIT.

35. Sayre diary, 28 Dec. 1899, and see entries for 29 May and 3, 4 Nov. 1899.

36. Hessen, *Steel Titan*, 97; see also JW to Linderman, 20 Apr. 1898, WP.

37. Hessen, *Steel Titan*, 145–62.

38. FWT to JW, 15, 27 Mar. 1901, Taylor Papers, SIT.

39. Concerning the absence of Wharton from Philadelphia 6–7 April 1901: On 5 April Wharton wrote Soule, the caretaker at Marbella, "If I go to Newport tomorrow it will probably be by rail." That Wharton left for Newport is attested to by Wenner, who upon receiving the communication from Taylor sent Taylor a note dated 6 April 1901 to the effect that Wharton would return on Monday (the eighth) and answer. WP.

40. Specifically, Nelson, *Frederick W. Taylor*, 101, Kakar, *Frederick Taylor*, 150. Copley in

Frederick W. Taylor, 2:152–53, does not specify the date on which the letter was sent to Linderman.

41. JW to H. P. McIntosh, 25 Mar. 1899, WP.

42. BICo Minutes of Bd., 29 Mar., 29 May 1899, *Iron Age,* 27 Apr. 1899, p. 13, Sayre diary, 2, 9, 15 Mar. 1899.

43. BICo Minutes of Bd., 29 May, 27 June 1899.

44. JW note (in letterbook), 28 March 1899, WP; Sayre diary, 29 April 1899.

45. *Iron Age,* 27 Apr. 1899, p. 3.

46. Scott, *Vickers,* 41–43, 46.

47. Sayre diary, 17 July, 15, 16 Aug. 1901, BICo Minutes of Bd., 15 Aug. 1901. Later, in a letter to Swank dated 27 May 1902, JW clarified his and Linderman's respective roles in the negotiations leading to the sale of Bethlehem Steel: "The small number of persons who owned a majority of that stock authorized me to sell their stock along with my own, but it was perfectly understood by all of us that every other stockholder must be given the opportunity of selling his stock at the same price as we might conclude to accept. I was not alone in this. In point of fact the deal which I had in hand came to naught, and my power to sell ended: The sale finally made to Mr. Schwab was negotiated by Mr. Linderman, the President of the Bethlehem Steel Co.—of course upon terms satisfactory to the above named majority—and every stockholder got the same price."

48. Linderman to JW, 31 Dec. 1902; Sayre to JW, 4 Jan. 1903, WP.

Chapter 17. The Jersey Ventures

1. Quoted in *Irish World* (New York), 25 Feb. 1893, in WB Scrapbook.

2. JW to E. Wright, 23 Mar. 1894, WP.

3. Geological Survey of New Jersey, *Annual Report of the State Geologist,* 1892, 253.

4. Ewing, *Atsion,* 18; JW Private Accts. 1885–98, entry of 1 Aug. 1891. Subsequent payments for the Raleigh tract were made 3 Sept. 1891 and 8 Apr. 1893. (This was his second large purchase of Raleigh properties. The first had been in 1873 and consisted of 4,083½ acres. See n. 39, chap. 5.)

5. JW to E. Wright, 21 June 1893, to Braddock, 16 Oct. 1893, WP; Ewing, *Atsion,* 19.

6. JW to E. Wright, 20 Mar. 1894, WP.

7. JW to E. Wright, 23 Mar., 1894; see also JW to E. Wright, 21 June 1893, 19 Nov. 1894, to Norton, 11 Oct. 1894, to Penrose, 26 Oct. 1894, to Braddock, 18 Jan. 1895, to Edwin S. Balch, 9 Apr. 1895, to Dr. Myers, 23 Feb. 1895, to Vermeule, 2, 5, 8, 11 Apr. 1895; JW, draft of a letter dated 20 Feb. 1899 to ed., *Public Ledger;* JW, MS "Pure Water" dated 20 June 1899, WP.

8. JW to Stearns, 6 May 1895, WP.

9. "Mr. Wharton's Scheme," *Public Ledger,* 15 May 1895, clipping in WP.

10. JW to H. S. Drake, 3 Sept. 1895; see also JW to Stearns, 15 May 1895 and form letter by JW dated 13 June 1895, WP.

11. JW to Trautwine, 25 Nov. 1896, to Bringhurst, 19 Jan. 1899, WP; see also Robert D. Bowden, *Boies Penrose: Symbol of an Era* (New York: Greenberg, 1937), 139.

12. JW to Emil Georgehin, 21 Feb. 1899, to Chas. G. Danach, 4 Nov. 1899, WP.

13. Vermeule to JW, 10 Nov. 1899, WP.

14. JW to H. G. Morrow, 23 Feb. 1900, WP.

15. The handbill is dated 10 Jan. 1900 and is with other writings on the subject of water in the WP.

16. JW to Trautwine, 13 Apr. 1900, WP.

17. JW to Morgan, 8 Oct. 1902, WP.

18. JW to E. Wright, 15 Apr. 1898, WP.

19. JW to Hon. Franklin Murphy, 2 June 1902, John R. and Oscar Foley to JW, 15, 24 Feb., 1904, JW to John R. and Oscar Foley, 16 Feb. 1904, WP.

20. Braddock to JW, 31 Jan. 1902, JW to Braddock, 1 Feb. 1902, WP.

21. "Haddonfield Man Has Plan to Make Atlantic a Seaport," letter to ed. from Isaac A. Braddock, paper and date unknown, clipping in WP; Lewis M. Haupt, Consulting Engineer, to JW, 2 Feb. 1904, WP.

22. JW to Etheridge, 12 Dec. 1901, to F. R. Meier, 8 Jan. 1906, W. C. Irons to JW, 1 Apr. 1904, C. W. Mathis to JW, 6 July 1903, Norton to JW, 15 Oct. 1903, WP.

23. Etheridge to JW, 4 June 1903, WP.

24. JW to Wendell P. Garrison, 28 Mar. 1898, WP.

25. Meier to JW, n.d.; see also Meier to JW, 15 Apr. 1902, WP.

26. Meier to JW, 25 Feb. 1903, WP.

27. Meier to JW, 4 May 1903, also Meier to JW, 6, 9, 21 Mar. 1903, WP.

28. Meier to JW, 18 Mar. 1904, WP.

29. JW to Wm. C. Sproul, 26 Apr. 1907. See also Meier to JW, 22 Mar., 13 Dec. 1904, JW to Meier, 19 Mar. 1904, 7 Jan. 1905, WP.

30. JW to Meier, 16 Mar. 1906, WP.

31. Hanson, "Joseph Wharton in New Jersey," 12: *History of Morris County, New Jersey,* 2:225–27.

32. JW to Nicoll, 7 Apr. 1897, WP.

33. Geological Survey of New Jersey, *Annual Report of the State Geologist,* 1897, 319–23.

34. Frank L. Dyer and Thomas C. Martin, *Edison, His Life and Inventions,* 2 vols. (New York and London: Harper & Bros., 1929), 2:501. Bryon M. Vanderbilt in *Thomas Edison, Chemist* (Washington, D.C.: American Chemical Society, 1971), gives an excellent account of Edison's experience in iron ore concentration, pp. 138–77.

35. Sayre in his diary for 19 May 1891 wrote of visiting the "Edson [*sic*] Concentrating Works": "Found a great plant and many interesting features in the crushing & separating plant. Mr. Edson the inventor was there. I was much pleased with him, he is a very pleasant man with great brains." See also JW to Kelly, 31 Jan. 1894 (2 letters), to Edison, 26 Nov. 1894, 21 May 1895, to Monell, 21 June 1906, WP.

36. Edison to JW, 9 Oct. 1894; JW to Edison, 10 Oct. 1894, WP.

37. JW to Edison, 13 Oct. 1894, 17 May 1895, WP.

38. Quoted in Dyer and Martin, *Edison,* 489–91.

39. JW to Kelly, 24, 31 Dec. 1895, WP.

40. Dyer and Martin, *Edison,* 493.

41. Vanderbilt, *Thomas Edison, Chemist,* 162–63. Wharton was under the impression that the order was for 50,000 tons: "Sam Adams [of the BICo] told me yesterday that Edison's works are now running and the concentrate going to Crane Co. who are said to have bought 50,000 tons of his ore bricks." JW to Kelly, 18 Dec. 1896, WP.

42. Dyer and Martin, *Edison,* 494–95.

43. JW to Kelly, 28 Dec. 1897, WP.

44. Bayley, *Iron Mines and Mining in N.J.,* 14.

45. For a description of Ball's magnetic separator, see "The Magnetic Concentration of Iron Ore in New Jersey," *Iron Age,* 22 Oct. 1903, 16–17.

46. JW to Kelly, 21, 24 Jan. 1899, WP.

47. Memo (in letterbook) JW to Kelly, 26 May 1899, JW to Nicoll, 13 May 1901, WP.

48. Bayley, *Iron Mines and Mining in N.J.,* 16.

49. Geological Survey of N.J., *Annual Report of the State Geologist,* for the years 1901, pp. 135, 142, 145–47; 1903, pp. 98, 99, 104–6; 1904, pp. 317–18; JW to C. Kirchhoff, 26 Feb. 1901, to Mahlor Pitney, 11 Apr. 1901, and many other letters, WP; Receipt signed by Wm. C. Sproul for Pond Fork Lands, Business Papers, WP.

50. "Joseph Wharton on the Iron Market," *The Iron Age,* 25 Oct. 1906, 1089; obit of JW in *Iron Age,* 14 Jan. 1909, 165.

51. Memorandum Concerning Wharton Steel Co. (in letterbook), 28 Mar. 1905, JW to Hon. E. H. Gary, 8 Nov. 1905, WP.

52. JW to Weiskopf, 31 Dec. 1904, to Gary, 15 Nov. 1905, to Frick, 29 Mar. 1906, to Schwab, 16 Oct. 1907, WP.

53. The American Iron and Steel Association, *Directory to the Iron and Steel Works of The United States,* 17th ed. (Philadelphia: 1908), 480; H. S. Morris to State Bd. of Assessors of N.J. (in letterbook), 6 Apr. 1908; H. C. Wenner for Wharton Steel Co. to King Stickle, 8 June 1908, WP.

54. JW Private Accts. 1885–98, s.v. "Fish Business."

55. JW to Miles, 18, 29 Sept. 1894, to Roosevelt, 6 Apr. 1898; form letter by JW (in letterbook), August 1894, WP.

56. The letterbooks in the WP contain a great deal of correspondence concerning the "fish business," mostly consisting of letters passing between JW on the one hand and Otis and Miles on the other.

57. "Joseph Wharton's Big Deal," *Philadelphia Bulletin*, 6 Mar. 1906, clipping in WP.

Chapter. 18. Far Western Gold

1. JW to ALW, 20 Apr. 1904, WP. The current and preferred spelling is "Eldorado." Wharton and Gracey, however, consistently spelled the word "El Dorado."

2. Bertrand F. Couch and Jay A. Carpenter, "Nevada's Metal and Mineral Production (1859–1940, Inclusive)," *Geology and Mining Series #38* (Reno: Nevada State Bureau of Mines, 1 Nov. 1943); 27; W. A. Chalfant, *Gold, Guns, & Ghost Towns* (Stanford: Stanford University Press, 1947), 159–62. Excellent maps of the area and a sketch of a cross section of the Techatticup Mine can be found in *Bulletin #62, Plate II*, Nevada Bureau of Mines (n.d.). The WP have color photographs of the Techatticup and Wall Street mine locations.

3. "The Southwestern Mining Company," a report to the board of trustees of the Southwestern Mining Company, 12 Feb. 1880, WP.

4. JW to Mills, 26 Mar. 1894, 4 June 1896, WP.

5. JW to Gracey, 15 Apr., 18 Oct. 1897, and see JW to Gracey, 16 July 1896, JW to G. B. Waterhouse, 18 Sept. 1896, WP.

6. JW to E. Sheridan, 6 Jan. 1902, WP.

7. JW to H. C. Stroup, 15 Oct. 1896, to Wilson M. Lambert, 7 Dec. 1896, Sample ballot for election of 1896, WP; J. Fritz to Swank, 7 Jan. 1897, Swank MSS, HSP.

8. JW to Linderman, 9 Dec. 1896, to G. K. Myers, 19 Dec. 1896, JW draft of speech delivered at the Academy of Music For Penrose, 22 Dec. 1896, WP.

9. JW to Tower, 10 Mar. 1897; see also JW to Tower, 15 June 1897, to Penrose, 15 Feb., 15 Mar. 1897, 1 Mar. 1898, JW to John Sherman, 20 Mar. 1897 (2 letters), WP.

10. JW to Gracey, 4 Jan. 1898, WP.

11. JW to Torreyson & Summerfeld, 14 Feb. 1898. The correspondence concerning transactions in acquiring the company is extensive. The most valuable information occurs in letters of JW to Gracey and to Torreyson & Summerfeld, 1896–98, WP.

12. In 1904 JW asked Gracey for the details of Avote's rampage. Gracey complied by sending JW a ten-page typed narrative of the affair as part of a letter dated 21 April 1904, WP: and see W. Ross Yates, "Frontier Justice in Eldorado: Charles Gracey's Story," *Nevada Historical Society Quarterly* 29, no. 2 (Summer 1986).

13. JW to ALW, 11 Mar. 1898, WP.

14. JW to ALW, 14 Mar. 1898, WP.

15. JW to ALW, 15 May 1907, WP.

16. JW to ALW, 20 Apr. 1904, WP.

17. JW to Gracey, 13 Apr. 1898, WP.

18. JW to Gracey, 17 Oct. 1898, and see JW to Gracey, 23, 25 Mar., 18, 25 Apr. 8 Nov. 1898, WP.

19. JW to Gracey, 26 Apr. 1898; see also JW to Torreyson & Summerfeld, 27 Apr. 1898, WP.

20. JW to Gracey, 11 Oct. 1898, to the White Hills Mining Co., 2 Dec. 1898, WP.

21. JW to Gracey, 5 Jan. 1900, and see JW to Gracey, 28 Mar. (to which is attached an agreement between JW & Gracey), 5 Apr. 1899, to F. W. Drawn & Co., 4 May 1899, WP.

22. JW to John Powers, 10 Apr. 1900, WP.

23. JW to Gracey, 12 May 1899, WP.

24. JW to J. Ball, 30 July 1901, WP.

25. JW to Gracey, 8 Jan., 5, 18, 25 Feb. 1902, 30 Aug. 1904, WP.

26. JW to ALW, 13 May 1907, WP.

27. With optimism characteristic of the time and place, one journal reported, "Could half the wonders of the Quartette be made public it would cause a world-wide sensation." "Review of the Mining Industry," *Mining and Engineering Review* 18, no. 4 (23 Jan. 1904): 13.

28. JW to ALW, 29 Apr. 1905, WP.

29. JW to Gracey, 11 June 1906, WP.

30. JW to Gracey, 27 Nov. 1906, WP.

31. Gracey to JW, 3 Dec. 1907; and see JW to Gracey, 23, 31 Oct. 1907, WP.
32. *Mining Science* (Denver), 28 May 1908, 520.
33. JW to W. E. Borah, 18 May 1904, WP. The correspondence concerning the gold-dredging venture in Idaho is extensive. Key items include: JW to Borah, 21 Sept. 1904, 21 Dec., 17 June 1905, to ALW, 21 Apr., 16 May 1905, to Norman Gratz, 2 Feb., 14, 24 Nov. 1905, 14 June, 1 Nov., 13 Dec. 1906, 29 May, 24 Oct. 1907, 28 Jan. 1908, to F. W. Estabrook, 13 Feb. 1908, to A. Monell, 9 Oct. 1906, WP.
34. JW to Estabrook, 13 Feb. 1908, WP.

Chapter 19. The Vigor of Old Age

1. Draft of letter to ed. of the *New York Times* dated 16 Jan. 1899, WP.
2. The correspondence passing between JW and the Thurston boys is extensive. The matter of the loans to William and Joseph Thurston is covered in a letter to JW to E. Coppée Thurston, 11 Feb. 1907, WP.
3. A. W. Morris journal, 24 Jan. 1909.
4. JW to ALW, 14 Jan. 1869, WP.
5. JW to Sheba, 25 June 1897, to Penrose, 7 Dec. 1897, WP.
6. JW to John A. Porter, 29 June 1897, to Roosevelt, 25 Nov. 1897, 7 July 1904, to Sen. Allison, 5 May 1898, Tower to JW, 29 Oct. 1901, 18 Jan. 1903, WP.
7. A. W. Morris journal, 13 Feb. 1907.
8. JW to Macfarlane, 12 May 1898, WP.
9. JW to Dr. M. U. Froncoso, 9 Nov. 1903, WP.
10. JW, Swarthmore Address of 1891, in Johanna Lippincott, *Biographical Memoranda*, 84.
11. JW, Swarthmore Address of 1888, in *Friends Intelligencer*, 23 June 1888, 386–88.
12. His pamphlet, *"Credo Quia Impossibile Est,"* was privately printed in 1898, copy in WP.
13. Hetty Smith to JW, 29 Feb. 1892. For another example of JW's lack of tolerance on religious issues see JW to Swain, 1 Aug. 1906, WP.
14. JW to John D. McPheran, 2 Oct. 1895, WP.
15. JW to Fleitmann, 3 July 1903, WP.
16. The correspondence is extensive. The following contain highlights: JW to Major Lockwood, 20 May, 24 June, 13 Nov. 1896, to "Dear Benjamin," 22 June 1896, to Hon. Joseph K. McCammon, 8 Dec. 1896, to ALW, 23 Mar. 1897, WP; S. L. Wright and C. M. Wright, *The Good Old Summertime.*
17. Tower to JW, 2 May 1907, WP.
18. Bernhard, Prince von Bülow, *Memoirs, Vol. 2: From the Morocco Crisis to Resignation, 1903–1909* (Boston: Little, Brown & Co., 1931), 38–39.
19. A. W. Morris journal, 11 June 1907.
20. JW to Carnegie, 30 Apr. 1907; see also Tower to JW, 5 May 1907, WP.
21. JW to ALW, 10 June 1907, Roger Haydock to JW, 8 June 1907, WP; A. W. Morris journal, 11 June 1907.
22. JW to ALW, 10 June 1907, WP.
23. JW to ALW, 15, 17 June 1907, ALW to JW, 14 June 1907, WP.
24. von Bülow, *Memoirs*, 2:119.
25. JW to Clothier, 20 June 1907, reprinted in *Friends Intelligencer*, 27 Feb. 1915, 132–33.
26. JW to ALW, 20 June 1907, WP.
27. JW to ALW, 23 June 1907, WP.
28. Mary Wharton to JW, n.d., ALW to JW, 4 July 1907, WP.
29. Cable from Dr. Sinclair, 17 July 1907, WP.
30. A. W. Morris journal, 17 July 1907.
31. Telegram, Tower to J. Lippincott, 17 July 1907, Sidney Hoyt to JW, 11 July 1907, Carnegie to JW, 8 July 1907, and other letters, WP.
32. JW to ALW, 22 July 1907, WP.
33. A. W. Morris journal, 6 Aug. 1907.
34. A. W. Morris journal, 4 Oct. 1907.
35. JW to Gracey, 11 Oct. 1907; see also JW to Gracey, 23 Oct. 1907, WP.
36. Quoted in a five-page typed and unsigned MS describing the crisis, WP, possibly written

by either Harrison S. Morris or J. B. Lippincott or the wife of one of them. Most information concerning the crisis comes from this MS and A. W. Morris journal, 21, 29 Oct., 13 Nov. 1907.

37. A. W. Morris journal, 13 Nov. 1907.

38. Quoted in ibid.

39. Ibid.

40. A. W. Morris journal, 17 Mar. 1908.

41. JW to Gracey, 28 Apr. 1908, WP.

42. JW to Gracey, 9 Aug. 1908, WP.

43. JW to Richards, 27 Sept. 1907, 3 June 1908; Richards to JW, 5 June 1908 and other letters, WP.

44. David Ferrier to JW, 16 Mar. 1908, Lauder Brunton to JW, 27 Aug. 1908, WP.

45. "A Christmas Present for Wharton Borough," *Iron Era* (Dover, N.J.), Dec. 24, 1908, 1, 7; "Gives Park to Philadelphia," *New York Times*, 24 Dec. 1908, p. 1, clippings in WP.

46. JW to De Lamar, 28 Oct. 1907, to J. D. Ellis, 27 Feb. 1908, WP.

47. JW to Gratz, 31 July 1908, WP.

48. JW to Gratz, 19 June 1908, WP.

49. Wenner to Mrs. Morris, n.d., Kelly to Mrs. Morris, 11 Jan. 1909, Carnegie to Mrs. Morris, 7 July 1910, WP.

Appendix: The Dry and Wet Processes of Making Nickel

1. JW Gap Journal.

2. The MS is in Box 42, WP. The handwriting is probably that of Fleitmann.

3. JW diary of a trip to Europe, 1873, WP.

Bibliography

Sources of Manuscripts and Related Material

The thousands of items which went into the making of this biography cannot be separately listed and still be meaningful. The reader could be lost in a forest. However, all but a few are in special collections maintained by libraries or museums which have more or less completely organized them according to subject.

First in importance among these collections of manuscripts is that of the Wharton Papers in the Friends Historical Library at Swarthmore College. Descendants of Wharton have created this extensive collection, which is arranged in eleven series: (1) *Family Papers*, including diaries, correspondence, legal documents, account books, and records of other sorts of Wharton's ancestors. Because many of the eighteenth-century ancestors were wealthy Quaker Philadelphia merchants, these papers contain much information concerning social and economic affairs in colonial Pennsylvania. Many items also deal with the Hicksite Separation. The letters of Wharton's parents, Deborah Fisher and William Wharton, are there, as are William Wharton's account books. (2) *Biographical Papers Concerning Joseph Wharton* include published articles, pamphlets, news items, etc., about him and his businesses. (3) *Anna L. Wharton Papers* have material concerning Wharton's wife and her ancestors, notably the Lovering and Corbit families. Also included is the extensive correspondence of Anna with husband, friends, and relatives. (4) *Correspondence of Joseph Wharton* contains letters sent to and received by him. Many are organized in folders according to senders and receivers. The series also has the letterbooks covering his businesses from 1893 until the time of his death. (5) *Writings of Joseph Wharton* have his most important publications as well as transcripts of testimony before various congressional committees. (6) *Business, Financial, and Legal Papers.* Much of the material is organized in folders by subject. In addition one finds here the ledgers and account books of his businesses to 1898. This is one of the most valuable parts of the collection, since the entries in the ledgers contain much information other than financial and also help a writer to determine with great accuracy the sequence of events. (7) *Swarthmore College Papers* contain correspondence and other documents concerning Wharton's long association with the college. (8) *Wharton School Papers* have letters and the indentures and related documents describing Wharton's motives and aims for the school. (9) *Wharton Estate Papers* include the letterbooks, accounts, and other material concerning Wharton's business enterprises maintained by his executors after his death. (10, 11) The final two series contain respectively memorabilia and reference materials kept by Wharton and his family.

The Friends Historical Library also has some uncatalogued material pertaining to Wharton: blueprints of lands on the Wharton Tract; correspondence in the 1900s between Wharton and the managers of his farms and other properties near Batsto and Atsion; and a large ledger kept by Samuel Rowland Fisher. Other useful material in the library includes genealogies of the Wharton and Fisher families; other genealogies; microfilms of records of Quaker (Hicksite) meetings; microfilms of minutes of the Board of Managers of Swarthmore College; a complete file of the *Friends Intelligencer;* books and manuscripts concerning various of Wharton's relatives and associates such as Susanna Dilwyn Parrish Wharton, Isaac Clothier, and Edward Magill; and much material defining the Quaker environment in which Wharton was reared.

Second in importance to the Friends Historical Library as a resource for understanding the life of Joseph Wharton is the manuscript room of the library of the Historical Society of Pennsylvania. Among its many collections are several small diaries of Deborah Fisher Wharton; letters of Joseph Wharton in the William D. Kelley papers; the diaries and journals of Samuel Rowland Fisher; documents concerning the businesses of the Wharton and Fisher families in the eighteenth century in the Family Papers (1728–1846) of Edward Wanton Smith, Correspondence (1817–1849) of Samuel Andrew Law, and the Family Papers (1732–1826) of Sarah A. Smith; papers of Joseph S. Lovering; the minutes of the board of directors of the Gap Mining Company; and miscellaneous relevant material in the Edward Carey Gardiner Collection and the Swank Manuscripts.

Other repositories with useful primary material are the Chester County (Pa.) Historical Society, which has records of the Walton family; the Lancaster County (Pa.) Historical Society, possessor of various publications concerning the Gap Nickel Mine; the Moravian Archives (Bethlehem, Pa.), which has the Registries of the Sun Hotel, miscellaneous material concerning the Pennsylvania and Lehigh Zinc Company, and a complete file of the newspaper *The Moravian;* the library of the Canal Museum (Easton, Pa.) to which, since the writing of this biography, the diaries of Robert

Heysham Sayre have been transferred; the libraries at Lehigh University, which house letters and publications concerning the Thurstons and the Coppées, part of the original manuscript of John Fritz's *Autobiography*, and a fine collection of books and periodicals dealing with industrial and economic developments in the United States during the period of Wharton's productive life; the Sterling Library at Yale University, whose Brush Family Papers contain seventy-seven letters written by Joseph Wharton; the library at the Stevens Institute of Technology, which has the collected papers of Frederick Winslow Taylor; the Manuscript Division of the Library of Congress, housing the papers of Wharton Barker and William E. Chandler, the latter having several letters by Joseph Wharton; and the Van Pelt Library of the University of Pennsylvania, which has files of *the Penn Monthly, The American*, other Phildelphia newspapers and journals, and numerous books dealing with various aspects of the environments in which Wharton lived.

The publications of the Batsto (N.J.) Citizens Committee were especially valuable for material concerning the pinelands.

Somewhat lesser amounts of material are found in the Patent Office of the U.S. Department of Commerce; the New Jersey Historical Society (Newark); the Newport (R.I.) Historical Society; the Public Library of Bethlehem, Pa.; the Peace Collection and main library at Swarthmore College; the library of the Franklin Institute; and the library of the American Philosophical Society.

A resource no longer available to scholars was the Schwab Memorial Library located in the corporate headquarters of the Bethlehem Steel Corporation, Bethlehem, Pa. When research for this biography was underway, the Schwab Library contained the minutes of stockholders meetings and of the board of directors of the Bethlehem Iron Company, lists of stockholders, and the minutes of the board of directors of the Saucon Iron Company. A recent reorganization of the Bethlehem Steel Corporation has resulted in the termination of this library and the distributing of its collections among various parties. As far as is known, the documents used in preparing this biography were returned to the legal department of the corporation and there remain.

Of signal utility has been material in the possession of Joseph Wharton's granddaughter, Mrs. Catharine Morris Wright, whose library at the Fox Hill Farm, Jamestown, Rhode Island, contains the remnants of Joseph Wharton's personal library, various memorabilia and documents, and especially the journal kept by Wharton's daughter Anna Wharton Morris.

General Works

Abrahams, Harold J. "The Sorghum Sugar Experiment at Rio Grande." *Proceedings of the New Jersey Historical Society* 83 (1965): 118–36.

The American Cyclopaedia: A Popular Dictionary of General Knowledge. 16 vols. New York: D. Appleton & Co., 1873–76.

The American (Philadelphia)

American Iron and Steel Association. *The Bulletin of the American Iron and Steel Association* 46, no. 15 (31 Dec. 1912).

———. *Directory to the Iron and Steel Works of the United States.* 17th ed. Philadelphia, 1908.

———. *Supplement to the Directory of the Iron and Steel Works of the United States.* Philadelphia, 1910.

Aykroyd, W. R. *The Story of Sugar.* Chicago: Quadrangle Books, 1967.

Baltzell, E. Digby. *Philadelphia Gentlemen: The Making of a National Upper Class.* Glencoe, Ill.: Free Press, 1958.

———. *Puritan Boston and Quaker Philadelphia: Two Protestant Ethics and the Spirit of Class Authority and Leadership.* New York: Free Press, 1979.

Barker, Wharton. *Bimetallism: On the Evils of Gold Monometallism and the Benefits of Bimetallism.* Philadelphia: Barker Publishing Co., 1896.

The Batsto Citizens Gazette.

Bayley, William S. *Iron Mines and Mining in New Jersey.* Vol. 7 of Final Report Series of the State Geologist, Geological Survey of New Jersey. Trenton: MacCrellish & Quigley, 1910.

Benjamin, Philip S. *The Philadelphia Quakers in the Industrial Age, 1865– 1920.* Philadelphia: Temple University Press, 1976.

Bethlehem (Pa.) *Daily Times.*

Bethlehem (Pa.) *Daily Times. Sesquicentennial Industrial Edition.* June 1892.

Biddle, Gertrude Bosler, and Sarah Dickinson Lowrie. *Notable Women of Pennsylvania.* Philadelphia: University of Pennsylvania Press, 1942.

Biographical Annals of Lancaster County, Pennsylvania. J. H. Beers & Co., 1903.

Blake, William P. "Nickel." In Albert Williams, Jr., *Mineral Resources of the United States, 1882.* Washington, D.C.: U.S. Geological Survey, 1883.

———. "Notes on the Metallurgy of Nickel in the United States." *JFI* 116 (1883): 60–67.

Boldt, Joseph R., Jr. *The Winning of Nickel: Its Geology, Mining, and Extractive Metallurgy.* Princeton: D. Van Nostrand Co., 1967.

Booth, James C. *The Encyclopedia of Chemistry: Practical and Theoretical, Embracing Its Applications to the Arts, Metallurgy, Mineralogy, Geology, Medicine, and Pharmacy.* Philadelphia: Henry C. Baird, 1850.

Bowden, Robert D. *Boies Penrose: Symbol of an Era.* New York: Greenberg, 1937.

Bowen, Eli. *The Pictorial Sketch-Book of Pennsylvania.* Philadelphia: Willis P. Hazard, 1852.

Boyd's Directory of Burlington County, N.J., 1895–96. Philadelphia: C. E. Howe, n.d.

Brodhead, J. Davis. *Historical Sketch of South Bethlehem.* South Bethlehem, Pa., 1885.

Browne, Junius H. "Queen of Aquidneck." *Harpers New Monthly Magazine* 49, no. 291 (August 1874); 305–20.

Bullard, John M. *The Rotches.* New Bedford, Mass., 1947.

Bülow, Bernhard Heinrich, Princeton. *Memoirs.* 4 vols., 1931–1932. Vol. 2: *From the Morocco Crisis to Resignation, 1903–1909.* Boston: Little, Brown & Co., 1931.

Burt, Nathaniel. *The Perennial Philadelphians: The Anatomy of an American Aristocracy.* Boston and Toronto: Little, Brown & Co., 1963.

Carey, Charles H. *History of Oregon.* Chicago and Portland: Pioneer Historical Publishing Co., 1922.

Carey, Henry C. *Principles of Social Science.* 3 vols. Philadelphia: J. B. Lippincott & Co., 1858.

Carpenter, Edward, and General Louis Henry Carpenter. *Samuel Carpenter and his Descendants.* Philadelphia: J. B. Lippincott Co., 1912.

Carter, Oscar C. S. "Artesian Wells as A Water Supply for Philadelphia." *JFI* 135, no. 1 (January 1893): 58–61.

Casson, Herbert. *The Romance of Steel: The Story of a Thousand Millionaires.* New York: A. S. Barnes & Co., 1907.

Chalfant, W. A. *Gold, Guns, and Ghost Towns.* Stanford: Stanford University Press, 1947.

Collins, Herman LeRoy. *Philadelphia, a Story of Progress.* 4 vols. New York, Philadelphia, and Chicago: Lewis Historical Publishing Co., 1941.

Comfort, William W. *Quakers in the Modern World.* New York: Macmillan Co., 1949.

Comly, John. *Journal of the Life and Religious Labours of John Comly, Late of Byberry, Pennsylvania.* Philadelphia: T. Ellwood Chapman, 1853.

Cope, Eliza, ed. *Philadelphia Merchant: The Diary of Thomas P. Cope, 1800–1851.* South Bend, Ind.: Gateway Editions, 1978.

Copley, Frank B. *Frederick W. Taylor, Father of Scientific Management.* 2 vols. New York and London: Harper & Bros., 1923.

Couch, Bertrand F., and Jay A. Carpenter. "Nevada's Metal and Mineral Production (1859–1940, Inclusive)." *Geology & Mining Series #38.* Publication of the Nevada State Bureau of Mines. Reno, 1943.

Davis, Allen F., and Mark H. Heller. *The Peoples of Philadelphia, A History of Ethnic Groups and Lower Class Life, 1790–1940.* Philadelphia: Temple University Press, 1973.

Dictionary of American Biography. 28 vols. New York: Charles Scribner's Sons, 1928–81.

Doherty, Robert W. *The Hicksite Separation: A Sociological Analysis of Religious Schism in Early Nineteenth Century America.* New Brunswick, N.J.: Rutgers University Press, 1967.

Dyer, Frank L., and Thomas Commerford Martin, with the collaboration of William Henry Meadowcroft. *Edison, His Life and Inventions.* 2 vols. New York and London: Harper & Bros., 1929.

Easton (Pa.) *Express*

Eberlein, Harold D., and Cortlandt Van Dyke Hubbard. *Portrait of a Colonial City: Philadelphia, 1670–1838.* Philadelphia: J. B. Lippincott Co., 1939.

Eliot, Charles W., and Frank H. Storer. "Arsenic as an Impurity of Metallic Zinc." *The American Journal of Science and Arts* (July–Nov., 1861): 380–94.

Ellis, Franklin, and Samuel Evans. *History of Lancaster County, Pennsylvania.* Philadelphia: Everts & Peck, 1883.

Emmons, S. F. "Geological Distribution of the Useful Metals in the United States." *Transactions AIME* 22 (1894): 53–95.

Encyclopaedia of Contemporary Biography of Pennsylvania. 3 vols. New York: Atlantic Publishing & Engraving Co., 1889–93.

Ewing, Sarah W. R. *Atsion, a Town of Four Faces.* Batsto, N.J.: Batsto Citizens Committee, 1979.

Fairbairn, William S. "Experiments to Determine the Properties of Some Mixtures of Cast Iron and Nickel." *JFI* 72 (1861): 93–97.

Feuchtwanger, Lewis. "Nickel and Its Uses in the Arts." *JFI* 96 (1873): 136–40, 204–13.

The First Hundred Years of the New Jersey Zinc Company. New Jersey Zinc Co., 1948.

Fisher, Sydney George. "The Diaries of Sydney George Fisher," ed. Nicholas Wainwright. *PMHB* 74, no. 2 (April 1952): 177–220; 88, no. 4 (Oct. 1964): 456–84; 89, no. 1 (Jan. 1965): 79–110.

Forbes, R. J. *Metallurgy in Antiquity.* Leiden: E. J. Brill, 1950.

Francis Wharton, a Memoir. Philadelphia: privately printed, 1891.

Frazer, Persifor, Jr. *The Geology of Lancaster County, Second Geological Survey of Pennsylvania: Report of Progress in 1877.* Harrisburg, 1880.

Friends Intelligencer and Journal.

Fritts, Peter. *History of Northampton County, Pennsylvania.* Philadelphia and Reading, 1877.

Fritz, John. *The Autobiography of John Fritz.* New York: John Wiley & Sons, 1912.

Geological Survey of New Jersey Annual Report of the State Geologist, separate reports for the years 1881–1909 and continuing. Trenton, N.J.

Glenn G. Munn's Encyclopedia of Banking and Finance. 7th ed. Boston: Bankers Publishing Co., 1973.

La grande encyclopédie. 31 vols. Paris: H. Lamirault et Cie, 1886–1902.

Hanson, Kenneth R. "Joseph Wharton in New Jersey." *New Jersey History* 86, no. 1 (Spring 1968): 3–13.

Henry, Matthew S. *History of the Lehigh Valley.* Easton, Pa.: Bixler & Corwin, 1860.

Hessen, Robert. *Steel Titan: The Life of Charles M. Schwab.* New York: Oxford University Press, 1975.

A History of Morris County, New Jersey. 2 vols. New York and Chicago: Lewis Historical Publishing Co., 1914.

Holbrook, Stewart H. *Iron Brew: A Century of American Ore and Steel.* New York: Macmillan Co., 1939.

Holley, A. L. "What is Steel?" *Transactions AIME* 4 (May 1875–Feb. 1876): 138–49.

Houston, R. G. "The Gap Copper Mines." *Journal of the Lancaster County Historical Society* 1 (1897): 283–98.

Howard-White, F. *Nickel: An Historical Review.* New York: Methuen, 1963.

Hughes, Thomas P. *Elmer Sperry: Inventor and Engineer.* Baltimore and London: Johns Hopkins Press, 1971.

Hunt, Robert W. "A History of the Bessemer Manufacture in America." *Transactions AIME* 5 (May 1876–Feb. 1877), 201–16.

Hussey, Miriam. *From Merchants to "Colour Men"—Five Generations of Samuel Wetherill's White Lead Business.* Philadelphia: University of Pennsylvania Press, 1956.

Ingalls, Walter R. *The Metallurgy of Zinc and Cadmium.* 1st ed. New York: Engineering and Mining Journal, 1903.

The Iron Age.

Jackson, C. T. "On the Manufacture of Zinc and Zinc White." *Proceedings of the American Association for the Advancement of Science* 4 (1850): 335–36.

James, E. J. Speech before the American Bankers' Association at Saratoga Springs, N.Y., 3 Sept. 1890. *Proceedings of the Convention of the American Bankers' Association* (1890): 20–33.

Jones, Rufus M. *The Later Periods of Quakerism.* 2 vols. London: Macmillan & Co., 1921.

Jordan, John W., ed. *Colonial Families of Philadelphia.* 2 vols. New York and Chicago: The Lewis Publishing Co., 1911.

Josephson, Matthew. *Edison.* New York: McGraw Hill Book Co., 1959.

Kakar, Judhir. *Frederick Taylor: A Study in Personality and Innovation.* Cambridge: MIT Press, 1970.

Kehl, James A. *Boss Rule in the Gilded Age: Matt Quay of Pennsylvania.* Pittsburgh: University of Pittsburgh Press, 1981.

Kemp, J. F. "The Nickel Mine at Lancaster Gap, Pennsylvania, and the Pyrrhotite Deposits at Anthony's Nose, on the Hudson," *Transactions AIME* 24 (Feb.–Oct. 1894): 620–33.

Kersey, Jesse. *A Narrative of the Early Life, Travels, and Gospel Labors of Jesse Kersey, Late of Chester County, Pennsylvania.* Philadelphia: T. Ellwood Chapman, 1851.

Lamborn, Leebert L. *Cottonseed Products: A Manual of the Treatment of Cottonseed for Its Products and Their Utilization in the Arts.* New York: Van Nostrand Co., 1904.

"Lancaster County Nickel Mines." in *Annual Report of the Secretary of International Affairs of the Commonwealth of Pennsylvania, 1874–1875, part III. Industrial Statistics,* 348–52. Harrisburg, 1876.

Laws of the Commonwealth of Pennsylvania, Sessions of 1851, 1855, 1860, 1861.

Lehigh Valley Railroad Annual Reports, 1852–6.

Levering, Joseph M. *A History of Bethlehem, Pennsylvania.* Bethlehem, Pa.: Bethlehem Times Publishing Co., 1903.

Lichty, Jean M. "Digging and Devotion at the Gap Nickel Mines Since 1857." *Journal of the Lancaster County Historical Society* 68 (1964): 121–26.

Lippincott, Bertram. *An Historical Sketch of Batsto, New Jersey.* Philadelphia: privately printed, 1933.

Lippincott, Joanna Wharton. *Biographical Memoranda Concerning Joseph Wharton, 1826–1909.* Philadelphia: privately printed and circulated by J. B. Lippincott, 1909.

Locher, Jack. "A History of Mining in Lancaster County, 1700–1900." *Journal of the Lancaster County Historical Society* 64, no. 1 (Winter 1960): 1–16.

Long, John D. "The Nickel Mines of Lancaster County." *Journal of the Lancaster County Historical Society* 80 (1976): 157–77.

McClure, A. K. *Old Time Notes of Pennsylvania.* 2 vols. Philadelphia: J. C. Winston Co., 1905.

McHugh, Jeanne. *Alexander Holley and the Makers of Steel.* Johns Hopkins Studies in the History of Technology, Thomas P. Hughes, general editor. Baltimore and London: Johns Hopkins University Press, 1980.

Magill, Edward H. *Sixty-Five Years in the Life of a Teacher, 1841–1906.* Boston and New York: Houghton Mifflin & Co., 1907.

Martindale, Joseph C. *A History of the Townships of Byberry and Moreland in Philadelphia, Pa.* Philadelphia: T. Ellwood Zell, 1867.

Metal Statistics 1972. 65th ed. New York: Fairchild Publications, 1972.

Miller, Benjamin L. *Lead and Zinc Ores of Pennsylvania.* Harrisburg: Department of Forests & Waters, 1924.

———. *Lehigh County, Pennsylvania: Geology and Geography.* Harrisburg: Department of Internal Affairs, 1941.

The Mining and Engineering Review (San Francisco).

The Mining Journal (London).

The Mining Magazine (New York).

Mining Science (Denver).

The Mining World (Chicago).

Morris, Anna Wharton. "Joseph Wharton: Discoverer of Malleable Nickel in the United States." *Germantown Crier* 5, no. 2 (May 1953): 7–8.

————. "The Romance of the Two Hannahs." *Bulletin of the Newport Historical Society* 46 (Oct. 1923): 1–33.

————. "Journal of Samuel Rowland Fisher, of Philadelphia," 1779–1781." *PMHB* 41, nos. 2, 3, 4 (1917): 145–97, 274–333, 399–457.

Munroe, H. S. "The Losses in Copper Dressing at Lake Superior." *Transactions AIME* 8 (May 1879–Feb. 1880): 409–43.

Myers, Richmond E. "The Story of the Zinc Industry in the Saucon Valley." *Rocks and Minerals*. The Official Journal of the Rocks and Minerals Assn. 10, nos. 2, 3, 4 (Feb., Mar., Apr. 1935): 17–21, 33–36, 56–59.

The National Cyclopedia of American Biography. 62 vols. 1893–1984. New York: James T. White & Co.

Nearing, Scott. *The Making of a Radical: A Political Autobiography*. New York: Harper & Row, 1972.

Nelson, Daniel. *Frederick W. Taylor and the Rise of Scientific Management*. Madison: University of Wisconsin Press, 1980.

Nevada Bureau of Mines. *Vertical Projection and Cross Sections through the Techatticup Mine, Bulletin 62, Plate II*, n.d.

Nevins, Allan. *Abram S. Hewitt: With Some Account of Peter Cooper*. New York and London: Harper & Bros., 1935.

New York Times.

Oaks, Robert F. "Philadelphians in Exile: The Problem of Loyalty during the American Revolution." *PMHB* 96, no. 3 (July 1972): 298–325.

Oberholtzer, Ellis P. *Philadelphia: A History of the City and Its People*. 4 vols. Philadelphia, Chicago, and St. Louis: S. J. Clarke Publishing Co., n.d.

Objects of Interest to Engineers and Others in and about Philadelphia. Philadelphia: The Engineers' Club of Philadelphia, 1893.

Overman, Frederick. *A Treatise on Metallurgy*. 6th ed. New York: D. Appleton & Co., 1868.

Pearse, John B. "Iron and Carbon, Mechanically and Chemically Considered." *Transactions AIME* 4 (May 1875–Feb. 1876): 157–78.

The Penn Monthly.

Pennypacker, Samuel W. *The Autobiography of a Pennsylvanian*. Philadelphia: John C. Winston Co., 1918.

Pepper, George Wharton. *Philadelphia Lawyer: An Autobiography*. Philadelphia and New York: J. B. Lippincott Co., 1944.

Percy, John. *Metallurgy, Vol. I. Fuel; Fire-Clays. Copper; Zinc; Brass, etc.* London: John Murray, 1861.

Peters, E. D., Jr. "The Sudbury Ore-Deposits." *Transactions AIME* 18 (May 1889–Feb. 1890): 278–89.

The American (Philadelphia).

Philadelphia as It Is in 1852. Philadelphia: Lindsay & Blakiston, 1852.

Phillips, John A. *A Manual of Metallurgy or Practical Treatise on the Chemistry of Metals*. London: John Joseph Griffin & Co., 1852.

Pierce, Arthur D. *Iron in the Pines, the Story of New Jersey's Ghost Towns and Bog Iron*. New Brunswick, N.J.: Rutgers University Press, 1957.

Porter, H. F. J. "How Bethlehem Became Armament Maker," *The Iron Age* 110 (23 Nov. 1922): 1339–41.

Prime, Frederick, Jr. "What Steel Is." *Transactions AIME* 4 (May 1875– Feb. 1876): 328–37.

Proceedings on the Inauguration of Swarthmore College. Philadelphia, 1889.

Pullman, J. Wesley. "The Produce of the Hibernia Iron-Mine, N.J. *Transactions AIME* 14 (June 1885–May 1886): 904–12.

Raistrick, Arthur. *Quakers in Science and Industry*. Newton Abbot, Devon, England: David & Charles (Holdings), 1968.

A Record of Accomplishment: 1848–1923. Privately printed by the New Jersey Zinc Co., 1924.

Reichel, William C. *The Crown Inn Near Bethlehem, Penna*. Philadelphia: privately printed, 1872.

Repplier, Agnes. *Philadelphia, the Place and the People*. New York: Macmillan Co., 1898.

Richardson, Leon B. *William E. Chandler, Republican*. New York: Dodd, Mead & Co., 1940.

Ritter, Abraham. *Philadelphia and Her Merchants, as Constituted Fifty to Seventy-Five Years Ago*. Philadelphia, 1860.

Roessler, A. R. "Nickel Linnaeite." *JFI* 89 (Jan.–June 1870): 85–86.

Sass, Steven A. *Pragmatic Imagination: A History of the Wharton School 1881–1981*. Philadelphia: U. of Pennsylvania Press, 1982.

Scott, J. D. *Vickers, a History*. London: Weidenfeld & Nicolson, 1962.

Scott, Leslie M. "The Yaquina Railroad." *Oregon Historical Quarterly* 16 (1915): 228–45.

Shapley, E. Cooper, Jr. *Legal Guide for Oil Companies and Stockholders: Including a Digest of the Mining Laws of Pennsylvania*. Philadelphia: Fowler & Moon, 1865.

Sipes, William B. *The Pennsylvania Railroad: Its Origin, Construction, Conditions, and Connections*. Philadelphia: Passenger Department, Pennsylvania Railroad, 1875.

Smedley, R. C. *History of the Underground Railroad in Chester and the Neighboring Counties of Pennsylvania*. New York: Negro Universities Press, 1968.

Smith, Anna Wharton. *Genealogy of the Fisher Family, 1682 to 1896*. Philadelphia: 1896.

Smith, Edgar Fahs. *Chemistry in America: Chapters from the History of the Science in The United States*. New York and London: D. Appleton & Co., 1914.

Smith, Ernest A. *The Zinc Industry*. Monographs on Industrial Chemistry. London and New York: Longmans, Green & Co., 1918.

Smith, Robert C. "Two Centuries of Philadelphia Architecture, 1700–1900." *Transactions of the American Philosophical Society* 43 (1953): 289–303.

Snowden, James R. *A Description of Ancient and Modern Coins in the Cabinet Collection of the Mint of the United States*. Philadelphia: J. B. Lippincott & Co., 1860.

South Bethlehem (Pa.) *Globe*.

Sperry, Francis L. "Nickel and Nickel-Steel." *Transactions AIME* 25 (1896): 51–61.

Stanwood, Edward. *American Tariff Controversies in the Nineteenth Century*. 2 vols. New York: Russell & Russell, 1903.

Swank, James M. *Notes and Comments on Industrial, Economic, Political and Historical Subjects*. Philadelphia: American Iron & Steel Association, 1897.

————. *Progressive Pennsylvania*. Philadelphia: J. B. Lippincott Co., 1908.

Tariff Acts Passed by the Congress of the United States from 1789 to 1909. H.R. Document #671, 61st Congress, 2d Session. Washington, D.C., 1909.

Terrill, Tom E. *The Tariff, Politics, and American Foreign Policy, 1874–1901*. Contributions in American History no. 31. Westport, Conn., and London: Greenwood Press, 1973.

Thompson, Erwin W., "The Manufacture of Cottonseed Oil." *Transactions ASME* 6 (Nov. 1884–May 1885): 414–36.

Thompson, John F., and Norman Beasley. *For the Years to Come, A Story of International Nickel of Canada*. New York and Toronto, 1960.

Thompson, Lewis. "On the Manufacture of Nickel" (reprinted from *Newton's London Journal*, Feb. 1863). *JFI* 75 (1863): 354–56.

Thompson, Robert Ellis. "Henry Charles Carey." *The Penn Monthly* (Nov. 1876), 816–34.

Thompson, Robert M. "The Orford Nickel Process." In Richard P. Rothwell, ed., *The Nickel Industry, Its Statistics, Technology and Trade in the United States and Other Countries*. 2 vols. New York: Scientific Publishing Co., 1893.

Tolles, Frederick B. *Meeting House and Counting House: The Quaker Merchants of Colonial Philadelphia 1682–1763*. Chapel Hill: University of North Carolina Press, 1948.

Townley, John M. "Early Development of El Dorado Canyon and Searchlight Mining Districts." *Nevada Historical Society Quarterly* 11, no. 1 (1968): 2–25.

Trego, Charles B. *A Geography of Pennsylvania*. Philadelphia: Edward C. Biddle, 1843.

U. S. Bureau of the Census. Eighth, Ninth, and Tenth Censuses of the United States (separate series). Washington, D.C., 1860, 1870, 1880.

Vanderbilt, Byron M. *Thomas Edison, Chemist*. Washington, D.C.: American Chemical Society, 1971.

Vermeule, Cornelius C. *Report on Water-Supply*. Vol. 3 of *Final Report of the State Geologist*, John C. Smock, Geological Survey of New Jersey. Trenton, 1894.

Wainwright, Nicholas B., ed. *A Philadelphia Perspective: The Diary of Sydney George Fisher Covering the Years 1834–1871*. Philadelphia: Historical Society of Pennsylvania, 1967.

————, ed. "Memoir of William Logan Fisher (1781–1862) for His Grandchildren." *PMHB* 99, no. 1 (Jan. 1975): 92–103.

Wall, Joseph F. *Andrew Carnegie*. New York: Oxford University Press, 1970.

Walton, Margaretta. *Diaries and Correspondence: Margaretta Walton, 1829–1904*. Edited by George A. Walton and J. Barnard Walton. 1962.

Ward, Townsend. "South Second Street and Its Associations." *PMHB* 4, no. 1 (1880): 42–60.

————. "Second Street and the Second Street Road and Their Associations," *PMHB* 4, no. 4 (1880): 401–31.

Watson, W. L. *History of Jamestown on Conanicut Island in the State of Rhode Island*. Providence, 1949.

Wharton, Anna H. *Genealogy of the Wharton Family of Philadelphia 1664 to 1880*. Philadelphia, 1880.

————. "The Wharton Family." *PMHB* 1 (1877): 324–29, 455–59.

Wharton, Francis. *A Digest of the International Law of the United States*. 3 vols. Washington, D.C., 1886.

Wharton, Joseph. *Speeches and Poems by Joseph Wharton*. Edited by Joanna Wharton Lippincott. Philadelphia: privately printed and circulated by J. B. Lippincott Co., 1926.

Wharton, Susanna Parrish, Comp. *The Parrish Family*. Philadelphia: George H. Buchanan Co., 1925.

Wharton, William, Jr., & Co., Inc. Catalogs of various products, 1887, et al.

Whitney, J. D. *The Metallic Wealth of the United States*. Philadelphia: Lippincott, Grambo & Co., 1854.

Widmer, Kemble, *The Geology and Geography of New Jersey*. vol. 19 in The New Jersey Historical Review. Princeton: D. Van Nostrand Co., 1964.

Wilbert, M. I. "Early Chemical Manufactures—A Contribution to the History of the Rise and Development of Chemical Industries in America." *JFI* (May 1904); 1–14.

Williams, Charles P. "Notes on the Method of Preparation of Zinc Oxide." *Transactions AIME* 5 (May 1876–Feb. 1877): 422–26.

Williams, Samuel T. "Man Behind A Name—Joseph Wharton," *The Philadelphia Forum* 28, no. 5 (Jan. 1949): 8–10.

Willig, H. Luther. "Two Notable Mining Industries of Lancaster County." *Journal of the Lancaster County Historical Society* 28, no. 1 (1924): 73–78.

Wright, Sydney L., and Catharine M. Wright. *The Good Old Summertime*. Privately printed, 1963.

Yates, W. Ross. "Frontier Justice in Eldorado: Charles Gracey's Story." *Nevada Historical Society Quarterly* 29, no. 2 (Summer 1986).

Yates, W. Ross, ed. *Bethlehem of Pennsylvania: The Golden Years, 1841–1920*. Bethlehem, Pa., 1976.

Yeoman, R. S. *A Guide Book of United States Coins*. 27th rev. ed. Racine, Wis.: Whitman Publishing Co., 1974.

Index